S0-AUQ-393

Jim Mora

Crazylegs Hirsch

Gene Hackman

(Quite)
A Few
Good Men

By John Gunn

Ernie Stautner

Hayden Fry

Bum Phillips

Copyright © 1992 John Alan Gunn

All rights reserved. No part of this book, in part or in whole, may be
reproduced, transmitted, or utilized, in any form or by any means,
electronic or mechanical, including photocopying, recording, or by any
information storage and retrieval system, without permission in writing
from the publisher, except for brief quotations in critical articles, books
and reviews.

International Standard Book Number   0-9631034-9-0

First Printing 1992

Special thanks to Frank Bisogno Sr. and Frank Bisogno Jr.

J&J Publishing
404 Brighton Springs
Costa Mesa, CA 92627

Table of Contents

The Cos, then a Navy corpsman, helped keep things loose as a trainer for the 1958 Quantico football team.

John Gunn, a retired Marine Corps Reserve colonel, first started following service football teams in World War II through the pages of the Chicago Tribune.

But he threw away all his records and clippings, for some reason, in high school.

Thirty years later, Gunn, a career newsman (Monmouth, Ill.; Galesburg, Ill.; Wilmington, N.C.; Richmond, Va.; Costa Mesa, Cal.; and Santa Ana, Cal.), found some old sports books on a Reserve assignment in Nevada.

Soon, he was poring through libraries at Camp Pendleton, El Toro, San Diego, North Island, Pensacola, Quantico, Camp Lejeune, Cherry Point, Headquarters Marine Corps, and Newport, R.I., plus newspaper microfilm.

Foreword

The Marine Corps estimates that $3\frac{1}{2}$ to 4 million men and women were Leathernecks at one time or another.

A lot of them were baseball fans; some preferred basketball; and others played or followed football. It just seems like a disproportionately high number fell in the latter category.

For whether Stateside, on Hawaii, in the South Pacific, in China, Japan, or Korea or at a dusty or grimy outpost somewhere, they'd pick up a football or something resembling one and throw it around.

Macho that they were, it was more fun to beat up on an Army team, a Navy outfit, an Air Force eleven or a civilian group. But if none was around, they didn't mind mixing it up with fellow Marines.

By and large, the football players were good men. One of their enemies was alcohol, and, later for some, the more potent hallucinogenic drugs of the '70s and '80s. A few might have chosen football over dodging bullets, but the relatively small size of the Corps made this less of a problem than in other services.

This compilation attempts to chronicle almost a century of football activity involving Marines or former Marines, their teams, their coaches, their successes, their losses, their stories.

The material comes from interviews, game programs, guides, newspaper clippings, microfilm, magazines, letters, yearbooks, histories, wire services, books and other sources.

But clippings yellow, memories fade and Marine PIO's occasionally were known to exaggerate or embellish. If a Marine had taken a 3-hour extension course at Notre Dame, he automatically was an All-American with the Fighting Irish.

A check of newspaper microfilm shows a lot of players labeled "college football stars" hadn't even lettered.

In some cases, one account might have Quantico winning the game; another might have Camp Lejeune the winner. Players' names and game facts at times were in dispute. Contradictions, inaccuracies and omissions abound.

And clerk-typists stationed overseas had other things to watch for, such as bullets or shells, while preparing game programs.

Against this background emerges a wide-ranging look at Marines and football, one not previously pieced together.

It's a cornucopia of immense — and often overlooked — contributions by Marines and the Marine Corps to football.

And vice versa.

One is reminded of not being able to see the forest through the trees. It's a shame this story wasn't told during the 1950's, '60s or '70s when so many Marines were in the football limelight one almost took their presence for granted.

Prelude To Heroism

The Marine Corps always has had a knack for picking hot, humid, lonely and swampy bases such as Camp Lejeune, Parris Island and Cherry Point for training.

Somehow, somebody slipped up during World War II and assigned Marines to Maui, then an unspoiled Hawaiian paradise.

True, it was only a respite between battles. But who was about to complain?

In the past of players on the Maui Marines team that 1944 season were the Marshalls, Saipan and Tinian invasions and numerous decorations for heroism.

They didn't know it, of course, but ahead was the hell of Iwo Jima where at least four of them would die and at least eight be wounded.

And the team — perhaps the most decorated in Marine history — couldn't even use the unit name, the 4th Marine Division, for security reasons, not wanting to let the Japanese know where they were or what they were doing. So the team was known as and described simply as the "Maui Marines."

It wasn't until the landing on Iwo on Feb. 19, 1945, that the Honolulu papers and wire services were permitted by censors to report, indeed, that the Maui Marines team actually represented the 4th Marine Division.

But what a season it was: the Central Pacific Armed Forces League title, five victories, no losses, a tie, and outscoring opponents, 164-6.

"The team was one of the most tenacious teams I have ever watched," said former Marine Ralph Most," who was brought up on Philadelphia Eagles games. "Smiley Johnson somehow psyched the team. Besides, we were mad at the world then."

The team had been formed on the orders of Maj. Gen. Clifton B. Cates, the division commander and onetime Tennessee letterman.

The coach was Lt. Col. LeRoy B. "Pat" Hanley, one of the famed Hanley brothers from Washington State. Hanley, in his 40s, won a Silver Star on Saipan. He had played on the Marines' fabled Mare Island team in the 1919 Rose Bowl and was the coach at Boston University from 1934-1941.

Maj. Frank Garretson, a Navy Cross winner and the assistant coach who later became a Marine general, wrote to his former Washington coach, Jimmy Phelan, for a playbook that was used during the season.

The players had won Silver Stars, Bronze Stars and Purple Hearts in the Pacific and wore the Presidential Unit Citation.

Recalls tackle Charles Fick of LaGrange Park, Ill., "The team started out as a rivalry between troops of the 4th in divided areas of Camp Maui."

And the East Gulchers, from the Infantry area and wearing red jerseys, faced the West Gulchers, from the Headquarters area and in blue jerseys, Oct. 11 in a game sponsored by the division Athletic and Morale Office, with Cates the honorary referee and Brig. Gen.

1

Franklin A. Hart, himself a football player at Auburn, the honorary umpire. A mimeographed program saved by Most listed 70 players.

Back Bob Schultz of Pewaukee, Wisc., said he "can never forget the Marines in the trees, on top of buildings, any place to view the (first) game," which ended in a 0-0 tie.

"The outcome of the game defies me," Fick said. "However, because it was such a remarkable game, higher echelon decided to hold trials between the personnel of both teams to create one team to represent the division."

The East won the rematch.

There were more than a few good men available from the college and pro ranks, plus some youngsters who would make a name during and after the war, such as:

■ Guard Howard "Smiley" Johnson, from the University of Georgia and the Green Bay Packers (1940-41). The winner of two Silver Stars, he was killed by artillery fire on Iwo, and a ballfield at Maui was named in his honor.

■ Si Titus, a Silver Star holder, was a center at Holy Cross and for the Brooklyn Dodgers (1940-42) and would join the Pittsburgh Steelers in 1945. He played at quarterback (blocking back in the single wing) for Maui.

■ Center Don Johnson was a standout at Northwestern and was with the Cleveland Rams in 1942.

■ Tackle Bill Smyth, a Marine V-12 trainee at Penn State in 1943, returned to the University of Cincinnati, and would play four seasons for the Los Angeles Rams.

■ Back Howard "Red" Maley, a Marine V-12 trainee at North Texas Agriculture in 1943, returned to Southern Methodist in 1945 before joining the Boston Yanks for two seasons.

■ Guard Jim Pearcy (Marshall), Johnson and backs Bill Kellagher (Fordham) and Bob Perina (Princeton) played for Pat Hanley's brother at El Toro on their way home late in 1945, and Pearcy and Kellagher followed Dick Hanley to the Chicago Rockets of the new All-America Football Conference in 1946. Perina would play five seasons in the AAFC and the NFL.

■ Tackle Norm McNabb helped Bud Wilkinson build his legend at Oklahoma in 1946, 1948 and 1949 and was captain of the 1950 national championship team. He would become president of Carl Albert Junior College in Oklahoma for 10 years.

■ End Al Thomas would letter at Northwestern from 1947-49 and play in a Rose Bowl game, before returning to the Marine Corps for keeps during the Korean War and be awarded three Silver Stars before retiring as a colonel.

And others would have made their name in football, too, but for the island campaigns and Iwo Jima.

Even Sgt. John Barberio, a combat correspondent who publicized the team during the 1944 season, died in the bitter Iwo campaign.

Wrote the Puuene Naval Air Station's Island Breeze: "Presenting ... one of the greatest football teams we've ever seen — pro, collegiate or service. This team was not only an outfit with skillful players and a splendid coach, it was above all an organization with indomitable spirit. ... We are very certain that these fighting men of the 4th Division had the greatest stamina and, above all, the finest team spirit of any organization we've ever seen."

"As we did our laps around the perimeter of the training area each morning," said Fick, "I, a youngster of 20, still was awed by playing with some of the stars I had only read about in the sports pages."

McNabb felt the same way. "As a young high school graduate, I was awed by their collegiate records."

There were other college standouts, among them end Ray Jenkins (Cornell), tackles W.A. Jones (George Washington), Tom Kinney (Syracuse) and Lew Ross (Clemson); guard Fraser Donlan (Manhattan), the holder of two Silver Stars who lost a leg on Iwo; and backs Dick Brown (Hardin-Simmons) and Bill Hallabrin (Ohio State and at Quantico in 1942).

After the island campaigns, the men were all muscle. Michels and Smyth at 220 pounds were the heaviest on the team.

The courage was unquestioned. Assistant Sam Mandich (West Virginia) also won a Silver Star, as did ends Bill Gaul and Bill Michels; tackles J.A. Alden, Ted Martino and John Sbordone (West Virginia Tech); center Pete Andrews; and backs Charles "Scooter" Anderson (Nebraska State Teachers), Edward Heath and James B. Wilson. Pearcy was awarded two Bronze Stars.

Befitting the magic of the season, a story on the team and its success, written by, of all people, 2nd Lt. Jim G. Lucas, a Tulsa Tribune newsman to become better known as a reporter and author ("Battle for Tarawa," "Dateline: Vietnam" and "Agnew: Profile in Conflict") was distributed by the Marine Corps in 1945.

On returning from Iwo, the survivors were called to a presentation by Cates.

"Each member of the team was presented a miniature bronze football, engraved with his name, position and the Pacific Ocean Area champion," Fick said. "This was something to be treasured by each of us. I sent mine home to my father (who had played for the Quantico Marines from 1919 to 1922.)"

And the story of the team didn't end on that idyllic island in 1944.

Four decades later, stories still were written about Johnson. The Green Bay Press-Gazette ran an anniversary piece in 1983 to mark the anniversary of his death ("Smiley's Example Worth Remembering," said the headline), and the February 1986 Leatherneck recalled some of his exploits (" 'Smiley' Johnson: A Team Player").

"The thing about Johnson was," wrote Don Langenkamp of the Press-Gazette, "he set examples in different ways. A dirt-poor orphan raised in the rural South, he had a lifelong friend in the Bible. But he didn't seem to annoy or antagonize people by his devotion to the Good Book, even in the rough-and-tumble environments of pro football and the World War II U.S. Marines."

Said the Leatherneck: "It was as a Marine, under combat conditions, that he proved his bravery. Because of his heroism, there are Marines today who will read and remember."

The same could be said of Anderson, Gaul and Simpson, who also died on Iwo.

Maui Marines 1944

Record: 0-0 Aiea Barracks, 12-6 Kaneohe Clippers, 19-0 Transient Center, 34-0 Ford Island, 48-0 Barber's Point, 51-0 Seabees. Record 5-0-1. Outscored opponents, 164-6, won Central Pacific Armed Forces League title.

Ends — Hank Acosta (Memphis State), J.H. Cotter (Citadel), Roy "Pappy" Crabaugh (Gonzaga), Chas. Fick, J.C. Floyd, Bill Gaul (KIA), Ray Jenkins (Cornell), Bill Michels (Holy Cross), D.E. Phelps, Salzbach, Bob Simpson (Wash. State-USC) (KIA), John Spear, E.F. Stull, Al Thomas (NU), Si Titus (Holy Cross)

Tackles — Jim Addie, J.A. Alden (Coast Guard Academy), G.R. Casey (Citadel), George DeBoef (William Penn), T.A. Johnson (USC), W.A. Jones (George Washington), Mark Kauffman, Tom Kinney (Syracuse), Ted Martino, Norm McNabb (Oklahoma), Edwin Parker, R.A. Ranker, Lew Ross (Clemson), John Sbordone (West Virginia Tech), Quinton Schaeffer, Bill Smyth (Notre Dame-Cincinnati-Penn State), Al Szymanski

Guards — Sandy Ball (Bluefield), H.P. Beaulieu, Mark Busser, Fraser Donlan (Manhattan), Lloyd Dosh (Gustavus-Adolphus), Ken Herbeck, Howard "Smiley" Johnson (Georgia) (KIA), J.S. Koenig, M. Lewis, Russell Martiq, Jim Pearcy (Marshall), V.A. Sarratore (Penn), Geo. Schuster, Joe Szarmack

Centers — Pete Andrews, Wayne Bloker (Bowling Green), Don Johnson (Northwestern), G.D. Regan (Penn), Chuck Schebor

Backs — B. Acker, Chas. "Scooter" Anderson (Nebraska State Teachers) (KIA), W.T. Askew, Frank Bausmith, Dick Brown (Hardin-Simmons), Quinton Burnette (Marquette), J.T. Colones (North Carolina), C.A. Del Bello, J.W. Dye, Bill Hallabrin (Ohio State), Chas. Edward Heath (Dartmouth), Don Hudson (Franklin & Marshall), Niles Joles, Bill Kellagher (Fordham), R.V. Kittle, Howard "Red" Maley (Southern Methodist-North Texas Agriculture), Bob Perina (Princeton), D.Y. Saylor, Bob Schultz, J.R. Smith, Art Sportore (Stetson), Tim Tyler (Rollins), Vic Uranowski, F. Whatley, James B. Wilson (Temple)

Also — Bob Austin, Jack Boenig, Tom Greene, Russ Handey, G.W., Harmeson, C. Rezzwicz, Ira Schaul

6th Base Depot 1944

Record: 0-14 Kaneohe NAS Klippers, 0-14 Hickam Field Fliers, 7-29 Aiea Barracks, 16-6 Waipio Amphibs, won at least one other game, lost at least one other (Central Pacific Area) (incomplete)
Coach: Lt. Bernard Gillespie (Scranton). **Assistant:** Lt. Major
Ends: Herman O'Kuinn, Teyema, Harle Walker. **Tackles:** Geo. Brown, Jim Julgen. **Guards:** Art Moskus, Alex Tucci. **Centers:** Harry Carson. **Backs:** Paul Fischer, Keith Grant, Jim Martin (Notre Dame), Miller, Horace Peeples, Warren. **Also:** Bob Jackman, Lee, Ed Roseborough (USF), Boyd Williams (incomplete)
(Peeples received a concussion during a kickoff in a game and died that night.)

Transient Center 1944

Record: 0-27 Kaneohe NAS Klippers, 6-12 (0-19) Maui Marines, 7-8 Ford Island NAS, 0-0 Aiea Barracks, lost to Barbers Point, 26-13 Seabees, 7-21 7th Air Force (Central Pacific Area) (incomplete)
Coach: Lt. Adam Kretowicz (Holy Cross)
Players: Ends: Christman, R. Palmer, Geo. Zellick (Oregon St.); **tackles:** E. Kulakowski, W. Kyle, Pyle, Bob Smith, L. Snyder; **guards:** J. Stephan, H. Wilson, Orv Zielaskowski (Oregon St.) (C); **centers:** A. Henry; **backs:** Couch, Darty, R. Davis, L. Lopez, Stroble, Frank Swiger, Jim Worst (Manhattan-Bucknell) (Navy All-Stars 1944) (incomplete)

Above And Beyond

The words Iwo Jima, Okinawa and heroism could be considered synonymous.

For on those desolate islands, Marines carved, clawed and scratched their way to the nation's very heart. The toll, of course, was high. But the heroism long will be remembered.

Football players, like farmers, merchants, professionals, teachers, students, government workers and those from other walks of life, helped defeat the Japanese.

Among the football players fighting on Iwo and Okinawa were these, according to "The Spearhead: 5th Marine Division" and the "History of the 6th Marine Division."

6th Marine Division (Okinawa)

Killed In Action

Aurel Bachiak (Eastern Kentucky) (Camp Lejeune 1943), Bob Bauman (Wisconsin), Chuck Behan (De Kalb Teachers) (Detroit Lions) (Camp Lejeune 1943), Tony Butkovich (Illinois-Purdue) (Camp Lejeune 1944), Bob Fowler (Michigan), Jim Green (Purdue), John Hebrank (Lehigh), Hubbard Hinde (SMU), Winston Hodgson (Georgia), Rusty Johnston (Marquette), Jerome Laue (Minnesota), George Murphy (Notre Dame) (Camp Lejeune 1943), John Perry (Wake Forest-Duke), Jim Quinn (Amherst), Dave Schreiner (Wisconsin), Larry Strawn (San Diego Marines 1944), Ed Van Order (Cornell)

Navy Cross

Behan, Perry

Silver Star

Fred Beans (Navy), Gus Camarata (Wartburg-Iowa State Teachers-Western Michigan) (Camp Lejeune 1944), Larry Halenkamp (Minnesota-Northwestern), Bob Herwig (California), Ted Ogdahl (Willamette-Pacific), Marv Plock (Nebraska), Spencer Silverthorne (Williams)

Two Bronze Stars

Frank Kemp (Yale)

Bronze Stars

Hank Bauer (baseball), Beans, Marv Bell (Marquette) (coach Camp Lejeune 1943), Harvey Brooks (Tufts), John Clifford (Notre Dame), Walter Moeling II (Penn), Tom Owen (Vanderbilt-North Carolina), O.K. Pressley (Quantico 1930-31, coach Quantico 1934, assistant San Diego Marines 1935, Norfolk Marines 1937), Hal Roise (Idaho) (San Diego Marines 1940), Odell Stautzenberger (North Texas Agriculture-Texas A&M), Ted Stawicki American-Morningside), Alex Wizbicki (Holy Cross-Dartmouth)

Letter of Commendation

John Bond (Texas Christian-North Texas Agriculture)

Purple Hearts

Tom Alberghini (Holy Cross), Joe Bartkiewicz (Indiana), Bauer, Bauman, Bob Beckwith (Connecticut) (Camp Lejeune 1943), Bill Bledsoe (USC), Fred Boensch (Stanford-California), Brooks, John Burroughs (Dartmouth), Frank Callen (St. Mary's), Camarata,

John Clark (Ohio University), Clifford, Tom Daly (Loyola of Los Angeles), Dunn, Mike Enich (Iowa), Len Fribourg (Ohio State), John Genis (Illinois-Purdue), Halenkamp, Patrick Hall (Louisiana State-Texas A&I), Allen "Scotty" Harris (Ohio State), Allen Hensley, Herwig, Bill Hofer (Notre Dame), George Jancosek, Eli Kaluger (Alabama-Miami of Ohio), Kemp, Bill Lazetich (Montana) (NFL) (same shell got him and Kemp), Steve Lewis (Yale), Dom Lisi, Wayne Marshall (Arkansas-Arkansas A&M), James McGillis, John McLaughry (Brown) (NFL), David Mears (Boston University), Tom Melcher (St. Joseph's), Bill Moates (Mississippi State-Duke), Moeling, Bob Neff (Notre Dame) (Camp Lejeune 1943), Ogdahl, Owen, George Pavalko (Villanova), Plock, Pressley, Stan Raytinski (Fordham), Jim Reeder (Ohio State), Bill Reynolds (Montana), Doctor M. Salmon (Oklahoma), Hugh Semple (Ohio Northern), Houstin Smith (Mississippi), Bob Spicer (Colorado), Stautzenberger, Stawicki, Charles "Pinky" Steed (Arkansas Tech-Arkansas A&M), Larry Sullivan (Notre Dame) (Camp Lejeune 1943), Bernie Tetek (Tulane-Purdue), Bruce Warren (Purdue), Bob Windish, George Witkowski, Jim Woodfin (Texas Christian-North Texas Agriculture) (Camp Lejeune 1944), Larry Yurkonis (Niagara) (Camp Lejeune 1944), Thomas Zapchenk

5th Marine Division (Iwo Jima)

Killed in Action

Wilmore Breaux (San Diego Marines 1943), Jack Chevigny (Notre Dame) (coach Chicago Cardinals 1932, Camp Lejeune 1943), Al Garcia (Santa Clara-Pacific), Brig Gardner (Utah-Colorado), Harry Lamport (Stanford), Robert McCahill (Marquette), Jack Lummus (Baylor) (New York Giants), Dwayne Mears (Pacific)

Wounded in Action

Edward Broussard (Louisiana Normal) (San Diego Marines 1943), Andy Chlebek (Notre Dame), Everett Dorr (Boston University), Robert Dunlap (Monmouth), Ed Kasky (Villanova) (NFL), Jim Myers (Tennessee-Duke), Ben Sohn (USC) (NFL), Bert Stiff (Penn), John Whelan (Boston College)

Medal of Honor

Dunlap, Lummus

Navy Cross

Harry Liversedge (California) (AEF 1918, Quantico 1920-24, asst. 1925-26, 29; asst. San Diego Marines 1930-31)

Silver Star

Clark King (Nebraska State), Myers

Distinguished Flying Cross

John Beckett (Jr.) (Navy)

Bronze Star

John Beckett (Sr.) (Oregon) (Mare Island Marines 1917, AEF 1918, coach Mare Island 1920, Quantico 1921-24, San Diego Marines 1925, 1931-32; athletic officer San Diego 1933; asst. East-West Game 1926), Tom Coll (St. Mary's), Robert Dethman (Oregon State), Milam Grevich (Minnesota-Nevada), George Stallings

Personnel

Headquarters Battalion: Beckett (Sr.), Hal Hirshon (UCLA), Stallings

26th Marines: Dethman, Dunlap, Tom Fields (Maryland)

27th Marines: Chevigny, Dorr, Kasky, Lummus, McCahill, Sohn, Stiff

28th Marines: George "Cotton" Gililland (San Diego State), Grevich, Liversedge, Mears, Myers, Whelan

13th Marines: Beckett (Jr.), Ed Kaminski (Univ. of San Francisco), Joe Muha (VMI) (NFL), Robert Thalman (Richmond)

5th Engineer Battalion: Ray J. Poppleman (Quantico 1927-28) (Maryland)

5th Motor Transport Battalion: Chlebek

5th Pioneer Battalion: Gardner

5th Joint Assault Signal Company: Townsend Hoopes (Yale)

2nd Armored Amphibian Tractor Battalion: John "Biff" Crawley (Kansas State)

11th Antitank Battalion: Coll, Pete Gorgone (Muhlenburg)

27th Replacement Battalion: Garcia, Richard Kelley (Minnesota), King, Lamport, Vic Ramus (USF)

Legacy From Guam

A Marine regiment on Guam almost could have fielded a football team of lieutenants.

At end, it could have started Dave Schreiner (Wisconsin, College Hall of Fame); at tackles, Bob Bauman (Wisconsin) and Frank Kemp (Yale), at guards, Charlie McAllister (Princeton) and Ray Segale (Oregon), at center, Bob Herwig (Cal, Hall of Fame), and in the backfield, Marv Plock (Nebraska), Bill Lazetich (Montana, two seasons in the NFL), Max Belko (USC) and Bill Hofer (Notre Dame).

All 10 but Kemp were second lieutenants.

A dispatch quoted Belko as saying, "Our football days are behind us. Of course, we could take our scrapbooks to Guam with us, but I don't think the Japs would be impressed."

Belko would be killed on Guam, Schreiner and Bauman on Okinawa.

With the 4th Marines on Guam

Alf Bauman (Northwestern) (NFL), Bob Bauman, Max Belko (USC) (KIA), Lee Bennett (Wayne-Michigan State), Jack Brennan, Clark, Clifford, Daly, Bill Doolittle (Ohio State), Fribourg, Hensley, Herwig, Hinde, Hofer, Lazetich, Paul Lentz (Guilford), McLaughry, Bob McNeil (Michigan State), John McTeer (USS New Mexico), Plock, Raytinski, Reynolds, Schreiner, Alan Shapley (Navy) (Quantico 1927-28, San Diego Marines 1932, asst. San Diego 33), Stawicki, Paul Szakash (Montana) (NFL)

Giving Their All

There was heroism on the home front, too.

Wounded Marines, at Klamath Falls, Ore., and Pocatello, Idaho, in particular, showed in 1944 that winning and losing on the football field were secondary to the game of life.

Klamath Falls

The Marine Corps Rehabilitation Center had some 85 wounded or sick personnel from the South Pacific with malaria, filariasis, mumu, elephantiasis and tropical ailments.

But a football team formed to help their recovery showed healthy signs, winning two, losing two and tying a game.

The Navy had assembled tropical-disease specialists at Klamath Falls to treat the Marines, using skiing, skating, basketball, hunting, hiking and other sports in addition to football in the regimen.

Capt. Jim Higgins (Trinity of Texas), a 6-1, 210-pound guard for the 1941 Chicago Cardinals and briefly with the '41 Quantico team, was assigned to Klamath Falls for treatment of malaria.

"There were some good football players, including several ex-collegiate players, and some tough Marines who could have played college ball," Higgins said.

Eight players weighed in at 200 or more.

The team, coached by Maj. Clyde Roberts, lost to Willamette, 33-14, and the California Ramblers, 13-0, but defeated Fairfield-Suisan AAS, 14-12, and Camp Beale, 8-0, and tied the Coast Guard Receiving Station, 6-6. A Nov. 12 rematch against Fairfield-Suisan was cancelled because of inclement weather.

"We though we had them (Coast Guard) beat, but their best back carried the ball every down for 75 yards — 2 to 5 yards at a time — to score and tie us just before the final gun," said Higgins, the Klamath Falls line coach.

The back? Emlen Tunnell (Toledo, Iowa), who would be a safety and kick returner for the New York Giants from 1948-58 and the Green Bay Packers from 1959-61. He is a member of the Pro Football Hall of Fame.

"We played some pretty good football at times, but it was a real coaching experience to know who could play each week," Higgins said. "I played and coached and even was hauled off to the hospital during the first quarter of one game with an acute attack of malaria."

Klamath Falls was ranked 46th in the country among military teams by one rating service, just a notch below more publicized MCAS Cherry Point.

Higgins would coach Lamar Tech (Texas) to a 59-38-4 record from 1953-62. The Cardinals would post the school's only undefeated record (8-0-2) under Higgins in 1957 and beat Middle Tennessee, 21-14, in the 1961 Tangerine Bowl. Higgins also would be men's athletic director 21 years and president of the Southland Conference. He retired as a colonel.

A program for the second Fairfield-Suisan AAS game listed James

Darnell and Bob Dravin at ends, Charles Taylor (205) and George Preston (215) at tackles, Bob Byrne and John O'Connor at guards, Harry Golden at center, Bernard Currie at quarterback, Frank Bancer and Jack Walters at halfbacks and Vince LaPaglia (200) at fullback.

The medics obviously were on to something: LaPaglia would play for Cherry Point in 1945.

Pocatello

At the Pocatello Naval Ordnance Plant, the Marine Barracks had 50 combat-tested Marines who had been released from a naval hospital but were on limited duty.

"None of us was in good physical shape, otherwise we would have been back in combat," said Archie B. Rackerby, the athletic officer as well as the executive officer, supply officer, PX officer, morale officer and other assignments.

Some had swollen glands from mumu or filariasis picked up in Samoa and various places; others had recurring malaria. And, of course, there were those with bullet and shrapnel wounds. But they could perform day-on, day-off security at the plant.

About two dozen Marines signed up in August to form a football team, augmented by half a dozen sailors.

"With no uniforms or equipment and the Marine Corps supply system had none to offer, I scrounged the Pocatello area for enough helmets, pants, jerseys, pads and shoes to field the team," said Rackerby, who also retired as a colonel.

Idaho Southern (now Idaho State) provided cast-off gear and uniforms. The Red Cross director at the Pocatello AAB turned over unneeded gear. And Pocatello High contributed used jerseys.

After an opening 27-0 loss to Idaho Southern, Ken Nolan, an air controller at the air base with minor-league football experience, volunteered to coach the Pocatello Marines team.

On short order, Rackerby had scheduled two games with Idaho State, two with Utah State and one each with Great Falls AAB, Hill Field and Ft. Warren.

The Ft. Warren game was cancelled, although the players grumbled.

"None of our Pocatello Marines was in good physical condition and, although they wanted to play ball and compete, I wasn't about to send them to slaughter by teams of physically fit pro material that outweighed them 50 to 100 pounds per man," Rackerby said.

Ft. Warren (5-4-1) had opened its season with a 21-20 victory over the NFL Brooklyn Tigers and also defeated Colorado, Colorado College and Idaho Southern (66-0). One service poll ranked it 24th in the country.

"When we explained the casualties that we already had in our first couple of games and the potential for more of our Pocatello Marines winding up in the hospital, the lads accepted the situation (cancelling the Ft. Warren game)," Rackerby said.

Against Colorado, Ft. Warren opened with players from Cornell, St. Thomas, Xaxier (La.), Santa Clara and Knoxville and had 16 others on the roster with college experience.

Pocatello apparently had only one player with such experience, tackle Bob Sarkisian (San Jose State).

But the Marines throughout the season played to the best of their physical ability.

"Sure, they lost most of their games but had a lot of fun doing it," Rackerby said.

Pocatello residents got behind the team and turned out for games, whose results were carried nationally by wire services and mentioned the city. And the air base band played "The Marine Hymn" as the team trotted on the field.

One rating service listed Pocatello as the 89th best military team in the country. The Marines simply could say they finished ahead of LaGarde Hospital, Bogue Field, Indiantown Gap, Knoxville Engineers, Camp Haan and Camp Beale, who were ranked below them.

The scores did not tell the real story of "these brave combat-veteran, physically impaired Marines ... against young, physically fit football players, mostly of college caliber," Rackerby said.

Klamath Falls (1944)

Record: 14-33 Willamette, 0-13 Cal Ramblers, 14-12 Fairfield-Suisan AAS, 8-0 Camp Beale, 6-6 Coast Guard Receiving Station (2-2-1). A second game with Fairfield-Suisan was called off.
Coach: Maj. Clyde Roberts (coach, MB Philadelphia)
Assistants: Capt. James Higgins (Trinity of Texas, Quantico), Capt. Ray Walters
Ends: Oscar Chapin, James Darnell, Bob Dravin, Delmar Hodson
Tackles: Joe Fiore, H.W. Hazen, George Preston, Steve Rauker, Charles Taylor
Guards: Walt Apt, Bob Byrne, Hosea Fowler, John O'Connor, Maurice Rothberg
Centers: Sam English, Harry Golden, Jack Walsh, C.J. Zabloski
Backs: Larry Albritton, Frank Bancer (Wake Forest), Tom Chance, Homer Chism, Bernard Currie, Ed Fadgen, G.R. Henne, Roy Hetland, Tom Hughes, Vince La Paglia, Mike Mastrorilli, Al McLaverty, Merlin Morehouse, Bill Salvador, Jack Walters

Pocatello (1944)

Record: 0-27 Idaho St., 6-34 Idaho St., 0-40 Utah St., 6-27 Utah St., 19-6 Great Falls AAB, 0-26 Hill Field (1-5). Ft. Warren game cancelled.
Coach: Cpl. Ken Dolan (USA).
Athletic officer: Lt. Archie Rackerby.
Ends: Elmer Beatty, Dan Compton, Frank Challinor USN, Bill Edwards, Vern Hooper USN, Lew Papin, Don Signor, Wes Wimberly
Tackles: Dave Maxwell, Maurice Pitt, Bob Sarkisian (San Jose State), Howard Schneeweis, N.H. Smith
Guards: Bill Brown, Preston Morris USN, Tom Peterson, Joe Wuycicki
Centers: John Cousans, Ray Mullen USN
Backs: John Bookin, Herman Celmer, Larry Conway, Don Cooper, Ray Dunkleberger, Walt Goldbach, Dick Hodgen, Fred Marks, Bill McCormick, Herman Morud USN, Harmon Noland, Noble Nussberger, Doyle Penton, Ed Rathbun, Wallace Seiheimer USN

Pocatello (1945)

Record: 6-36 Montana, 0-65 Nevada, 0-45 Utah St., 0-52 Utah St., 0-36 Farragut Navy (0-5)
Coach: not available. **Assistants:** not available
Roster: not available

The Boys of Autumn

Driving past the bland military architecture of the Marine Corps Air Station at El Toro, one hardly can envision a time when the Southern California airfield was a Notre Dame or Green Bay of football.

But, for a period in the mid-1940s, it was. And, blush, the fly-boys, not the grunts, got the most ink.

Coached by Lt. Col. Dick Hanley, who had played at Mare Island and Washington State and coached the Haskell Indians and Northwestern, and led by future (College and Pro) Hall of Fame back Elroy "Crazlegs" Hirsch, the 1945 El Toro team:

■ Won 8 and lost 2 — both to Fleet City, the nation's No. 1 service team.

■ Reportedly tried to schedule Minnesota, Navy and the Great Lakes Naval Training Station.

■ Reportedly offered to play Army and its famed backs, Glenn Davis and Doc Blanchard, for the national title.

■ Reportedly sought a benefit game with the National Football League champion, despite the Marines' training restrictions.

■ Faced controversy all season over Hanley's two-platoon offense.

■ Was accused of dirty football.

■ Broke a 16-game winning streak of the Air Training Command, 7-0, on literally a Hollywood finish, a 38-yard deflected pass play in the last 46 seconds.

■ Almost moved in midseason to Santa Barbara.

■ Had difficulty in scheduling college-varsity opponents.

■ Tackled and injured Heisman Trophy winner Frank Sinkwich of Georgia, playing for the 2nd Air Force, virtually ending his career.

■ Beat USC and UCLA (twice) in scrimmages.

■ Dismissed Kenny Reese, a back who dropped a punt on his own 5 in the first Fleet City game.

■ Played the team barber, Jim Tanner, in routs and even let him attempt some points-after-touchdown.

Despite the peaks and valleys, the Flying Marines — and there reportedly were only eight flying Marines on the team — consistently ranked No. 2 in the nation among service teams and had 36 players who had played pro football or would after returning from World War II. And this was the era of two-way players and small rosters.

The fame was nationwide. The Chicago Tribune, for example, gave extensive play, partly because of Hirsch and the many Midwesterners.

Interest in the team throughout Southern California was such that Los Angeles radio station KMPC broadcast some games.

Football magazines carried glowing accounts.

The team, consisting primarily of Marines with infantry-oriented or aviation-support MOS's, included:

■ Hirsch, who starred as a sophomore at Wisconsin in 1942, as a Marine V-12 trainee at Michigan in 1943, and at Camp Lejeune in 1944 in between OCS requirements. He would score 15 touchdowns in his lone El Toro season.

■ All-Pro tackle Wilbur "Wee Willie" Wilkin (St. Mary's) of the Washington Redskins, who stood 6-6 and at times weighed 290.

■ End-guard Bob Dove (Notre Dame), a 1941 and 1942 All-American and the 1942 Knute Rockne Trophy winner who would play nine pro seasons.

■ Quarterback Paul Governali (Columbia All-American), the 1942 Maxwell Trophy winner who was elected to the College Hall of Fame in 1986.

And the swashbuckling crew attained even more visibility in 1946 when 17 players from the 1944 and '45 El Toro teams formed the nucleus of the ill-fated Chicago Rockets of the new All-America Football Conference.

According to "Crazylegs: A Man and His Career," the Rockets "gave me $1,000 for signing and a contract for $6,000. I was flush."

Hanley lasted only two games and sued owner John Keeshin, a trucking owner and executive, for slander and $100,000. Years later, he won his case — but received only $1, according to a published report, after an initial award was reduced. Still, he was vindicated.

Hanley argued that Keeshin said the Rockets players voted "32-1 against (his) retention."

A triumvirate including Dove and Wilkin then coached until Oct. 29. Pat Boland, assisted by Ernie Nevers, a former Marine officer, took over for the remainder of the season.

Hanley had signed a three-year contract as coach and general manager in February 1945. Bill Hachten, a member of the 1945 team and an All-America guard at California in 1944 as a Marine V-12 trainee, said, "Hanley was to sign up as much of the team as he could. The various arrangements were being made. And Keeshin showed up out here."

Amid recurring news reports, Hirsch denied Oct. 17 that he had signed.

Governali, who tied a college record with 19 TD's, signed with Buffalo in October. He had been the Brooklyn Dodgers' No. 1 draft choice in 1943.

Keeshin announced in November that he had signed a "large percentage" of the El Toro team to '46 contracts.

"Don't worry about Hirsch. He'll be with us," Keeshin told Denver writers.

"I haven't even seen a contract," Hirsch told newsmen.

According to a Denver paper, Keeshin "previously announced he held his (Hirsch's) check for $900, endorsed by Hirsch, as a down payment on the lad's services."

Keeshin, the paper also said, "reportedly has been very free with his checks to El Toro boys and is also said to be saving them with the endorsements thereon."

Keeshin also said he had signed Capt. George Franck, a Minnesota All-American, away from the New York Giants. But he misspoke badly regarding Franck.

Hirsch signed in late March 1946.

In some games the Rockets, who played in Chicago's Soldier's Field, would start as many as seven former Marines. The Santa Ana Register headlined the opener: "Rockets (El Toro) Make League Debut."

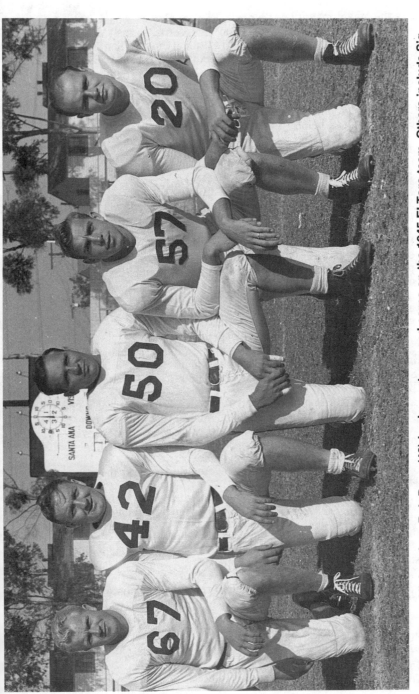

Notre Dame All-American Bob Dove (42) leads a veteran end corps on the 1945 El Toro team. Others include Sig Sigurdson (left, Pacific Lutheran), Pat Lahey (John Carroll), Bob Hein (Kent State) and Frank Quillen (Penn). All would play in the NFL or AAFC

In the meantime, at least a dozen El Toro players would return to the college ranks for the 1946 season: end Verne Gagne (Minnesota), tackles West Matthews (UCLA), Ed Sprano (Univ. of San Francisco), Ed Stacco (Colgate) and Bob Tulis (Texas A&M), guards Hachten (Stanford), John Hyle (Cornell) and Joe Venturi (Millikin); center Dick Handley (Fresno State), and backs Kit Kittrell (Baylor), Mickey McCardle (USC), Joe Scott (Univ. of San Francisco) and Ken Smock (Purdue). Chuck Page and Jerry Whitney would play for UCLA in 1947 after lettering at USC before Marine service.

And Bill Kennedy would be an assistant to former Marine officer Maurice "Clipper" Smith at USF in 1946.

Two who didn't return to the college ranks were backs Walt Clay and Ernie Lewis.

Said the "1946 Football Prevues," "Before Clay and Lewis signed with the Rockets, bowl talk was common at Colorado. Since their departure bowl talk has stopped." The team finished 5-4-1.

Hanley often stressed that the Flying Marines' pro reputation, at times, was overemphasized, and that the majority of his players had college eligibility remaining. A check of NFL rosters showed only 13 players in the two seasons had played pro ball, and seven of those but one season.

A group of University of Oregon alumni would seek out Hanley, a native of the state, as head coach in 1947. But Jim Aiken, then at Nevada, was chosen to succeed Tex Oliver.

■

It was a rollicking, fun-loving, boisterous, rough, macho group — about half-officer, half-enlisted — that played under the El Toro name in 1945. Some had fought in the South Pacific. Hanley had served also in World War I.

"You couldn't complain," end Pat Lahey (John Carroll) said, "because of the rank. So we used (Maj.) Ernie Nevers as a sounding board."

Nevers, in his early 40s, was considered by some the best ever to play football. The onetime Stanford back was elected to the College and Pro Halls of Fame.

Hirsch said there was a "great togetherness among the officers and enlisted. We never wore our bars."

LA and Hollywood were nearby. Hirsch later would star in three films, including "Crazylegs" and "Unchained," which would premiere in Wausau, Wis., and Jacques O'Mahoney, who tried out as end, would become more famous as Jock Mahoney and Yancey Derringer.

And there were Pacific Coast League games on Sundays under assumed names. (See separate chapter)

The war was over.

If the Brooklyn Dodgers of baseball were the Boys of Summer, these were the Boys of Autumn.

■

The Flying Marines would have won more than eight games in 1945 if the Coast Guard Pilots, Ft. Bliss, Norman NAS, Luke Field, Iowa Pre-Flight, Camp Beale, Amarillo AAB, Camp Cooke and semi-pro San Joaquin Cowboys hadn't cancelled for various reasons. None was in El Toro's class.

14

Hanley, the veteran, was a master strategist and tactician off the field as well as on.

There was a "blood and guts" intersquad game on the airfield itself, one survivor said, apparently to impress Army or the NFL champion.

Bob MacLeod, an All-America back at Dartmouth, was on the 1944 El Toro team ranked 16th in the final Associated Press poll. He recalled that Hanley's pep talks included "fake telegrams from the commandant of the Marine Corps."

MacLeod, a member of the College Hall of Fame, was the Chicago Bears' No. 1 draft pick in 1939.

Lahey, who played on the '44 and '45 teams, said the telegrams told the players flatly, "The next time (you mess up) you'll catch the next boat to the next action place."

Jean "Cheesie" Neil, one of the Marines' greatest all-around athletes with the San Diego Marines in the 1930s, was fooled by another Hanley ploy.

Hanley invited Neil's Camp Pendleton Boat Basin team up to play the El Toro "second string."

Out trotted Wilkin, Hirsch, Governali, Dove, Gagne, etc.

The score was 61-0. Hanley got his headlines.

"On my return," Neil lamented, "Gen. H.M. Smith held up the newspaper and gave me the worst chewing-out I ever got. And I've had some."

To many, the H.M. stood for Howling Mad.

Smith, in retaliation, decreed that Camp Pendleton no longer would furnish El Toro with players such as the 6-2, 188-pound Hirsch, who would score 405 points and intercept 15 passes as a back and wide receiver in two pro leagues.

∎

El Toro, even with the cutoff, had enough on hand to win five straight before the nationally publicized 48-25 loss to the Fleet City Navy of Pleasanton, Cal., and Illinois' Buddy Young in front of more than 60,000 witnesses (some say 90,000 because of servicemen let in at halftime) at the LA Memorial Coliseum. The game decided the national service title.

The game had been moved from Santa Barbara to accommodate a larger crowd.

After the game, Hanley said Young "is the greatest runner I've ever seen in 30 years of football — bar none."

The Los Angeles Times wrote: "In the wildest scoring duel the Coliseum ever housed, the Fleet City Bluejackets remained unbeaten (13-0-1) by whipping the El Toro Marines, 48-25, before 55,000 pop-eyed spectators. TD's piled up so rapidly for a while that the scoreboard smoked."

The San Francisco Chronicle saw it this way: "The greatest game 60,000 had ever seen — fittingly for the service championship of the United States — ended in the dramatic dark in this gargantuan bowl with Fleet City's famous Blue Jackets smashing the courageous challenge of the fighting Flying Marines of El Toro by the sensational score of 48-25."

The Associated Press added: "With the incredible Buddy Young featuring one of the greatest offensive exhibitions ever seen in the Coliseum, the Fleet City Bluejackets outscored the El Toro Marines, 48-25, to clinch the unofficial national service title before 59,143. ..."

But the LA Herald Examiner's Vincent X. Flaherty hit from the flanks. "Never have I seen an individual (Young) totally humiliate 11 topflight performers so woefully. He ran away from them. Made them look like novices."

El Toro had taken a 6-0 lead, only to have Young return the kickoff 94 yards for a touchdown.

Young returned a punt 77 yards for another TD. Yet, El Toro led, 25-21, in the third quarter before Young's third TD on a run of 25 yards. Then Fleet City's reserve strength began to tell.

There had been charges the week before that Fleet City was loading up by importing the nucleus of the Pearl Harbor Navy team.

"I want it known that we are not complaining about the addition of these men," Hanley said before the game. "We should do the same if we had the chance. More power to the sailors."

Afterward, Hanley remarked: "We just ran out of gas. They had too much reserve strength for us and wore us down. Do you realize they employed 16 backs?"

Because of a fit of pique by Lt. Gen. Roy Geiger, line replacements from the FMF Pacific team in Hawaii such as Bill Blackburn, Ralph Cleo Calcagni, Dick Huffman, Elmer "Buck" Jones, Fred Negus, Joe Signaigo and John Yonakor, all to play in the NFL or AAFC, by and large were shipped instead to Japan or China for occupation duty.

As a result, Kennedy (Michigan State), a blocking back, and Handley had to play 60 minutes against Fleet City. Hirsch was in for 57.

Overshadowed in defeat was Governali, who completed 29 of 45 passes for 228 yards and three touchdowns. And several passes were dropped, including two for apparent touchdowns by Lafayette King (Georgia) early in the game.

Governali "received as big an ovation as Young when he finally came off the field," the Times reported.

Oddly, El Toro led in first downs, 17-14. Hirsch (twice), Clay and Whitney scored for El Toro. Hirsch also returned a kickoff 61 yards but didn't score.

Surprisingly, 15 Flying Marines, Young and five Fleet City teammates joined forces for at least two postseason games: Jan. 20, 1946 against the Hollywood Bears, champions of the Coast League, and Feb. 10 against the Kenny Washington All-Stars. The opponents relied heavily on former 4th Air Force (March Field) players.

■

A number of combat veterans such as Capt. Hugh Gallarneau (Stanford All-American, Bears) and Franck played early in the '45 season before returning to civilian life and the NFL. Gallarneau had been awarded a Bronze Star, and Franck flew 17 missions before his Corsair was shot down in a raid on Wotje atoll in the Marshall Islands.

After crash-landing, Franck floated in a life raft 2½ hours before being picked up by a motor whaleboat while a Navy destroyer dispatched to the rescue slugged it out with Japanese coastal-defense guns.

Fourteen fighters from the 4th MAW protected Franck. "The best job of running interference I ever had."

Gallarneau, a key part of the famed T-formation backfield that carried the Indians to victory in the 1941 Rose Bowl game, would be an All-Pro in

ST. MARY'S NAVY PRE-FLIGHT
VERSUS
EL TORO FLYING MARINES
18 November 1945

$.244 Selling Price
.006 Sales Tax
TOTAL PRICE........ **25c**

1946 and be elected to the College Hall of Fame. Franck had been the Giants' No. 1 draft pick in 1941.

Backs Frank Balasz (Iowa) and Mort Landsberg (Cornell) and Tulis also were released on discharge points before mid-season.

Some Marines played the entire campaign. Capt. Jim Pearcy (Marshall), a guard; Lt. Don Johnson (Northwestern), a center, and backs Bill Kellagher (Fordham) and Lt. Bob Perina (Princeton) joined El Toro on returning to the States in November after recuperating from the fighting on Iwo, where Pearcy was awarded two Bronze Stars and Johnson a Bronze Star. The four had played for Pat Hanley's undefeated Maui (4th Division) Marines in 1944.

Lt. Wally Williams (Boston University), a back; Capt. Andy Droen (St. Olaf), a center, Capt. Claude Pieculewicz (Fordham), a back, and Lt. John Wickham (Tulsa), a tackle, among others, also were back from the South Pacific.

For that era, the line was big. Wilkin was listed at 270 but weighed more. End Frank Quillen (Penn) was 225, Gagne and Bob Hein (Kent State) 210, and Dove and Lahey 205. Tackle Harley McCollum (Tulane All-American) weighed 240, Wickham 245, Tulis 238, Chuck Huneke 218, Sprano 215, Stacco 210 and Matthews 205. At guards, Tony Sumpter (Cameron) was 215, Hyle 212 and Pearcy 205. At center, Sam Brazinsky (Villanova) was 208 and Handley 205.

The backfield had ample size, with Balasz at 225, Lewis 212, Kellagher 212 and Jack Lee (Carnegie Tech) 205.

Dick Hanley, who had begun coaching at Haskell Institute in 1923, was accused of being a Neanderthal for using the double-wing formation, as he had in 1944. He did employ a platoon offense — one of the double wing, the other the up-and- coming T-formation. Programs even listed which players would run which offense.

But he pleased neither side.

A tongue-in-cheek headline in the Flight Jacket, the base newspaper, followed the first loss to Fleet City: "El Toro Alumni Demand Resignation of Coach Hanley After Fleet City Bluejackets Humble Marines, 21-7."

And critics complained that his talent-laden teams won two games in 1944 by a mere touchdown and three in 1945.

Dick Hanley's official title was director of combat conditioning for the Marine Corps. As such, he at times had the pick of officers and men passing through West Coast bases for his staff and was in a position to hear about good players.

For example, four members of the unbeaten 1943 Recruit DI's team at MCB San Diego — Clay, guard Joe Daugherty (Tulsa), Lewis and center Carl Perkinson (Duke) — wound up at El Toro in 1944. Kittrell had played for the Recruit Depot Clerks.

More importantly, however, as director Hanley helped prepare many thousands of Marines for combat. As such, he might have had as much effect on the outcome of the war as anyone in Washington or Hawaii.

While Dick Hanley's national reputation was as a coach, he knew a few things about carrying the ball.

In 1918, at Mare Island, he might have set a Marine scoring record for Al Carmichael, Joe Bartos and Skeet Quinlan to shoot at in the late 1940s.

No one will know because record keeping was hit-or-miss. It is known he scored nine TD's in five games for which records were available. But Mare Island, with only 15-20 players, also won five other games, by 39-0, 68-0, 89-0, 32-14 and 12-7 margins, and Dick Hanley might have had multi-TD games.

He lettered at Washington State in 1915, a season the Cougars beat Brown, 14-0, in the Rose Bowl; and 1916, 1917 and 1919, when he was captain. The teams went 22-4-1.

Because of the flu, he missed the 1919 Rose Bowl game when Mare Island (10-1) lost to Great Lakes and George Halas, 17-0.

Dick Hanley, elected to the school's Hall of Fame in 1986, played with the NFL Racine Legion Legion in 1924 amidst his duties at Haskell.

When the Marine Corps called up Coaches Bernie Bierman, Dick Hanley, Pat Hanley, Ray Hanson and others in January 1942, the news was played on Page 1 by some papers, an indication of the seriousness of the war situation.

And it was a patriotic family. Dick, Pat and Harold Hanley, who all lettered at Washington State, played on the 1918 Mare Island team. Pat, who contracted malaria on Guadalcanal, received a Silver Star on Saipan and would retire as a colonel. Lee Hanley, who lettered under his brother at Northwestern in 1928-30, served in WWII. Dick's son, Bob, a Denver lawyer listed in "Who's Who," served in the Corps from 1942 to 1964, retiring as a lieutenant colonel.

Making headlines, and money, for the program in 1944 and 1945 was Maj. Ben Finney, business manager, showman, team spokesman, ticket seller, etc., who had been wounded in World War I and would serve during the Korean War before retiring from the Reserve in 1960.

Finney, a morale officer, suggested to Dick Hanley in 1944 that they form a Marine team from air bases within Marine Fleet Air West Coast (Marfair), including Santa Barbara, El Centro, Mojave, Miramar and Corvallis, Ore.

El Toro, commissioned March 17, 1943, offered a "plethora of air transportation and a stadium in Santa Ana that could be used as a home field," said Finney. He was an author, movie producer, leading man in the silents, big-game hunter and fisherman, rider on the Graf Zeppelin's maiden flight, and friend of Hemingway, F. Scott and Zelda Fitzgerald, Alexander Woolcott, Bogart and Harpo Marx.

"Many of the senior officers were about my age and a lot of them I had known from World War I, making it easy to do a lot of things that would have been impossible for a boot."

Statistics confirm how well Dick Hanley and Finney did:

Besides the 36 past and future pros on the 1945 team, there were 26 on the 1944 squad. In addition, during the two seasons Dick Hanley had at his disposal three Pro Hall of Fame members; five College Hall of Fame members; 33 draft choices, including four No. 1's and two No. 2's; five All-Pros; seven Pro Bowl selectees; 25 with service-football experience; eight first-team All-Americans; 12 College All-Star Game selectees; 10 East-West Game players; and 15 Marine V-12 players from the 1943 season.

El Toro was the home base in 1944 as the Flying Marines went 8-1. The 1945 team was set to play out of MCAS, Santa Barbara, but the city of Santa Ana asked at the last minute that the Flying Marines stay.

The opener, a 13-12 victory over the Hollywood Rangers, drew 10,000. But as Santa Ana Junior College resumed football practices, conflicts arose over the use of the Santa Ana Municipal Bowl. Again, the Marines threatened to move before the furor was settled.

Controversy dogged Dick Hanley, who had posted a 74-33-8 record at Haskell (1923-26) and Northwestern (1927-34) plus tying for two Big Ten titles.

He made a special appearance before the Northern California Sports Writers Assn. in San Francisco on Oct. 1, denying that dirty play was the reason El Toro couldn't schedule college teams. It didn't play a college varsity team in 1944 or 1945.

"I never taught a questionable or unsportsmanlike tactic in my life, and wouldn't I be a sucker to start now?"

Dick Hanley could have cited — but apparently didn't — travel restrictions, the small number of colleges fielding teams or that collegians could not play against pros.

Coach Bill Reinhart of Fleet City noted, "Col. Hanley is not noted for timid football."

But Coach Bernie Masterson of St. Mary's Pre-Flight observed later in the season that their game was "one of the cleanest service games we have ever played."

The knee injury to Sinkwich in an admittedly rough game at Colorado Springs, Colo., brought the charges to the surface again. Ironically, Sinkwich had washed out of boot camp at Parris Island because of flat feet.

Dick Hanley, besides calling on his coaching staff, used a brain trust for advice, scouting or expertise during the season and especially before the second Fleet City game. News accounts mentioned, among others, Nevers, Capt. Cliff Battles, Capt. James Orville Tuttle, brother Pat Hanley — a respected college coach in his own right; Lt. Col. (later general) Rivers Morrell Jr. (Navy); Capt. Tim Moynihan (Notre Dame, Chicago Cardinals) and Lt. Harry Wright (Notre Dame).

Dick Hanley had a knack for being quoted, but also for outlandish statements, such as the T-formation "would pass away as teams learned to defense it" and two-platoon football was "un-American."

And yet Dick Hanley could be an enigma.

Said Huneke, who played for three colleges, two pro teams and two seasons for Dick Hanley, "I never met another man like him. He was proud ... caring ... treated everybody equal. When we traveled, we were well taken care of. He never taught dirty football. I know the reports must have hurt him."

Added Hirsch: Hanley was "tough outside, with a big heart inside."

When the Coast Guard Pilots could not scout El Toro in 1944, Dick Hanley sent play diagrams to the coach.

A look at highlights of the two seasons:

1944

Record: 13-7 Fleet City, 56-0 Fairfield AB, 51-0 Beaumont Hospital, 6-0 San Diego NTC, 14-20 March Field, 14-0 Fleet City, 51-7 Coronado, 42-0 Ft. Bliss, 60-0 CG Pilots (8-1)

Coach — Lt. Col. Dick Hanley (Washington St., Mare Island)

Assistants — Cliff Battles (West Virginia Wesleyan), James Orville Tuttle (Phillips-Oklahoma City)

Ends — Bob Dove (Notre Dame), Harry Durham (Southern Teachers), Dick Evans (Iowa), Verne Gagne (Minnesota), Bob Hein (Kent State), Pat Lahey (John Carroll), James "Moe" Richmond (LSU, Southwestern Louisiana), Sig Sigurdson (Pacific Lutheran), Noah Waters

Tackles — Relden Bennett (LSU), John Brandt (Marquette), Jim Claffee (Purdue), Clyde Hall, Chuck Huneke (St. Mary's of Texas, Wyoming, St. Benedict's), Harley McCollum (Tulane), Lloyd McDermott, Dom Papaleo (Cherry Point), Frank Ramsey (Oregon St.), Ernie Stautner (Cherry Point), Guy Way, Wee Willie Wilkin (St. Mary's)

Guards — Larry Broering (USC), Joe Daugherty (Tulsa, MCB San Diego), Paul Davis, Sy Fuhrman (USC), Julian Pressley (Texas), Joe Ruetz (Notre Dame, St. Mary's Pre-Flight), Tony Sumpter (Cameron), Tuttle, Joe Venturi (St. Mary's of Texas), Hugh Ward

Centers — Al Crosby (Georgia), Dick Handley (Fresno St., USC), Carl Perkinson (Duke, MCB San Diego), Bernie Smith (Tulane), Roland Whalen (LSU, Rochester)

Backs — Frank Balasz (Iowa), Battles, Walt Clay (Colorado, MCB San Diego), Lynn Cryar, Phil Dufault (Bradley), Chuck Fenenbock (UCLA), Paul Governali (Columbia), Gordon Gray, Don Griffin (Illinois), John Hanna (Santa Clara), Charles Horvath (Penn), Jim Jones (Kent State), Bill Kennedy (Michigan St.), Ernie Lewis (Colorado, MCB San Diego), Bill Martinson, Bob MacLeod (Dartmouth), Mickey McCardle (USC), Tony Minetto (Pacific, Redlands), Walt Ott, Simon Palumbo, Charles Robinson, Bill Schroeder (Wisconsin), Ken Smock (Purdue), Harry Squatrito (Fordham), Jim Terrell (Oklahoma), Harry Wright (Notre Dame)

This was the only Marine team ever to finish in the Top 20, and was picked even though the base was only 1½ years old, most selectors' votes were from the East and Midwest, and games on Pacific time missed some newspaper deadlines east of the Mississippi. (College and service teams were ranked together in the 1943 and '44 seasons.)

Like the '45 team, it had difficulty scheduling opponents because of its reputation. Arguments still rage whether the '44 or '45 team was the best.

Former pros such as future Hall of Fame back Battles (West Virginia Wesleyan) and 210-pound guard Tuttle (Oklahoma City) provided the needed maturity. MacLeod, a true flying Marine, was back from the South Pacific, where with VMF-212 he shot down a Japanese plane in June 1942. Others, such as teen-ager Ernie Stautner (6-1, 230), a No. 2 draft pick of the Pittsburgh Steelers in 1950 and future Pro Hall of Fame tackle, soon would be headed to combat.

And it was a team of contrasts.

Gagne would be a four-time Big Ten heavyweight wrestling champion at Minnesota, 1948 Olympian and longtime pro wrestler and promoter. Even in his 60s in the 1980s, Gagne would rush into the ring if son Greg, also a pro wrestler, was menaced by villains.

McCardle would go into the movie industry.

Yet, 200-pound guard Joe Ruetz (Notre Dame, All-Navy at St. Mary's Pre-Flight), an aviator and later coach at St. Mary's and general secretary and six years the athletic director at Stanford, was a pre-med student and did graduate study in anthropology.

Wilkin would teach mathematics and social studies to retarded children in Deer Lodge, Mont.

MacLeod would become editor/publisher of Teen magazine, vice president of the Petersen Publishing Co., publisher of Harper's Bazaar and Seventeen magazines and be listed in "Who's Who." Tackle Frank Ramsey (Oregon State), 240, would become president of the Medford (Ore.) Coca Cola Co.

The Flying Marines were athletic. Clay; Dick Evans (Iowa), a 6-3, 205-pound former NBL player; Chuck Fenenbock (UCLA), Hein, Huneke, Lewis, Julian Pressley (Texas), Bill Schroeder (Wisconsin), Sig Sigurdson (Pacific Lutheran), Jim Terrell (Oklahoma) and Tuttle were on the 1944-45 station basketball team. The coach? Former Minnesota grid standout Dale Rennebohm. The assistant? Ramsey.

MacLeod also had played in the NBL. Matthews was a boxer, Lewis a shot-putter, and Pressley and Fenenbock, among others, baseball standouts.

There were a few growing pains. A game program, for example, still could not be located 40 years later. (By 1945, the programs were flowing regularly.)

El Toro opened with a 13-7 victory over Fleet City as Dove and Clay scored TD's. In a 56-0 triumph over Fairfield AAB, Fenenbock, Schroeder, Smock, Kennedy and Tony Minetto (Pacific, Redlands) each scored once, and Lewis and MacLeod twice.

A 52-0 pasting of the Beaumont Army Hospital followed as Battles, also a future selection to the College Hall of Fame; Fenenbock, Terrell, Lewis, Don Griffin (Illinois) and Pressley each scored once and MacLeod twice. Fenenbock scored as El Toro beat NTC San Diego, 6-0.

Then came a 20-14 loss to March Field as the other fliers took a 20-0 lead. Gagne and Battles, the NFL rushing leader in 1932 and '37, scored but a rally fell short.

The San Francisco Chronicle described the March Field game thusly: 'Strictly as advertised, maybe even a little more physical than expected, the 4th Air Force gridders slugged it out with a vicious El Toro Marine eleven before 16,000 chattering, screaming fans, largest athletic response in Riverside history. ... It was the roughest exhibition of hairy-chested, man-sized football I've ever seen," said the writer.

Seven El Toro and six March Field players were carried off the field.

The Flying Marines resumed winning ways, beating Fleet City, 14-0, as Schroeder and Clay scored. In a 51-7 rout of ATB Coronado, Griffin, Fenenbock, Tuttle, McCardle, Governali and Clay scored once and Balasz twice.

Then came a 42-0 rout of Ft. Bliss. MacLeod and McCardle each scored once, and Griffin and Pressley twice. The score might have been higher but for a harrowing plane ride to El Paso.

"It was the first plane ride for most," Huneke said. "We aborted the takeoff the first time down the runway. We taxied. Then the pilot yelled, 'Hey, will some of you big guys move up to the front?' "

The Flying Marines closed with a 60-0 shellacking of the Coast Guard Pilots, who had received the El Toro plays. Handley, Schroeder and MacLeod each scored once, and Griffin and Fenenbock (one a 99-yard run) three times each.

22

Wilkin and Dove were first-team Coast All-Service by United Press, and Battles, still a threat at 34, second team.

"I've never seen anyone in as good a shape," Huneke said. "His legs were all muscle. He would hurt students (in training) without meaning to."

Dick Hanley had introduced the T late in the season to complement the Pop Warner double wing (one of only a handful of teams in the country still using it) and the short punt.

Fenenbock led in scoring with 51 points. Griffin had 50, MacLeod 30, Clay 25, Pressley 19, Lewis and Schroeder 18, Battles 13, and Balasz and McCardle 12.

The Flying Marines were considered for the Sun Bowl but did not receive the bid. (Southwestern of Texas and the University of Mexico did.)

Efforts were unsuccessful for a Nov. 11 or Dec. 3 game with Randolph Field in the LA Coliseum. The Texas air-base team, led by All-America back and 1942 All-Pro Bill Dudley (Virginia), won all 12 games, scoring 508 points to the opponents' 19.

A Dec. 2 game with Bainbridge (Md.) Navy at San Diego also fell through. Bainbridge, led by teen-age running sensation Charlie "Choo Choo" Justice, won all its 10 games.

Battles would take over as Brooklyn coach in mid-1946 and in 1947 coach Hein, Huneke and Perina from the '45 El Toro team plus former Marines Al Akins, Saxon Judd, Bernie Nygren, Tex Warrington and Garland "Bulldog" Williams.

Daugherty (Univ. of San Francisco), Gagne, Handley, Dom Papaleo (Boston College), Perkinson, McCardle, James "Moe" Richmond (LSU), Smock, Harry Squatrito (Fordham), Stautner (Boston College) and Hugh Ward (Loyola of LA), among others, would play college ball in 1946, Lloyd McDermott at Kentucky starting in 1947 and Guy Way at UCLA in 1950. Way also would play at Great Lakes NTS in 1946 and Camp Pendleton in 1951.

By the time he reached the pros, the 6-foot McDermott weighed 240.

1945

Record: 13-12 Hollywood Rangers, 68-0 LA Bulldogs, 7-21 Fleet City, 61-0 Camp Pendleton, 20-9 Second Air Force, 7-0 Air Training Command, 20-0 San Diego NTC, 7-0 St. Mary's Pre-Flight, 40-7 Fort Warren, 25-48 Fleet City (8-2)

Coach — Lt. Col. Dick Hanley (Washington St., Mare Island)

Assistants — Bob Dove (Notre Dame), Mickey McCardle (USC), Wee Willie Wilkin (St. Mary's)

Ends — Dove, Carl Ellis, Verne Gagne (Minnesota), Ralph Harmon (Northeast Oklahoma), Bob Hein (Kent State), Ralph Heywood (USC), Lafayette King (Georgia, Cherry Point), Pat Lahey (John Carroll), Jacques O'Mahoney (Iowa), Frank Quillen (Penn), Sig Sigurdson (Pacific Lutheran), James White (Virginia)

Tackles — Joe Bechtold (Notre Dame), Bob Clarke, Ed Hardy (William & Mary, Cherry Point), Chuck Huneke (St. Mary's of Texas, Wyoming, St. Benedict's), West Matthews, Harley McCollum (Tulane), Ed Sprano, Ed Stacco (Colgate), Bob Tulis (Texas A&M), Norm Verry (USC), John Wickham (Tulsa), Wilkin, George Worthen (Utah)

Guards — Francis Crimmins (Auburn, Georgia Pre-Flight), Bill Hachten (Stanford, California), John Hyle (Georgetown, Cherry Point), Dick Jamison (USC), Bill Kennedy (Michigan St.), Guy Knebel, Jim Pearcy (Marshall, Maui Marines), Julian Pressly (Texas), Tony Sumpter (Cameron).

Centers — Sam Brazinsky/Bray (Villanova, Cherry Point), Al Crosby (Georgia), Larry Davis (Dayton, Penn State, Cherry Point), Andy Droen (St. Olaf), Dick Handley (Fresno State, USC), Don Johnson (Northwestern, Maui Marines)

Backs — Frank Balasz (Iowa), Frank Boyd (Riverside JC-Oregon), Al Clark (Boston Univ.), Walt Clay (Colorado, MCB San Diego), Don Ezell (TCU, North Texas Agriculture), George Franck (Minnesota, Corpus Christi NAS), Hugh Gallarneau (Stanford), Paul Governali (Columbia), Walt "Mouse" Halsall (South Carolina, Cherry Point), Elroy Hirsch (Wisconsin, Michigan, Camp Lejeune), Bill Kellagher (Fordham, Maui Marines), Milford "Kit" Kittrell (Baylor, MCB San Diego), Mort Landsberg (Cornell, North Carolina Pre-Flight), Jack Lee (Carnegie Tech, Georgia Pre-Flight), Ernie Lewis (Colorado, MCB San Diego), McCardle, Bill McDaniel (Schreiner), Tony Minetto (Pacific, Redlands), Chuck Page (Santa Ana JC-USC), Bob Perina (Princeton, Maui Marines), Claude Pieculewicz (Fordham), Ken Reese (Alabama, Cherry Point), Roger Roggatz (Drake, Eagle Mountain Lake), Bill Schroeder (Wisconsin), Joe Scott (Texas A&M), Ken Smock (Purdue), Aubrey Van Loo (Pacific of Ore.), Joe Venturi (St. Mary's of Texas), Jerry Whitney (Ventura JC-USC), Walt Williams (Boston Univ.), Len Wilson

In the opener at Santa Ana Municipal Bowl against Hollywood, Franck and Dove scored the TD's and Dove the deciding extra point. The program even listed a "Double Wing Back Team" and "T-Team."

In the 68-0 romp over the Los Angeles Bulldogs, Hirsch carried four times — for TD's of 31, 58, 52 and 81 yards and more than 220 yards rushing. Franck and Page both scored twice, and Kittrell and Lahey once.

But Fleet City won, 21-7, before 25,000 at Kezar Stadium in San Francisco as El Toro scored on a Clay-Hirsch pass play of 54 yards. Kennedy went 60 minutes. Gallarneau played the first half, then flew to Chicago to join the Bears the next day.

Hanley spoke of Fleet City having the "three greatest lines in the country."

Hirsch and Whitney each scored twice, and Page, King, Kittrell, Clay and Williams once in the 61-0 rout of Pendleton. Williams was some 35 pounds lighter than when he won 11 letters in college as a result of South Pacific duty.

A crowd of 10,000 turned out at Colorado Springs as El Toro won, 20-9, over the 2nd Air Force. Hirsch scored twice and Lewis once. The losers, with Bulldog Turner, Tom Fears, Ray Evans and Dick Barwegan, in addition to Sinkwich, were arguably history's best 3-7 team.

The Marine plane couldn't make the return flight because of mechanical trouble. An Air Force plane "brought us back," Hachten said. "The pilots never had been to El Toro. It was foggy and with the mountains real scary."

There were 35,000 on hand at the Coliseum to see the victory over the Air Training Command (formerly Randolph Field). Wrote a Los Angeles paper:

"A storybook touchdown gave a storybook finish to the game, and netted El Toro a storybook upset over a Skymaster eleven that was working on a two-year winning streak.

"With 46 seconds remaining and nothing but goose eggs on the scoreboard, the underdog Marines had a 'beachhead' on the Skymasters' 38-yard line.

"Governali, whose sensational passing had brought the fans to their feet and the opposition to its knees time after time, fired a long one at Dove, who was waving down on the 15. Herm Rohrig and Pat McHugh went high into the air to deflect the 'bomb' only to have it carom into the mitts of Hirsch.

"Hirsch, narrowly missing the sideline stripe, scooted for a touchdown."

Whitney had been stopped on the 1-foot line as the first half ended. Gen. Smith even sent congratulations and a "well done."

Hirsch, Governali and Kelleher scored TD's in a 20-0 victory over NTC San Diego in an away Armistice Day game.

The 7-0 victory over St. Mary's Pre-Flight before 35,000 at Kezar was as physical as the Fleet City games. St. Mary's, which tied Fleet City, 13-13, had lost quarterback Frank Albert (Stanford) but was able to use officers and former pro standouts such as Len Eshmont, Parker Hall, John Kuzman, Ray Mallouf, Jim McDonald, Ray Riddick, Bob Titchenal and John Woudenberg against service opponents. A 70-yard Governali-Lewis pass play with three minutes left pulled out the victory. It was the first penetration of St. Mary's territory.

The 40-7 triumph over Ft. Warren, at Denver before 23,000 in a Victory Bond game, saw Hirsch score twice, and Lewis, Page, Kellagher and Kittrell once each. Keeshin watched his future charges before putting his foot in his mouth with the Denver reporters.

El Toro and March Field, after their bruising '44 battle and with Dick Hanley and 4th Air Force coach Paul Schissler locked in a publicity battle, never did get together. Said Finney: "We'll play for money, marbles or chalk, in dungarees or barefoot."

So deep was the El Toro talent that the unheralded Scott (Texas A&M), a back, would be the Giants' No. 2 draft pick in 1948 and lead the NFL that season with a 28.5-yard kickoff-return average. One was for 99 yards.

Don Ezell (Texas Christian, North Texas Agriculture), Ralph Heywood (USC All-American), Perina and Williams would become colonels. Ezell, Heywood, McCardle, Page, Reese, Smock, Way and Williams, among others, also would serve during the Korean War, where Smock would receive a DFC and Williams a Bronze Star.

In civilian life, Dr. Hachten would become a professor and director of the School of Journalism and Mass Communications at Wisconsin, write four books and be listed in "Who's Who." Perina would be a prominent Madison, Wisc., lawyer. Gallarneau would be a Hart Schaffner & Marx VP. And Dick Hanley would manage a successful Chicago insurance agency.

The camaraderie would continue. Reunions and newsletters would keep the players in touch through the years, with California and Texas as well as Illinois and Wisconsin the favored states of residence.

■

The fame of the Flying Marines extended even into the 1946 football magazines.

"Football Prevues," for example, mentioned that Texas A&M had "an excellent crop of guards with a newcomer, Odell Stautzenberger, junior college transfer who starred with last year's El Toro Marines, likely to crowd out" competitors. Meanwhile, "Street & Smith's Yearbook" reported that Stautzenberger of the El Toro Marines "may crack the starting lineup."

"Street & Smith" reported also that "Marine sergeant Nelson Greene has just shown up at Tulsa. He is a 258-pounder and a No. 2

tackle on Dick Hanley's El Toro Marines."

Since both went on to brief pro careers, El Toro could *well* have used them against Fleet City.

■

Tragically, Wilkin's twin sons, John and Christopher, were killed in a 1965 car accident. John had lettered in football at Stanford in 1963.

But the El Toro names lived on, too. Gagne's son also lettered in football at Wyoming in 1970. Joe Venturi's son, Rick, was an assistant coach at Purdue and Illinois and head coach at Northwestern from 1978-80. He joined the Indianapolis Colts as an assistant in 1982. Son John coached an Illinois prep champion and son Tom was an assistant at Northwestern, Missouri, Eastern Illinois and Illinois State.

Chuck Page's son, Toby, was a quarterback at USC in 1966 and 1967. A grandson, Robert, was a Dartmouth linebacker in the late '80s.

Kennedy's son, Marty, lettered in football at Eastern Michigan in 1977 and '78.

Pro backgrounds (1944)

B Frank Balasz, Green Bay Packers 1939-41, Chicago Cardinals 1941, 1945
B Cliff Battles, Boston Braves 1932, Boston Redskins 1932-36, Washington Redskins 1937
B Walt Clay, Chicago Rockets 1946-47, Los Angeles Dons 1947-49
E Bob Dove, Rockets 1946-47, Cardinals 1948-53, Detroit Lions 1953-54
E Dick Evans, Packers 1940, Cardinals 1941-42, Packers 1943
B Chuck Fenebock, Lions 1943, 1945, Dons 1946-48, Rockets 1948; Calgary (CFL) 1950
B Paul Governali, Boston Yanks 1946-47, New York Giants 1947-48
B Don Griffin, Rockets 1946
C Dick Handley, Baltimore Colts 1947
E Bob Hein, Brooklyn Dodgers 1947
T Chuck Huneke, Rockets 1946-47, Dodgers 1947-48
E Jim Jones, pre-season Lions 1941
E-G Bill Kennedy, Lions 1942, Boston Yanks 1947
E Pat Lahey, Rockets 1946-47
B Ernie Lewis, Rockets 1946-48, Chicago Hornets 1949
B Bob MacLeod, Chicago Bears 1939
T Harley McCollum, New Yank Yankees 1946, Rockets 1947
T Lloyd McDermott, Lions 1950, Cardinals 1950-51
T Frank Ramsey, Bears 1945
G Joe Ruetz, Rockets 1946, 1948
B Bill Schroeder, Rockets 1946-47
E Sig Sigurdson, Colts 1947
T Ernie Stautner, Pittsburgh Steelers 1950-63
G Tony Sumpter, Rockets 1946-47
G James Orville Tuttle, Giants 1937-41, 1946
T Wilbur "Wee Willie" Wilkin, Redskins 1938-43, Rockets 1946

Pro backgrounds (1945)

Balasz, Clay, Dove, Governali, Handley, Hein, Huneke, Kennedy, Lahey, Lewis, McCollum, Schroeder, Sigurdson, Sumpter, Wilkin
C Sam Brazinsky, Buffalo Bisons 1946; Hamilton (CFL) 1947
B George Franck, Giants 1941, 1945-47
B Hugh Gallarneau, Bears 1941-42, 1945-47
G Bill Hachten, Giants 1947
E Ralph Heywood, Rockets 1946, Lions 1947, Boston Yanks 1948, New York Bulldogs 1949
B Elroy "Crazylegs" Hirsch, Rockets 1946-48, Los Angeles Rams 1949-57
C Don Johnson, Cleveland Rams 1942
B Bill Kellagher, Rockets 1946-48
E Lafayette "Dolly" King, Buffalo Bisons 1946, Buffalo Bills 1947, Rockets 1948, Hornets 1949
B Mort Landsberg, Philadelphia Eagles 1941, Dons 1947
B Jack Lee, Steelers 1939
G Jim Pearcy, Rockets 1946-48, Hornets 1949

26

B Bob Perina, New York Yankees 1946, Dodgers 1947, Rockets 1948, Bears 1949, Colts 1950
E Frank Quillen, Rockets 1946-47
B Ken Reese, Charlotte (Dixie) 1946; Lions 1947
B Joe Scott, Giants 1948-53
T Ed Stacco, Lions 1947, Redskins 1948
T Bob Tulis, Lions 1948
T Norm Verry, Rockets 1946-47
B Wally Williams, Rockets 1946, Boston Yanks 1947
T John Wickham, pre-season Rockets 1946

All-Pros
Cliff Battles 1933, 1936-37; Hugh Gallarneau 1946; Elroy Hirsch 1951, 1953; Ernie Suautner 1956, 1958; Wee Willie Wilkin 1941-42

Pro bowl
Frank Balasz 1940, Bob Dove 1951, Hugh Gallarneau 1941-42, Elroy Hirsch 1952-54, Ernie Stautner 1953-54, 1956-62; James Orville Tuttle 1939-40, Wee Willie Wilkin 1940, 1942 (2 games)

Draft selections
Frank Balasz, Packers — 16th round, 1939
Relden Bennett, Boston — 16th round, 1944
Walt Clay, Giants — 10th round, 1946
Bob Dove, Redskins — 3rd round, 1943
Vern Gagne, Bears — 14th round, 1947
George Franck, Giants — 1st round, 1941
Hugh Gallarneau, Bears — 4th round, 1941
Paul Governali, Dodgers — 1st round, 1943
Don Griffin, Packers — 12th round, 1944
Bill Hachten, Giants — 11th round, 1947
Ralph Heywood, Lions — 3rd round, 1944
Elroy Hirsch, Rams — 1st round, 1945
Dick Jamison, Bears — 21st round, 1944
Lafayette King, Rams — 5th round, 1946
Kit Kittrell, Giants — 21st round, 1944
Mort Landsberg, Steelers — 20th round, 1941
Jack Lee, Steelers — 10th round, 1939
Ernie Lewis, Eagles — 7th round, 1946
Bob MacLeod, Bears — 1st round, 1939
Mickey McCardle, Packers — 4th round, 1944
Harley McCollum, Redskins — 4th round, 1942
Lloyd McDermott, Packers — 6th round, 1950
Dom Papaleo, Bears — 4th round, 1950
Frank Ramsey, Bears — 5th round, 1938
Ken Reese, Eagles — 29th round, 1945
Moe Richmond, Boston — 21st round, 1944
Joe Scott, Giants — 2nd round, 1948
Ed Stacco, Redskins — 16th round, 1945; Lions, 23rd round, 1946
Ernie Stautner, Steelers — 2nd round, 1950
Bob Tulis, Lions, 29th round, 1947
Norm Verry, Packers, 7th round, 1943
Jerry Whitney, Dodgers — 25th round, 1945
Harry Wright, Redskins — 11th round, 1943

Service football
NAS Corpus Christi 1942: George Franck
Georgia Pre-Flight 1942: Francis Crimmins, Jack Lee
North Carolina Pre-Flight 1942: Mort Landsberg
St. Mary's Pre-Flight 1942: Joe Ruetz (All-Navy selection)
Cherry Point 1943: Sam Brazinsky, Lafayette King, Dom Papaleo, Kenny Reese, Ernie Stautner
Recruit DI's (San Diego) 1943: Walt Clay, Joe Daugherty, Ernie Lewis, Carl Perkinson
Recruit Clerks (SD) 1943: Kit Kittrell
Camp Lejeune 1944: Elroy Hirsch
Cherry Point 1944: Brazinsky, Larry Davis, Walt Halsall, Ed Hardy, John Hyle, King, Reese
Eagle Mountain Lake 1944: Roger Roggatz
Maui Marines 1944: Don Johnson, Bill Kellagher, Jim Pearcy, Bob Perina

All-Americans (first team)

Bob Dove 1941-42, George Franck 1940, Hugh Gallarneau 1940, Paul Governali 1942, Bill Hachten 1944, Ralph Heywood 1943, Bob MacLeod 1938, Harley McCollum 1939

Coaches

Cliff Battles, Dodgers 1946-47; co-coach, FMF Pacific 1945; assistant, Columbia 1938-43, 1946-56

Frank Boyd, assistant, Ewa Marines 1946

Bob Dove, co-coach, Rockets 1946; coach, Hiram 1962-68; assistant, Detroit, Youngstown 1969-89

Dick Evans, MCAS Santa Barbara 1945, NTC San Diego 1953; assistant, Long Beach CC, Nevada, Notre Dame; Cardinals, Cleveland Browns, Eagles, Packers, New England Patriots

Don Ezell, assistant, Camp Pendleton 1947

Paul Governali, San Diego State 1956-60

Ralph Heywood, 3rd Marines 1954, MCRD San Diego 1955

Bill Kennedy, assistant, Univ. of San Francisco 1946

Jack Lee, El Toro 1946, Ford Island 1947, Edenton 1949, Cherry Point 1951

Joe Ruetz, St. Mary's 1950; assistant, St. Mary's, Stanford

Ernie Stautner, assistant, Steelers 1963-64, Redskins 1965, Dallas Cowboys 1966-88

James Orville Tuttle, co-coach FMF Pacific 1945; Oklahoma City 1948-49; assistant, New York Yankees, Oklahoma

Joe Venturi, Illinois High School Coaches Football Hall of Fame

Norm Verry, El Camino CC 1952-60

Wee Willie Wilkin, co-coach Chicago Rockets 1946

Wally Williams, Hawaii Marines 1953-54, Parris Island 1955

Harry Wright, Portland Univ. 1949, Kings Point 1958-63

Administrative

Paul Governali, San Diego State; Elroy Hirsch, GM, assistant to the president, Rams; AD, Wisconsin 1969-87; Joe Ruetz, AD Stanford 1972-78; Wally Williams, Western Carolina

College All-Star Game

Frank Balasz 1939, Dick Evans 1940, George Franck 1941, Vern Gagne 1949, Hugh Gallarneau 1941, Paul Governali 1943, Don Griffin 1946, Ralph Heywood 1946, Elroy Hirsch 1946, Bob MacLeod 1939, Joe Ruetz 1938, Norm Verry 1946

Dick Hanley, assistant 1934

East-West Game

Bob Dove 1943, Paul Governali 1943, Don Griffin 1946, Bob MacLeod 1939, Mickey McCardle 1947, Joe Scott 1945, Ed Stacco 1947, Ernie Stautner 1949, Norm Verry 1943, Harry Wright 1943

Dick Hanley, assistant 1927-37, 1945

V-12 trainees (1943)

Bill Hachten, **California**; Ed Stacco, **Colgate**; Elroy Hirsch, **Michigan**; Don Ezell, **North Texas Agriculture**; Frank Quillen, **Penn**; Larry Davis, **Penn State**; Tony Minetto, **Redlands**; Roland Whalen, **Rochester**; James "Moe" Richmond, **Southwestern Louisiana**; Dick Handley, Ralph Heywood, Dick Jamison, Mickey McCardle, Paul Page, Norm Verry, **USC**

Those Crazy Legs

He's one of the most famous football players at the University of Wisconsin, yet Elroy Hirsch played only his sophomore season at Madison.

He had been a sensation at Wausau High School in Wisconsin, scoring 85 and 110 points his final two seasons. The 5-10, 122-pound Hirsch was third string and played but four minutes as a prep soph.

Four years later, he burst into national prominence, leading the unheralded Badgers to an 8-1-1 record and No. 3 national ranking in 1942 and acquiring the nickname "Crazylegs."

Wrote Francis Powers of the Chicago Daily News after a 13-7 victory over Great Lakes Navy: "Hirsch ran like a demented duck. His crazy legs were gyrating in six different directions all at the same time during a 61-yard touchdown run that solidified the win."

By 1943, Hirsch was a Marine V-12 trainee at Michigan, led the No. 3-ranked football team in scoring with 68 points and also lettered in basketball, track and baseball — the only Wolverine ever to win four in one school year.

One Saturday he jumped 24-2¼ to win the broad jump in a triangular meet and an hour later hurled a one-hitter against Ohio State. The Chicago Cubs expressed interest.

He played for Camp Lejeune in 1944 as military duties permitted and in 1945 was the star of the El Toro Flying Marines.

After signing with the new Chicago Rockets, according to "Crazylegs: A Man and His Career," Hirsch "hurried home to ask Ruth Stahmer to marry him.

"Her dad was a tough, old-world minister with one very special daughter.

" 'I understand you want to marry my Ruth. What do you intend to do with your life,' " he asked.

" 'Pro football. I just signed with the Chicago Rockets.' And, so help me, his very next question was: 'But what are you going to do for a living?' "

Hirsch had two years of eligibility left at Wisconsin when turning pro. He scored two TD's and was named the most valuable player as the College All-Stars defeated, ironically, the Rams, 16-0, in 1946.

Three injury-prone years did follow with the downtrodden Rockets, including a back injury, torn ligament in the right leg and a fractured skull in an October 1948 game against the Cleveland Browns.

Still, most players would be envious of Hirsch's 1946 statistics for the Rockets: rushed 87 times for 226 yards and a TD, completed 12 of 20 passes for 156 yards and a TD, caught 27 passes for 343 yards and 3 TD's, returned 17 punts, one for a TD, and handled 14 kickoffs, one for a TD. He intercepted six passes as the unpredictable and controversy-marred Rockets went 5-6-3.

Hirsch and the Rockets (1-13) tailed off in 1947. He carried only 23 times for 51 yards and a TD, his only pass was incomplete, he caught

10 passes for 282 yards and three TD's, and handled two punts and six kickoffs.

In his abbreviated 1948 season, Hirsch carried 23 times for 93 yards, caught 7 passes for 101 yards and a TD and handled two punts and a kickoff. He had two interceptions. The hapless Rockets again went 1-13.

The losing seasons were Hirsch's first as a collegian, Marine or pro. He would play on only one other with an under-.500 mark, the 1956 Rams.

A series of headaches resulted from the fractured skull and his coordination was marginal at best just prior to signing with the Los Angeles Rams. He had been the Cleveland Rams' No. 1 draft pick in 1945.

The move to Los Angeles, a winning atmosphere and a plastic helmet to protect him brought #40 immediate dividends. Hirsch carried 68 times for 287 yards and two TD's, caught 22 passes for 326 yards and four TD's, and intercepted two passes in 1949.

Switched permanently to wide receiver in 1950, Hirsch led the league in scoring (102 points), receptions (66), yardage (1,495) and average (22.7) in 1951. Ten of the 17 TD's were on bombs. He was named All-Pro in 1951 and 1953 and selected to the Pro Bowl three times.

In his AAFC/NFL career, he caught 387 passes for 7,029 yards and 60 touchdowns. He retired in 1957 and later was the Rams' general manager.

He also would become athletic director at Wisconsin, not realizing the athletic department had a $200,000 deficit.

Wrote David Condon of the Chicago Tribune: "Hirsch wasn't Wisconsin's first choice. The Badgers would have preferred to sign St. Jude, that patron of impossible causes."

Wrote the Los Angeles Times in a takeoff on the "Music Man:" "We got trouble. I say trouble. Right here in Madison. Trouble. That starts with 'T' and translates into football. But, there's a salesman in town. No, the name isn't Prof. Harold Hill, and he isn't selling band instruments. The name is Elroy Hirsch. ... 'Crazylegs' and he's selling spirit. Crew cut, smiling, collegiate rah-rah spirit. And you know, the people are buying it."

■

The Sept. 7, 1945 base paper at El Toro noted that "Lt. Hirsch has been 'visiting' at the base the past week, watching the local grid squad work out. He is stationed at Camp Pendleton."

Soon he was to run wild for the Flying Marines.

"When I learned that Hirsch and (Mickey) McCardle were in San Diego waiting to board a transport for overseas duty, I flew to Washington to have their orders changed," said Maj. Ben Finney, business manager of the El Toro team. "What the hell, the war was over. I'm not at all certain they ever knew just what had happened."

Swamp Success

But for a war, they could have fielded some pretty good teams at Camp Lejeune in 1943 and 1944.

Of course, World War II had priority, so football took a back seat at the hot, humid, swampy, primitive and remote base in coastal North Carolina.

But look at the players who passed through — five of them No. 1 draft picks — although not necessarily playing:

■ Quarterback Angelo Bertelli of Notre Dame, the Heisman Trophy winner in 1943, a No. 1 pick and a member of the College Hall of Fame.

■ Halfback Elroy "Crazylegs" Hirsch, who had played at Wisconsin in 1942 as a sophomore and at Michigan in 1943 as a Marine V-12 trainee. A No. 1 pick, he was destined for membership in both the College and Pro Halls of Fame after being with the Chicago Rockets from 1946-48 and the Los Angeles Rams from 1949-57.

■ Halfback Alvin Dark, who had starred at Louisiana State in 1942 as a sophomore and at Southwestern Louisiana in 1943 as a Marine trainee before attaining fame as a baseball player and manager.

■ Guard Chuck Drulis (Temple), who had played for the Chicago Bears in 1942, and would return from 1945-49 and be with the Green Bay Packers in 1950 and later be a coach of the St. Louis Cardinals.

■ Navy dentist Bill Osmanski, a former Bears' star who took a liking to the Corps, briefly coached the 1944 team and stayed with the Marines through bitter Pacific campaigns.

■ John Yonakor, an All-America end at Notre Dame in 1943, and No. 1 draft choice, whose son, Rich, starred as a basketball player at North Carolina. Yonakor played for the Cleveland Browns from 1946-49, the New York Yankees in 1950, Montreal (Canadian Football League) in 1951 and the Washington Redskins in 1952.

■ Back Johnny Podesto, an All-American at Pacific in 1943 and a No. 1 draft pick.

■ Back Tony Butkovich, an All-American at Purdue in 1943 and a No. 1 draft choice.

■ Tackle Pat Preston, an All-American at Duke in 1943.

■ Lt. Jack Chevigny, who played for Knute Rockne at Notre Dame but was better known as the coach at the University of Texas and of the NFL Chicago Cardinals. He would die on Iwo Jima.

(George Franck, an All-America back at Minnesota who played for the New York Giants and was a Marine aviator in World War II, got to know Chevigny on a boat to Iwo. On the day Chevigny died, Franck said "no" to his request to sit and talk in a shell hole.

("I told him the hole scared the heck out of me," said Franck. "His reply was that lightning never hits the same place twice. Less than 10 minutes later he was wrong. That still scares me today.")

■ And four future All-Pros: Drulis (1948), back Joe Geri (1950), Hirsch (1951, 1953) and guard Joe Signaigo (1949).

One had to have served at "Swamp Lagoon" to know how lonely and isolated it can be — even today. But in 1943 the base was in its second year of existence and had only basic facilities at best. Godforsaken was a term applied as much as any.

So the military and athletic powers-to-be decreed that a "big time" football team — a "million-dollar club on paper" — would be formed to entertain the troops and keep them on base.

If the Marines got some publicity out of it, so be it!

Brig. Gen. Henry L. Larsen, commanding general of the base, was an admitted sports enthusiast.

According to the base paper, the New River Pioneer, he "declared himself in support (of football), adding his wish that the Marines might use this undertaking as a way to make Camp Lejeune famous throughout sports circles in the same manner as the famous Quantico teams of the 1920s."

Some 175 turned out and an initial cut was made to 48 (18 of them officers). The Leathernecks (also Devil Dogs) had size: The line averaged 202, the backfield 191, although only tackle John Baklarz (Tempe Teachers) (230 pounds) and reserve tackle Charles Cann (235) were above 225.

A 10-game schedule was arranged, with seven at the base. (A game with Wake Forest was cancelled.)

Practices weren't to start until 5 p.m., which did minimize some heat problems. There was no admission charge to the games, but the public wasn't invited.

And who's to argue with success? The 1943 game against undefeated Bainbridge Navy and its famed teen-age speedster, Charlie Justice, drew an estimated crowd of 20,000 to the new football field. (A pickup game with Camp Davis in 1941 had drawn 15,000.) Cynics would suggest there was nothing else to do or nowhere else to go. Jacksonville, N.C., isn't Jacksonville, Fla.

Overall, the '43 and '44 teams won 12, tied 1 and lost four — three of the losses to Bainbridge, undefeated in 1943 and ranked No. 5 nationally in 1944 (among colleges as well as service teams), the other to Marine-studded Duke, ranked seventh nationally in 1943.

Both seasons got off to erratic starts, which had their repercussions.

In 1943, there were "equipment delays, transfers and other unavoidable factors" that affected the start of the season, according to the team's media guide.

And after the red and gold lost to Duke, 40-0, and to powerful Bainbridge, 9-0 (on a pass from Bill De Correvont to Howard "Red" Hickey and Harvey Johnson's fourth-quarter field goal), Chevigny came aboard as coach. Coach Marv Bell, a player (1933-35) and assistant at Marquette and Bronze Star winner in the Pacific, then became an assistant. It had been Bell's unenviable task to try to blend players with diverse backgrounds in the single wing, double wing, the T and other formations into one offense.

The remainder of the schedule was softer. The likes of the North Carolina B team, Ft. Monroe, Norfolk Marines and the Jacksonville Naval Air Station provided opposition, plus legitimate toughies Camp Davis and North Carolina Pre-Flight.

The Marines, with four regulars from Notre Dame's 1942 team, a good mix of Big Ten, major-college and pro players, and two stud Coast Guardsmen (Minnesota end Bob Fitch was All-Service), won six of their final seven games, and tied the other, to finish at 6-2-1.

Tackle George Speth (Murray State) had played for the Detroit Lions in 1942, and back Russ "King" Cotton (Texas Mines) for the Brooklyn Dodgers in 1941 and the Pittsburgh Steelers in 1942).

Center Joe Sabasteanski (Fordham) would play for the Boston Yanks from 1946-48 and the New York Bulldogs in 1949, and back Ray Terrell (Mississippi) for the Browns in 1946-47 and the Baltimore Colts in 1947.

Ends Chuck Behan (De Kalb Teachers and Lions) and George Murphy (Notre Dame), and guard Aurel Bachiak (Eastern Kentucky) also would die in the Pacific campaigns, on Okinawa, where much of the '43 team was sent as part of the 6th Marine Division. Behan was awarded the Navy Cross for heroism.

But 1944 was the season of peaks and valleys.

The announcement that there even would be a team wasn't made until Sept. 13, and the season was not to interfere with training. How prophetic!

The season opened uneventfully with a 6-0 victory over Duke's JV. But then Osmanski, who is in the College Hall of Fame for his play at Holy Cross, was to be transferred a week before the 53-7 loss to Bainbridge.

"The general wanted me to stay as coach," Osmanski said. "I did refuse the offer and said I'd stay with the Marine Corps — which I did. Then our 1st and 6th Divisions were sent to Guadalcanal, Okinawa, Guam and Nagasaki."

So it was back to the drawing boards.

Besides being a staging area for troops, Lejeune was a halfway house for officer candidates. Many trainees from the football-oriented 1943 V-12 class had gone to boot camp at Parris Island in June and to Lejeune for Officer Candidate Applicants School (OCA) in August, awaiting assignment to an overcrowded OCS at Quantico. But they weren't allowed to play football.

Candidates dribbled to Quantico, mostly by age. Of the five OCA companies, only A and B had departed by October. Many candidates went through OCA again.

"Most of the OCA talent (Hirsch, Art Honegger, Bruce Gelker, Sam Robinson, Chuck Dellago, Bernie Meter, Joe Signaigo, Gaspar Urban, Bill Gray, Grady Martin, Julie Rykovich, etc.) was in D Company," recalled Farnham Johnson, an end with Wisconsin in 1942 and with Michigan in 1943 as a Marine V-12 trainee. He was in E Company ("Kiddie Kamp").

Because of the pasting by Bainbridge, Johnson said, the "D Company commander, Capt. R.C. 'Maxie' Maxwell Jr., a former Georgia end who was decorated in the Pacific, was able to convince the CG that the OCA's should be turned loose."

"While Maxie got the ban lifted, we were only allowed to practice one hour (including the round-trip time from the barracks or in the field). This forced Coach Frank Knox to field two units, one from the old camp team, and the other of OCA's."

This worked until just before the second Bainbridge game when Knox tried to blend the best of the two teams (in five practice sessions), a move that didn't fly although the sailors' margin was cut to 33-6.

For the finale against Camp Mackall, Knox reverted to the two-unit program, which produced a 52-6 victory.

"I'm not inferring that Mackall was Bainbridge, however," Johnson admitted.

Coach Knox, only a private despite being the nephew of the Secretary of the Navy, and 34-year-old assistant Charlie Malone (Texas A&M and the Redskins) even had to suit up one game. Knox had played at Illinois under Bob Zuppke, toured Japan with Pop Warner's troupe in the '30s and played guard for the Lions from 1934-36.

Podesto, who also starred two seasons at St. Mary's (Calif.), completed 11 of 22 passes for a base-record 142 yards in the first Bainbridge game but was injured and did not play again that season. However, despite his abbreviated season, he was selected on Bainbridge's second all-opponent team.

Hirsch, in half a season, averaged 7.2 yards a carry, and the team won the five games against light opposition and had the loss against Bainbridge to close a 6-2 campaign.

And there was size aplenty, in contrast to the '43 edition. Tackles included Charles White (225), Bill Ward (220), Ted Johnson (245), Mike Hines (Notre Dame) (250), John Kozlowski (Villanova-Rochester) (220) and Angelo Giannini (220), ends Paul McKee (220), Oliver Poole (220) and Yonakor (230), and back Jack Guthrie (St. Mary's) (220).

End Charles Getchell (Temple) had been with the Philadelphia Eagles in 1943, and would play for the Colts in 1947.

In addition, 13 others would play pro ball after the war: Johnson, for the Bears in 1947 and Rockets in 1948; McKee (Syracuse-Rochester) for the Redskins in 1947-48; Poole (Mississippi-North Carolina) for the Yankees in 1947, the Colts in 1948 and the Lions in 1949; Yonakor; tackle Urban (Notre Dame) for the Rockets in 1948; Ward (Washington State-Washington) for the Redskins in 1946-47 and the Lions from 1947-49; guard William "Spot" Collins (Texas-Southwestern of Texas) for the Yanks in 1947; Signaigo (Notre Dame) for the Yankees from 1948-50; center Gray (Oregon State-USC) for the Redskins in 1947-48; back Bob David (Villanova) for the Rams in 1947-48 and the Rockets in 1948; Geri (Georgia) for the Steelers from 1949-51 and the Cardinals in 1952; Hirsch, and back Rykovich (Illinois-Notre Dame) for the Buffalo Bills in 1947-48, the Rockets in 1948, the Bears from 1949-51 and the Redskins in 1952-53.

In addition, back Bill Aldridge (Oklahoma A&M) would be drafted in the 30th round by the Packers in 1945; back Gus Camarata (Wartburg-Western Michigan-Iowa State Teachers) by the Lions in the 12th round in 1947; tackle Dellago (Minnesota-Northwestern) in the fourth round by the Eagles in 1945; end Martin (SMU-Arkansas A&M) by the Redskins in the 21st round in 1945; back Robinson (Washington) in the sixth round by the Eagles in 1945; and end Jack Tracy (Washington) in the fifth round by the Packers in 1944.

With overseas orders and confusion surrounding the status of the officer candidates, many players got in only one or two games, and the roster was lengthy. If participation was the goal, it was met; at least 105 Marines — some of them Guadalcanal veterans — got into games during the '44 season.

But Bertelli, Butkovich, Dark and Preston weren't allowed to play. Neither were Joe Andrejco (Fordham-Dartmouth), Chuck Bodley and John Burroughs (Dartmouth), Guy Cassels (West Virginia-Rochester), Hugh "Shot" Cox (North Carolina), Keith Curry (San Diego State-TCU-North Texas Agriculture), Earl Maves (Wisconsin-Michigan), Carl Schiller (Montana-Western Michigan), Bert Stiff (Penn), Frank Sweeney (West Chester-Franklin & Marshall), Barney Werner (Syracuse-Rochester), nor Norm West (Eastern Oregon-Pacific). All but Stiff had played college ball as Marine V-12 trainees in 1943.

By Christmas Eve, Butkovich — the Cleveland Rams' top pick in 1944 — was playing football on Guadalcanal in a game called the Mosquito Bowl. On April 18, 1945, Cpl. Butkovich was killed in action on Okinawa.

1943

Record: 0-40 Duke, 0-9 Bainbridge NTC, 26-0 North Carolina B team, 51-0 Ft. Monroe, 20-7 Jacksonville NAS, 14-0 Camp Davis, 55-6 Norfolk Marines, 14-14 North Carolina Pre-Flight, 13-6 Jacksonville NAS, 13-6 Camp Davis. (6-2-1). game with Wake Forest canceled. 20,000 attended Bainbridge game.

Coaches: Lt. Marv Bell (Marquette), Lt. Jack Chevigny (Notre Dame) (KIA)

Assistants: Bell, Lt. Don Fleming (Creighton), Ted Johnson, Lt. Bill MacKay (Houston), Lt. Jack Thurner (North Carolina State), Lt. Al Tillman (NYU)

Ends: Chuck Behan (De Kalb Teachers) (KIA), Bill Dawson (Baldwin-Wallace), Bob Fitch USCG (Minnesota), J.B. Frey (Quantico), Hank Maliszewski (Duquesne), Al Mannino (Iowa), Bill Meyer, Dick Mitchell, Ed Murphy (Holy Cross), George Murphy (Notre Dame) (KIA), Charles Reid (Cincinnati), Dick Stalnaker, Francis Wirt

Tackles: John Baklarz (Tempe Teachers), George Bytsura (Duquesne), Charles Cann, Angelo Giannini, John Heard (Oklahoma), James Meek USCG (West Texas), Bob Neff (Notre Dame), George Speth (Murray State), Larry Sullivan (Notre Dame)

Guards: Auriel Bachiak (Eastern Kentucky) (KIA), Bob Beckwith (Connecticut), John Bochynski (Temple), Chuck Drulis (Temple), Stan Erickson (Georgetown), Don Fetter (Ohio State), Gus Fracassi, Alex Leugo (Purdue), Leon Mandelbaum (North Carolina State), Tom Ponsalle (Georgetown)

Centers: Bob Cales (Western Kentucky), Charles Cooper (Hofstra), John Greer (Colgate), John Lanahan (Notre Dame), Paul Murphy, Joe Sabasteanski (Fordham)

Backs: Dom Anicito, Walt Bergman (Colorado A&M), John Brown (Florida), Matt Constable (Ohio University), Jim Cotton (Texas Mines), Payul Dubenetzky (Temple), Cowboy Ferris (Montana), Fleming (p-c), Ed Ford, Tom Hall (Shurtleff), Clarage Irby (Auburn), Frank Kiesecker (Manhattan), Alex Kleinhenz, Allan Lang (Xavier of Ohio), Bill Peace (Duke) (Jacksonville NAS 1942), Jim Phillips (Northwestern), Gil Purucker (Peru Teachers), Ray Savage (Evansville), Ed Sexton, Ray Terrell (Mississippi) (Jacksonville NAS 1942, Quantico 1949-50, assistant Quantico 1951, asst. 12th Marines 1954), Albin Vaznelis (Morehead State)

1944

Record: 6-0 Duke JV, 7-53 Bainbridge Navy, 33-0 Camp Detrick, 33-0 Kinston MCAS, 41-0 Bogue Field, 26-0 Ft. Monroe, 6-33 Bainbridge Navy, 52-6 Camp Mackall. (6-2).

Coaches: Lt. Bill Osmanski USN (Holy Cross), Pvt. Frank Knox (New Hampshire-Illinois)

Assistants: Cpl. Ted "Swede" Johnson, Pfc. Stan Kucab (Scranton), Lt. E.B. Lerch (Ohio State), Pfc. Charlie Malone (Texas A&M), Capt. John Winberry (Notre Dame)

Ends: Ken Daniels (Maryland-Emory & Henry-North Carolina), Dorso, Bill Few (Pensacola), Charles Getchell (Temple) (coach El Toro 1951, assistant 1952), Ernie Gottlieb, John Grout (Yale) (Cherry Point 1945), Farnham Johnson (Wisconsin-Michigan), Bill LaFleur (Dayton-Penn State) (MCRD San Diego 1950-51), Larry Lynch (Notre Dame), Malone (p-c), Grady Martin (SMU-

Arkansas A&M), Paul McKee (Syracuse-Rochester) (Hawaii Marines 1945), Bob Miller, Newton, Hank Olshanski (Wisconsin-Michigan), Oslovski, Oliver Poole (Mississippi-North Carolina), Edmunds Powell (Duquesne), Charles Reed, Ed Roark (Washington), Vic Ruffenbach, Paul Steel, Todd, John Tracy (Washington), Ulstad, John Yonakor (Notre Dame) (Hawaii Marines 1945)

Tackles: George Alevizon (CCNY), Bruce Gelker (Santa Ana JC-USC), Angelo Giannini, Mike Hines (Notre Dame), Johnson (p-c), Steve Kitis, John Kozlowski (Rochester), Larry Smith (Akron), Harry Treglawney (North Dakota State-Western Michigan), Gaspar Urban (Notre Dame) (Hawaii Marines 1945, assistant Camp Lejeune 1951), Bill "Smiley" Ward (Washington State-Washington),, Charles White (Tennessee)

Guards: Earl Braunlich (Bucknell), Vince Carlesimo (Villanova), W.H. "Spot" Collins (Texas-Southwestern of Texas), Culo, Chuck Dellago (Minnesota-Northwestern) (Camp Pendleton 1951), Bill Evans, Gus Fracassi, Sy Fuhrman (USC) (El Toro 1944, Hawaii Marines 1945), Cecil Gordon, Bernie Meter (Notre Dame), George Meyers (Washington) (Camp Pendleton 1945), Joe Signaigo (Notre Dame) (Hawaii Marines 1945), Tony Zullo (Tufts)

Centers: Bill Gray (Oregon State-USC) (Hawaii Marines 1945), John Greer (Colgate), Carroll Hauptly, Don Henderson (Tennessee Tech), Dan Hirsch (Memphis State), "Black Mike" Kerns (Villanova-Penn State), Murphy, Mario Pera (Santa Clara-Pacific), Bill "Potch" Pottenger (Springfield, Mo. Teachers) (assistant Camp Pendleton 1951), Scott Schuster (Ohio University-Michigan), Jim Sullivan (Notre Dame), Jim Woodfin (TCU-North Texas Agriculture)

Backs: Bill Aldridge (Oklahoma A&M), Balough, Batory, Gus Camarata (Wartburg-Western Michigan-Iowa State Teachers), Bob David (Notre Dame-Villanova) (Hawaii Marines 1945), Ken "Whitey" Davis (Cornell) (Georgia Pre-Flight 1942), Joe Ferem (St. Mary's-Pacific) (Hawaii Marines 1945, Camp Pendleton 1951), Cowboy Ferris (Montana), Ed Ford, Joe Geri (Georgia) (Cherry Point 1945), George Graves (Penn), Jack Guthrie (St. Mary's), Harris, Elroy "Crazylegs" Hirsch (Wisconsin-Michigan) (El Toro 1945), Art Honegger (California) (Camp Pendleton 1945), Clarage Irby (Auburn), John Kelly (Western Michigan), Bob Kettlewell, Alex Kleinhenz, Mike Kostynick (Manhattan-Bucknell), Bruce Locke (NW Mississippi JC), Lowry, George Lund (Springfield), Bob Madden (Xavier of Ohio), Doug Miller (Santa Monica JC-USC), Nick Milosevich (Southern Illinois-Western Michigan), Ellis Paulk (Mercer), Bill Peace (Duke) (Jacksonville NAS 1942), Bob Phillips, Johnny Podesto (St. Mary's-Pacific) (Hawaii Marines 1945), Mike Rakowski, Pat Richard (Ohio State), Sam Robinson (Washington), Julie Rykovich (Illinois-Notre Dame) (Hawaii Marines 1945), Tilden Smiley, Sowle, Paul Weaver (Penn State), Mack Winter (West Texas), Larry Yurkonis (Niagara)

Also: John Hickey, Russ Hillegass, Russ Jones, John Massarella

The Marine Corps also publicized its football program on postcards

What Might Have Been

There were big plans afoot for the 1945 season at Camp Lejeune.

This schedule had been announced:

Sept. 23: North Carolina; **Sept. 29:** Duke (Griffith Stadium, Washington); **Oct. 7:** Cherry Point; **Oct. 19:** at North Carolina Pre-Flight; **Oct. 21:** Camp Peary; **Oct. 28:** Air Training Command; **Nov. 11:** at Camp Peary; **Nov. 18:** Camp Davis; **Dec. 9:** at Cherry Point

But demobilization and other factors resulted in cancellation of the program.

Maj. Lonnie McCurry (Texas Tech) had been announced as head coach, with Capt. Jim Higgins (Trinity of Texas, Chicago Cardinals, 1st MarDiv 1943, Klamath Falls assistant 1944) as assistant.

According to Higgins, later the football coach and athletic director at Lamar, he reported to Lejeune in the spring of 1945 after recovering from malaria at a Klamath Falls, Ore., treatment center.

As athletic director, "I was ordered to assemble and coach a team and make a suitable schedule. Money was no object, and they promised (and delivered) the clout to order in any football-playing Marine I could find."

Prospects looked good "for a full schedule of good games," Higgins said, adding that Elroy "Crazylegs" Hirsch and Pat Harder, two former Wisconsin stars, were potential team members. Then the Marine Corps "decided that, with an impending invasion of Japan looming, it was no time for Marines to be playing football."

Marines he had recruited "received orders overseas," as did Higgins, who was to report to the 5th Division.

A base intramural program was arranged instead. Among players were ends Thurman Owens (Tulane, Southwestern Louisiana, Cincinnati, Camp Pendleton 1951), Don O'Neil (Denison, Missouri Valley, Pendleton 1951) and backs Pete Sultis (Rice, Southwestern Louisiana) and Bob Gary (Texas A&M). Art Young (Springfield, Dartmouth) was a coach.

Montford Point was the lone Lejeune team to play an outside schedule (see separate chapter).

1945

No base team. Maj. Lonnie McCurry (Texas Tech) was to have been coach, with Capt. Jim Higgins (Trinity of Texas) (assistant Klamath Falls 1944) the assistant, before the schedule was canceled.

Montford Point played a nine-game schedule against black colleges and teams.

1946

No base team.

1947

Record: 13-6 USS Roosevelt, 12-7 Little Creek. (2-0). A 2nd MarDiv all-star team, made up of players from five teams, won the Group I Atlantic Fleet title with the victory over the Roosevelt. The 2nd MarDiv also beat Little Creek but was eliminated from further title contention because it had not played a "representative" schedule, a decision that obviously upset the Lejeune community. **Coach:** NA. **Assistants:** NA. **Players:** NA

What Potential!

But for a scorelist in The Official NCAA Football Guide, the exploits of the 1943 team at Cherry Point might have been forgotten — and become one of the Corps' great untold stories.

It is a positive story about some teen-agers who went off to war.

A story of tapping potential, not untapped potential.

The guide simply gave the scores of the four games the Flyers won and the two they lost. It said the coach was a Lt. Bill Hopp.

All well and good. But that was it.

The Marine Corps had no clippings. No base newspapers were available. No other football publications carried information on the team other than to say as one did the team was based at Cherry Pointe. Wire-service stories were brief. Four decades later, the military opponents were difficult to come by.

Someone thought Hopp might be related to the famous Nebraska Hopps, Johnny and Harry, but that tip proved groundless.

Another thought Hopp was from Minnesota. But he wasn't in the school's lettermen's list although he was mentioned as a leading guard candidate in the 1941 Illustrated Football Annual.

"No assay of the (Gophers') line is complete without considering guard Bill Hopp (185) and ... , furious charging guards, providing reserve strength."

"Sorry, but the Alumni Office does not have any info on Bill Hopp," the university said.

Oh well, the air station at Cherry Point — more often than not called Cheerless Point — was only a year old, and the team couldn't have been of much importance, right?

Wrong.

It took several years to piece together the background and to locate some of the players.

What players!!!

■ They were young then, but tackles Leo Nomellini, 19, and Ernie Stautner, 18, both would be elected to the Pro Hall of Fame, and Nomellini — an All-American in 1948 and 1949 — to the College Hall of Fame.

■ End Lafayette King (Georgia) played for the Buffalo Bisons (1946) and Bills (1947) and the Chicago Rockets (1948) and Hornets (1949) in the All-America Football Conference.

■ End Herb Siegert, 19, was a guard for Illinois from 1946-48, captained the team in '48 and was with the Washington Redskins (1949-51) and Detroit Lions and New York Yanks in 1951.

■ Guard Jim Cullom, 18, played for Cal from 1946-49, for the New York Yanks in 1951, for the Quantico Marines in 1951 after being recalled, and fought again — in Korea. (He and Siegert served together in the South Pacific but faced each other in a 1951 NFL game.)

■ Guard Dom Papaleo starred with Stautner at Boston College from

1946-49, and the 223-pounder was drafted by the Bears in the 4th round in 1950.

■ Center Sam Bray (Villanova) also played for the Bisons in 1946 and in the Canadian Football League.

"My real name is Brazinsky," Bray admitted. "When I entered Villanova as a freshman, they shortened my name to Bray."

■ Back Hugo Marcolini returned to play at St. Bonaventure and for the Brooklyn Dodgers in 1948.

And there were others with college experience.

Correspondence with Cullom on an unrelated matter provided the breakthrough.

"We had a bunch of good ones on the team," Cullom recalled. "Hugh Gallarneau (Stanford, Chicago Bears, College Hall of Fame) played half a game that year. He came out of the stands to help the cause against Ft. Lee, Va."

But the presence of Nomellini and Stautner was the story.

"Nomellini, who had never played high school ball in Chicago, was discovered on guard duty by Hopp, who recruited him to football, then to Minnesota," Cullom said.

Ronald Mendell and Timothy Phares, in their "Who's Who in Football," called Nomellini a "ferocious and intimidating defensive tackle."

That he was. "Leo the Lion" was an All-Pro six times, played in 10 Pro Bowls, and appeared in 174 consecutive games for the 49ers from 1950-63 — and 266 overall.

If that wasn't enough, he and Art "Boom Boom" Michalik, another former Marine and 49ers player, teamed to form a devastating tag team in pro wrestling.

As for Stautner, he was the "toughest SOB I ever knew," said Cullom, as a mark of respect. And he had played against quite a few.

Former pro coach Buddy Parker called Stautner "as tough as any man who ever played."

"Who's Who" described him as a "tremendously strong, aggressive, durable defensive tackle. He had huge, punishing hands."

Stautner played in nine Pro Bowls and was All-Pro twice while playing for the Steelers from 1950-63, during which he recovered 21 fumbles and in 1962 recorded three safeties.

After being an assistant with the Steelers and Redskins, Stautner joined the Dallas Cowboys' staff in 1966 for a two-decade stay and was an architect of the famed "Doomsday Defense." TV coverage often picked up Stautner and ex-Marine Jim Myers on the sideline with Coach Tom Landry.

Besides being teen-age tackles together at Cherry Point, there were remarkable parallels between Nomellini and Stautner. Both came to this country from Europe. Nomellini was born in Lucca, Italy, Stautner in Calm, Bavaria.

Both played the same years of college ball and hit the National Football League in 1950 to last 14 seasons.

And they were almost teammates on the 49ers. San Francisco, then with the AAFC, made Stautner its top choice in 1949 but the selection was thrown out because he was not a senior. One shudders to think of them operating on the same line.

"Three Hall of Famers ain't bad," Cullom would say, referring to the two linemen and Gallarneau.

As for duty, the "story was that if you were good you went to El Toro; if not, you went to war," lamented Cullom. "I went to war."

Stautner and Papaleo played for El Toro in 1944 before being shipped out, and Brazinsky, King and back Kenny Reese (Alabama) in 1945.

Nomellini fought on Saipan and Okinawa.

Center Joe Bottalico (William & Mary) was killed on Iwo Jima.

The pros obviously thought highly of the players, too. Nomellini was the 49ers' No. 1 pick in 1950, Stautner the Steelers' No. 2 in 1950, King the Rams' No. 5 in 1946, back John Sims (Tulane) the Miami Seahawks' No. 19 in 1947, and Reese the Eagles' No. 29 in 1945.

Cullom and Siegert even were drafted twice. Cullom was the Redskins' No. 24 pick in 1949 and No. 17 in 1950. Siegert was the 49ers' 29th pick in 1948 and the Redskins' 18th in 1949.

By the time they had stopped growing, Brazinsky was 6-1, 215; Cullom 5-11, 235; King 6-3, 195; Marcolini 6-0, 203; Nomellini 6-3, 259; Siegert 6-3, 216, and Stautner 6-1, 230.

It took microfilm of the Raleigh (N.C.) News & Observer to confirm the lineup — awesome in potential — that otherwise might have been considered part of someone's imagination and never been heard of again.

1943

Record: 0-20 Camp Lee, 39-0 Wilmington CG, 68-6 Wake Forest Army Finance School, 20-0 Richmond AAB, 40-0 Camp Butner, 0-19 Greensboro AAB. (4-2)

Coach: Lt. E.W. "Bill" Hopp (Minnesota) (Iowa Pre-Flight). **Assistants:** NA

Ends: Lafayette King (Georgia) (El Toro 1945), Nash, Herb Siegert (Illinois)

Tackles: Leo Nomellini (Minnesota) (College and Pro Halls of Fame), Ernie Stautner (El Toro 1944) (Boston College) (Pro Hall of Fame)

Guards: Jim Cullom (Cal) (Quantico 1951), Dom Papaleo (El Toro 1944) (Boston College), Sakshaugh, Bob Stone

Centers: Joe Bottalico (William & Mary) (KIA), Sam Brazinsky (Villanova) (El Toro 1945), Retrosi, Ward

Backs: John Atwood (Wisconsin), Hugh Gallarneau (Stanford) (College Hall of Fame), Ed Gallik (Duquesne), Engle, Kunda, Hugo Marcolini (St. Bonaventure), Ken Reese (Alabama) (El Toro 1945; MCAS Santa Barbara 1945), John Richter (Michigan), John Sims (Tulane) (Georgia Pre-Flight 1942), Bill Smillie

---

(leader) Who's got the team?
(crowd) Quantico!
(leader) Who?
(crowd) Quantico!
(leader) Who?
(crowd) Team! Team! Team!

A Quantico cheer

Fewer V-12 Headlines

The Marine V-12 All-Americans from 1943 had moved on, and with them most of the headlines for the 1944 season.

Hundreds of Marine trainees who had bolstered college-football ranks in the 1943 season were now in boot camp, in OCS, at a duty station or headed overseas. For some, Iwo Jima was only four months away as the 1944 season got under way in the States.

And there weren't as many V-12 programs. The Marines had dropped units at Arizona Teachers (Flagstaff), Emory, Gustavus-Adolphus, Millsaps, North Texas Agricultural and Northwestern on March 1, 1944.

For the most part, the '44 Marine V-12 trainees had been underclassmen a year earlier. Their ranks were bolstered by enlisted men, some with combat in the Pacific.

But the Marine Corps didn't have the same impact as in 1943 when eight of the top 20 teams in the final Associated Press poll had their V-12 units. And three others with units could have been ranked in the Top 20.

There were impact players in 1944 but they were the exception rather than the rule. Frank Bauman was a second-team All-America end at Purdue, Gordon Berlin a second-team All-America center at Washington and Bill Hachten a second-team All-America guard at California.

Billy Cromer of Arkansas A&M led the nation in scoring with 11 touchdowns through Oct. 21 and was third as of Nov. 1 although he had played in just six games.

Future All-Americans included back Chalmers "Bump" Elliott of Purdue, later to be honored at Michigan, and tackle Jim Turner of Pacific, later to be honored at California.

There were future pros: back Gene Hubka (Bucknell), tackle Ed Stacco (Colgate), tackle John Kerns (Duke and North Carolina), back Earl "Dixie" Howell (Muhlenburg), back Jim Camp (North Carolina), back Achille "Chick" Maggioli (Notre Dame), guard Bob David (Villanova) and end Gail Bruce (Washington).

Future college coaches included Elliott (Michigan), Chuck Klausing (Indiana of Pa. and Carnegie-Mellon), Camp (George Washington) and Frank Lauterbur (Toledo and Iowa).

Future generals included Ken McLennan and Thurman Owens, both of Southwestern Louisiana, and Harold Hatch of Oberlin. Future colonels included Wilcomb Washburn (Dartmouth) and Lou Futrell (USC).

Another trend emerged in the 1944 season: some Marines who fought on Guadalcanal and in other campaigns had recovered from war wounds and returned to civilian life. A number of them headed to college, and despite pieces of shrapnel here and there, to the football fields.

Four former Marines, Marine Reservists or Marine trainees received various All-America mention in 1944.

Hachten and Stacco would play for the famed El Toro Marines in 1945, and the names of Bob Buel, Simon Degulis, Dick Enzminger, Rudy Flores, Ernie Hargett, Howell, Tony Messina, Don O'Neil, Owens, Ken Peck, Dick Piskoty, George Rusch, John Seiferling, Wayne Steele and Duane Whitehead, among others, would turn up on postwar Marine teams. Glenn Rodney, a Silver Star winner, would coach Marine teams in the 1950s.

And, as in 1943, some V-12 players left for boot camp Nov. 1, 1944, leaving small squads even smaller. Some also were transferred to other V-12 units as the Marines, seeing a dwindling enrollment and — at one point — the long-term need for officer candidates lessening, consolidated units. Pacific alone lost 25 players.

The original 40 units had declined to 13, as the Corps shut down its V-12 training at Arkansas A&M, Bowling Green, Bucknell, Colorado, Denison, Duke, Franklin & Marshall, Louisiana Tech, Miami (Ohio), Muhlenburg, Notre Dame, Occidental, Pacific, Redlands, Rochester, Penn State, Southwestern Louisiana, Washington and Western Michigan.

Besides Kerns, others playing for two teams were Bob Albrecht (Bucknell and Dartmouth); Jim Seel (Bucknell and Yale); Don Canfield (Colorado and Purdue); Don Farrand (Colorado and Michigan); Nick Fusilli (Dartmouth and Yale); Jim Artley (Duke and Michigan); Allan Edgar and Jim Ellis (Duke and North Carolina); Tony Kurowski (Penn State and Princeton); and Allen Bush, Clay Hendricks, Tom O'Shaughnessy, Rodney, Jim Shattuck and Neil Zundell (Princeton and Western Michigan).

Fusilli played for Dartmouth one week — and against Dartmouth a week later.

1945

More and more veterans returned, some joining teams as late as October and November. A number had been decorated.

Knox's Bill Heerde, at 33, was believed to be the oldest college player that season.

The pared-down V-12 ranks had turned more and more to former enlisted men, with the colleges having primarily 17-year-olds, 4-F's, honorably discharged or those in designated fields of study to choose from. Jim Boswell (Oberlin), a Little All-America selection, had 11 TDs prior to Nov. 1.

There were only seven future pro draft selections: tackle Wendell Beard (California), Albrecht, back Francis O'Brien (Dartmouth), tackle Ted Hazelwood (North Carolina), ends Bob Heck and Norm Maloney (Purdue) and guard Vic Vasicek (USC).

Zundell was captain of Princeton's football and basketball teams and a catcher on the baseball team.

Beard, Degulis, Heck, Rusch and Bill Teefey would play on postwar Marine teams.

V-12 players (1944)

Arkansas A&M: Terrel Allen, Bob Boehlow, Chandler, Bill Conger ('43), Billy Cromer (A&M '43/North Texas 1946-47), Faber, Wilton Ferrell, Stan Green (Oklahoma/San Diego Marines 1943/Illinois 1946), Norman Stilwell.

Bowling Green: William Burns, Al Dimarco (Creighton/Bowl. Green '43), Joe Henry, Mel Houle (Gustavus-Adolphus), John Jeremiah ('43), Carl Jones, Cliff Jones, Charles Joyce, Brenton Kirk ('43), Jack Lewis, Ed Lonjak, Don Mohr (Baldwin-Wallace/Bowl. Green '43), G. Schmidt (Valley City), J. Schmiedt (Gustavus-Adolphus), Al Taves (Creighton)

Bucknell: Bob Albrecht (Marquette/Dartmouth 1944-46), Ralph Grant ('43), Les Heinz, Gene Hubka ('43, 1946), Howard Lawson (Drexel), Jim Powell (Franklin & Marshall), John Rendall, Jim Seel (Bucknell '43/Yale 1944), Wayne Steele (Syracuse/Bucknell '43), Felix Wade (Mississippi St.), Al Yannelli

California: Ed Anderson, Ed Barnett (Santa Clara/Cal '43), Bill Bryant ('43), Jim Gierelich (Occidental/Cal 1945), Jack Groff (San Diego St.), Bill Hachten (2nd team all-American) (Stanford/Cal '43/Stanford 1946), John Higgins, Pete Janopaul (Occidental), Dick Madigan (Stanford/Cal '43/Stanford 1946), George Rasmussen (Stanford/Cal '43)

Colgate: Joe Burczak (1942-43), Dick Kreter (1942-43), George McKibbon, Art Pollock (Syracuse), John Rawitser, Bill Raynor, Don Ross, John Sellon (1946), Jim Smyth (1942-43, 1945-46), Ed Stacco (1942-43, 1946), Tom Stroock, Anderson Williamson

Colorado: Don Canfield (Colorado '43/Purdue 1944), Don Farrand (Michigan 1944), Jim Price (Baylor/Colorado '43, 1946)

Colorado College: Charles Osborne (Tennessee/San Diego Marines), John Seiferling (Utah St./Colo. College '43/Fresno St. 46), John Zeigler ('43, 1946)

Cornell: Wilbur Dameron (Harvard/Cornell '43), Charles Davidson ('43), Simon Degulis (1945), Grant Ellis (Penn/Cornell '43/Penn 1946), Frank McArthur, Bob Scully (1945)

Dartmouth: Bob Albrecht (Marquette/Bucknell 1944/Dartmouth 1945-46), Bill Bennett (Manhattan/Dartmouth '43), Jim Biggie (1945-46), Darrel Braatz (Marquette/Canisius 1946), Nick Fusilli (Yale 1944, 1946), Gordon Grant, N. Roger Hammond, Bob Harvey ('43, 1945), Joe Hayes, Al Martin, George Rusch (1945-46), Harold Swanson (1945), Wilcomb Washburn ('43, 1947), Art Young (Springfield/Dartmouth '43, 1946)

Denison: Don O'Neil (Missouri Valley)

Duke: Jim Artley (Michigan 1944), George Balitsaris (Tennessee/Duke '43/Tennessee 1946-48), Allan Elgar (Iowa/North Carolina 1944/Marquette 1946-47), Jim Ellis (North Carolina 1944), John Kerns (Ohio Univ./North Carolina 1944, Ohio 1945-46), Bob McNeely, David Owen (Western Reserve), E.C. Suhling (Virginia), Garland Wolfe ('43, 1946)

Franklin & Marshall: Bob Buel (Wisconsin), Bill Iannicelli (Catawba/F&M '43, 1947)

Georgia Tech: Jim Dorough (South Georgia/Tech '43), George Hills ('43, 1945), J.T. Landry, Billy Williams (1945, 1947)

Louisiana Tech (3-5-1): R.D. Burnham, R.K. Clough, Howard Helfrich, Oscar Stewart, L.E. Weber

Miami (Ohio): Dick Enzminger (1946), Dick Piskoty (1946-47)

Michigan: David Adams, Jim Artley (Duke 1944), George Babe, George Burg (1945-46), Don Farrand (Colorado 1944), Bob Nussbaumer ('43, 1945), Art Renner ('43, 1945-46), John Weyers

Muhlenburg: Jim Devlin (Lebanon Valley/Muhlenburg '43), George Duplaga, Earl "Dixie" Howell (Mississippi 1947-48), John McKay, Bill Moreland (Waynesburg/Muhlenburg '43)

North Carolina: John Blair (Virginia), Boyce Box (West Texas 1946), Jim Camp (Randolph-Macon/N.C. 1945-46), Dallas Davis, Allan Elgar (Iowa/Duke 1944/Marquette 1946-47), Jim Ellis (Duke 1944), Jim Godwin, John Kerns (Ohio Univ./Duke 1944/Ohio 1945-46), Monte Koppel (Georgia Tech), Tom Lane ('43), Art Lowe, Bill Walker (1945), Walt Ward (North Texas Agri.)

Notre Dame: Achille "Chick" Maggioli (Illinois 1946-47), George Terlep (apparently took Navy option).

Oberlin: Harold Hatch (Monmouth), Frank Lauterbur (Oberlin '43/Mount Union 1946-48).

Pacific: Bob Canter, Charlie Cooke (San Francisco CC), W.A. Cousins (Humboldt), Ed Fennelly (Univ. of San Francisco), Ray Jaeger (Univ. of San Francisco/Pacific '43), Fred Klemenok (Univ. of San Francisco/Pacific '43/USF 1946-48), Joe Kokes, Keith Lukens, Gordon Medlin, Tony Messina (California), Bill Millhaupt (Santa Clara/Pacific '43), Bob Muenter (Univ. of San Francisco/Pacific '43), Dick Payne (San Jose St.), Vince Rutherford, Don Semon, Darrell Smith, Jim Turner (San Francisco CC/Pacific '43/Cal 46-49; All-American).

Penn State: Bruce Allen (Nebraska), Al Auer (Ohio Univ./Penn St. '43), Earl Bruhn (Minnesota 1945-46), Ed Bush (Minnesota/Northwestern '43), George Chambers (Transylvania), Chuck Klausing (Penn St. '43/Slippery Rock 1946-47), Tony Kurowski (Princeton 1944), Bill Larson (Northwestern), Frank Martenis ('43), Dick McCown ('43), Ed Meyer, Dan Orlich (Northwestern '43),

43

Allen Richards (Cincinnati/Penn St. '43/Cincinnati 1946), John Schlesinger (Nebraska), Paul Swiggum (Northwestern), Ted Wilhelm

Princeton: Fred Allen, Randall Boeing, Allen Bush (West. Michigan 1944/Princeton 1945/West. Michigan 1946-47), Jim Carman, Bill Christmas, Bill Cupelo, Lou Faust, Clay Hendricks (Simpson/West. Michigan 1944), Tony Kurowski (Penn St. 1944), John Melvin, Tom O'Shaughnessy (West. Mich. 1944, 1946-47), Al Pedracine, Glenn Rodney (SW Missouri/West. Michigan 1943-44), Jim Shattuck (West. Michigan 1944/Princeton 1945), Neil Zundell (Utah/San Diego Marines/West. Michigan 1944/Princeton 1945-46)

Purdue: Frank Bauman (All-American) (Illinois/Purdue '43//Illinois 1946), Don Canfield (Colorado 1943-44), Stan Dubicki (Shurtleff/Purdue '43), Chalmers "Bump" Elliott (Purdue '43/Michigan 1946-47; All-American); Tom Hughes (Missouri/Purdue '43, 1945; All-American), Morris Kaastad ('43, 1946), Jim Lockwood (1945), Gordon Logan (1945), Olin Lougheed ('43), Walt Poremba (Case/Purdue '43), Leonard Schipferling

Redlands: Stan DeForde ('43), Jack Schiefer (Univ. of San Francisco/Redlands '43/USF 1946)

Rochester: Bill Adler (Northwestern '43)

Southwestern Louisiana: Glenn Allen, Maury Babin ('43), J.S. Cargile, Dave Cook (Rice), L.A. Colquitt, Ray Day (Arizona St. Tch.), Warren Fortier, Ernie Hargett, Joe Klune ('43), Dudley LeBlanc, Ken McLennan, Van Molkenbuhr (Santa Clara 1946-47), Jim O'Neil (Nevada), Thurman Owens (SW La. '43/Cincinnati 1947-49), Ken Peck (Flagstaff 1943/Stanford 1947, 1949), Jim Shamblin, Charlie Stewart, Bob Wachs (Colorado College/SW La. '43), Jack Whitmire, Bob Winship (Loyola of LA/Flagstaff '43/Loyola 1946-48)

Southwestern (Texas): Rudy Flores (Southwestern 1945/Texas), Billy Latch, Ed McFarland ('43).

USC: Bob Hanley, Lou Futrell (Fresno St./USC '43), Fran Johnson (Michigan St.), Doug MacLachlan (UCLA), George Pauly, Marshall Romer ('43, 1946), L. Merritt Thomas (Colorado 1943), Bob Venn (Fresno St.), Duane Whitehead ('43, 1946).

Villanova: Bob David (Notre Dame/Villanova '43, 1946)

Washington: Gordon Berlin ('43, 1946-47), Gail Bruce ('43, 1945-47), Don Cowan, Charles Dines, Bruce Meyers, Bob Moore ('43, 1945), Fred Osterhout (1945)

Western Michigan: Jim Benson, Allen Bush (Princeton 1944-45/West. Michigan 1946-47), Len Dovalovsky, Jim Henderson, Clayton Hendricks (Simpson/Princeton 1944), Phil Igoe, Mallett Jackson, Charles Kalbfleish ('43), Cliff Keddie (1946), Reuben Leiske, Ed Mendrysa, Gerald Nelson, Tom O'Shaughnessy (Princeton 1944/West. Michigan 1946-47), Wayne Pease (Princeton 1945), Glenn Rodney (SW Missouri/West. Michigan '43/Princeton 1944), Jim Shattuck (Princeton 1944-45), John Stotlar (Southern Illinois), Martin Stimac, Joe Wagner, Ben Wall (Central Michigan/West. Michigan '43), Neil Zundell (Utah/San Diego Marines/Princeton 1944-46)

Yale: Dana Dudley (Harvard), Nick Fusilli (Dartmouth 1944/Yale 1946), Frank Gillis ('43, 1945), Jim Seel (Bucknell '43, 1944)

Among the former Marines and former trainees playing were:

Dartmouth: Dick Bennett, Carl McKinnon (1942, 1945)

Duke: Tom Davis (3rd team all-American) (1941-43)

Georgia: Al Perl (Youngstown)

Georgia Tech: Rolands Phillips (Texas A&M/Tech '43, 1946-47)

Minnesota: Bob Graiziger (Minnesota 1942-43, 1945; tried out at Northwestern in 1943); Vic Kulbitski (Minnesota 1941-42/Notre Dame '43/Minnesota 1945), Rudy Sikich (1941), Wayne Williams (1942-43, 1945)

Murray St.: Johnny Underwood (1942)

Notre Dame: Pat Filley (2nd team All-American) (1941-43), Art Mergenthal (Xavier/Bowl. Green '43)

Pacific: Jim Watson (1942-43)

Pennsylvania: George Savitsky (2nd team All-American) (1945-47)

Southern Methodist: Earl Cook (1945-47)

Texas: Harold Fischer (3rd team All-American) (Texas 1941-42/Southwestern of Texas '43), Jack Sachse (Texas 1941-42/Southwestern of Texas '43)

UCLA: Jack Boyd (Rice/UCLA 1943, 1945)

USC: Earl Audet (Georgetown/USC '43)

1945 Trainees

California: All-Coast Wendell Beard (New Mexico) (pros) (Quantico 1949, Camp Pendleton 1951, asst. Parris Island 1953, asst. Pendleton 1958) (2 Bronze Stars), Steve Dotur, Ken Gerner, Jim Gierlich (Occidental/Cal 1944), Web Jessup, Keith Jackson, Leo McIntyre, Elden Mohn (San Jose st.), Dave Tennebaum.
(Roster but no Navy-Marine breakdown)
Pro draftee: Beard.

Colgate: Jim Cox (Indiana), Bill Deming, Oscar Eggeson, Fernand Gilles, Don Kreitz (Minnesota), Milt McClure (Georgia), Bob McNutt, George Nilsen (Muhlenburg), Elvin Nordmark (Colgate 1943, 1946), John O'Donnell (Muhlenburg), Ray Otis, Ken Scheel, Allen Short, Paul Thompson, Bill Wetten (Swarthmore), Frank Worland (Illinois).

Colorado College: Harry Hoth (Cherry Point), G.H. Sims (San Diego Marines), Lars Watson (San Diego Marines 1944) (Colo. College 1946-47)
(Roster but no Navy-Marine breakdown)

Cornell: Frank Adey, Bill Best, Tom Blatchford, Al Caleen, Bob Coniff, Amos Cook, Simon Degulis (Cornell 1944) (Quantico 1948, Camp Pendleton 1949) (Letter of Commendation), Harold Devold, Bill Farrar, Bob Glaser, Herb Glatzer, Bob Gover, Harold Oenick, Bill Petruzel, Roy Pneumann, Jack Rakiski, R.K. Schwieger, Bob Scully (Cornell 1944), Ray Sikanis, Bernard Simon, John Skawski, Bob Smith, Bill Speece, Rube Stevens, Norris Walkup, John White, Julius Woznicki, Gil Zwicki

Dartmouth: Frank Aberle, Bob Albrecht (Marquette/Bucknell 1944/Dartmouth 1944, 1946), Wayne Andreas, David Barr, S.J. Baudhuin, Jim Biggie (Dartmouth 1944, 1946), Billie Boyd, John Daly, Jack Deutsch, Al Gould, Bob Harvey (Dartmouth 1944), Barry Marks, Francis O'Brien (Dartmouth 1946-47), Atherton Phleger, George Rusch (Dartmouth 1944, 1946), John Sullivan, Harold Swanson (Dartmouth 1944), Tom Tormey
Pro draftees: Albrecht, O'Brien

Georgia Tech: Roster but no Navy-Marine breakdown

Michigan: George Burg (Michigan 1944, 1946), Jim Foltz (Toledo 1946-48), Norm Rabbers, Reg Sauls, Dennis Youngblood

North Carolina: Burl Bevers, John Colones, R.V. Cox, Ted Hazelwood (UNC 1946-48) (pros), John Lineweaver, W.R. McIntyre (Rockhurst), Ed Mead, Bob Oliphant, Haworth Parks, Bill Rainey, Jim Rogers, M.D. Sims, Henry Stowers, Bill Teefey (Richmond) (1st Marine Division 1944/Camp Lejeune 1950), Bill Walker (UNC 1944), Ralph Widell
Pro draftee: Hazelwood

Oberlin: Little All-American Jim Boswell, who scored 11 TDs prior to Nov. 1 (San Diego Marines 1943)

Princeton: Don Black (Wittenberg), Al Bush (West. Michigan 1944/Princeton 1944/West. Michigan 1946), John Callahan, Art Goodman, Charles Johnson (Nevada), Theodore Margossisan, Gil McCormich, Wayne Pease (West. Michigan 1944), Alex Prezioso (Notre Dame), Ernest Ransome (Princeton 1946), R.H. Rister, Jim Shattuck (West. Michigan 1944/Princeton 1944), Dave Supple, Claude Watts, Neil Zundell (Utah/West. Michigan 1944/Princeton 1944, 1946) (San Diego Marines 1943)
Zundell was captain of the Tigers' football and basketball teams and a catcher on the baseball team.

Purdue: Paul Gilbert, Bob Heck (Purdue 1946-48) (pros) (Quantico 1950), Tom Janes, Jim Lockwood (Purdue 1944), Gordon Logan (Purdue 1944), Norm Maloney (Purdue 1946-47) (pros), Bill Richey, Dick Smith (Arizona St.)
Pro draftees: Heck, Maloney

USC: Frank Bruner, Jay Coghlan, John Davis, James Duke, Bob Henderson, Ken Krause, Bill Nelson, Jack Nichols, Bill Olney, Leon Randell, Fred Thomas, Vic Vasicek (Texas 1946-48) (pros), Reggie Whitlock, Ervin York.
Pro draftee: Vasicek

Villanova: John Childers, Frank Geleskie, John Gladscott, Ed Lawless (Penn 1944, 1946-47), John Peters
(Have roster but no Navy-Marine breakdown)

Yale: Frank Gillis (Yale 1943-44)
(Roster but no Navy-Marine breakdown)

Others

In addition, there were a number of Marines — some of whom had fought in the South Pacific — and former trainees playing during the 1945 season:
Alabama: Joe Gambrell (Alabama 1946), Dick Gibson
Auburn: Summie "Sonny" Poss (Duke 1943)
Baylor: Wayne Franks (San Diego Marines 1943)
Boston College: Steve Helstowski
Brown: Jim Lalikos (Northeastern/Villanova 1943/North-South Game 1945/Brown 1946)
California: Ed Welch (Cal 1943)
Dartmouth: John Costello (Dartmouth 1947), Carl McKinnon (Dartmouth 1942, 1944)

Denver: Doug Shouldice
Detroit: Jack Murphy (TCU)
Duke: Kelly Mote (South Carolina 1942/Duke 1943, 1946) (pros)
Illinois: Bill Krall, Wes Tregoning (Illinois 1941/Notre Dame 1943), Mac Wenskunas (Illinois 1942, 1946) (coaches)
Iowa: Tom Hand (Iowa 1943)
Kansas St.: Jim Durham
Knox: Bill Heerde (Knox 1939-40; at 33, perhaps the country's oldest player)
LSU: Andy Kosmac (LSU 1942)
Michigan: Bob Nussbaumer (Michigan 1943-44) (pros), Art Renner (Michigan 1943-44, 1946)
Michigan St.: Chet Kwiatkowski
Minnesota: Earl Bruhn (Penn St. 1944/Minnesota 1946), Bob Graiziger (Minnesota 1942-44), Bob Hanzlik (Wisconsin 1942/Michigan 1943), Vic Kulbitski (Minnesota 1941-42/Notre Dame 1943/Minnesota 1944) (pros), Charles Judd Ringer (Minnesota 1940-41) (Iowa Pre-Flight 1942) (DFC); Wayne Williams (Minnesota 1942-44)
Mississippi: Roland Dale (Mississippi 1947-49) (pros) (coaches)
Nevada: Ron Barker, Ralph "Happy" Reed
North Carolina: Jim Camp (Randolph-Macon/UNC 1944) (pros) (coaches)
Northwestern: Jack McKenzie (Drake 1942/Northwestern 1946) (pros)
Ohio University: John Kerns (Ohio 1942/Duke-UNC 1944/Ohio 1946) (pros)
Oklahoma: Hal Schreiner
Oregon: Gene Gillis, Elliott Wilson (Oregon 1940-41; team captain declared ineligible because of '37 season at Nebraska)
Oregon St.: Bob Gromackey
Pennsylvania: All-American George Savitsky (Penn 1944, 1946-47) (pros)
Purdue: All-American Tom Hughes (Missouri/Purdue 1943-44) (coaches)
San Diego St.: Bill Martinson
SMU: Earl Cook (SMU 1944, 1946-47) (pros), second-team All-American Tom Dean (SMU 1942/Arkansas A&M 1943) (pros); Howard "Red" Maley (SMU 1941-42/North Texas Agriculture 1943/North-South Game 1945) (Maui Marines 1944) (pros)
Stanford: Dick Munroe (Stanford/Cal 1943)
Syracuse: Pete Morrow (Syracuse 1942/Colgate 1943), Roger Robinson (Syracuse/Rochester 1943/Syracuse 1946) (coaches)
Temple: George Waltzer
TCU: James O'Neal (TCU 1942/Southwestern of Texas 1943) (pros), Ray Newton
Tulsa: Pat Patrick
UCLA: Jack Boyd (Rice/UCLA 1943-44)
Virginia: Sam Fray (North Carolina 1943/Virginia 1946)
Wake Forest: Harry Clark (Wake Forest/Duke 1943/Wake Forest 1946-47)
Washburn: Leroy Harmon
Washington: Gail Bruce (Wash. 1943-44, 1946-47) (pros), Jack Laughner, Bob Moore (Wash. 1943-44), third-team All-Coast Fred Osterhout (Wash. 1944)
Washington St.: Charles Wilson (Ward Island Marines 1942)
Coaches: Bernie Bierman (Minnesota), Tuss McLaughry (Dartmouth)
Pro draftees: Boyd, Bruce, Camp, Cook, Dean, Hanzlik, Hughes, Kerns, Kosmac, Kulbitski, Lalikos, McKenzie, Maley, McKinnon, Mote, Nussbaumer, Renner, Robinson, Savitsky, Wenskunas.

Makris Wins at Bolling

Former Marine George Makris ran up a 47-4-2 record in five seasons as coach of the Bolling AFB Generals in Washington, D.C.

Makris, who played at Wisconsin, had 10-0, 10-1, 11-0, 8-1-1 and 8-2- records from 1955-59. Bolling dropped football in 1960.

Against Quantico, Makris won two, lost two and tied one.

Breaking Color Line

A mid an era of segregation, a black team from Montford Point was the only one at Camp Lejeune playing an outside football schedule in 1945.

A base varsity team loaded with (white) college all-stars cancelled its program because of demobilization and other service teams dropping schedules. Instead, an intramural schedule was arranged.

Ben Whaley of the 1945 Montford Point team is believed to be the first black Marine in pro football. After playing at Virginia State, he was a guard with the Los Angeles Dons of the All-America Football Conference in 1949.

Whaley also would be head football and basketball coach at Hampton.

The identity of the first black Marine to play on a Marine-base varsity team is not known. But tackle Rufus Williams played at Camp Lejeune in 1949, guard Tom Reeves (Shaw), back Calvin Clark and Williams at Lejeune in 1950, and end John Scott (Tennessee St.) at Camp Pendleton; guard Harold Bradley (Iowa) at MCRD San Diego; back Elmer Tolbert, Reeves and back Paul Woodard (Shaw) at Lejeune; and Williams at Quantico in 1951.

In 1952, black players included end Gene "Tiny" Lipscomb and Tolbert at Pendleton; tackle Bob Brown (Florida A&M), tackle Art Davis (Alabama St.), tackle Willie McClung (Florida A&M), Reeves, back Orville Williams (Butler) and Woodard at Lejeune; end Harold Turner (Tennessee St.), back Tom Carodine (Boys Town and Nebraska) and Bradley at San Diego; end Bill Best (Florida A&M) and back Russ Murphy (Winston-Salem) at Cherry Point; and back Al Rowe (Tennessee St.) at El Toro.

Bradley would play four seasons in the NFL, Davis with the 1953 Chicago Bears, McClung seven NFL seasons and with Hamilton (CFL) in 1962, Turner with the 1954 Detroit Lions and Carodine tried out with the Cleveland Browns in 1954.

Lipscomb, of course, would grow and bulk up to 6-6, 284 and as "Big Daddy" would in the NFL 10 seasons and be an All-Pro choice three times and play in three Pro Bowls.

Carodine, Davis and Williams in 1952 may have been the first blacks chosen on Leatherneck's All-Marine teams.

By 1953, blacks were better represented on Marine varsity teams and a number through the years used their Marine football experience as a springboard to the NFL, CFL, AFL and WFL.

Ed Fletcher (San Diego St.), a member of the 1954 MCRD San Diego team, in 1953 was one of the early blacks in OCS. He retired as a Reserve colonel.

■

The Montford Point Panthers won five, lost three and tied one in 1945, and a check of newspapers showed that most carried the team name as Camp Lejeune, not Montford Point, in score lists. One football guide referred to "Camp Lejeune (colored)."

The losses were to the famed Tuskegee AAF Warhawks (5-2), coached by Lt. Bill Bell (Ohio State), and the Godman Field (Ky.) Bombers (7-1).

The Panthers defeated two college teams, Benedict and Fayetteville, and scheduled two semi-pro teams to help fill out the schedule. They defeated the Charlotte Bees twice, and defeated and tied the Atlanta All-Stars.

According to the Official 1946 NCAA Guide, the other black service-football teams of 1945 were MacDill (Fla.) AAF, Ft. Benning, Randolph (Texas) AAF, Ft. Leonard Wood (Mo.), Jacksonville (Fla.) NAS, Norfolk NTS, Galveston . NS, Robins (Ga.) AAF, Aberbeen (Md.) Proving Ground, Ft. McClellan (Ala.) and Camp Plauche (La.)

Record: 0-27 Tuskegee AAF, 0-26 Tuskegee AAF, 0-12 Godman Field, 46-0 Benedict, 20-0 Fayetteville St., 21-0 Charlotte Bees, 13-6 Charlotte Bees, 7-7 Atlanta All-Stars, 33-6 Atlanta All-Stars (5-3-1)

Coach: Capt. Wojiak

Linemen: John W. Davis, Henry Harris, John Harris, Wilbur T. Hunter, Albert L. Jackson, Thomas H. Lee. William Newman. Elwood Nichols, Nobles. Robinson. Svlvester Salters, Paul Stephens, James V. Stewart, Orville V. Trabue, Ben Whaley, Art Wimbley

Backs: Ernest R. Booker, Leroy Collins, Willie Hill, Peter Jackson, Willie Jackson, Hilton Keith John H. "Bubber" Moore, Edwin E. Pettiford, Dene Qualls, Charles R. Richardson, Aaron B. Sims.

Former Marine Tony Elliott was a big man — literally — as a 1980s nose tackle for the New Orleans Saints.

Best 0-4 Team Ever

The 1944 Maui Marines, with their bucolic setting and 5-0-1 record, must have used up Hawaii's luck quota because nothing went right for the 1945 Fleet Marines team.

Blessed with depth and ability (36 players were picked in prewar or postwar NFL drafts), the Pacific Marines had to be the best 0-4 team the Marine Corps ever produced.

Or for that matter, one of the best 0-4 teams — anywhere and at any time.

Murphy's Law took its toll but had nothing to do with running back Billy "Spook" Murphy, who had starred at Mississippi State and Duke and later would be football coach and athletic director at Memphis State.

How bad was it?

It was so bad that Lt. Gen. Roy S. Geiger, commanding general of Fleet Marine Force, Pacific, presumably embarrassed at having to face admirals and generals from other services at the officers' clubs and lounges after the Pearl Harbor team's demise, refused to book a game with the fabled El Toro Marines for the Corps' championship.

It was so bad a Stars and Stripes article said the Marines were "starving for victory."

It was so bad, recalled end Bob Rennebohm (Wisconsin-Michigan), "that the first half of the alphabet was sent to China and the second half to Japan for occupation duty. A few stayed at Pearl Harbor and others who had been in combat and had enough points were sent home."

So Alvin Dark, Bump Elliott (Purdue), George Grimes (Virginia-North Carolina), Jim Loflin (LSU-Southwestern Louisiana) and others went to China.

A Stars and Stripes story reported that Dark, "an apple-cheeked youngster whose 19 points led the 1st Marines to a 66-44 basketball victory over the USS Tatum in Shanghai, seems to be that rare type which stands out in every sport he approaches." Elliott scored 14 points and Grimes 4 in the game.

Meanwhile, Bill Milner (South Carolina-Duke), Jim Myers (Tennessee-Duke), Hosea Rodgers (Alabama-North Carolina), Joe Signaigo (Notre Dame) and others were assigned to Japan.

So much for losing twice to the Navy and twice to the Army Air Forces.

No offense, and that was part of the problem, but *this* still was a team.

It boasted nine prewar or postwar, first-team All-Americans (ends Herb Hein of Northwestern and John Yonakor of Notre Dame, tackles Dick Huffman of Tennessee, Art McCaffray of Pacific and Darrell Palmer of Texas Christian, guard Milner, and backs Elliott, later of Michigan; Johnny Podesto of Pacific and Jim Turner, later of California).

It had the cream of the crop from the Marines' 1943 V-12 program.

Back Bill Maginnis (Tulane) recalls "listening to stories by (backs) Jack Verutti and Podesto about playing for Amos Alonzo Stagg at Pacific." McCaffray, Turner and back Joe Ferem also had been instrumental in Pacific's national ranking that season.

Ten had played, for varying periods, for Camp Lejeune in 1944.

The Fleet Marines' players, almost to a man lieutenants, were mostly 21 to 24 in age and in their prime. Thirty-four would play postwar college ball.

There was ample size, especially for the 1940s. For example, tackle Willard Lynch weighed 250; Huffman 235; 6-5 center Bill Blackburn (Rice-Southwestern Louisiana) and tackle Bill Pearson (Franklin & Marshall) 230, and six others in the 220-225 range.

Their record as pros was admittedly impressive:

■ Among the ends, Paul McKee (Syracuse-Rochester) played for the Washington Redskins in 1947-48; Ray Poole (Mississippi-North Carolina) for the New York Giants from 1947-52, and Yonakor for the Cleveland Browns from 1946-49, the New York Yankees in 1950, in Canada in 1951 and for the Redskins in 1952.

■ Among the tackles, Cleo Calcagni (Penn-Cornell) was with the Boston Yanks in 1946 and the Pittsburgh Steelers in 1947-48; Huffman with the Los Angeles Rams from 1947-50 and seven seasons in Canada; McCaffray (also of Santa Clara) for the Steelers in 1946, and Palmer for the Yankees from 1946-48 and the Browns from 1949-53.

■ Among the guards, Gaspar Urban (Notre Dame) was with the Chicago Rockets in 1948; Jones (Wake Forest-Franklin & Marshall) for the Buffalo Bisons in 1946 and the Detroit Lions in 1947-48; John Magee (Rice-Southwestern Louisiana) for the Philadelphia Eagles from 1948-55; Milner for the Bears from 1947-49 and the Giants in 1950; John Perko (Minnesota-Notre Dame) for the Bisons in 1946; and Signaigo for the Yankees from 1948-50.

■ Among the centers, Blackburn toiled for the Chicago Cardinals from 1946-50 and two seasons in Canada, and Fred Negus (Wisconsin-Michigan) for the Rockets in 1947-48, the Chicago Hornets in 1949 and the Chicago Bears in 1950.

■ Among the backs, Blondy Black (a 9.7 sprinter at Mississippi State) played for the Bisons in 1946, and the Buffalo Bills and Baltimore Colts in 1947; Bob David (Villanova) for the Rams in 1947-48 and the Rockets in 1948; Pete Gorgone (Muhlenburg) for the Giants in 1946; Bill Gray (Oregon State-USC) for the Redskins in 1947-48; Grimes for the Lions in 1948; Rodgers for the Los Angeles Dons in 1949, and Julie Rykovich (Illinois-Notre Dame) for the Bills in 1947-48, the Rockets in 1948, the Bears from 1949-51 and the Redskins from 1952-53.

Another half-dozen had pro tryouts.

So what went wrong?

One possibility might have been a "lack of cohesiveness and confidence in the Notre Dame box formation we were using," according to Milner. "Cliff Battles took over as head coach right before the first game and continued what the first coach had installed."

1000-75-20
012/222

HEADQUARTERS, TRANSIENT CENTER,
FLEET MARINE FORCE, PACIFIC,
FLEET POST OFFICE, SAN FRANCISCO,

12 October, 1945

TRANSIENT CENTER SPECIAL ORDER)
                                :   Assignment,
NUMBER.................170-45)

1.   Effective this date the below named officers are relieved of their
uties with Headquarters and Service Battalion and are assigned to Casual Battalion for duty as Permanent Personnel with the Fleet Marine Force, Pacific, Athletic Association:

Maj CHURCH, Charles R., USMCR. (014654) 2dLt LABOVITZ, Harry., USMCR. (043568)
Capt RANDALL, Roy E., USMCR. (017431)   2dLt LEHMKUHL, Donald C., USMCR. (043569)
2dLt DANA, John P., USMCR. (041170)   2dLt LOFLIN, James T., USMCR. (043222)
2dLt DARK, Alvin R., USMCR. (043135)

2.   Effective this date the below named officers are relieved of their
duties with Replacement Battalion, and are assigned to Casual Battalion for duty
with the Fleet Marine Force, Pacific, Athletic Association as Football Players on
the Fleet Marine Force, Pacific, Football Team:

FIRST LIEUTENANTS
BLACK, "J""T"., USMCR. (029153)
BLACKBURN, William W., Jr., USMCR. (036362)
BLACKSTONE, Billy D., USMCR. (029752)
GERMANN, Kenneth G., USMCR. (032358)
GORGONE, Peter., USMCR. (031677)
MYERS, James A., USMCR. (037622)

SECOND LIEUTENANTS
ARMSTRONG, Henry N., USMCR. (044232)
BOYLE, John T., USMCR. (043849).
BUSCEMI, Joseph A., USMCR. (044263).
BUSH, Albert J., USMCR. (043863)
CALCAGNI, Ralph C., USMCR. (041151)
CHRISTENSEN, Lawrence N., USMCR. (043870)
CZEKAJ, Edward., USMCR. (043132)
DAVID, Robert J., USMCR. (045003)
DEAN, John B., USMC. (044293)
ELLIOTT, Chalmers W., USMCR. (046980)
FEREM, Joseph P., USMCR. (044705)
FUHRMAN, Seymour., USMCR. (045246)
GRAY, William R., Jr., USMCR. (044721)
GRIMES, George S., USMCR. (043924)
HALLIDAY, Sid M., USMCR. (043927)
KASPRZAK, Donald T., USMCR. (043558)

SECOND LIEUTENANTS (CONTINUED)
LIVELY, Charles L., USMCR. (043575)
MC CAFFRAY, Arthur J., USMCR. (041295)
MC CAIN, William C., USMCR. (044380)
MC KEE, Paul H., USMCR. (045063)
MAGEE, John W., Jr., USMCR. (044773)
MARSHALL, Magness W., USMCR. (043989)
MERCER, Walter E., Jr., USMCR. (044785)
MILNER, Charles E., USMCR. (040186)
MURPHY, Billy J., USMCR. (039214)
NEGUS, Frederick W., USMCR. (043600)
PARKER, Keith D., USMCR. (041320)
PERKINS, Robert L., USMCR. (043264)
PERKO, John F., USMCR. (043615)
PODESTO, John., USMCR. (039640)
RENNEBOHM, Robert B., USMCR. (044828)
RODGERS, Rosen W., USMCR. (043600)
RYKOVICH, Julius A., USMCR. (044836)
SIGNAIGO, Joseph S., USMCR. (044842)
TEAGUE, Edward L., Jr., USMCR. (043668)
TURNER, James B., USMCR. (047138)
TYNDALL, Lon., USMCR. (043327)
URBAN, Gasper G., USMCR. (044871)
VERUTTI, Jack L., Jr., USMCR. (044064)
WELDON, Howard., USMCR. (043685)

BY ORDER OF COLONEL WHEELER:

H. A. VERNET, Jr.,
Lieutenant Colonel, U.S. Marine Corps Reserve,
Executive Officer.

Distribution "A", less FMF,Pac.

Dark "worked hard, as did a lot of the others," Milner continued, "but the right ingredients were not there.

"We all felt that the Air Force and Navy teams had the advantage by employing the T-formation."

But there wasn't a Fleet Marines coach schooled in the T, or many on the team manning skill positions who were that acquainted with the formation.

Battles, whose running carried him into both the Pro and College Football Halls of Fame, and James Orville Tuttle, a lineman from Oklahoma City University who had starred for the Giants from 1937-41 and returned in 1946, coached the team. Both had been player-coaches for Dick Hanley's El Toro Marines in 1944. The Flying Marines had used the double wing and short punt formations most of the season.

Tuttle's hand was seen in the Giants' 1946 draft, when Jones was the No. 2 pick, Rodgers No. 3, tackle Al Bush (Georgia-Duke) No. 12, tackle Stan Stapley (Utah and later Brigham Young) No. 15, Loflin No. 19 and back Dick Kelley (Minnesota) No. 20.

The athletic officer, Maj. Roy Randall, an All-American at Brown and a coach before and after the war for 27 years at Haverford (Pa.) College, coached until Battles reported.

True, the Navy had players such as backs Charlie "Choo Choo" Justice, Steve Lach, George McAfee and Bob Sweiger plus linemen Vince Banonis, Russ Letlow and Buster Ramsey. The Army Air Forces had backs Bill Dudley and Indian Jack Jacobs and lineman Martin Ruby.

But 0-4?

The leadership was there.

Perhaps the most renowned Marine was Dark, who made football headlines as a sophomore at LSU in 1942 and at Southwestern Louisiana in 1943 as a Marine trainee.

Street & Smith's 1946 Football Pictorial Yearbook noted, "One of the great athletes in LSU history, Dark was expected back from Marine Corps duty in China in time to answer the September call at Baton Rouge. Dark punts, passes and runs with the best in the Southeast. At least he did four years ago. If this boy comes through, LSU will be even tougher than last season."

But, of course, Dark reported instead to the Boston Braves baseball team for 15 games, was seasoned at Milwaukee of the American Association in 1947 and was the National League Rookie of the Year in 1948, when he hit .322 for Boston and fielded .983 at shortstop.

Eventually Dark managed in the major leagues and in 1986 was named director of player development for the Chicago White Sox.

South Carolina also came up short in 1946. The Street & Smith guide say the "Gamecocks' line will be hard to crack with All-American Bill Milner ... back from service."

Milner starred instead for Duke, where he played as a Marine trainee in 1943.

Elliott (Michigan), Murphy, Myers (Iowa State, Texas A&M, Dallas Cowboys), Poole (Northwest Mississippi) and Eddie Teague (Guilford, The Citadel), among others, went into coaching, and Ed Czekaj (Penn

State), Elliott (Iowa), Murphy, Poole and Teague, among others, became athletic directors.

Myers had won a Silver Star and been wounded on Iwo Jima, where Gorgone, Kelley and others had fought. Murphy had been awarded the Bronze Star on Okinawa.

"Maj. Charles Church (a California basketball coach) was the prime officer behind the organizing of the team and was its chief officer," said Rennebohm. "We had been together for some time at an officers' rest camp at Nanakuli ... but the orders came through well into the season."

Transient Center Special Order 170-45, issued Oct. 12, has to be one of the Corps' more interesting documents. Church, Randall, Dark (serial number 043135), Don Lehmkuhl (043569) and Loflin (043222), among others, "are relieved of duties with Headquarters and Service Battalion and are assigned to Casual Battalion for duty as Permanent Personnel with the Fleet Marine Force, Pacific, Athletic Association."

Six first lieutenants and 40 first lieutenants, a veritable "Who's Who," also were "relieved of their duties with Replacement Battalion, and assigned to Casual Battalion for duty with the FMF, Pacific, Athletic Association as football players on the FMF, Pacific, Football Team."

Section 3 of the order assigned 1st Lt. Andrew Philip (036885), the former Illinois Whiz Kid and later All-Pro, to the FMF basketball team.

And, not forgetting baseball, the Marines "informally assigned Ted Williams to us as it was the best place for him to work out, play handball, etc. and start getting ready to go back to the Boston Red Sox the next spring," Rennebohm recalled.

Five years later, at least 13 players — Henry Armstrong, Czekaj, Ferem, Hein, Lehmkuhl, Loflin, McCaffray, Milner, Podesto, Rodgers, Signaigo, Teague and Urban — were recalled to active duty during the Korean War, for a much bigger game.

FMF Pacific 1945

Record: 0-13 Navy, score of second game not available; 0-13 Army Air Forces, score of second game not available. Won 0, lost 4.

Ends: Joe Buscemi (Illinois-Purdue), Ed Czekaj (George Washington-Penn State), Sy Fuhrman (USC), Sid Halliday (Southern Methodist-Arkansas A&M), Herb Hein (Minnesota-Northwestern), Jim Loflin (LSU-Southwestern Louisiana), Paul McKee (Syracuse-Rochester), Ray Poole (Mississippi-North Carolina), Bob Rennebohm (Wisconsin-Michigan), John Yonakor (Notre Dame).

Tackles: Henry Armstrong (Rice-Southwestern Louisiana), Al Bush (Georgia-Duke), Cleo Calcagni (Penn-Cornell), Larry Christensen (Washington State-Washington), Dick Huffman (Tennessee), Charles Lively (Arkansas-Arkansas A&M), Willard Lynch (UCLA), Art McCaffray (Santa Clara-Pacific), Jim Myers (Tennesee-Duke), Darrell Palmer (Texas Christian), Bill Pearson (Franklin & Marshall), Stan Stapley (Utah), Gaspar Urban (Notre Dame).

Guards: John Boyle (Maryland-Colgate), Elmer Jones (Wake Forest-Franklin & Marshall), Nelson Klaus (Missouri), Don Lehmkuhl (Iowa-Purdue), John Magee (Rice-Southwestern Louisiana), Bill Milner (South Carolina-Duke), John Perko (Minnesota-Notre Dame), Joe Signaigo (Notre Dame).

Centers: Bill Blackburn (Rice-Southwestern Louisiana), John Dean (Navy), Bill McCain (Mississippi State-Duke), Fred Negus (Wisconsin-Michigan).

Backs: John "Blondy" Black (Mississippi State), Ron Cahill (Holy Cross), Alvin Dark (LSU-Southwestern Louisiana), Bob David (Notre Dame-Villanova), Chalmers "Bump" Elliott (Purdue), Joe Ferem (St. Mary's-Pacific), Ken Germann (Columbia), Pete Gorgone (Muhlenburg), Bill Gray

(Oregon State-USC), George Grimes (Virginia-North Carolina), Don Kasprzak (Columbia-Dartmouth), Dick Kelley (Minnesota), Bill Maginnis (Tulane), Wayne Marshall (Arkansas-Arkansas A&M), Walt Mercer (Fordham-Dartmouth), Billy Murphy (Mississippi State-Duke), Keith Parker (Missouri-Purdue), Bob Perkins (Lamar-Rice-Southwestern Louisiana), Johnny Podesto (St. Mary's-Pacific), Hosea Rodgers (Alabama-North Carolina), Julie Rykovich (Illinois-Notre Dame), Eddie Teague (North Carolina State-North Carolina), Jim Turner (San Francisco CC-Pacific), Lon Tyndall (LSU-Southwestern Louisiana), Jack Verutti (St. Mary's-Pacific), Howard Weldon (Alabama-North Carolina), Jim Worst (Manhattan-Bucknell)

NFL draftees: Black, Blackburn, Bush, Calcagni, Dark, David, Elliott, Gray, Grimes, Halliday, Huffman, Jones, Kasprzak, Kelley, Lively, Loflin, Magee, McCaffray, McKee, Milner, Murphy, Myers, Negus, Palmer, Perko, Podesto, Poole, Rennebohm, Rodgers, Rykovich, Signaigo, Turner, Urban, Verutti, Weldon, Yonakor.

1946 and/or 1947 college ball: Armstrong, Buscemi, Bush, Christensen, Czekaj, David, Dean, Elliott, Ferem, Gray, Grimes, Halliday, Hein, Huffman, Kasprzak, Lehmkuhl, Lively, Loflin, Magee, McCain, McKee, Milner, Murphy, Myers, Negus, Poole, Rennebohm, Rodgers, Rykovich, Signaigo, Stapley, Turner, Urban, Verutti.

Transient Center 1945

Record: 6-0 Ford Island NAS, 0-7 Aiea Barracks, won at least two other games, lost at least one other (14th Naval District League) (incomplete)
Coach: Lt. Bill Michels (Holy Cross) (Maui Marines 1944)
Assistants: Mike Kerns (Villanova-Penn St., Camp Lejeune 1944), Lt. Carl Meadows (Transylvania), Sgt. W.H. Pickett
Ends: Bob Buel (Wisconsin-Franklin & Marshall), John Poulos; **tackles:** Bud Carpenter (Rhode Island); **guards:** Chic Cherico, Cork Corkery, Dick Voris (San Jose St.); **centers:** Sonny Boy Watson; **backs:** Barker, Sam Cohagan, Stan Dubicki (Shurtleff-Purdue), Miller, Streble, Tate, Zimmer (incomplete)

Service Command 1945

Record: 35-2 Ft. Shafter, 6-42 Kaneohe NAS Klippers, won at least one other game, lost at least three others (14th Naval District League) (incomplete)
Coach: Lts. Majer and McAlister
Assistants:
Guards: Korff, Tucci. **Backs:** Barbee, Fred Broeg, Brown, Tommy Davis, Eitson, Herman O'Quinn, Bill Warren. Also: Kirk, Murdock.
(incomplete)

Pearl Harbor Marines 1945

Record: 7-6 Ft. Shafter, lost at least four games (14th Naval District League) (incomplete)
Coach: Lt. Phil Cohen. **Assistants:** Claude Chappel, Red McCarthy (Illinois), Dan Perkins,
Ends: White. **Tackles:** Butler. **Centers:** Fiene. **Backs:** Devlin (incomplete)

Maui Marines (5th Amtrac Bn.) 1945

Record: 13-44 Leialums (incomplete)
Coach: Lt. Joe Reece (Clemson). **Players:** not available

Elliott Elected to Hall

Former Marine Chalmers "Bump" Elliott was among the first players inducted into the Rose Bowl Hall of Fame.

Elliott, who played at Purdue and Michigan and with the 1945 FMF Pacific team, was honored in 1989 for his play in Michigan's 49-0 victory over USC in the 1948 Rose Bowl game.

Outside Distractions

It was difficult to focus on football at MCAS Santa Barbara, what with the azure Pacific nearby, the natural beauty of the area, a most moderate climate and the war being over.

In its one season of varsity competition in 1945, the Bombers won seven and tied once in an 11-game schedule against college, service and semipro competition. They were ranked No. 40 nationally among service teams by the Williamson Rating Service. Not too shabby.

One loss was by five points and another by seven. Had the Bombers been based at a more military surrounding, could they have won nine times?

The turnover was rapid, with players reporting from the South Pacific and from El Toro and others being honorably discharged. By and large, the players — principally ground-support personnel rather than aviators — had little college varsity experience.

Of the 34-man roster listed for the Minter Field game, backs Walt Halsall, Tony Minetto, Ken Reese and Roger Roggatz were among the few who had stamped on them what today would be called Division I experience.

However, at least a dozen had a service-football background.

Of the 34, only four were under 20; only two were over 25.

A year later, end Ed Hamilton was playing at Arkansas, tackle West Matthews at UCLA, tackle Ed Sprano and guard Joe Daugherty up the coast at the University of San Francisco, guard Jack Hyle at Cornell, center Carl Perkinson at Duke, back Eli Maricich at Georgia and back Dan Radakovich at Montana.

Tackle Lloyd McDermott, who as a teen-ager weighed 235 at Santa Barbara, would play for Kentucky from 1947-49, the Detroit Lions in 1950 and the Chicago Cardinals in 1950-51.

Reese (Alabama), who had played at Cherry Point in 1943-44, would be with Charlotte (Dixie League) in 1946 and the Lions in 1947.

Dick Evans was the Santa Barbara coach most of the season. He had lettered at Iowa from 1937-39 and been selected for the College All-Star Game. He was with the Green Bay Packers in 1940, Chicago Cardinals in 1941-42, Packers in 1943 and nationally-ranked El Toro Marines in 1944. Evans also played in the National Basketball League.

He brought some of the '44 El Toro team with him, and a piqued Flying Marines coach Dick Hanley sent more in the fall of 1945. Actually, the Marines at one point considered moving the famed El Toro team to Santa Barbara as a result of a dispute with the city of Santa Ana over stadium practice time.

Evans later was an assistant at Nevada and Notre Dame, coached Navy teams in Japan and San Diego and was a pro assistant with the Cardinals, Cleveland Browns, Philadelphia Eagles, Packers and New England Patriots.

The base had toyed with the idea of a team in 1943 when pros George Franck, Dolph Kissell and Mort Landsberg were aboard. But flight-training requirements did not permit a schedule, according to the commanding officer. He just happened to be Col. L. H. Sanderson, a renowned aviator who had been a football player at Montana and with a Mare Island Marine team in the Rose Bowl.

Record: 7-7 Pacific, 25-0 Minter Field, 20-12 Albany Navy, 14-19 Nevada, 6-0 Fresno State, 42-0 Cal Poly SLO, 40-7 Compton JC, 6-13 Hondo AAB, 25-0 Compton JC, 32-0 San Joaquin Cowboys, 7-34 NTC San Diego (7-3-1)

Coaches: Ed Beinor (Notre Dame), Dick Evans (Iowa, El Toro 1944)

Assistants: not available

Athletic officer: Capt. Lloyd Trout (Millersville)

Ends: W.L. Cornwell, J.P. Duncan (Coffeyville JC), D.B. Gallagher, Ed Hamilton (Arkansas), W.C. Jordan, McKay, R.L. Pourchot, Watley

Tackles: Trotzky Kalnin (St. Mary's, NAS Jacksonville 1943), A.L. Kracik, West Matthews (El Toro 1945, UCLA), Lloyd McDermott (El Toro 1944, Kentucky), M.E. Ploman (Iowa State), C.J. Roberts, Smith, Ed Sprano (El Toro 1945, Univ. of San Francisco), G.E. Twitchell (St. Mary's)

Guards: G. Blagg, W. Brozowsky (Scranton), C. Caruso, Joe Daugherty (Tulsa, MCB San Diego 1943, El Toro 1944, Univ. of San Francisco), Gasper, Jack Hyle (Georgetown, Cherry Point 1944, El Toro 1945, Cornell), A.B. Molson, Simpson, C.C. Vasey, F.J. Wierciock

Centers: Forester, M.L. Katich, Carl Perkinson (Duke, MCB San Diego 1943, El Toro 1944)

Backs: C.C. Collum, Lynn Cryar (El Toro 1944), P.K. Davis (Rice), E.J. Giddings (Minnesota), Walt "Mouse" Halsall (South Carolina, Cherry Point 1944, El Toro 1945), Charles Horvath (Penn) (El Toro 1944), J.J. Jankowski (Missouri), W.E. Kreisle (Purdue), F.M. Kunka (Alabama), Hank Little, Eli Maracich (Georgia), Tony Minetto (Pacific, Redlands, El Toro 1944-45), Walt Ott (El Toro 1944), Dan "Bunny" Radakovich (St. John's of Minnesota, Montana), Ken Reese (Alabama, Cherry Point 1943-44, El Toro 1945), Rogger Roggatz (Drake, Eagle Mountain Lake 1944, El Toro 1945), Jim Terrell (Oklahoma, El Toro 1944).

Former Notre Dame players gather at Camp Lejeune: (first row) Joe Signaigo, Jim Sullivan, Mike Hines, Bernie Meter; (top row) Gaspar Urb Julie Rykovich, Bob David, John Yonakor.

Kinston's Two Teams

T he Kinston Marines fielded football teams only two seasons. And both won two games in abbreviated schedules.

Playing as MAG-91, the Fliers — also known as the Corsairs — beat the North Carolina Pre-Flight B and Bogue Field in 1944 before the schedule was canceled after the fifth game because group personnel were transferred to Congaree, S.C.

The top player arguably was back Chris "Duke" Iversen, who had played at Oregon in 1940 and '41, at NAS Jacksonville in 1942 and 1943, at Oregon in 1946 and with the New York Giants in 1947, New York Yankees in 1948 and 1949 and the New York Yanks in 1950 and '51. He scored 12 of Kinston's first 15 points in 1944.

The 1945 team defeated Ft. Monroe and Camp Mackall. Two players, in particular, would be heard from after the war.

Back Lloyd Merriman would star at Stanford in 1946 but then head for major-league baseball and be recalled for combat flying in Korea. Charles Bradshaw, after playing four seasons at Kentucky, would go into coaching and head up the programs at Kentucky and Troy State 14 years.

1944

Record: 7-0 N.C. Pre-Flight B, 8-0 Bogue Field, 0-62 Maxwell Field, 0-0 Norfolk Navy, 0-33 Camp Lejeune (2-2-1).

Player-coaches: Chris "Duke" Iversen (Oregon, NAS Jacksonville 1942-43), Lou Campbell (Southwestern Louisiana)

Assistants: George Hanna (Denison), Bob Olson (Miami of Fla.)

Ends: Bill Allen, Al Bown, Joe Cramer, Stan Duganz (Montana), Frank Kennedy, Bill Przewoznik

Tackles: Blois Grissom (Georgia), Joe Lorkiewicz, Joe Moreau, Olson, Sam Stark, Bill Taylor, John Walmsley (West Virginia)

Guards: Campbell, Tex Curl, Joe Dzielak, Hanna, Sam Marcus, Gerald Rhodes

Centers: Bob Reherman, Charlie Saunders (Texas A&M), Ted Urban

Backs: Ed Barry, Bill Botterbusch, Vince Burger, Jim Cramer, Iversen, George Lowery (Washington & Lee), Bill Lyerla (Pittsburg Teachers), Stan Malkasian (Northeastern), Jim Norvell (Western Illinois, NAS Jacksonville 1943), Jim Peterson, Bill Sicilia, Billy Smith, Ray Zakutynski

1945

Record: 13-7 Ft. Monroe, 0-21 Catawba, 6-10 Oak Grove Marines, 6-9 N.C. JC, 6-0 Camp Mackall (2-3).

Coach: not available. **Assistants:** not available.

Ends: not available. **Tackles:** not available. **Guards:** not available. **Centers:** Charlie Bradshaw (Kentucky). **Backs:** Lloyd Merriman (Stanford, NAS Norman 1944). **Kicker:** Daken)
(INCOMPLETE)

Tough Times at Bogue

B ogue Field made more headlines by losing one game
than it did in the remainder of its two abbreviated
seasons.

The eastern North Carolina base, an auxiliary field for Cherry
Point, fell before the Duke Blue Devils, 76-0, in 1945.

The game was held in the Eastern time zone, which meant it was
completed in time for the major Atlantic Coast and Midwest papers to
carry the game account —such as it was.

And since Duke had beaten South Carolina the previous week, 60-0,
some papers put the 76-0 victory on the front sports page. The 76 points
was a Duke school record. The Blue Devils (6-2) lost only to national-
champion Army and to Navy that season.

But Bogue Field (1-2) could say it really wasn't that bad, pointing to
a victory over the Oak Grove Marines and losing to Little Creek by the
same 6-0 score. It was ranked No. 56 by the Williamson Rating
Service, ahead of other Army, Navy, Air Force and Marine teams.

The team in 1944 and 1945 had virtually no college experience. Back
Bob Heer had played freshman ball at North Dakota State and for
Iowa Pre-Flight in 1942 and would return to State for the 1946 and 1947
seasons.

And the '44 team (0-2) didn't have size, either. A center, Cassidy,
was the heaviest at 206 pounds.

1944

Record: 0-41 Camp Lejeune, 0-8 MCAS Kinston (0-2)
Coach: not available. **Assistants:** not available
Ends: Durham, France, Hader, Mayberry, Squittieri, Vinnerman
Tackles: Anderson, Cox, Earnhart, Kuhn, George Preston, Wyman
Guards: Berry, Hoover, Kane, Matheson, Peloquin, Stickles
Centers: Cassidy, Linderman, Lovelace
Backs: S. Bogas, Callahan, G. Freytag, J. Jackson, T. Kane, C. King, E. Luther, L. Mathie, W.
Monfort, R. Rees, R. Young

1945

Record: 0-6 Little Creek, 0-76 Duke, 6-0 Oak Grove Marines (1-2)
Coach: not available. **Assistants:** not available.
Ends: B.J. Baenen, T. Doyle, Joe Hartman (Fordham), C. Helberg, J. McCormick, Geo. Preston,
M. Sobeiack
Tackles: E. Beinberg (Washington), B. Burwell, Jim Cozad, G.A. Elminger (Holy Cross), N. Pace,
W. Vanderbrook, E. Yukeanavage
Guards: Dave Asbell, A. Bennett, R. Hovis, J. Huey, J. Hurford, J. Jones, W. Kane (Minnesota),
Bill Silver, G. Visci
Centers: F. Crane (Amherst), L. Daily, J. Munson (Wooster), J. Tigan
Backs: L. Allen, M. Bethea (Auburn), R. Carroll, R. Cranston, R. Fairman, Bob Heer (North
Dakota State, Iowa Pre-Flight 1942), L. Mathie, G. McGuire, J. Rushforth, R. Rutley (Canisius), J.
Taylor, E. Uhl, J. Urbach (South Dakota). W. Watson (Tampa), C. Williford, J. Wolf

Stateside Raiders

The Ward Island Raiders won two games in 1943 but can't be accused of a soft schedule. Quite the contrary. The Marine team, using enlisted players entirely and honoring the exploits of Carlson's Raiders, opened with a 54-0 loss to Southwestern University and followed with 39-9 and 53-14 losses to Randolph Field.

But Southwestern, using Marine trainees from the 1942 Texas and Baylor teams, was of Top 10 quality and finished with a 10-1-1 record, beating Texas, Rice and New Mexico and tying Tulsa. The loss was to Marine-studded Southwestern Louisiana. But for losing eight first-stringers and five second-stringers to Parris Island on Nov. 1, the Pirates might have finished in the AP's Top 10.

Randolph Field, led by quarterback Glenn Dobbs (Tulsa), won nine, lost once and tied Texas, 7-7, in the Cotton Bowl.

Back at its level, Ward Island beat Abilene AAF and Camp Hearne but lost to Blackland AAF.

Ward Island was coached by S/Sgt. Don Plato (Colgate, St. Lawrence), a guard at Quantico in 1941 and NAS Jacksonville in 1942. He would coach the Cherry Point team in 1946 and later at Drake.

The Southwestern opener was unusual in that Marine met Marine.

"The Pirates, called the 'all Southwest Conference' team by the Corpus Christi Caller-Times, sloshed and slid to an easy victory in Buccaneer Stadium amid a drizzling rain," one account said.

Approximately 5,000 fans, "most of them Marines and sailors from Ward Island, flocked to the stadium where they braved an intermittent rain.

" ... Though the wet weather prevented either team from attempting many passes, there was plenty of running, and the Raiders' line was no match for the Pirates' brick-wall line."

Blocking back Chet Holewinski (Michigan State) might have been the only player with major-college experience. End Charles Wilson would return to Washington State for the 1945 season.

Record: 0-54 Southwestern of Texas, 9-39 Randolph Field, 14-53 Randolph Field, 14-0 Abilene AFB, 6-19 Blackland Field, 32-0 Camp Hearne (2-4). Camp Livingston game cancelled.
Coach: S/Sgt. Don Plato (Colgate, St. Lawrence, Quantico 1941, NAS Jacksonville 1942)
Assistant: S/Sgt. Red Monson
Ends: Bob Baker (Rice), Charles Wilson (Washington State)
Tackles: Walter Bartels, Egert, Bob Kuyper (Michigan), Schwitzer, Charles Wiethoff (Minnesota)
Guards: Angelo Alfieri (Brooklyn), Fred Robinson, Vuckovitch
Centers: Bob Benham (Morris-Harvey)
Backs: R. Adams, Rod Gervais (Purdue), Jim Harms (Minnesota), Bill Helm (Wisconsin), Chet Holewinski (Michigan State)
Others: Dick Geyser, Ben Howard (Tennessee), Dick McGrath (Marquette), Merlin Rikola (Ely JC)

Squadron Battle

Better late than never, say members of the 1945 Marine Air Warning Squadron-8 (touch) football team.

Forty-two years after winning the 2nd Marine Air Wing championship on Okinawa, MAWS-8 received a plaque and congratulatory letter from Maj. Gen. M.P. Sullivan, commanding general of the wing.

"... Although I was not able to personally attend your championship game with MAWS-6, I was 12 at the time, I have read the press reports on the contest and feel that it is one that would have rivaled any of the Super Bowls," Gen. Sullivan wrote.

'... I fully understand and appreciate the team's inability to participate in the winner's trip to Japan or to remain on the island for gold footballs. Given the same circumstances, I would also have foregone the formalities for an opportunity to head home."

A theater championship also was at stake as MAWS-8 defeated MAWS-6, 9-6, on Jan. 20, 1946 in what was called the "Shootout at the Oki Corral." Lou Mackey decided the game with a 21-yard field goal in the last seconds.

MAWS-6 had been the best team on the island's east coast. The undefeated MAWS-8 team had defeated Army, Navy, Seabee, Army Air Force and other Marine teams in Okinawa's Southern Division in the fall of 1945.

"Missing from MAWS-8's lineup that day was one of its biggest guns, Ernie Johnson, pass catcher par excellence and a tough defender," said a May 1989 Leatherneck story. "Johnson was heading home for discharge, but MAWS-6 was not aware of his absence.

"MAWS-8 Coach 'Pappy' Potter pulled a slight change-of-letters trick to deceive MAWS-6. He had Harold Hasenmeyer play in Johnson's place and stenciled J-O-H-N-S-O-N on Hasenmeyer's green skivvy T-shirt. This permitted our passer to ignore Hasenmeyer, who was triple-teamed, and hit (Chet) Cieslinski and others for several long gainers."

Johnson would post a 40-23 record in nine seasons as a relief pitcher with the Boston Braves in 1950 and '52, the Milwaukee Braves from 1953-58 and Baltimore Orioles in 1959. He would have a 3.77 ERA in 273 games.

He also would become administrative assistant to the president, and public-relations director of the Milwaukee Braves, and director of broadcasting and an Atlanta Braves announcer, retiring after the 1989 season.

Guard John Petercuskie of MAWS-8 would play at East Stroudsburg (Pa.) and be a college assistant at Dartmouth, Boston College, Princeton and Harvard, and a pro assistant with the Cleveland Browns. In 1989, he joined the staff at Liberty (Va.).

On Jan. 1, MAWS-6 and MAWS-8 had combined forces to defeat an Army team, 20-6, also at Point Dog.

An Army major "tried to sandbag us," said Potter. "From bases as far as the Philippines to depots in Japan, a formidable Army team — mostly, if not all, former football players from the NFL — was hurriedly assembled. The team practiced a few days and declared itself fit for battle, ready to show the Marines how the game should be played."

An island (Army) paper wrote that a "wanton, violent war-like game was won by a gang of wild Marines. ... And it can only be described as 'out-of-control' madness. ... Such play should be outlawed ... or officials should be permitted to enforce the rules rather than being ignored and threatened. Oddly, tackling was not permitted. This rule was enforced and even accepted by the Marine ruffians. ..."

"I've been told that small fortunes were made on games played by MAWS-8's football team," said the commanding officer in 1946, Capt. Frank Casserly of South Laguna, Cal., who retired as a colonel.

The MAWS-8 personnel continued to hold reunions into the '90s.

MAWS-8
Coach: Joe "Pappy" Potter
Linemen: Chet Cieslinski, Dan D'Attilio, Harold Hasenmeyer, Lou Mackey, Porky Mituzas, John Petercuskie, Bernie Reynolds
Backs: Dutch Brong, Dick Decker   K Vern Gill
(incomplete)

MAWS-6
Coach: not available
Line: Eddie Depesky, T.J. Flynn, Eddie Herlein, La Manna, Tuffy Marino, Corky Orkiswski, Gimper Palonis
Backs: Bill Decker, Bill Ehler, John Harris, Ace Rawlings
(incomplete)

L.A. Reservists Persevere

M aj. Gen. L.H.M. Sanderson, a commanding general at MCAS, El Toro, made a DC-3 available to transport the 1948 Los Angeles Marine Reserve football team to games.

However, after the Marine Reserve team defeated El Toro, 6-0, Sanderson, a former football standout at Montana and with Mare Island and the All-Marines, had mixed emotions.

"Here I gave you a plane all year and you came and beat us."

Fortunately, perhaps, the Marine Reserve team had driven the 50 miles to the game.

Record: 6-0 MCAS El Toro, 13-26 Palo Verde JC, 0-28 MCRD San Diego, 21-6 El Centro JC
(incomplete)
Coach: George "Cotton" Gilliland (San Diego St.)
Assistants: Len Fribourg (Ohio St.), Bob McNeil (Michigan St., Quantico assistant 1951)
Ends: Bilby, Earl, Johnson
Tackles: Brown, R. King, Wilbur
Guards: W. King, Ralston, Perez
Centers: Arias, Lewis
Backs: Brawner, Jack Dunn, Livingston, Bill Stelle, Stankin
(incomplete)

How They Hit in '46

The Illinois-Wisconsin game in 1946 was dubbed the "Battle of Marine Lieutenants" and was typical of many that fall where former Leathernecks lined up on both sides of the ball.

Illinois had ends Frank Bauman and Joe Buscemi, tackle Mike Kasap, guard Alex Agase, center and captain Mac Wenskunas and back Julie Rykovich, who were commissioned through the V-12 program in the latter half of WWII. Wisconsin countered with backs Wally Dreyer, Earl Maves and Jack Wink, ends Farnham Johnson, Hank Olshanski and Bob Rennebohm, guard John Gallagher and center Fred Negus.

Fueling the rivalry was that four of those Illini had played for Purdue as Marine trainees in 1943 and the Wisconsin group wore Michigan uniforms.

Pride also was involved.

Wrote Henry J. McCormick in a Madison, Wisc., paper just before the game (won by Illinois, 27-21), "Every Wisconsin athlete on this year's team who was in Marine training at Michigan went on to earn his commission."

He added of the game: "The beachhead to be secured will be the gridiron at Memorial Stadium in Champaign, Ill. ... You now how those Marines are. Or haven't you ever heard them tell how good they are — and then go out and prove they speak the truth. ... ?"

Illinois had other former Marines, tackle John Genis, end Stan Green, backs Bill Krall and Chick Maggioli and guard Herb Siegert, players who helped the Illini win the Big Ten title and open the Rose Bowl series against the West Coast schools with a 45-14 victory over UCLA.

The 1946 Illustrated Football Annual referred to the "Marine-studded" team and "leakproof Leatherneck line" at Illinois, saying the players had come "From the Halls of Montezuma to the plains of Illinois."

Carrying out the theme, the magazine said, "Back from Iwo and Okinawa, home from Purdue and Notre Dame (where Wenskunas and Rykovich had played), came seven valiant Marines to put a devildog bite in Illinois football."

But what else could be expected after the Corps from 1942-45 took hundreds of thousands of men, from the city and farm, and ran them ... and ran them ... and turned out superbly conditioned Marines.

Despite postwar partying and the return to civilian status, there wasn't enough time for all of them to lose their edge before the 1946 season, and by and large they had the situation well in hand.

Typical of their spirit was the example of Boston University's Everrett Dorr, who could play only on kicking downs because of shrapnel in his leg from Iwo Jima.

Stanford lineman Fred Boensch played with a special helmet designed to protect a sniper's wound from Okinawa.

Bernie Gallagher, a standout lineman at Penn, erroneously had been reported killed on Okinawa.

And there were funny moments, too.

End Ed Kaminski of San Francisco and tackle Cyclone Sullivan of Nevada were about to mix it up in a game. "I know you," said one of them, "from a foxhole on Okinawa."

Of course, many Marines did not return, such as backs Tony Butkovich (Illinois-Purdue) and Johnny Perry (Wake Forest-Duke), who were killed on Okinawa, plus countless others killed or wounded on Iwo Jima and in other Pacific campaigns.

How good were these former Marines?

■ Agase, back Charlie Conerly (Mississippi), guard Weldon Humble (Rice), tackle Thurman McGraw (Colorado A&M), tackle Leo Nomellini (Minnesota), end Barney Poole (Army) and 30-year-old tackle Alvin 'Moose" Wistert (Boston University) would be elected to the College Hall of Fame. Guard Artie Donovan (Boston College), Nomellini and tackle Ernie Stautner (Boston College) would be chosen for the Pro Hall of Fame.

■ Agase, tackle Dick Huffman (Tennessee), Humble and tackle George Savitsky of Penn were first-team All-Americans in 1946. Poole and tackle Bill Milner (Duke) were second-team, and Bernie Gallagher, quarterback Mickey McCardle (USC) and end Ray Poole (Mississippi) were third-team.

■ Pity the Associated Press as it tried to name its Lineman of the W eek. For example, nominees the week of Oct. 5 included Agase, Boensch, Jackson Bush (Georgia), Spot Collins (Texas) and Huffman.

For the week of Oct. 12 the voters had to consider, among others, Collins, Weldon Edwards of Texas Christian, Bill Hachten (Stanford), Sid Halliday (SMU), Ray Poole and Jim Sid Wright (SMU). For the week of Nov. 12 the contenders included Edwards, Humble, Ray Poole and Wright. Bernie Gallagher was the Lineman of the Week against Virginia, Humble for the week of Nov. 16 and Joe Sultis (Rice) for the week he faced Texas.

■ San Francisco always has been a Marines' town, and 11 former Leathernecks took part in the 1947 East-West Game.

■ Thirty-six were chosen in the 1947 NFL draft, and 26 by the All-America Football Conference. Bernie Gallagher was Chicago's special selection in the AAFC draft, Conerly was picked in the second round, end Ray Kuffel (Marquette), back Lloyd Merriman (Stanford) and Collins in the third round; and Humble, back Joe Andrejco (Fordham) and Wright in the fourth round. In the NFL draft, tackle Nelson Greene (Tulsa), Merriman and Savitsky were picked in the third round; center Bill Gray (Oregon State), back Duke Iverson (Oregon), tackle Bill Smyth (Cincinnati) and tackle Carroll Vogelaar (San Francisco) in the fifth round.

This is not to say there weren't problems adjusting to college life. How does a coach discipline players who had fought through hell on Okinawa or Iwo Jima? How does he maintain a relationship with former Marines who lost friends or were wounded in combat? What about smoking? What about the wives and children? And alcohol, not cocaine, was the most dangerous addiction of that era.

Col. Bernie Bierman USMCR, who served in both World War I and II. had little success with his iron-hand policy after returning to coach at Minnesota. But he wasn't the only one.

And how does a Bill Miklich adjust to playing at Idaho after last lettering in 1941? Apparently very well, because he was drafted by the New York Yankees in the 13th round of the All-America Football Conference draft.

Tackle Thurman Owens of Cincinnati, who would be recalled for the Korean War, went on to become a general.

And there were other leaders sprinkled among the teams. For example, these were among the decorated Marines in the Pacific:

■ **Silver Star:** Gus Camarata (Iowa Teachers), Larry Halenkamp (Minnesota) and Jim Myers (Tennessee).

■ **Distinguished Flying Cross:** Jack Sloan (Cal).

■ **Bronze Star:** Dee Andros (Oklahoma), Bill Doolittle (Ohio State), Les Dugan (Niagara), Milam Grevich (Minnesota), Billy Murphy (Mississippi State), Tom Owen (Vanderbilt), Odell Stautzenberger (Texas A&M) and Alex Wizbicki (Holy Cross).

Three of the nation's most publicized backs did not compete again in the college ranks. Alvin Dark, who starred at LSU in 1942 and Southwestern Louisiana in 1943, signed a baseball contract after returning from China. Elroy "Crazylegs" Hirsch also gave up two years of eligibility to sign a pro football contract. All-American Pat Harder, also of Wisconsin, turned pro.

Others giving up eligibility to play for pay included center Bill Blackburn (Rice-Southwestern Louisiana), tackle Art McCaffray (Santa Clara-Pacific) and end John Yonakor (Notre Dame).

And there were broken hearts along the way. Alabama expected back Hosea Rodgers to return, but he went to North Carolina, where he had played as a V-12 trainee in 1943. South Carolina was looking for Milner to come back, but he opted for Duke, where he, too, had played in 1943 as a V-12er. And there were others.

But 33 players from the lieutenant-laced Pearl Harbor Marines team of 1945 were playing college ball in 1946, as were 10 from the 1944 El Toro powerhouse (8-1) and 12 from the fabled 1945 team (8-2).

And guard Ben Whaley played for Virginia State in a career that three years later apparently made him the first black Marine to play for the pros.

Minnesota had at least nine former Marines, several of whom had played as trainees at Northwestern.

The University of San Francisco, coached by former Capt. Clipper Smith USMCR, had eight.

Villanova had eight. So did Baylor, Duke and Rice.

When Quantico took the field against Davis & Elkins, Coach Austin Shofner learned that his team was facing seven former Marines.

California, Mississippi State and Stanford also had seven each, and Dartmouth, Mississippi, Missouri, USC and and Western Michigan six each.

Stanford could start a former Leatherneck forward wall of Jim Cox and Boensch at tackles, Hachten and Dick Madigan at guards, and Dick Flatland at center.

In the Tangerine Bowl against Maryville, Catawba started six. Colgate, Michigan, Notre Dame, Purdue and St. Mary's each had five on the roster.

Obviously some recruiting went on in the Pacific in between battles, but in many cases the players simply picked up where they left off.

"It seems Smith has found a number of ex-Gyrenes as well as other GIs more than willing to cast their lot with him (at USF)," said the Illustrated Football Annual.

Besides Bierman and Smith, former Marines who were head college coaches included Ray Hanson (Western Illinois), Tuss McLaughry (Dartmouth) and Roy Randall (Haverford).

In retrospect, however, it might have been in coaching, not on the playing field, that the former Marines would make their greatest impact. From the ballfields of 1946 would come such future college coaches as Agase, Andros, Charlie Bradshaw, Jim Camp, Jerry Carle, Collins, Doolittle, Dreyer, Dugan, Chalmers "Bump" Elliott, Bob Hatch, Don Henderson, Chuck Klausing, Frank Lauterbur, Mike Lude, Murphy, Myers, Roger Robinson, Max Spilsbury, Bob Thalman, Dick Voris, Wenskunas, Wink and Ray Yagiello.

In the pro ranks, John North would become a pro head coach, and Agase, Don Doll, Brad Ecklund, Lauterbur, Jim Martin, McGraw, Myers, John Petercuskie, Smyth, Stautner and Voris pro assistants.

Among the many playing that 1946 season were:

ALABAMA: Johnny August, Gri Cashio, Joe Gambrell, John Staples; **ARIZONA:** Fred Knez, Max Spilsbury; **ARKANSAS:** Ed Hamilton, Charles Lively, Herman Lubker, Joyce Pipkin; **ARMY:** Barney Poole; **AUBURN:** Marv Hewlett, Tom McKinney.

BALL STATE: Jim Stone; **BAYLOR:** R.L. Cooper, Bill Craven, James Erwin, Wayne Franks, Jim Griffin, Bob Henderson, Gordon Hollon, Kit Kittrell; **BOSTON UNIVERSITY:** Harry Botsford, Everett Dorr, Bob Hatch, Alvin Wistert; **BOSTON COLLEGE:** Artie Donovan, Bob Mangene, Dom Papaleo, Ernie Stautner; **BRIGHAM YOUNG:** Stan Stapley; **BROWN:** Jim Lalikos; **BUCKNELL:** Gene Hubka

CALIFORNIA: Wendell Beard (injured), Jim Cullom, Bob Dal Porto, Lou Jurkovich, Jack Sloan, Jim Turner, Ed Welch; **CANISIUS:** Darrell Braatz; **CATAWBA:** M.L. Barnes, Harold Bowen, Jim Dickey, Don Hanley, Lynn Hunter, Leland Littleton, Vernon Ramsey, C.M. Tarleton, Ray Yagiello; **CINCINNATI:** Thurman Owens, Allen Richards, Bill Smyth; **CLEMSON:** Lew ross: **COLGATE:** Neil Dooley, Elving Nordmark, John Sellon, Jim Smyth, Ed Stacco; **COLORADO:** John Dean, Jim Price, Bob Spicer; **COLORADO A&M:** Thurman McGraw; **COLORADO COLLEGE:** Lars Watson, John Zeigler; **COLUMBIA:** Don Kasprzak; **CONNECTICUT:** Len Arntsen; **CONWAY TEACHERS:** Mike Malham; **CORNELL:** Matt Bolger, Ted Hapanowicz, John Hyle

DARTMOUTH: Bob Albrecht, Jim Biggie, Bob McLaughry, Francis O'Brien, George Rusch, Art Young; **DAYTON:** Joe Accrocco, Milt McGuire, Bill Powers, Joe Zoul; **DENVER:** Joe Cribari, Bob Hazelhurst, Tom Saracino; **DUKE:** Frank Inman, Leo Long, Buddy Luper, Bill Milner, Kelly Mote, Carl Perkinson, Herman Smith, Garland Wolfe

EAST STROUDSBURG: John Petercuskie; **EAST TEXAS:** Jim Cody

FORDHAM: Joe Andrejco, Joe Ososki, Harry Squatrito; **FRANKLIN & MARSHALL:** Frank Sweeney; **FRESNO STATE:** Jackie Fellows, Dick Handley, Rex Schroeder, John Seiferling

GEORGE WASHINFGTON: Paul Weber; **GEORGIA:** Jackson Bush, Joe Geri, Eli Maracich, Garland Williams; **GEORGIA TECH:** Roland Phillips, Jim Still

HARDIN-SIMMONS: Dick Brown; **HARVARD:** Cleo O'Donnell; **HILLSDALE:** Mike Lude; **HOLY CROSS:** Alex Wizbicki

IDAHO: John Dana, Carl Kilsgaard, Bill Miklich, Wil Overgaard; **INDIANA:** Joe Bartkiewicz, Joe Polce; **IOWA TEACHERS:** Gus Camarata

KANSAS STATE: Grover Nutt; **KENTUCKY:** Charlie Bradshaw

LAFAYETTE: Bill Greenip; **LSU:** Holley Heard, Jim Loflin, James "Moe" Richmond; **LOYOLA (LA):** John Machado, George Vercelli, Bob Winship

MARQUETTE: Allan Elgar, Ray Kuffel, Carl Schuette; **MARYLAND:** Fred Jackson, Bob Stuart; **McMURRY:** F.G. Hoefer; **MIAMI (Fla.):** Bob McDougal; **MIAMI (Ohio):** Dick Enzminger, Dick Piskoty; **MICHIGAN:** George Burg, Fenwick Crane, Chalmers "Bump" Elliott, Art Renner, Paul White; **MICHIGAN STATE:** Vince Mroz; **MISSISSIPPI:** Charlie Conerly, Cecil Dickerson, Bill

Erickson, Oliver Poole, Ray Poole, Houstin Smith; **MISSISSIPPI STATE:** Jim Arnold, Kermit "Rosey" Davis, John Grace, Bill McCain, Mike Mihalic, Bill Moates, Billy Murphy; **MISSOURI:** Verlie Abrams, Jim Austin, Ken Bounds, Jim Darr, Leo Milla, Bernard Pepper; **MONTANA:** Dan "Bunny" Radakovich, William Reynolds; **MONTANA STATE:** Len "Bud" Seelinger; **MOUNT UNION:** Frank Lauterbur; **MUHLENBURG:** Bob Mirth

NAVY: Ken Schieweck; **NEBRASKA:** Ed Nyden, Joe Partington, Sam Vacanti; **NEVADA:** Bob "Cyclone" Sullivan; **NEW YORK UNIV.:** Gus Autieri, Roxy Finn; **NIAGARA:** Frank Buran, Les Dugan; **NORTH CAROLINA:** Jim Camp, Ted Hazelwood, Hosea Rodgers; **NORTH CAROLINA STATE:** Bert Dressler, Fred Miller, Bernie Watts; **NORTH DAKOTA STATE:** R. Heer; **NORTH TEXAS:** Billy Cromer; **NORTHWESTERN:** Jerry Carle, Frank Genovese, Jack MacKenzie; **NOTRE DAME:** Gus Cifelli, Jim Martin, Bernie "Bud" Meter, Joe Signaigo, Gaspar Urban.

OHIO UNIV.: John Kerns, Chris Stefan; **OHIO STATE:** Bill Doolittle, Fred "Curley" Morrison; **OKLAHOMA:** Dee Andros, Norm McNabb; **OKLAHOMA A&M:** Bill Aldridge; **OREGON:** Brad Ecklund, Duke Iverson, Sam Ramey; **OREGON STATE:** Martin Chaves, Bill Gray, Lee Gustafson, Ted Ossowski.

PENN: Grant Ellis, Bernie Gallagher, Ed Lawless, George Savitsky; **PENN STATE:** Ed Czekaj, Bill Kyle, Paul Weaver, Bob Williams; **PITTSBURGH:** Sam Haddad; **POMONA:** John Jaqua; **PRINCETON:** Ernest Ransome, Herb Warden, Neil Zundell; **PURDUE:** Bob Heck, Morris Kaastad, Don Lehmkuhl, Norm Maloney, Ken Smock.

REDLANDS: Keoth Broaders, Ben Mansell; **RICE:** Henry Armstrong, Virgil Eikenberg, Weldon Humble, John Magee, Charles Malmberg, Fred Noble, Joe Sultis, Windell Williams; **RICHMOND:** Bob Thalman.

ST. BONAVENTURE: Hugo Marcolini; **ST. LOUIS:** Stancel James, Vern Kenny, Harry Sortal, Pete Wismann; **ST. MARY'S:** Ray Ahlstrom, Frank Callen, Joe Ferem, Jack Flagerman, Jack Verutti; **SAN DIEGO STATE:** Keith Curry, Val Robbins; **SAN FRANCISCO:** Joe Daugherty, Ed Kaminski, Fred Klemenok, Ed Roseborough, John Sanchez, Jack Schiefer, Ed Sprano, Carroll Vogelaar; **SAN JOSE STATE:** Bruce Clarke, Bob Creighton, Dick Voris; **SANTA BARBARA STATE:** John Pickarts; **SANTA CLARA:** Ed Barnett, Bart Gianelli, Val Mohlenhuhr; **SCRANTON:** Sal Cicotelli; **SLIPPERY ROCK:** Chuck Klausing; **SMU:** Lloyd Baxter, Earl Cook, Sid Halliday, Jim Sid Wright; **STANFORD:** Ainslie Bell, Fred Boensch, Jim Cox, Dick Flatland, Bill Hachten, Dick Madigan, Lloyd Merriman; **SYRACUSE:** Paul McKee, Roger Robinson.

TEMPLE: Paul Dubenetzky, George Waltzer; **TENNESSEE:** George Balitsaris, Dick Huffman, Jim Myers; **TENNESSEE TECH:** Don Henderson; **TEXAS:** W.H. "Spot" Collins, Vic Vasicek; **TEXAS A&M:** Odell Stautzenberger, Bob Tulis; **TEXAS CHRISTIAN:** Weldon Edwards, Pete Stout, Elmer Tidwell; **TEXAS TECH:** J.W. Coats, Cal Steveson; **TEXAS WESTERN:** Lew Hartzog; **TOLEDO:** Jim Foltz, Dave Hardy; **TULANE:** Mike Balen, Art Porter, John Sims; **TULSA:** Nelson Greene, Charles McGinley, Art Ramage (injured).

UCLA: Carl Benton, West Mathews, Jim McConnaughy, Xavier Mena; **USC:** Don Doll, Si Fuhrman (injured), Mike Garzoni, Mickey McCardle, Marshall Romer, Duane Whitehead; **UTAH STATE:** Dick Howard.

VANDERBILT: Fred Hamilton, John North; **VILLANOVA:** Ed Berrang, Tom Clavin, Bob David, Bill Dost, Zig Gory,, Mel Downey, George Pavalko, Bob Polidor; **VIRGINIA:** Sam Fray, George Grimes; **VIRGINIA STATE:** Ben Whaley; **VIRGINIA TECH:** John "Greek" Maskas.

WAKE FOREST: Harry Clark, Otis "Bo" Sacrinty; **WASHINGTON:** Gordon Berlin, Gail Bruce, George Meyers, Sam Robinson; **WESLEYAN:** John M.R. Morton; **WESTERN MICHIGAN:** Al Bush, Clifton Brown, Cliff Keddie, Nick Milosevich, Tom O'Shaughnessy, Carl Schiller; **WEST TEXAS:** Boyce Box, Cloyce Box, Mac Winter; **WEST VIRGINIA:** Ambrose Zugel; **WILLIAM & MARY:** Jim McDowell; **XAVIER** (Ohio): John Picciano; **YALE:** Enrico Cipolaro, Nick Fusilli, Emory Larson Jr.

Also: Montana St.: Cliff Brisbin, Neil Brooks, Gene Miles. Oklahoma: John Rapacz. USF: Joe Scott

And some former Marines didn't make it back until the 1947 season, or even 1948, because of returning late to the States, war wounds, practice injuries, the adjustment to college, attendance at a junior college, etc.

Back Bernie Rohling of Vanderbilt, captain-elect of the '46 Vanderbilt team who was wounded on Iwo Jima, did not play until 1947. Neither did linemen Jack Faulkner (Miami of Ohio) nor Abe Gibron (Purdue), later to be pro coaches.

Others who returned for the 1947 season included:

W.E. Anderson (Massachusetts), Joe Brady (Dartmouth), Larry Christensen (Washington State), John Costello (Dartmouth), Carol Cox (Clemson), Roland Dale (Mississippi), Hank Ennen (UCLA), Henry George (Western Michigan), Marv Hess (Utah), Dick Hoffman (West Virginia), Earl Howell (Mississippi), Carroll Huntress (New Hampshire), George Kiesel (Michigan), Otto Kofler (Washington State), Bill LaFleur (Penn State), Jim Liber (Xavier), Frank Marcus (Florida State), Joe McCrane (Army), Lloyd McDermott (Kentucky), Carl McKinnon (Dartmouth), John Miskiewicz (Penn State), Chuck Page (UCLA), Lenox Palin (Princeton), Keith Parker (Missouri), Ken Peck (Stanford), Jim Pittman (Mississippi State), Dick Rash (San Diego State), Bill Renna (Santa Clara), Jay Roundy (USC), Joe Sadonis (Fordham), Bill Sheridan (Santa Clara), Ray Stackhouse (Xavier), Al Thomas (Northwestern), Wilcourt Washburn (Dartmouth), Jim Whipple (Stanford), Jerry Whitney (UCLA), Billy Williams (Georgia Tech), Bob Windish (Georgetown) and Joe Zuzga (Xavier).

Also: Jim Reed (Texas Tech)

Coaches: Bierman, Hanson, Jim Lee Howell (Wagner), John McLaughry (Union), Tuss McLaughry, Randall.

Tackle John Sanchez made his mark at USF, Redlands and in the NFL.

A Title at Miramar

The Marine Corps Air Station at Miramar had but one varsity football team. But it was a memorable season. And how many teams had a star back with silver leaves on his shoulders?

The Tigercats won six games, captured the 11th Naval District title, tied for the West Coast Naval Aviation Athletic Conference title, were ranked 21st nationally by the Williamson Rating Service among service teams and lost only to NAS Alameda, 16-0.

Following on the heels of two awesome basketball teams at the San Diego area base, Miramar was tested in only one other football game, a 15-13 victory over NTC San Diego. The other victory margins were 32, 58, 19, 34 and 13 points.

The Tigercats also scrimmaged San Diego State and Santa Barbara State.

Not unexpectedly, the player-coach went by "Wild Bill." He was Lt. Col. William Clasen, also known as "Swede," a back at Indiana, at Pensacola and who would suit up again at NAS Patuxent River in 1947. He had been awarded a DFC during two South Pacific tours.

In a 19-6 victory over El Toro, Clasen scored the Miramar touchdowns on runs of 5, 20 and 5 yards. He also scored against NAS North Island, the Submarine Raiders (on a pass) and against NTC (on a pass).

Joe Sharman at 160 pounds was an all-around back while 225-pound fullback Joe Pillon, another DFC holder, had played at St. Mary's Pre-Flight and would play later for El Toro and Cherry Point.

End Bob Logal, after an All-Marine season at El Toro in 1947, jumped all the way to the Buffalo Bills of the All-America Football Conference two years later without college experience. He was among 13 ends on the 41-man Miramar roster.

Guard Joe Polidori would play for El Toro from 1947-50 and Camp Fisher in 1953 and coach the 1st Marine Division team in Korea in 1954 and MCRD San Diego in 1956.

The Marine Air West headquarters was moved to El Toro on Nov. 1, although the football team continued to play out of Miramar. At least six Miramar players would compete for El Toro in 1947.

Record: 32-0 San Diego Naval Hospital, 64-6 NAS Seattle, 19-0 NAS North Island, 0-16 NAS Alameda, 34-0 Submarine Raiders, 15-13 NTC San Diego, 19-6 MCAS, El Toro (6-1)
Coach: Lt. Col. William Clasen (Indiana, Pensacola 1939)
Assistants: Lt. Jim Hull (Kentucky Teachers), Lt. Jim Tuma
Ends: Nathan Kines, Bob Logal, Del Miller, Charles Metzlaars (Indiana, Butler), Simon Villoreal
Tackles: Al Leick, Ed Miller (Rice), Morris
Guards: George Poff, Joe Polidori, Petersen
Centers: Ed Brown, Jack Wells
Backs: Bill Chesak (Wisconsin, Texas Western), Classen, Jim Hall, Jack Harris, Charles Iorg, Bill Jacobs, Jay Miller, George Pillon (Detroit, St. Mary's Pre-Flight), Jack Phillips, Joe Sharman, Jack Statham
Kicker: Jim Zimmer

In The Beginning

Little did Lt. Col. Austin "Shifty" Shofner realize what he was setting in motion when he cumshawed equipment and uniforms for a Quantico football team in 1946.

While he was not at the Virginia base to see the results, the Quantico teams posted 12-1, 13-0 and 11-3 records in the succeeding seasons, captured three All-Navy titles and scored 400 or more points each year in an awesome display of power.

But the beginnings were humble.

"I was a battalion commander," Shofner said, "and about the middle of August in 1946 the chief of staff of Marine Corps Schools, Col. Edwin A. Pollock, sent for me. He said the commanding general, Maj. Gen. Clifton B. Cates (like Shofner a former Tennessee letterman) wanted to see me."

The general was blunt.

"He told me that Quantico was going to have a football team that fall and that he had selected me to be the head cooach," Shofner said.

The man Cates had selected was captured by the Japanese with the 4th Marines on Corregidor, escaped and was evacuated by submarine, and fought on Peleliu and other Pacific islands. He is the holder of the Distinguished Service Cross, the Legion of Merit and two Silver Stars. After retirement, he became a prominent businessman in Shelbyville, Tenn.

"I asked about players," Shofner said.

"He said for me to find them.

"I asked about a schedule.

"He said for me to draw it up with Col. Russ Honsowetz, the post special services officer."

"I asked about equipment.

"He said there was none as there had been no team at Quantico during World War II, and it was up to me to find it and buy it.

"I asked about assistant coaches.

"He said for me to select them and they would be so ordered.

"I asked where the practice field was.

"He told me to locate one."

So much for the power of positive thinking.

"I had a lot to do in a few short days," Shofner remembers. "I found a nice grassy area that Gen. Cates approved over the objections of polo players — as I had selected the polo field."

But another problem arose.

"Medical personnel said the field was unsafe due to tetanus — from horse droppings. But the team doctor assigned to me was a Navy captain who was a quarterback at Alabama. He quickly overcame the tetanus problem."

As for equipment, no money was available on such short notice.

"I called a former Tennessee teammate, Herman D. 'Breezy' Wynn, and explained my problem," Shofner related.

Wynn owned the Southern Athletic Company, a large manufacturer of athletic equipment.

"He came through by taking shoulder pads, etc., from *each* of his customers to give us game and practice equipment.

"But I was unable to locate football shoes anywhere, even though one of the biggest athletic dealers in the East in Philadelphia was a Marine Reserve officer.

"I phoned Breezy and he came through again.

"He told the Marine Reserve officer in Philadelphia he was having labor problems at his factory that made the athletic uniforms, and he (the officer) might not be able to order the hundreds of ordered uniforms if the Quantico Marines football team did not get the game and practice shoes needed."

Needless to say, the Marines obtained them.

"Within an hour, the Marine Reserve officer phoned, saying he was happy to report he had just located additional shoes and could ship our order the following day," Shofner said.

But there was the matter of finding players.

"Besides articles in the Marine paper, post orders, etc., requesting all interested in playing to turn in their names and organizations, I visited formations, selling the program and discussing football with all interested parties," said Shofner. "I also heard of a few players at other East Coast stations, and Gen. Cates had them transferred to Quantico if they wanted to join the team."

Honsowetz, just back from North China where he had served under Cates, said the general told him: "I can stand to lose to a Marine team and even a Navy team once in a while, but I *cannot* stand to lose to the Army or Air Force," after a 30-6 loss to Ft. Belvoir.

Lt. Col. George Bowman, a back who had lettered at Louisiana State from 1932-35, played on the San Diego Marines team in 1938 and who later would become a major general, served as the backfield coach.

And they even called on Brig. Gen. Elmer Hall (ret.), one of the Marines' most famous coaches, under whom Shofner, Honsowetz and Bowman had played at San Diego, to give a pep talk to the squad of approximately 60.

With the war over, bases and stations were starting football programs and scheduling was worked out — even in late August and early September.

And under the circumstances, a 3-8 record probably was about as much as could be expected. The victories came against the Army's Ft. Monroe (39-7), Norfolk Navy (19-0) and MCAS Cherry Point (25-0).

'I was most pleased with the team," said Shofner, "as it had a lot of character. We started from scratch and kept scratching all season."

As the Quantico Sentry noted, "There are no All-Americans on this squad and only a few who list college experience."

Four losses were by a touchdown and no one ran wild against the Marines. With a mixture of youngsters and war veterans, some of whom won the Silver Star and Bronze Star in combat, Quantico even extended unbeaten All-Service champion Ft. Benning before losing in Georgia, 15-6.

That seemed to be the spark.

"Ft. Benning had a number of West Point players, including All-America guard John Green and back John Sauer," Shofner recalled. "On paper, we should not have been on the same field."

Benning, with player-coach Bill Meek (Tennessee), end Walt Kersulis (Illinois), tackle Jack Stroud (Tennessee) and back Hillard Shands (Texas), was rated a 30- to 40-point favorite.

The showing against the Army team was the foundation for the great Quantico teams to follow. ■

The "LSU Connection" made its presence felt again in 1947 as Lt. Col. Marvin "Moose" Stewart took over the coaching reins.

Stewart, a center for the Tigers from 1934-36 and an All-American in 1936, was a teammate of Bowman and Honsowetz on the 1938 San Diego Marines team and had been player-coach of the USS Arizona team in 1939. George Halas thought enough of Stewart to make him the Bears' No. 2 choice in the NFL's second draft in 1937.

Capt. R.H. "Hap" Spuhler, the athletic officer, was a former Duke athlete and future George Mason University athletic director, who helped arrange schedules and brought Sammy Baugh, Andy Farkas and Wayne Millner of the Redskins down for spring practice. And Stewart went to the Redskins' summer camp.

The Quantico team looked good on paper and Gens. Cates and Pollock went to Lexington, Va., for the opener against Washington & Lee.

The Generals won, 13-0.

"I thought you said we had a great team," Cates said. "I should make you (Honsowetz) and the team walk back to Quantico."

He was recalling the example of Gen. Smedley Butler, who had done just that after a galling, 6-0 loss at VMI in 1923 that broke the Marines' 16-game winning streak. Butler had expected a 40-0 victory.

"Football is like war," Butler bellowed. "Who in hell wants to lose a war."

The loss to Washington & Lee gave little portent of what was to come during the 1947 season, however.

Because 12 straight Quantico victories followed, culminating in a 26-0 triumph over the Alameda (Cal.) Naval Air Station before 18,000 in San Diego for the All-Navy title. The Marines bottled up Hall of Fame back Joe Perry that day, something few teams ever did.

"The Devildogs established a beachhead on his right arm," said the San Diego Union. "He spent most of the afternoon studying cloud formations."

Perry started his record-breaking pro career the following season with the San Francisco 49ers.

The Marines rolled up 444 points, including routs of 53-0 against Ft. Eustis, 57-0 against Ft. Lee, 56-0 against Ft. Benning and 47-0 against Cherry Point, to be the highest scoring team in the nation.

Benning was undefeated, untied and unscored upon going into the game, and the loss shattered the Doughboys' 17-game victory streak.

With a defense that gave up but 63 points and recorded seven shutouts, it was natural that comparisons began to the great All-Marine teams of the 1920s.

Joe Bartos, who had played at Annapolis and was destined to become one of the Marines' greatest backs ever, scored 15 TDs.

In reality, it was a quick team but not a big one, even for that era. Tackle Joe Donahoe (Navy) was the heaviest at 225, and no one else was above 215. There were 15 players from the 1946 team to lend experience.

So dominant was Quantico that it gained 5,096 yards during the season to but 1,504 for opponents.

Honors followed. Bartos, back Tom Barrington (a sailor), guard Pat Boyle (Wisconsin-Michigan), center Bill Jesse (Montana-Navy) and 19-year-old tackle Clem Thomas were selected on the All-Marine team by Leatherneck magazine, and five on the second team.

And Quantico's red clay hills were not just a training ground for troops: End Charles Walker (Wabash), Donahoe, Jesse and tackle Ted Stawicki (American-Morningside) all became Marine varsity coaches.

■

After a 12-1 record, what does a team do for an encore?

It wins all 13 games, and that's what the Quantico Marines did in 1948 as they again captured the Middle Eastern Service Conference title, defeated MCRD San Diego, 21-0, before 15,000 in Norfolk, Va., for the All-Navy title and routed Ft. Bragg, 40-7, in College Park, Md., for the All-Service title.

An argument could be made that at 13-0 this was one of the greatest Marine teams of all time.

The team's winning streak reached 25, breaking marks set by the Mare Island Marines in World War I and Parris Island in the 1920s.

End Bernie Kaasmann, who played on the 1948, 1949 and 1950 teams, says the '48 season was the most enjoyable, "primarily because of the personnel. It was a congenial group and had a lot of fun along the way."

There was not an "abundance of highly touted college players and most of the enlisted personnel had little or no college experience," said Kaasmann, a Bronze Star winner who later was an assistant coach at Camp Lejeune and Quantico.

Bartos scored 86 points as Quantico rolled up 419 points, and quarterback Rudy Flores (Southwestern of Texas) completed 54 of 100 passes for 875 yards and 12 TDs after passing for more than 1,000 yards in 1947.

Besides the one-sided victory over Ft. Bragg, Quantico rolled over Ft. Benning, 64-0; Patuxent Naval Air Test Center, 59-0, and Parris Island, 51-7.

No other Marine team ever won 13. The other besides the '47 Quantico team to win 12 was the 1963 San Diego Marines team.

The defense, permitting but 56 points, including four TDs in the final 12 games, was perhaps the Marines' best since 1917, when Mare Island did not allow a touchdown in the regular season. Quantico blanked nine opponents.

Little wonder that tackles Charles Abrahams, Bartos, Flores and end Ernie Hargett, in addition to Jesse, were named All-Marine, and three to the second team.

The depth was such that Coach Hal Harwood (Navy) could employ four units in some games.

"We did not have an offensive team and defensive team, rather we ran sort of a two-team system," said Kaasmann. "We called them the Red team and the Gold team. They generally alternated a quarter at a time."

This time the Leathernecks boasted of more size and a line averaging 208. For example, at tackle Harwood, a naval aviator, could use Bob Prather (271), Don Boll (242), later a lineman at Nebraska and with the Washington Redskins, and Joe Alston (232). (Boll broke an ankle against Bolling AFB and missed more than half the season.) Stawicki at guard was 228 and Jesse at center, although but 190, was in the second of his five All-Marine seasons. Bartos was a solid 210.

And the Leathernecks were known outside the East Coast, too:

■ The Williamson Rating Service, in an unusual but realistic move, placed Quantico among the nation's top 50 college teams.

■ Quantico was considered for the Refrigerator Bowl game in Chicago, and turned down a bid to the Silver Bowl in Mexico City.

■ Bill Stern broadcast the All-Navy title game on NBC, and famed sportswriter Grantland Rice, who had covered some All-Marine games in the '20s, took the game in, too.

■

What better way to start the 1949 season that to have the president, Harry S. Truman, toss the coin to open the game with Virginia Polytechnic Institute (now Virginia Tech) at Alexandria, Va.

And the scarlet and gold, coached again by Harwood, rolled to a 33-14 victory, extending their winning streak to 26.

The following week Virginia Military institute was a 14-7 victim, and the streak reached 27.

That was the high-water mark.

The following week, Xavier (Ohio), which split the 26 games against the Marines in their long series from 1926 and 1972, won handily, 29-7, before 25,000 in Cincinnati. This wasn't just any Xavier team. The Musketeers beat Arizona State in the Salad Bowl to cap a 10-1 season.

"We had a good ball club but probably weren't as balanced and deep," said Kaasmann. "In 1948 we had Joe Bartos and Red Schuett running out of the same backfield but both were lost after the season."

Quantico nevertheless scored 400 points, posted an 11-3 record (six opponents were from the college ranks) and was the All-Navy champion again with a 14-13 victory over Bartos and an augmented Camp Pendleton team before 11,000 on a bleak day in the Los Angeles Coliseum.

(The All-Navy championship was dropped in 1950, partly because of the Korean War commitments, but no doubt in part because Marine teams won all three titles and a Leatherneck team beat a Leatherneck team in the final in both 1948 and 1949. In addition, the Navy brass must have squirmed to see seven Annapolis players aiding Quantico's 1948 team and no less than 13 in 1949.)

The tackle corps was strong again. Prather slimmed down to 250, Wendell Beard (New Mexico-California) was a mean 230 and Cas Ksycewski (Catholic) 227.

Jesse, tackle Randy Lawrence (Navy) and guard Bernie Norem, 20, were named All-Marine, and five players were placed on the second team.

The three-year 12-1, 13-0 and 11-3 records were among the best in Marine annals.

But the success was short-lived. The nation would be in an undeclared war before the 1950 season opened.

1946

Record: 0-6 Aberdeen Proving Ground, 6-14 Davis & Elkins, 39-7 Ft. Monroe, 7-13 MCAS Cherry Point, 0-7 Bainbridge NTS, 6-30 Ft. Belvoir, 6-20 Ft. Eustis, 19-0 Norfolk Navy, 6-15 Ft. Benning, 25-0 MCAS Cherry Point, 6-20 Bainbridge NTS. (3-8).

Coach: Lt. Col. Austin Shofner (Tennessee) (MCB San Diego 1939, assistant 1940)

Assistant: Lt. Col. George Bowman (LSU) (MCB San Diego 1938)

Ends: R.O. Evans (Villanova), Dave Foos (MCB San Diego 1939-40, Ed Fraver, Don Hedican, Tom Hodges, Jack Lerond (Cal), Mike McEvoy, Art Rosecrans

Tackles: John Barath, James "Goon" Davis, John Gillen, Dan Jones, Ed O'Connor (Maryland), Clem Thomas (Tennessee), Kid Walton

Guards: Don Bazemore, Charles Bouey, Levern Butterbaugh, Bronko Gromko USN, Fred Jarvis, Laws, Jim Mariades (Pitt-Penn State), Rocky McClintock USN, Nick Nichols, Denny Quinlan, Dave Puzzoli (Alabama)

Centers: Art Kalaka (NYU), Ted Stawicki (American-Morningside)

Backs: Scooter Alessi, Russ Arnaud, Walt Atkinson, Ray Baker, Glenn Barrington USN (Miami of Ohio), Arnie Bryson (Duke), Bob Dove (Ohio State), Doug Foreman (LSU), Dag Gall, Guy Procilo, Murphy Pucylowski (Navy Plebes), Jay Santo (Slippery Rock), Art Schmagel (Maryville Teachers) (El Toro 1946), Bill Sigler (p-c) (North Carolina-Michigan), Denny Stith (St. Louis) (Iowa Pre-Flight), Bill Tidwell (Auburn), George Wood

1947

Record: 0-13 Washington & Lee, 15-13 Ft. Belvoir, 53-0 Ft. Eustis, 29-0 Davis & Elkins, 57-0 Ft. Lee, 20-6 Patuxent NAS, 56-0 Ft. Benning, 33-0 Bainbridge Navy, 27-13 Parris Island, 46-6 Bolling Field, 47-0 Cherry Point, 35-12 Jacksonville NAS (playoff), 26-0 Alameda NAS (All-Navy title). (12-1). Won Middle Eastern Service Conference title. Barrington, Bartos, Boyle, Jesse and Thomas All-Marine; Bazemore, Dawson, Donahoe, Dove and Messina second team.

Coach: Lt. Col. Marv "Moose" Stewart (LSU) (MCB San Diego 1938, player-coach USS Arizona 1939)

Assistants: Lt. Leon Bramlett (Navy), Lt. Bill Sigler (North Carolina-Michigan), Maj. H.E. "Buck" Wertman (Ohio University)

Ends: Sam Clavenger, Tom Dawson, Tom Hardin, Ernie Hargett (Southwestern Louisiana), Mike McEvoy, Russ Schaeffer, Alex Stirling, Joe Vosmik, Charles Walker (Wabash)

Tackles: Jim "Goon" Davis, Joe Donahoe (Navy), Joe Eagle, John Gillen, Bernie Norem, Ed O'Connor (Maryland), Ted Stawicki (American-Morningside), Clem Thomas (Tennessee)

Guards: Don Bazemore, Ray Bender, Don Bordinger, Pat Boyle (Wisconsin-Michigan), George Galbraith, John Lynch, Jim Mariades (Pitt-Penn State), Lou Prete, Fred Ritter, Pete Stoffelenen (Great Lakes 1947)

Centers: Bill Jesse (Montana-Navy), Art Kalaka (NYU), Richard Lubs, Artis Mills, Claude Mounts

Backs: Glenn Barrington USN (Miami of Ohio), Joe Bartos (Navy), Jim Brewer, Jim Bright, Levern Butterbaugh, John Buyers, Don Clement, Bob Dove (Ohio State), Rudy Flores (Southwestern of Texas-Texas), John Johnson, Harold McKenna, Tony Messina (Cal-Pacific), Jack Place (William & Mary), Guy Procilo, Frances Pucylowski (Navy Plebes), Jim Santo (Slippery Rock), Art Schmagel (Maryville Teachers) (El Toro 1946), Denny Stith (St. Louis) (Iowa Pre-Flight), Curt Ward

1948

Record: 44-27 Ft. Belvoir, 18-0 Camp Lejeune, 7-0 Wayne (Mich.), 33-0 Bolling Field, 64-0 Ft. Benning, 59-0 Patuxent NAS, 26-15 Xavier (Ohio), 26-0 St. Francis (Pa.), 51-7 Parris Island, 12-0 Bainbridge Navy Prep School, 21-0 Little Creek (playoff), 21-0 MCRD San Diego (All-Navy title), 40-7 Ft. Bragg. (13-0). Abrahams, Bartos, Flores, Hargett and Jesse were all-Marine; Ambrogi, Prather and Wimberg were second team.

Coach: Maj. Hal Harwood (Navy)

Assistants: Maj. Ralph "Bud" Boyer (Navy), Capt. Joe Donahoe (Navy), Capt. Charles Walker (Wabash)

Ends: Clarence Friesen, Ernie Hargett (Southwestern Louisiana), Bernie Kaasmann, Fred Kenworthy, Harold Krug (Camp Lejeune 1947), Ed Leach (Indiana), Ray Pfeifer (Camp Pendleton 1947) (Rice), Bob Smith (Navy) (KIA), Carl Strauss, Ken Wilson, Herb Zalophany

Tackles: Charles Abrahams (Simpson) (El Toro 1946-47), Joe Alston, Larry Ashman (Bucknell), Al Batorski, Don Boll (Nebraska), Donahoe (p-c), Larry Drennan (Oklahoma A&M), Bob Prather, Sam Selbe, Ed Selva (Jacksonville NAS 1946, Pensacola 1947), Bill Turk (Purdue)

Guards: Simon Degulis (Cornell), Milan Devecka (Waynesburg), Jerry Fly, Jim Mariades (Pitt-Penn State), John McGuigan, Bernie Norem, Doug Phillips (Norfolk NAS), Ted Stawicki (American-Morningside), Bristol Steele, Paul Stephenson, Pete Stoffelenen (Great Lakes 1947), Mel Weigler, Jim Wimberg

Centers:v Ed Arbaczawki (PH Marines), Les Grulich, Lou Hernandez, Bill Jesse (Montana-Navy), Fred McGiffin, Henry Schneph, J.O. Williams (Citadel)

Backs: Dick Ambrogi (Penn-Navy), Joe Bartos (Navy), Clarence Camp, Rudy Flores (Southwestern of Texas-Texas), Gail Graham, George Greco (Guam Marines), Joe Hamden, Wilmer Hixson (Yuba JC), Jim Levendusky, Maurice Long (Fallbrook NAD), Richard Lynn, Harold McKenna, Tony Messina (Cal-Pacific), Ben Moore (Mississippi College-Texas-Navy), George Mullaney, Roy Russell (Navy), Ray Schuett (Illinois State) (PH Marines), Bob Scott, Joe Tamillo, Edgar Turnipseed (Mississippi), Goode Wilson

1949

Record: 33-14 Virginia Poly, 14-7 Virginia Military, 7-29 Xavier (Ohio), 54-0 Bolling AFB, 33-14 Wayne (Mich.), 26-47 West Virginia, 26-7 Ft. Belvoir, 68-0 Patuxent NAS, 7-23 Camp Lejeune, 27-19 Niagara, 33-13 Norfolk Navy, 24-0 Little Creek, 34-14 Camp Lejeune (playoff), 14-13 Camp Pendleton (All-Navy title at LA Coliseum). (11-3). Xavier snapped Marines' 27-game winning streak but Quantico scored 400 points during season. Xavier had a 10-1 record and beat Arizona State in Salad Bowl. President Truman threw coin for VPI game. With team trailing, Tom Parsons stole handoff against Niagara and ran 93 yards for TD. Scrimmaged Mt. St. Mary's and Villanova. Jesse, Lawrence and Norem All-Marine; Abrahams, Cordle, Flores, Greco and McElroy second team.

Coach: Maj. Hal Harwood (Navy)

Assistants: Maj. Ralph "Bud" Boyer (Navy), Lt. Pat Boyle (Wisconsin-Michigan), Capt. Bill Chip (Duquesne-Navy), Capt. Joe Donahoe (Navy), Maj. J.T. Hill (Navy)

Ends: George Cordle (Camp Pendleton 1947, Pensacola NAS 1948), Al Haliwell, Bernie Kaasmann, Ed Leach (Indiana), Ruben Longoria, Bob McElroy (Navy), John McGinty, Dave Petros, Paul Reigert, Bob Smith (Navy) (KIA), Carl Strauss, John Wiles, Ken Wilson

Tackles: Charles Abrahams (Simpson) (El Toro 1946-47), Wendel Beard (New Mexico-Cal), Jim Beeler (Navy) (KIA), Larry Drennan (Oklahoma A&M), Joe Eagle, Umberti Gigli (China Marines 1947, Camp Lejeune 1948), Cecil Jones, Cas Ksycewski (Catholic), Randy Lawrence (Navy), Bob Prather, Ray Snyder, Ervin York

Guards: Gene Baldoni, Bill Eysenbach (Parris Island 1948), Hiplis, Bob Hunt (Navy), Leroy Johnson, Bernard Norem, Doug Phillips (Norfolk NAS), Mike Radatz, Paul Santillo (Youngstown), Ken Schieweck (Northwestern-Navy), Bristol Steele, Paul Stephenson, Jim Wimberg

Centers: Harry Boyd, Bill Jesse (Montana-Navy), Tom Parsons (Navy), George "Socko" Vavrek (Cherry Point 1947-48)

Backs: Dick Ambrogi (Penn-Navy), Ken Bott (Navy, Rudy Flores (Southwestern of Texas-Texas), Fred Grabowsky, George Greco (Guam Marines), Joe Hamden, Wilmer Hixson (Yuba JC), Henry Hoppe, Ed Johnson, Cal Killeen (Bucknell-Navy), Clinton King, Maurice Long (Fallbrook NAD), Bob Maiden (Colorado State Teachers), Mel McKenzie, John Merricks (Marshall), Ben Moore (Mississippi College-Texas-Navy), Dick Negri, Adolph Plank, Carl Robb, Ed Romankowski, Roy Russell (Navy), Dick Schargus, Ray Terrell (Mississippi) (Jacksonville NAS 1942, Camp Lejeune 1943), Edgar Turnipseed (Mississippi)

All In The Family

A young back, Hugh "Red" Kriever, had been a standout on the 1948 and 1949 teams at Parris Island and the 1950 Quantico team. After another season at Quantico in 1952, he was recruited by Louisville and lettered for the Cardinals.

Years later, Kriever succeeded Bill Justice as assistant superintendent of the Pinellas County schools in Florida. Justice had been Quantico's 1951 coach.

Different Field of Battl

The events of June 25, 1950 in Korea had an obvious impact on Marine Corps football.

Some players who might have been on 1950 teams were among the first sent to Korea to try to stem the invasion from the north.

Schedules were in limbo as military officials from all services were unsure whether their bases could field teams, and to what extent.

And the Corps' focus obviously had to be on the undeclared war, not on a sport played in the fall.

Still, Quantico's 1950 entry was among the Marines' best — and most famous — primarily because of a publicized T-formation quarterback from the College of the Pacific in Stockton, Cal., one Eddie LeBaron.

The 5-7, 165-pound signal caller had started to catch the nation's attention as a 16-year-old performer for Amos Alonzo Stagg in 1946, the coach's last year at Pacific. Little All-America and All-America honors followed.

LeBaron was a private in Company C of the 12th Amphibian Tractor Battalion in Stockton when the Marine Reserve was mobilized in the summer of 1950. He accepted a commission in August and, while on leave, led the College All-Stars to a 17-7 upset of the Philadelphia Eagles in the annual classic in Chicago's Soldier Field.

He checked into the Washington Redskins' training camp for two exhibition games — he had been their No. 10 draft choice — before his leave ended.

With the help of holdovers from the 1949 Quantico team, new officers from the college football ranks through the NROTC and Platoon Leaders Class programs, and World War II officers recalled to active duty, Quantico posted a 9-2 record against an almost all-college schedule.

Showing the Leathernecks' depth, the passenger list for a United Air Lines' charter flight to California listed a party of 56, including coaches and trainers. Of the group, 22 were lieutenants, a tipoff to the talent.

LeBaron, only 20, hardly had time to learn the plays before an opening 34-13 loss to Xavier (Ohio).

"His gridiron debut was far from auspicious," the Quantico Sentry observed. "He and several other starters had just reported and had little time for practice. Xavier bombed the locals, with the Musketeers' line granting little time for LeBaron's patented double-spin handoffs and attempts to pass."

But Quantico was not to lose again until the final game of the season, a 37-14 loss to, appropriately, Pacific, in the Valley Bowl at Stockton on Dec. 2, a game in which Quantico led, 14-9, at halftime. The victory boosted Pacific's record to 7-3-1.

Offsetting some of the grim news from the Far East that fall were headlines telling of Quantico victories over Bolling Air Force Base (55-0), Virginia Tech (61-21), Waynesburg (41-7), Niagara (34-13), Dayton

(7-0), Scranton (41-21), Youngstown (33-14), Camp Lejeune (42-7) and Tampa (48-0), good enough for the No. 1 ranking among the nation's service teams by the Williamson Rating Service.

The games at Butler Stadium also provided a badly needed diversion for the Marines and the Marine community at Quantico as the war widened.

For example, an estimated 15,000 turned out for the Lejeune game, matching future College Hall of Fame quarterbacks LeBaron and Harry Agganis, a Boston University star also mobilized that summer by the Marine Reserve.

But the "expected duel between the pair failed to materialize as LeBaron and Company scored early and often en route to the easy win," according to the Quantico Sentry.

Another expected duel fell through when a Dec. 9 game with the Marine Corps Recruit Depot of San Diego had to be cancelled because of Korean war commitments. San Diego, ranked No. 2 in the Williamson ratings, won all 11 games and scored a Marine-record 524 points. Coached by ex-Quantico end Charles Walker, the Depot team featured back Skeet Quinlan, who rushed for 1,080 yards and scored 23 TDs; quarterback Rudy Flores and Bill Jesse, an All-Marine center at Quantico in 1947, 1948 and 1949.

The game potentially could have been one of the greatest involving Marine teams, but had to join the what-might-have-been category with a 1945 game that never materialized between the famed El Toro Flying Marines and the FMF Pacific (Pearl Harbor) Marines.

As for LeBaron, "Maybe being smaller actually helped me," he told one interviewer. "It might have made me work harder to concentrate on making up for my size. I might not have gone so far if I had been big."

There was nothing small, of course, about LeBaron's accomplishments.

■ At Pacific, "Excellent Eddie" completed 204 of 430 passes for 3,841 yards and a school-record 49 TDs. The Tigers posted 10-1, 7-1-2 and 11-0 records from 1947-49, and in 1949 were ranked 10th in the country, ran up a national-record 575 points and three times scored 75 or more.

■ At Quantico, No. 40 (also his college number) completed 71 of 144 for 1,279 yards and 14 TDs in 1950, besides punting for a 43-yard average, and was named Service Player of the Year by the Washington Touchdown Club.

■ In the National Football League, the "Little Magician" completed 897 of 1,796 attempts for 13,399 yards and 104 TDs, and rushed 202 times for 650 yards and nine TDs while playing for the Redskins from 1952-53 and 1955-59 and the new Dallas Cowboys from 1960-63. (He played for Calgary of the Canadian Football League in 1954.)

The pro passing yardage alone is equivalent to 7½ miles.

LeBaron, the Rookie of the Year in 1952, the NFL passing leader in 1958 and a Pro Bowl selection in 1956, 1958, 1959 and 1963, later was a lawyer, businessman and TV commentator before becoming general manager (1977-82) and executive vice president/chief operating officer (1982-85) of the Atlanta Falcons. The Sporting News named him its Football Executive of the Year in 1980.

Hal Harwood (Navy), who had directed Quantico to a 13-0 record in 1948 and 10-3 mark in 1949, may have done his best coaching job with the 1950 team, considering the circumstances, the distractions and the strength of the schedule.

Nine Annapolis players were on hand, plus newcomers such as end Bob Heck (Purdue), guard Wit Bacauskas (Columbia), and backs Bob Farrell (Holy Cross), Don Ferguson (Iowa State) and Earl Roth (Maryland).

Two old hands from the V-12 program of World War II also lent skill and experience: 6-3, 233-pound center Len "Tuffy" McCormick (Baylor and Southwestern of Texas) and back Hosea Rodgers (Alabama and North Carolina). Both literally were old pros, too: McCormick had played for the Baltimore Colts in 1947-48 and Rodgers for the Los Angeles Dons in 1949. Heck was with the Chicago Hornets in 1949.

End Bob McElroy (Navy), tackle Randy Lawrence (Navy), guard Paul Stephenson, backs Bill Hawkins (Virginia Military Institute and Navy), LeBaron and Rodgers were All-Marine selections.

Hawkins led the team with 11 TDs, Farrell rushed for 519 yards and five TDs and McElroy caught 38 passes for 686 yards and six TDs.

And, for the record, there was this tackle named Kelley.

"Yes, the Paul Kelley from Villanova who was a member of the 1950 Quantico team and the Marine commandant are one and the same," Gen. Kelley said. "In all candor, however, I must admit that on this illustrious team I was little more than a scrub.' "

Kelley was among three players on the '50 team destined for the stars. Assistant coach Charles Cooper, who had made stops at Ole Miss and Navy, and back Cal Killeen (Bucknell and Navy) both would serve as three-star generals.

Other players from the '50 team also went on to serve in Korea, and some even in Vietnam.

"LeBaron was a Marine first and a football player second," the Quantico Sentry noted. "Within five months, he was far removed from the adoring and cheering fans in Butler Stadium, serving as a platoon leader in Korea, where he was twice wounded and awarded the Bronze Star for heroism in combat."

From the 1950 team, Cooper was awarded the Silver Star in Korea; and end Bernie Kaasmann, Killeen, tackle Cas Ksycewski (Catholic), Lawrence, Roth and assistants Bill Chip (Navy), Joe Donahoe (Navy) and J.T. Hill (Navy) the Bronze Star.

Quantico players and coaches from the 1947, 1948 and 1949 teams also were cited for Korean heroism.

But between 1950 and the truce in July 1953 word also would come back of former players such as tackle Jim Beeler (Navy) of Quantico's 1949 team being killed in action in Korea.

Tackle Byron Chase (San Diego State), a Silver Star winner from the 1951 Quantico team, and back Gene Stewart (Mississippi State) from the '52 Quantico team, a 26th-round draft choice of the Philadelphia Eagles, also would be reported as KIA.

And Bob Smith (Navy), an end for Quantico in 1948 and 1949, was was among 2,500 Americans listed as missing in action in Southeast

Asia. The status was changed 10 years later in 1979 to a presumptive finding of death. A daughter, Robin, who was a television producer, continued to try to spotlight the plight of her father and the MIA's.

1950

Record: 13-34 Xavier (Ohio), 55-0 Bolling AFB, 61-21 Virginia Tech, 41-7 Waynesburg, 34-13 Niagara, 7-0 Dayton, 41-21 Scranton, 33-14 Youngstown,, 42-7 Camp Lejeune, 48-0 Tampa, 14-37 Pacific. (9-2). Game with MCRD San Diego cancelled because of Korean War commitments. Hawkins, Lawrence, LeBaron, McElroy, Rodgers and Stephenson All-Marine; Farrell, Heck, Ksycewski and Parsons second team.
Coach: Maj. Hal harwood (Navy)
Assistants: Maj. Bill Chip (Duquesne-Navy), Lt. Charles Cooper (Mississippi-Navy), Maj. Joe Donahoe (Navy), Maj. J.T. Hill (Navy), Bill Justice (Rollins) (MCRD San Diego 1950)
Ends: Art Cotton, George Cordle (Camp Pendleton 1947, Pensacola NAS 1948), Gene Foxworth (Holy Cross), Harrison Frasier (Navy), Bob Heck (Purdue), Imhof, Bernie Kaasmann, Bob McElroy (Navy), Bill McCurdy, Ken Wilson
Tackles: Bill Chelette, Joe Conroy, Sheldon Dunlop, Jack Fraka, Bert Gigli (China Marines 1947, Camp Lejeune 1948), Orion Hingst, Art Jolicouer, Cas Ksycewski (Catholic), Randy Lawrence (Navy), Murray Nelson, Fred Paige, Bob Prather
Guards: Wit Bacauskas (Columbia), Neil Blanchard, Alex Dermer, John Greer, Paul McMahon, Macon Pharr, Dave Ridderhoff (Navy), Paul Santillo (Youngstown), Paul Stephenson, Joe Ternyik, Don Weinacht
Centers: Harry Boyd, Len "Tuffy" McCormick (Baylor-Southwestern of Texas) (Georgia Pre-Flight), Tom Parsons (Navy), George "Socko" Vavrek (Cherry Point 1947-48)
Backs: Len Aloy (Parris Island 1947-49), Jim Bradley, Bob Farrell (Holy Cross), Don Ferguson (Iowa State), George Greco (Guam Marines), Lyle Harman, Bill Hawkins (VMI-Navy), Ed Johnson, Paul X. Kelley (Villanova), Cal Killeen (Bucknell-Navy), Hugh Kriever (Louisville) (Parris Island 1948-49), Eddie LeBaron (Pacific), Jim LeVoy, John Merricks (Marshall), Ben Moore (Mississippi College-Texas-Navy), Hosea Rodgers (Alabama-North Carolina), Ed Romankowski, Earl Roth (Maryland), Roy Russell (Navy), Ray Terrell (Mississippi) (Jacksonville NAS, Camp Lejeune 1943), Keith Woods

Football Bolsters Recruiting

T he recruiting value of Marine football was demonstrated in the eight-game series between Quantico and Holy Cross from 1951 to 1964.

Holy Cross won five of the games: 39-14 in 1951, 7-0 in 1955, 13-0 in 1956, 33-14 in 1957 and 16-0 in 1964. Quantico triumphed 27-18 in 1952, 17-0 in 1953 and 7-6 in 1963.

But a stream of Crusaders players opted for Marine officer programs. Among those to perform for Quantico were:

1952: John Cullity, Bill DeChard, George Foley, John Feltch and Dick Murphy
1953: Chet Millett and Vic Rimkus
1954: Joe Harrington, Rimkus and Pat Ryan
1955: Bob Dee
1956: Dee, Bernie Taracevicz
1957: Jim Allegro, Jim Cavanaugh, Joe Murphy and Taracevicz
1958: Tony Santaniello and Bob Tortorella
1959: Dave Stecchi, Santaniello
1961: Barry Bocklet
1962: Bocklett, Kes Desmarais
1963: Hank Cutting, Dennis Golden, Pat McCarthy and Jack Whalen
1964: Cutting, Golden, Ken Mahieu, McCarthy and Whalen
1965: Bill Sexton

A Puzzling Season

The 1951 Holy Cross game program warned: "The Marines have landed: 39 former collegians, eight of whom have pro experience and four who played with the College All-Stars, make up part of the Quantico Marines' roster."

Not mentioned was that the team had two All-Americans (one of whom was destined for the College Hall of Fame).

The Leathernecks could field 11 players drafted by National Football League and All-America Football Conference teams.

And there was an 80-man squad, 57 of whom were officers.

Heady stuff.

But the team won five and lost six. What happened?

Said Weldon Humble, a Pro Bowl guard recalled to active duty for the Korean war, "With fellows from so many different teams and systems, it was bound to take longer for us to get organized. ... It's usually been a fumble or pass interception that has cost us the game," he told a Cleveland paper.

Quantico had gotten off to a 1-4 start.

An ambitious Quantico game program said the "roster shows 27 states and one territory represented. As on many another grid muster roll, California leads with 11 men."

According to the program, schools represented were Stephen F. Austin, Brown, California, Cal Poly, Colgate, Colorado, Dartmouth, Detroit, Drake, Duke, Duquesne, Franklin & Marshall, Florida State, Furman, Gettysburg, Idaho, Iowa State, Kansas, Marquette, Middlebury, Mississippi, Mississippi Southern, Navy, Niagara, Northwestern, Oregon, Oregon State, Pittsburgh, Princeton, Rice, San Diego State, USC, Scranton, South Carolina, Stanford, St. Bonaventure, St. Lawrence, Syracuse, Tufts, Tulane, Virginia, William & Mary, Washington and Wyoming.

The coach was Capt. Bill Justice, one of a number of players and coaches mobilized with the Marine Reserve in 1950 and 1951. Justice, brother of famed back Choo-Choo Justice of North Carolina, had posted a 26-4 record from 1947-49 as coach at Clearwater (Fla.) High and was an assistant with the 1950 Quantico team. A Rollins gridder and graduate, he had served with the 2nd Marine Division during World War II.

After scrimmaging North Carolina and Virginia, Quantico lost to Xavier (Ohio), 12-7, in the opener. But Xavier finished with a 9-0-1 record.

A 21-14 loss to Dayton was followed by a 28-7 victory over Bolling Air Force Base. But losses to Parris Island, 20-14, and to Ft. Jackson, 21-13, brought the record to 1-4. To their credit, the Marines won four of the final six games.

Said one observer: "Gen. Franklin Hart was the base commander and attended most of the football practices. It was a very tough and demanding situation for Justice and his staff to have the CO second-guess every move."

Hart had been a reserve at Auburn (then Alabama Poly) and was a football junkie.

Injuries also hurt the team. Tackle Carl Kilsgaard (Idaho), who had played for the Chicago Cardinals before being recalled and earning All-Marine honors for the MCRD San Diego in 1950, was hurt in the opener.

"The doctors thought I had a ruptured spleen, but fortunately that wasn't the problem but it ended my football days," said Kilsgaard, who had spent three years in the South Pacific in World War II.

"I got out in March 1952. The Cardinals wanted me to come back, but when you are 28 years old it's tough to be a rookie again so I did not try football any more," said Kilsgaard.

Back Bob Farrell (Holy Cross), Quantico's leading rusher in 1950, and end Bob Scott (Stanford), who had played at Parris Island in 1950, also were lost early in the season.

Despite the problems, the veteran Leathernecks, with eight players returning from the 9-2 team of 1950 and at least 11 members 25 years or older, were ranked eighth among service teams late in the season by the Williamson Rating Service and finished 12th in the rankings of Touchdown Tips.

The team had a powerful 1-2 punch at quarterback. Dick Flowers (Northwestern), who would be with Quantico again in 1952 and with the Baltimore Colts in 1953, completed 48 of 101 attempts for 796 yards. "Wingin' Willie" Weeks of Iowa State, an 18th-round draft pick of the Philadelphia Eagles, completed 41 of 100 for 687 yards.

Earl "Dixie" Howell (Mississippi), a 9.7 sprinter who had played at Muhlenburg in 1944 as a Marine V-12 trainee and with the Los Angeles Dons in 1949, scored eight touchdowns. Bob Tougas (Providence), who had played for the minor-league Providence Steamrollers, rushed 98 times for 475 yards. Bill Samer (Pitt) caught 10 passes for 206 yards and two TDs to lead the receivers.

But Humble, a Marine captain, was the franchise-type player. He had been a standout at Rice in 1941 and 1942, and at Southwestern Louisiana in 1943 as a Marine V-12 trainee. He was selected on seven All-America teams on returning to Rice in 1946.

The Cleveland Browns traded five players to the Colts for Humble in 1947 and he played for the AAFC and NFL champions from 1947-50, closing his pro career with the Dallas Texans in 1952.

"Those college boys are scrappy, but not so hard to move around as those big pros," Humble once said.

A member of the College Hall of Fame, Humble was selected All-Marine in 1951 and on the first team by the Armed Forces Press Service. He also was chosen the Service Player of the Year by the Washington Touchdown Club.

Tougas also was an All-Marine selection and Flowers an AFPS first-team choice.

And the talent didn't stop there:

■ Center Ray Wietecha (Northwestern), after playing for Quantico in 1952, starred with the New York Giants from 1953-62, during which he started 133 straight games, was All-Pro in 1958, was chosen for four Pro Bowls and started in five NFL title games.

(Since then, Wietecha has been an assistant coach and scout for the Los Angeles Rams, Green Bay Packers, Giants, Buffalo Bills, Colts, and the Blitz and Wranglers of the United States Football League.)

■ Guard Jim Cullom (California), who played as a teen-ager at MCAS Cherry Point in 1943 and served in the South Pacific, started the 1951 season with the NFL New York Yankees before reporting to Quantico. Within a year, he, along with many of the team members, was fighting in Korea. A number of them were decorated for heroism.

■ Tackle Art McCaffray (Santa Clara) was an All-America guard at Pacific in 1943 as a Marine V-12 trainee and was with the Pittsburgh Steelers in 1946. He was among those mobilized for the Korean war.

■ Tackle Ed Sharkey (Duke-Nevada) had played for the Yankees from 1947-50. After his release from active duty, the durable lineman was with the Browns in 1952, the Colts in 1953, the Eagles in 1954-1955, the San Francisco 49ers in 1955-1956, and closed his pro career with British Columbia of the Canadian Football League in 1957-1958.

■ Tackle Jim Crawford (Mississippi) had been drafted in the 20th round by the Chicago Bears and back Jay Roundy (USC) in the 11th round by the Giants.

1951

Record; 7-12 Xavier (Ohio), 14-21 Dayton, 28-7 Bolling AFB, 14-20 Parris Island, 13-21 Ft. Jackson, 21-14 St. Bonaventure, 35-15 John Carroll, 13-20 Camp Lejeune, 13-0 Navy JV, 14-39 Holy Cross, 67-6 Ft. Myer. (5-6). Lackland AFB game cancelled. Humble and tougas All-Marine; McCaffray second team.

Coach: Capt. Bill Justice (Rollins) (MCRD San Diego 1950)

Assistants: Lt. Carl Benton (Northwestern State-Southwestern Louisiana-UCLA), Andy Farkas (Detroit) (civilian), Capt. Cas Ksycewski (Catholic), Capt. Bob McNeil (Michigan State) (asst. coach LA Marine Reserves 1948), Lt. Hosea Rodgers (Alabama-North Carolina), Ray Terrell (Mississippi) (Jacksonville NAS 1942, Camp Lejeune 1943), Lt. Jim Woodside (Temple-Rochester).

Ends: Killiam Blackman, Dick Bunting, George Cordle (Camp Pendleton 1947, Pensacola NAS 1948), Art Cotton, Tom DeStefano (St. Lawrence), Bob Hennelly, Bob Levin (Occidental), Stan Lewza (St. Bonaventure), Joe Peterson, Jim Pinkerton (South Carolina), George Rusch (Dartmouth), Bill Samer (Pitt), Bob Scott (Stanford) (MRD San Diego 1951), Dick Shanor (Wyoming), Doug Van Metre (Colorado), Syd White (Virginia)

Tackles: Byron Chase (San Diego State) (KIA), Bill Chelette, Jim Cullom (Cherry Point 1943) (California), Dan De Neico (Colorado), Bob Donley, Jim Hanker (Oregon State), Art Hargrove (South Carolina) (Parris Island 1948-50), Carl Kilsgaard (Idaho) (MCRD San Diego 1950), Joe Kirinic, Art McCaffray (Santa Clara-Pacific), Wil Overgaard (Idaho), John Tillo (Iowa State), Frank Turner, Rufus Williams

Guards: John Chernak (Brown), George Ciampa, Jim "Tank" Crawford (Mississippi), Tom Dockery, Weldon Humble (Rice-Southwestern Louisiana), Charles Johnson, Bob Langan, Ray Lung, Frank Marcus (Florida State), Al Neveu (Parris Island 1949-50), Vince Peroni (Furman), Dolph Simons (Kansas), Art Skinner (Notre Dame), Vince Vetrano (Colgate)

Centers: Rineldo Borg (USC), Tom Chesnut, George Coleman (San Diego State), Alex Krousz, Bruce Rehn (Washington), Fran Reichel, Ed Sharkey (Duke-Nevada), Fred Tullai (Temple-Maryland) (Parris Island 1948, Camp Lejeune 18949), Vernon Vick, Ray Wietecha (Michigan State-Northwestern)

Backs: Len Aloy (Parris Island 1948-49), Bennett, Jim Bradley, Aubrey Elam, Bob Farrell (Holy Cross), Don Ferguson (Iowa State), Art Filson (San Diego State), Dick Flowers (Northwestern), Red Gallo (Marquette), Don Hardey, Bill Hawkins (VMI-Navy), Howie Hostetler (Oregon), Earl "Dixie" Howell (Muhlenburg-Mississippi), Bob Jones, Bob King, Hugh "Red" Kriever (Louisville) (Parris Island 1948-49), Joe Krulock (Scranton), Joe Makarewicz (Drake), Chris Markey (California), Doug Mason, Lynn McKelvey (Florida State), John O'Loughlin (St. Lawrence), Bob O'Malley, Ken Peck (Flagstaff-Southwestern Louisiana-Stanford), Jack Place (William & Mary) (Camp Lejeune 1950), Ted Podolak, Lee Rosa, Jay Roundy (USC), Bob Tougas (Providence), Bill Weeks (Iowa State), Duane Whitehead (USC)

Eight Wasn't Enough

As Johnny Carson might say, how tough was the competition Quantico faced in 1952?

Damn tough.

Although the Virginia Marines had 12 players drafted by NFL teams, with tackle Jim Weatherall a No. 1 pick; eight with past or future pro playing experience; two destined for stardom in the National Football League (All-Pro center Ray Wietecha and Pro Bowl end Jim Mutscheller), two to make their mark in coaching (Leon "Bud" Carson and John Mazur), and 12 back from the 1951 team, they lost three times.

As a matter of fact, they were only third best among East Coast Marine teams.

Quantico lost, 22-13, to Parris Island (9-3-1), a team that scored a near-record 505 points that season; to Camp Lejeune (7-3) in a game televised by CBS, and to Bolling Air Force (10-1), 14-6.

Oh yes, Bolling — the No. 1 service team in the country — had a Big Ten look with the likes of end Dorne Dibble and quarterback Al Dorow of Michigan State, and backs Mel Groomes (Indiana) and Walt Klevay (Ohio State).

Still, the season wasn't a washout. Maj. Charles Walker's predominantly officer team won eight. Among the victims were Fordham, Xavier and Holy Cross for a sweep of college opponents. Four Army teams were defeated as well as MCAS Cherry Point.

And Quantico was ranked as the sixth best service team in early November by the Williamson Rating service.

While Parris Island and Lejeune had top-drawer teams, and might have won anyway, Quantico was hampered by a 50-50 officer-enlisted rule, which meant some of its better players had to sit out some downs.

Recalls Harold Brinson (Tulane), a Lejeune player who later became president of Southern Arkansas University:

"I visited with a Tulane teammate, Billy Joe Harper, prior to the Quantico game. Joe was telling me about all the material Quantico had. ... He really was not taking us too seriously and was not bragging at all when he acted as if there would be no contest.

"Of course, Joe probably forgot the rule concerning officers and enlisted men that was in effect at the time."

Lejeune won, 25-2.

"I went around to try to find Joe after the game and I didn't find him. I haven't seen him since. When I do, I'll ask him what happened," Brinson chuckled.

Perhaps there was *too* much talent.

Staff Sgt. Larry Ashman of the Office of Public Information at Quantico saw it this way:

"Ordinarily, a coach in Walker's togs might well be quite excited over having a large cast of football notables. But, understandably, Charlie's biggest worry as he goes into his first year at the Quantico helm is just how he is going to effect complete coordination in his backfield and line with men who have played and experienced a multitude of football offenses, ranging from the straight T to the old Kanisha spread."

Walker did have to blend players from 65 cities, 36 states and 32 colleges.

After four weeks of "sporadic practice sessions determined by training requisites and necessities for men in the Korea action, the eleven remained as one of the 'mystery' teams of Quantico history," Ashman wrote.

There was no mystery, however, about the talent.

Besides Weatherall, an All-American at Oklahoma, NFL clubs had drafted Mutscheller, a second-team All-American at Notre Dame and a 1952 All-Marine selection; end Jack Nix (USC); tackles Ken Barfield (Mississippi), John Feltch (Holy Cross) and Bob Werckle (Vanderbilt), a Bronze Star winner in Korea; guard Ken Huxhold (Wisconsin); Wietecha (Northwestern), and backs Bill DeChard (Holy Cross), John Kerestes (Purdue), Jay Roundy (USC), and Gene Stewart (Mississippi State), who would be killed in Korea.

Weatherall played for Edmonton (Canada) in 1954, the Philadelphia Eagles from 1955-57, the Washington Redskins in 1958, and the Detroit Lions in 1960-61; Barfield for the Redskins in 1954; Huxhold for the Eagles from 1954-58; and Wietecha for the New York Giants from 1953-62.

Nix, who played for the San Francisco 49ers in 1950 and Saskatchewan (Canada) in 1951, coached the Camp Fisher (Japan) Marines in 1953 and later was a back judge in NFL games.

Carson, who lettered at North Carolina, would coach at Georgia Tech (1967-71) and was the defensive architect for the Pittsburgh Steelers, Los Angeles Rams, Baltimore Colts, Kansas City Chiefs and New York Jets. Mazur, a Notre Dame product who played for British Columbia (Canada) in 1954, coached the New England Patriots (1970-72) and was an assistant with three other pro teams.

Weatherall and Mutscheller, who scored 10 touchdowns, were first-team All-Service selections of the Armed Forces Press Service.

And the team was awash with players of Division I caliber.

At the ends, Walker, a Wabash graduate who was awarded the Bronze Star in Korea, could use Harper, Jack Lockett (Oklahoma), John McDonald (Dartmouth), Joe Rilo (Villanova) and Bob Scott (Stanford). Combined with Mutscheller, the contingent gave Quantico certainly the deepest set of ends and perhaps the best end play in Marine history.

Guards included Ben Amsler (South Carolina), George Foley (Holy Cross) and Len Stewart (Fresno State). Besides Wietecha, the centers included George Coleman (San Diego State), Sam Greenawalt (Penn), Dick Murphy (Holy Cross) and Wint Winter (Kansas).

Other backs included Fred Bates (San Diego State), Joe Caprara (Notre Dame), John Cullity (Holy Cross), Dick Flowers (Northwestern), Walt Mawyer (Memphis State) and All-Marine Don Scott (Villanova). Flowers and Weatherall were members of the 1952 College All-Star team and Flowers was with the Colts in 1953. Caprara ran 99 yards for a TD in the finale against Ft. Belvoir.

And there was size. Feltch weighed in at 237, Weatherall 235, Coleman 234, Barfield 232, tackle Bob Stephenson 231, end Joe Peterson 227 and tackle Dave Harvey (VMI) 226.

And the kicker, at age 30, was an old pro: Ralph Heywood, an All-America end at USC in 1943 who had played for the Chicago Rockets, Lions, Boston Yanks and New York Bulldogs, before being recalled for the Korean War. Heywood, who remained in the Corps, retired as a colonel and commanded the 26th Marines in Vietnam.

And the young enlisted were tops. Tackle Stan Dwyer lettered at Northwestern from 1954-56; guard John Eldridge at Northwestern from 1955-56 and back Hugh "Red" Kriever at Louisville in 1953.

The loss to Bolling came in the opener. The Marines had won 46-6, 33-0, 54-0 and 55-0 romps before the Air Force started to upgrade Bolling's program. The Marines also won, 28-7, in 1951, but the 1952 game marked the start of perhaps the most physical, demanding and publicized series in service-football history. The games often decided the national championship, and Bolling had a 34-game winning streak snapped in 1956.

Mutscheller, Amsler, Carson and DeChard teamed to take Nix's Camp Fisher team to a 1953 Rice Bowl victory in Tokyo.

Mutscheller then joined the Colts in 1954 for the first of his eight NFL seasons in which the 6-1, 213-pounder would catch 220 passes for 3,684 yards (a 16.7-yard average) and 40 TDs, and start the 1958 and 1959 NFL title games won by Baltimore.

At Notre Dame, Mutscheller had caught 35 passes for 426 yards and seven TDs in 1950, and 20 passes for 305 yards and two TDs in 1951.

No look at the '52 season, however, would be complete without mention of the game matching Holy Cross against Quantico and its five Crusaders' alumni: Cullity, DeChard, Feltch, Foley and Murphy.

"The return of Dick Murphy poses a situation unique in Holy Cross history," said the game program. "It means not only the pitting of Holy Cross man against Holy Cross man. It also matches brother against brother, and Marine against Marine, inasmuch as Dick's brother, John 'Tiger' Murphy, spearheads the Crusaders' defensive line.

" 'Tiger' was a Marine before Dick was. He entered Holy Cross a year after his younger brother because of serving a hitch on active duty. A year ago (1951) they were teammates," the program noted.

Five players competing for Holy Cross, which lost, 27-18, would play for Quantico in later years.

They were All-America guard Chet Millett; end Joe Harrington, tackle Vic Rimkus and quarterback Pat Ryan, 1954; end Bob Dee 1955-56.

The game program, appropriately, had referred to Holy Cross as a "sister Marine base in a modest sort of way."

1952

Record: 6-14 Bolling AFB, 14-7 Xavier (Ohio), 28-0 MCAS Cherry Point, 7-22 Parris Island, 7-2 Ft. Eustis, 21-8 Fordha m, 48-7 Indiantown Gap, 2-25 Camp Lejeune, 42-21 Ft. Jackson, 27-18 Holy Cross, 41-6 Ft. Belvoir. (8-3). Mutscheller and Scott All-Marine.
Coach: Maj. charles Walker (Wabash) (MCRD San Diego. 1949-50)

Assistants: Maj. Ray "Stormy" Davis (Hardin-Simmons), Andy Farkas (Detroit) (civilian), Capt. Hosea Rodgers (Alabama-North Carolina), Capt. Bill Sigler (North Carolina-Michigan) (asst. MCRD San Diego 1949), Maj. Denny Stith (St. Louis) (Iowa Pre-Flight), Wally Williams (Boston University) (El Toro 1945)

Ends: Art Cotton, John Coyne (Pitt), Bill Joe Harper (Tulane), Jack Lockett (Oklahoma), John MacDonald (Dartmouth), Jim Mutscheller (Notre Dame), Jack Nix (USC), Joe Peterson, Joe Rilo (Villanova), Bob Scott (Stanford) (San Diego Marines 1951), Art Skinner (Notre Dame)

Tackles: Al Adams (USC), Ken Barfield (Mississippi), Bob Brady (Ball State), Stan Dwyer (Northwestern), John Feltch (Holy Cross), Art Hargrove (South Carolina) (Parris Island 1948-50), Dave Harvey (VMI), Bob Stephenson, Frank Turner, Jim Weatherall (Oklahoma), Bob Werckle (Vanderbilt)

Guards: Tom Acuff (Southwest Texas), Ben Amsler (South Carolina), John Costa, John Eldridge (Ball State-Northwestern), George Foley (Holy Cross), Ken Huxhold (Wisconsin), Ed Johnson (Tufts), Don Mitchell (Penn State), Dave Rodgers (Eastern Kentucky), Len Stewart (Fresno State)

Centers: George Coleman (San Diego State), Sam Greenawalt (Penn State), Dick Murphy (Holy Cross), Ray Wietecha (Michigan State-Northwestern), Wint Winter (Kansas)

Backs: Fred Bates (San Diego State), Bill Bonsall (Temple), Joe Caprara (Notre Dame), Bud Carson (North Carolina), John Cullity (Holy Cross), Bill DeChard (Holy Cross), Dick Flowers (Northwestern), LaVaughn Gehring, Dick Grabiak (Indiana of Pa.), Dave Hallberg, Howie Hostetler (Oregon), John Kerestes (Purdue), Hugh "Red" Kriever (Parris Island 1948-49) (Louisville), Joe Makarawicz (Drake), Eddie Marr, Arch Martin, Walt Mawyer (Memphis State), John Mazur (Notre Dame), Jack McCoy (Niagara), Bob Miller, John Mitchell (Erskine), Ray Pendergraft (Morehead), Jay Roundy (USC), Eddie Salata, Don Scott (Villanova), Don Southerland, Gene Stewart (Mississippi State) (KIA), Ray Wires (Evansville)

Kicker: Ralph Heywood (USC) (El Toro 1945)

Army, Air Force Ties

West Point and the Air Force Academy have had a few football ties to the Corps.

Chris Stanat of Army was a Quantico back in 1962 and '63 and Bill Zadel a Quantico tackle in 1965.

Perhaps that was a payback for the Corps sending end and Marine V-12 trainee Barney Poole (College Football Hall of Fame) to West Point in 1944 and former Marines Joe McCrane (1947-49) and Vic Pollock (1949-50, 1952).

Tackle Neal Roundtree of the Air Force Academy played for Quantico in 1961 and 1962 and MCRD San Diego in 1963. He had been selected for the U.S. Bowl all-star game in Washington, D.C., in 1961.

On the other end of the scale, back Gene Filipski was a standout Army back before receiving All-America honors at Villanova in 1952 and playing with Quantico in 1954-55 and Calgary in the Canadian Football League from 1958-61.

Jay Robertson (Northwestern), a Quantico center in 1964 and assistant coach in 1965, joined the Army coaching staff in the 1980s after serving at Notre Dame, Wisconsin, Northern Illinois and Northwestern.

Hi rickety hoop-te-do (slow)
Hi-rickety hoop-te-do (faster)
Hi rickety hoop-te do (faster)
Quantico Devildogs, SOCKEROO!

A Quantico cheer

Corps' Best, Anyway

Quantico's 1953 team could well have been dedicated to the Marine recruiter.

He'd had three years since the start of the Korean War to beat the bushes — and the campuses — for officer candidates who, coincidentally, could play football. And he had done his job well, quite well thank you, with the Platoon Leader Class, NROTC and Officers Candidate Course programs turning out prospects in near-record numbers.

Of course, he had no way of knowing that the cease-fire talks begun in July 1951 would result in an end to the fighting July 27, 1953, at a time the coaches and some players were starting workouts for the '53 season.

But peacetime took away some urgency of the training and let the Marine Corps Schools at Quantico shift some of its focus to football. And, let there be no misunderstanding, this was to be *the* team.

The team didn't — and couldn't — live up to the impossible expectations ballyhooed as early as the spring, but still compiled a 10-3 record, falling just one game short of the national service title.

Said Street & Smith's FOOTBALL magazine: "The Leathernecks are blessed with a squad of experienced college and pro players who should make Quantico a dreaded foe. Ball carriers come a dime a dozen at this huge post and linemen who know their way around a football field are stumbling over each other to make the team."

And Marine public information officers distributed advance stories on Quantico's prospects, a photo of four players from the pro ranks and another photo of those who had captained college teams.

Maj. Charles Walker (Wabash), who in three seasons at MCRD San Diego and Quantico had posted 8-2, 11-0 and 8-3 records, also was blessed with an influx of players who had played for other Marine teams in 1952.

Everyone was thinking Big.

But not all the All-Americans and all-conference players counted upon reported, and reality set in quickly as Quantico lost the opener, 9-6, to MCAS Cherry Point, generally a doormat of Marine football.

The upset may rank as the greatest in Marine history.

But there was too much talent on hand, and the Leathernecks ran off seven victories before losing to Ft. Jackson (S.C.), 9-7. The Golden Arrows (8-1-1) featured All-America guard Ray Beck of Georgia Tech and lost only to Bolling Air Force Base.

Again, the Holy Cross game proved a highlight of the schedule. The Marines downed the Crusaders, 17-0, before 22,000 in Worcester, Mass. A Boston paper said the difference was "Walker using 38 players and substituting full teams as units midway through each quarter."

"The star-spangled Marines, older and more experienced and finely conditioned and eager, simply had too much of everything," the paper said.

Quantico, after the Ft. Jackson loss, beat Ft. Lee, Ft. Belvoir (coached by a young Al Davis), and Camp Pendleton, 21-14, for the All-Marine title before 14,000 in San Diego.

The victory earned Quantico a bid to the Poinsettia Bowl, although in retrospect and to paraphrase a joke, first prize should have been a bye and second prize the trip to San Diego.

The opponent was Ft. Ord, perhaps the finest service aggregation ever assembled.

The result was predestined: the California team, helped by six fumble recoveries, walloped Quantico, 55-19, for the All-Service title — a defeat for the Marines akin to the 48-25 loss by MCAS El Toro to the Fleet City Navy in the Los Angeles Coliseum in December 1945.

Ft. Ord, by beating Great Lakes, 67-12, in the Jan. 1 Salad Bowl, closed a 13-0 season in which it scored 524 points and trailed only twice, after losing exhibitions to, yes, the Los Angeles Rams and San Francisco 49ers. Its roster read like a "Who's Who."

Back Ollie Matson (University of San Francisco), enshrined in both the College and Pro Halls of Fame and for whom the Rams traded nine players, played 14 pro seasons.

Ends Ed Henke (USC) and Cliff Livingston (UCLA) were pros for 11 seasons, quarterback Don Heinrich (Washington) for eight seasons, halfback Dave Mann (Oregon State) three seasons, and linebacker Pat Cannamela (USC) was with the Dallas Texans in 1952.

"Quantico may have been the pride and joy of Eastern service football but they left little, if any, impression on West Coast fans as the Warriors ran over, around and through the All-Marine champs," said one game account.

The loss not withstanding, Quantico's '53 aggregation generally is mentioned when the roll is called of great Marine teams.

The backfield was one of the strongest any Marine team ever fielded.

Quarterback John Fry had lettered at Baylor (1947-50). Halfbacks included John Pettibon of Notre Dame (1949-51), a defensive starter on the 1949 national championship team; John Idzik of Maryland (1947-50), Jackson King of Colgate (1949-51), Bob Meyers of Stanford (1950-51) and Jim Parker of Baylor (1948-50). Fullbacks included John Amberg of Kansas and John Mounie of Duke (both 1948-50).

Meyers was a second-team All-Service selection in 1953; Amberg was All-Marine and the Washington Touchdown Club's Service Player of the Year.

Amberg was with the New York Giants in 1951-52, Meyers with the 49ers in 1952, and Pettibon a teammate of Cannemela's with the Texans in 1952, and such was their renown that drill instructors hesitated to take their 7th OCC on forced marches.

"Look," said one DI. "These guys just came out of pro football, and are in incredible shape. They could go on for 100 miles and march us into the ground. We can't let that happen."

And they didn't.

Pettibon, because of playing for Notre Dame and Coach Frank Leahy, was the best known nationally.

Public-address announcers would intone: "At righhtt hhaallffbbaacckk, ffrromm NNottrre DDammmme, JJohhhhhnnnn PPettttiibbbbonn."

And the crowds would cheer.

And Pettibon, who played for a Marine team in Japan in 1954 and in the NFL for three seasons after his release from active duty, would be the most sought-after Marine before and after games, befitting his All-Service status and his 5.2 rushing average.

Amberg was the workhorse, carrying for 347 yards in 95 carries during the regular season and for 124 yards in 15 carries against Camp Pendleton.

"When the other team had the ball, Amberg was one of the Virginians' best pass defenders," said the Leatherneck.

During the regular season, Fry completed 41 of 86 passes for 524 yards, and passed for two TDS against Ft. Eustis, Parris Island and Camp Pendleton, and TDs against Dartmouth and Ft. Ord.

The rest of the team wasn't too shabby, either:

■ **Ends:** They were almost as deep as the 1952 team. Walker could call on All-American Frank McPhee (Princeton), an All-Service selection in 1953; Ken MacAfee (Alabama), a second-team All-Marine selection who later caught 79 passes for 1,160 yards and 18 TDS in six NFL seasons; Bob Trout (Baylor), a Detroit Lions' draft choice; Jim Baldinger (Navy), and Paul Andrew and David Hood (both of Cal).

McPhee's "outstanding defensive abilities helped the champs hold their opposition to a meager 43 points during regular-season play," the Leatherneck observed.

■ **Tackles:** Depth and experience abounded in Roscoe Hansen (North Carolina and the Philadelphia Eagles); Tony Kramer (Dayton), Edwin Lee (Kansas); Tom Roche (Northwestern), a Baltimore Colts' draft choice; Paul Stephens (South Carolina), and Walt Viellieu (Purdue).

■ **Guards:** Again, depth and experience were available in Chuck Cusimano (LSU), All-American Chet Millett (Holy Cross), Tom Roggeman (Purdue), Pete Reich (Dartmouth), Pete Simmons (San Diego State), Al Viola (All-Marine in 1953 and in 1952 at Camp Lejeune) and Gene Watto (Fordham).

■ **Centers:** This was the lone position without predominant Division I experience. Other than Jess Berry (South Carolina) and Jim Erkenbeck (San Diego State), the candidates had Division II or III backgrounds.

Seven Quantico performers had played for other Marine teams. Hansen, Idzik and MacAfee had helped Parris Island to a 9-3-1 record in 1952; Viola and back Al Hoisington were with Camp Lejeune, and Harris with Camp Pendleton, where he scored 120 points. Back Fred Rippel (Bradley) had played for Pendleton in 1951.

After his return to civilian life, Viola lettered at Northwestern from 1955-57, guard John Eldridge at Northwestern from 1955-56, Harris at Georgia from 1954-55, quarterback Steve Piskach at Detroit from 1956-57 and Rippel at Iowa State from 1955-56.

But just as tantalizing was the "What Might Have Been" aspect to the 1953 season.

The Street & Smith preview, based on a Quantico news release, listed almost enough players to man another base team, players who through transfer, training, injury, medical problems, delays or other reasons, weren't available.

Among them were "backs Dick Foster and R.C. Allen of Vanderbilt, Bobby Gantt and Ernie Liberatti of North Carolina, George Kinek of Tulane and (All-American) Rick Casares of Florida; ends Ben Roderick and Bob Hines of Vanderbilt, Bennie Walser and Glenn Nickerson of North Carolina and Bill Owens of Colgate; tackles Tom Higgins of North Carolina, Jim Howe of Northwestern, Buford Long of Florida and Erwin Fox of Boston University; guards Tom Seeman of Notre Dame and Tom Hardy of North Texas; and center Bobby Kelley of West Texas."

Ironically, Kinek, playing for Cherry Point, figured in the upset victory over Quantico.

All the while back Bob Mathias, a driving force on Stanford's 1952 Rose Bowl team, Olympic decathlon champion in 1948 and 1952, and later a congressman, was on base at Quantico but was heavily committed to appearances on Capitol Hill and the nearby Washington scene in behalf of the Marine Corps, the Olympics and athletics.

A report circulated that the Marine Corps, because of his time away from training, was having difficulty writing a fitness report on Mathias. The solution reportedly was to grade him average or below average in physical condition and appearance, a rating that obviously would not affect Mathias' promotion chances.

As could be expected of men with leadership potential, a number went into coaching and athletic administration:

■ Idzik was the coach at the University of Detroit from 1962-64, and an assistant with five pro teams over a 16-year span.

■ Roggeman became an assistant at Purdue, Arizona and USC.

■ Erkenbeck was an assistant at four colleges and later served on staffs of the Canadian Football League, United States Football League, New Orleans Saints and Dallas Cowboys.

■ Center Bob Peck (Stetson) would be the athletic director at Williams College.

And, yes, quarterback John Fry eventually dashed into a Texas telephone booth, Clark Kent-style, changed uniforms and emerged as Hayden Fry, the nationally-known football coach at Southern Methodist (1962-72), North Texas (1973-78) and Iowa (1979-). He hauled in a number of coaching honors and led the Hawkeyes to Top 10 rankings and the Rose Bowl (twice), the Peach Bowl, Gator Bowl, Freedom Bowl and Holiday Bowl.

But the team's legacy, apart from Fry's success, lives on in another fashion:

■ MacAfee's son, Ken Jr. (6-4, 249), was a tight end at Notre Dame from 1974-77, and an All-American three seasons, won the Walter Camp Award and placed third in the Heisman Trophy voting in 1977.

■ Baldinger's sons literally were big men in the NFL. Rich (6-4, 281), a tackle-guard born at Camp Lejeune, and defensive end-tackle Gary

(6-3, 260) played at Wake Forest, and center-guard Brian (6-4, 261) at Duke, before turning pro.

■ Fry's sons, Randy, Zach and Kelly, played for him at North Texas.

■ Roggeman's son, Buck (6-1, 240), was a guard at Stanford.

■ Tackle Bob Norman's son, Tim (6-6, 274), was a lineman at Illinois and in Canada, the USFL and with the Bears.

Like they said, the accommodations at Quantico weren't much, but, oh, that water. ...

1953

Record: 13-6 Xavier (Ohio), 31-0 Dayton, 17-0 Holy Cross, 28-7 Ft. Belvoir, 7-9 Ft. Jackson, 16-12 Bolling AFB, 21-0 Ft. Eustis, 9-0 Ft. Lee, 6-9 Cherry Point, 35-0 Parris Island, 3-0 Camp Lejeune, 21-14 Camp Pendleton (All-Marine title), 19-55 Ft. Ord (Poinsetta Bowl). (10-3). John Amberg named Service Player of the Year by Touchdown Club of Washington. Amberg, McPhee, Pettibon and Viola All-Marine; MacAfee and Meyers second team.

Coach: Maj. Charles Walker (Wabash) (coach San Diego Marines 1949-50)

Assistants: Maj. Ray "Stormy" Davis (Hardin-Simmons), Maj. Paul Lentz (Guilford), Maj. Bill Sigler (North Carolina-Michigan) (asst. San Diego Marines 1949), Capt. Al Thomas (Northwestern) (Maui Marines 1944)

Ends: Paul Andrew (California), Jim Baldinger (Navy), John Coyne (Pitt), David Hood (California), Merrill Jacobs (St. Mary's-San Francisco State), Ken MacAfee (Alabama), Frank McPhee (Princeton), Don Southerland, Bob Trout (Baylor)

Tackles: Bob Brady (Ball State), Russ Burns, Roy Colquitt (Idaho), Roscoe Hansen (North Carolina) (Parris Island 1952), Tony Kramer (Dayton), Edwin Lee (Kansas), John Naylor (Texas), Bob Norman, Vic Rimkus (Holy Cross), Tom Robinson, Tom Roche (Northwestern), Paul Stephens (South Carolina), Bob Stephenson, Walt Viellieu (Purdue)

Guards: Charles Cusimano (Louisiana State) (San Diego Marines 1952), John Eldridge (Ball State-Northwestern), Chet Millett (Holy Cross), Don Mitchell (Penn State), Marv Peterson (Utah State), Tom Roggeman (Purdue), Pete Reich (Dartmouth), Pete Simmons (San Diego State), Al Viola (Georgia-Northwestern) (Camp Lejeune 1951-52), Gene Watto (Fordham)

Centers: Jess Berry (South Carolina), Tony DiPaolo (Bloomsburg), Jim Erkenbeck (San Diego State), Bob Loving (McMurry), Bob Peck (Stetson), Gerry Wenzel (Indiana-St. Joseph's)

Backs: John Amberg (Kansas), John Hayden Fry (Baylor), Dick Grabiak (Indiana of Pa.), Charlie Harris (Georgia) (Camp Pendleton 1951-52), Al Hoisington (Pasadena JC) (Camp Lejeune 1952), John Idzik (Maryland) (Parris Island 1952), Jackson King (Colgate), Labat, Bob Meyers (Stanford), Bob Miller, John Mounie (Duke), Dick Neveux (Detroit), Jim Parker (Baylor), Jophn Pettibon (Notre Dame), Steve Piskach (Toledo-Detroit), Fred Rippel (Bradley-Iowa State) (Camp Pendleton 1951), Eddie Salata, Rex Simonds (Bowling Green), Russ Smale, Stan Sterger (Indiana) (Parris Island 1953), Dan Stewart, Edwin Wood

Others: Joe Gleason, Tom Payne (Santa Clara), George Tinsley

Why He Wears Shades

Fellow coaches joke about the sunglasses worn by Iowa coach Hayden Fry, saying he wears them even to an evening social event.

But Fry, a former Quantico and 3rd Marine Division All-Stars quarterback, discussed the subject on his WHO/AM radio show in Des Moines.

"I've worn the shades since I nearly lost my eyesight on a recruiting trip out in west Texas and New Mexico. I got caught in a blizzard, one of the few they've ever had between Odessa (Texas) and Hobbs (N.M.). and I had to hang my head out the (car) window to see. It really affected my eyes. My shades are prescription glasses. I have to wear them to see the scoreboard."

10-2, 8-3 Not Bad

The names Beckett, Hall, Hanley, Harris, Harwood, Overgaard, Stawicki, Trometter and Walker dominate any list of the outstanding Marine coaches.

As does the name of Lt. Col. John T. (or "J.T.") Hill.

In four seasons at Parris Island (1951-52) and at Quantico (1954-55), Hill, an Annapolis man, won 36 games, lost 10 and tied one. He coached the 1951 team to an All-Marine title, his 1952 team was the second-highest scorer in Marine history with 505 points, his teams were nationally ranked at Quantico, and, overall, he coached 19 players who earned All-Marine honors.

His 1954 edition, for example, posted a 10-2 record and was ranked No. 4 by the Williamson Rating Service and third in another poll.

His 1955 crew wound up 8-3 and with a Williamson ranking.

Hill, a lineman at Navy from 1939-41, won the the Bronze Star in Korea and would be awarded the Legion of Merit in Vietnam.

A game program, almost matter-of-factly, noted that Hill, an assistant at Quantico in 1949-50, "received his first taste of the game while playing guard at Buchtel High in Akron, Ohio, his hometown. He attended Kiski Prep in Saltsburg, Pa., for one year and in 1938 went to the Naval Academy, where he starred on the Middie varsity for three years running, at the guard slot."

While not as flamboyant as a Dick Hanley, Hill was just as successful, ranking eighth in Marine career coaching victories, and third overall in percentage (.783), behind only Bull Trometter (.884) and Elmer Hall (.860).

Quantico's 1953 team perhaps is best remembered for its quarterback, John Hayden Fry of Baylor, later to be a nationally known coach.

And in 1954 Quantico had back Vince Dooley, who was destined for coaching greatness at the University of Georgia. Dooley, the 1953 captain at Auburn, was named the Most Valuable Player in the Gator Bowl, played in the Senior Bowl and was selected for the College All-Star Game (where he intercepted a Bobby Layne pass).

But Dooley reinjured a knee (hurt as a sophomore against Mississippi) in the second game of the 1954 season, a game in which he threw a TD pass. A year later, he started his coaching career as a Parris Island assistant.

Asked why he chose Dooley as Georgia's coach, Athletic Director Joel Eaves once said: He's an "outstanding player, on offense and defense; unusually successful assistant varsity coach and head freshman coach; a disciplinarian (two years active duty as a Marine officer); a gentleman and scholar (a master's in history)."

At Georgia, Dooley established a 183-71-10 record through the 1986 season, and his teams won the national title in 1980 and six Southeastern Conference titles, and played in 18 postseason games. Dooley was chosen Coach of the Year in 1980 by the NCAA and in 1982 by Chevrolet-WTBS.

The preseason spotlight in 1955 was on guard J.D. Roberts of Oklahoma, the Outland Trophy winner in 1953, an All-American and the Lineman of the Year. Roberts, who played for Hamilton of the Canadian Football League in an injury-abbreviated 1954 season, was an assistant at five colleges before becoming a pro assistant. He coached the New Orleans Saints from 1970-72.

According to "Who's Who in Football" (Ronald L. Mendell and Timothy B. Phares), Roberts, 5-10 and 190, "played so well against Notre Dame in 1953 that Irish coach Frank Leahy wrote him a personal letter of congratulations."

A year later as an assistant, Roberts was asked what made a good guard.

"A man has to be physically tough ... mentally ready ... have the desire to play ... and have the right reactions. ... Every man on that field is having a battle, if he has to take out a man, it stems out, is he tougher than the man who has to be taken out of the play?"

As Hill had predicted, the '54 season got off to a slow start with victories over Xavier and Detroit sandwiched around losses to Bolling Air Force Base (9-1-1), 25-14, and Ft. Belvoir (7-1-1), 16-6.

Hill had been quoted in Street and Smith's 1954 FOOTBALL Yearbook as saying, "Our prospects aren't as good as in the past, principally because the caliber of service football has improved tremendously in the past few years. Boys like Notre Dame's John Pettibon, Stanford's Bob Meyers, Princeton's Frank MacPhee and the New York Giants' John Amberg — outstanding two-way performers last year (1953) — will be playing against us this season."

(Actually, Amberg and Pettibon wound up overseas and MacPhee at Camp Pendleton. Meyers was the workhorse of the Camp Lejeune team.)

But once the Quantico Marines were good, they were very, very good.

"I said before the fall practices began that I wanted a team that wanted to play football," Hill told the Quantico Sentry. "I think I've got one. I've never coached a finer, more willing bunch of boys."

Paced by All-Marine and All-Navy selections Don Bingham (Sul Ross) at halfback, Steve Eisenhauer (Navy) at guard and Steve Piskach at quarterback, Hill's 1954 team closed in runaway fashion by winning its final eight games, most of them one-sidedly.

In that span, the Marines scored 320 points, an average of 40 a game, with a diversified offense.

(The All-Marine championship game was not held.)

The numbers game was impressive.

Before being injured, Piskach, who played freshman ball at Toledo, completed 33 of 66 passes for 652 yards and 10 touchdowns. Ted Keller (Randolph-Macon), who stepped in, hit on 29 of 46 passes for 497 yards and eight TDs as the other half of a powerful 1-2 punch.

Said the Leatherneck: "Piskach proved to be the field general of the year when he lifted a doddering ball club into the win column and kept it there against tough competition."

Bingham gained 406 yards in 66 carries, a 6.1 average, caught 16 passes and scored 90 points. Against Parris Island, he scored five times. Bill Roberts (Dartmouth) gained 582 yards in 90 carries, a 6.5-yard average, and had eight TDs. Before an injury, Bill Tate (Illinois) rushed for 178 yards in 45 carries. (The trio all played at Camp Lejeune in 1955.)

Bingham, said the Leatherneck, "has been described with straight-face accuracy as 'touchdown happy.' In Bingham's book, there seemed to be only one thing to do with a handoff or a pitchout — score. And he did. Often."

Fullback Fred Franco (Navy), "off to a slow start, came on like a house-a-fire toward the middle of the season to win a starting berth, grind out 244 yards and score 30 points," said one writer. "As a linebacker, he has an uncanny sense for diagnosing plays."

Gene Filipski (Army and an All-American at Villanova in 1952) rambled for 180 yards in 32 carries before an ankle injury.

Incredibly, according to Street & Smith, the backfield could have even been deeper. "Midsummer found Hill also expecting Bob Mathias, Stanford's fine back, and Larry Grigg, who scored Oklahoma's winning touchdown in the Orange Bowl."

Mathias, however, did not play for Quantico in 1953 or 1954.

But they were hardly missed. The backfield probably was as impressive as 1953's and the depth compensated for the injuries. Hill could use an A unit and a B unit.

The line on the line was impressive, too. Besides Eisenhauer, an All-American at Navy in 1952-53, Hill had these troops from major colleges:

■ **Ends:** Joe Harrington (Holy Cross), second-team All-American Don Penza (Notre Dame) and Howie Pitt (Duke).

■ **Tackles:** Jesus Esparza (New Mexico A&M), Lou Florio (Boston College), Jack Hamber (San Jose State), Vic Rimkus (Holy Cross) and Joe Wojtys (Purdue).

■ **Guards:** Pat Cacace (Boston College), Bob Hallett (Bowling Green) and Marv Peterson (Utah State).

■ **Centers:** Dick Petty (USC) and Jim Rawley (Iowa State).

■ **Backs:** Ed Mioduszewski (William & Mary), Ray Powell (Oklahoma), Pat Ryan (Holy Cross), Rex Simonds (Bowling Green) and Dick Zotti (Boston College).

The only apparent weakness was size. Florio was 230, tackle Jerry Groome (Fordham) 228, tackle Bill Keepper (Illinois Wesleyan) 225 and Rimkus 225.

However, the team capitalized on speed — and smartness.

Besides Dooley, Keller (a 104-57-6 record from 1964-81 at Randolph-Macon), Tate (Wake Forest 1964-68), and back Bill Dando (John Carroll 1964, University of Buffalo 1978-86), were college head coaches, and several players became assistants.

A tipoff on the talent was the interest by pro teams and scouts.

Bingham, back Alex Bravo (Cal Poly San Luis Obispo), Esparza, Filipski, Mioduszewski (also known as Meadows), Penza, Pitt and Rimkus had been drafted by NFL teams. And Bingham (Chicago Bears 1955-56), Bravo (Canada 1956, Los Angeles Rams 1957-58,

re Pages • Authentic Experts

FOOTBALL

YEARBOOK

'IKE" EISENHAUER
NAVY GUARD

MID-WEST
BIG TEN
MID-AMERICAN
OHIO CONFERENCE
By Tommy Devine

THE EAST
IVY LEAGUE
YANKEE CONFERENCE
By Jesse Abramson

DEEP SOUTH
By Walter Stewart

SOUTHWEST
BORDER • LONE STAR
GULF • TEXAS
By Flem Hall

SKYLINE
ROCKY MOUNTAIN
By Jack Carberry

BIG SEVEN
MISSOURI VALLEY
NORTH CENTRAL
By Bob Busby

SOUTHERN
   CONFERENCE
NEW CONFERENCE
MARINE CORPS
By Jack Horner

PACIFIC COAST
SO. CALIFORNIA
   CONFERENCE
CALIF. COLLEGIATE A A
By Paul Zimmerman

PROFESSIONAL
   FOOTBALL
WESTERN DIVISION
EASTERN DIVISION
By Harry MacNamara

SCHEDULES

SELECTORS' CHART

ACTION PHOTOS

COLLEGE AND PRO ROUNDUPS

Oakland Raiders 1960-61), Filipski (Giants 1956-57, Canada 1958-61), Mioduszewski (Baltimore Colts 1953) and Bill Roberts (Green Bay Packers and Rams 1956, Canada 1957) played professionally.

But the younger members also continued to play. Dando, tackle Emerson Dromgold and Piskach all lettered at the University of Detroit, a team they had played against. Quantico defeated the Titans, 20-0, in 1954.

The 1955 season:

The team potentially was one of the most experienced in Marine history because at least eight players had taken advantage of freshman eligibility in 1951 and lettered four times at major schools, and at least a dozen three seasons.

End Tom Izbicki won letters at Boston College from 1951-54, tackles E.P. "Buddy" Lewis at Arizona and Frank Morze at Boston College, guard Don Tate at Illinois, centers John Damore at Northwestern and Dick Frasor at Notre Dame, and backs Don Daly at Eastern Kentucky, All-Marine selection Worth "A Million" Lutz at Duke and Buddy Rowell at Penn State.

And there was a University of Wisconsin flavor in center Mike Cwayna and backs John Dixon, Glenn "Buzz" Wilson and Jerry Witt.

A mid-season slump — losses to Ft. Belvoir, 13-7; Holy Cross, 7-0, in the rain, and Bolling AFB, 20-14, in a span of four games — spoiled a 3-0 start and 4-0 finish. Bolling won all 10 games.

"The Marines had entered the 1955 football picture without the services of 12 of their 1954 standouts," noted Street & Smith's FOOTBALL Yearbook. "Hill also is mourning the loss of Piskach, who is ineligible (because he had played two seasons). ...

"This sounds as if the Virginia Leathernecks will have a rough go of it. Maybe so, but as in the past, Quantico is hoping to come up with another powerhouse."

And it did.

Franco returned and received All-Marine and All-Sea Service honors as did Hamber. Filipski was back. And Keller. And five others from the '54 team.

Eight players had been drafted by NFL teams, and Damore would play for the Bears in 1957 and 1959.

And the recruiters sent these major-college players:

■ **Ends:** Bob Dee (Holy Cross), Dick Gagliardi (Boston College), Tom Hague (Ohio State) and Sig Niepokoj (Northwestern).

■ **Tackles:** Mike Giddings (Cal) and Frank Pavich (USC). (Giddings later coached Utah and the WFL Hawaii Sun, was an NFL assistant and president of Pro Scout Inc. of Newport Beach, Cal.)

■ **Guards:** Ralph Denton (Wichita), Joe Mattaliano (Boston College), Ed Patterson (North Carolina), J.D. Roberts — a first-team Armed Forces Press Service selection — and Ralph Torrance (Duke).

■ **Center:** John Palmer (Duke)

■ **Backs:** Jack Ging (Oklahoma) and Gordie Kellogg (Rice).

And throw in NAIA All-Americans Wayne Buchert and Bob Ward, both of Whitworth (Wash.). Ward later was an assistant for the Dallas Cowboys.

Again, the Achilles' heel was size. Other than Morze (285), only Giddings (228), Lefferts (225) and Pavich (220) were 220 or heavier.

Franco was mentioned in many of the headlines and named the Most Valuable Player of the Navy Times' All-Sea Service team.

Franco and Hamber "played the same side, making Quantico's left side almost impregnable," said the Navy Times, which noted that Franco had not been called for a penalty.

Hamber, said the Leatherneck, is "big, rugged and speedy. He was usually one of the first men downfield on kickoffs and punts."

But the after-Marine life of three players was just as fascinating:

■ Dee, a 19th-round draft pick of the Washington Redskins in 1955 but not nationally acclaimed, grew from a 6-3, 210-pounder at Quantico to a 250-pound defensive end for the Boston Patriots. He was credited with scoring the first TD in the new American Football League when he recovered a fumble in the end zone.

He had played for the Redskins in 1957-58 before being cut in 1959. But the American Football League was founded and Dee appeared in 112 consecutive regular-season games during his 1960-67 stay with the Patriots and was selected for the 1962, 1964, 1965 and 1966 Pro Bowl games. The Patriots retired his No. 89.

■ Ging's name might not be as familiar as Dooley's. But his face and voice are from his years as an actor, most notably perhaps as Lt. Quinlan on TV's "Riptide."

A 1985 Los Angeles Times article suggested that "few people in Alva., Okla., would have predicted that Ging would become a television actor, that Clint Eastwood and Jack Nicholson would attend his wedding, or that he would have Lee Majors as a longtime friend, and Robert Redford as a neighbor."

The Times also observed that Ging "has had various identities ... among them University of Oklahoma football player, single parent, nightclub owner, Crosby golf tournament winner, Clint Eastwood Celebrity Tennis tournament champion and Malibu real estate salesman."

A high school All-American at 150 pounds, Ging played three seasons as a halfback and defensive back for Bud Wilkinson's Sooners, and in the Canadian Football League in 1954. He convinced the Marines to accept him despite three knee operations and a shoulder separation.

(Son Adam, an infielder, was traded by the San Diego Padres to the New York Mets in the December 1986 baseball trade involving outfielder Kevin McReynolds.)

■ The 6-5 Morze, a No. 2 pick of the San Francisco 49ers in 1955, still was learning to cope with his size at Quantico and at Camp Lejeune in 1956. But he adapted quickly and had a distingushed pro career with the 49ers from 1957-61, the Cleveland Browns from 1962-63 and the 49ers again in 1964.

Morze was another in a long line of Marine linemen the likes of Artie Donovan, Abe Gibron, Big Daddy Lipscomb,,Thurman McGraw, Leo Nomellini, Ernie Stautner, Wee Willie Wilkin and Ray Wietecha.

1954

Record: 20-7 Xavier (Ohio), 14-25 Bolling AFB, 20-0 Detroit, 6-16 Ft. Belvoir, 46-13 MCAS Cherry Point, 33-19 Ft. Eustis, 26-19 Camp Lejeune, 39-21 Parris Island, 61-14 Great Lakes NTC, 34-6 Ft. Lee, 40-7 Ft. Monmouth, 41-11 Ft. Jackson. (10-2). Ranked No. 4 by the Williamson Rating Service. Don Bingham scored 90 points. Bingham, Eisenhauer and Piskach All-Marine; Fullam and Hamber second team.

Coach: J.T. Hill (Navy) (coach Parris Island 1951-052)

Assistants: Lt. Norm Manoogian (Stanford), Maj. Rick McMullen, Jim Quinn (Fordham) (asst. Parris Island 1952), Capt. Roy Whitlock

Ends: Don Cropper (Camp Pendleton), Paul Crowley (Harvard), Don Fullam (Navy), Joe Harrington (Holy Cross), Don Penza (Notre Dame), Howie Pitt (Duke), Bob Plackett (Maryland), Gene Sparks, Fred Voss (Carleton)

Tackles: Bill Bodmer, Emerson Dromgold (Detroit), Jesus Esparza (New Mexico A&M), Lou Florio (Boston College), Wayne Fransom (Michigan), Maury Gilbert (Camp Lejeune 1947, Pearl Harbor Marines 1948-49), Jerry Groome (Fordham), Jack Hamber (San Jose State), Bill Keepper (Illinois Wesleyan) (Parris Island), Vic Rimkus (Holy Cross), Joe Wojtys (Purdue), Bob Ward

Guards: Pat Cacace (Boston College), Len De Augustine (Lock Haven), Steve Eisenhauer (Navy), Buddy Griffin (South Carolina), Bob Hallett (Bowling Green), Marv Peterson (Utah State), Jim Schenk (Kentucky), Jack Traband, John Washington (Oklahoma), Ray Wichus

Centers: Tony Correnti (Navy), Dick Petty (USC), Tony DiPaolo (Bloomsburg), Jim Rawley (Iowa State), Jim Tomko, Bob Warner

Backs: Roger Beattie (Camp Lejeune 1950), Don Bingham (Sul Ross), Alex Bravo (Cal Poly Pomona), Bill Dando (Univ. of San Francisco-Detroit) (Memphis NAS 1953), Vince Dooley (Auburn), Gene Filipski (Army-Villanova), Fred Franco (Brown-Navy), Bill Groetz (Kent State), Norm Hisler (Houston), Ted Keller (Randolph-Macon), Bob Lamphere (Wisconsin), Cleo Lee, Eddie Marr, Ed Mioduszewski (William & Mary), Steve Piskach (Toledo-Detroit), Ray Powell (Oklahoma), Bill Roberts (Dartmouth), Pat Ryan (Holy Cross), Rex Simonds (Bowling Green), Stan Sterger (Indiana) (Parris Island 1953), Bill Tate (Illinois), Dick Zotti (Boston College)

1955

Record: 21-7 Xavier (Ohio), 27-6 Ft. Eustis, 21-0 Parris Island, 7-13 Ft. Belvoir, 0-7 Holy Cross, 27-7 Camp Lejeune, 14-20 Bolling AFB, 49-14 Great Lakes NTC, 32-7 Ft. Lee, 13-0 Ft. Monmouth, 27-0 Ft. Jackson. (8-3). Ranked among top 10 by Williamson, but position not available. Franco, Hamber and Lutz All-Marine; Damore, Dee, Filipski, Hague and Roberts second team. Franco MVP of Navy Times' All-Service team. Quantico potentially one of Marines' strongest of any era, with at least eight players winning four letters at Division I schools, and at least a dozen three letters.

Coach: Lt. Col. J.T. Hill (Navy) (coach Parris Island 1951-52)

Assistants: Lt. Bill French (Notre Dame), Capt. Jim Quinn (Fordham) (asst. Parris Island 1952), Capt. Don Spencer, Maj. Roy Whitlock

Ends: Bob Dee (Holy Cross), Ken Dement (Southeast Missouri), Dick Gagliardio (Boston College), Tom Hague (Ohio State), Herm Howard (Virginia Union), Tom Izbicki (Boston College), Chuck Kirkhoff (Xavier), Jim LaRussa (Miami of Fla.), George Murphy (Fordham) (Camp Lejeune 1955), Sig Niepokoj (Northwestern), John Rushing (Redlands)

Tackles: Emerson Dromgold (Detroit), Mike Giddings (Cal), John Hamber (San Jose State), George Lefferts (Idaho), E.P. "Buddy" Lewis (Arizona), Frank Morze (Boston College), Frank Pavich (USC), John Traband

Guards: Will Conatser (Cincinnati), Ralph Denton (Wichita), Maurie Gilbert (Camp Lejeune 1947, Pearl Harbor Marines 1948-49), Joe Mattaliano (Boston College), Ed Patterson (North Carolina), Mal Patterson (Southeastern Louisiana), J.D. Roberts (Oklahoma), Don Tate (Illinois), Ralph Torrance (Duke), John Washington (Oklahoma)

Centers: Mike Cwayna (Wisconsin), John Damore (Northwestern), Dick Frasor (Notre Dame), John Palmer (Duke)

Backs: Pete Bruni, Wayne Buchert (Whuitworth), Don Daly (Eastern Kentucky), Bill Dando (Univ. of San Francisco-Detroit) (Memphis NAS 1953), John Dixon (Wisconsin), Gene Filipski (Army-Villanova), George Fowler, Fred Franco (Brown-Navy), Jack Ging (Oklahoma), Vince Jazwinski (Brown), Don Julie (Wisconsin), Ted Keller (Randolph-Macon), Gordon Kellogg (Rice), Worth 'A Million" Lutz (Duke), Jim Milne (Missouri), Buddy Rowell (Penn State), Bob Ward (Whitworth), Glenn "Buzz" Wilson (Wisconsin), Jerry Witt (Wisconsin), Ray Wrabley (St. Vincent's)

Win, Or Lose, Nine

Hal Harwood would be finding out in the 1956, 1957 and 1958 seasons whether author Thomas Wolfe's assessment of coming home was correct.

Harwood, now a lieutenant colonel, had been the incredibly successful coach of the Virginia team almost a decade earlier, fashioning a 12-1 record and the All-Service title in 1948, an 11-3 mark and the All-Navy title in 1949 and a 9-2 record and No. 1 ranking among service teams in 1950.

Improving upon that success would be difficult. And it was.

With nine Rice players on the roster, Quantico won 9, lost 3 and was ranked No. 3 among service teams in 1956. A highlight was a 7-6 victory over Bolling Air Force Base, ending a 34-game winning streak and handing the top-ranked Flyers, stocked with Notre Dame players, their only loss.

But everything seemed to go wrong in 1957, and the Leathernecks won 3, lost 9 and tied 1. The number of losses was the most in the base's history.

But the football world tilted in 1958, and Quantico won 9, lost 3 and tied 1, a record more commensurate with Harwood's.

And 1958 would be remembered, too, as the season that a young Navy corpsman helped out as a trainer.

His name? Bill Cosby.

Before he became a big name in the entertainment world and the biggest in television, Cosby went to Temple and lettered in football, and in track and field, and later picked up a master's and doctorate.

And in small-world fashion, Cosby played football at Temple for former Marine George Makris, who had coached at Bolling from 1955-59.

"My wife and I went back East one year," Harwood recalled, "and Bill was entertaining at a local night club. So we went.

"We sent Bill a note before the show, saying hello and wishing him well."

Cosby, always the showman but in the Harwoods' debt, dedicated the show to them, saluted them, thanked them, made them stars of the show, too.

The Harwoods had found Cosby places to sleep and sandwiches to eat on road trips in 1958 — a time when such were difficult for blacks to find,

Like the elephant, Cosby hadn't forgotten.

Harwood, a former Marine enlisted man, was a center at Navy in 1938-40, commanding officer of VMA-251 in Korea and VMF-312 at Cherry Point, and wore the Distinguished Flying Cross, Bronze Star with Combat "V" and five Air Medals.

The 1958 season also found the Marines in the national spotlight with a 13-12 victory over 19th-ranked Rutgers (8-0), believed to be the only Marine victory over a Top 20 college team. It was Rutgers' only loss.

A national magazine called Quantico "a collection of old men." The average age was an "old" 22.

The three Harwood seasons also were marked by name players. In 1956, for example, Ron Beagle, a Navy All-American in 1954 and 1955, and Bob Dee, destined for greatness in the American Football League, were among the ends. Navy's captain, John Hopkins, a tackle, was to be awarded two Bronze Stars in Vietnam and become a Marine general. Assistant coach J.D. Roberts (Oklahoma) had won the Outland Trophy and was Lineman of the Year in 1953, and assistant John Phil Monahan, captain of the Navy team that beat Mississippi, 21-0, in the 1955 Sugar Bowl, also would become a Marine general.

Name players in 1957 included end Jim Mora (Occidental), later to be a USFL and NFL coach; Hopkins and All-America guard Sam Valentine (Penn State), who also starred on the 1958 team.

The 1956 season:

"Returning starters and reserves provide an excellent nucleus for Harwood's team," noted Street & Smith's FOOTBALL Yearbook. "His big problem is replacing Fred Franco (Navy) at fullback and All-American Gene Filipski (Villanova). The Leathernecks were hardest hit at guard in the line."

But Harwood had the talent from major colleges:

■ Besides Beagle, an All-Marine, All-Navy and All-Service selection, and Dee at end, he utilized Dick Gagliardi and Dick Lucas, both of Boston College; Tom Kisselle (Bowling Green) and Sig Niepokoj (Northwestern). Lucas played with the Pittsburgh Steelers in 1958, sat out parts of two seasons because of a knee injury, signed with the Washington Redskins and was traded to the Philadelphia Eagles, for whom he played from 1960-63. He was a reserve on their 1960 NFL title team.

■ Besides Hopkins, the Marines had Fred Campbell (Duke), an 18th-round draft pick of the Chicago Cardinals; and 225-pound Eddie Rayburn and 238-pound Orv Trask, both of Rice, at tackles. Rayburn played with Montreal of the Canadian Football League in 1958, and Trask with the Houston Oilers in 1960-61 and the Oakland Raiders in 1962.

■ Guards included All-Marine Fred Bucci (Columbia); 228-pound Jim Lohr (Southeast Missouri), a 26th-round draft pick of the Baltimore Colts; John Miller (USC), Jim Neville (North Carolina), Tom Siragusa of Rice and Bernie Taracevicz of Holy Cross.

■ All-Marine and All-Navy selection John Damore (Northwestern), 220, and Don Wilson (Rice) headed the center contingent. Damore was with the Chicago Bears in 1957 and 1959.

■ Backs were plentiful. The Marines could use All-Marine Doug Cameron (Texas); Gordie Kellogg, John Nisbet and Thurlo Rogers, all of Rice; Bobby Lee (New Mexico); All-Marine selection Worth "A Million" Lutz (Duke); Emidio Petrarca (Boston College), an 18th-round draft pick of the Detroit Lions; Buddy Rowell (Penn State) and Tom Troxell (Miami of Ohio).

The team had a kick to it in the person of 5-5, 138-pound Tad Weed, who was a publicized leg man at Ohio State and who kicked 12 extra points and three field goals for the Steelers in 1955. His PAT was the difference in the victory over Bolling.

And there was talent from other directions. Tackle Don Deskins (Adelphi), a 225-pounder, had starred for the 1st Marine Division team in Korea in 1954 and the Hawaii Marines in 1955. He would letter at Michigan in 1958-59 and play with the Raiders in 1960.

Quarterback John Shearer had been an NAIA All-American at Shepherd in 1955, and was drafted by the Colts in the 26th round. Back Bob Ward was an NAIA All-American at Whitworth in 1954.

Put these pieces together and the 9-3 record emerged. The Leathernecks opened with two victories before losing to Ft. Eustis, 13-9; they won three before losses to Holy Cross, 13-0, and Camp Lejeune, 9-6; they closed with four victories.

And the offensive statistics were startling. Eight backs rushed for more than 100 yards, led by Cameron, 454 in 81 carries; Kellogg, 450 in 57 for an astounding 7.9 average; Lutz 288 in 84; and Ward, 241 in 39. Shearer completed 36 of 86 passes for 557 yards and five touchdowns, and Lutz 28 of 68 for 340 yards and three TDs. Dee caught 18 passes for 236 yards and two TDs, Lucas 13 for 270 and four TDs, and Gagliardi 12 for 177 yards and a TD.

Back Lew Erber (Montclair State) could not play because of injuries. "I spent most of that season in Bethesda Naval Hospital with a pinched nerve that caused a temporary paralysis in my left arm.".

He was to become an assistant at five colleges and with four pro teams. Lohr would be the coach at his alma mater from 1974-83 and Ward an assistant with the Dallas Cowboys.

The expectations of the usual outstanding season were evident at the postseason banquet. Lt. Gen. Merrill Twining, commandant of the Marine Corps Schools, attributed a comment — "I have one request: win, that's all I ask" — to Maj. Gen. Smedley Darlington Butler, a colorful, controversial figure who brought Quantico into the football world in the 1920s.

And few had even heard then of Al Davis.

The 1957 season:

A switch of 35 points in six games would have given Quantico a 9-4 record rather than the surprising 3-9-1 finish. For example:

■ The Marines lost one game by five points to Ft. Lee, 12-7.

■ They lost four games by six points, to Little Creek, 12-6; Boston College, 13-7; Eglin Air Force Base, 12-6; and Hamilton Air Force Base, 12-6, in a "sea of mud and water" in the Valor Bowl in Chattanooga, Tenn.

■ They tied Camp Lejeune, 26-26.

A penalty here ... an interception there ... a fumble ... a missed tackle ... a botched block ... added to the frustrating season.

The Leathernecks led opponents in first downs, 155 to 119; in yards rushing, 2,064 to 1,938; in passing yardage, 1,321 to 1,226; in passes intercepted, 19 to 18; in punting average, 35.3 to 31.5, and in fewest yards penalized, 497 to 626.

But the telling statistics were the fumbles. Quantico fumbled 72 times and lost the ball 41 times; opponents fumbled 41 times and gave up possession 23 times. In pro terms of today, the fumbles and interceptions resulted in a turnover ratio of minus-17, one clue to the 3-9-1 record.

The recruiters hadn't jumped ship. Harwood had operatives primarily from major schools:

■ At ends, Allen Bliss (Miami of Ohio), a 26th-round draft pick of the Cleveland Browns; Fred Carew (Boston University); Joe Losack (Texas); Lucas, an All-Marine selection; Don Martin (Kansas), Mora, Bob Morman (Northwestern), Tom Richardson (Syracuse) and Darrell Sorrell (Duke).

■ At tackles, Jim Allegro and Joe Murphy (both of Holy Cross), 240-pound Dwight Barnhill (Wichita), Ron Botchan (Occidental); Don Stoeckel (Ohio State); Hopkins, an All-Marine and All-Navy selection; Jim Royer (Navy) and Trask. Botchan played with the Los Angeles Chargers in 1960 and the Oilers in 1961.

■ At guards, Bucci, an All-Marine selection again; Bob Cupit, an NAIA All-American at Upsala; John Dekleva (Colorado A&M); Bill Fackleman (Colgate), Chet Franklin (Utah), Bill Parker (Vanderbilt), Earl Shumaker (Penn State) and Valentine.

■ At center were Bob Berguin (Nebraska); Frank Black (Kansas), a high school All-American; Don Karnoscak (Colorado), John O'Rourke (Pacific), Ted Ringer (Northwestern), Bill Saye (Georgia) and Taracevicz, all of whom had lettered three seasons in college. The contingent, had it all been available at one time, would have been the deepest in Marine history.

■ The backfield included Dick Broderick (Fordham), Shearer, Don Swanson (Minnesota) and John Wolff (Colorado A&M) at quarterback; Ray Alberigi (Penn State), Frank Jeske (Northwestern), Herb Nakken (Utah), a fifth-round draft choice of the Los Angeles Rams, and Tom Reis (Boston College) at halfbacks; and Cameron, an All-Marine selection again, Charlie Laaksonen (Syracuse) and Ray Murray (George Washington) at fullback.

Cameron collected 517 yards in 88 carries to lead ground gainers again and Reis picked up 412 in 83 carries. In passing, Broderick completed 29 of 62 for 506 yards and four TDs, Shearer 27 of 76 for 374 yards and five TDs, and Wolff 18 of 51 for 282 yards and two TDs. Lucas had another banner year in receiving (18 receptions for 321 yards and three TDs) and Alberigi caught 8 for 204 yards.

In 1961, recounted the NFL Alumni magazine, the Eagles had a favorite goal-line play.

"The team would pull its regular tight end, Bobby Walston, and replace him with Lucas, who was a few inches taller and 20 pounds heavier.

" 'Nick Skorich (the coach) put me in because I was a better blocker than Bobby,' " Lucas said, " 'but it just so happened that instead of blocking I would catch a touchdown pass on a simple, quick look-in pass.' "

Lucas caught eight passes that season, but five were for touchdowns. Walston caught 34 but two were for scores.

The turnover of players in 1957 was quite high by Quantico standards ... throw in a few injuries ... a lack of size ... leads that

102

slipped away ... and you had problems.

Harwood used approximately 80 players during the season as lieutenants were whisked in and out of The Basic School.

Compounding the situation was the loss of nine players, including tackle Bob Loughridge, an Oklahoma tri-captain in 1955, because of a "communications problem" with their company. The players reported to the team but were unable to keep up with their football schedule plus the nightly assignments their CO required to make up for their absences in the afternoons.

Another player Harwood couldn't use because of injuries was Royce Flippin, a high school All-American, a star back at Princeton, a 27th-round draft choice of the Redskins and later the athletic director at MIT. He became a Harwood assistant coach.

And other than Barnhill and Trask, tackle Greg "Fat Daddy" Thomasson (Arkansas State), 255, was the lone player over 225 — a light squad even by 1957 standards.

The schedule was tougher. Quantico did not play Ft. Benning, Ft. Belvoir, Parris Island, Xavier and Ft. Monmouth, teams it defeated in 1956, and added Ft. Knox, Eglin AFB and Detroit, teams it lost to in 1957.

But the team had character — as well as characters. There was Mora. Franklin would coach at three colleges and with four pro teams. End Walt Nadzak (Denison) would be the coach at Juniata (1969-76) and Connecticut (1977-82) and the athletic director at The Citadel. Royer would coach at four colleges and for three pro teams and become pro-personnel director of the New York Jets. And Swanson would be one of California's most successful high school coaches at Temple City.

The 1958 season:

Cosby made a winner of NBC in the 1980s, and while there's no scientific evidence that his work as a trainer was solely responsible for Quantico's turnaround, the record does show that the Leathernecks turned a 3-9-1 mark in 1957 to a more-normal 9-3-1 record in 1958.

Harwood, of course, was a man driven to reverse the only team of his to finish below .500.

And he had the horses — and the necessary luck.

To start with, he had 10 returnees from the 1957 team that wasn't as bad as the record might indicate, among them key players such as Franklin, Laaksonen, Losack, Thomasson and Valentine, all of whom were chosen All-Marine.

And the newcomers were impressive:

■ At ends, besides Losack, were Nick Germanos (Alabama) and Bob Timberlake (Oklahoma).

■ At tackles, besides Thomasson, were Tony Anthony (Navy), an All-Marine selection; Barnhill, Ron Cherubini (Villanova), 280-pound Harvey Koudela and Paul Ward (Whitworth). Cherubini, a Bronze Star winner in Vietnam, coached Camp Lejeune in 1965 and Quantico in 1966. Ward played for the Lions in 1961-62.

■ At guards, besides Franklin, were Tony Santaniello and Bob Tortorella (both of Holy Cross) and Tony Stremic of Navy, an All-

Marine and All-Service selection.

■ At center/linebacker were Bob Adelizzi (Dartmouth) and Valentine, an All-Navy and All-Service selection.

■ In the backfield, besides Laaksonen, were Alberigi, Claude "Bo" Austin (George Washington), a 13th-round draft choice of the Redskins; John Fritsch (Maryland), Harry Jefferson (Illinois) and Gene Roll (Missouri).

Like Ernie Cheatham, Charlie Weber and others before him, guard Bobb McKittrick "did not play at Quantico while at Basic School, though they tried to force me to," he said. "The Basic School CO saw that I was transferred into the company with the football players, but I still chose not to play."

The loss was the Marine Corps'. McKittrick, a member of Oregon State's 1957 Rose Bowl team, went on to coach at two colleges and with three NFL teams.

The Leathernecks, with only three players 225 or heavier and outweighed in most contests, opened with a 13-6 victory over Ft. Belvoir before 18,000; won two; lost to Detroit again, 26-13; won two, lost to national service champion Eglin AFB, 27-20; won a game; tied Bolling, 0-0; won two; lost to Camp Lejeune, 13-6, and won the finale.

Harwood could leave as a winner.

1956

Record: 47-0 Ft. Benning, 33-0 Ft. Belvoir, 9-13 Ft. Eustis, 39-0 Ft. Lee, 49-0 Parris Island, 27-13 Xavier (Ohio), 0-13 Holy Cross, 6-9 Camp Lejeune, 20-6 Boston College, 7-6 Bolling AFB, 34-0 Ft. Monmouth, 27-7 Little Creek NAB. (9-3). Broke Bolling's 34-game winning streak. Rated No. 4 by Williamson. Nine players from Rice. Beagle, Bucci, Cameron, Damore and Lutz All-Marine; Dee, Kellogg and Rayburn second team.

Coach: Lt. Col. Hal Harwood (Navy)

Assistants: Lt. Andy Androlewicz (St. Louis-Missouri) (Camp Lejeune 1955), Maj. Ernie Hargett (Southwestern Louisiana), Capt. Bob McElroy (Navy) (asst. Pensacola NAS 1951), Lt. John Phil Monahan (Navy), Lt. J.D. Roberts (Oklahoma)

Ends: Ron Beagle (Navy), Bob Dee (Holy Cross), Dick Gagliardi (Boston College), Bob Harrison (Rice), Tom Kisselle (Bowling Green), Jim LaRussa (Miami of Fla.), Dick Lucas (Boston College), Sig Niepokoj (Northwestern), Danny Risher (Mississippi State), Dick Widdows (Shepherd)

Tackles: Fred Campbell (Duke), Don Deskins (Adelphi) (1st MarDiv 1954, Hawaii Marines 1955), Bob Hickettier, John Hopkins (Navy), Jim Lohr (Southeast Missouri), Don Moran (Pepperdine), Eddie Rayburn (Rice), Orv Trask (Rice)

Guards: Fred Bucci (Columbia), Ron Ebberts (Emporia), John Miller (USC), Jim Neville (North Carolina), Clyde Perrere (Tulane-Mississippi State), Jim Pokipla (Denver), Billy Redding (Texas A&M-Austin), Tom Siragusa (Rice), Bernie Taracevicz (Holy Cross)

Centers: Jerry Bishop (Wake Forest) (Parris Island 1954-55), John Damore (Northwestern), Ed Johnson (Pittsburgh) (Far East), Don Wilson (Rice)

Backs: John Beagall (Waynesburg), Pete Bruni, Doug Cameron (Texas), Mark Chitijian (Rice), Lew Erber (Montclair), Gordie Kellogg (Rice), Bobby Lee (New Mexico), Worth "A Million" Lutz (Duke), Jim Manley (Penn), John Martin (Parris Island 1954-55), Merlyn Murphey (Southern Methodist), John Nisbet (Rice), Bill Ortman (Haverford), Bob Ortman (9th Marines 1955), Emidio Petrarca (Boston College), Tom Reis (Boston College), Thurlo Rogers (Rice), Les "Buddy" Rowell (Penn State), John Shearer (Shepherd), Don Stankus (Shippensburg), Sid Swann, Henry Talamantz (Baylor), Tom Troxel (Miami of Ohio), Bob Ward (Whitworth)

Kicker: Tad Weed (Ohio State)

1957

Record: 6-12 Little Creek NAB, 29-13 Norfolk Navy, 33-7 Pensacola NAS, 7-13 Boston College, 27-6 Ft. Eustis, 7-26 Ft. Knox, 6-12 Eglin AFB, 14-33 Holy Cross, 26-26 Camp Lejeune, 0-33 Detroit, 6-38 Bolling AFB, 7-12 Ft. Lee, 6-12 Hamilton AFB (Valor Bowl). (3-9-1). Great Lakes game cancelled. Bucci, Cameron, Hopkins and Lucas All-Marine; Alberigi, Mora, Reis, Ringer and Royer second team.

Coach: Lt. Col. Hal Harwood (Navy)
Assistants: Capt. Wit Bacauskas (Columbia) (Camp Lejeune 1951, Pensacola NAS 1952, player-coach Edenton MCAF 1954, Pensacola 1956), Royce Flippin (Princeton), Maj. Ernie Hargett (Southwestern Louisiana), Capt. Bob McElroy (Navy) (asst. Pensacola 1951), Capt. Ben Moore (Mississippi College-Texas-Navy) **Ends:** J.B. Bennett (Northeast Oklahoma), Allen Bliss (Miami of Ohio), Fred Carew (Boston University), Bill Hutcheson (Northwest Missouri), Joe Losack (Wharton JC-Texas), Dick Lucas (Boston College), Don Martin (Kansas), Charles McLennan (VMI), Jim Mora (Occidental), Bob Morman (Northwestern), Walt Nadzak (Denison), Dan Rankin (Hillsdale), Tom Richardson (Syracuse), Jim Smiley (Oklahoma), Darrell Sorrell (Duke), Ed Walsh (Penn Military)
Tackles: Jim Allegro (Holy Cross), Dwight Barnhill (Wichita), John Bednash (Scranton), Jerry Bishop (Wake Forest) (Parris Island 1954-55), Ron Botchan (Occidental), Jim Cerasoli (Brown), Dick Guy (Ohio State), John Hopkins (Navy), John Maher (Harvard), Joe Murphy (Holy Cross), Jim Royer (Navy), Don Stoeckel (Ohio State), Greg Thomasson (Arkansas State), Orv Trask (Rice), Wes Wharton (Texas Western)
Guards: Steve Banks (Toledo) (Memphis NAS), Fred Bucci (Columbia), Jim Cavanaugh (Holy Cross), Bob Cupit (Upsala), John Deklava (Colorado A&M), Vern Ellison (Oregon State), Bill Fackleman (Colgate), Chet Franklin (Utah), Bill Parker (Vanderbilt), Herb Paschen (Princeton), Joe Pollino (Syracuse), Paul Roush (Navy), Jim Schwartz (Xavier), Earl Shumaker (Penn State), Sam Valentine (Penn State)
Centers: Bob Berguin (Nebraska), Frank Black (Kansas), Don Karnoscak (Colorado), John O'Rourke (Pacific), Ted Ringer (Northwestern), Bill Saye (Georgia), Bernie Taracevicz (Holy Cross)
Backs: Ray Alberigi (Penn State), Dick Broderick (Fordham-Michigan State), Tal Broughton (Davidson), Doug Cameron (Texas), Jim DeFabio (Dayton), Ron Furman (Denver), Doug Hibbs (Cal), Dick Jannoni (Vermont), Frank Jeske (Northwestern), Bob Johnston, Art "Buddy" Jones (Arkansaas), Charles Laaksonen (Syracuse), Ray Murray (George Washington), Herb Nakken (Utah), Paul Naumann (Valparaiso), Tom Reis (Boston College), Morris Rogers (Texas A&M), John Shearer (Shepherd), Mike Sikora (Connecticut), Sid Swann, Don Swanson (Minnesota), Bob Sylvia (Boston University), Bill Williams (Yale), Art wilson (Columbia), John Wolff (Colorado A&M)

1958

Record: 13-6 Ft. Belvoir, 26-0 Pensacola NAS, 31-20 Xavier (Ohio), 13-26 Detroit, 50-28 Northern Michigaan, 30-6 Ft. Dix, 20-27 Eglin AFB, 33-0 Lockbourne AFB, 0-0 Bolling AFB, 13-12 Rutgers, 19-13 Villanova, 6-13 Camp Lejeune, 14-0 Ft. Lee. (9-3-1). Rutgers (9-0) was 19th-ranked at the time. The Belvoir game drew 18,000. Harry Jefferson scored 78 points, carried 129 times for 981 yards. After upsetting Rutgers, a national magazine called Quantico a "collection of old men." (The average age was 22). Anthony, Franklin, Jefferson, Laaksonen, Losack, Stremic, Thomasson and Valentine All-Marine; Adelizzi, Alberigi, Cherubini, Germanos, Magilligan, Santaniello, Seager and Timberlake second team.
Coach: Lt. Col. Hal Harwood (Navy)
Assistants: Wit Bacauskas (Columbia) (Camp Lejeune 1951, Pensacola 1952, player-coach Edenton MCAF 1954, Pensacola 1956), Bob McElroy (Navy) (asst. Pensacola 1951), Maj. Tony Messina (Cal-Pacific) (asst. Parris Island 1949-50), Ben Moore (Mississippi College-Texas-Navy), Lt. Ted Ringer (Northwestern)
Trainer: Bill Cosby (Temple)
Ends: Jack Barrett (East Texas), J.B. Bennett (Northeast Oklahoma), Nick Germanos (Alabama), Jim Kane, Bob Long (St. Mary's of Minn.), Joe Losack (Wharton JC-Texas), Neil Molsbee (Hawaii Marines 1957), Bob Timberlake (Oklahoma), Don Waits (Pearl River JC-Southern Mississippi)
Tackles: Tony Anthony (Navy), Steve Banks (Toledo) (Memphis NAS), Dwight Barnhill (Wichita), Ron Cherubini (Villanova), Joe Jones (Iowa), Harvey Koudela (Parris Island), John Koontz (Tennessee), Cas Kudla, Greg Thomasson (Arkansas State), Paul Ward (Whitworth)
Guards: Joe Breidenstein (Notre Dame), Art Broering (Vanderbilt), Chet Franklin (Utah), Vic Muzzi (Stetson), Dick Oelerich (Purdue), Frank Prusch (Bloomsburg), Tony Santaniello (Holy Cross), Tony Stremic (Navy), Al Strickland (Austin), Bob Tortorella (Holy Cross)
Centers: Bob Adelizzi (Dartmouth), Barnie Delp (Purdue), Hugh Harkrider (Texarkana JC-North Texas), Bob Roche (St. Francis-Pitt), Sam Valentine (Penn State)
Backs: Ray Alberigi (Penn State), Claude "Bo" Austin (George Washington), Tim Etter (VMI), John Fritsch (Maryland), Harry Jefferson (Illinois), Dave Kindt (Ball State), Don Laaksonen (Syracuse), Jim Lorenz (Pasadena JC-Cal), Larry Magilligan (Holy Cross-Hofstra), W.H. McCullough (Lehigh), Gerry McGuire (St. John Fisher), Denny Pardee (Case) (Pensacola NAS 1957), Dick Potter (Cornell College), Bill Reisert (Notre Dame), Charles Rogers (New Mexico Highlands), Gene Roll (Missouri), Tom Sacramone (New Haven), Don Seager (Boston College), Dale Thibault (Westminster of Utah), George Weimer (Hofstra), Bill Williams (Yale), John Wuenschel (Stetson)

That 90-0 Bowl Victory

What can you say about a team that wins all 11 games? And what can you say about a team that romps to a 90-0 victory in a bowl game to decide the national service title?

You can say awesome if you're talking about the 1959 Quantico team.

One of 10 undefeated, untied Marine teams in history, the Leathernecks rolled over the Holyoke (Mass.) Merchants, 31-15; Ft. Lee, 34-7; Ft. Bragg, 27-6; Ft. Dix, 41-0; Ft. Gordon, 50-12; Bolling AFB, 15-3; Xavier (Ohio), 23-21; Ft. Campbell, 29-7; Camp Lejeune, 22-21; Ft. Belvoir, 48-14; and McClellan Air Force Base by an amazing 90-0 score in the Shrimp Bowl in Galveston, Texas.

The victory over Bolling ended a series that since 1951 had been one of service football's most intense. The Flyers gave up football in 1960.

And the loss spoiled Camp Campbell's 9-1 season.

The bowl victory over McClellan obviously caught the nation's attention.

The California team wasn't supposed to be a patsy, having won 9 of 11. However, an analysis of McClellan's schedule points up one of football's greatest mismatches and, indeed, how a shrimp of a bowl resulted.

Consider that McClellan's victories had been over the Alameda Naval Air Station (twice), Moffett Field, Santa Clara, a college JV team, a semipro team, Treasure Island Navy, San Quentin Prison and the Alameda Marine Reserve, hardly a world-class schedule.

Surprisingly, the Shrimp Bowl promoters had a history of matching the best service teams but went over the cliff with McClellan.

The Flyers' losses, incredibly, were to Oregon Tech, a small-college team, and to the Pacific JV. Not the College of the Pacific JV, but the University of Pacific JV in Oregon.

And they had lost in 1958 to Camp Pendleton, 87-0.

The ideal matchup would have been Quantico against the San Diego Marines (10-0), but a schedule conflict prevented what could have been one of the great games in Marine history. The jury was out, on the West Coast, anyway, about Quantico being the best in the land.

Still, a bowl victory over McClellan is a bowl victory — and is counted as such in the record books.

Coach Wil Overgaard had succeeded Hal Harwood as coach, and in three seasons would win 29 games and lose but 6 at Quantico. He had fought with the 4th Marine Division in the South Pacific as an enlisted man in World War II, then played four seasons as a tackle at Idaho and won the Bronze Star in Korea.

Vietnam, of course, lay ahead, and some of his 1959-61 players would be in the forefront of the early combat. Back John Prichard (Navy), a Bronze Star winner, would die in the Southeast Asia war, apparently the first Quantico player killed since back Gene Stewart of the 1952 team in Korea.

Overgaard had played on the 1951 Quantico team and readied himself with coaching assignments at Parris Island, Little Creek and Camp Lejeune. He already had a 20-9-3 record as a head coach.

With 10 players back from Harwood's 9-3-1 team of 1958 and the usual influx of major-college talent, the success was not a surprise.

"With this array of talent in the starting eleven, plus a bench loaded with outstanding football players, the coaches expect great things from their charges this season," the Quantico Sentry reported before the season-opener.

The Leathernecks boasted experience, depth and speed, but lacked size. The line averaged 210, the backfield 184 and only four players were 225 or heavier.

But, as they say, three out of four ain't bad.

Overgaard had available:

■ Ends such as All-Marine selection Holly Hollingshead (Mississippi State) and Dave Stecchi (Holy Cross).

■ Tackles that included Dwight Barnhill (Wichita), playing his third season; 235-pound Ron Cherubini (Villanova), Quantico's 1966 coach and a Bronze Star winner in Vietnam; 230-pound Jerome Havrda (Boston College), 230-pound Jerry Kershner (Oregon), Don Rhoda (Nebraska) and Dick Theer (Iowa), a Silver Star and Bronze Star winner in Vietnam.

■ Guards that included Jim Hardin (Western Kentucky), All-Marine selection John McGinley (Notre Dame), Cliff McGraw (Rice), All-Marine and All-Navy selection Tom Meehan (Boston College), Tony Santaniello (Holy Cross) and All-Marine selection Tony Stremic (Navy).

■ Centers that included Bill Feind (Missouri) and All-Marine selection John Yohn (Gettysburg), who played with the Baltimore Colts in 1962 and the New York Jets in 1963.

Besides the extraordinary strength at tackles and guards, Overgaard had a backfield with a Southern flavor any coach could envy:

■ At quarterback was Overgaard's version of The Lettermen: John Fritsch (Maryland), Tom Maudlin (USC), who was with Toronto of the Canadian Football League in 1962 and Montreal in 1963; Glenn St. Pierre (Missouri) and Bob Schwarze (The Citadel), named the team's Most Valuable Player.

■ At the halfbacks were All-Marine and All-Navy selection King Dixon (South Carolina), the coach at MCRD San Diego in 1964 and at Quantico in 1968, and a Bronze Star winner in Vietnam; Dan Droze (North Carolina), Ed Post (Duke), Don Seager (Boston College) and All-Marine selection Stu Vaughan (Utah).

■ And at fullback were All-Marine selection Phil Dupler (Duke), an 18th-round draft choice of the Chicago Bears; and Dave Pratt (Dartmouth).

Dixon was another in a line of Quantico standouts named the Service Player of the Year by the Washington Touchdown Club.

Cherubini, Fritsch, 225-pound tackle Cas Kudla, halfback Dennis Pardee, guard Frank Prusch, halfback Charles Rogers, Santaniello,

Seager and Stremic, in addition to Barnhill, had played at least one season with Quantico.

Rogers got his kicks. He supplied the last-period field goal that was the difference in the Xavier game and his extra point with 2:00 remaining helped to defeat Camp Lejeune.

In addition, Quantico picked up end Percy Price, halfback Stewart Flythe and Post after the Hawaii Marines gave up football and fullback Ed Lynch from Ft. Meade.

The Marines also had been taking along Jiggs, an English bulldog that was the team's mascot, on bus trips in 1958 and 1959. But Jiggs developed an offensive habit resulting from a bodily function and his travels soon stopped.

On the Galveston trip, recalls a member of the party, the "team went on a tour of a local brewery and when they came back it was time for practice. Overgaard had them line up for wind sprints and they got down in their three-point stances."

Those who had partaken at the brewery fell on their faces.

But the newcomers as well as the veterans had a picnic in the McClellan game. Flythe returned a fumble 90 yards for one of his two touchdowns; Vaughan returned an interception 53 yards for one of his two TDs; Pardee scored twice; Maudlin threw two TD passes; and end Bill Caley (Dartmouth), Rogers, Hollingshead, halfback Joey Allen (Baylor) and Seager scored six-pointers; and even Cherubini caught a TD pass.

Fullback Chuck Blowers (2), back Allen Davidson, Hollingshead, Lynch, Rogers and Stecchi (2) either kicked extra points or scored on two-point conversions.

Shades of the 1940 Chicago Bears!

The 1960 season:
After winning a 90-0 bowl game, what can a coach do for encore? Not much, really.

Overgaard coached Quantico to a 9-2 record in 1960, a season acceptable in most quarters but one not quite up to 1959's 11-0.

Still, the Virginia Leathernecks walloped Pensacola Navy, 36-6, in the first Missile Bowl in Orlando, Fla., and the San Diego Marines, 36-6, in the Leatherneck Bowl for the All-Service title in San Diego, so there was no dispute this time over who was No. 1.

(The dispute was over luggage. San Diego gave out 42 pieces of luggage to the visiting Quantico team. But the Virginia Marines brought a party of 60. After a series of strained phone calls between the bases, Quantico diplomatically accepted the 42 pieces but purchased 18 suitcases after returning to Virginia.)

And wrap Quantico victories over the D.C. Collegians, 39-0; Ft. Campbell, 42-7; Lycoming, 33-0; Ft. Dix, 42-8; Ft. Lee, 38-6; Camp Lejeune, 36-15; and Ft. Belvoir, 41-16, around losses to two longtime nemeses, Xavier, 28-20, and the University of Detroit, 28-7.

The Xavier loss snapped a 16-game winning streak. It was a case of deja vu for Capt. Bernie Kaasmann, a Quantico assistant. He had been an end on the 1949 team when the Musketeers had ended a 27-game Quantico winning streak.

And, yes, the Marines scrimmaged a school named Penn State. Perhaps you've heard of the Nittany Lions.

Overgaard had more than a few old hands to build around: Hollingshead and Price at ends; Havrda at tackle; Hardin at guard; Yohn and Jerry Knapper at center; and Blowers, Dixon, Flythe, Maudlin, Post, Rogers, St. Pierre, Schwarze and Vaughan in the backfield.

Some coaches would have settled just for that.

But the Marine officer training programs also brought in the usual number of blue-chip players, such as:

■ Steve Meuris (Denver), Ben Robinson (Stanford) and Larry Stewart (Illinois) at ends.

■ Gordon Batchellor (Princeton), Reggie Powe (Villanova), Mason Rose (New Mexico), 225-pound Jim Swofford (Duke), Larry Wagner (Vanderbilt) and Art Wallace (Florida State) at tackles. Wagner, a Boston Patriots' draft choice, had spent the preseason with the New York Titans.

■ Ken Sadler (Tennessee), Dal Shealy (Carson-Newman) and Roger Zensen (Virginia) at guards. Shealy later was an assistant at five schools and the coach at Mars Hill (N.C.) in 1969, Carson-Newman from 1970-73 and Richmond from 1980-86, where his Spiders made Division 1-AA waves.

■ And Jerry D'Avolio (Connecticut), Jim Hefferman (Toledo), Chuck Latting (Iowa State and Pensacola Navy); All-Marine selection Bob Marshall (Kansas), the team's leading scorer with 60 points; Don Magee (San Diego State) and Bob Miller (Lenoir-Rhyne) in the backfield.

The stage was set and all Overgaard had to do was send them into battle. So what if it was one of the lightest teams fielded in that era at Quantico — only two players weighing in at 225 or more?

Dixon, a high school All-American; Maudlin and Yohn were All-Marine and all-Navy selections, and Hollingshead an all-Marine choice.

Dixon thrived on the pressure games. He scored touchdowns on runs of 16 yards, 7 and 1 and on a 68-yard pass play in the big game against San Diego. He was the MVP of the Pensacola game, scoring twice, once on a 95-yard kickoff return. He also had scored three times against Ft. Dix, including an 82-yard TD.

Maudlin, chosen as the Sea Service MVP, ran for five TDs and passed for 11, and at one point had completed 66 of 109 passes.

And Overgaard got the most of several others without major reputations. Howard Caughron, for example, started at end and Dolphus Milton at guard.

Thus, for another season the best was not in the West.

The 1961 season:

Take away a Dixon and a team is bound to feel it.

And send Blowers, Caughron, Marshall, Meuris, Robinson, Rogers and Rose to the Pensacola Navy team; Hardin, Latting, Miller, back John Parrinello (Rochester), Price, Schwarze and Wagner to Camp Lejeune; and Fritsch, Hollingshead, Magee, Maudlin and Yohn to MCRD San Diego. ... and you've been hit hard.

Despite this, Overgaard directed the Leathernecks to a 9-4 record, a tie for second place in the East Coast Conference and to within a whisker of a third consecutive All-Service title.

After an exhibition loss, Quantico won 8 of 10, losing to Baldwin-Wallace, 18-7, and Villanova, 34-0. After a 19-0 loss to Camp Lejeune, Quantico defeated Ft. Belvoir but lost to Ft. Eustis, 25-24, in the second Missile Bowl in Orlando.

"This was a rematch because Quantico had defeated Ft. Eustis, 9-7, earlier in the season," Kaasmann said. "Quantico took an early 18-0 lead, only to be defeated by a point in a real thriller."

(The first game was nip-and-tuck, too. A Quantico safety with 5:00 to play was controversial. Then a disallowed Eustis TD later was approved to give the Wheels a 13-9 victory, but that, too, was overruled and the 9-7 score stood again.)

The loss to Lejeune, a team augmented by former Quantico players, ended a 21-game winning streak against service opposition.

From his 1960 team, Overgaard retained Stewart, guard Bob Davis, Milton, All-Marine selection Wallace; center Brian McNeeley, a high school All-American; Flythe, back Bob Johnson and back Jim Ross.

The recruiters didn't forget Overgaard, however, sending four Navy players: tackle Frank Butsko, an All-Marine selection, and backs Harry Dietz, Fred Palumbo and Prichard, plus:

■ Ends Jerry Huml (Cornell College), Lynn Oxenreider (Princeton) and Frank Weber (Lenoir-Rhyne).

■ A large tackle contingent, in 228-pound All-Marine selection Ed Heuring (Maryland), 230-pound Neal Rountree (Air Force Academy), John Spivey (Florida State) and Art Whittier (Virginia Tech). Heuring, a 16th-round draft choice of the Chicago Bears, had played with Montreal of the Canadian Football League and had a tryout with the Denver Broncos. He must have picked up some tips from Overgaard because Heuring posted a 15-6 record as Quantico's coach in 1969-70.

■ Guards Tom Cusick (Holy Cross), 225-pound Jose Gacusana (Nebraska) and All-Marine selection George Zadjeika, 18, who would play at North Carolina from 1965-68.

■ Center Ken Kestner (Florida State).

■ Backs John Arms (Southwest Louisiana), Berry Bocklet (Holy Cross), Ralph Kincaid (William Jewell), a second-team NAIA All-American; Glen Kirk (Austin), Dan Luecke (Notre Dame), and a Bucknell backfield nucleus of Paul Terhes, Bruce Nealy and George Salinger. Terhes, a Little All-America quarterback, was drafted in the eighth round by the Colts and the seventh round by the New England Patriots and had spent the preseason with the AFL team.

Arms, ironically, was Pensacola's quarterback in its 1960 Missile Bowl loss to Quantico.

For the first time since 1949, though, the team had to make extensive use of enlisted players because of manpower limitations, and a number of the new officers hailed from Division I-AA type and small colleges such as Eastern Kentucky, Juniata, Lake Forest, St. Lawrence and Wabash instead of the usual outpouring from Big Ten, Big Eight and Southwest Conference schools.

As such, it may have been Overgaard's best coaching performance.

1959

Record: 31-15 Holyoke (Mass.) Merchants, 34-7 Ft. Lee, 27-6 Ft. Bragg, 41-0 Ft. Dix, 50-12 Ft. Gordon, 15-3 Bolling AFB, 23-21 Xavier (Ohio), 29-7 Ft. Campbell, 22-21 Camp Lejeune, 48-14 Ft. Belvoir, 90-0 McClellan AFB (Shrimp Bowl). (11-0). The victory over McClellan, in Galveston, Texas, incredibly was for the All-Service title. King Dixon was named Service Player of the Year by the Touchdown Club of Washington. Dixon, Dupler, Hollingshead, McGinley, Meehan, Stremic, Vaughan and Yohn were All-Marine.

Coach: Capt. Wil Overgaard (Idaho) (Parris Island 1953, assistant PI 1954 and Little Creek 1955, coach Little Creek 1956 and Camp Lejeune 1957-58)

Assistants: Lt. Tony Anthony (Navy), Ernie Brown (Kansas State) (Pensacola 1954-55, Camp Lejeune 1956, asst. Lejeune 1957), Tony Messina (Cal-Pacific) (asst. Parris Island 1949-50), Lt. Bob Timberlake (Oklahoma)

Ends: Dwight Barnhill (Wichita), Ed Brinkley (Virginia Tech), Bill Caley (Dartmouth), L.J. Carmody, Mel Christman (Stetson-Florida State), Dan Cone (Florida), Levaine "Holly" Hollingshead (Mississippi State), Percy Price (Hawaii Marines 1958), Dave Stecchi (Fordham-Holy Cross)

Tackles: Ron Cherubini (Villanova), Bill Duchaine, Jerome Havrda (Boston College), Jerry Kershner (Oregon), Harvey Koudela (Parris Island), Cas Kudla, Don Rhoda (Nebraska), Dick Theer (Iowa), Jan Tupper (Oklahoma)

Guards: Carl Gipson (Oklahoma), Jim Hardin (Western Kentucky), Renzie Lamb (Hofstra), John McGinley (Notre Dame), Cliff McGraw (Rice), Tom Meehan (Boston College), Frank Prusch (Bloomsburg), Tony Santaniello (Holy Cross), Tony Stremic (Navy)

Centers: Bill Branner (Mississippi State), Bill Feind (Missouri), Jerry Knapper, John Yohn (Gettysburg)

Backs: Joey Allen (Baylor), Chuck Blowers (Florida), Allen Davidson, King Dixon (South Carolina), Dan Droze (North Carolina), Phil Dupler (Duke), Stewart Flythe (St. Paul's) (Hawaii Marines 1958), John Fritsch (Maryland), Phil Inglee (Davis & Elkins), Ed Lynch (Springfield) (Ft. Meade 1958), Tom Maudlin (USC), Dennis Pardee (Case) (Pensacola NAS 1957), Ed Post (Duke) (Parris Island 1956, Hawaii Marines 1957-58), Dave Pratt (Dartmouth), Charles Rogers (New Mexico Highlands), Glenn St. Pierre (Missouri), Bob Schwarze (Citadel), Don Seager (Boston College), Stu Vaughan (Utah)

1960

Record: 39-0 D.C. Collegians, 42-7 Ft. Campbell, 33-0 Lycoming, 42-8 Ft. Dix, 20-28 Xavier (Ohio), 7-28 Detroit, 38-6 Ft. Lee, 36-15 Camp Lejeune, 41-16 Ft. Belvoir, 36-6 Pensacola NAS (Missile Bowl in Orlando, Fla), 36-6 MCRD San Diego (Leatherneck Bowl in San Diego). (9-2). Loss to Xavier snapped a 16-game winning streak. Scrimmaged Penn State. Dixon, Hollingshead, Marshall, Maudlin and Yohn All-Marine.

Coach: Wil Overgaard (Idaho) (Parris Island 1953, assistant PI 1954 and Little Creek 1955, coach Little Creek 1956 and Camp Lejeune 1957-58)

Assistants: Lt. Dave Ash (Illinois), Capt. Ernie Brown (Kansas State) (Pensacola 1954-55, Camp Lejeune 1956, asst. 1957), Capt. Bernie Kaasmann (asst. Camp Lejeune 1955-57), Maj. Tony Messina (Cal-Pacific) (asst. Parris Island 1949-50), Lt. Stu Vaughan (Utah)

Ends: Howard Coughron (Tennessee), John Fitzgerald (West Chester), Holly Hollingshead (Mississippi State), Steve Meuris (Denver), Percy Price (Hawaii Marines 1958), Ben Robinson (Stanford), Larry Stewart (Illinois), Dick Trafus (St. Thomas)

Tackles: Gordon Batchellor (Princeton), Jerome Havrda (Boston College), Reggie Powe (Villanova), Max Rhodes (Mississippi State), Mason Rose (New Mexico), Jim Ruffini (Bridgewater of Mass.), Jim Swofford (Duke), Larry Wagner (Vanderbilt), Art Wallace (Florida State)

Guards: Bob Davis, Jim Hardin (Western Kentucky), Dolphus Milton, Ken Sadler (Tennessee), Dal Shealy (Carson-Newman), Roger Zensen (Virginia)

Centers: Jerry Knapper, Brian McNeely (Michigan State) (Camp Lejeune 1958), Pete Peterson (Brigham Young), Jack Throckmorton (Rice), John Yohn (Gettysburg)

Backs: Charles Blowers (Florida), Jerry D'Avolio (Connecticut), King Dixon (South Carolina), Stewart Flythe (St. Paul's) (Hawaii Marines 1958), Jim Hefferman (Toledo), Bob Johnson (Nebraska Wesleyan), Chuck Latting (Iowa State) (Pensacola NAS 1959), Bob Marshall (Kansas), Tom Maudlin (USC), Don Magee (San Diego State), Bob Miller (Lenoir-Rhyne), John Parrinello (Rochester), Ed Post (Duke) (Parris Island 1956, Hawaii Marines 1957-58), Chuck Rogers (New Mexico Highlands), Jim Ross, Bob Schwarze (Citadel), Glenn St. Pierre (Missouri)

Record: 20-19 North Carolina A&T, 7-18 Baldwin-Wallace, 33-2 Ft. Benning, 32-9 Ft. Campbell, 13-8 Ft. Dix, 15-0 Morrissey Club, 0-34 Villanova, 9-7 Ft. Eustis, 40-8 Ft. Devens, 28-0 Holyoke Merchants, 0-19 Camp Lejeune, 38-8 Ft. Belvoir, 24-25 Ft. Eustis (Missile Bowl). (9-4). Lost 30-0 exhibition to Columbia Colts of UFL. Tied for second in East Coast Conference. Defeated Ft. Eustis in first game on controversial safety. Butsko, Herring, Wallace abnd Zadjeika All-Marine.

Coach: Wil Overgaard (Idaho) (Parris Island 1953, assistant PI 1954 and Little Creek 1955, coach Little Creek 1956 and Camp Lejeune 1957-58)

Assistants: Lt. Dave Ash (Illinois), Capt. Ernie Brown (Kansas State) (Pensacola 1954-55, Camp Lejeune 1956, asst. 1957), Capt. Bernie Kaasmann (asst. Camp Lejeune 1955-57), Capt. Jim Quinn (Fordham) (asst. Parris Island 1952, Camp Lejeune 1958; coach Lejeune 1959)

Ends: John Graybeal (Eastern Kentucky), Brian Harting, Jerry Huml (Cornell College), Harold Krause (Juniata), Lynn Oxenreider (Princeton), Thom Perkins (Arkansas), Ron Richardson (St. Lawrence), Carl Sommers (Missouri), Larry Stewart (Illinois), Frank Weber (Lenoir-Rhyne)

Tackles: Frank Butsko (Navy), Frances Cuddy (Navy Prep), Ed Heuring (Maryland), Bob Panzer (Wabash), Ray Pace (Texas Tech), Neal Rountree (Air Force Academy), Bob Solakoff, John Spivey (Florida State), Art Whittier (Virginia Tech)

Guards: Ed Abel (Notre Dame), William Baumeister, Tom Cusick (Holy Cross), Bob Davis, Joe Gacusana (Nebraska), George Herring (North Texas), Bill Hitchcock (Lake Forest), Dolphus Milton, Jerry Peery (Central Oklahoma), Art Wallace (Florida State), Bob Wellens, Don Williams (East Carolina), Joe Yetter (Miami), George Zadjeika (North Carolina)

Centers: Frank Collins (Penn), Ken Kestner (Florida State), Brian McNeely (Michigan State) (Camp Lejeune 1958), Harry Zimmerle

Backs: John Arms (Southwest Louisiana) (Pensacola NAS 1960), Jon Barton (Texas Christian), Barry Bocklet (Holy Cross), Harry Dietz (Navy), Dave Edmunds (William & Mary), Darrell Fitts (Alabama), Stewart Flythe (St. Paul's) (Hawaii Marines 1958), John Harris (Eastern Kentucky), Bob Johnson (Nebraska Wesleyan), Ralph Kincaid (William Jewell), Glen Kirk (Austin), Dan Luecke (Notre Dame), Clarence Lyons (Tennessee), Tony Mandina (East Texas), Bruce Nealy (Bucknell), Fred Palumbo (Navy), John Prichard (Navy) (KIA), Jim Ross, George Salinger (Bucknell), Paul Terhes (Bucknell), Ray Tidwell (Brigham Young), Dillard Weaver, Beau Wynn

Quantico Wins 27 Straight

Quantico won a Marine-record 27 straight games in the 1947, 1948 and 1949 seasons.

The streak was broken before 25,000 in Cincinnati by Xavier (Ohio), 29-7.

Quantico, coached in 1947 by Lt. Col. Marv "Moose" Stewart (LSU) and in 1948 and 1949 by Maj. Hal Harwood (Navy), lost its first game of the 1947 season to Washington & Lee, 13-0, but won its other 12 games; took all 13 in 1948; and captured the first two in 1949.

Parris Island, coached by Lt. Emory "Swede" Larson (Navy), was unbeaten in 20 games during the 1925-27 seasons, winning 17 and tying Mercer, High Point and Presbyterian.

The streak ended at Franklin Field in Philadelphia in the last game of the 1927 season when the All-Army team won, 39-12.

Mare Island won 18 straight in the 1917 and 1918 seasons before losing to Great Lakes Navy, 17-0, in the 1919 Rose Bowl game.

California oranges,
Texas cactus,
We play Lejeune
Just for practice!

A Quantico cheer

Football Amid Crises

Quantico's 1962 and 1963 players found themselves in somewhat the predicament of the 1939 and 1940 teams at Marine Corps Base, San Diego, and those in the Corps' stateside football programs in 1949.

Something was going on in the world, but no one was exactly sure what it meant.

The United States had military advisers in South Vietnam and President Kennedy said in 1962 that they would fire if fired upon. By late 1963 U.S. troops in the Southeast Asia country totaled more than 15,000 and aid to South Vietnam that year exceeded $500 million. And, of course, in 1964 things got worse.

But the Marines had been through several wars and while it was not business as usual at Quantico there was a sense of meaning business.

Maj. Jim Quinn (Fordham), a Bronze Star winner, had succeeded Wil Overgaard as coach in 1962 and would coach the Leathernecks to a 5-2 record before the final five regular-season games were cancelled because of the Cuban missile crisis.

And in 1963 Quantico won the national service title with a 10-1 record, although two games were cancelled after the assassination of the president.

These were not the easiest of times.

Still, with key returning players, a strong enlisted cadre and new officers from the college ranks, Quinn called on his coaching experience as an assistant at Parris Island in 1952, Quantico in 1954-55 and 1961, and Camp Lejeune in 1958, and as the head man at Lejeune in 1959 (a 7-3 record), to lead his men through troubled times.

Some 200 turned out initially.

The 1962 crew lost only to Miami (Ohio), 16-0, and Ft. Benning, 14-3. Miami (8-2-1) hardly was a pushover, later defeating Purdue, 10-7, and losing to Houston, 49-21, in the Tangerine Bowl. The Doughboys (11-0) were mythical national service champions.

And there was support (again) from the higher-ups. The team flew in the general's plane when it was available, and left and returned to the music of a Marine band.

Favoring a pro-type slot offense with the accent on the passing game, Quinn had a a pair of quarterbacks in Tom Singleton (Yale) and Paul Terhes (Bucknell) who had the arms and size to carry out his game plans.

For example, both passed for touchdowns in the victories against North Carolina A&T and Ft. Dix.

The Ft. Dix game also was a memorable one for tackle Fred Kienel (Georgia Tech). The score was tied when linebacker Cosmo Piccolo (Boston University) hit the quarterback and the ball popped into Kienel's hands.

"Since I was already moving in the direction of the goal line, I continued the march," he recalled. Teammates blocked, and the "80-

113

yard run took me about 12 seconds, but we scored. I got a lot of ribbing."

Quantico won, 49-7.

Singleton (6-1, 200) was All-Ivy League and All-East, while Terhes (6-0, 200) was a Little All-American who was with the Boston Patriots before joining Quantico midway through the '61 season.

And there were 11 returnees: All-Marine Walt Zadjeika and Lynn Oxenreider (Princeton) at ends; All-Marine Frank Butsko (Navy) and Neal Roundtree (Air Force Academy) at tackles; Bill Baumeister, George Herring (North Texas) and Dolphus Milton at guards; and Barry Bocklett (Holy Cross), John Prichard (Navy) and Jim Ross plus Terhes in the backfield.

Add to that such major-college newcomers as:

■ Ron Bartlett (Syracuse), Bob Federspiel (Columbia) and Ray Ratkowski (a high school All-American, Notre Dame and the Patriots) at ends.

■ Kes Desmarais (Holy Cross), Joe Eilers (Texas A&M and later of the Canadian Football League), Kurt Gegner (Washington), Kienel and Dick Lucas (Memphis State) at tackles.

■ Rich Crain (Duke), Doug Graham (California), Bob Lozier (New Mexico) and Piccolo at linebackers and guards.

■ Jim Davis (Oklahoma), a Patriots' draft choice, and Arden Esslinger (Iowa State) at center.

■ And Herman Brauch (Colgate), John Clancy (The Citadel), Jay Dale Evans (Kansas State and the Denver Broncos), Walt Flowers (Mississippi State), Ron Roemer (Indiana), Walt Spainhour (North Carolina), Chris Stanat (Army) and Tony "Mad Anthony" Wayne (Penn State), a 9.7 sprinter, in the backfield.

In addition, back Mike Long (Brandeis) had played for the Patriots.

Besides North Carolina A&T and Ft. Dix, Quantico beat Ft. Lee, Ft. Campbell and the University of Tampa.

The Tampa game was so rough in the first half that "Quinn ran onto the field at halftime and grabbed the Tampa coach by the arm and told him 'we would soak the field in blood — in particular, theirs' — if the dirty play continued," Kienel said.

There wasn't much improvement in the second half, but Quantico won, 32-3.

With the depth and experience on hand, and for perhaps the first time in Quantico history some size, the Leathernecks might have won 10 or more. Cancelled were games with Ft. Belvoir, Ft. Devens, Ft. Eustis, Camp Lejeune and the Morrissey Club team, plus potential Missile Bowl and Leatherneck Bowl contests for All-Service honors.

Lozier was named the most valuable lineman and Singleton the most valuable back.

Coaches Hal Harwood and Overgaard had turned out winners with light but fast players. Quinn, however, could call on guard Mike Giacinto, a high school All-American and discus standout, and Roundtree, both 240; Kienel and Oxenreider, both 235; and end Bill Bartles (North Dakota State), Desmarais and Lucas, all 230, among others.

The 1963 season:

Ft. Eustis, by a 13-0 score, was the only team to down Quantico in a season topped by a 13-10 victory over MCRD San Diego in the Missile Bowl in Orlando, Fla., for the All-Service title. Singleton passed to Brauch for a TD pass play covering 26 yards, and Dave Hayes (Penn State) ran in from the 1 to defeat San Diego.

The Leathernecks defeated three college teams: Xavier (Ohio), Holy Cross and Villanova, and six other service teams: Ft. Bragg, Ft. Lee, Ft. Campbell, Ft. Dix, Ft. Devens and Ft. Benning. The Ft. Belvoir and Camp Lejeune games were cancelled.

Quinn lost one quarterback in Terhes but retained Singleton and gained another top signal-caller in All-East selection Pat McCarthy (Holy Cross), a 19th-round draft choice of the Patriots.

Despite injuries, Singleton gained 447 yards in 106 carries during the regular season and completed 32 of 56 passes for 305 yards. In addition, he punted for a 39-yard average.

Quinn also acquired some needed defensive backs to shore up a 1962 weakness.

"The thing that stood out about the team was its rock-iron defense," Leatherneck magazine commented.

So tough was the defense that opponents scored 57 points all season, and three were shut out. Only Ft. Eustis scored as many as 13.

Quinn retained a key nucleus from the 1962 team: Zadjeika (for a third season) at end, Eilers at tackle, Jack Everett (Arkansas State) and Milton (for a fourth season) at guards, Davis at center, and Brauch, Clancy, Ross (for a fourth season), Stanat and Wayne in the backfield.

The additions were top-drawer, too, such as:

■ Mike Youngquist (Oregon State) at end.

■ Dennis Golden (Holy Cross), a 16th-round Dallas Cowboys' draft pick; Henry Gotard (Villanova), who had signed with the Denver Broncos; George Lombardo (Boston University) and Jack Whalen (Holy Cross) at tackles.

■ Little All-American Ron Eckert (Upsala), Jay Huffman (Penn State), who had signed with the Philadelphia Eagles; Pete Optekar (Navy), a former Marine buck sergeant; and Steve Turkalo (Boston University) at guards.

■ Hank Cutting (Holy Cross), Hayes, an 8th-round draft pick of the Colts; Jay McNitt (New Mexico) and Tom O'Rourke (Villanova), who had signed with the Broncos.

The hopes admittedly were high. The Quantico Sentry, before the opener of what was to have been games on 12 consecutive weekends, said, "The word at Marine Corps Schools is that Quinn has the horses to bring Quantico its third national service championship in the last five years."

The line wasn't quite as heavy as 1962's, with Gotard (240) and Eilers (230) the big men. But in the backfield Brauch, Cutting, Hayes, Singleton, Stanat and Jack Wallace all were at least 200.

Davis, Eilers, Huffman, Optekar, Singleton and Whalen were All-Marine selections. Davis was selected as the team's most valuable lineman and Hayes, with eight TDs, was the most valuable back.

Eilers, said Leatherneck, "was one of the most consistent tackles at Quantico over a two-year period and is an exceptional blocker and defender."

So Quinn closed out three seasons with a 22-6 mark and spawned some coaches.

Eckert was the head man in Quantico's last seasons in 1971-72; Golden at Framingham (Mass.) College from 1974-81, and McNitt at Fort Lewis (Colo.) College from 1971-81.

But the 1962 and 1963 seasons would be remembered best for the players' heroism in Vietnam, where many of them fought.

Clancy, Gotard and Lombardo, among others, were on active duty a quarter of a century later.

Huffman won two Silver Stars.

Prichard and Spainhour were killed.

1962

Record: 28-12 North Carolina A&T, 0-16 Miami of Ohio, 13-7 Ft. Lee, 22-19 Ft. Campbell, 49-7 Ft. Dix, 3-14 Ft. Benning, 32-3 Tampa. (5-2). Five games (Ft. Belvoir, Ft. Devens, Ft. Eustis, Camp Lejeune and Morrissey Club) cancelled because of the Cuban missile crisis. Miami had beaten Purdue, 10-7.

Coach: Maj. Jim Quinn (Fordham) (asst. Parris Island 1952, Camp Lejeune 1958; coach Lejeune 1959)

Assistants: Lt. Dave Ash (Illinois), Capt. Vern Ellison (Oregon State) (Camp Lejeune 1958), Capt. Howard "Tank" Long (Tulane-Arkansas State-Arkansas Tech) (Okinawa 1957). **Scout:** Roy Stephens (Arizona)

Ends: Bill Bartles (North Dakota State), Ron Bartlett (Syracuse), Bill Cervenak (Iowa State), Bob Federspiel (Columbia), Jim Madden, Gerald Obendorfer, Lynn Oxenreider (Princeton), Bernard Ozlins (St. Vincent's), Ray Ratkowski (Notre Dame), George Zadjeika (North Carolina)

Tackles: Frank Butsko (Navy), Ken Desmarais (Holy Cross), Joe Eilers (Texas A&M), Kurt Gegner (Washington), Jim Jakubowski (Michigan State-Miami of Ohio), Fred Kienel (Georgia Tech), Dick Lucas (Memphis State), Neal Rountree (Air Force Academy), Dave Thompson (Tufts)

Guards: William Baumeister, Rich Crain (Duke), Bob Everett (Arkansas State), Mike Giacinto (Notre Dame), Doug Graham (California), George Herring (North Texas), Bob Lozier (New Mexico), Dolphus Milton, Cosmo Piccolo (Boston University)

Centers: Jim Davis (Oklahoma), Tommy Davis, Bob Downard, Arden Esslinger (Iowa State), John Tucker

Backs: Barry Bocklet (Holy Cross), Herman Brauch (Colgate), John Clancy (Citadel), Jay Dale Evans (Kansas State), Walt Flowers (Mississippi State), Bill Gray (Coffeyville JC-Arkansas State), Jim Honeywell, Don Jeisy (Arizona State), Mike Long (Brandeis), John Prichard (Navy) (KIA), Ron Roemer (Indiana), Jim Ross, Tom Singleton (Yale), Walt Spainhour (North Carolina) (KIA), Chris Stanat (Army), Warner Terhes (Bucknell), Anthony Wayne (Penn State), Bill Wheeler

1963

Record: 9-7 Xavier (Ohio), 18-6 Ft. Bragg, 14-0 Ft. Lee, 41-0 Ft. Campbell, 54-6 Ft. Dix, 42-6 Ft. Devens, 7-6 Holy Cross, 7-3 Ft. Benning, 0-13 Ft. Eustis, 16-0 Villanova, 13-10 San Diego Marines (Missile Bowl in Orlando, Fla). (10-1). Captured national service title. Cancelled Ft. Belvoir and Camp Lejeune games because of the assassination of President Kennedy. Davis, Eilers, Huffman, Optekar, Singleton and Whalen All-Marine. Clancy, Gotard and Lombardo on active duty in 1986.

Coach: Maj. Jim Quinn (Fordham) (asst. Parris Island 1952, Camp Lejeune 1958; coach Lejeune 1959)

Assistants: Capt. Vern Ellison (Oregon State) (Camp Lejeune 1958), Capt. Howard "Tank" Long (Tulane-Arkansas State-Arkansas Tech) (Okinawa 1957), Capt. Roy Stephens (Arizona)

Ends: Dick Bainbridge (Gettysburg), Larry Knott (Colorado Western), Dick Rockstad (Lewis & Clark), Ted Uritus (John Carroll), Mike Youngquist (Oregon State), George Zadjeika (North Carolina)

Tackles: Charles Coe (Brown), Joe Eilers (Texas A&M), Dennis Golden (Holy Cross), Henry Gotard (Villanova), Bill Hatcher (Parris Island, Camp Lejeune 1962), George Lombardo (Michigan

State-Boston University), Jack Whalen (Holy Cross)

Guards: Ron Eckert (Upsala), Jack Everett (Arkansas State), John Gutter (Rhode Island), Jay Huffman (Penn State), Dolphus Milton, Peter Optekar (Navy), Steve Turkalo (Boston University), Mike Wydo (St. Vincent)

Centers: Jim Beery (Harvard), Jim Davis (Oklahoma),

Backs: Rick Bainbridge, Herman Brauch (Colgate), John Clancy (Citadel), Hank Cutting (Holy Cross), Frank Finizio (Rhode Island), Dave Hayes (Penn State), Bill Killian, Pat McCarthy (Holy Cross), Darrell McKibban (Redlands), Dennis Mudd (St. Joseph's), John/Jay McNitt (New Mexico), Tom O'Rourke (Villanova), Jim Ross, Marty Sheveling (Culver-Stockton), Tom Singleton (Yale), Chris Stanat (Army), Jack Wallace (Ohio State), "Mad Anthony" Wayne (Penn State)

Also: Al Gerwig, Jim Johnson, Dan Knurek

Ted Stawicki coached Camp Pendleton Parris Island, the Hawaii Marines and 3rd Marine Division All-Stars.

Rolling Right Along

There was an (undeclared) war going on, and football, by necessity, had to take a back seat — again.

The tipoff was that over the next five seasons — 1964 through 1968 — Quantico would have five head coaches. The Marine Corps generally could not keep an officer at the same duty station for three years during this period because of commitments in Southeast Asia and changes in the nature and length of assignments.

As a result:

■ Capt. Vern Ellison directed the 1964 team. He had lettered three years at Oregon State for Tommy Prothro and played in the 1957 Rose Bowl game. A 12th-round draft pick of the Pittsburgh Steelers, he manned a tackle position at Camp Lejeune in 1958 and was a Quantico assistant in 1962-63.

The record was 2-6-1 and it marked the beginning of the end for most of the service competition. Opponents Ft. Bragg, Ft. Lee, Ft. Benning, Ft. Eustis, Ft. Campbell and the San Diego Marines gave up football after the 1964 season.

Camp Lejeune dropped it after the 1965 season.

The Pensacola Navy, the last service opponent for Quantico, continued through the 1970 season.

■ Maj. Joe Caprara (Notre Dame), a back at Quantico in 1952 and at Lejeune in 1953, was recalled to active duty and coached Quantico to a 6-4 record in 1965, with seven opponents from the college ranks. Caprara was perhaps remembered best for a 99-yard run against Ft. Belvoir in the final game of the '52 season.

■ Ron Cherubini (Villanova), a Quantico tackle in 1958-59, a stalwart at Lejeune in 1959, the Lejeune coach in 1965 and a Bronze Star winner in Vietnam, was at the helm in 1966 when a 5-2-2 record was posted.

■ Lt. Col. Frank Marcus (Florida State), a back on Quantico's 1951 team, a decorated WWII and Korean War veteran, and a Bronze Star winner in Vietnam, took over the reins in 1967 for a 2-8 record. He also had been recalled to active duty.

■ King Dixon (South Carolina), a back on Quantico's 1959 and 1960 teams, coach of the Okinawa team in 1961 and MCRD San Diego in 1964, and a Bronze Star winner in Vietnam, called the shots in 1968 during a 4-7 season.

But if the traditional rivalries with the service opponents were ending, a new relationship with college football was beginning, with Quantico ultimately playing 10- and 12-game schedules.

In the 1920s, the All-Marine teams playing out of Quantico and Philadelphia took on predominantly college schedules, some seasons entirely on the road. During the 1930s, teams at the Virginia base occasionally played smaller colleges, but it was not until the late '40s and '50s that Quantico began to schedule major-college teams again. And in 1958 the Marines even knocked off a Top 20 foe (Rutgers).

Through the years the athletic programs proved to be one of the best ways not only to publicize the Corps but also to recruit enlisted personnel and officers.

For example, the eight-game Quantico-Holy Cross series between 1951-64 resulted in a number of Crusaders' players joining the Corps. Playing for Quantico were: John Cullity, Bill DeChard, George Foley, John Feltch and Dick Murphy in 1952; Chet Millett in 1953; Joe Harrington, Vic Rimkus and Pat Ryan in 1954; Bob Dee in 1955; Dee and Bernie Taracevicz in 1956; Jim Allegro, Jim Cavanaugh, Joe Murphy and Taracevicz in 1957; Tony Santaniello and Bob Tortorella in 1958; Dave Stecchi and Santaniello in 1959; Barry Bocklet in 1961; Bocklet and Kes Desmarais in 1962; Hank Cutting, Dennis Golden, Pat McCarthy and Jack Whalen in 1963; Ken Maheu, Cutting, Golden, McCarthy and Whalen in 1964; and Bill Sexton in 1965.

A 1950s' football rivalry with Boston College also resulted in a number of the Eagles' players becoming Marines.

The majority of the schedules in the 1964-68 seasons were on the road, good for recruiting but bad for a team's won-loss record.

With an unpopular war being fought thousands of miles away in Asia, the appearance of a Quantico team, quite often an accompanying Marine band, players' relatives and supporters, generally created a most favorable impression in the community ... and extensive media coverage.

And thus the football program continued.

■ In 1964, Quantico played at Ft. Lee, Va.; Cincinnati; Worcester, Mass.; Ft. Eustis, Va.; Ft. Campbell, Ky.; and San Diego.

■ In 1965, Quantico played at Toledo; Cincinnati; Huntington, W.Va.; Dayton; Villanova, Pa.; and Camp Lejeune.

■ In 1966, Quantico played at Xavier, Memphis State, Pensacola, Toledo, and Camp Lejeune (Angelo State).

■ In 1967, Quantico played at Williamsburg, Va.; Cincinnati; Bowling Green, Ohio; Akron, Beaumont, Texas; Villanova, Pa.; and Marquette, Mich.

■ In 1968, Quantico played at Clinton, S.C.; Cincinnati; Des Moines, Iowa; Pensacola; Marquette, Mich.; Villanova, Pa.; and Fairfield, Iowa.

The 1964 season:

Ellison, the architect of Quantico's sturdy defense in 1963, faced a formidable task.

Although hopes were high, as usual, the manpower and chemistry weren't as strong as in previous seasons and the prospect of a war-to-be in Southeast Asia obviously was unsettling.

Ellison retained 14 from the 1963 national-champion team: end Dennis Mudd (St. Joseph's), tackles Golden, Henry Gotard (Villanova) and Whalen; guards Ron Eckert (Upsala), John Gutter (Rhode Island), Jay Huffman (Penn State), Dolphus Milton (a fifth season) and Steve Turkalo (Boston University), and backs Cutting, Dave Hayes (Penn State), Bill Killian, McCarthy and Darrell McKibban (Redlands).

But the player pipeline temporarily was blocked. The only players arriving from major colleges were end Mahue, tackle Gene Carrington (Boston College), guard Tom Holden (Navy), center Jay Robertson (Northwestern) and backs Lou Chiarolanza (Villanova), John Snider (Syracuse), Tom Teigen (Minnesota) and Terry Terrebone (Tulane).

The quality was there.

But not the quantity. (The "squad's initial turnout was sparse," according to the Quantico Sentry.)

Or the size. (Other than tackle Jake Jimerson (245), Carrington (235) and Golden (230), there was no one else over 220, and the Leathernecks generally were outweighed.)

As the Sentry noted, "The national service title is a big burden to carry. Every game the Quantico Marines play, their title is at stake."

Ellison's team defeated Ft. Lee and Camp Lejeune, tied Ft. Bragg, and lost to Xavier, Holy Cross, Ft. Benning, Ft. Eustis, Ft. Campbell and MCRD San Diego.

"The going turned out to be much rougher than the year before," the Leatherneck noted. "Forced to rebuild ... the squad lacked the explosive and all-around backfield of former years.

"On the other hand, their record of 2-6-1 was deceiving insofar as it was not a true indication of the team's ability or toughness on defense."

The San Diego loss in the finale was heartbreaking — and typical of the season. It came on a field goal in the last five seconds.

Hayes had scored on a 4-yard run with 1:49 to play and, going for broke, McCarthy passed to back Hank Hatch (Harvard) for two points and a 22-21 lead. But a 1963 Quantico quarterback, Tom Singleton, drove San Diego into position for the winning three-pointer.

Hayes, the top ball rusher and an All-Marine selection, was "one of the bright spots in an otherwise light-hitting backfield ... possessing great power with good speed," said the Leatherneck.

Huffman, named the area's top service player for the second year, was a repeat All-Marine selection.

"Many feel there is no better defensive center in service football," the Leatherneck commented. "In one game, the 6-1, 210-pounder accounted for 14 tackles."

He would be awarded two Silver Stars in Vietnam.

Golden, a third All-Marine selection, "was another consistent performer ... on either defense or offense," the Leatherneck said.

The 1965 season:

"It's not uncommon," noted Memphis State's media guide," when a team loses its quarterback via (a) graduation, (b) injury or other natural causes. ... Quantico lost its signal-caller to Viet Nam.

Considering the world situation, Quantico may lose additional players to the same place."

But after defeats by Toledo, Xavier and Marshall, Quantico — "untried but talented," according to the Sentry — closed with a 6-1 record, and the victories over Pensacola and Camp Lejeune brought a mythical national service championship.

The scarlet and gold also rolled over Dayton and Villanova, lost to Bradley and knocked Memphis State out of a possible Liberty Bowl berth, 20-14.

As usual, the Leathernecks had to rely on speed and athletic ability rather than size. Caprara had only two players over 225: Carrington and guard Bill Zadel (Army), both at 230.

But the defensive line did average 220 and Quantico retained Hatch and John Kopka (Bridgeport) at ends; Carrington and Jimerson at tackles; Holden at guard, Glenn Custar (East-Central Oklahoma at center), and young George Fitzgerald, Killian, shot-putter Roger Schmitt, Snider and Gene Sutton in the backfield.

"Quantico may not face a defense any tougher than our own," Caprara told a reporter.

The recruiters funneled these players to Caprara:

■ Ends Tom Cox (Murray State); Woody Gilliland (West Texas), a Bronze Star winner in Vietnam; Fred Jones (Oregon State), Steve Lawrence (Yale) and Sexton.

■ Tackle John Breiten (Colgate)

■ Guards Bruce Capel (Illinois), Ed Conti (Syracuse), John Lucas (Louisville) and Ed Stuckrath (Penn State).

■ Backs Granny Amos (Virginia Military), Mike Cotten (Texas), Jim McGowan (Boston College), Dave McInturff (West Texas) and Steve Szabo (Navy).

Amos, named the area's outstanding service player, rushed for 526 yards in 106 carries and scored six times.

With San Diego giving up football, Quantico landed 6-3, 220-pound end Mike Gail and 5-11, 220-pound guard Ron Meyer, plus back John Dixon (Central State) from Okinawa.

In addition, rotating duty assignments brought to Quantico backs Jay Dale Evans (Kansas State and the Denver Broncos) from the 1962 team and Jack Wallace from the '63 squad.

So the pieces eventually fell into place.

Perhaps the most intriguing player was 6-1, 205-pound fullback Moses Denson, who played high school ball in Akron, Ohio.

The media guide described him as a "latecomer to football" who developed into a "real find." Denson had competed in the Marine Corps Schools' intramural league in 1964, scoring 17 TDs in seven games.

After his enlistment, he attended Maryland State and played pro ball with Montreal of the Canadian Football League from 1970-72 and for the Washington Redskins, 32 miles up the road, from 1974-75.

At 215 pounds he ran the ball, caught passes and returned kickoffs.

The 1966 season:

"The football situation at Quantico is, in a word, flexible," said Memphis State's media guide. "The general uncertainty stems from the war in Vietnam.

"Quantico officials are sure they will field a team but do not know who will be their coach or who will play for him. The program is expected to come into focus late in the summer."

Despite such beginnings, and a slow start (a 1-2 record), Cherubini's team did not lose in the final six games, defeating Pensacola (in the last 45 seconds), Angelo State, Drake and Lamar and tying Toledo and Northern Michigan.

To start with he had 11 veterans:

■ Gail, Bill Hardey and Don Ross (Wiley) at ends; Bob Harrington at tackle; Jones, Bill Miller and Ron Timpanaro (John Carroll) at guards; and Denson (for three games), Dixon, Fitzgerald (his third season), and Wallace in the backfield.

■ End Herb Brooks from Camp Lejeune's final '65 team; 31-year-old tackle Troy Perkins (Arkansas Baptist), guard Roger Grooms (Cincinnati) and back Jim Pyle (Wartburg), two-year performers at MCRD San Diego; and back Tom O'Rourke (Villanova) from Quantico's 1963 team.

And, with a war on, the officers and selected enlisted poured in by the thousands as the Corps' strength swelled to more than a quarter of a million. Cherubini snagged:

■ Ends Emmett Michaels (Villanova) and Tony Rocco (Indiana).

■ Tackles Ron Buschbom and Stan Holmes (Navy), Francis Cuddy (Rhode Island), Bryan Duniec (Illinois) and Bob Zvolerin (Tennessee).

■ Guards Fred Fugazzi (Missouri Valley), a 20th-round draft choice of the Boston Patriots; Jim Rapp (Indiana) and Cliff Yoshida (Cal Poly Pomona).

■ Centers Ron Hartnett (Navy) and Dave Snyder (Florida State).

■ Backs George Cheek (Georgia); Gene Hardman (Navy); Ed Kesler (North Carolina), a 16th-round pick of the Pittsburgh Steelers; Tom Longsworth (Miami of Ohio), Mike Parker (Arkansas), Mike Payte (Houston), Bill Peters (Brown), Alan Richards (Oregon State) and Jerry Ward (Bowling Green, and Richmond of the Continental Football League).

True to tradition, the squad was mean but lean, with Perkins (250) the only player over 225 to see extensive playing time.

Longsworth, playing with two cracked ribs, scored three times and gained 117 yards in 29 carries against Lamar, but the team balance was best shown at awards time. Fitzgerald, a teen-ager, was named MVP; Longsworth and Hartnett the top offensive players; Hartnett and Perkins the top defensive players; and Payte — who intercepted five passes — the best area service player.

Longsworth led ground gainers with 647 yards in 163 carries and scored six TDs. Ward was the leading scorer with eight TDs and 18 conversions for 66 points, and as a passer completed 72 of 183 attempts for 813 yards. Michaels caught 31 passes for 344 yards.

The 1967 season:

Twelve potential starters and 10 reserves were transferred in August, moves that set the tone for a rugged season.

Even the victories came with difficulty: 3-0 over East Tennessee and 12-10 over Parsons in the finale.

Marcus "was faced with a monumental rebuilding job," a season review noted — an understatement.

The Leathernecks opened with a 38-7 loss at William & Mary, coached by Marv Levy. Losses followed to Xavier, Bowling Green, Akron, Lamar, Villanova and Northern Michigan.

Even Pensacola defeated Quantico, for the first time, 20-14, as Heisman Trophy winner Roger Staubach (Navy) led the come-from-behind victory by completing 18 of 35 passes for 237 yards and two TDs. The Marines drove to the Pensacola 9 in the closing minutes but couldn't score against a team that had former Quantico players Cuddy, Duniec, Longsworth and Ward.

Veterans returning included ends Brooks ('66), Cox ('65), Hardey ('65-66) and Michaels ('66); tackles Ed Dear (Temple) ('65); guards Cheek ('66), Clarence Harris (Grambling) ('66); and backs Mike Jordan (Idaho) ('66), Pyle ('66), Richards ('66) and Szabo ('65).

There wasn't much quantity to count on from the new officers, who were being rushed through training on their way to Vietnam. Among those available were tackle Harris Elliott (Syracuse) and Bob Laravie (Dayton), guards Ancer Haggerty (Oregon State) and Steve Radich (Cal), and backs Fred Cobb (Virginia Tech), Tom Cruickshank (Utah State), Floyd Hunter (USC), Tony Kozarsky (North Carolina State and Richmond of the CFL), Ron Oyer (Syracuse) and Tom Trovato (Oregon).

That forced Marcus into utilization of players from smaller colleges such as Central Washington, Centre, DePauw, Millikin, Occidental, Sul Ross and Wabash, and enlisted Marines not too long out of high school. He was playing a Division I schedule — and did not have a home game until Oct. 28. By then the record was 0-7.

There was no NFL or AFL experience.

The offense never did get untracked, scoring five TDs in the first five games, and 10 all season. It was shut out three times.

The defense was hard-pressed, although 6-4, 250-pound tackle Mike McCoy of Indianapolis, Ind., received glowing reports. But the other starters weren't that much heavier than their 1947 counterparts.

Opponents outrushed the Marines, 1,490 yards to 502; outpassed them, 1,357 yards to 1,015, and led in first downs, 160-98.

Still, the victory over maverick Parsons (6-3-1) took out some of the sting. The Marines used a field goal, safety, blocked kick and conversion to beat the small Iowa college that went big time in football before closing a few years later. Parsons' other losses were by a point to East Carolina and Idaho.

Kozarsky, exciting at 5-8, 175 pounds and a Bronze Star winner in Vietnam, was Quantico's leading rusher with 285 yards in 81 carries, while John Carr gained 208 in 76 carries.

Cobb completed 49 of 130 passes for 620 yards and a TD, Trovado 23 of 66 for 380 yards and a score. Michaels caught 13 for 206 yards and a TD. Cruickshank had five interceptions.

The 1968 season:

Dixon, in his mind, no doubt would have lugged the ball himself, and traded some of the victories from his 1959 and '60 playing days at Quantico, or the '61 Camp Hansen and '64 San Diego teams he coached, for a better '68 record.

His Marines, off to a 1-5 start, recovered somewhat but had to settle for victories over Drake, Wisconsin-Milwaukee, East Tennessee and Wisconsin-Superior, against losses to Presbyterian, Xavier, Pensacola (and Staubach), Northeast Louisiana, Northern Michigan, Villanova and Parsons.

He built the attack around Bob Hill, a young quarterback from Akron, Ohio, who ran and passed for 1,167 yards and a combined 11 TDs, and the team around the usual mixture of players from the 1967 team, veterans back from Vietnam, new officers and young enlisted.

But with the demanding road schedule, he could only accomplish so much.

For continuity, he had Brooks, who led receivers with 26 catches for 336 yards and two TDs, Carr and Gary Nelson at the ends; Laravie, Charles Norstrand and Dick Oldendick at tackles; Hartnett, Jones and Milton at guards; Dick Craddock (Northeast Missouri) at center; and Cruickshank, Harris and Szabo in the backfield.

But the war siphoned off many potential candidates, leaving these newcomers:

■ Rikki Aldridge (USC) and Mike Rosborough (Pitt) at the ends.

■ Joel Trachtenburg (Utah) at tackle, and Marv Ferguson and Walt Weaver (SMU) and Gunnar Hagen and Steve Hinds (Washington) at guards.

■ Ed Blecksmith (USC), Andy Heck (Wake Forest) and Tom Krebs (Virginia), a Bronze Star winner in Vietnam, in the backfield; and kicker Jim Stotz (Illinois).

There just weren't enough bodies to compete, though the flesh was willing to try.

Dixon had some size in Harris (230 pounds) at linebacker; Craddock (231) and Jim Robinson (240) at center; 230-pound Alex Mobley (Edward Waters), Wade Reece (230), Gary Kasten (230), Norstrand (267) and Steve Mandreger (244) at defensive tackles, and Oldendick (255) at offensive tackle.

But only three had college varsity experience.

In reviewing the 1964-68 seasons, there were two particular circumstances regarding the players:

■ A number of them made their marks in coaching. Golden was head coach at Framingham State from 1964-71; Jay McNitt a '64 assistant, head coach at Fort Lewis (Colo.) from 1971-81; Szabo an assistant at seven colleges and head coach at Edinboro (Pa.) from 1985-86; Craddock head coach at Northeast Missouri from 1979-82 and at Western Illinois from 1983-86; and guard Tom Kurucz of the 1968 team an assistant at five schools, including South Carolina, and head coach at the University of Chicago in 1979.

■ Guard Ray Shands (1964) was a college and pro assistant; Robertson an assistant at five schools, including Notre Dame and

Army; Yoshida an assistant at four schools; Parker an assistant at four schools, including Texas; back Steve Bernstein (1967) an assistant at four schools, including Colorado; Cruickshank an assistant at two schools; and Ted Unbehagen (a 1968 assistant) an assistant at four schools, including Houston.

■ And lest they not be forgotten, Holden of the 1964 and '65 teams, tackle Gene McMullen (Penn State) and Capel of the '65 team, assistant Ron Brown (Montana State) of the '65 team and Cobb of the '67 team were killed in Vietnam.

1964

Record: 0-0 Ft. Bragg, 34-0 Ft. Lee, 7-17 Xavier (Ohio), 0-16 Holy Cross, 6-14 Ft. Benning, 0-14 Ft. Eustis, 6-31 Ft. Campbell, 28-0 Camp Lejeune, 22-24 San Diego Marines. (2-6-1). Golden, Hayes and Huffman All-Marine.

Coach: Vern Ellison (Oregon State) (Camp Lejeune 1958)

Assistants: Lt. Mike Giacinto (Notre Dame) (coach Okinawa 63), Capt. Howard "Tank" Long (Tulane-Arkansas State-Arkansas Tech) (Okinawa 1957), Lt. Terry Looker (Gettysburg), Lt. John/Jay McNitt (New Mexico)

Ends: Clyde Drewett (Northwest Louisiana), Garland Jones (Austin Peay-Howard), John Kopka (Bridgeport), Ron Mahue (Holy Cross), Dennis Mudd (St. Joseph's), Dave Van Singel (Ripon)

Tackles: Gene Carrington (Boston College), Dennis Golden (Holy Cross), Henry Gotard (Villanova), Jake Jimerson (Arizona State), Joe McArthur (Fayetteville), Mike O'Rourke (Delaware), Jack Whalen (Holy Cross)

Guards: Jack Davis (Northeast Oklahoma), Ron Eckert (Upsala), John Gutter (Rhode Island), Tom Holden (Navy) (KIA), Jay Huffman (Penn State), Joe Kovacevich (New Mexico-Upper Iowa), Dolphus Milton, Ken Renaud (Alma), Ray Shands (Tulsa-Central Oklahoma), Jim Shumaker (Virginia Military), Paul Sullivan (Univ. of San Francisco), Steve Turkalo (Boston University)

Centers: Glenn Custar (East-Central Oklahoma), Marc Glasgow (Ohio University), Jay Robertson (Northwestern)

Backs: Lou Chiarolonza (Villanova), Hank Cutting (Holy Cross), George Fitzgerald, Dale Harkins (West Virginia), Hank Hatch (Harvard), Dave Hayes (Penn State), Jim Holley (Colorado Mines), John Juul (Louisiana State), Bill Killian, Pat McCarthy (Holy Cross), Darrell McKibban (Redlands), Pat Norton (Sacramento JC), Gerald Philpot (Ohio University), Roger Schmitt (Michigan), John Snider (Syracuse), Gene "K.O." Sutton (Atsugi NAS 1953), Tom Teigen (Minnesota), Terry Terrebone (Tulane), Gerald White (Connecticut)

1965

Record: 0-9 Toledo, 12-28 Xavier, 9-10 Marshall, 10-0 Dayton, 37-0 Pensacola NAS, 36-12 Camp Lejeune, 32-7 Villanova, 14-7 Camp Lejeune, 7-14 Bradley, 20-14 Memphis State. (6-4). Amos, Breiten, Capel, Conti, Cotten, Cox, Holden, Lawrence, McGowan, Meyer, Stuckrath and Szabo All-Marine.

Coach: Maj. Joe caprara (Notre Dame) (Camp lejeune 1953)

Assistants: Capt. Ron Brown (Los Angeles Valley JC-Montana State) (coach Okinawa 1962; assistant MCRD San Diego 1963-64; was to have been SD coach in 1965 but sport dropped) (KIA), Capt. Art "Buddy" Jones (Arkansas), Lt. Terry Looker (Gettysburg), Capt. Chuck McLennan (Virginia Military), Lt. Jay Robertson (Northwestern), Lt. Ted Uritus (John Carroll)

Ends: Tom Cox (Murray State), Bill Cunnif (East Carolina), Bill Dorsch (Illinois), Mike Gail (MCRD San Diego 1964), Woody Gilliland (West Texas), Bill Hardey (Pasadena JC), Hank Hatch (Harvard), Fred Jones (Oregon State), John Kopka (Bridgeport), Steve Lawrence (Yale), Tom Mullam, Bob Rogers (Miami of Ohio), Bill Sexton (Holy Cross)

Tackles: Bob Bokelman (Virginia), John Breiten (Colgate), Gene Carrington (Boston College), Ed Dear (Temple), Jake Jimerson (Arizona State), Ken Gay, Gene McMullen (Penn State) (KIA), Harold Pelak, Pete Work (DePauw), Bill Zadel (Army)

Guards: Bruce Capel (Illinois) (KIA), Ed Conti (Syracuse), Larry Evans (Wake Forest), Dave Gillespie (Navy), Bob Harrington (Auburn), Tom Holden (Navy) (KIA), Ray Kinkead (Southeast Missouri), John Lucas (Louisville), Ron Meyer (Mesa JC) (MCRD San Diego 1963-64), Bill Miller (Indiana), Ed Stuckrath (Penn State), Ron Timpanaro (John Carroll), Jeff Warner (Iowa State)

Centers: Glenn Custar (East-Central Oklahoma), Joe Mark-Anthony (Hofstra), Steve Yocum (American River JC)

Backs: Granny Amos (Virginia Military), Frank Bentley (Weber State), Mike Cotten (Texas), Moses Denson (Maryland State), John Dixon (Central State of Ohio) (Okinawa 1964), Jay Evans (Kansas State), George Fitzgerald, Franklin Kaaa (Weber State), Bill Killian, Jim McGowan (Boston College), Dave McInturff (West Texas), Don Ross (Wiley), George Rouf, Roger Schmitt (Michigan), Ed Schriber (William Jewell), John Snider (Syracuse), Jim Stewart (Southern Illinois), Gene "K.O." Sutton (Atsugi NAS 1963), Steve Szabo (Navy), Jack Wallace (Ohio State) (Okinawa 1964)

1966

Record: 3-14 Xavier, 10-7 Marshall, 14-21 Memphis State, 21-17 Pensacola, 35-9 Angelo State, 21-13 Drake, 14-14 Toledo, 7-7 Northern Michigan, 30-26 Lamar. (5-2-2)

Coach: Ron Cherubini (Villanova) (Camp Lejeune 1960, Lejeune coach 65). **Assistants:** NA.

Ends: Herb Brooks (Lejeune 1965), Ron Crane (Cal Poly), Mike Gail (San Diego Marines 1964), Bill Hardey (Pasadena JC), Bill Link (William Jewell), Emmett Michaels (Villanova), Don Prichard (SMU), Claude Reinke (Sam Houston), Tony Rocco (Indiana), Don Ross (Wiley), Larry Taylor (Missouri Valley) and Bob Vaughn.

Tackles: Ron Buschbom (Navy), Francis Cuddy (Rhode Island), Bryan Duniec (Illinois), Eddie Fuller, Bob Harrington (Auburn), Stan Holmes (Navy), Dick Oldendick, Troy Perkins (Arkansas Baptist) (San Diego Marines 1963-64) and Bob Zvolerin (Tennesee).

Guards: Jim Rapp (Indiana), Rene Rizzo (Wisconsin-River Falls), Eric White (Lenoir-Rhyne) and Cliff Yoshida (Cal Poly Pomona).

Linebackers: Fred Fugazzi (Missouri Valley), Roger Grooms (Cincinnati) (San Diego Marines 1963-64), Gene Hardman (Navy), Fred Jones (Oregon State), Ken Lloyd, Bill Miller (Indiana), Bob Nunnally (Stephen F. Austin), Dave Snyder (Florida State) and Ron Timpanaro (John Carroll).

Centers: John Francis (St. Norbert), Toby Griggs, Ron Hartnett (Navy), Pat Rogers (Santa Clara) and John Swatek (Missouri).

Backs: Bob Busse (Wisconsin), Wendell Cayton (BYU), George Cheek (Georgia), Moses Denson (later at Maryland State), John Dixon (Central State of Ohio) (Far East 1964), George Fitzgerald, Charles Gilmer (Mt. Union), Clarence Harris (Grambling), Gene Jenkins (Lincoln), Mike Jordan (Idaho), Ed Kesler (North Carolina), Tom Longsworth (Miami of Ohio), Tom O'Rourke (Villanova), Mike Parker (Arkansas), Mike Payte (Houston), Bill Peters (Brown), Jim Pyle (Wartburg) (San Diego Marines 1963-64), Alan Richards (Oregon), Warner Robertson (Eastern Utah JC), Jim Vinson, Jack Wallace (Ohio State) and Jerry Ward (Bowling Green).

1967

Record: 7-38 William & Mary, 18-20 Xavier of Ohio, 0-29 Bowling Green, 0-20 Akron, 6-41 Lamar, 16-41 Villanova, 0-27 Northern Michigan, 3-0 East Tennessee, 14-20 Pensacola, 12-10 Parsons. (2-8).

Coach: Lt. Col. Frank Marcus (Florida St.)

Assistants: Capt. Gene Carrington (Boston College), Lt. Larry Doak (Chattanooga), Lt. Woody Gilliland (West Texas), Lt. Jim Scroggins (Austin Peay)

Ends: Herb Brooks (Camp Lejeune 1965), John Carr (Arkansas), Tom Cox (Murray State), Dick Dinkle (Tulane), Henry Dorsey (Morris-Brown), Bill Finnegan (Univ. of San Francisco), Bill Hardey (Pasadena JC), Emmett Michaels (Villanova), Gary Nelson (Glendale JC) and Larry Wood.

Tackles: Gus Cardwell, Richard Craddock (Northeast Missouri), Ed Dear (Temple), Harris Elliott (Syracuse), Charles Girdwood (Wabash), Gary Harwood (Central Washington), Ed Hepp (Navy), John Kent (DePauw), Bob Laravie (Dayton), Bob Lynch, Francis Mangrum, Mike McCoy, Charles Nordstrand (Notre Dame), Bob Pearce, Bob Silver (Findlay), Barrett Williams and Adolph Winkelbauer (East Tennessee).

Guards: Dave Beaty (Navy), Kim Butts (Millikin), Terry Johnston (Los Angeles St.) and Phil Jones (Indiana).

Linebackers: George Cheek (Georgia), Chris Dixon, Ancer Haggerty (Oregon), Clarence Harris (Grambling), Paul McGrath (Villanova) (KIA), Steve Radich (California), Nathaniel Wood and Tom Wyffels (Mankato).

Centers: Dick Gresham (Alabama), John Ferrigno (South Carolina), Brian Leahy (Boston College) and Charles Stanfield (Sul Ross).

Backs: Bob Archer (C.W. Post), Steve Bernstein (Cerritos JC-Occidental), Brown, Ray Clatworthy (Navy), Fred Cobb (Virginia Tech) (KIA), Tom Cruickshank (Utah St.), Clayton Davis, Jim Goebel (Navy), Floyd Hunter (Orange Coast JC-USC), Charles Isaacs (Centre), Mike Jordan (Idaho), Tony Kozarsky (North Carolina St.), John Mars (Colorado-Washington of Mo.), Ron Oyer (Syracuse), Jim Pyle (Wartburg) (San Diego Marines 1963-64), Harold Reynolds (Omaha), Al Richards (Oregon), Ray Stevens, Steve Szabo (Navy), Trom Trovato (Monterey JC-Oregon) and Voyten. **Kicker:** Bronco Belichesky.

126

Record: 0-10 Presbyterian, 12-28 Xavier, 33-31 Drake, 7-31 Pensacola, 0-13 Northeast Louisiana, 0-47 Northern Michigan, 41-12 Wisconsin-Milwaukee, 23-20 East Tennessee, 13-27 Villanova, 7-13 Parsons, 7-3 Wisconsin-Superior. (4-7)

Coach: King Dixon (South Carolina) (coach Okinawa 1961; player-coach San Diego Marines 1962, assistant 1963, coach 1964).

Assistants: Capt. Rick Crain (Duke), Capt. Woody Gilliland (West Texas), Capt. John Gutter (Rhode Island), Maj. Jim Hardin (Western Kentucky), Capt. Mike Parker (Arkansas), Sgt. Ted Unbehagen (Texas A&I).

Ends: Rikki Aldridge (USC), John Baker, Herb Brooks (Camp Lejeune 1965), Steve Campbell (Mississippi College), John Carr (Arkansas), Aubrey Lewis (Lejeune 1965), Jim Mlady, Gary Nelson (Glendale JC) and Mike Rosborough (Pittsburgh)

Tackles: Bill Bennett (Indiana St.), John Carden, Grant Foster (Concord), Gary Kasten, Bob Laravie (Dayton), Steve Mandreger, Alex Mobley (Edward Waters), Earl Norman, Charles Nordstrand (Notre Dame), Dick Oldendick, Wade Reece and Joel Trachtenburg (Utah)

Guards: Bob Bingaman (Monmouth), Gene Bowen, Paul Cindrich (Colorado St.), Joe Dowda (Howard Payne), Marv Ferguson (SMU), Ray Guttendorf, Gunnar Hagen (Washington), Ron Hartnett (Navy) and Charles Towne (Miami of Fla.).

Linebackers: Greg Bankston (Georgia), Luther Boone, Larry Gillen (Idaho St.), Steve Hinds (Washington), Clarence Harris (Grambling), Fred Jones (Oregon St.), Leonard Moore (Jackson St.), Robert Thomas (Southwestern Louisiana) and Walt Weaver (SMU).

Centers: Dick Craddock (Northeast Missouri), Gregory Ex and Jim Robinson (Oklahoma)

Backs: Cal Armstrong (Imperial Valley JC), Phil Ayers, Ron Beard (Texas Southern), Bruce Bell (Montgomery JC), Ed Blecksmith (USC), Jeff Brown, John Clark (Quonset Point, Camp Lejeune), Jerry Collins, Dennis Crowley (Morehead), Tom Cruickshank (Utah St.), Bob Cruse, Larry Curella (Louisville) (MCAS Beaufort), Bob Debnam (West Texas), Al Dunphey, John Glenn (USS Topeka), Andy Heck (McCook JC-Wake Forest), Bob Hill, Willie Hinton (Hawaii Marines), Tom Krebs (Virginia), Dave Low, Bob Mullen (Macalester), John Nelson, Oran Owens (McNeese), Ralph Sinke (Texas Tech), Paul Smith (California Western), Steve Szabo (Navy) and James Williams

Kickers: Jack Lowe (Angelo St.), Jim Stotz (Illinois) and Bruce Sturgess (Miami of Fla.) (Camp Lejeune)

Back Al Carmichael, just out of Gardena (Cal.) High, starred at MCAS El Toro in 1947 and 1948, then went on to fame at Santa Ana JC, USC and in the NFL

On the Home Front

If you were looking for an ideal Quantico coach, you'd like him to have come from a major conference, say the Atlantic Coast Conference.

You'd like him to have some pro experience and background.

You'd like him to have played at Quantico.

You'd like him to have some coaching experience.

Amazing, isn't it, how these qualifications all seem to fit Capt. Ed Heuring, the Quantico coach in 1969 and 1970?

He lettered as a tackle at Maryland from 1954-56, played for Montreal of the Canadian Football League three seasons and briefly with the Denver Broncos of the American Football League before an injury, was an All-Marine selection at Quantico in 1961 and coached Camp Hansen (Okinawa) to an undefeated season and the Far East championship. Heuring had served a year in Vietnam.

His 1969 team won nine and lost two with a high-powered offense whose lowest point total until the 10th game was 19 points ... and a defense that held eight opponents to nine points or fewer.

And his 1970 team won six and lost four, including a 44-6 victory over Pensacola in what proved to be Quantico's last appearance against a service team.

His 1969 team had a strong nucleus from the '66, '67 and/or '68 teams: ends Rikki Aldridge (USC), Chuck Girwood (Wabash), Tony Kozarsky (North Carolina State) and Robert Mullen (Macalester); tackles Grant Foster (Concord), Francis Mangrum and Leonard Moore (Jackson State); guards Greg Bankston, Kim Butts (Millikin), Harris Elliott (Syracuse), Tom Kurucz (Defiance), Dolphus Milton (his seventh season) and Steve Radich (California); and backs Bobby Hill and Ron Oyer (Syracuse).

Some had returned from Vietnam, where Mullen won the Silver Star and Bronze Star, and Kozarsky, guard Lynn Oehling (Mount Union) and end Marshall "Skip" Wells (Washington of St. Louis) the Bronze Star.

With a start like that, the addition of players such as ends Jerry Allen (Alabama State), Roger Calderwood (Arizona) and Jim McNamara (Tennessee), tackles Mike Pritchard (Arizona State) and Pat Shea (North Carolina), guards Bry Lake (Brigham Young) and Mike Sweatman (Kansas), center Mike Zoffuto (West Texas), and backs Willie Belton (Maryland State), Charles Burt (Wisconsin), Larry Curella (Louisville), Mike Davis (Tampa), Jerry Kinnikin (Illinois State), Tom Kmetovic (Colorado), Stan Quintana (New Mexico) and Eli Smith (Grambling) made the Leathernecks formidable.

There was pro-caliber material to work with again.

Kozarsky and Moore had been with Richmond of the Continental Football League, Quintana with the Minnesota Vikings and Las Vegas of the CFL, and Smith with the Los Angeles Rams.

Belton, a 200-pound 9.5 sprinter who had a 99-yard TD against Presbyterian, would play for the Atlanta Falcons in 1971-72 and the St.

Louis Cardinals in 1973-74. Back Glenn Ellison, troubled by injuries at Arkansas, would be with the Oakland Raiders in 1971 and Jacksonville of the World Football League in 1974.

Elliott, Quintana and Sweatman had been selected for the East-West Game in San Francisco.

And the young enlisted were talented. Hill had run and passed for 1,167 yards for the Leathernecks in 1968, and threw for four TDs against Drake. Ronnie Erb was a publicized prep back in Virginia.

Although outweighed just like previous Quantico teams, Heuring did have some size in tackles Carroll Davis (240), Mike Fauver (230), Howard Jarvis (240), Mangrum (235) and Pritchard (235), guard Dennis Ewing (San Francisco State) (230) and linebacker Bob Martin (Parsons) (230).

Quantico roared to a 7-0 start with Burt at the controls, defeating Presbyterian, Tennessee-Martin, Northeast Louisiana, Pensacola, Parsons, Northern Michigan and Wisconsin-Milwaukee; lost to Tampa, defeated Gustavus-Adolphus, lost to old nemesis Xavier and closed by beating Delta State.

Kinnikin, an excellent kicker, led the scoring with 46 points and Allen had 42.

The 1970 season:

Talk about a streaky team!

The Leathernecks got off to an 0-2 start against Northern Arizona and Eastern Michigan in what could be called a geographic schedule; defeated Fairmont State, Pensacola Navy and Northeast Louisiana to run the record to 3-2; lost to Northern Michigan and Xavier (again) as the record slipped to 3-4; then downed Wisconsin-Superior, Delta State and Parsons to close at 6-4.

(A potential seventh victory evaporated when Federal City College of Washington canceled its game.)

There were 12 familiar faces to make the offense and defense go: Allen, George Cox, Jim Goebel (Navy), Jim Lange (Gustavus-Adolphus) and McNamara at ends; Fauver and Mike Maehl (Northern Illinois) at tackles; Lake at guard; and Ellison, Kmetovic, Quintana and Joe Whitney in the backfields.

Augmenting them were these newcomers:

■ Ends Gary Barnes (Northern Arizona) and Tom Higgins (Texas).

■ Tackles Sam "Buck" Baker, Dave Freeman (William Jewell) and William Upshaw (Northern Arizona).

■ Linebackers Danny Hale (West Chester), Jerry Humble (Western Kentucky) and Jerry Steffen (St. Thomas).

■ Guard Mike Roof (UCLA and Pensacola) and center Bill Broderick (Navy).

■ Backs Mike Bixiones (Richmond), Dennis Kucharek (Eastern Michigan), Daynor Prince (Parsons), Les Steckel (Kansas) and Fred Wolf (Illinois).

■ Kicker Vern Albery (Muskingum), who had a tryout with the Dallas Cowboys.

The team was explosive. In its final eight games, only Northern Michigan held the Leathernecks under 20 points. Prince, with a prince of an arm, completed 124 of 227 passes for 1,687 yards and 12 TDs.

Ellison bulled his way for 564 yards on 150 carries. Albery kicked for 45 points, Ellison scored 44 and Lange 30.

Prince was the MVP. His pass to Allen beat Pensacola in the last 28 seconds and his pass to Ellison nipped Northeast Louisiana in the last 11 seconds.

And this was a team that could mix it up, with Baker (6-5, 251), Gene Clark (235), Fauver (229), Freeman (228), Mike Lynch (6-5, 243), Maehl (265), Bill Smith (235), Ken Sorenson (Northwest Missouri) (235), Upshaw (232) and Dallas Whitewing (237) at tackles; linebacker Gene Anderson at 226; center Wes Hodges (Millikin) at 245; and Ellison 240 at fullback.

What happened to some of the players after their return to civilian life?

Baker went back to Georgia for the 1972-73 seasons and played with Jacksonville of the World Football League in 1974-75. .... Freeman played at West Texas in 1972. ... Hale was an assistant at four schools before becoming head coach at West Chester (Pa.) · ...
Ellison turned pro. ... and Quintana coached at New Mexico.

Steckel, of course, coached the Minnesota Vikings in 1984, and was quarterbacks and receivers coach for the New England Patriots in 1985-86.

"I know I'm young (38) and following the legend of Bud Grant," Steckel told USA Today before the 1984 season. "But I've led 210 Marines and 80 Vietnamese soldiers into combat so don't talk to me about being a head coach."

He was the youngest NFL coach that year.

"When Steckel — the unmarked face, the gleaming teeth, the perfect hairdo, the outspoken Christian — talks of being street tough, it is difficult to comprehend," St. Paul Pioneer Press writer Patrick Reusse noted.

"My wife, Chris, says the same thing," retorted Steckel.

As for Vietnam, "I figured if I was going in the service, I wanted to be with the best, so I enlisted in Marine officers training," Steckel said, in a wide-ranging interview. "I was young and not married and Vietnam was the preoccupation of my generation. If we were going to fight a war, I wanted to be a part of it — to experience it, to test myself in those conditions. My views of what went on in Vietnam may not be the same now as when I was young, but my year there was one of the greatest of my life. I wouldn't give up my Vietnam experience."

Steckel played for Quantico on Saturdays, and was into co-ed touch football in Washington's Potomac Park on Sundays.

"That's where I met my wife."

After his Marine tour, he turned down a Nixon administration appointment supervising youth programs and instead took a "$150-a-month job as a graduate assistant in football at Colorado."

From there he went to the Naval Academy — where he had been rejected as a midshipman because of his physical exams — and to the San Francisco 49ers as an assistant.

He also obtained a master's degree in sports administration at the College of St. Thomas, stayed in the Marine Reserve as a lieutenant colonel and was a sought-after motivational speaker for the Fellowship of Christian Athletes.

While a Vikings' assistant (1979-83), Steckel also had been recommended by a search committee for the head coaching job at the University of Minnesota.

"Some people describe me as perfectionist and a workaholic," he commented after his appointment. "I say, 'What's wrong with a guy who works had and tries to do a good job?' "

But Steckel was in the public eye almost immediately following reports of an Ironman competition in training camp and his portrayal as a taskmaster. The players competed for $30,000 in prizes, including a new car, in the eight-event Ironman competition.

He filmed recruiting commercials for the Corps, saying, "Being on a Marine team is no different from being on a football team. They both demand discipline and tough training."

But he soon backed off from comparing his job as coach to his days as a lieutenant in Vietnam — at the urging of his wife.

She said "it was a war long gone. She said when people read the word Vietnam they'll think about a lost son or loved one. ... The fewer times I bring it up, the better," Steckel said.

He started long-overdue financial, career and chemical-dependency counseling for the Vikings' players.

But Steckel faced problems, too. The Vikings were getting old, there were injuries, and the front office — on an economy kick — made few efforts to sign top draftees or to trade for veterans.

Steckel received a vote of confidence in November from General Manager Mike Lynn, despite a 3-9 record, on the basis of an internal study conducted by a private consulting firm. But he was fired less than a month later after closing with a franchise-worst 3-13 record.

"I think to blame Les Steckel by himself is a mistake," Lynn said. "When you're in this sort of situation, everyone connected with this organization is to blame, from the management to the equipment managers."

The Associated Press said "like the good commander he is, he refused to quit, to step down gracefully, choosing instead to go down with the ship."

Steckel released a statement, thanking the Vikings "for the opportunity to work with a good group of people. ..."

"I knew, realistically, within a few months, my opportunity to be a head coach in the NFL had been damaged by the media more than anything else," Steckel told The Sporting News in January 1986. "By distortion. The feedback I get all the time is, 'You're not like that.' "

But he proved to be a survivor. The Patriots reached the Super Bowl his first season and got to the the playoffs again in 1986 with an 11-5 record before losing to the Denver Broncos, 22-17.

1969

Record: 41-21 Presbyterian, 29-14 Tennessee-Martin, 20-7 Northeast Louisiana, 44-6 Pensacola NAS, 25-7 Parsons, 21-7 Northern Michigan, 42-3 Wisconsin-Milwaukee, 19-45 Tampa, 21-6 Gustavus-Adolphus, 7-9 Xavier, 10-3 Delta St. (9-2)

Coach: Capt. Ed Heuring (Mayland) (coach Okinawa)

Assistants: Steve Bernstein (Cerritos JC-Occidental) (asst. Okinawa 1968), Howard George (Hawaii Marines 1954-55, Camp Lejeune 1957-59, Severn River Naval Command 1961-63), Ed Kesler (North Carolina), Mike Parker (Arkansas), John Turner (Virginia Military) (asst. Okinawa 1968), Cliff Yoshida (Cal Poly) (coach Okinawa 1968)

Ends: Rikki Aldridge (USC), Jerry Allen (Alabama St.), Bob Buckner (Texas-Arlington), Roger Calderwood (Arizona), George Cox, Mike Daly (Temple), Chuck Girwood (Wabash), Dave Hunt (Arkansas), Jim Johnson (Sequoias JC) (Okinawa 1968), Tony Kozarsky (Noth Carolina St.), Tom Lange (Gustavus-Adolphus), Richard Lowe (Morehouse), Francis Mangrum, Jim McNamara (Tennessee), Robert Mullen (Macalester) and Marshall Wells (Washington of Mo.)

Tackles: Frank Blakemore (Cal Poly), Ed Craig, Carroll Davis (Oklahoma St.), Dennis Ewing (San Francisco St.), Mike Fauver (Mississippi St.), Grant Foster (Concord), Howard Jarvis, Mike Maehl (Northern Illinois), Jim Medley (Western Kentucky), Leonard Moore (Jackson St.), Bob Pfeiffer, Mike Pritchard (Arizona St.), Pat Shea (North Carolina) and K. Wawsyniak

Guards: Kim Butts (Millikin), Jim Ford (William Jewell), Tom Kurucz (Defiance), Ralph Lake (BYU), Rod McCoy and Lynn Oehling (Mt. Union).

Linebackers: Greg Bankston (Georgia), Charles Deardorff (East Stroudsburg), Harris Elliott (Syracuse), Larry Gillen (Idaho St.), Bob Martin (Parsons), Dolphus Milton, Steve Radich (California), Fred Smith (North Carolina A&T), Mike Sweatman (Kansas) and Larry Warren (Huron).

Centers: Bob Olmstead (Tampa), Reggie Simon (Virginia Union) and Mike Zoffuto (West Texas)

Backs: Phil Anderson (Dana), Willie Belton (Maryland St.), Charles Burt (Wisconsin), Larry Curella (Louisville) (MCAS Beaufort 1968), Julian Davis, Mike Davis (Tampa), Glenn Ellison (Arkansas), Ron Erb, Wayne Frahn (Franklin & Marshall), Bobby Hill, Jerry Kinnikin (Illinois St.), Tom Kmetovic (Colorado), Walter Odes, Ron Oyer (Syracuse), Stan Quintana (New Mexico), Eli Smith (Grambling), Ray Stevens, Steve Struble (Arkansas St.), Dave Tomeo (Arizona Western JC), Jim Wager (Fullerton JC), Joe Whitney and Jeff Zorn (Wooster)

1970

Record: 3-25 Northern Arizona, 0-23 Eastern Michigan, 38-14 Fairmont, 28-21 Pensacola, 21-20 Northeast Louisiana, 6-13 Northern Michigan, 27-35 Xavier (Ohio), 27-9 Parsons, 28-18 Wisconsin-Superior, 20-13 Delta St. (6-4)

Coach: Ed Heuring (Maryland) (coach Okinawa)

Assistants: Lt. Gary Barnett (Southwest Missouri), Lt. Mike Davis (Tampa), Capt. Ron Eckert (Upsala) (coach 8th Marines 1967-68), First Sgt. Howard George (Hawaii Marines 1954-55, Camp Lejeune 1957-59, Severn River Naval Command 1961-63), Lt. Pat Shea (North Carolina), Lt. Jim Troppmann (Stanford)

Ends: Jerry Allen (Alabama St.), Gene Andrews (Georgia), Gary Barnes (Northern Arizona), Danny Choate, George Cox, Jim Goebel (Navy), Tom Higgins (Texas), Tom Lange (Gustavus-Adolphus), Jim McNamara (Tennessee) and Fred Vossekiul (Central Michigan).

Tackles: Sam Baker (Georgia), Gene Clark, Don Fauver (Mississippi St.), Dave Freeman (Texas-Arlington and William Jewell; later at West Texas), Paul Jones (Southern), Bruce Kirry (Central Washington), Mike Lynch, Mike Maehl (Northern Illinois), Curtis Mitchner, Jim Revels (Dana), Cal Roberson (Southern), Jimmy Roberts (Tampa), Rick Sizemore (BYU), Bill Smith (Mississippi St.), Ken Sorenson (Northwest Missouri), Bob Sponcil (Butler), William Upshaw (Northern Arizona) and Dallas Whitewing.

Guards: Charles Constance, Allen Davis (Wenatchee Valley JC), Roger Eberhardt (William Jewell), Ed Foster (Northland), Brye Lake (BYU), Bob May (West Chester), Jim Williams and John Withers (Eastern Oregon).

Linebackers: Gene Anderson (Penn St.), Jim Freland (Xavier of Ohio), Danny Hale (West Chester), Wilson Hawkins (Norfolk St.), Jerry Humble (Western Kentucky), Mike Roof (UCLA) (Pensacola 1968-69), Ken Sheeler and Jerry Steffen (St. Thomas).

Centers: Bill Broderick (Navy), Wes Hodges (Millikin) and Frank Ray.

Backs: Rod Alexander (Ferris), Mike Bixiones (Richmond), Mike Caulk, Rogers Coleman, Pete D'Achille (Ursinus), Bob Dudley, Glenn Ellison (Arkansas), Bruce Evans (San Fernando St.), Tom Kmetovic (Colorado), Dennis Kucharek (Eastern Michigan), Lynn Lowder (Northern Illinois), Aubrey McNutt (Abilene Christian), Terry Murray (Navy), Hap Myers (Hope), Larry Orlando, Larry Payne (Pasadena JC), Skip Pound, Daynor Prince (Parsons), Stan Quintana (New Mexico), Willie Ransom, Ed Sandrick (John Carroll), Les Steckel (Kansas), Harold Thigpen, Joe Whitney, D.J. Williams (Taft JC) and Fred Wolf (Illinois). **Kicker:** Vern Albery (Muskingum)

When you're up, your're down,
When you're down, you're down,
When you're up against Quantico,
You're upside down!

A Quantico cheer

132

All Good Things ...

O ld-timers generally worried when things were going well in the Marine Corps: It meant that the higher-ups were plotting to change things around — usually for the worse.

And, like all good things, the expected happened and the Marine Corps' football program was scrapped, a program that at Quantico alone had resulted in approximately 335 victories since 1919.

But not before Capt. Ron Eckert (Upsala) directed the Marines, based at Quantico and with at least 14 players and two assistants back from Vietnam, to a 9-3 record in 1971 that included an 18-17 victory over Prairie View in the Astrodome. And as a major, Eckert coached the Leathernecks to an 8-4 record in 1972.

A 17-7 record in two seasons against a national college schedule.

A crowd of 11,000 for the final home game against South Dakota State.

After the last home game, Gunnery Sgt. Russ Thurman of the base Public Affairs Office wrote for the Quantico Sentry: "It wasn't just any loss. It was a loss that marked the last Marine varsity football game at Butler Stadium. ... The record has been written. The ink is dry. No matter what the past or future, the book, when taken down from the back shelf and dusted, will read: Final Home Game — Marines 21, South Dakota State 24."

United Press International noted that "several NCOs still hoped that, somehow, the Marines will return to the gridiron next year. Marine recruiters say football also can be a persuasive tool in attracting talented athletes."

UPI added that Quantico "is dropping its program just when it seemed to be on the upgrade."

A game with Syracuse had been planned for 1973.

And a three-game series with small-college power Delaware had been set for 1973-75.

Sure enough, the Marine Corps couldn't stand prosperity.

A program that brought the Marine players to numerous campuses across the country, and brought countless players to Butler Stadium and the Marine Corps Schools, was stopped. Finis.

Gen. Robert E. Cushman, the commandant, told the Navy Times in August: "Upon completion of the 1972 schedule, the varsity program will be terminated. This stems from a recommendation of a special football study panel after an in-depth review of the program. It was determined that current financial support from the central Marine Corps Recreation Fund and personnel support from Headquarters Marine Corps was no longer in the best interest of the Corps."

At least the Marines were able to take their last hurrah in the manner of a Carl Yastrzemski or a Julius Erving.

"You think they won't be sky-high for this one?", said Xavier coach Tom Cecchini. "When you play college ball, you always remember your last game more than any other."

And the Marines, as might be expected, went out as a class act, defeating Xavier, 34-0.

The headline in the Quantico Sentry read: "XAVIER BOWS IN GRID FINALE: MARINES EVEN LONG SERIES."

(The team used the name Marine Corps in the final two seasons.) The series, started in 1926, wound up a 13-13 tie.

Ironically, Xavier dropped football after the 1973 season.

In those final two seasons, the Marine Corps teams opposed 19 colleges from Alabama, Arkansas, Colorado, Illinois, Louisiana, Massachusetts, Michigan, Minnesota, New York, Ohio, Oklahoma, Pennsylvania, South Dakota and Texas.

The 1971 season:

The Marines closed with a roar, winning nine of the last 10 as rifle-armed quarterback Daynor Prince (Parsons) completed 176 of 344 passes for 2,292 yards and 15 TDs.

This was on top of his 124-of-227 passing for 1,687 yards and 12 TDs in 1970.

His 1971 season and combined 1970-71 marks are believed to be Marine records.

Les Steckel, who had served in Vietnam and would coach the Minnesota Vikings and be a New England Patriots assistant in 1985-86, was a threat as a runner and pass receiver, rushing for 429 yards in 141 carries for five TDs and catching 28 passes for 295 yards and two TDs.

"The (Vikings) players get on me about having been a hack player," Steckel told the St. Paul Pioneer Press before the 1984 season, "but I wasn't. I had a respectable career at Kansas and, later, I was the leading rusher for the Quantico Marines."

(Actually back Karl Schwelm (Navy) was with 484 yards in 130 carries.)

Still, Steckel, among other things, is the answer on the Wisconsin-Superior campus to this trivia question: Which NFL coach scored two TDs against the Yellowjackets? He did in a 29-18 Quantico victory in 1970.

Mike Sweatman, a teammate at Kansas, coach of the Okinawa Devil Dogs in 1970, a Marines assistant in 1971 and Steckel's outside linebackers coach with the Vikings, said he understood why Steckel's talk was peppered with Marine analogies.

"The Marines have a tremendous influence on you," said Sweatman, later an assistant with the New York Giants. "There's no such thing as an ex-Marine," he said to the Minneapolis Star and Tribune.

The Marines' passing attack was extremely efficient in 1971. Pete Kimener (Holy Cross) caught 45 passes for 455 yards and a TD, Tom Lange (Gustavus-Adolphus) 35 for 545 yards, Schwelm 34 for 489 yards and seven TDs, and George Cox 21 for 326 yards and four TDs.

Schwelm, as a running back and pass catcher, scored 60 points as the team posted at least 13 points in every game, and more than 30 in three outings. Back Alex Bearfield accounted for 35 points, Cox 24, kicker Vern Albery (Muskingum and a tryout with the Dallas

Cowboys) 22, and Prince and Johnny Harrison, who carried for 301 yards in 67 carries, 18 each.

Considering the caliber of opposition, the defense held up its end(s), allowing 0, 6, 8, 17, 17, 19, 7, 8, 10 and 0 points the final 10 games. Linebacker Charles Sherrill (Appalachian) led in tackles with 36, tackle Glen Fleming (Jackson State) and linebacker Bill Lanham had 33 each, linebacker Gene Johnson (Harding) 32 and end Mike Daly (Temple) 29.

Eckert had been around, as a guard for Quantico in 1963-64, coach of the 8th Marines at Camp Lejeune in 1967-68 (a 23-3 record), two tours in Vietnam, and as a Quantico assistant in 1970.

The Quantico media guide described him as "likable, demanding, meticulous and personable."

Before entering Upsala, according to the guide, "In 1958 I went to see the Quantico Marines play. I had heard so much about the Marine team, and I was so impressed with the Marines on that team ... that I knew I wanted to be a Marine. I'm sure there are people today (1972) that are affected the same way by this team."

To start with, he had 15 players with prior Quantico experience:
■ Ends Roger Calderwood (Arizona), Cox, Daly and Lange.
■ Tackles Sam "Buck" Baker and Jimmy Williams.
■ Guards Dave Freeman and Rick Sizemore (Brigham Young).
■ Linebackers Danny Choate, Danny Hale (West Chester) and Ken Sheeler.
■ Backs Rogers Coleman, Prince and Dennis Williams, plus Albery.

Calderwood, Cox, Daly and Sheeler were Vietnam veterans.

And Eckert had ample beef for the cross-country schedule in ends John Dalton (230) and Pat Ryan (235), tackles Dwayne Adams (225), Baker (250), Fred Brutsche (Penn Military) (230), Roy Crawford (Troy) (225), Don Dwyer (245), Fleming (230), Seton Siff (DePauw) (240), Greg Sundby (Augustana of S.D.) (225), Carl Whitesell (280), Jimmy Williams (235) and George Yeager (Lock Haven) (250); guards Freeman (230) and Sizemore (225); linebacker Hale (225); and center John Bringer (Northeast Missouri) (225).

Surprisingly, the majority of these heavyweights came from the officer ranks, although 23 of the 50 players listed in the Livingston game program were enlisted.

Dalton, Siff, Sundby and Yeager had served in Vietnam.

And Eckert picked up Kimener, who was awarded two Silver Stars and a Bronze Star in Vietnam; linebackers John Mauzey (Illinois) and Mike Zizzo (Villanova); and backs Joe Belasco (Villanova) and Jeff Simonds (Iowa State).

The talents extended beyond the football field, too: Steckel was a boxer, Baker a wrestler and Schwelm a lacrosse standout.

Baker returned to Georgia, where he lettered two seasons, and played two years with Jacksonville of the World Football League.

The team was colorful in another way, too, as the uniforms were different. Instead of the traditional red and gold, the Marines had home jerseys of royal blue with white lettering, with the away jerseys white with red lettering. Both had the word "Marines" across the front and the Marine emblem on both sleeves.

The trousers were royal blue with red stripes down the sides, similar to the dress uniform. The socks were red, white and blue.

The 1972 season:

The Marine were establishing a tradition of top quarterbacking as well as winning.

Tom Maudlin, John Arms, Paul Terhes, Tom Singleton, Pat McCarthy, Bob Hill and Prince had played starring roles during the 1960s and into the '70s. This time it was Mike Jay (Wyoming), who completed 84 passes in 189 attempts for 1,224 yards and nine touchdowns (three against Akron). After his tour ended, he lettered at Texas A&M from 1973-75 and was seen on national television as the Aggies (10-2) lost to USC in the 1975 Liberty Bowl, 20-0.

"A feeling of cautious optimism surrounds those connected with the team," said a writeup in Villanova's guide. "Not because of the upcoming schedule, to be sure, since it is probably the toughest to face a Marine eleven in many a year, but because there is the possibility that at least 25 members of last year's 9-3 squad will be returning, including 11 starters."

Eckert scheduled scrimmages with Carson-Newman, Elon and Richmond to prepare for the regular season.

And after a 3-3 start, the Marines roared down the stretch, defeating Villanova, Northern Michigan, Eastern Illinois and Akron, losing to South Dakota State and closing with the victory over Xavier.

They knew how to move the ball, scoring 56 points against Eastern Illinois, 43 against Arkansas-Pine Bluff and the 34 against Xavier. Kicker Bob Nasby (St. John's) was the leading scorer with 56 points, Simonds had 30. Rod Alexander (Ferris) scored three times against Arkansas-Pine Bluff and wound up with 24 points, as did Jay, Willie Williams and Belasco.

The Akron game program said Williams' "forte is speed, which the Leathernecks have used to good advantage in punt and kickoff returns. The 197-pound speed merchant returned a kickoff 95 yards for a TD against Northern Michigan and sped 64 yards with an Eastern Illinois punt."

And the Vietnam veteran scored on a 68-yard pass play against Xavier.

The passing attack was amazingly balanced: Pat Holder (Abilene Christian) caught 24 for 241 yards, Bill Degan (New Hampshire) 19 for 248 yards and two TDs, Simonds 16 for 205 yards and two TDs, Willie Williams 16 for 287 yards and two TDs, Paul Smith (Western Carolina) 15 for 230 yards and a TD and big-play Bobby Joe Easter (Middle Tennessee) 10 for 256 yards and a TD.

Easter also led rushers with 439 yards in 100 carries, Jay had 91 plays from scrimmage for 319 yards (including a 78-yard run against Xavier and a 59-yard romp against Eastern Illinois), Alexander 96 carries for 307 yards, Simonds 72 for 281 and Harrison 43 for 155.

Some regular quarterbacks would have settled for Belasco's stats as the backup: 39 of 70 for 499 yards..

The balance between rushing and passing was shown by the 1,184 yards rushing and 1,262 in passing during the first eight games.

The defense knew its way around, too, shutting out Akron and Xavier, and holding Northeast Louisiana, Gustavus-Adolphus, Arkansas-Pine Bluff, C.W. Post, Villanova and Northern Michigan to 10 or fewer points. Johnson led in tackles with 88, Crawford had 59, Lanham 58, linebacker Jim Cedarstrom 56, end Tommy Tate (West Texas) 54, linebacker John Craig (Central Washington) 45 and linebacker George Russell 40. Cedarstrom picked off six interceptions, and Jerome Bailey (William Penn) and Russell four each.

The numbers told the story.

Eckert had enough old hands from former Quantico teams to virtually assure a successful season even before it opened: Adams, Mike Bambauer (Cal Poly) and Greg Boice (Oregon Tech) at ends; Crawford, Bob Ingrum, Stan Kabala, Jimmy Roberts (Tampa), David Smalls (a Vietnam veteran) and Scott Williams at tackles; Brutsche, David Champagne and Sizemore (for a third season) at guards; Buddy Briley (Northwest Oklahoma), Craig, Arthur Hardy (Johnson C. Smith), Johnson, Lanham and Russell at linebackers, Alan Hartman (Michigan Tech) at center, and Bailey, Gary Barnes (Northern Arizona and a Vietnam veteran), Belasco, John Deleo, Harrison, Sam Reed (Tampa), Simonds, Charles Williams (Seton Hall) and D.J. Williams, a Vietnam veteran, in the backfields.

Graduate schools and the pro ranks had siphoned off most of the name players. But Eckert was able to rely successfully on players from Division I-AA and Division II schools, and of the 58 players listed on the game program for Northeast Louisiana, 28 were enlisted. Eckert's use of enlisted in both 1971 and '72 was perhaps the most extensive at Quantico since the 1950 season.

There was adequate size: Adams (228) at end, Boice (230), Dom Gray (Morgan State) (240), Kabala (225), Roberts (225), Smalls (225), Barry Steele (New Mexico) (270), Scott Williams (235) and Robert Wilson (West Chester and Pottstown of the Continental Football League) (230) at tackles; Russell (228) at linebacker; Brutsche (228) and Sizemore (225) at guards, and Fred Hill (Texas Southern) (225) at center.

He also added Bob Brown (Northern Arizona) and Don Kelly (Richmond) at ends; Harold Harris (Knoxville), Tom O'Brien (Navy) and Roger Wiedeman (Murray State) at guards; John Kavcar (Kent State) at center; Jerry Balsley (Navy), Gary Capehart (Boston University), Ozzie Fretz (Navy), Bobby Hensley (Eastern Kentucky), Bill Lantow (West Texas), Terry McNeil (Winston-Salem), Maynard Pierce (Western Carolina) and Lon Troxel (College of Idaho) in the backfields; and Doyle Brunson (Sacramento State) as a punter.

Curiously, there were four players on the team named Williams plus an assistant by that name.

The 1971 and '72 teams, besides being known for the Marines' final teams, produced a number of coaches.

From the '71 team, Hale was an assistant at Colgate, Bucknell and Vermont and the head coach at West Chester (Pa.);
Steckel an assistant at Colorado and Navy before joining the staff of the San Francisco 49ers; Sweatman an assistant at Tennessee, Kansas and Tulsa plus Edmonton of the Canadian Football League; Thom

Park an assistant at Maryland, Connecticut, West Chester and The Citadel; and assistant Mike Zoffuto an assistant at West Texas in 1972.

From the '72 team came assistant John Morello to be an assistant at Pacific and San Diego State; O'Brien to be an assistant at Navy and Virginia; Sweatman; and Troxel to be assistant at San Jose State, Idaho State, Idaho and Cal State Northridge.

After the closing Xavier game, Thurman wrote: "Thus went the final game, with everybody giving their all to go out in style. ... It was fitting that the Marines played their last game against one of their oldest rivals.

"Now it's over — the last huddle has broken, the last TD scored, the last cheer sounded, the last win recorded and the last team gone."

As Yogi Berra might have said, it *was* over now.

1971

Record: 13-19 Northeast Louisiana, 20-28 Eastern Michigan, 13-0 Southeast Louisiana, 24-6 Xavier (ohio), 23-8 Springfield, 13-17 Livingston, 18-17 Prairie View, 32-19 East-Central Oklahoma, 34-7 Southwest Minnesota, 31-8 Northern Michigan, 21-10 Gustavus-Adolphus, 28-0 Fort Lewis (Colo.) (9-3)

Coach: Capt. Ron Eckert (Upsala) (coach 8th Marines 1967-68).

Assistants: Lt. Terry Davis (Panhandle), Lt. Ev Keene (Boise JC-Rhode Island) (asst. Okinawa 1970), Lt. Thom Park (Brown-West Chester) (p-c Okinawa 1970), Lt. Mike Sweatman (Kansas) (coach Okinawa 1970), Lt. Mike Zoffuto (West Texas)

Ends: Dennis Blake (Okinawa 1970), Greg Boice (Oregon Tech), Roger Calderwood (Arizona), Dave Champagne, John Collins, George Cox, John Dalton, Mike Daly (Temple), Willis Holcombe (Baldwin-Wallace), Pete Kimener (Holy Cross), Tom Lange (Gustavus-Adolphus), Pat Ryan, Karl Schwelm (Navy) and Scott Williams (Notre Dame).

Tackles: Dwayne Adams (Northern Arizona), Sam Baker (Georgia), Fred Brutsche (Penn Military), Michael Coffron (Tennessee-Martin), Roy Crawford (Troy St.), Don Dwyer (Ohio St.), Glenn Fleming (Jackson St.), Seton Siff (DePauw) (Okinawa 1970), Greg Sundby (Augustana of S.D.) (Okinawa 1970), Carl Whitesell, Jimmy Williams and George Yeager (Lock Haven).

Guards: Mike Bambauer (Shasta JC-Cal Poly), Pete Connolly, Dave Freeman (Texas-Arlington and William Jewell; later at West Texas), Bob Ingrum (Southwestern Louisiana-Tennessee), Stan Kabala, Dick Sizemore (BYU), David Smalls and Grant Sparks (Kearney).

Linebackers: Denny Choate, Roy Grover, Danny Hale (West Chester), Art Hardy (Johnson C. Smith), Gene Johnson (Harding), Bill Lanham (Concord-West Virginia Tech), John Mauzey (Illinois), Dick Musmanno (Cornell), George Russell (Georgia), Ken Sheeler (Appalachian), Rick Sherrill (Appalachian), Radford Taylor (Angelo-Howard Payne) and Mike Zizzo (Villanova) (Okinawa 1970).

Centers: John Bringer (Northeast Missouri), Alan Hartman (Michigan Tech) and James Ross.

Backs: Jerome Bailey (William Penn), Alex Bearfield (Kaneohe Bay 1970), Joe Belasco (Villanova), Buddy Briley (Northwestern Oklahoma), Rogers Coleman, Harold Dean, John Deleo, Bert Fortuna (Drake), Johnny Harrison, Bill Mills, Sean O'Keeffe (Manhattan), Pete Pelissier (Bridgeport), Daynor Prince (Parsons), Sam Reed (Tampa), Jeff Simonds (Iowa St.), Les Steckel (Kansas), Bob Sweat (Richmond) (Okinawa 1970), Charles Williams (Seton Hall) and D.J. Williams (Taft JC).

Kickers: Vern Albery (Muskingum) and John Craig (Central Washington). **Also:** John Young (West Chester)

1972

Record: 6-10 Northeast Louisiana, 14-6 Gustavus-Adolphus, 43-7 Arkansas-Pine Bluff, 15-28 Jacksonville St., 16-10 C.W. Post, 7-21 Eastern Michigan, 13-7 Villanova, 20-6 Northern Michigan, 56-14 Eastern Illinois, 24-0 Akron, 21-24 South Dakota St., 34-0 Xavier. (8-4).

Coach: Maj. Ron Eckert (Upsala) (coach 8th Marines 1967-68).

Assistants: Lt. Ev Keene (Boise JC-Rhode Island) (asst. Okinawa 1970), Lt. John Morello (San Francisco CC-Pacific), Capt. Terry Murray (Navy) Lt. Mike Sweatman (Kansas) (coach Okinawa 1970), Lt. Radford Taylor (Angelo-Howard Payne), Lt. C.O. Williams (Southern-UC Santa Barbara) Lt. John Young (West Chester)

Ends: Dwayne Adams (Northern Arizona), Mike Bambauer (Shasta JC-Cal Poly), Greg Boice (Oregon Tech), Bob Brown (Northern Arizona), Riley Carrington, Bill Degan (New Hampshire), Ed Evans (Frostburg), Pat Holder (Abilene Christian), Don Kelly (Richmond), Steve Mayfield, Paul Smith (Western Carolina), Mike Tanner, Tommy Tate (Eastern Arizona JC-West Texas) and Willie Williams (East Texas)

Tackles: Roy Crawford (Troy St.), Dominic Gray (Morgan St.), Bob Ingrum (Southwestern Louisiana-Tennessee), Bob Jonischkies (Rice), Stan Kabala, Jimmy Roberts (Tampa), David Smalls (Northeastern JC-New Mexico), R.F. Turbyfill (Catawba), Scott Williams (Notre Dame) and Bob Wilson (West Chester).

Guards: Fred Brutsche (Penn Military), David Champagne, Harold Harris (Knoxville), Mark Severson, Richard Sizemore (BYU), Russ Waddell (Texas A&M) and Roger Wiedeman (Murray St.)

Linebackers: Buddy Briley (Northwestern Oklahoma), Cornelius Callahan (Frostburg), Walt Cashwell (North Carolina), James Cedarstrom (Arizona), John Craig (Central Washington), Burrell Godbolt (Okinawa 1971), Arthur Hardy (Johnson C. Smith), Gene Johnson (Harding), Bill Lanham (Concord-West Virginia Tech), Dick Lawrence (Delta JC), Howard Merrick (Catawba), Tom O'Brien (Navy) and George Russell (Georgia).

Centers: Alan Hartman (Michigan Tech), Fred Hill (Texas Southern) and John Kavcar (Kent St.)

Backs: Rod Alexander (Ferris), Jerry Bailey (William Penn), Jeri Balsley (Navy), Gary Barnes (Northern Arizona), Joe Belasco (Villanova), Gary Capehart (Boston Univ.), Bob Cox (Texas Lutheran), John Deleo, Bobby Easter (Middle Tennessee), Ozzie Fretz (Navy), John Harrison, Chris Hawkins, Bobby Hensley (Eastern Kentucky), Mike Jay (Wyoming; later at Texas A&M), Bill Lantow (West Texas), Jerry Lyons (William Penn), Gerald McIntyre, Terry McNeil (Winston-Salem), Ken Petkovich, Maynard Pierce (Western Carolina), Sam Reed (Tampa), Jeff Simonds (Iowa St.), Bruce Sindewald (Northern Michigan), Lon Troxel (College of Idaho), Charles Williams (Seton Hall) and D.J. Williams (Taft JC).

Kickers: Doyle Brunson (American River JC-Sacramento St.), Dick Ewaldson (Mankato), Dave Morgan (Catawba) and Bob Nasby (St. John's).

1973

Football dropped.

Football And The Olympics

A few Marine footballers found their way to the Olympics.

Among them were (Gen.) Harry Liversedge (Cal, AEF 1918, Quantico 1920, All-Marines 1921-24, Al-Marines assistant 1925-26 and 1929, MCB San Diego assistant 1930), third in the shotput in 1920; Dick Hyland (Stanford), rugby in 1928; Bob Mathias (Stanford), the 1948 and 1952 Olympic decathlon champion; Vern Gagne (Minnesota, El Toro 1944-45), wrestling in 1948; Howard George (Hawaii Marines 1954-55, Camp Lejeune 1957-59, Severn River Naval Command 1961-63, Quantico assistant 1969-70), wrestling in 1960; and Percy Price (Hawaii Marines 1958, Quantico 1959-60), boxing in 1960.

Pinky Newell (Purdue) was a trainer for three U.S. Olympic teams.

Leatherneck Imprint at Bates

Bates College in Lewiston, Maine, decided that one Marine coach wasn't enough. Actually, two weren't, either.

Bob Hatch was the football coach from 1952-72. At one point, Bob Peck, a former Quantico athlete, was the baseball coach and William Leahey, a former Marine, the basketball coach.

San Diego 1942-46

1942

No base team

1943

Six teams competed in a round-robin schedule at Balboa Park and Point Loma that was open to the public. The Recruit Depot DI's won with a 5-0 record. Ernie Lewis, who would play for El Toro in 1944-45 and four seasons in the All-America Football Conference, was the top scorer with 30 points; Johnny Monroe with 24 was second.

Recruit Depot DI's
Coach: Sgt. J.D. Nicolini
Ends: NA. **tackles:** Stan Green (Oklahoma), Dick Kelley; **guards:** NA; **centers:** Carl Perkinson (Duke); **backs:** Walt Clay (Colorado), Larry Declusin (St. Mary's), Ernie Lewis (Colorado), E.J. York
Also: Ray Babich, Floyd Bishop, Dave Casper, Steve Chivaro, Joe Daugherty (Tulsa), Lyle Ebner, Charles Furman, Wyatt Harding, Gerald Hart, Travis Hughes, Vern Kenny, Mike Meca, Carroll Parrott, Clyde Peeples, Howard Price, William Roberson, Lee Williams, Howard Wimberly

Service Battalion
Coach: MarGun W.F. Durocher Jr. **Backs:** Anthony Amendola (KIA), L. Ferrante, E.W. Franks (Baylor)

Depot Clerks
Coaches: Lt. Doyle New, Pfc. Ray Dawson (Stanford); **Backs:** Mike Gonzales, Milford "Kit" Kittrell (Baylor)

Guard Battalion
Coaches: Lt. Wildred Strong, MarGun Dave Eastes, Pfc. Leroy Foster (New Mexico)
Ends: Cowan; **centers:** Charles Gatewood (Baylor), Neil Zundell (Utah); **backs:** David Wyatt; **Also**: Wilmore Breaux (KIA), Ed Broussard (Louisiana Normal), Henry Corda (Salinas JC), George Dunbar, Al Pileggio, Ken Scheel (Arizona), Pete Spily (St. Mary's), George Vaigh (North Texas Agriculture), Al Wilson

Headquarters Battalion
Coach: Lt. Don Strong (Michigan); **ends:** Doyle Cofer (Indiana), Henry Reynolds (Mississippi St.); **tackles:** Jack Bellamy, H.R. Callahan, Roy Ward (Tulsa); **guards:** Jim Crawford (Nebraska), P. Dean; **centers:** F.D. Smith (Santa Clara); **backs:** Jim Boswell (Oberlin), Joe Hebel, Johnny Monroe, Rudolph Pugh

Signal Battalion
Coaches: Capt. Charles Eddinger, Lt. R.E. Alexander, T/Sgt. C.F. Kent, Pvt. E.S. Yon
Ends: Frank Gates, Murrell, Ralph Robinson, John Wedberg; **tackles:** Bill Duke (Texas A¢&M); **guards:** George Crilly (USC); **centers:** Dave Pennebaum; **backs:** Blaine Aston, Ted Broeg (Missouri), Wilmar Martineson, Bill Oubre, Al Richmire, Al Widmer (incomplete)

1944

There was no base team. Among the players on battalion teams were:
Ends: Steve Mihalic, Dave Pacillas, Ernie Seiner, Lowell Tucker, C.E. Woodard; **tackles:** NA; **guards:** Jerry Fly; **centers:** Phil Cowper; **line:** Jim Gill, Hoffmaster, Bernie Iassugna, Joe Kaster, Pickarzyk, Jim Simms, William Oakley, Lars Watson (Colorado College), Wayne Wilton; **backs:** Warren Arnold, Bob Campbell, Myron Dornboos, Herb Hew, Jack Huber, Ray Isham (Texas A&M), Vernal "Nippy" Jones (baseball), Joe Jurges, William Kilgore, John McCullough, Dee Moore (baseball), Vic Smith, Jay Snelling, Johnny Staten (Nebraska Wesleyan), Larry Strawn (KIA), Bob Telander (Northwestern)

1945

No base team.

1946

No base team

The Train Starts Up

What better way to keep alive the tradition of those pre-World War II teams at San Diego than to call upon some of the very players to revive the program in 1947?

In one of the Marines' shrewdest moves, they selected CWO Robert "Bull" Trometter, a standout on the 1936, 1937, 1938, 1939 and 1940 teams, as coach of the Marine Corps Base's first program since 1940.

Before he returned to the civilian world in 1960, Trometter coached Marine Corps Base and Marine Corps Recruit Depot teams to 46 victories against but 6 losses, and his winning percentage of .884 is the highest in Marine annals.

Trometter, who played freshman ball at St. Mary's and later for the San Diego Bombers of the old Pacific Coast Professional Football League, lined up WO Don Gibson, a back on the 1935-36-37-38-39-40 San Diego teams, and lineman Warren "Lockerbox" Jones from the 1937-38-39 teams as assistants.

Tackle Martin Barber was on the 1939-40 teams and back Bob Rann on the 1940 squad that lost only at Oregon, 12-2, in a near-hurricane.

There were postwar parallels in the programs at Quantico and San Diego, just as there were in the two decades before the war.

Quantico and the All-Marine teams put the Corps on the football map in the 1920s, particularly with their dominance in the President's Cup series.

But after Quantico de-emphasized the sport in the early 1930s, San Diego literally picked up the ball and ran with it, playing before crowds of 75,000 in Berkeley, almost defeating California-Southern Branch (now UCLA) and turning out dozens of would-be generals and colonels in the late 1930s.

In the '40s, Quantico had gotten the jump again. Coach Austin Shofner and Athletic Officer Russ Honsowetz, with the backing of Gen. Clifton B. Cates, had resumed a program in 1946 and by 1947 the Virginia team was rolling to a 12-1 record and the All-Navy title. In the process, they scoured the Corps for many of the best players.

Trometter's wasn't an easy task. There were only a few players with college experience at San Diego as opposed to Quantico's reliance on Annapolis graduates, aviators and college-caliber players.

The team was light. Tackle Fred Williams at 205 pounds was among the heavyweights.

And it had a string of injuries. Maj. Rex Williams, an assistant coach, had to suit up at one point when the ranks thinned.

So Trometter had to rely initially on the best men turned out in boot camp, a wealth of contacts, superior scouting and his instincts.

Camp Pendleton also returned to the football wars in 1947, making the West Coast competition for players as intense off the field as the programs were on it. (The teams scrimmaged but did not meet in a game.)

San Diego admittedly cranked up the football fever with a schedule that wasn't to be confused with Division I. But Trometter and the Marines had a dream, and that journey — extending to 186 games before the sport was dropped in 1965 — had to start somewhere.

The early going was rocky. A 7-6 loss to the San Diego Naval Training Center and a 21-19 loss to DesPac were sandwiched around a 39-6 victory over the USS Tarawa.

Trometter, although in his 30s, did his part, throwing two TD passes against the Tarawa team and three in the DesPac game, plus contributing his usual punting artistry.

But Trometter now had come up with some kind of runner for his single- and double-wing offenses. Volney "Skeet" Quinlan, who played freshman ball at Texas Christian, in the coming years would be a threat every time he carried the ball — from any part of the field — in the college and professional ranks as well. And he held up his end on defense, too.

The 5-11, 170-pound Quinlan missed the NTC game and saw but brief action against DesPac but compiled awesome statistics as the Marines closed by defeating the semipro San Diego Bulldogs, 68-0; San Diego Naval Training Station, 53-6; Terminal Island, 33-19; Ream Field, 32-7; Del Mar Marines, 40-0, and SubForce, 55-0, to close with a 7-2 record.

Against SubForce, San Diego had a 701-54 yardage advantage in total offense.

Quinlan scored the first 33 points against Del Mar and wound up with 131 points on 18 touchdowns and 23 extra points.

Bob Sloan, a Texan like Quinlan, scored 10 TDs. The former Texas A&M freshman could beat you as a runner, pass receiver or defender.

Quinlan was a first-team selection on Leatherneck's initial All-Marine team, and guard Ed Galloway and back Gene Moore (Ada Teachers) were second-team in a season in which Quantico also led in publicity.

Said Leatherneck: "Time after time, Quinlan broke up what might have been close games with his elusive pigskin packing. ... He was one of the few triple-threat men operating in this season of specialists and his excellent performance of all three tasks made him dangerous opposition."

Moore, who was wounded on Peleliu and Okinawa, scored 24 points as did back Mark Rainer (Auburn-Duke), a Bronze Star holder who would be the San Diego coach in 1951.

The team averaged 38 points a game against suspect opposition, but the two losses were by the margin of conversions and who was to argue with success?

Football had landed again in San Diego.

The 1948 season:

With a year of playing and planning behind them, Trometter and the staff were ready to move up in the football world.

And how they did!

Before the season was over, the upstart scarlet and gold rode a 15-game winning streak and, augmented by 11th Naval District players, even challenged favored Quantico — who else? — for Marine supremacy. Quantico won, 21-0, at Norfolk, Va., for the All-Navy title, with sportswriter Grantland Rice and actress Terry Moore among the spectators. But it took a team with a 12-0 record carrying a 24-game winning streak to corral San Diego, now known as the Marine Corps Recruit Depot.

As Leatherneck put it, "Both teams qualified to battle it out on the top rung of the football ladder by whipping everything within Navy circles, as well as Marine, on their respective coasts."

Quinlan, who rushed for 105 yards in 21 carries and completed 3 of 5 passes for 74 yards against a bigger Quantico team, was named the game's most valuable player.

In one year Trometter had turned San Diego from an unknown quantity into a service power.

He had Quinlan back, himself and Jones as player-coaches, plus 13 from his 1947 team as more than 150 turned out in the summer.

And this time around Trometter had a defense, one so good opponents were shut out in the first five games and scored but four TDs during the regular season.

The team was heavier, for one thing. At the tackles, Jim Delaney was 210, Bob Havard 205 and Leroy Meisner 200; at the guards, Jones 220, and Donald Norvell and Hans Jacobsen both 200; at center, Don Gray, 205, and in the backfield Don "Skip" White, who scored four TDs, 200.

Only one team came within five points of the Marines during the regular season as they downed the San Diego Bulldogs, 26-0; San Diego Naval Training Center, 13-0; Los Angeles Marine Reserves, 28-0; SubForce, 44-0; North Island Naval Air Station, 14-0; PhibPac (Coronado), 19-14; DesPac, 19-9 (before 18,000); Terminal Island, 19-7, and the Hawaii All-Stars, 39-0, before 15,000 in the All-Navy playoffs.

A potential 10th victory fell through when a contest against MCAS El Toro was dropped because of a conflict with the playoffs.

At least three players would go on to the college ranks: center Vern Sampson at USC from 1953-55, Quinlan at San Diego State in 1951 and White at Fresno State in 1949 and 1951-52. All three were recalled for the Korean War.

Quinlan scored 17 TDs for 102 points in 1948, and Leatherneck selected him, Moore and guard Bill Butler on the All-Marine team, and guard John Gregerson on the second team.

"Aptly nicknamed by his teammates 'Smedley,' " said the Leatherneck, "Butler is a lineman's lineman. Weighing only 185 pounds, he fitted in perfectly with Trometter's double-wing stratagems. ... As co-captain, he was an inspiring leader. San Diego's line functioned best when he was in there."

Other comments by Leatherneck:

■ Gregerson, the "other watch-charm guard ... at 175 pounds was almost as much of a fire-horse in Trometter's line."

■ Quinlan, averaging 7.6 yards a carry, "has now, in Trometter's word, 'the coolness under fire that comes only with experience.' ... He is equally adept at operating from the signal-calling spot or one of the halfback posts. Skeet is a fine passer, punter and placekicker."

■ Moore "is one of those unsung lads, often overlooked by the fans; but not by teammates, observers and students of the game. For he's the lad who springs 'em loose on those long runs. The guy who helps linemen open larger holes, the lad that people don't see cutting down the incoming end or defensive backs.

"At fullback, he's also the lad they call on when they want those 2, 3 or 4 'sure' yards. Moore packed only 180 pounds, not too much for a bulling back, but he knows how to use it."

Four selections. But the team deserved better.

1947

Record: 6-7 San Diego NTC, 39-6 USS Tarawa, 19-21 DesPac, 68-0 San Diego Bulldogs (semi-pro), 53-6 San Diego NTS, 33-19 Terminal Island, 32-7 Ream Field, 40-0 Del Mar Marines, 55-0 SubForce. (7-2)

Coach: CWO Robert "Bull" Trometter (St. Mary's)

Assistants: Don Gibson, Warren "Lockerbox" Jones (Pearl Harbor Navy), Maj. Rex Williams.

Ends: T.W. Anderburg, Bob Cobb, T.A. Edwards, Walt Helling, Jones (p-c), R.M. Kinney, Ed Kirkpatrick, Don McAlexander, M.E. McIlroy, R.L. Mitchell, Hal Robertson, Gene Roche, M. Skaggs, Lonnie White and Jim Wilde.

Tackles: R.J. Adams, Martin Barber, R.J. Botdorf, P.P. Castro, John Deck, Warren Marques, McCullough, Don Meagher, Leroy Meisner, Ed Payton and Fred Williams.

Guards: W.H. Brown, Bill Butler, W..A. Cline, Hiram Crosby, V.D. Durand, Bob Gallagher, Ed Galloway, Marlan Knobbs, H.D. Mitchell and Watson.

Centers: Herb Cline, Jim Copeland (Baylor), Bill Farnum, J.F. Garlington and J.I. Hayes.

Backs: Jack Carter, Walt Coysong, Ivan Duhick, Luther Durham, Gibson (p-c), Goodwin, Greenlee, J.G. Hicks, Walt Kilbourn, McIntyre, Gene Moore (Ada Teachers), Allyn Nelson, Volney "Skeet" Quinlan (TCU; later at San Diego St.), Howie Priest, Mark Rainer (Auburn-Duke) (Coronado NAB), Bob Rann (Michigan St.) (coach Pendleton 1945), Jerry Ruse, Bob Sloan (Texas A&M), Gordon Strand and W.A. Wysong.

1948

Record: 26-0 San Diego Bulldogs (semi-pro), 13-0 San Diego NTC, 28-0 Los Angeles Marine Reserves, 44-0 SubForce, 14-0 North Island NAS, 19-14 PhibPac, 19-9 DesPac, 19-7 Terminal Island, 39-0 Hawaii All-Stars (playoff), 0-21 Quantico (All-Navy title). (9-1). El Toro game canceled.

Coach: CWO Robert "Bull" Trometter (St. Mary's)

Assistants: Jelly Farrell, WO Don Gibson, WO Warren "Lockerbox" Jones (Pearl Harbor Navy)

Ends: Hank Batterton, Bob Bell, Bob Cobb, Jones, Don McAlexander, Clarence Robb, Harold Robertson, Harold Waller and Milt Wiltfang.

Tackles: Jim Delaney, Bob Havard, Winnie Henson, Jesse Hodges (Butler), Leroy Meisner, Joe Moulton and Walt Sims.

Guards: Bill Butler, Bob Gallagher, John Gregerson, Hans Jacobsen (Drake), H.D. Mitchell and Chief Wilde.

Centers: Vern Sampson (later at USC).

Backs: Jack Carter, Paul DiCorpo, Murray Grant (USN), Claude La Bean, Stan Main, Rich McCune, Gib Meyer, Gene Mooore (Ada Teachers), Bill Noble, Howard Priest, Volney "Skeet" Quinlan (Texas Christian; later at San Diego St.), Jerry Ruse, Gordon Strand, Trometter, Don "Skip" White (later at Fresno St.). **Kicker:** Chief Saunkos.

Touchdown Terrors

I t was almost a tossup in 1949 and 1950 whether the football or basketball teams at MCRD San Diego were scoring the most points.

Coach Robert "Bull" Trometter, who revived the San Diego football program in 1947 and 1948, had traveled 45 miles up the road to Camp Pendleton to be an assistant coach with the West Coast Navy champion but had left the cupboard full of players.

Capt. Charles Walker (Wabash), fresh from playing an end position at Quantico in 1947 and being an assistant there in 1948, guided San Diego to:

■ An 8-2 record in 1949, a Marine-record 485 points, an average of 48.5 points a game and the co-championship of the 11th Naval District.

■ An 11-0 record in 1950, a total of 524 points — breaking the mark set the previous season — an average of 47.6 points a game, 100 points against North Island NAS and the 11th Naval District title.

It was one of 10 Marine teams ever to go undefeated and untied.

The 524 points in 1950 stand as the most ever scored by *any* Marine team. Mare Island racked up 454 in 1918, Parris Island 467 in 1926, Quantico 444 in 1947 and Parris Island 505 in 1952.

But San Diego couldn't even lay claim to being the best Marine team of 1950. Quantico, led by All-America quarterback Eddie LeBaron (College of the Pacific) was ranked No. 1 by the Williamson Rating Service. San Diego was No. 2. A scheduled Dec. 9 game between the powers was canceled because of Korean War commitments. (The opening game with PhibPac also had been canceled.)

Don Gibson and Warren "Lockerbox" Jones, who had played for the Marine Corps Base teams in the 1930s and assisted Trometter in the first two postwar seasons, stayed on at San Diego in 1949 to ease the transition. They were joined by Bill Sigler (North Carolina-Michigan), a player-coach at Quantico in 1946 and an assistant in 1947. As an NROTC instructor, he was an assistant at Vanderbilt in 1948.

Oh, yeah, back Volney "Skeet" Quinlan returned. All-Marine his first two seasons, he would be even better in 1949, scoring 27 touchdowns for San Diego in nine games and rushing for 1,055 yards in 107 carries.

Against Treasure Island and the San Diego Naval Training Center he scored five times; against North Island and MCAS El Toro he had four TDs.

"Something new has been added," noted the Leatherneck, "Coach Walker brought his T-formation with him.

"During the spring practice session the San Diegans took to the 'T' like a gang of beagle puppies to their first feeding of ground round steak."

Still, a 19-13 loss to Parris Island in the first Boot Bowl game in South Carolina took some luster off the season. The Islanders' victory was not a fluke as they bottled up San Diego's T-formation attack and led in first downs, 14-5, and total yardage, 322-201.

The other loss was to Pomona College, 34-28, in the last 28 seconds.

But most of the victories were no-contest: 64-0 over Camp Cooke, 79-0 over Treasure Island, 89-0 over TraPac, 32-19 over Terminal Island, 32-7 over the Naval Training Center, 67-0 over North Island, 47-0 over El Toro and 34-20 over Ft. Bliss.

The schedule-makers, however, were unable again to mollify the egos involved and arrange for San Diego and Pendleton — the West Coast's leading Marine teams — to report to the same field on the same day. (They didn't meet until 1951.)

Trometter had headed the program in the right direction, and Walker had 23 things to show for it in his first season: ends Hank Batterton, Bob Bell, Harold Robertson and Milt Wiltfang; tackles Jim Delaney, Bob Havard, Jesse Hodges, Leroy Meisner and Bob White; guards Bill Butler, Bob Gallagher, Hans Jacobsen and Chief Wilde; center Vern Sampson; and backs Paul DiCorpo, Murray Grant, Claude La Bean, Stan Main, Gib Meyer, Bill Noble, Quinlan, Jerry Ruse and Gordon Strand, all from the '48 team.

And Dorsey Tisdale, a back on the 1948 Jacksonville Naval Air Station team, reported to San Diego.

While Quantico siphoned off the top officer candidates, and Pendleton had an excellent mix of former Quantico and San Diego players plus enlisted standouts, San Diego continued to rely on the youngsters leaving boot camp. Sigler apparently was the lone player who had lettered in college. He and Ruse handled quarterback duties.

But Walker proved equal to the challenge posed by the inexperience. And so did Havard, Butler and Quinlan, among others.

Havard, said the Leatherneck which selected him All-Marine, "is a husky 235-pounder who can amble downfield with the halfbacks. He's responsible for many of Quinlan's long runs, throwing key blocks at the right time. He's also good in the line, offensively and defensively."

Butler, a second-team All-Marine selection, "is one of those good little men who can make it tough on a big guy. (He) charges fast, hard and low, then comes up under the other guy. (He) diagnoses plays very well and is a ballhawk," said the Leatherneck.

Gibson, a Japanese POW for four years after his capture in the Philippines, was a calming influence on young Quinlan.

And there wasn't much that hadn't been said about Quinlan on the occasion of his third All-Marine selection. Leatherneck noted simply that the triple-threater "topped his 7.6 yards ball-hauling average of last season and was instrumental ... in helping Pendleton beat DesPac in their big second meeting (in the playoffs)."

(He scored four TDs while he and 15 teammates augmented Pendleton for the All-Navy playoffs. Two came in the 32-14 victory over DesPac before 20,000; the others were in a 68-0 rout of the Hawaii All-Stars; he did not score in a 14-13 loss to Quantico at the Los Angeles Coliseum for the All-Navy title. Overall, he averaged 9.2 yards a carry for the season and scored 31 times.)

Pendleton and San Diego had tied for the West Coast Navy Conference title, but Pendleton got the playoff berth on a controversial 4-1 vote of member bases.

The 1950 season:

There was no way opponents were going to stop this depot team because of:

■ The old hands from former years: Bell, tackles Delaney, Floyd McLellan, Meisner (for a fourth season) and Ray Tillman; guards Butler (for a fourth season), Dick Engelson, Hodges (for a fourth season) and Jacobsen, who would be the San Diego coach in 1960; centers Bob Collins and Sampson; and backs Ron Burroughs, Marinelli (who had changed his name from DiCorpo), Meyer and Tisdale, who would carry 89 times for 472 yards and score eight TDs.

■ The return of Quinlan for a fourth All-Marine season. He had been released from active duty and enrolled at Corpus Christi University but was recalled after the Korean War broke out.

Incredibly, he would set more records, scoring 138 points on 23 TDs, and gaining 1,080 yards on 104 carries, catching 10 passes for 303 yards, returning eight interceptions for 205 yards, and handling 29 punts for 594 yards and 11 kickoffs for 260 yards, for a total of 2,442 yards. In addition, he completed 3 of 8 passes for 53 yards.

Quinlan "is also a heads-up defensive man," Leatherneck said, "and writers on the West Coast claim he is one of the best they have seen in years. Bill Schuette, coach of San Diego State, claims it was his defensive work rather than offense that beat them."

It "would be difficult as well as foolhardy to even think of leaving Quinlan off an all-star selection," the Leatherneck said.

■ The addition of center Bill Jesse (Navy), All-Marine in 1947, 1948 and 1949, and quarterback Rudy Flores (Southwestern of Texas), quarterback at Quantico those seasons, during which the Marines compiled a 36-4 record.

"For three years running, Jesse was the No. 1 center in Marine football while at Quantico," said the Leatherneck, "and now, while at San Diego, like wine, he seems to improve with age. While only 190 pounds, he ranks with the best at backing up the line and on pass defense. Jesse is a lineman's lineman and one of the most popular service players ever seen on the West Coast or East Coast, for that matter."

Flores would complete 30 of 80 passes for 619 yards and 10 TDs.

■ The windfall of young players turning up. "The threat of the draft brought many potential college players into the Marine Corps as recruits," said the Leatherneck, "and many recent college graduates in a reserve status were called to active duty."

The reservists, volunteers and enlisted personnel with obligated time called up that summer and fall included tackle Walt Ashcraft (USC), who returned to the Trojans in 1952 and was a 26th-round draft choice of the Washington Redskins in 1953; Sampson, who rejoined San Diego late in the season and played for USC from 1953-55; back Paul Chess, who would return to Pitt and letter in 1951-52; quarterback McKinley Harding (Houston); back Mike Michon, who would letter at Houston in 1956-57; back Don White, who would go back to Fresno State for the 1951-52 seasons, and 17-year-old Morton Moriarity, an end who played for Texas in the mid-'50s and was drafted in the 15th round by the Philadelphia Eagles in 1957.

147

■ The addition of tackle Carl Kilsgaard (Idaho), who had played in the East-West Game, the 1950 College All-Star Game and for the Chicago Cardinals in September when he received his orders. An All-Marine selection, he "is the 'old pro' type, and rightly so," said the Leatherneck. "After three years of wartime service, he returned to his native Idaho and played four years of varsity ball." The Cardinals had made him a fifth-round pick.

■ The play of All-Marine end Dan Brogee. Said Leatherneck: "While a good pass receiver, he is better known among the opposition as a hard offensive blocker and great defensive man."

Butler and Delaney were second-team All-Marine selections.

■ Some size, for a change. Tillman was 250, Ashcraft and tackle Gene DeMartini (University of San Francisco) 245, Delaney and Kilsgaard 235, tackle Sherwood Fleming and center Alva Thompson 234, fullback John Hatley 225, tackle Tom Snowden 222, and tackle Stuart Barbour and fullback Harvey Solon 220.

Quinlan wasn't the only offensive threat. Halfback John "Rocky" Alcock gained 422 yards in 64 carries and scored six times. Eighteen-year-old end Don Brand also scored 36 points, catching 10 passes for 230 yards. Kicker Ted Hopper contributed 41 points.

The season was not without its moments:

■ A 43-0 victory over Ft. Bliss was called with 11 minutes to play because of a rainstorm.

■ North Island, in the 100-0 loss, ran for but 17 yards and passed for 6.

■ The rivalry against San Diego State resumed after a 10-year lapse, with the Marines winning, 28-14.

■ San Diego avenged its 1949 loss to Parris Island with a 57-18 victory in the second Boot Bowl and took possession of the Boondocker trophy.

■ The Marines also avenged their other loss in 1949 with a 28-7 victory over Pomona, and beat a third college team, Occidental, 35-20.

■ The team was so deep that Harding, the back-up to Flores, was chosen on the San Diego Evening Tribune's second All-West Coast team. San Diego placed six each on the first and second teams.

■

Two men, in particular, Quinlan and end Jimmie Howard, would be heard from after their MCRD careers.

Quinlan was released from active duty in August 1951 and played for San Diego State that fall before leaving the squad late in the season because of what were termed financial difficulties. He was drafted in the fourth round by the Los Angeles Rams in 1952 and played five seasons in the National Football League:

■ **1952:** He rushed 52 times for the Rams for 224 yards and a TD, caught 14 passes for 265 yards and two TDs, was 0 for 4 as a passer, returned 14 punts for 167 yards and ran back 17 kickoffs for 440 yards.

■ **1953:** In his best pro season, he carried 97 times for 705 yards and four TDs, caught 17 passes for 260 yards and two TDs, completed 2 of 4 passes for 60 yards and returned two kickoffs for 38 yards.

148

■ **1954:** He carried 82 times for 490 yards and four TDs, caught 18 passes for 324 yards and two TDs, completed 1 of 2 passes for 34 yards, returned a punt for 4 yards and ran back four kickoffs for 69 yards.

■ **1955:** The playing time decreased as he carried 15 times for 70 yards, caught 19 passes for 245 yards and returned a punt 55 yards for a TD.

■ **1956:** Now with the Cleveland Browns, he closed out his pro career with 12 carries for 25 yards, caught seven passes for 87 yards, returned 14 punts for 50 yards and ran back 12 kickoffs for 256 yards.

Said a former opponent: "At 5-11 and 170 pounds, you can't carry the ball on every other down in the NFL. If he had been used as a specialist, he could have played five more years — and maybe more."

Howard, a 21-year-old, 6-3, 207-pounder from Burlington, Iowa, would be awarded the Silver Star in Korea and the Medal of Honor for heroism in Vietnam.

1949

Record: 64-0 Camp Cooke, 79-0 Treasure Island, 28-34 Pomona College, 89-0 TraPac, 32-19 Terminal Island, 32-7 San Diego NTC, 67-0 North Island NAS, 13-19 Parris Island (Boot Bowl), 47-0 El Toro, 34-20 Ft. Bliss. (8-2)

Coach: Capt. Charles Walker (Wabash) (Quantico 1947, assistant 1948)

Assistants: Don Gibson (now a civilian), Warren "Lockerbox" Jones (Pearl Harbor Navy), Lt. Bill Sigler (North Carolina-Michigan) (Quantico 1946, assistant 1947)

Ends: Hank Batterton, Bob Bell, Wiley Haynes, Clarence Robb, Harold Robertson and Milt Wilfang.

Tackles: Jim Delaney, Bob Havard, George Hanson, Jesse Hodges (Butler), Lloyd McLellan, Leroy Meisner, Claude Tillman and Bob White.

Guards: Bill Butler, Dick Engleson, Bob Gallagher, Hans Jacobsen (Drake), Angus Norvell, Jack Roznos, Bob Trail and Chief Wilde.

Centers: John Pennington, Vern Sampson (later at USC)

Backs: Ron Burroughs, Bob Collins, Paul DiCorpo, Murray Grant (USN), Claude La Bean, Stan Main, John Melvin, Gib Meyer, Bill Noble, Johnny O'Brien, Billy Olson (Howard Payne-Corpus Christi Univ.), Volney "Skeet" Quinlan (Texas Christian; later at San Diego St.), Jerry Ruse, Sigler, Lou Smolik, Gordon Strand and Dorsey Tisdale (New Mexico) (Jacksonville NAS). **Kicker:** Billy Megrue.

1950

Record: 43-0 Ft. Bliss, 75-0 Terminal Island, 100-0 North Island NAS, 28-14 San Diego St., 28-7 Pomona College, 29-0 SubPac, 26-13 San Diego NTC, 35-20 Occidental, 57-18 Parris Island (Boot Bowl), 41-7 El Toro MCAS, 62-7 AirPac. (11-0)

Coach: Capt. Charles Walker (Wabash) (Quantico 1947, assistant 1948)

Assistants: Capt. Pat Boyle (Wisconsin-Michigan) (Quantico 1947, assistant 1948-49), Capt. Charles Greene, Capt. Bill Sigler (North Carolina-Michigan) (Quantico 1946, assistant 1947)..

Ends: Bob Bell, Don Brand, Dan Brogee, Ray Creighton, Jimmie Howard (Medal of Honor), Jim Loflin (LSU-Southwestern Louisiana) (Fleet Marines 1945), Gene Metz, Morton Moriarity (later at Texas) and Horace Murdock.

Tackles: Walt Ashcraft (USC), Stu Barbour, Jim Delaney, Carl Kilsgaard (Idaho), Gene DeMartini (Univ. of San Francisco), Floyd McLellan, Leroy Meisner, George Salazar (Pacific), Fleming Sherwood, Tom Snowden, Ray Tillman and Marv Wilkerson.

Guards: Bill Butler, Dick Engelson, Johnny Van Ert, Dale Hall, Jesse Hodges (Butler), Ted Hopper, Hans Jacobsen (Drake), Bill LaFleur (Dayton-Penn State) (Camp Lejeune 1944), Marv Merritt and Bill Schultz.

Centers: Bob Collins, Bill Jesse (Montana-Navy) (Quantico 1947-49), Al Marquette, Vern Sampson (later at USC) and Alva Thompson.

Backs: John Alcock, Ron Burroughs, Paul Chess (Pitt), Dick Denney, Dan Dougherty, Rudy Flores (Southwestern of Texas) (Quantico 1947-49), Howard Garlinger, McKinley Harding (Houston), John Hatley, Bill Justice (Rollins) (assistant Quantico 1950), Cheney Close (William Jewell), Paul Marinelli, Gib Meyer, Mike Michon (Rice; later at Houston), Mike O'Mattick (Pitt), Volney "Skeet" Quinlan (Texas Christian; later at San Diego St.), Harvey Solon (South Dakota-Minnesota), Rube Swanson (St. Cloud), Dorsey Tisdale (New Mexico) (Jacksonville NAS 1948), Don "Skip" White (Fresno St.) and Larry Workman. **Also:** Carl Hannah.

One, And Only, Skeet

There was only one Volney "Skeet" Quinlan.

A teen-ager from Grand Prairie, Texas, the 6-foot, 170-pounder burst onto the Marine scene in 1947, scoring 18 TDs and 23 extra points for 131 points and sparking San Diego's first post-war entry to a 7-2 record. And he missed the opener because of an injury.

In 1948, Quinlan scored 17 TD's for 102 points as the Recruit Depot went 9-1, its loss to Quantico, 21-0, for the All-Navy title.

In 1949, Quinlan scored a Marine-record 27 TD's for 162 points and rushed 107 times for 1,055 yards as the depot won eight and lost two. (He also scored four TD's while augmenting Camp Pendleton in the All-Navy playoffs.) He was promoted to sergeant just after the season ended.

His enlistment up, Quinlan left the Corps after the '49 season and enrolled at Corpus Christi University. But he, and many others, were recalled in the summer of 1950 after the outbreak of the Korean War. He scored 23 TD's for 138 points and rushed 104 times for 1,080 yards that season as San Diego won all 11 games.

In his four seasons, Quinlan, who also was a passer and receiver of note, led the depot to a 35-5 record as he scored 85 TD's, 23 extra points and 533 points.

But some say he was just as good a defender.

Leatherneck, in selecting him on its All-Marine team for the fourth time in 1950, said Quinlan was a "heads-up defensive man, and writers on the West Coast claim he is one of the best they have seen in years."

Quinlan was released again in 1951 and played that fall for San Diego State. The Aztecs, behind future Marines Jim Erkenbeck and Art Preston, had a 10-0-1 record. Quinlan, joining an established team, was not the star although he led the team in kickoff and punt returns.

Still, he was a No. 4 draft choice of the Rams in 1952 and played with the Rams from 1952-56, closing out with the Cleveland Browns in 1956.

His pro numbers were dazzling, too: He rushed 258 times for 1,514 yards (a 5.9-yard average) and nine TD's; he caught 75 passes for 1,181 yards (a 15.7 average) and six TD's; he handled 30 punts for 276 yards (a 9.2 average) and a TD; and returned 35 kickoffs for 803 yards (a 22.9 average).

■

Scoring-wise, the closest thing to Quinlan based on three or more seasons was back Joe Bartos (Navy), who scored 90 points for Quantico's All-Navy champion in 1947, 86 points for Quantico's All-Navy champion in 1948 and 80 for Camp Pendleton's All-Navy runner-up in 1949.

Charles Harris (Georgia) had one standout season, scoring 120 points for Pendleton in 1952.

Records are incomplete as to whether Dick Hanley of Mare Island's famed and high-scoring 1918 team might have set a single-season record.

A Breathing Spell

There were San Diego teams that had lost as many games, or more, and others that would, but the 1951 season for all its accomplishments would be remembered for losing to Parris Island — twice.

Like Quantico, which posted a 5-6 record with an all-star cast, MCRD San Diego fell short of expectations despite a 6-5 record and a berth in the All-Marine final.

"MCRD is well set for another 'winning' season," said a season preview.

True, the scheduled had been upgraded, to wit:

■ A 28-13 loss to a Arizona State (6-3-1), a school trying to shed the image of Tempe Teachers and in the process making a national name for itself. With the defeat went San Diego's 13-game winning streak.

■ A 34-18 loss to San Diego State (10-0-1), another up-and-coming school that scored 385 points that season. Volney "Skeet" Quinlan, an All-Marine back at MCRD in 1947, 1948, 1949 and 1950, played for the Aztecs, as did Art Preston, the school's career scoring leader who would play for MCRD in 1953.

■ A 27-14 loss before 22,000 to the San Diego Naval Training Center (8-3), the All-Navy champion featuring end Bucky Curtis (Vanderbilt).

And Parris Island, the East Coast Marine champion, was hardly a soft touch. J.T. Hill's All-Marine champion, led by quarterback Sam Vacanti (Iowa-Purdue-Nebraska), posted a 9-2 record and scored 399 points.

The Islanders won the Boot Bowl game, 16-9, at Savannah, Ga., and the title game, 30-13, at Parris Island to hand San Diego its third straight loss in the series in the Southeast. They also had won the initial Boot Bowl, 19-13, at Savannah in 1949.

But the Depot had talent, too. Coach Mark Rainer (Auburn-Duke), a Bronze Star holder who was a back on the 1947 MCB team and for West Coast Navy champion Camp Pendleton in 1949, could call on:

■ Thirty players from the 11-0 San Diego team of 1950. Guard Bill Butler played part of a fifth season before his discharge. End Bob Bell, guards Jesse Hodges and Hans Jacobsen, center Vern Sampson and backs Paul Marinelli and Gib Meyer were playing their fourth seasons at "old MCRD U.".

■ Six who had been drafted, or would be, by National Football League teams, another who would play in the NFL and one who would go to the Canadian Football League.

■ Five others from major colleges: ends Harry Kahuanui (University of Hawaii) and Bob Scott (Stanford), tackle Rudy Trbovich (Purdue), guard Frank Epstein (Notre Dame) and back Sanford Ceckler (SMU).

Of course, there *was* a war going on and Rainer and Coach Bill Justice of Quantico had much in common to commiserate about. Transfers, releases and uncertainty related to Korea caused major distractions.

Rainer, indeed, was to have been the backfield coach, but the head coach-designate, Pat Boyle (Wisconsin-Michigan), was transferred. Boyle was an All-Marine guard at Quantico in 1947, a Quantico assistant in 1948-49 and a San Diego assistant in 1950.

Still, MCRD was ranked No. 6 among service teams late in the season by the Williamson Rating service, and No. 11 by Touchdown Tips. It was the West Coast Marine champion and runner-up for the 11th Naval District title.

And Depot players took turns with those from Pendleton and NTC to play 20 minutes each against the Los Angeles Rams before 18,000 in a preseason benefit game. (MCRD was outscored, 13-0.)

Despite the loss of Quinlan in August, the Depot rolled up 363 points and the six victories came easily: 53-0 over MCAS El Toro, 101-0 over Moffett Field (as 12 players scored TDs), 84-7 over Pomona-Claremont College (as 12 again had TDs), 20-9 over North Island Naval Air Station (before 20,000 at the Rose Bowl), 12-0 over Camp Pendleton (16,000 watched the long-awaited first meeting) and 26-6 over PhibPac (Coronado).

The 101 points against Moffet Field is believed to be a Marine record, surpassing the 100 against the North Island NAS in 1950.

Quarterback Tom Kingsford (Montana) had been the nation's 15th-ranked college passer in 1950 when he completed 84 of 184 for 1,362 yards and 10 TDs. (No. 3, Bill Weeks of Iowa State, and No. 11, Dick Flowers of Northwestern, shared 1951 signal-calling duties at Quantico.)

And the Depot added Dick Ellis (San Francisco State) for its own solid 1-2 punch at quarterback. Even Ellis' back-up, Milt Price, threw for five TDs.

Among the returnees was 6-1, 190-pound center Bill Jesse (Navy), All-Marine at Quantico in 1947, 1948 and 1949 and at San Diego in 1950. He would be selected a record fifth time in 1951.

Also back were 6-2, 198-pound end Milt Moriarity and 5-11, 185-pound back Mike Michon, who would be second-team All-Marine selections in 1951.

The Devildogs could muster plenty of size on offense and defense. Tackle Tom Loman at 285 pounds was one of the heaviest players ever to represent the Marine Corps. Tackles R.T. Durham and Claude Tillman were 250; tackle Gene DeMartini (University of San Francisco) 245; tackle Walt Ashcraft (USC) 240; tackle Marv Beguhl (Idaho), tackle Pat Flanagan (Marquette) and center Alva Thompson 235; tackle Volney Peters (USC) and Trbovich 225; and tackle Stu Barbour, back John Hatley, end Harold Kilman (Texas Christian) and guard Jim Little 220. Fourteen others were at least 200.

Ashcraft was a 26th-round draft choice of the Washington Redskins in 1953, Flanagan a 14th-round pick of the New York Giants in 1951, Kilman a 27th-round pick of the Rams in 1950, Kingsford a 24th-round pick of the San Francisco 49ers in 1951, Moriarity a 15th-round pick of the Philadelphia Eagles in 1957 and Peters a 13th-round pick of the Chicago Cardinals in 1951.

Peters, surprisingly not an All-Marine selection although he was named the outstanding lineman in the naval district, developed into a standout pro lineman, joining the Cardinals for the 1952 and 1953 seasons, and playing for the Redskins from 1954-57, the Eagles in 1958, the new AFL Los Angeles Chargers in 1960 and the Oakland Raiders in 1961.

Beguhl played for CFL's Saskatchewan in 1954.

Kingsford would coach the Southern Utah teams from 1967-77.

New players also made a difference:

■ Guard Ed Brown (6-2, 210), an All-Marine selection. His aggressiveness, said Leatherneck, "won him a starting berth on San Diego's team and a well-deserved berth on the All-Marine squad. Limited to high school experience, big Ed played his first year at the guard spot for a service club like a seasoned veteran, turning in a durable performance in a tough league."

■ Kahuanui (6-4, 215) played in the 1949 East-West Game and was a 1951 All-Marine selection. "Better known to California fans as 'Murphy,' Honolulu's Kahuanui ... was a giant in the 'Diego line," said Leatherneck, "shining consistently on defense and offense. Other ends had better receords for pass receiving but Kahuanui's spirited team play rated him invaluable to San Diego's mighty attack."

At the end of the season, Leatherneck noted, Jesse "hung up his '41' and departed ... for the Korean hinterlands. Jesse ... this year turned in another stellar performance, particularly on defense, to get the nod" as the only player selected All-Marine five times.

Peters, Durham and Marinelli received All-Marine honorable mention.

Unfortunately, guard Harold Bradley (Iowa) wasn't able to join the scarlet and gold until late in the season. Earlier, he might have made a difference. The 6-2, 230-pound lineman would play for the Cleveland Browns from 1954-57 and the Eagles in 1958.

The five losses equaled the totals posted by the 1924, 1930, 1938 and 1956 San Diego teams. The 1932 team lost six times, the 1955 squad seven times.

1951

Record: 13-28 Arizona St., 53-0 MCAS El Toro, 101-0 Moffet Field, 18-34 San Diego St., 84-7 Pomona-Claremont, 20-9 North Island NAS, 12-0 Camp Pendleton, 9-16 Parris Island (Boot Bowl), 26-6 PhibPac, 14-27 San Diego NTC, 13-30 Parris Island (All-Marine title). (6-5)

Coach: Capt. Mark Rainer (Auburn-Duke) (Camp Pendleton 1949)

Assistants: Rudy Flores (Southwestern of Texas) (Quantico 1947-49), Robert "Bull" Trometter (St. Mary's) (asst. Pendleton 1949), Capt. R.C. Weber (Albright)

Ends: Bob Bell, Bill Bortz, Dan Brogee, Tom Evans, Harry Kahuanui (Univ. of Hawaii), John Kapotan, Hal Kilman (TCU), Al Marquette, Marv Merritt, Mort Moriarity (later of Texas), Bob Scott (Stanford) (Quantico 1951) and Terry Sweet.

Tackles: Walt Ashcraft (USC), Stu Barbour, E.B. Carney (Bradley) (Pendleton 1949), Gene DeMartini (Univ. of San Francisco), Bob Durham, Pat Flanagan (Marquette), Tom Loman, Volney Peters (USC), Don Thompson, Claude Tillman and Rudy Trbovich (Purdue).

Guards: Harold Bradley (Iowa), Ed Brown, Bill Butler, Frank Epstein (Notre Dame), Jesse Hodges (Butler), Ted Hopper, Hans Jacobsen (Drake), Jim Little, Bill LaFleur (Dayton-Penn State) (Camp Lejeune 1944), Bob Myers and Tom Self.

Centers: Marv Beguhl (Idaho), Bob Collins, Bill Jesse (Montana-Navy) (Quantico 1947-49), Fred Lewis (Colorado), Vern Sampson (later at USC) and Alva Thompson.

Backs: Clayton Bieck (Pepperdine), Jack Brannen (Long Beach CC), Sanford Cleckler (SMU), Charles Davis (Cal), Dick Denney, Dan Dougherty, Dick Ellis (San Francisco St.), Flores, Howard Garlinger, Phil Haas (Lawrence), McKinley Harding (Houston), John Hatley, C.S. Johnson, Milt Kadlec, Tom Kingsford (Montana), Cheney Close (William Jewell), Paul Marinelli, Gib Meyer, Mike Michon (Rice; later at Houston), Milt Price, Tim Porter, Bob Richardson, Dorsey Tisdale (New Mexico) (Jacksonville NAS 1948) and Larry Workman.

One Of The Best

Take a wand. Assemble — at their prime — the two best Marine teams ever fielded and have them play for the Championship of the 20th century.

One team would have to be the famed El Toro Flying Marines of 1945, featuring Wee Willie Wilkin, Bob Dove and Vern Gagne in the line, Paul Governali at quarterback and Crazylegs Hirsch at halfback.

The other could be the Quantico team of 1948 or 1959.

Or the San Diego team of 1940 or 1959.

Poll 10 pro scouts, and they'd probably vote, 11-0, to go with the 1952 All-Marine champion team at MCRD San Diego. For that *one* game, anyway.

This was a team generally overlooked when talking about the great ones, but it dripped with pro talent — a No. 1 draft pick and a No. 2 — plus size, speed, linebackers, and, most importantly a T-formation quarterback.

Marine teams were notorious through the '40s and '50s for having more talent but often sticking to the single wing and double wing while opponents ran over and around them with their 'T' attacks. Even El Toro had aroused controversy in 1945 for having a double-wing unit as well as a T-unit.

The Marine teams simply did not go with the flow.

But the Depot in 1952 had quarterback Ed Brown, fresh from the University of San Francisco's 9-0 team of 1951 and the East-West Game. Brown, of course, became much more widely known in his 12 National Football League seasons.

But it was difficult for San Diego to gain much respect that season. San Diego, the All-Marine champion, placed but four players on Leatherneck's All-Marine selections. Parris Island, the runner-up, had 11 honored! And Camp Lejeune had five!

Curiously, Maj. Bruce Clarke, the Depot coach, had not coached a Marine team previously and would not in the future.

But, as they say, 7-1 ain't bad.

The Leathernecks opened with a 66-0 trouncing of MCAS El Toro, a 45-13 whipping of North Island Naval Air Station and a 39-20 drubbing of PhibPac and quarterback Billy Wade (Vanderbilt and 13 seasons in the NFL). Wade and Brown would be Chicago Bears teammates in 1961.

Then came a rugged five-game stretch.

The Depot gained a measure of revenge by defeating Parris Island, 21-12, in a Boot Bowl game televised by CBS. The Islanders had won both the Boot Bowl and All-Marine title games in 1951.

San Diego rolled over Camp Pendleton, 42-33, in a wild one.

The Leathernecks blasted San Diego State, 51-21, also avenging a 1951 loss.

They defeated a good Brooke Army Medical Center team from Texas, 21-15.

Then came one of the great games ever played in San Diego, as the Naval Training Center — ranked No. 2 by Williamson Rating Service — outlasted the Devildogs, 27-21, in a contest that could have gone either way. A 75-yard pass play from back Verl Lillywhite (USC and four seasons with the San Francisco 49ers) to end Bucky Curtis (Vanderbilt) was a key.

But give credit where it's due. NTC (11-3) scored 578 points, more than any Marine team in history. The losses were to the Los Angeles Rams, 10-0; USC, 20-6; and No. 1-ranked Bolling Field, 35-14, in the first Poinsettia Bowl for the All-Service title. The training center, loaded with college and pro standouts, closed with an 81-20 rout of the 101st Airborne in the Salad Bowl.

Clarke had played at Fresno State in 1939-40, then competed at San Jose State in 1946-47 after Marine service in WWII. Whatever his formula, whatever his coaching philosophy, whatever his methods, they worked.

There was a good base to build upon. Back from the bittersweet 1951 season were ends Bob Bell (for a fifth year), Tom Evans, Marv Merritt and Mort Moriarity; tackles Marv Beguhl (Idaho), Harold Bradley (Iowa) and Rudy Trbovich (Purdue), guards Ed Brown and Frank Epstein (Notre Dame); and backs Sanford Cleckler (SMU), Dick Ellis (San Francisco State), McKinley Harding (Houston), Tom Kingsford (Montana) and Mike Michon.

Beguhl would play for Saskatchewan (Canada) in 1954, and Bradley for the Cleveland Browns from 1954-57 and the Philadelphia Eagles in 1958. Kingsford was a 24th-round draft choice of the 49ers in 1951, and would coach 11 seasons at Southern Utah. Moriarity would be a 15th-round pick of the Eagles in 1957.

But it was the newcomers who turned a potentially good team into a great one:

■ Back-linebacker Rob Goode (Texas A&M), a 6-4, 220-pound No. 1 draft choice who had played in the 1946 and 1949 East-West Games and the 1949 College All-Star Game. He had been the Washington Redskins' leading rusher in the 1949, 1950 and 1951 seasons. After a season at MCAS El Toro, he returned to the Redskins for the 1954-55 seasons and finished up with the Eagles in '55. Three decades later, he still was the sixth leading rusher in Redskins' history with 2,247 yards in 519 carries, and ranked sixth for a single season with 951 yards in 1951.

■ Tackle Randy "Tex" Lawrence, a mainstay in 1949 and 1950 at Quantico, where he was All-Marine both seasons, and a Bronze Star winner in Korea.

■ Center-linebacker Bob Griffin (Arkansas), a 6-3, 240-pound No. 2 pick of the Rams in 1951 who was chosen for the '51 College All-Star Game. After a season at Pendleton, he played for the Rams from 1954-57, the Detroit Lions in 1958, Calgary of the Canadian Football League in 1959, and the St. Louis Cardinals and Denver Broncos in 1961. Later, he was an assistant with Calgary, the Broncos and the Atlanta Falcons and a scout for the Dallas Cowboys.

■ Ends Sam Duca (Arizona State), Dick McKee (Missouri) and Harold Turner (Tennessee State), who played for the Lions in 1954.

■ Tackle J.T. "Tex" Seaholm (Texas). After two seasons at MCAS Cherry Point, he was drafted in the 13th round by the Bears in 1954, lettered at Texas in 1956-57, and played at Calgary in 1958. And guard Chuck Cusimano (LSU), and center John Bergamini (St. Mary's).

■ Backs Tom Carodine (Boys Town and Nebraska), Ron Hoenisch (Wisconsin) and Mike Ryan (Minnesota).

But it was the linebackers and quarterback Ed Brown — there also was lineman Ed Brown, All-Marine in 1951 — who made the difference. Brown's 1952 performance, and a season at Pendleton in 1953, were but a preview of what was to come.

Brown, a No. 6 Chicago draft pick in 1952, quarterbacked the Bears from 1954-61 and to a Western Conference title in 1956, the Pittsburgh Steelers from 1962-65 and wound up as an insurance policy for the Baltimore Colts' playoff chances in '65.

As a passer, he completed 949 of 1,987 attempts for 15,600 yards and 102 TDs in his NFL career.

As a runner, the 6-2, 209-pound Brown gained 920 yards in 265 carries and scored 14 times

As a kicker, he averaged 40.3 yards on 493 punts.

Carodine, an All-Marine selection, rushed for more than 1,000 yards and scored 12 TDs — four against San Diego State — in the eight-game schedule. He also returned the opening kickoff 93 yards for a score against Parris Island. Said Leatherneck: "At 6-feet, 185 pounds, (he) is a speedy, hard-running, aggressive player. Once past the line of scrimmage he was hard to bring down." Carodine had a tryout with the Browns in 1954.

The 6-1, 195-pound Lawrence, San Diego's other All-Marine selection on offense, "is one of the better blockers in the business," said Leatherneck.

Goode and Griffin, All-Marine selections on defense, "are given a large part of the credit for the Depot's fine 7-1 record," said the Leatherneck.

As well they should.

1952

Record: 66-0 MCAS El Toro, 45-13 North Island NAS, 39-20 PhibPac, 21-12 Parris Island (Boot Bowl), 51-21 San Diego St., 21-15 Brooke Army Medical Center, 21-27 San Diego NTC. (7-1)

Coach: Maj. Bruce Clarke (Fresno St.-San Jose St.)

Assistants: Lt. Art Filson (San Diego St.) (Quantico 1951), Maj. Maurice Flynn (Rhode Island), Capt. Mark Rainer (Auburn-Duke) (Camp Pendleton 1949), Lt. Dick Rockenback (Illinois St.), Capt. Joe Stribling (Hardin-Simmons) and Bull Trometter (St. Mary's) (assistant Pendleton 1949)

Ends: Bob Bell, Sam Duca (Arizona St.), Tom Evans, Dick "Rusty" McKee (Hutchinson JC-Missouri), Marv Merritt, Mort Moriarity (later at Texas), Don Taylor and Harold Turner (Tennessee St.)

Tackles: Marv Beguhl (Idaho), Harold Bradley (Iowa), Bill Lammes (West Texas), Randy "Tex" Lawrence (Navy) (Quantico 1949-50), J.T. "Tex" Seaholm (Texas) and Rudy Trbovich (Purdue)

Guards: Ed Brown, Bob Conklin, Chuck Cusimano (LSU), Frank Epstein (Notre Dame), Bob Griffin (Arkansas) and George Lockett

Centers: John Bergamini (St. Mary's) and Earl Riley (St. Ambrose)

Backs: Ed Brown (Univ. of San Francisco), Arnold Burwitz (Arizona), Camillo Capuzzi (Cincinnati), Bob Carew (Hamline), Tom Carodine (Loyola of LA-Nebraska), Sanford Ceckler (SMU), Dick Ellis (San Francisco St.), Rob Goode (Texas A&M), McKinley Harding (Houston), Ron Hoenisch (Wisconsin), Herb Hunter (Tennessee St.), Earl Jackson, Tom Kingsford (Montana), Mike Michon (Rice; later at Houston), Mike Ryan (Minnesota) and Mike Serna (Compton JC-Cal Poly)

Winning Continues

After 7-2, 9-1, 8-2, 11-0, 6-5 and 7-1 records, what does a team do for an encore at San Diego?

Well, the 1953 team, despite heavy losses from the '52 season, maintained the winning record with four victories, three losses and two ties by, some said, using mirrors.

But there would be no postseason playoff berth, the honor going to Camp Pendleton despite a 13-13 tie with the Devildogs. Pendleton had a 4-1-1 record in the 11th Naval District, San Diego a 2-1-2 mark.

Such '52 players as ends Bob Bell and Harold Hunter, tackle Harold Bradley (for a game), guards Bob Conklin and Earl Riley, linebacker Bob Griffin, quarterback Ed Brown (a 1953 second-team All-Marine selection) and backs Tom Carodine, Dick Ellis, Herb Hunter and Mike Ryan played for West Coast Marine champion Pendleton this time around. Back-linebacker Rob Goode was an All-Marine selection at MCAS El Toro, tackles Sam Duca (a 1953 All-Marine selection) and J.T. Seaholm keyed Cherry Point's surprising season, and guard Chuck Cusimano played for All-Marine champion Quantico.

Coaching the Devildogs was Capt. Art Ramage, who had played for Coffeyville JC and Tulsa before World War II and returned to Tulsa for the 1946 season. Like many, he was called back for the Korean War and was an assistant with Parris Island's high-scoring teams of 1951-52.

The schedule-makers didn't do Ramage any favors:

■ The opener was a 33-0 loss to Ft. Ord, the All-Service champion and perhaps the strongest military team ever assembled. Led by back Ollie Matson (University of San Francisco) and quarterback Don Heinrich (Washington), the Warriors won all 13 games and ran up 524 points in the process. They lost exhibition games to the Los Angeles Rams and San Francisco 49ers.

■ The third game was a 20-7 loss to Ft. Bliss (4-2-1), which featured tackle Marion Campbell (Georgia), later a pro player and coach.

■ The final game was a 28-0 loss to the San Diego Naval Training Center (7-2), the third loss in a row to the sailors, who again featured end Bucky Curtis (Vanderbilt). The victory was NTC's 19th straight over 11th Naval District opposition. The NTC coach was former Marine Dick Evans (Iowa, Green Bay Packers, Chicago Cardinals, El Toro Marines and National Basketball League).

On paper the 1953 Depot team couldn't carry the '52 team's helmet liner. But in between those three defeats came victories over the USC Spartans, MCAS El Toro, PhibPac and San Diego State, all by 13 points or fewer, and a tie against North Island NAS as well as Pendleton.

Ramage had but seven returning players: end Don Taylor, tackle Bill Lammes, guard Frank Epstein (Notre Dame), center John Bergamini (St. Mary's), and backs Arnold Burwitz, Camillo Capuzzi and Ron Hoenisch (Wisconsin). He had to be a miracle-worker because the flow of college material slowed down.

Tackles Dewey Wade (Kansas State) and Phil Muscarello (Mississippi Southern), guard Jack Lordo (Missouri) and backs Jim Marinos (California) and Art Preston (San Diego State) were the only three-year Division I standouts reporting. Otherwise, the new players largely had played freshman ball or, in a few cases, lettered as sophomores before enlisting just ahead of being drafted.

Preston had played against the Devildogs in 1950 and 1951. Drafted in the 21st round by the Rams in 1952, he held the school's career scoring record of 192 points for more than 35 years but opted instead for a baseball career in the Boston Red Sox organization.

Wade was drafted in the 25th round by the 49ers in 1955 and had a tryout in 1956.

But Ramage was able to mold a winning season from the veterans and youngsters. And there were a few jewels of raw talent here and there:

■ End Joe Young (St. Benedict's-Marquette) would be drafted in the 24th round by the Chicago Bears in 1955. He would play briefly in Canada and for the Denver Broncos of the new American Football League in 1960-61.

■ Back Harold Jackson (Southern), who was drafted in the 29th round by the New York Giants in 1955.

It was a young team, as evidenced by Young playing at Arizona in 1956-57, guard Joe Logan at Mississippi State from 1956-58, and back John Giangiorgi at Bradley in 1956-57.

Shut out twice during the season, the Devildogs almost were shut out in the All-Marine selections, too. Bergamini, on the second team, was the lone San Diego player selected as the East Coast Marine teams, for whatever reason, dominated the picks, again. Muscarello and Burwitz received honorable mention.

The Navy Times looked on more favorably, however. Lordo and Muscarello were second-team All-Sea Service selections. And Preston was a third-team Williamson Service All-American team choice.

1953

Record: 0-33 Ft. Ord, 26-13 USC Spartans, 7-20 Ft. Bliss, 21-16 MCAS El Toro, 13-13 Camp Pendleton, 14-14 North Island NAS, 9-7 PhibPac, 14-7 San Diego St., 0-28 San Diego NTC. (4-3-2)

Coach: Capt. Art Ramage (Coffeyville JC-Tulsa) (assistant Parris Island 1951-52)

Assistants: Lt. Jim Delaney (Fallbrook NAD 1951, Guam 1952), Lt. Hans Jacobsen (Drake), Capt. Randy "Tex" Lawrence (Navy) (Quantico 1949-50), Robert "Bull" Trometter (St. Mary's) (assistant Pendleton 1949).

Ends: Larry Cooley (Vanderbilt), John Flippen (Wyoming), Max Hawkins, John Kammerman (Utah St.), George Kendall, Bob Kirkpatrick (Tennessee), Don Price, Ralph Studebaker, Don Taylor and Joe Young (St. Benedict's-Marquette; later at Arizona).

Tackles: Sam Craig, Ray Darling, Jack Davis (Oklahoma), Ezra Gordon (Victoria JC), Bill Lammes (West Texas), Bill Lehman (Mississippi Southern), Phil Muscarello (Mississippi Southern), Rudy Trbovich (Purdue) and Dewey Wade (Kansas St.)

Guards: Bill Banaga (San Diego CC), Luther Borgeson, Don Davis, Frank Epstein (Notre Dame), Joe Logan (Mississippi State) and Jack Lordo (Missouri).

Centers: John Bergamini (St. Mary's) and Cecil Parker.

Backs: Ed Alario, Otis Bealmear (Oklahoma), Arnold Burwitz (Arizona), Camillo Capuzzi (Cincinnati), Stan Carr, Tom Danforth, A.T. DeVaughan (Bishop) (Barstow 1951-52), John Giangiorgi (Loras; later at Bradley), Ron Hoenisch (Wisconsin), Charles Holliday (Sam Houston), Harold Jackson (Southern), Bill Kellar, George Kendall (SMU), Jim Marinos (California), Ed Ostrowski, Art Preston (San Diego St.), Rodger Rosenquist and George Stevenson (UCLA).

Depot Overachieves

Quantico could play its All-Americans and fledgling officers, but San Diego showed in 1954 that its way could win, too, thank you.

Relying heavily on enlisted men plus college players with freshman or sophomore football experience at best, the Depot rolled to an 8-3 record — and the 11th Naval District title.

A showdown with Quantico to settle, among other things, who had the better idea did not materialize, however, because the All-Marine title series, started under Navy auspices in 1947, was canceled.

For the fourth time in as many seasons, San Diego had a new coach, Maj. John Crawley, who brought the needed experience to mold these youngsters into a winning combination. A guard at Kansas State in 1936-37, he had been an assistant coach at his alma mater in 1948, and an assistant at Camp Pendleton on returning to active duty in 1949. He would have been the Pendleton coach in 1950, but the schedule was dropped because of Korean War commitments. Crawley had coached Camp Lejeune to an 8-3-1 record in 1953.

A look at a San Diego game program no doubt impressed opponents because of the players' college affiliations, and the coaching staff with the help of the public information office probably encouraged the ploy for whatever psychological edge it might bring.

But, in truth, few of the players had lettered, and, of those who did, it often was for but a year.

Only five players had lettered twice at a major school and apparently none for three seasons.

And, of course, some players had come into the Corps directly from high school.

The listings of Tennessee, USC, Wyoming, Miami, Oklahoma, LSU, Illinois, Missouri and Michigan State on the programs were mainly window dressing.

But Crawley and his staff were equal to the challenge.

The Devildogs opened with victories over the Barstow Marines and Cal Poly San Luis Obispo (breaking a 12-game winning streak); lost to PhibPac, 26-19; defeated Camp Pendleton; lost to San Diego State, 14-0; beat New Mexico A&M; lost to Ft. Ord, 27-14, and closed the regular season with victories over North Island Naval Air Station, Fresno State and the San Diego Naval Training Center.

San Diego won a playoff game from Pendleton, 26-19, for the 11th Naval District title before 7,500, for the 8-3 record.

The commandant rejected a bid for the Depot to replay Ft. Ord in the postseason Lettuce Bowl.

Which on a football level probably wasn't too bad a ruling, at that. The Warriors, loaded with college and pro standouts such as quarterback Jim Powers (USC and four seasons with the San Francisco 49ers) and back Sam Baker (Washington Redskins), posted a 10-3-1 record. However, two of the losses were to the 49ers and Los Angeles Rams.

Crawley inherited just seven players from the 1953 team: ends Bob Kirkpatrick and Joe Young (St. Benedict's-Marquette), tackle Ezra Gordon (Victoria JC), guard Joe Logan (Mississippi State), and backs Camillo Capuzzi, John Giangiorgi (Loras) and Harold Jackson (Southern).

Which meant starting almost from scratch.

But in poured the youngsters.

At tackle for example, Crawley landed quality players such as Wayne Bock, Dick Fouts, Jim Howe and George Palmer.

Bock, a high school All-Stater in Illinois, had played freshman ball at Illinois and would be drafted in the fifth round in 1957 by the Chicago Cardinals. He was with the Cardinals for parts of the 1957, 1958 and 1959 seasons and briefly with Toronto of the Canadian Football League in 1960 and the Rams in 1961 during an injury-plagued career.

Fouts, who had played freshman ball at Missouri, would be drafted in the 22nd round by the Rams in 1956, and had a tryout with LA in 1956. But it was in Canada that Fouts found his niche, at Toronto from 1957-61, British Columbia from 1962-66, Toronto again in 1967 and BC again from 1968-69.

Howe had lettered at Northwestern in 1950-51 and was with Jim Mutscheller, Ernie Cheatham and Bud Carson on the Camp Fisher (Japan) team that won the Rice Bowl in 1953. Palmer lettered at Iowa in 1952.

At guard the Devildogs had three who had lettered in 1952: George Allen and Ken Anglin, both at Texas, and Logan.

"Coaches acclaimed Allen 'Diego's most valuable player," said the Leatherneck, which selected him All-Marine.

There was strength at center in Jim Cauthron (Arkansas) and Fred Martin (Arizona), both of whom had lettered twice.

In the backfield, it was pretty much the same picture: Ed Fletcher (San Diego State) and Bob Warren (Arkansas) had lettered twice, and Carl Gunn (Arkansas) and Dick Washington (Notre Dame) once.

Fletcher, who led the Aztecs in interceptions and punt returns in 1952, was one of the first black officers in the Corps and retired as a Marine Reserve colonel.

Washington's playing time was limited at Notre Dame in that 1953 national championship season because he was the back-up at right half to — of all people — Heisman Trophy winner Johnny Lattner. Washington, like several Devildogs teammates, would play in Canada, with Calgary in 1958 and Hamilton briefly in 1959.

Young would be drafted in the 24th round by the Chicago Bears in 1955, play with the Hawaii Marines in 1955, Saskatchewan (CFL) and the Tucson Rattlers in 1958 and the Denver Broncos of the American Football League in 1960-61. Jackson was drafted in the 29th round by the New York Giants in 1955.

"Mighty Joe Young," an All-Marine selection, "with a scant year of high school ball, two years of college play to his record, finished his second season with the recruiter depoteers fashionably by scoring two touchdowns and setting the ball in position for a third (against Pendleton)," said the Leatherneck. "... The big receiver was a consistent performer all season." He also was a Navy Times' All-Sea Service choice.

Crawley's work paid other dividends as Cauthron, guard Russ Mather and Jackson received second-team All-Marine honors.

How young was the team?

End Lindsey Hubby lettered at USC in 1956-57, Young at Arizona in 1956-57, Mather at Wyoming in 1957, Palmer at Fresno State in 1956-57, Logan at Mississippi State from 1956-58, center Larry Yonkee at Wyoming in 1957, Giangiorgi at Bradley in 1956-57 and back Bob Moneymaker at San Diego State in 1956.

1954

Record: 40-0 Barstow Marines, 23-3 Cal Poly SLO, 19-26 PhibPac, 20-0 Camp Pendleton, 0-14 San Diego St., 33-7 New Mexico A&M, 14-27 Ft. Ord, 34-0 North Island NAS, 20-0 Fresno St., 19-13 San Diego NTC, 26-19 Camp Pendleton. (8-3)

Coach: Maj. John Crawley (Kansas St.) (assistant Pendleton 1949; coach Camp Lejeune 1953)

Assistants: Lt. Hans Jacobsen (Drake), Art Ramage (Coffeyville JC-Tulsa) (assistant Parris Island 1951-52), Capt. Ken Schieweck (Navy) (Quantico 1949, Lejeune 1951), Royal Walker (Wisconsin-Columbia College)

Ends: Bob Black, Gerald Harper (San Francisco St.), Bob Kirkpatrick (Tennessee), Lindsey Hubby (USC) and Joe Young (St. Benedict's-Marquette; later at Arizona)

Tackles: Wayne Bock (Illinois), Richard Fouts (Missouri), Ezra Gordon (Victoria JC), Jim Howe (Northwestern), Russ Mather (Wyoming), George Palmer (Iowa; later at Fresno St.) (Pendleton 1954), Bob Reis (Miami) and Clark Wasson (Oklahoma)

Guards: George Allen (Texas), Ken Anglin (Texas), Phil Kruzick (St. Benedict's), Joe Logan (Mississippi St.) (Pendleton 54), Joe Stranger (Pendleton 1949) and Allan Strangeland (Arizona)

Centers: Jim Cauthron (Arkansas), Fred Martin (Arizona) and Larry Yonkee (Wyoming)

Backs: Jim Boggess (LSU), Bob Bohn (Tulsa), Camillo Capuzzi (Cincinnati), Ed Fletcher (San Diego St.), John Giangiorgi (Loras; later at Bradley), Carl Gunn (Arkansas), Darrell Guttormson (Augustana of S.D.), Harold Jackson (Southern), James Jackson (Bishop), Carl Lutes (Arkansas), Fred Magett (Michigan St.), Dick McKown (Arizona), Bob Moneymaker (El Camino JC-Santa Barbara St.; later at San Diego St.), Bob Warren (Arkansas) and Dick Washington (Notre Dame).

Reserve Col. James Higgins (Trinity of Texas) played with Chicago Cardinals before signing up prior to Dec. 7, 1941. He later was football coach and athletic director at Lamar (Texas).

Jekyll-Hyde Season

Would the real 1955 San Diego Recruit Depot team stand up? Was it the one that lost its first seven games — some badly — and was outscored, 211 to 80?

Or was it the team that made one of Marine football's more remarkable turnarounds and won the final two games?

And it wasn't just the victories, but the way the Devildogs defeated San Diego State, 32-0, and the San Diego Naval Training Center, 51-6.

As Leatherneck put it, the "Devildogs, hampered by injuries to key players, got off to a slow start and managed to pick up speed only at the tail end of the season.. ... These (two) wins salvaged a measure of success in an otherwise dismal season."

Maj. Ralph Heywood, a USC All-America end in 1943, presided over the Jekyll and Hyde season marred by injuries and transfers.

"The Marines have played spotty football this year," a November game program commented, "looking like world-beaters on occasions. Their line is big enough, averaging 220 pounds a man, and has done the most work. The trouble lies in injuries to the backfield stars. Fullback Dick Washington and halfback Fred Magett, both standouts last season, have started slowly and been sorely missed."

Washington and Magett, when healthy, formed a solid 1-2 offensive punch, with Magett scoring 42 points — including a 90-yard TD against Pendleton — and Washington 40.

True, there was a Murphy (a center from Heidelberg) on the team, but that hardly explains why so much went so wrong at the outset.

Heywood, a 6-2, 200-pounder, had joined the famed El Toro Marines for the latter part of their 1945 season and then joined the Chicago Rockets of the All-America Football Conference in 1946 (as did half the El Toro team), the Detroit Lions in 1947, the Boston Yanks in 1948 and the New York Bulldogs in 1949.

He returned to the Corps in 1952, punting for Quantico that season and coaching the 3rd Marines in Japan in 1954. Heywood commanded the 26th Marines in Vietnam and retired as a colonel.

There were pluses and minuses that 1955 season:

■ Heywood retained only nine from the 8-3 team of 1954: end Russ Mather, tackles Dick Fouts and George Palmer (Iowa); guards George Allen (Texas) and Joe Stranger, center Jim Cauthron (Arkansas) and backs Bob Bohn, Magett and Washington (Notre Dame.)

■ There were no ends with major-college experience.

■ The frontline tackles (Fouts, Palmer, Bill Frank and Walt Schneiter of Colorado) were impressive.

■ Allen was the lone guard with a major-college background.

■ With Cauthron and Ernie Cheatham (Loyola of Los Angeles, the Pittsburgh Steelers and the Baltimore Colts), the center position was in good hands.

■ Washington was the lone back with much of a Division I background.

■ There was some size in 18-year-old end Frank Snyder (6-6, 225) and tackles Conrad Margowski (6-4, 230), 19-year-old Allan Moore (238) and Schneiter (225). But they all had not been tested and the overall team speed was not worth writing to Washington about.

Allen and Washington received second-team All-Marine honors from Leatherneck, and Allen was a second-team All-Sea Service selection by the Navy Times.

Heywood was forced to rely heavily — as were the coaches in 1953 and 1954 — on players bearing potential but with high school or college freshman backgrounds. Ten of them hadn't reached their 20th birthdays.

For example, end Willie Allison, 19, a 6-5 Baylor freshman player, would be drafted in the 18th round by the Baltimore Colts in 1961.

The 6-5, 240-pound Fouts, a Missouri freshman player drafted in the 22nd round by the Los Angeles Rams in 1956, would play 13 seasons in the Canadian Football League.

Washington also would put in parts of two seasons in Canada.

But, just as in 1954, the college listings on game programs were more impressive than the backgrounds represented. Indiana, Wyoming, Alabama, Nebraska, UCLA, Michigan State, USC, California and LSU, in truth, referred to freshman teams.

On the other hand, some of the younger players would return to college. Mather would letter at Wyoming in 1957, Frank at Colorado in 1961-62 after two seasons with the Hawaii Marines, Palmer at Fresno State in 1956-57, guard Walt Beddeo at Denver in 1959-60 and guard Bill Hannah at Alabama from 1957-59.

Frank, 6-5, 226 pounds and just 17, was drafted in the 18th round by the Dallas Cowboys in 1964 and would play for British Columbia (CFL) in 1963, the Cowboys in 1964, Toronto from 1965-68 and Winnipeg from 1970-76, or 13 seasons in all.

The 6-2, 230-pound Cheatham ("Big Ernie") literally was destined for the stars. After being drafted by the Steelers in the 21st round in 1951 and starring for Camp Fisher (Japan) in 1953, he put in his season as an NFL linebacker and returned to the Corps, which gladly took him back. He also was a San Diego player-coach in 1956, when he earned All-Marine honors as a tackle; won the Navy Cross and Legion of Merit in Vietnam, was selected as a brigadier general in 1957, and commanded the 1st Marine Division at Camp Pendleton on his way to a third star.

He and assistant Walt Cook (William Jewell) were forced to suit up during the '55 season after a siege of injuries.

Hannah, another in the line of football Hannahs from Alabama, returned to Alabama for the three seasons before beginning a coaching career at Lompoc and La Puente highs in California, then moving up to San Bernardino Valley Junior College. He had joined Cal State Fullerton for the 1971 season only to be killed in a 1971 plane crash that took the lives of two other coaches and the pilot.

Opening with Ft. Ord would start any team off in the wrong direction. The Warriors, 57-18 winners, rolled to a 12-2 record (the losses were to the Rams and Ft. Sill) behind the likes of backs Jim Powers (USC), Paul Cameron (UCLA), Sam Baker (Washington

Redskins) and end Ron Miller (USC), later to head the Walt Disney Co.

The Devildogs then lost to the California Ramblers, 22-13; Cal Poly San Luis Obispo, 44-12 (after being tied at 12 in the fourth quarter); Fresno State and Darryl Rogers, 20-0; North Island Naval Air Station, 21-16; Camp Pendleton, 34-14; and Hamilton AFB (a 9-1 record), 19-7.

But the Devildogs recovered to beat the Aztecs in a game played in fog, as Marv Fiorini passed to Don Scott on a 24-yard TD pass play, Bohn ran 31 yards for a score and passed to Allison on a 36-yard TD play, John Willman passed to Mather on a 62-yard TD play and Magett scooted 26 yards for a score.

Prophetically, the game program noted that the "rivalry between the Marines and State College is a long one and Heywood shouldn't have too much trouble getting his men up for this game." He didn't.

And then the Devildogs fattened up on the training center, a nemesis, with Magett gaining 126 yards in 10 carries and Dick Pickett (Idaho) 90 in 13 tries. Magett, Washington and Pickett each scored twice.

But the plays of the day were TD passes of 1 and 4 yards from Bohn to Fouts, who lined up as a tackle-eligible. Fouts also had scored a TD on defense against Ft. Ord.

The Rams obviously had their eye on Fouts.

1955

Record: 18-51 Ft. Ord, 13-22 Cal Ramblers, 12-44 Cal Poly SLO, 0-20 Fresno St., 16-21 North Island NAS, 14-34 Camp Pendleton, 7-19 Hamilton AFB, 32-0 San Diego St., 51-6 San Diego NTC. (2-7)

Coach: Maj. Ralph Heywood (USC) (El Toro 1945) (Quantico 1952, coach 3rd Marines 1954)

Assistants: Lt. Ernie Cheatham (Loyola of LA) (Camp Fisher 1953), Lt. Walt Cook (William Jewell) (assistant 1st MarDiv 1954), Capt. Joe Polidori (Miramar MCAS 1946, El Toro 1947-50, Camp Fisher 1953, coach 1st MarDiv 1954)

Ends: Willie Allison (Baylor), Jerry Baum (Indiana), Jack Kasson, Russ Mather (Wyoming), Pete Neiter (Lancaster JC), Jim Scott and Frank Snyder (Chico St.)

Tackles: Dick Fouts (Missouri), Bill Frank (later at San Diego CC, Colorado), Conrad Margowski, Allan Moore (Alabama), Jerry O'Donnell (Dayton), George Palmer (Iowa; later at Fresno St.) (Camp Pendleton 1954) and Walt Schneiter (Colorado)

Guards: George Allen (Texas), Walt Beddeo (Nebraska; later at Denver), Bill Hannah (Alabama), Lew Kearney (Simpson), Olsen, Joe Schloderer (East LA JC-UCLA), Joe Stranger (Pendleton 1949), John Wynne (Michigan St.) (Camp Lejeune 1952, Hawaii Marines 1954)

Centers: Jim Cauthron (Arkansas), Cheatham (p-c), Howard Conrad (St. Mary's-USC) (Ft. Ord, Ft. Bragg), Bob Gray (Prairie View) and Frank Murphy (Heidelberg) (Great Lakes)

Backs: Bob Bohn (Tulsa), Cook (p-c), Marv Fiorini (California), Frank Gilbert, Charles Golden (Eau Claire St.), Bill Hall (San Diego JC), Jerry Jones (Marshall), Fred Magett (Michigan State), Frank Miller (William Jewell-Kansas), Dick Pickett (Idaho), Don Scott (Connecticut), Jim Summers, Dick Washington (Notre Dame), Jim Wherry (LSU), John Willman (North Dakota St.) and Jack Young (Texas Tech)

Cole Letters at UCLA

UCLA linebacker Randy Cole might have been the only former Marine playing Division I football in 1991.

He had played regimental ball at Camp Pendleton and at Santa Monica CC.

Oh, For More Backs

After seven seasons with the T-formation, San Diego returned to the single wing in 1956.

But the backfield wasn't big, and it wasn't fast.

So, despite a line called the "Iron Monsters" that almost to a man played pro ball or was drafted by an NFL team, the Devildogs had another sub-.500 season, winning four, losing five and tying San Diego State, 19-19.

At the ends, 6-5, 215-pound Wilson Allison would be an 18th-round draft choice of the Baltimore Colts in 1961, and 6-3, 222-pound Ron Aschbacher (Oregon State), a 10th-round pick by San Francisco in 1955, had played briefly with the 49ers.

At tackle, 6-4, 235-pound Ernie Cheatham (Loyola of Los Angeles) had been drafted in the 21st round by the Pittsburgh Steelers in 1951, and been with the Steelers and Colts in 1954 before returning to active duty.

Tackle Bill Frank, a 6-5, 235-pounder, would be drafted in the 18th round by Dallas, be with the Cowboys in 1964 and play 13 seasons in the Canadian Football League.

Tackle John Klotz (Penn Military), a 6-5, 250-pounder, was drafted in the 18th round by Los Angeles in 1956 and would be with the Rams briefly in 1958. He would play for the New York Titans from 1960-62, the San Diego Chargers in 1962, the New York Jets in 1963 and the Houston Oilers in 1964.

And 6-4, 235-pound tackle Hank Schmidt (USC) would be a sixth-round pick of the 49ers, play for them in 1959-60, the Chargers from 1961-64, the Buffalo Bills in 1965 and the Jets in 1966.

At guards, 6-2, 219-pound John Gremer (Illinois) would be drafted by the Oilers in 1960; 6-1, 225-pound Ted Karras (Indiana) would be with the Steelers in 1958-59, the Chicago Bears from 1960-64, the Detroit Lions in 1965 and the Rams in 1966, and 6-2, 230-pounder John Coyne (Clarion) was drafted in the 20th round by the Rams in 1956.

At center 6-3, 220-pound Mike Connelly (Pasadena JC) would play for the Cowboys from 1960-67 and the Steelers in 1968, and 6-0, 220-pound Lou Hallow, an NAIA All-American at East Carolina, was drafted in the 26th round by the Rams in 1955 and would be with the Boston Patriots briefly in 1961.

The line, on an individual basis, may have been the best ever fielded in Marine football.

How, you say, could this team lose — and lose five times at that.

Frankly put, the backfield couldn't measure up to the Depot's Quinlan-Goode-Brown-Carodine-Washington standards.

Coach Joe Polidori, with the '56 line but the '52 or '54 Depot backfield instead, probably could have gone unbeaten using a T, a single wing, a double wing or even a quadruple wing.

True, there was potential in the '56 backfield. Alvin Hall, for example, gained 101 yards in 8 carries and had a 43-yard TD against Occidental, and returned a punt 56 yards for a score against San Diego

State. He would play for the Rams from 1961-63.

Dick Pickett (Idaho) was a second-team All-Marine choice, gaining 705 yards in 159 carries and scoring nine TDs despite missing two games. He picked up 134 yards in 29 carries against Occidental, and scored four times and gained 153 yards in 31 carries against UC Santa Barbara. He and Allison teamed on a 61-yard TD pass play against Pomona.

But largely the backs were just out of high school, had played freshman ball or hailed from Division II and Division III schools.

And the game-program listings and news stories denoting Alabama, Baylor, South Carolina, Washington, Colorado, Northwestern, Purdue and UCLA often referred, unfortunately, to freshman ball.

Ten players were teen-agers.

In the final analysis, it probably mattered little what formation was used by Polidori, who came up through the ranks and would be awarded the Bronze Star in Vietnam. The schedule, as usual, was challenging. And Polidori felt strongly that the talent best matched the single-wing requirements and stuck with his gutty, albeit controversial, move.

There were 12 holdovers to build with: Allison, Jack Kasson and Pete Neiter (Lancaster JC) at ends, Cheatham, Frank, Conrad Margowski and Allen Moore at tackles; 6-0, 215-pound Bill Hannah at guard and Bill Hall, Pickett, Joe Schloderer and John "Jug" Willman in the backfield.

Polidori had been around, as a guard for the MCAS Miramar team in 1946, for MCAS El Toro from 1947-50 and for Rice Bowl champion Camp Fisher in 1953, and coached the 1st Marine Division team in Korea to an 8-1 record and the 8th Army Conference title in 1954. He had been a San Diego assistant in 1955.

Said a San Diego writeup in the Fresno State game program, "One could say it (San Diego) will be a 'green' team — only five of its members have ever played under the single-wing formation. It'll be a big team in the forward wall, but small, and not too fast, in the backfield. It is doubtful that it will be fully synchronized with its new formation until the middle of the season."

And that was the case.

The Depot defeated Pomona-Claremont, 32-7, in the opener; lost to Fresno State and Darryl Rogers by an unusual 2-0 score; but recovered to down Occidental, 27-6, with the Tigers' touchdown coming on a pass from Jack Kemp to Jim Mora, two persons of considerable fame in later years.

Hamilton Air Force Base and Pepper Rodgers pulled out a 19-13 victory; the tie game with the Aztecs followed; Cal Poly San Luis Obispo and John Madden won, 27-8, and Camp Pendleton (an 8-1 record) rolled to a 52-20 triumph.

Continuing the see-saw pattern, San Diego whipped the North Island Naval Air Station, 38-6, but lost to its nemesis, the San Diego Naval Training Center, 33-15, in the finale. The two games also wrote finis to football at both North Island and the training center, which had opposed Marines teams since the 1920s.

Again, those Devildogs came back for a closing 25-14 victory over Santa Barbara in the Citricado Bowl at Escondido.

Cheatham, later to be a lieutenant general, was an All-Marine selection. Said the Leatherneck: "(He was) a player of the rough and tough school. ... Not one to 'dog' it, he decisively ... earned his place on the first team with his play on the field." He was also a first-team Armed Forces Press Service pick and second team All-Sea Service.

In the final two regular-season games, Cheatham and Hallow even caught TD passes on tackle-eligible plays. Hallow was on the receiving end of a 20-yard pass play against North Island. Cheatham's was for 47 yards against the training center, a feat he no doubt regaled his staffs with for years.

And at least five Devildogs would be heard from later in the college ranks: Connelly (Utah State), Frank (Colorado, 1961-62), Gremer (Illinois, 1959), Hannah (Alabama, 1957-59) and Schmidt (Trinity of Texas, 1958).

Hannah would die in a 1971 plane crash on his way to a football scouting assignment.

1956

Record: 32-7 Pomona-Claremont, 0-2 Fresno St., 27-6 Occidental, 13-19 Hamilton AFB, 19-19 San Diego St., 8-27 Cal Poly San Luis Obispo, , 20-52 Camp Pendleton, 38-6 North Island NAS, 15-33 San Diego NTC, 25-14 UC Santa Barbara (Citricado Bowl). (4-5-1)

Coach: Capt. Joe Polidori (Miramar MCAS 1946, El Toro 1947-50, Camp Fisher 1953; coach 1st MarDiv 1954)

Assistants: Capt. Ernie Cheatham (Loyola of LA) (Camp Fisher 1953), Lt. Walt Cook (William Jewell) (assistant 1st MarDiv 1954), Lt. (USN) Dan Garza, Lt. Phil Moyles

Ends: Wilson Allison (Baylor), Ron Aschbacher (Oregon St.), Wyllis Fisher (Bradley), Jack Kasson, Ron Jones (3rd MarDiv), Pete Neiter (Lancaster JC), Lim Salser

Tackles: Cheatham (p-c), Bill Frank (later at San Diego CC, Colorado), John Klotz (Penn Military), Conrad Margowski, Allen Moore (Alabama), Al Plaskey (South Carolina), Henry Schmidt (USC; later at Trinity of Texas)

Guards: Charles Brady (Washington), John Coyne (Clarion), John Gremer (Illinois), Bill Hannah (Alabama), Lee Herald (Palomar JC), Ted Karras (Purdue-Indiana), Jim Nill

Centers: Mike Connelly (Pasadena JC-Washington St.; later at Utah St.), Lou Hallow (East Carolina), Charles Halstead

Backs: Paul Christopherson (Montana St.), Mike Contreras (Palomar JC), Tom Cook (William Jewell), Walt Cook (p-c), Dick Dobbs (Colorado), George Guidry, Alvin Hall, Bill Hall (San Diego JC), Bob King (Northwestern), Fred McLean (Ottawa), Fred Nelson (Midwestern), Larry Patzer (Purdue), Dick Pickett (Idaho), Frank Pirman (St. Norbert's), Joe Schloderer (East LA JC-UCLA), Ed Seybold (La Crosse St.), Larry Williams, John Willman (North Dakota St.).

Marine Vs. Marine in S.C.

An upset of the 1990 season was The Citadel's 38-35 victory over South Carolina, probably costing the Gamecocks (6-5) a bowl bid.

The Citadel's athletic director was Walt Nadzak, a former Quantico end; South Carolina AD was King Dixon, a former Quantico back.

Trometter Heard From

They were singing "Happy Days Are Here Again" as well as the "Marines' Hymn" at San Diego in 1957.

And that's no bull.

Or maybe it was, because in this case the legendary Robert "Bull" Trometter had returned to the coaching arena.

Why all the excitement? Partly because Trometter, when he retired, had the highest winning percentage (.884) of any Marine coach in history with his 46-6 record. Partly because Trometter's teams were exciting.

After 2-7 and 4-5-1 records, the Depot was thirsting for a winner. And did it get one — and two — and three — from Trometter!

■ The Devildogs won nine straight in 1957 before losing to Bolling Air Force Base, 28-7, in the Shrimp Bowl at Galveston, Texas, for the national service title.

■ The Devildogs posted a 10-2 record in 1958, defeating Camp Lejeune, 62-22, in the first Leatherneck Bowl for the All-Marine title.

■ The Devildogs were unbeaten (10-0) in 1959, defeating Bolling AFB, 41-14, in the Leatherneck Bowl. (A game with unbeaten Quantico for the All-Marine title could not be arranged.)

Who in the world was this Trometter, now in his third decade of San Diego football?

■ From 1936-40 he had been a runner and world-class kicker on the Marine Corps Base teams of C. McL. Lott and Elmer Hall that had 6-3-1, 4-4-2, 7-5-1, 11-0 and 9-1 records, and played for San Diego in the West Coast Professional Football League. (He also competed in basketball and baseball at MCB.)

■ As a coach, he had presided over the resurrection of San Diego football in 1947 and 1948 with 7-2 and 9-1 records, respectively.

■ Trometter had been a San Diego assistant from 1951-53 before launching the three-year dynasty in the latter part of the decade.

(He also had been an assistant coach for Camp Pendleton's 1949 West Coast Marine champion and coached the Naval Amphibious Base at Coronado to a 7-1-1 record in 1954.)

The man had the credentials.

He obviously had found quite a few good men for the Depot — backs Coach Joe Polidori badly needed in 1956.

And Trometter installed the split-T formation. As a result:

■ Aunt Gertie probably could have won two games with the returnees from the '56 season, including the nucleus of the "Iron Monsters" of the line: end Ron Aschbacher; tackles John Coyne, John "Moose" Klotz and Hank Schmidt; guards Charles Brady, John Gremer and Ted Karras; center Mike Connelly; and backs Tom Cook, George Guidry, Alvin Hall and Fred Nelson.

How good were the "Iron Monsters?" During the regular season, San Diego rushed for 3,382 yards; the opponents wound up with 608.

■ Seven players had been drafted by NFL teams, two would after their Marine tours and a 10th by the new American Football League.

Aschbacher (Oregon State), 6-3, 225 pounds, was picked by the San Francisco 49ers (No. 10 in 1955), end Darryl Rogers (Fresno State), No. 24 by the Los Angeles Rams in 1957; end Jack Stillwell (Northwestern), No. 20 by the Cleveland Browns in 1957; Coyne (Clarion), 6-2, 245, No. 20 by the Rams in 1956; Klotz (Penn Military), 6-4, 261, No. 18 by the Rams in 1956; Schmidt (USC), 6-4, 253, No. 6 by the 49ers in 1958; tackle John "Tiny" Scott (Ohio State), 6-4, 260, No. 26 by the Pittsburgh Steelers in 1959; Gremer (Illinois), 6-2, 225, by the Houston Oilers in 1960; back Jack Hays (Trinity of Texas), No. 11 by the 49ers in 1959; and back Ken Lutterbach (an NAIA All-American at Evansville), No. 24 by the Chicago Bears in 1957.

Aschbacher was with the 49ers briefly in 1955; Rogers would have tryouts with the Rams in 1959 and the Denver Broncos in 1960; Stillwell would have a Boston Patriots' tryout in 1960; Klotz would play five seasons in the American Football League; Schmidt would put in eight seasons in the NFL and AFL; the 6-1, 240-pound Karras (Indiana), brother of Alex and Lou, would play nine NFL seasons; the 6-3, 225-pound Connelly (Pasadena JC) would play nine seasons in the NFL; Hall would be with the Rams three seasons; Lutterback would have tryouts with Toronto (Canadian Football League) in 1960 and the Buffalo Bills in 1961; and Scott would have a tryout with the Steelers in 1960 and play for the Bills in 1960-61.

Rogers, of course, went on to a "State of the art" coaching career at Hayward State (1965), Fresno State (1966-72), San Jose State (1973-75), Michigan State (1976-79) and Arizona State (1980-84), resulting in 129 victories, 84 losses and 7 ties. His Spartans won a share of the Big Ten title in 1978 and he directed teams in the Camelia Bowl (1968), Mercy Bowl (1971) and Fiesta Bowl (1983).

(The Mercy Bowl was staged to help the families of three football coaches and a pilot killed in a plane crash. One victim was ex-Depot guard Bill Hannah.)

Then in 1985 Rogers joined former Marines Bill Arnsparger, Jack Chevigny, Chuck Drulis, Rick Forzano, Abe Gibron, Jim Lee Howell, John Mazur, Jim Mora, Ernie Nevers, John North, Bum Phillips, John Ralston, J.D. Roberts, Clipper Smith and Les Steckel as a head coach in the NFL, guiding the Detroit Lions.

■ If that talent wasn't enough, the Depot profited from the college ranks, adding ends Pete Covington (Arkansas) and 6-2, 215-pound Jim "Piggy" Robinson (Fisk); 6-3, 215-pound tackle Ray Fisher (Eastern Illinois), center Ed Strange (Kentucky), and backs Dale Boutwell (Arkansas), Bob Garner (Fresno State), Bob Liles (Wichita State), Ernie Merk (USC), Jim Pyles (San Diego State), Ed Snider (Fresno State), Lee Taylor (Fresno State) and Pete Walski (UC Santa Barbara).

Ironically, Pyles, Rogers, Walski and others had played against the Devildogs as collegians.

Fisher would play with the Steelers in 1959 and briefly in 1960, and the Dallas Cowboys in 1961; Garner would be with the Los Angeles Chargers in 1960 and the Oakland Raiders from 1961-63; and Merk would be with the Steelers briefly in 1959.

■ Additionally, Trometter picked up end Merrill Jacobs (St. Mary's-San Francisco State), who had played for Quantico, the 1st Marine Division and the Hawaii Marines; tackle George Lefferts (Idaho), 6-2, 230, who had played for Quantico and Camp Pendleton; tackle Buddy Lewis (twice a captain at Arizona), 6-0, 215, with Quantico and Pendleton experience; and guard Eddie Johns (San Diego State), also a former Pendleton standout.

■ And the younger players had college and pro potential. Covington would play at Northeast Louisiana in 1959, Gremer at Illinois in 1959, Connelly at Utah State and center John O'Grady at Wyoming in 1958.

In addition, a Trinity of Texas connection bagged Schmidt for 1958, and end Don Peltier, Boutwell and Hays for later seasons.

Nine MCRD players weighed in at 225 or more.

But how did all this talent just happen to wind up at San Diego?

Admittedly, Trometter, a chief warrant officer, had contacts throughout the Corps. For example, Trometter's teammates and assistant coaches on the MCB teams in the 1930s included George Bowman, Odell Conoley, Lowell English, Rivers Morrell, Ray Murray, Ben Robertshaw, George R.E. Shell, Austin Shofner, Joe Stewart, Gay Thrash, Harvey Tschirgi and Lew Walt. (For the unitiated, they all became generals. And a number of MCB teammates were colonels.)

Also, Camp Pendleton did not field a varsity team in 1957, easing the competition for key players.

But Trometter's strengths were in organizing, evaluating talent, attention to detail, promoting, scheduling, public relations, motivating and looking out for his players as well as his superior coaching instincts.

Almost three decades later at a 1986 Marine athletes reunion in San Diego, many of those turning up had ties to Trometter and were there to pay allegiance to their coach.

MCRD had beaten the Barstow Marines, 42-12, in an Armed Forces Day game to close spring drills that '57 season.

And "optimism is the word for the 1957 edition," said a team media guide, citing the "new coaching staff, new system (split-T) and the most outstanding group of newcomers to be assembled on the San Diego gridiron in several years."

In the fall, the Depot never looked back as it roared to a 78-0 victory over Malmstrom Air Force Base in the Oyster Bowl in South Bend, Wash., in a game mandated by a Northwest congressman. The Marine commandant declined to intercede in the politicking. In retrospect, the airmen wished he had. Boutwell scored three times, and Hall and Liles twice each.

Hamilton Air Force Base (9-1-1 for the season) and Pepper Rodgers lost their only game, 27-20, as Hall scored twice. The Marines struggled to defeat a weak Ft. Bliss team, 14-7, then steamrollered Fresno State, 53-0, as Boutwell, Hall, Merk and Pyles each scored twice.

San Diego State was a 20-7 victim as ex-Aztec Pyles bulled for 159 yards in 17 carries and Hall for 122 in 15 attempts.

The Hawaii Marines went down, 20-13; the University of San Diego, 41-0; and Travis Air Force Base, 72-0, as Hall returned the opening kickoff 80 yards for one of two TDs. Walski, who was introduced to the split-T that fall, scored four times and Merk twice.

Cal Poly San Luis Obispo and John Madden were defeated, 27-14, as Hall had 92- and 48-yard TDs and gained 211 yards in 15 carries.

And the Devildogs beat the Hawaii Marines for a second time, 32-7, to close the regular season.

It was like "old home week" in the Hawaii games because ends Wilson Allison and Lim Salser, tackles Bill Frank and Joe Schloderer, center Wyllis Fisher and backs Larry Patzer and John "Jug" Willman were former MCRD players.

In trying to hold down the score against USD, Trometter sent in Willie Moore, the trainer and depot boxing coach, who, according to the base paper, the Chevron, "was closer to 40 than he cares to admit." He went in for one play but returned at the behest of teammates. "He barely missed a shoestring catch of one short pass," the Chevron reported.

(Both North Island Naval Air Station and the San Diego Naval Training Center had given up football.)

Bolling, coached by former Marine George Makris and unbeaten in 10 regular-season games, boasted a lineup dominated by former pros and Notre Dame players (Ralph Guglielmi, Joe Heap, Don Schaeffer and Dan Shannon) that probably could have held its own against a second-division NFL team.

Bolling held Hall in check (17 yards in 7 rushes) and the Devildogs scored only on Walski's 65-yard interception return.

Hall had been the main man for Trometter during the regular season, rushing for 898 yards in 108 carries and scoring 14 TDs. He often teamed with Walski at quarterback, Merk, who gained 551 yards in 71 carries, at halfback and Pyles, who rushed for 459 yards in 54 carries, at fullback.

The combination may have been the only entire backfield ever chosen All-Marine.

Karras, Lewis, Schmidt, Stillwell and Strange also were selected All-Marine on the expanded 22-man team. (Karras was a first-team choice of the Armed Forces Press Service and the Navy Times, Hall and Strange were second-team Navy Times selections and Hall a second-team AFPS choice. Karras was the runner-up for the Navy Times' MVP award.) And Gremer, Jacobs and Robinson were on the second All-Marine team.

Leatherneck called Stillwell a "speedy flankman who also possesses an aptitude for catching passes." Lewis, the magazine said, was a "strongpoint in the bulky line and missed being a unanimous choice by two votes." Karras, said Leatherneck, was a "tough, aggressive lineman. Foes learned too late that he experienced little trouble in moving his 240 pounds with remarkable ease." Strange, the magazine said, "reported late but rounded into playing condition and proved to be the answer to Trometter's acute center problem."

Hall, said Leatherneck, "has limited experience, but the vote of confidence he received was indicative of his ability. Bothered with a bad ankle in 1956, he still managed to emerge as the Devildogs' best back. The pro-laden Bolling team was the only 1957 opponent to effectively contain his outside slants." Merk, the magazine said, "is a versatile back, noted for his power running. He is an excellent blocker, and a top-notch defensive player." Pyles, the "leading ground gainer for San Diego State in 1955 ... would prefer to run over an opponent than go around him," said the Leatherneck. "Pyles also was one of Trometter's most effective blockers." .

Trometter, as usual, had done his homework and mended all the fences and Leatherneck couldn't overlook the Depot as it had in some seasons. And with nine on the All-Marine team, three on the second team and three honorable mentions, it didn't.

1957

Record: 78-0 Malmstrom AFB (Oyster Bowl), 27-20 Hamilton AFB, 14-7 Ft. Bliss, 53-0 Fresno St., 20-7 San Diego St., 20-13 Hawaii Marines, 41-0 Univ. of San Diego, 72-0 Travis AFB, 27-14 Cal Poly SLO, 32-7 Hawaii Marines, 7-28 Bolling AFB (Shrimp Bowl). (10-1)

Coach: Bull Trometter (St. Mary's) (assistant Camp Pendleton 1949, coach Coronado NAB 1954)

Assistants: Lt. Eddie Johns (San Diego St.) (Pendleton 1956), Lt. Don McAlexander, Capt. Frank Pirman (St. Norbert's)

Ends: Ron Aschbacher (Oregon St.), Claude "Skip" Brock, Pete Covington (Arkansas; later at Northeast Louisiana), Homer Green, Merrill Jacobs (St. Mary's-San Francisco St.) (Quantico 1953, 1st MarDiv 1954, Hawaii Marines 1955-56), Chuck Limbach (USC), Bill Morgan (Xavier of La.), Don Peltier (Trinity of Texas), Jim "Piggy" Robinson (Fisk), Darryl Rogers (Long Beach CC-Fresno St.), Jack Stillwell (Northwestern)

Tackles: John Coyne (Clarion), David Evans, Ray Fisher (Eastern Illinois), John Klotz (Penn Military), George Lefferts (Idaho) (Quantico 1955, Pendleton 1956), Buddy Lewis (Arizona) (Quantico 1955, Pendleton 1956), Bob Mountjoy (Central Missouri), Hank Schmidt (USC; later at Trinity of Texas), John "Tiny" Scott (Ohio St.)

Guards: Charles Brady (Washington), Dick Fulk (Western Illinois), John Gremer (Illinois), Dick Henigan, Ed Hook (College of Idaho), Johns (p-c), Ted Karras (Purdue-Indiana), Jim Lassiter (Colorado), Felix Mallett (Long Beach CC), Bill Patton (USC), Bill Price

Centers: Mike Connolly (Pasadena JC-Washington St.; later at Utah St.), Don McGovern, John O'Grady (Wyoming), Don Salio (USC), Ed Strange (Kentucky)

Backs: Clarence Baity, Dale Boutwell (Arkansas; later at Trinity of Texas), Elbert Bullock (Fresno St.), Tom Cook (William Jewell), Bob Garner (Fresno St.), George Guidry, Alvin Hall, Jack Hays (Trinity of Texas), Bob Liles (Wichita St.), Ken Lutterbach (Evansville), Ewing McLaren (Florida), Russ McLean (Ferris), Ernie Merk (USC), Fred Nelson (Midwestern), Jim Pyles (San Diego St.), Charles Smith, Jack Smith (Lafayette), Ed Snider (Fresno St.), Lee Taylor (Citrus JC-Fresno St.), Pete Walski (UC Santa Barbara), Bill Welch (Pittsburgh), Willie Williams

Hanley A Famed Trial Lawyer

Bob Hanley, son of Dick Hanley, coach of famed El Toro Flying Marines, was a Chicago trial lawyer known nationally for winning a large jury verdict in 1980.

He was lead counsel for MCI Communications Corp. in an antitrust case against AT&T in which MCI won $1.8 billion.

Hanley, a Marine Reserve lieutenant colonel, died in September 1991.

All-Marine Champion

For Coach Robert "Bull" Trometter, 1958 was an off season in that he lost two games!

Imagine, two losses, and that tied his career high of 1947. Other coaches should have such a bad year.

True, his San Diego Devildogs won 10 games — and the All-Marine title — but the record does show that two of his six Marine coaching losses (in 52 games) came that season.

Besides the two losses in 1947 and 1958, he'd lost once in 1948 and once in 1957, all at San Diego. His 1959 Depot team would go undefeated. (He also lost once while coaching a Navy team in 1954.)

With Trometter, losses were news and occurred at the hands of Arizona teams: 25-13 at Arizona State-Flagstaff, and 28-7 to the Tucson Rattlers, not your everyday minor-league team.

Northern, coached by former Marine Max Spilsbury, was hardly a soft touch, closing with an 11-1 record, its loss to Northeast Oklahoma, 19-13, in the NAIA Holiday Bowl in St. Petersburg, Fla.

Trometter's predominantly enlisted Devildogs defeated four college teams, two semi-pro teams, three military teams and closed with a 62-22 whipping of Camp Lejeune before 18,000 in San Diego's first Leatherneck Bowl that benefitted the Navy Relief Society.

Trometter had 20 players back from the (10-1) team of 1957 that played for the national service title and added a mix of players with college and service experience.

But All-Marine players such as Ted Karras, Buddy Lewis (now an assistant coach), Hank Schmidt and Ed Strange, second-team selections John Gremer and Merrill Jacobs, plus Ron Aschbacher, John Coyne, John Klotz and Mike Connelly, were difficult to replace. And, with a lighter team, minimal college experience at guard and center, and a slowdown in reinforcements, the Devildogs weren't as strong as in 1957.

But they still were stronger than 10 opponents.

"The Devildogs will have no All-Americans or near All-Americans in their lineup (for the Leatherneck Bowl)," commented the base paper, the Chevron, "but boast a well-rounded squad that will be dangerous. ... In addition to a host of good running backs, the Depot's team has an aerial attack that can click well enough to keep the opposing defense honest, and a line that many consider better than last year's."

The 20 returnees included:

■ Ends Pete Covington (Arkansas), Charles Limbach, Jim "Piggy" Robinson (Fisk), Darryl Rogers (Fresno State) and John Stillwell (Northwestern).

■ Tackles Ray Fisher (Eastern Illinois), now up to 240 pounds, and 265-pound John "Tiny" Scott (Ohio State).

■ Guards Elbert Bullock and Felix Mallett.

■ Backs Dale Boutwell (Arkansas), Skip Brock, Bob Garner (Fresno State), Alvin Hall, Bob Liles (Wichita State), Ken Lutterbach (Evansville), Ernie Merk (USC), Jim Pyles (San Diego State), Ed

Snider (Fresno State), Lee Taylor (Fresno State) and Pete Walski (UC Santa Barbara).

But Trometter was able to bring in only six Division I-type players: tackles Art Anderson (Idaho), John Glover, Dick Loncar and Bob Whitlow (Arizona); halfback Billy Martin and quarterback Vern Valdez (University of San Diego). Camp Pendleton resumed football and no doubt siphoned off some players.

Anderson, another in a line of Vandals to compete in Marine athletics, would play for the Chicago Bears in 1961-62, and the Pittsburgh Steelers in 1963 and briefly in 1964.

The 6-2, 220-pound Glover had JC experience and played for Camp McGill in 1955 and the Hawaii Marines in 1956-57. He was an All-Marine selection in 1957. Said the Leatherneck: "Early in the season, the Hawaii Marines threatened the San Diego Marines before bowing by one touchdown. Glover's line play that day was beyond reproach."

Trometter was the opposing coach. They say a bull elephant never forgets. Glover played for Trometter in '58.

Loncar, who played freshman ball at Notre Dame and at Camp Pendleton in 1955-56, would play for Northeast Louisiana in 1959, be drafted by the Steelers in the 29th round and be with Pittsburgh briefly in 1960.

Surprisingly, Whitlow and Martin, who both reported without fanfare, would turn out to have the longest pro careers.

Whitlow, to be converted to a pro center, would play for the Washington Redskins in 1960-61, the Detroit Lions from 1961-65, the Atlanta Falcons in 1966, briefly with the Los Angeles Rams in 1967 and the Cleveland Browns in 1968.

Martin, a speedster who played freshman ball at Minnesota, would be drafted by the Buffalo Bills in the 30th round in 1961, and be a kick returner for the Bears from 1962-64 and continue the San Diego/Canadian Football League connection at Edmonton in 1965, Toronto in 1966 and Winnipeg in 1968.

Lutterbach played briefly at Toronto in 1960, another of the ex-MCRD players such as Marv Beguhl, Wayne Bock, Dick Fouts, Bill Frank, Bob Griffin, Tom Maudlin, J.T. "Tex" Seaholm, Dick Washington and Joe Young to head north in the '50s and '60s.

Valdez would play for the Rams in 1960, the Bills in 1961 and the Oakland Raiders in 1962.

The Devildogs had other pro-type talent, too.

Stilwell had been drafted by the Browns (20th round) in 1957, and Scott would be a 1959 Steelers' selection (26th round). Oddly, Lutterbach (Bears) and Rogers (Rams) both were selected in the 24th round of the 1957 draft. Rogers, of course, went on to be a nationally known college and pro coach.

From 1959-64, Fisher, Garner, Hall, Lutterbach, Merk, Rogers, Scott and Stilwell either had pro tryouts in the National Football League or the American Football League or played one or more seasons.

But the days of the 1956-57 "Iron Monsters" were gone. In their place in 1958 were the "Mighty Mites."

Balance was the keyword on offense.

Rogers scored on 78- and 11-yard scoring runs in the loss at Flagstaff. Five players had TDs in a 33-0 romp over the semi-pro

Eagle Rock AC; three scored TDs in a 20-6 victory over Fresno State; four had TDs in a 27-0 victory over the University of Hawaii; Hall scored twice in a 19-6 triumph over the Hawaii Marines; Valdez had the TD against the Rattlers; Pyles scored twice against his alma mater, including a 97-yarder, in a 25-0 victory over San Diego State; Martin scored twice in defeating (8-3) Hamilton Air Force Base, 18-14; Martin scored three TDs in a 34-6 rout of Camp Pendleton; Martin scored twice to help defeat the semi-pro Montebello Rhinos; and five players scored in a 35-0 triumph over the University of San Diego.

The 62-22 pasting of Lejeune wasn't as close as the score indicated, with the lead 48-0 at one point.

According to Leatherneck, the game, "Billed as being played for the mythical championship of the Marine Corps, seemed to pit opponents of more or less equal strength." And the base paper, the Chevron, reported that Lejeune actually was favored "because of an advantage in experience and weight."

Lejeune, with a 7-2-1 regular-season record and led by Ron Beagle and Jim Mora, defeated favored Quantico, 13-6, for the East Coast Marine title.

But San Diego had all the fun. Martin had the kind of a field day only a Marine could appreciate: a TD run of 23 yards, TD run of 22 yards and a TD on a 79-yard pass play involving Valdez. Lutterback scored twice and kicked six conversions. Stilwell caught two TD passes.

San Diego rushed for 338 yards, Lejeune but 20, an indication of the one-sidedness.

The game also marked the return of Hall, who had been injured at mid-season.

Leatherneck again knew the score and picked Stillwell, Scott, Bullock, Valdez, Martin, Hall and Pyles on the All-Marine 'A' team.

In addition, Robinson, Glover, Rogers and Merk were selected on the All-Marine 'B' team.

Robinson also was a first-team Navy Times selection, Pyles was on the second team and Glover the third.

1958

Record: 19-25 Arizona State-Flagstaff, 33-0 Eagle Rock AC (semi-pro), 20-6 Fresno State, 27-0 Univ. of Hawaii, 19-6 Hawaii Marines, 7-28 Tucson Rattlers (minor-league), 25-0 San Diego State, 18-14 Hamilton AFB, 34-6 Camp Pendleton, 34-7 Montebello Rhinos (semi-pro), 35-0 Univ. of San Diego, 62-22 Camp Lejeune (Leatherneck Bowl). (10-2)

Coach: Bull Trometter (St. Mary's) (assistant Camp Pendleton 1949, coach Coronado NAB 1954)

Assistants: Capt. Hans Jacobsen (Drake) (assistant Barstow Marines 1957), Lt. Buddy Lewis (Arizona) (Quantico 1955, Pendleton 1956)

Ends: Ernest Brooks (Hawaii Marines 1957), Pete Covington (Arkansas; later at Northeast Louisiana), Charles Limbach (USC), C.D. Pomajevich, Jim "Piggy" Robinson (Fisk), Darryl Rogers (Long Beach CC-Fresno St.), Jack Stilwell (Northwestern)

Tackles: Art Anderson (Idaho), Bill Cole, Ray Fisher (Eastern Illinois), John Glover (Camp McGill 1955, Hawaii Marines 1956-57), Dick Loncar (Notre Dame; later at Northeast Louisiana) (Pendleton 1955-56), John "Tiny" Scott (Ohio St.), Bob Whitlow (Arizona)

Guards: Dick Austin, Bill Bradley, Elbert Bullock (Fresno St.), Ernest Delco (Pendleton 1955-56), Felix Mallett (Long Beach CC)

Centers: Rex Collins, Doug Day, Don Geddes

Backs: Norm Adams, Dale Boutwell (Arkansas; later at Trinity of Texas), Skip Brock, Charles Butler, Al Chapman, Bob Garner (Fresno St.), Alvin Hall, Bob Liles (Wichita St), Ken Lutterbach (Evansville), Billy Martin (Minnesota), Ernie Merk (USC), Jim Pyles (San Diego St.), Ed Snider (Fresno St.), Lee Taylor (Citrus JC-Fresno St.), Vern Valdez (Antelope Valley JC-Univ. of San Diego), Pete Walski (UC Santa Barbara)

Undefeated Season

Former Marine Ted Williams was a classic example of an athlete retiring at the top.

At age 42, the Splendid Splinter hit .316 for the Boston Red Sox in 1960, with 29 homers, 72 runs batted in and a .645 slugging percentage in his final season.

Robert "Bull" Trometter was an example of a coach going out at the top, guiding San Diego to a 10-0 record in 1959 before closing a Marine career than began in the mid-1930s.

He left with a 16-game winning streak, a 1957-59 mark of 30 victories and three losses, two Leatherneck Bowl triumphs and an overall 46-6 Marine coaching record at San Diego, retiring in July 1960 to coach at nearby University High.

Of more importance, Trometter — who somehow as a running back at the former Marine Corps Base picked up the nickname "Bull" despite a 5-11, 175-pound frame — had a positive influence on hundreds of young men passing through the Recruit Depot. And, for many, this special relationship continued for three decades.

A funny thing had happened on the way to that 1959 season — and it proved to be a key to the Devildogs' success. While San Diego and Quantico are as far apart in many approaches as they are in miles, Quantico for the first time in postwar football sent a nucleus of a team to San Diego — not to play the Depot but to play *for* the Depot.

The East Coast team that rolled up a 9-3-1 record in 1958, including a 13-12 victory over 19th-ranked Rutgers, contributed nine players to San Diego's unbeaten 1959 edition:

Ends Jackie Barrett (East Texas) and Nick Germanos (Alabama and a 1956 Senior Bowl player), tackles Greg Thomasson (Arkansas State) and Paul Ward (Whitworth), center Bob Adelizzi (Dartmouth), and backs Claude "Bo" Austin (George Washington), Charles Laaksonen (Syracuse), Jim Lorenz (California) and Gene Roll (Missouri).

And, with a powerful 1-2 halfback punch of Alvin Hall and Billy Martin, the Depot did go on a roll, defeating the semipro Anaheim Rhinos, 36-19, in the opener as Martin scored on a 101-yard kickoff return and 56-yard pass play. Overall, he gained 58 yards on 10 carries, caught four passes for 83 yards, returned two kickoffs for 119 yards and a punt for 44 yards.

The Depot beat Fort Carson (twice), as six players scored in a 42-2 triumph, while quarterback Vern Valdez (University of San Diego) was the main man in a 40-0 victory, completing scoring passes of 29 and 39 yards, running 57 yards for a TD and returning an interception 2 yards for a score.

Fresno State fell, 13-6, as Hall gained 110 yards in 21 carries and scored a TD. The Devildogs' 27-7 victory ended Hamilton Air Force Base's four-game winning streak. Hall scored twice in a 40-14 victory over the University of San Diego. Bob Keyes (University of San Diego) put on a show against the semipro Eagle Rock Athletic Club in a 21-9 victory, rushing for 182 yards in 12 carries and scoring three TDs, including a 90-yard TD run.

Against Moffett Field, Trometter tried to hold down the score, even attempting six field goals in the second half of a 46-0 victory. Bill Leroy scored twice and Bob Liles (Wichita State) completed scoring passes of 73 yards to Bob Wright and 36 yards to Austin.

Then came the shocking 64-6 rout of San Diego State in the regular-season finale as the Depot rushed for 508 yards and passed for 145, and all 41 Devildogs in uniform played. Hall scored on a 72-yard run and 36-yard interception, and Walt Kelly had two TDs. It was a bittersweet victory, however, because the Aztecs' coach was Paul Governali, Columbia's College Hall of Fame quarterback who starred for the El Toro Flying Marines in 1944-45.

In the Leatherneck Bowl before 20,000, the Devildogs polished off Bolling Air Force Base, 41-14, scoring three TDs in the first four minutes. For the day, Hall registered three TDs and rushed for 91 yards in 11 carries, and Martin scored twice.

Bolling, coached by former Marine George Makris, entered the game with an 8-1-1 record and since late in the 1951 season had posted a 78-8-3 mark. (Three of the losses and one tie were at the hands of Quantico.)

Yet, it was a poignant moment, not only for Trometter who was coaching his last Marine team but also for Bolling, which dropped football after the '59 season.

San Diego couldn't claim the national service title because Quantico (11-0) also was undefeated. The Virginia team had defeated Bolling, 15-3, and walloped McClellan Air Force Base, 90-0, in the Shrimp Bowl.

Regrettably, a game between San Diego and Quantico — potentially one of the best ever involving Marine teams — could not be arranged. Quantico blamed San Diego. ... San Diego blamed Quantico. ...

Besides the Quantico reinforcements, Trometter retained 15 from the 1958 team:

End Ernie Brooks; tackles Art Anderson (Idaho), John Glover and Bob Whitlow (Arizona); guards Dick Austin, Bill Bradley, Bill Cole and Chris Pomajevich; centers Ron Collins and Doug Day; and backs Al Chapman, Hall, Liles, Martin and Valdez.

With Camp Pendleton dropping football, San Diego picked up guard Mike Brown and center Don "Duke" Karnoscak (Colorado) from its 1958 team.

But there weren't many replacements for the Depot from the college ranks, as was also the case in 1958, with backs Keyes, Jim McGuire (Arizona) and Ray Yoast (University of San Diego) the principal additions. End Carroll Roberts also was a key newcomer.

How good were the Devildogs? They didn't trail until the Eagle Rock game, the seventh of the season. Besides the 41 players in the San Diego State game, Trometter used reserves freely in other contests.

A tipoff to the team's talent was the pros' interest.

Austin was drafted in the 13th round by the Washington Redskins and had a tryout in 1957. Martin would be drafted by the Buffalo Bills on the 30th round in 1961 and play three seasons in the National Football League and three in the Canadian Football League.

Trometter made sure the scouts were aware of the others' abilities.

Anderson would play parts of four NFL seasons. Ward would be with the Chicago Bears briefly in 1961, Detroit in 1961-62 and the Lions briefly in 1963. Whitlow would put in eight NFL seasons. Karnoscak would be wih the Denver Broncos briefly in 1960. Hall would be with the Los Angeles Rams three seasons. Keyes would be an Oakland Raider in 1960 and a San Diego Charger briefly in 1961. Back Jesse Murdock would play for the Raiders and Bills in 1963 and be with the Bills briefly in 1964, a year before he died. Valdez was a member of the Rams in 1960, the Bills in 1961 and the Raiders in 1962.

Leatherneck magazine was impressed, too, selecting Anderson, Brooks, Chapman, Glover, Hall, Karnoscak, Roberts, Valdez and Whitlow as All-Marine.

But in an embarrassing oversight, Martin was not chosen. Otherwise, the entire San Diego backfield would have been picked for the third year in a row.

It was the third honor for Glover, who was All-Marine in 1957 with the Hawaii Marines and second team in 1958 with the Depot.

The Navy Times took note, too, naming Karnoscak the Most Valuable Player on the All-Service team, and awarding first-team berths to Hall and Valdez.

Valdez, said the Navy Times, is the "man who made the Devildogs go. The former Little All-American hit on 25 of 62 passes for 536 yards and nine touchdowns (although) San Diego was primarily a running team — 1,064 yards passing to 3,059 rushing. He had a 3.3 rushing average, was the team's leading punter with a 35.3 yard average and was the leading pass interceptor (six) of a team which grabbed off 23 enemy aerials."

With the undefeated season, Trometter couldn't have *written* a better script than the one he acted out in 1959, or had a better hand to play.

1959

Record: 36-19 Anaheim Rhinos (semipro), 42-2 Ft. Carson, 13-6 Fresno St., 27-7 Hamilton AFB, 40-14 Univ. of San Diego, 40-0 Ft. Carson, 21-9 Eagle Rock AC (semipro), 46-0 Moffett Field, 64-6 San Diego St., 41-14 Bolling AFB (Leatherneck Bowl). (10-0)

Coach: Robert "Bull" Trometter (St. Mary's) (assistant Camp Pendleton 1949; coach Coronado NAB 1954)

Assistants: Capt. Hans Jacobsen (Drake) (asst. Barstow Marines 1957), Lt. Buddy Lewis (Arizona) (Quantico 1955, Pendleton 1956)

Ends: Jackie Barrett (East Texas) (Quantico 1958), Ernie Brooks (Hawaii Marines 1957), Nick Germanos (Alabama) (Quantico 1958), Carroll Roberts, Lou Watson (Pratt JC-Kansas), Bob Wright

Tackles: Art Anderson (Idaho), John Glover (Camp McGill 1955, Hawaii Marines 1956-57), Greg Thomasson (Arkansas St.) (Quantico 1958), Paul Ward (Whitworth) (Quantico 1958), Bob Whitlow (Arizona).

Guards: Dick Austin, Bill Bradley, Mike Brown (Pendleton 1958), Bill Cole, Cal Fackrell, Dave Frederick, Chris Pomajevich, Tom Totuske.

Centers: Bob Adelizzi (Dartmouth) (Quantico 1958), Ron Collins, Doug Day, Duke Kornoscak (Colorado) (Quantico 1957, Pendleton 1958).

Backs: Bo Austin (George Washington) (Quantico 1958), Art Brakefield, Al Chapman, Billy Charles, Alvin Hall, Walt Kelly, Bob Keyes (Univ. of San Diego), Bill Leroy, Bob Liles (Wichita St.), Billy Martin (Minnesota), Charles Laaksonen (Syracuse) (Quantico 1957-58), Jim Lorenz (Pasadena JC-California) (Quantico 1958), Jim McGuire (Arizona), Jesse Murdock (later at Cal Western), Gene Roll (Missouri) (Quantico 1958), Vern Valdez (Antelope Valley JC-Univ. of San Diego), Ray Yoast (Riverside CC-Univ. of San Diego).

The Beat Goes On

Hans Jacobsen found out in succeeding Robert "Bull" Trometter in 1960 a little of what Gene Bartow would go through in taking over for John Wooden at UCLA in 1975.

True, the national spotlight wasn't on Jacobsen as it was on Bartow, but the military and civilian community in San Diego can be rather critical, too.

Trometter had posted 10-1, 10-2 and 10-0 records before retiring, and All-Marine players such as ends Ernest Brooks and Carroll Roberts, tackles John Glover and Bob Whitlow, center Don Karnoscak, and backs Al Chapman and Vern Valdez had moved on.

But Capt. Jacobsen proved equal to the challenge, guiding the Recruit Depot to an 8-2 record, a season that included a successful two-game Eastern swing, the losses to the University of San Diego, 21-20, and to Quantico (a 9-2 record) in the third Leatherneck Bowl, 36-6.

The victory by the Toreros ended a 21-game winning streak stretching over three seasons, while the victory by Quantico settled the All-Marine and national service titles.

Jacobsen, after entering Drake, had followed the right road map to the coaching position. He was a guard on the 1948, 1949, 1950 and 1951 San Diego teams that had a combined 34-8 record; and was a San Diego assistant in 1953-54; at Barstow in 1957, and again at San Diego in 1958-59.

A strong nucleus remained, including the explosive halfback combination of 6-0, 185-pound Alvin Hall and 5-11, 190-pound Billy Martin, who scored 27 touchdowns between them.

Incredibly, Hall — an All-Marine selection in 1957, 1958 and 1959 — was not chosen for a fourth time by Leatherneck magazine, which selected 11 players instead of the 22 as in 1959. He had rushed for 525 yards in 73 carries and scored 90 points. What did a guy have to do to be recognized?

Part of the problem might have stemmed from the 1959 All-Marine selections when Martin was passed over. Martin rushed for 684 yards in 83 carries and scored 90 points in 1960, and possibly was picked over Hall to right the earlier wrong.

The foulup deprived Hall of tying back Volney "Skeet" Quinlan of San Diego (1947-50) for being All-Marine four times. Guard Bill Jesse of Quantico (1947-49) and San Diego (1950-51) was the only five-time selection.

Hall at least was a Navy Times' All-Sea Service selection in 1960, as was Martin.

Jacobsen also retained 13 from the 1959 team: Ends Nick Germanos (Alabama) and Lou Watson; tackles Art Anderson (Idaho), a 6-3, 238-pounder, and Paul Ward (Whitworth), a 6-3, 245-pounder; guards Dick Austin and Dave Frederick; and backs Art Brakefield, Billy Charles, Walt Kelly, Jim Lorenz (California), Jesse Murdock, Gene Roll (Missouri) and Ray Yoast (University of San Diego).

Anderson and Ward would be All-Marine selections, Anderson a first-team All-Sea Service pick and Ward, a shot-putter and hammer thrower, a second-team choice.

As in 1959, the Depot landed some players with service experience: end Earl Allen (Camp Pendleton) and John Lee (two seasons at Camp Lejeune); center Bob Roche (Quantico); and backs Al Daniels (two seasons with the Hawaii Marines), John Robert Fritsch of Maryland (two seasons at Quantico) and Gerry McGuire of St. John Fisher (Quantico).

Add to the equation 6-3, 245-pound tackle Bill Meglen (Utah State), guard Donn Carswell (Stanford), who would be selected All-Marine, and back Kelton Winston (Wiley), plus a big ol' tackle also named John Robert Fritsch. By the time he would try out for the Kansas City Chiefs at age 28 in 1964, Fritsch was listed as 6-4 and 260. (He also was with the Chiefs in 1965.)

The Depot's growing reputation was making it difficult to attract college opponents and there were few military teams left to play.

Cal Poly San Luis Obispo was the victim in the opener, 26-10, as Martin ran 78 yards for a TD and three others scored. The semipro San Fernando All-Stars lost, 45-6, as Martin ran 80 yards for a score and returned a punt 90 yards for another, and Hall and Murdock scored twice.

The Devildogs defeated the semipro Eagle Rock Athletic Club, 20-15; downed Ft. Belvoir, 48-0, in Virginia as Hall scored three times (once on an 80-yard run) and Martin twice; and beat Camp Lejeune, 28-8, in North Carolina as Martin scored twice.

San Diego State was a 33-0 victim of the Devildogs' passing attack with Winston catching three TD passes and Bob Alexander two. The game was the last for Aztecs coach Paul Governali, a former Marine. His teams had tied the Depot once and lost four times in his five seasons.

Whitman was defeated, 34-0, as Martin caught two TD passes; and Eastern New Mexico fell, 54-7. The Depot rushed for 409 yards and passed for 199. Martin gained 156 yards in 10 carries and Fritsch passed for two TDs.

In the loss to the University of San Diego, Hall scored twice and Martin returned a kickoff 82 yards for a TD.

Lorenz completed 63 of 103 attempts and had nine TD passes. Hall caught 18 passes for 133 yards and Martin 16 for 202.

(The Depot even fielded a B team, losing to Los Angeles Pacific, 40-12, and Southern California College, 56-0.)

The varsity had plenty of pro potential.

Hall — at age 28 — would join the Rams for three seasons, beginning in 1961. Martin would put in six years in the National Football League and Canadian Football League.

Lee, an all-around athlete, had been drafted by the Baltimore Colts in the 14th round in 1955.

Meglen, a 22nd-round pick of the Los Angeles Rams in 1959, had tryouts with the San Diego Chargers in the 1960 preseason and again in 1963.

Anderson would play three seasons in the NFL, and Ward parts of three seasons.

Murdock would put in a season in the AFL.

(In at least two cases, the ages listed on Marine programs appear to be younger than the players actually were, possibly to enhance the players' pro prospects.)

One of the success stories was the development of the 6-0, 195-pound Winston, who would be drafted by the Chicago Bears in the ninth round in 1962 while a Marine as a result of his Depot play. One of his traits was persistency. Winston tried out for the Bears in 1964 and the Rams in 1966, at age 26 joined the Rams as a defensive back and kickoff returner for the 1967 and 1968 seasons and was with the Rams briefly in 1969.

1960

Record: 26-12 Cal Poly San Luis Obispo, 45-6 San Fernando All-Stars, 20-15 Eagle Rock AC, 48-0 Ft. Belvoir, 28-8 Camp Lejeune, 20-21 University of San Diego, 33-0 San Diego St., 34-0 Whitman, 54-7 Eastern New Mexico, 6-36 Quantico (Leatherneck Bowl). (8-2)

Coach: Capt. Hans Jacobsen (Drake) (assistant Barstow Marines 1957)

Assistants: Jackie Barrett (East Texas) (Quantico 1958), Chuck Laaksonen (Syracuse) (Quantico 1957-58).

Ends: Bob Alexander, Earl Allen (Arizona St.-Flagstaff) (Camp Pendleton 1956), Nick Germanos (Alabama) (Quantico 1958), Jack Gravitt (Baylor), John Lee (Georgia Tech) (Camp Lejeune 1954-55), Chris Pomajevich, Lou Watson (Pratt JC-Kansas).

Tackles: Art Anderson (Idaho), Terry Conley (Indiana), John Fritsch, Bill Meglen (Minnesota-Utah St.), Ray Petersen (UC Davis), Paul Ward (Whitworth) (Quantico 1958).

Guards: Dick Austin, Dom Bruno (Pearl River JC), Donn Carswell (Stanford), Dave Frederick, Ron Post, Bo Raney (Abilene Christian), Tom Totuske.

Centers: Ira Black (Prairie View), Bob Roche (St. Francis-Pittsburgh) (Quantico 1958, Okinawa)

Backs: Art Brakefield, Billy Charles, Al Daniels (South Dakota) (Hawaii Marines 1956-57), Dick Eschbach (California Western), John Fritsch (Maryland) (Quantico 1958-59), Alvin Hall, Walt Kelly, Jim Lorenz (Pasadena JC-California) (Quantico 1958), Billy Martin (Minnesota), Gerry McGuire (St. John Fisher) (Quantico 1958), Jesse Murdock (later at California Western), Curt Plott (Occidental) (Pendleton assistant), George Robb, Gene Roll (Missouri) (Quantico 1958), Kelton Winston (Wiley), Ray Yoast (Riverside JC-Univ. of San Diego).

Running back Cleveland Jones, former standout running back at Oregon State and MCRD San Diego, went into social work in California

Lieutenants Lead Way

Q uantico to the rescue!
There was a time when them were fighting words.
The Virginia and California branches of the Corps in the past had little in common, and at times hated each other's guts. But the times had changed. Or was it that San Diego had faced reality?

Whatever, with the Marines' supply of college players dwindling, the Recruit Depot gladly accepted these young Quantico lieutenants — who also could play some pretty good football.

In the 1961 season, the Depot would call on seven players with Quantico experience, and four of them would be selected All-Marine.

The Devildogs simply couldn't have posted an 8-3 record without them.

Allen "Scotty" Harris, who had won two Bronze Stars in Korea and was a veteran of Marine coaching, picked up the march from Hans Jacobsen with a blend of players having Quantico, MCRD, college, service or high school experience.

The Quantico contingent numbered end Holly Hollingshead (Mississippi State; Quantico 1959-60), 6-1, 230-pound tackle Tony Anthony (Navy) (Quantico 1958), guard Tony Stremic (Navy) (Quantico 1958-59), 6-0, 225-pound center John Yohn (Gettysburg) (Quantico 1959-60), and backs John Fritsch (Maryland) (Quantico 1958-59), Don Magee (San Diego State) (Quantico 1960) and Tom Maudlin (USC) (Quantico 1959-60).

Returning Devildogs were ends Earl Allen, Jack Gravitt, John Lee (Georgia Tech) and Lou Watson; tackles Terry Conley, 6-3, 245-pound John Fritsch, 6-3, 245-pound Bill Meglen (Utah State) and 6-3, 238-pound Ray Petersen (UC Davis), guards Dom Bruno, a 5-9, 225-pounder, and Ron Post; center Bo Raney (Abilene Christian), and backs Billy Charles, Al Daniels, Dick Eschbach (California Western), Fritsch and Kelton Winston (Wiley).

Newcomers included end Jack Faris (Penn State), 6-4, 238-pound tackle Larry Hunt (San Jose State) and 6-1, 225-pound tackle Bob Moss (San Diego State).

Guard Ken Beverlin would play for Northern Iowa after his Marine tour, and back Perry Rodrique at Brigham Young.

But the prize catch was a back with but high school experience, Brad Hubbert, who at age 20 was 6-2, 205. By the time he had played two more seasons at MCRD in 1962 and 1963, two at Arizona in 1965 and 1966, and joined the San Diego Chargers in 1967, Hubbert would be a 227-pound fullback.

He was awesome as a Chargers' rookie, rushing for 643 yards in 116 carries and two touchdowns and catching 19 passes for 214 yards and two TDs.

Injuries slowed him in 1968, a season in which he gained 119 yards in 28 carries and scored twice.

But he displayed his old form in 1969, rushing for 333 yards in 94 attempts and scoring four times, and closed his pro career with the Chargers in 1970 by gaining 175 yards in 48 carries and scoring a TD.

The Devildogs opened with a 41-16 victory over the University of Mexico as six players scored TDs; defeated the Eagle Rock Athletic Club, 28-21, as Winston scored two TDs; the San Fernando All-Stars, 32-0, as Raney kicked two field goals; the University of San Diego, 37-0, as Winston scored two TDs and Maudlin threw three TD passes; and Cal Poly Pomona, 28-14, as four scored TDs, before losing to Pacific, then an independent, 12-9.

The Depot also downed Cal Poly San Luis Obispo, 28-20, as four scored TDs, and Lewis & Clark, 22-20, as Maudlin threw two TD passes.

But the Pensacola Naval Air Station Goshawks spoiled the Leatherneck Bowl, 21-15, before a crowd of 25,102. The only good news was that Pensacola was a predominantly Marine team. There were 27 Leathernecks on the squad, including seven who had played for Quantico.

Idaho State was a 28-6 victim in the teams' first meeting, before the climactic closer, an 18-13 loss to San Diego State. The Aztecs' first-year coach was Don Coryell, who had been successful at Ft. Ord and Whittier and guided the Aztecs to a 7-2-1 mark in 1961. In 12 seasons at State, Coryell would fashion a 104-19-2 record. In later years, of course, Coryell would be the coach and offensive genius behind the NFL St. Louis Cardinals and San Diego Chargers.

Besides Hubbert, four other players had been drafted by the pros or would be after their Marine football. Lee was picked in the 14th round by the Baltimore Colts in 1955, Faris in the 14th round by the Washington Redskins in 1958, and Meglen in the 22nd round by the Los Angeles Rams in 1959. Winston would be a ninth-round choice of the Chicago Bears in 1962, and Hubbert in the seventh round as a future by the Chargers in 1966.

Meglen had 1960 and '63 tryouts with the Chargers. Hollingshead would play briefly with the Pittsburgh Steelers in 1962. Yohn would be with the Colts in 1962, and the New York Jets in 1963 and briefly in 1964. Fritsch, the tackle, would have tryouts with the Kansas City Chiefs in 1964 and 1965. And Winston would play parts of five NFL seasons.

Maudlin would pass for Toronto of the Canadian football league in 1962 and Montreal in 1963.

What a '61 season Maudlin had put in for the Depot, completing 116 of 233 passes for 1,769 yards and rushing for 131 yards. Little wonder he was selected All-Marine. He is "considered one of the finest signal callers ever to don Marine grid togs," said Leatherneck magazine.

Winston, also named All-Marine, gained 755 yards in 130 carries, scored 11 TDs and six extra points, and caught 22 passes for 359 yards. He led "in every offensive department except passing and pass receiving," said the Leatherneck.

Hollingshead, another All-Marine, caught 27 passes for 497 yards and five TDs as the primary receiver although missing two games.

Stremic, a "bulwark on defense throughout his team's winning season" according to Leatherneck, and Yohn also were All-Marine selections.

Neither Maudlin nor his Depot teammates were selected for a Navy Times' All-Service team, however, only because the publication did not select one.

1961

Record: 41-16 Univ. of Mexico, 28-21 Eagle Rock Athletic Club, 32-0 San Fernando All-Stars, 37-0 University of San Diego, 28-14 Cal Poly Pomona, 9-12 Pacific, 28-20 Cal Poly San Luis Obispo, 22-20 Lewis & Clark, 15-21 Pensacola NAS (Leatherneck Bowl), 28-6 Idaho State, 13-18 San Diego State. (8-3)

Coach: Allen "Scotty" Harris (Ohio State) (coach Okinawa, Hawaii Marines 1958; assistant at Camp Lejeune, Camp Pendleton 1953-54)

Assistants: Donn Carswell (Stanford), Vern Rosene (Iowa State Teachers), Mike Wiggins

Ends: Earl Allen (Arizona St.-Flagstaff) (Pendleton 1956), Jack Faris (Penn st.), Tom Gallagher (Carroll), Jack Gravitt (Baylor), Holly Hollingshead (Mississippi St.) (Quantico 1959-60), John Lee (Georgia Tech) (Camp Lejeune 1954-55), Lou Watson (Pratt JC-Kansas), Neil Wright (Lincoln)

Tackles: Tony Anthony (Navy) (Quantico 1958), Terry Conley (Indiana), John Fritsch, J.E. Howard, John Hunnicutt (Colorado St.), Larry Hunt (San Jose St.), Bill Meglen (Minnesota-Utah St.), Bob Moss (San Diego St.), Ray Petersen (UC Davis)

Guards: Ken Beverlin (Iowa State Teachers); Jim Breen (Eastern Michigan), Dom Bruno (Pearl River JC), Alan Goodman, Darryl Lasater (San Diego CC), Ron Post (Riverside JC), Vic Snider (UC Santa Barbara), Tony Stremic (Navy) (Quantico 1958-59), Jim Wells (Twentynine Palms Marines 1958-59)

Centers: Jim Allen, Ray Eaglen, Bo Raney (Abilene Christian), John Yohn (Gettysburg) (Quantico 1959-60)

Backs: Billy Charles, Al Daniels (Hawaii Marines 1956-57) (South Dakota), John Dear, Dick Eschbach (California Western), John Fritsch (Maryland) (Quantico 1958-59), Brad Hubbert (later at Arizona), Lenahan, Ben Lett (Okinawa), Gene Lewis (Porterville JC), Don Magee (San Diego St.) (Quantico 1960), Lonnie Matthews, Tom Maudlin (USC) (Quantico 1959-60), Eddie Nailon, Fred "Tank" Moore (Twentynine Palms Marines 1960), Perry Rodrique (Southeast Louisiana; later at Brigham Young), Joe Shepard (Miles), Barney Williams (Paris JC), Kelton Winston (Wiley).

Coach Bill Arnsparger gained renown as a pro assistant with Baltimore Colts, head coach with the New York Giants and head coach at LSU.

184

The Talent Runs Deep

The San Diego Marines made their mark all right in 1962, and the players themselves would be doing it for the next decade.

Coach Scotty Harris' Leathernecks won eight — including a 16-7 victory over the Pensacola Naval Air Station in the annual Leatherneck Bowl and a 34-6 rout of Don Coryell's San Diego State Aztecs — against two losses during a predominantly college schedule.

The team had character (some spelled that characters). But what the players accomplished after San Diego was just as interesting. For example:

■ Guard Mike Montler, a scrawny 185-pounder on graduating from high school, already had bulked up to 6-5, 240 pounds and with the Depot experience would take his talents to Colorado (1966-68) and to the pro ranks.

At Colorado, he was the captain as a senior, won All-America honors as a tackle and was a member of the Blue-Gray, Hula, Senior Bowl and College All-Star squads.

Montler perhaps is best remembered as a member of the 1977 Denver Broncos team that played in the Super Bowl. In the process he became at least the fifth Marine to play in the Super Bowl, joining Gary Larsen, Mike Mercer, Cornelius Johnson and Howard Kindig.

Montler was a center and offensive guard and tackle for the Boston (and New England) Patriots from 1969-72 and the Buffalo Bills 1973-76, and closed out with the Detroit Lions in 1978.

A 1976 Bills media guide noted that Montler, the "oldest man on the roster," had started "every game at center for the second straight year and ran his consecutive string to 35 straight starts." It noted that he didn't miss a game in 1974 "despite a painful leg injury." Montler had become a starter in the ninth game of the '73 season.

■ Any story has to mention kicker Herb Travenio (Texas College), for whom life began at 30. He had been with the 1st Marine Division team in Korea as far back as 1954. Surprisingly, his best years were ahead as Travenio would kick for the San Diego Chargers in 1964-65. He converted all 40 extra-point tries in 1965 and 18 of 30 field-goal attempts.

■ End Gary Henson (Colorado) also would head to the pro ranks, performing as a kick returner for the Philadelphia Eagles in 1963.

■ Back Brad Hubbert would wind up at Arizona for the 1965 and '66 seasons, then star for another San Diego team, the Chargers of the American Football League, from 1967-70. In 1967, he rushed for 643 · yards.

■ Back Kelton Winston (Wiley) would become a pro figure, playing with the Los Angeles Rams in 1967 and 1968.

■ Tackle John Fritsch, 6-3, 255, would try out with the Kansas City Chiefs in 1964 and 1965, and tackle Bill Meglen (Minnesota-Utah State), 6-2, 255, had tryouts with the Chargers in 1960 and 1963.

■ Guard Ron Smeltzer would letter at West Chester (Pa.) in 1964-65-

66 before embarking on a coaching career that would take him as an assistant to Colorado, UC Santa Barbara and the Canadian Football League as well as a successful tour in the California high school ranks.

■ Besides Montler and Smeltzer, guard Ken Beverlin would head for the college ranks, Beverlin at the State College of Iowa in 1964, and tackle Paul Ehrmann (Cal Poly San Luis Obispo) and back Perry Rodrique (Southeastern Louisiana) at Brigham Young in 1965.

■ Quarterback John Arms (Southwestern Louisiana), playing for his third service team, would become a colonel, and back King Dixon (South Carolina), San Diego's head coach in 1964 and a Bronze Star winner in Vietnam, would retire as a lietenant colonel to oversee family business interests.

The '62 success came as no surprise what with 23 returnees: ends Earl Allen (Arizona State-Flagstaff), Jack Faris (Penn State), John Gravitt and Neil Wright (Lincoln); tackles Terry Conley, Fritsch, Meglen and Bob Moss (San Diego State); guards Beverlin, Dom Bruno (Pearl River JC), Eddie Nailon, Ron Post and Tony Stremic (Navy); center Bo Raney (Abilene Christian); and backs Billy Charles, Hubbert, Ben Lett, Don Magee (San Diego State), Fred "Tank" Moore, Rodrique, Joe Shepard (Miles), Barney Williams (Paris JC) and Winston.

As a result, the "only novice in the Devildogs' front line was rough and tough Don Nelson, who won the starting center berth," according to the base paper, the Chevron.

And, as in recent Devildog seasons, no one had to ask, "Where's the beef?"

"The Marines held a big edge in weight (against Long Beach State)," the Chevron noted, "with eight tackles going over 230 pounds and five over 250."

Harris had played baseball at Ohio State, won two Bronze Stars in Korea and been an assistant and head coach of Marine teams in Hawaii and at Camp Pendleton and Camp Lejeune. His Devildogs opened with victories over Long Beach State, 39-0; Cal Poly San Luis Obispo, 35-0, and the San Fernando All-Stars, 59-6, before a 14-7 loss to Pacific.

They won south of the border, 16-0, over the University of Mexico before 45,000, then lost to Cal Poly Pomona, 12-10. Cal Poly would lose once in 10 games.

Victories followed over New Mexico Highlands, 10-7, on Travenio's last-minute field goal; Pensacola, before a crowd of 19,000; and San Fernando State, 41-0. Pensacola, with several Marines on the roster, would post an 8-2 record.

Buoyed by the addition of back Cleveland Jones, who had completed recruit training, the Leathernecks won the finale from the crosstown Aztecs as Dixon scored three TDS. Jones, a 5-3, 150-pound speedster, was the last player cut by the Dallas Cowboys in 1961. He played several post-San Diego seasons with Southern California minor-league and semi-pro teams.

San Diego State had won eight straight for second-year coach Coryell to close with an 8-2 record. This loss, plus a 16-12 setback in 1963, rankled Coryell and the school, and the teams did not play in the

Depot's final 1964 season.

Rodrique was the leading ground gainer in 1962 with 549 yards in 111 carries, and Winston picked up 507 in 92 attempts.

Magee, at quarterback, completed 31 of 64 attempts for 430 yards, and Arms 29 of 66 for 364. Allen was the leading receiver with 18 catches for 237 yards. Faris, a 14th-round draft pick of the Washington Redskins in 1958, had 12 receptions for 173 yards.

Dixon and Winston both scored 36 points, and Travenio 25.

As good as the season was, even more lay ahead in 1963.

1962

Record: 39-0 Long Beach St., 35-0 Cal Poly San Luis Obispo, 59-6 San Fernando All-Stars, 7-14 Pacific, 16-0 Mexico, 10-12 Cal Poly Pomona, 10-7 New Mexico Highlands, 16-7 Pensacola NAS (Leatherneck Bowl), 41-0 San Fernando St., 34-6 San Diego St. (8-2)

Coach: Allen "Scotty" Harris (Ohio St.) (coach Okinawa, Hawaii 1958; assistant at Camp Lejeune, Camp Pendleton 1953-54)

Assistants: Jimmie Howard (Medal of Honor winner), Marty Lewis (San Diego Naval Training Center), Tom Molen (Montana St.), Pete Petersen

Ends: Earl Allen (Arizona St.-Flagstaff) (Pendleton 1956), John Cook (West Texas), Jack Faris (Penn St.), Jack Gravitt (Baylor), Gary Henson (Colorado), Bob Owens, Neil Wright (Lincoln)

Tackles: Terry Conley (Indiana), Jack De Priest, Paul Ehrmann (Cal Poly SLO; later at Brigham Young), John Fritsch, Bill Meglen (Minnesota-Utah St.), Bob Moss (San Diego St.), Dave Wetzell

Guards: Ken Beverlin (Iowa State Teachers), Dom Bruno (Pearl River JC), Mike Montler (Colorado), Eddie Nailon, Ron Post, Ron Smeltzer (later at West Chester), Tony Stremic (Navy) (Quantico 1958-59), Jim Wankum (Hancock JC)

Centers: Ray Eaglin, Dave Edmondson (Cal Poly SLO), Don Nelson (Minnesota), Bo Raney (Abilene Christian), Barrett Williams

Backs: John Arms (Southwestern Louisiana) (Pensacola 1960, Quantico 1961), Jack Armstrong (Ohio St.), Bill Charles, John Dear, King Dixon (South Carolina), (Quantico 1959-60, coach Okinawa 1961), Dave Edmunds (William & Mary) (Quantico 1961), Ron Everett (Texas A&M), Brad Hubbert (later at Arizona), Cleveland Jones (Oregon), Ben Lett (Okinawa), Don Magee (San Diego St.) (Quantico 1960), Fred "Tank" Moore (MCB Twentynine Palms 1960), Dick Nawotcyzinski (Montana St.), Perry Rodrique (Southeastern Louisiana; later at Brigham Young), Joe Shepard (Miles), Barney Williams (Paris JC), Kelton Winston (Wiley)

Kicker: Herb Travenio (Texas College) (1st MarDiv 1954)

Former Marine football figures Ed Arnold (left, El Toro) and Gen. Thomas Riley (center, Norfolk Marines) gather at a 1989 business promotion in California. Arnold is a Los Angeles TV sportscaster, Riley an Orange County public official

Victorious 12 Times

When three backs and your placekicker are selected All-Marine, the chances are you had quite an offense as well as *some* team.

Those presumptions were valid concerning the 1963 San Diego Marines, winners of 12 straight before a 13-10 loss to Quantico in the Missile Bowl at Orlando, Fla., a game that decided the national service title and the All-Marine championship.

To put the season in perspective, one other Marine team (Quantico in 1947) ever won 12 times and one (Quantico in 1948) captured 13.

Maj. Allen "Scotty" Harris, the coach, had directed the Devildogs to an 8-2 record in 1962 and, with a number of familiar faces and bodies returning, hopes were high anyway. The 429 points against 13 opponents simply were frosting on the cake.

And this put the '63 team in the company of other potent Marine outfits: Mare Island, 454 points in 1918; Parris Island, 467 in 1926; Quantico, 444 in 1947; Quantico, 419 in 1948; Quantico, 400 in 1949; San Diego, 485 in 1949; San Diego, 524 in 1950; and Parris Island, 505 in 1952.

There had been San Diego teams, perhaps, with more talent, but the chemistry, speed, size and balance of the 1963 team were just right for a schedule that had eight college opponents.

Carrying over a four-game winning streak from 1962, the Leathernecks opened with a 42-0 victory over the University of Mexico, as Cleveland Jones (Oregon) scored three times, followed by triumphs over Long Beach State, 23-14; Arizona State-Flagstaff, 40-7, and Lincoln (Mo.), 27-6.

Then it was off to Farmington, N.M., for a 33-12 victory over the Lackland Air Force Base Warhawks in the Petroleum Bowl.

Returning to the college scene, the Depot rolled over Cal Poly Pomona, 37-6; Cal Poly San Luis Obispo, 41-14, behind Hugh Oldham's three TDs; and Pacific, 24-6. The Pacific and Cal Poly victories avenged San Diego's only '62 losses.

A 43-12 shellacking of the semipro San Fernando All-Stars was a tuneup for a 44-7 victory over the Pensacola Naval Air Station before 24,091 in the Leatherneck Bowl, one of the largest home crowds in history for any Marine game. Oldham scored three TDs, including one of 78 yards; Glen Kirk (Austin) scored twice and quarterback Erroll Yeager (Murray State) threw two TD passes. Pensacola was not exactly dog meat, either, finishing with a 9-2 record.

The Depot also downed San Diego State, 16-12, for the unofficial city title as Perry Rodrique (Southeastern Louisiana) scored from the 2 with 1:00 left. Coach Don Coryell's Aztecs were led by quarterback Rod Dowhower, later a college and pro coach, and closed with a 7-2 record.

A 49-7 victory over the semipro South Bay Athletic Club set the stage for the Missile Bowl game pairing San Diego (12-0), riding a 16-game winning streak, and Quantico (9-1), loser only to Ft. Eustis, 13-0.

Yeager passed to Oldham for a TD and 31-year-old Herb Travenio (Texas College) kicked the extra point and a field goal, but they couldn't offset a Tom Singleton to Herm Brauch pass for 26 yards for a Quantico TD and Dave Hayes' 26-yard TD run.

Leatherneck magazine chose Jones, Oldham, Rodrique and Travenio, who wound up with 10 field goals and 38 conversions for 68 points, as All-Marine. Surprisingly, no member of an offensive line that obviously controlled the line of scrimmage or a defensive unit that gave up but 16 touchdowns in 12 regular-season games was picked. Quantico had five linemen chosen. Like they say, San Diego didn't get much respect!

Harris, a combat and Marine-coaching veteran, did not have to start from ground zero that season, what with 18 back from the 8-2 team of 1962: ends Ray Eaglin, Jack Gravitt and Dick Nawotcyznski (Montana State); tackles John Fritsch, massive Mike Montler and Bob Moss (San Diego State); guards Paul Ehrmann (Cal Poly San Luis Obispo), Eddie Nailon and Ron Post; center George Edmondson (Cal Poly SLO); and backs John Armstrong, King Dixon (South Carolina), Brad Hubbert, Rodrique, Joe Shepard (Miles), Barney Williams (Paris JC), Kelton Winston (Wiley); and Travenio.

But what helped turn a good team into a great one was the infusion of players with service experience: tackle Neil Rountree (Air Force Academy) and center Lance Piccolo (Boston University) from Quantico's 1962 team; center Jack Eatinger from Pensacola, and tackle Troy Perkins (Arkansas Baptist) and backs Kirk, Oldham, John Proctor (San Diego City College) and Yeager with Okinawa experience.

Another key was Yeager's stepping in right away at quarterback to succeed Don Magee and John Arms of the '62 squad.

The team was as big and deep as any the Marines have produced, to wit: Montler weighed 260; Fritsch 255; Ehrmann and Rountree 250; guard John Wyffels, Moss and tackle Max Newberry (Napa JC), 245, Post, 240; Piccolo, Perkins and Nowatcyznski, 235; guard Dennis Couse, tackle Dick Banky and Gravitt, 230; and Eaglin, 225. No team scored more than 14 points against the Depot.

During the regular season, San Diego had one of the more powerful 1-2-3 Marine punches ever, with Rodrique rushing for 740 yards in 120 carries, Jones —with 9.8 speed in the 100 and the team MVP — for 623 yards in 62 attempts (an average of 10 yards a carry) and Oldham for 607 yards in 66 carries.

Rodrique, said Leatherneck, "was the type of powerful fullback which every football team needs."

As might be expected, Montler moved on to Colorado and the pro ranks. Hubbert, Winston and Travenio each put in at least two seasons in the pros and Fritsch received a pro tryout.

But the strangest twist was that Banky, Newberry, Ehrmann, back Bob Cain and Rodrique all wound up at Brigham Young for the 1965 season.

1963

Record: 42-0 Univ. of Mexico, 23-14 Long Beach St., 40-7 Arizona St.-Flagstaff, 27-6 Lincoln, 33-12 Lackland AFB (Petroleum Bowl), 37-6 Cal Poly Pomona, 41-14 Cal Poly San Luis Obispo, 24-6 Pacific, 43-12 San Fernando All-Stars, 44-7 Pensacola (Leatherneck Bowl), 16-12 San Diego St., 49-7 South Bay AC, 10-13 Quantico (Missile Bowl). (12-1)

Coach: Allen "Scotty" Harris (Ohio St.) (coach Okinawa, Hawaii 1958; assistant at Camp Lejeune, Camp Pendleton 1953-54)

Assistants: Ron Brown (Los Angeles Valley JC-Montana St.) (coach Okinawa 1962) (KIA), King Dixon (South Carolina) (Quantico 1959-60, coach Okinawa 1961), Jimmie Howard (Medal of Honor winner), Tom Molen (Montana St.)

Ends: Gerald Brown (Utah St.), M. Copeland, Ray Eaglin, Jack Gravitt (Baylor), Prince Hearns, Dick Nawotcyznski (Montana St.), Bill Rogers (Dakota Wesleyan), Murry Wallace

Tackles: Dick Banky (later at Brigham Young), John Fritsch, Mike Montler (later at Colorado), Bob Moss (San Diego St.), Max Newberry (Napa JC; later at Brigham Young), Troy Perkins (Arkansas Baptist) (Camp Pendleton, Okinawa), Neil Rountree (Air Force Academy) (Quantico 1961-62)

Guards: Bob Cimini, Dennis Couse, Paul Ehrmann (Cal Poly SLO; later at Brigham Young), Ron Meyer (Mesa JC), Eddie Nailon, Ron Post, John Reilly (Maryland), John Wyffels

Centers: Jack Eatinger (Notre Dame) (Pensacola NAS 1962), George Edmondson (Cal Poly SLO), Roger Grooms (Cincinnati), Lance Piccolo (Boston University) (Quantico 1962), Al Walker (Texas)

Backs: Jack Armstrong (Ohio St.), Bob Cain (later at Brigham Young), Mike Davis, Dixon (p-c), John Dorsey, Al Garner (American River JC), Brad Hubbert (later at Arizona), Cleveland Jones (Oregon), Glen Kirk (Austin) (Quantico 1961, Okinawa 1962), Hugh Oldham (Okinawa 1962), John Proctor (San Diego CC) (Okinawa), Perry Rodrique (Southeastern Louisiana; later at Brigham Young); Joe Shepard (Miles), Barney Williams (Paris JC), Kelton Winston (Wiley), Errol Yeager (Murray St.) (Okinawa 1962)

Kicker: Herb Travenio (Texas College) (1st MarDiv) 1954

Chuck Dickerson paid dues in Continental League, CFL, USFL and WFL and 20 years in college ranks before being on staff of Buffalo's 1991 and '92 Super Bowl teams.

Helluva Way To Go

If you have to go, 10 and 1 is the way to do it.

The Marine Corps Recruit Depot in 1964 closed out a varsity-football program that had begun in the early 1920s with 10 victories against the one loss — and the All-Marine championship.

It was a crazyquilt schedule that involved five service teams, two semipro teams and four college teams (one of them in Mexico). The eyes of Texas also were on the Depot because, for whatever reason, four opponents hailed from the Lone Star State.

The loss was to Lackland Air Force Base, 10-3.

The Devildogs posted two bowl victories: 14-7, over Ft. Hood in the Petroleum Bowl at Farmington, N.M., and 15-6 over the Pensacola Naval Air Station in the seventh and final Leatherneck Bowl at San Diego.

They also played before a University of Mexico crowd of 50,000, perhaps the largest to see any Marine team since 1945 when El Toro and the Fleet City Navy tangled for the national service title at the Los Angeles Coliseum.

And San Diego went out in style with a dramatic 24-22 victory over Quantico for the All-Marine title and bragging rights that went with it.

The victory — on Jim Pyle's 17-yard field goal with five seconds left after he earlier had missed three attempts — also was the 45th straight at home.

But perhaps the team would be remembered just as much for sending eight players to the 1965 Brigham Young squad.

One of them, end Phil Odle, was the only Devildog drafted by the pros, a possible tipoff that the team had a group of overachievers.

Odle, perhaps the best Marine wide receiver since Crazylegs Hirsch, played for the Cougars from 1965-67, was drafted in the sixth round by Detroit in 1968, and was with the Lions from 1968-70.

Catching passes from Virgil Carter and Marc Lyons, Odle had 46 receptions for 657 yards and 11 TDs in his first season at BYU; 60 passes for 920 yards and 5 TDs his second season, and 77 passes for 971 yards and 9 TDs his final season. He was selected for the Hula Bowl, the Coaches All-American Bowl and the East-West Game.

He didn't enjoy that much success as a pro, however. Playing behind Earl McCullouch, Billy Gambrell and Larry Walton for three seasons, his six receptions for 71 yards in 1968 were his best totals.

Six Depot players received All-Marine honors: tackle Dick Banky, guard Paul Ehrmann (Cal Poly San Luis Obispo), and the backfield of quarterback Tom Singleton (Yale), Frank Finizio (Rhode Island), Cleveland Jones (Oregon) and Perry Rodrique (Southeastern Louisiana).

Finizio edged Rodrique, 483 yards to 480, for rushing honors, and Jones ran for 389. Singleton, named the team's Most Valuable Player, ran and passed for a combined 1,437 yards.

Ironically, Singleton in 1963 had directed Quantico to a 10-1 record and passed for a touchdown as the Virginia team defeated San Diego,

13-10, in the Missile Bowl for the national service title.

Singleton, said the Leatherneck, "on more than one occasion used his cool generalship to turn apparent defeats into stirring wins." For example, against Lamar, he "passed to Rodrique with only 27 seconds left. It was good for a score and a 33-28 victory." Against Quantico, Singleton "took his team downfield in the closing seconds and got close enough for a field goal to give the Devildogs a hard-fought 24-22 victory."

Jones, noted a game program, is a "little man with the lion's heart, playing against comparative mammoths." He stood 5-5 and weighed 160.

Rodrique scored three TDs against both the San Diego Sabres and Montana. He "had two unbeatable assets," according to Leatherneck: "a good pair of hands, and speed with power."

Finizio, a 5-8, 197-pound battering ram, "got into league action by accident," said the Leatherneck. "An injury forced Dixon to shift his regular fullback to halfback, and he put Finizio in as an experiment. Neither turned out to be sorry."

Banky, Ehrmann, tackle Max Newberry (Napa JC), and backs Casey Boyette, Bob Cain, Rodrique and Barney Williams (Paris JC) joined Odle at BYU a year later.

Tom Hudspeth, the "Cougar coach, raided the San Diego Marines and came up with several gems," said the 1965 Street & Smith Football magazine.

He needed a quick fix, because BYU had gone 3-6-1 in 1964 and hadn't had a winning season since 1958. He got it. The Cougars posted a 6-4 record and won the Western Athletic Conference title in 1965, and followed with an 8-2 record in 1966.

Capt. King Dixon (South Carolina), the Devildogs' coach, had a strong nucleus back from the 12-1 team fielded by Coach Allen "Scotty" Harris in 1963 in Gerald Brown (Utah State), Al Garner (American River JC) and Dick Nowatcyznski (Montana State) at ends; Banky, Bob Moss (San Diego State), Newberry and Troy Perkins (Arkansas Baptist) at tackles; Ehrmann, Ron Meyer (Mesa JC), Al Walker and John Wyffels (injured in the preseason) at guards; Jack Eatinger, Jack Gravitt, Roger Grooms (Cincinnati), John Reilly (Maryland) at center-linebacker; and Cain, John Dorsey, Jones, Glen Kirk (Austin), John Proctor (San Diego JC), Rodrique, Bill Rogers (Dakota Wesleyan) and Williams in the backfields.

Emblematic of the times, the team had a decided JC flavor, as well as a wealth of experience from the service ranks in end Bill Cervenak (Quantico 1962), end Dave Culmer (Camp Lejeune 1949, El Toro 1950-52, Lejeune 1956 and El Toro 1960), Perkins (Okinawa, Camp Pendleton), guard Jim Jakubowski (Quantico 1962), guard Bob Lozier of New Mexico (Quantico 1962), Eatinger (Pensacola 1962), Finizio (Quantico 1963), Kirk (Quantico 1961, Okinawa 1962), Proctor (Okinawa), Singleton (Quantico 1962-63) and Anthony Wayne of Penn State (Quantico 1962-63).

Culmer, in his prime, had been one of the Corps' top all-around athletes.

There was no questioning the team's size. Perkins was 6-1 and 260 pounds; tackle P.J. Nepote (San Mateo JC), 6-4, 252; Ehrmann and Moss, 6-1, 250; Newberry, 6-2 and 250; tackle Mike Workman (Cal Poly SLO), 6-3, 245; tackle Mike McCoy (Cal Poly SLO), 6-3, 240; Banky, 6-5, 235; Cervenak, 6-4, 230; guard Jim Nelson, 6-2, 230; Meyer, 230; Nowatczynski, 6-2, 225; and end Mike Gail, 6-4, 225.

Banky "helped save many games with his deadly hitting," the Leatherneck said, and he "was a major reason his team wound up with 10 wins."

Ehrmann was a "mainstay on the offensive line at guard," according to the Leatherneck. ... "He gave Singleton good pass protection when time was essential."

1964

Record: 24-0 San Fernando All-Stars, 26-0 San Diego Sabres, 14-7 Ft. Hood (Petroleum Bowl), 58-6 Univ. of Mexico, 3-10 Lackland Air Force Base, 33-28 Lamar, 16-3 North Texas, 29-21 Ft. Sill, 43-7 Montana, 15-6 Pensacola NAS (Leatherneck Bowl), 24-22 Quantico. (10-1)

Coach: Capt. King Dixon (South Carolina) (Quantico 1959-60; coach Okinawa 1961)

Assistants: Lt. Ron Brown (Los Angeles Valley JC-Montana St.) (coach Okinawa 1962) (KIA), Cpl. Jack Gravitt (Baylor), Sgt. Jimmie Howard (Medal of Honor holder), Lt. Tom Molen (Montana St.), SSgt. Jim Morton (Memphis NAS), John Wynne (Michigan St.) (Camp Lejeune 1952, Hawaii Marines 1954, 1956)

Ends: Gerald Brown (Utah St.), Bill Cervenak (Iowa St.) (Quantico 1962), Dave Culmer (Camp Lejeune 1949, El Toro 1950-52, Lejeune 1956, El Toro 1960), Mike Gail, Al Garner (American River JC), Gerry Griffith (Sam Houston), Dick Nowatcyznski (Montana St.), Phil Odle (later at Brigham Young), Jim Thompson

Tackles: Dick Banky (later at Brigham Young), Mike McCoy (Cal Poly San Luis Obispo), Bob Moss (San Diego St.), P.J. Nepote (San Mateo JC), Max Newberry (Napa JC; later at Brigham Young), Troy Perkins (Arkansas Baptist) (Okinawa, Camp Pendleton), Mike Workman (Cal Poly SLO)

Guards: John Barnes, Paul Ehrmann (Cal Poly San Luis Obispo; later at Brigham Young), Jim Jakubowski (Michigan State-Miami of Ohio) (Quantico 1962), Bob Lozier (New Mexico) (Quantico 1962), Mike McGarry, Ron Meyer (Mesa JC), Jim Nelson, Al Walker (Texas), John Wyyfels

Centers-linebackers: Vic Duncanson (Cincinnati), Jack Eatinger (Notre Dame) (Pensacola NAS 1962), Gravitt (p-c), Roger Grooms (Cincinnati), John Reilly (Maryland), Mike Tribe (Baylor), Bob Vaughn (San Diego St.), Wynne (p-c)

Backs: Rich Beber, Casey Boyette (Northeastern Louisiana; later at Brigham Young), Bob Cain (later at Brigham Young), Sonny Calta (Kansas St.), John Dorsey, Frank Finizio (Rhode Island St.) (Quantico 1963), Larry Hostetler (Wyoming), Cleveland Jones (Oregon), B.C. Kelly (Prairie View), Glen Kirk (Austin) (Quantico 1961, Okinawa 1962), Jim Morehead, John Proctor (San Diego CC) (Okinawa), Jim Pyle (Wartburg), Perry Rodrique (Southeastern Louisiana; later at Brigham Young), Bill Rogers (Dakota Wesleyan), Tom Singleton (Yale) (Quantico 1962-63), Tony Wayne (Penn St.) (Quantico 1962-63), Barney Williams (Paris JC)

Bull's Players Turn Out

Some 250 former Marines turned out at San Diego in January 1986 for a football reunion.

Many of them were players from Coach Bull Trometter's famed 1957-59 teams that won 30 and lost 3.

Unfortunately, It Ends

The San Diego schedule is canceled because of the "uncertain times and future."

The statement could have been issued in 1965 in connection with dropping the Devildogs' football program because of Vietnam commitments.

Actually, it was issued in August 1941 — under remarkably similar circumstances — when the Marine Corps Base (San Diego) dropped its football program with World War II approaching.

In 1941, the legendary Elmer Hall was to have been the coach, and games had been scheduled with Whittier, Redlands, Fresno State, Santa Barbara State, San Diego State, San Jose State, Willamette, College of the Pacific and an Army team.

In 1965, Lt. Ron Brown (Los Angeles Valley JC-Montana State) was to have been the coach. He had been the coach on Okinawa in 1962, and a Devildogs assistant in 1963-64, and assisted Quantico that 1965 season after San Diego canceled its program.

He would be killed in action in Vietnam.

Games had been scheduled with the University of Mexico, the semipro San Diego Sabres, Lamar, Quantico, Camp Lejeune, West Texas and Pensacola in the Leatherneck Bowl, with others to be added.

There was another similarity.

San Diego, in dropping the 1941 schedule (and not resuming football until 1947), was coming off an 11-0 record under Hall in 1939 and a 9-1 record in 1940 — the loss at Oregon, 12-2, in a near-hurricane.

San Diego, in dropping the 1965 schedule, was coming off a 12-1 record under Harris and a 10-1 mark under Dixon.

This time, however, the football program would not resume.

Put On Your Own Bowl

You can go to a bowl game, or hold one of your own.

MCRD San Diego, not totally satisfied with service-bowl arrangements and wanting to do something for its fans, sponsored Leatherneck Bowls from 1958 through its last season of competition in 1964.

And the Marines won five of the games: 62-22 over Camp Lejeune in the inaugural; 41-14 over Bolling AFB in 1959; 16-7 over NAS Pensacola in 1962; 44-7 over Pensacola in 1963 and 15-6 over Pensacola in 1964.

The losses were to Quantico, 36-6, in 1960 and to Pensacola, 21-15, in 1961.

Big Can Mean Better

The recruit depot at San Diego had a number of physically imposing players in the early 1950s who went on to the NFL or AFL.

One didn't mess around with Bob Griffin, Volney Peters, Rob Goode, Harold Bradley, Joe Young or Wayne Bock.

Camp Pendleton's 1953 line was legendary, too: Eugene "Big Daddy" Lipscomb at 265 pounds, Pat Flanagan and Earl Riley, 255; Harold Turner, 246; Ray Suchy 240, Harold Bradley and John Feltch, 230, and Len Stewart 220.

In the mid-'50s, the Corps saw to it that as many of its best physical specimens as possible would wind up at San Diego.

In 1956, for example, MCRD could call on such linemen as John Klotz (6-4, 261), Hank Schmidt (6-4, 253), John Coyne (6-2, 245) Ted Karras (6-1, 240), Ernie Cheatham (6-4, 235), Bill Frank (6-5, 235) and Conrad Margowski (6-4, 235).

In 1957, the depot could field Karras, Klotz, Schmidt, Coyne, John Scott (6-4, 260) and Ray Fisher (6-2, 240).

In 1958, Coach Bull Trometter could line up with Fisher, Scott, Sam Robinson (5-8, 230), John Glover (6-2, 220), Bob Whitlow (6-1, 215) and Art Anderson (6-3, 210).

In 1961, Coach Scotty Harris had at his disposal John Fritsch (6-3, 255), Bill Meglen (6-3, 245), Larry Hunt (6-4, 238), Ray Petersen (6-3, 238), Tony Anthony (6-1, 230) and John Yohn (6-0, 225).

In 1963 Harris — with one of the heaviest Marine teams ever — utilized Mike Montler (6-5, 260), Troy Perkins (6-1, 260), Max Newberry (6-2, 250), Paul Ehrman (6-1, 250), Neal Rountree (6-4, 250), Bob Moss (6-1, 250), John Wyffels (6-0, 245), Ron Post (6-0, 240), Dick Banky (6-5, 235), Dick Nawotczynski (6-2, 235), Lance Piccolo (6-0, 235), Jack Gravitt (6-2, 230) and Fritsch.

In San Diego's last season in 1964, Coach King Dixon could call on Ehrman, Newberry, Banky, Moss, Perkins, Nawotczynski, P.J. Nepote (6-4, 252), Mike Workman (6-3, 245), Mike McCoy (6-3, 240), Ron Meyer (5-11, 230), Jim Nelson (6-2, 230), Bill Cervenak (6-4, 230) and Mike Gail (6-4, 225).

Back in Business

Camp Lejeune returned to the football wars in a hurry, posting a 7-4 record in 1948 and capturing the East Coast Marine, 6th Naval District and South-Central Naval Group titles in 1949.

Joe Missar (Villanova), coach of the 1941 Quantico team who would be awarded a Bronze Star in Korea, supervised the re-entry in 1948 as the North Carolina Marines called on a combination of officers with combat and college experience, players with a service-football background and the usual talents of division enlisted personnel.

Tackle Charles Dawson received All-Marine honors and end Umberto Gigli (215) and Claude Hipps, both from the 1947 China Marines team, earning second-team honors. Hipps returned to Georgia for the 1949-51 seasons and played with the Pittsburgh Steelers in 1952-1953. Gigli played for Quantico in 1949-50 and was back with Lejeune in 1951.

End Loren Burnett (Rice); tackles Paul Blasko (Cornell, Quantico), a Silver Star winner on Guam, and 220-pound Mitch Sadler (Rice); and guards Nick Canzona (St. Mary's of Minnesota) and Stone Quillian (Rice, player-coach at Little Creek), added the needed maturity.

Burnett, Quillian and Sadler were 3 of the 25 Rice players to sign up with the Marines in 1941.

Canzona would be awarded a Silver Star in Korea and a Legion of Merit in Vietnam; Quillian would receive two Silver Stars, a Bronze Star and a Letter of Commendation in Korea and a Legion of Merit in Vietnam.

Back Bob Gault would be awarded a Silver Star and Bronze Star in Korea, and Gil Hershey (Norfolk Marines), the son of the Selective Service director, would be the recipient of a Bronze Star and Letter of Commendation in Korea.

And 235-pound tackle Joe Ward (1st Naval District) would help out in 1948 and 1949.

The losses were to unbeaten Quantico, 18-0; the Ft. Bragg All-Americans (9-1), 27-21, after a penalty on the game's last play, and Little Creek, 6-0. A Lejeune crowd of 10,000 watched the Bragg game.

But the stage was being set for bigger things as Lejeune posted 53-0, 42-0, 59-0, 34-0, 40-13, 78-0 and 33-6 victories against primarily service opposition.

■

Fifteen players returned for the 1949 season, and a 10-2 record and 364 points under Coach Bruno Andruska (Iowa) followed.

The Marines also picked up ends Lou Darnell (Pearl Harbor Marines) and Ernie Hargett (Southwestern Louisiana, 2 seasons at Quantico), a Bronze Star winner in Korea; guard Jim Mariades (Pittsburgh, Penn State, 3 seasons at Quantico), recipient of the Silver Star on Iwo Jima, DFC in Korea and Air Medal in Vietnam; and back Art Husband (Wake Forest, 2 seasons at Parris Island), among others.

One highlight of the season was a 23-7 victory over favored Quantico (11-3), the Virginia base's first loss to a service team in 18 games. Back Dick Stein (Fresno State), Canzona and back Joe Bertholf scored TD's in what some observers still consider one of the major upsets in Marine annals. Quantico, however, beat Lejeune, 34-14, in the playoffs on its way to the All-Navy title.

Another highlight was a 7-0 Thanksgiving Day victory over Parris Island before 10,000.

Hargett and Stein were All-Marine. Stein averaged 47 yards a punt.

Darnell would play at North Carolina in 1951 and 1952, center Owen Rudd at Kentucky in 1951 and center Fred Tullai (Parris Island) at Temple in 1955.

The other loss was to Ft. Bragg, 28-0.

1948

Record: 19-26 Campbell College, 53-0 Philadelphia Naval Base, 0-18 Quantico, 42-0 Norfolk Marines, 59-0 USS Mississippi, 21-27 Ft. Bragg, 0-6 Little Creek, 34-0 Kindley AFB, 40-13 Cherry Point, 78-0 USS Coral Sea, 33-6 Parris Island. (7-4). Tom Dawson All-Marine; Gigli and Claude Hipps second team.

Coach: Joe Missar (Villanova) (coach Quantico 1941)

Assistants: Capt. John Paul (sassistant Parris Island 1947), Maj. Ray Portillo

Ends: Loren Burnett (Rice), Tom Dawson (Quantico 1947), Jim Gallo, Ed Jenkins, Dick Moledor, Leo Moody, Norris Morris, Rollin Park, Herman Romero, Joe Vosmik (Quantico 1947), Westfall

Tackles: John Barto, Paul Blasko (Cornell) (Quantico 1941-42), Charles Dawson, Umberto Gigli (China 1947), Mitch Sadler (Rice), Steve Vedeskas, Joe Ward (1st NavaL District 1947)

Guards: Byron Bakewell (Penn State), H.E. Bare, Nick Canzona (St. Mary's of Minn.-Notre Dame-Cornell) (Pearl Harbor Marines 1946), Henry Lay, Stone Quillan (Rice) (player-coach Little Creek 1947), Leroy Siville, George Sparks

Centers: Burl Bevers, Harry Black, Joe Harbin, Bob Marshall, Jack Overholt

Backs: Mike Ameen, R.W. Bayless, Ray Chispuzio, Bob Gault (Illinois), Gil Hershey (Army) (Norfolk Marines), Claude Hipps (Georgia) (China 1946-47), Frances Hipps (Georgia) (China 1946), Frank Maksin, Martin, Lawrence Miller, James Ptak, William Romey, George Slater, Richard Stein (Fresno State), Ralph Wood, Steve Zakjula

Also: Bradfield, Hampton, Little, Steepe

1949

· **Record:** 41-0 Campbell College, 14-7 Ft. Jackson, 0-28 Ft. Bragg, 81-0 Ft. Lee, 54-0 4th Naval District, 29-0 Cherry Point, 40-0 Jacksonville NAS, 23-7 Quantico, 21-0 Little Creek, 7-0 Parris Island, 40-0 Boston Navy Yard (playoff), 14-34 Quantico (playoff). (10-2). East Coast Marine champion and 6th Naval District title holder. Lost to Quantico in All-Navy semifinals. Had handed Quantico its first loss to a military team in 18 games. Hargett and Stein All-Marine.

Coach: Maj. Bruno "Andy" Andruska (Iowa)

Assistants: Lt. Mike Ameen (Boston Univ., Miami), Capt. Jim Gallo (Colgate), Lt. Bob Hamilton (Pittsburgh), Maj. Dick Opp (Northeastern, Navy), Capt. John Paul (Cornell College, asst. Parris Island 1947)

Ends: Dave Culmer, Lou Darnell (North Carolina, Pearl Harbor Marines 1946-48), Charles Davidson, Tom Dawson (Quantico 1947), Bob Donley, Ernie Hargett (Southwestern Louisiana) (Quantico 1947-48), Mel Hawk, Bob Hennelly, Ewald Vom Order

Tackles: John Barto, Charles Dawson, Mike Kobak, Harry Romers, Don Smith, Joe Ward (1st Naval District), Rufus Williams

Guards: Bob Angus, Byron Bakewell (Penn State), Nick Canzona (St. Mary's of Minn.-Notre Dame-Cornell) (Pearl Harbor Marines 1946), John Gregarson, Henry Lay, James Mariades (Pitt-Penn State) (Quantico 1946-48), Lou Pichon, Stone Quillan (Rice) (player-coach Little Creek 1947), George Sparks

Centers: Norris Martin, Dick McMullen, Owen Rudd (Kentucky), Fred Tullai (Temple-Maryland) (Parris Island 1948)

Backs: Joe Bertholf, Bob Gault (Illinois), Gil Hershey (Army) (Norfolk Marines), Gil Hickoff, Art Husband (Wake Forest) (Parris Island 1947-48), Sid Klinepeter, Frank Maksin, Leo Moody, John Nettingham, Oscar Robinson, Mel Serres, Dick Stein (Fresno State), Ed Strickland, Bill Ward, Steve Zakula

Reserves To Rescue

The Korean War had broken out. Second Division and base personnel had to focus on minefields not playing fields. There didn't seem to be enough players available for a 1950 football team at Camp Lejeune, and the schedule was on the brink of being cancelled.

To the rescue ... came the Organized Marine Reserve.

Called up in the summer, the reservists, particularly those from New England units, provided the quality as well as the needed quantity to continue the football program.

And, although some regulars and reservists were available only for short periods because of the war effort, the Marines won seven, lost two and tied a game during the regular season and defeated Kessler Field, 32-7, in the Electronics Bowl at Biloxi, Miss.

The record might have been more impressive, but games against Ft. Bragg, Atlantic Christian and Warner Robins AFB were called off.

As it was, Lejeune was ranked No. 3 among service teams (behind Quantico and MCRD San Diego) by the Williamson Rating Service. The losses were to Tampa, 13-7, and Quantico, 42-7, in the heralded matchup of Lejeune's Harry Agganis and Quantico's Eddie LeBaron. The tie was against Cherry Point, 0-0.

Ironically, Tampa was coached by 1942 Heisman Trophy winner Frank Sinkwich (Georgia), who washed out of boot camp at Parris Island because of flat feet.

At Biloxi in the bowl inaugural, Agganis, a southpaw from Boston University, ran for three TD's, passed for a fourth and scored two extra points.

The New England connection was evident on the sideline, too.

Assisting head coach Maj. Bruno Andruska (Iowa), for example, were Lt. Harry Botsford (Boston University), Lt. "Big Jim" Landrigan (Holy Cross, Dartmouth, Baltimore Colts), Maj. Dick Opp (Northeastern, Navy) and Capt. Wally Williams (11 letters at Boston University, El Toro Marines, 2 pro seasons).

The jewel, of course, was young Agganis, "The Golden Greek," who had completed his sophomore season at BU (55 completions in 110 attempts for 762 yards and 15 TDs) and arrived at Lejeune just in time to quarterback the 1950 team.

Agganis, a future selection to the College Football Hall of Fame, would be a second-team All-Marine selection by Leatherneck but Lejeune's only one. (The first-team quarterback was another future Hall of Famer, LeBaron.)

Agganis attracted attention, too. The Parris Island paper devoted more space to him (a column, a sports cartoon, headline and No. 1 play in the story) than to a preview of the Thanksgiving Day game.

On the field, Lejeune as part of the New England connection, among others, also could call on Botsford (218) and Tom Lavery (Boston University), 212, at ends; George Ladeau (Springfield) and Landrigan (6-4, 238) at tackles; Don Brawn (Maine), Jerome Combs (Holy Cross)

"WHY THEY ALL PICK AGGANIS" BY COACH BUFF DONEL

football
stars

25c

500 Sportswriters
pick five best
passing backs

AGGANIS, Boston
HEINRICH, Washington
McKOWN, T.C.U.
SAMUELS, Purdue
SCARBATH, Maryland

HARRY AGGANIS

1952

DELL

and Bob Herson (Rhode Island) at guards; Jim O'Connell (Holy Cross) at center; and Williams in the backfield.

Returning from the 1949 team (10-2) were end Lou Darnell (Pearl Harbor Marines), tackles Bob Donley, Don Smith (215) and boxer Rufus "Rufe" Williams (220); guards Byron Bakewell, Henry Lay and Lou Pichon; center Fred Tullai; and backs Bill Minahan and Steve Zakula.

Also reporting from various posts were end John Schuetzner (Pacific Fleet, Great Lakes, South Carolina), 214-pound end Bill Teefey (Richmond, 1st Marine Division, North Carolina), tackles Ed O'Connor (2 seasons at Quantico), 220, and Leslie Molnar (260), guard Wayne Steele (Syracuse, Bucknell); and backs Grover "Red" Martin (William & Mary), Russ Picton (Temple, 2 seasons at Parris Island) and Jack Place (Quantico, William & Mary).

Agganis would be at BU for the 1951 and '52 seasons; Darnell at North Carolina in 1951-52, O'Connor at Maryland in 1952 and Tullai at Temple in 1955.

Agganis would be the Cleveland Browns' No. 1 draft choice in 1952, Schuetzner the Detroit Lions' 24th pick that year and O'Connor the Pittsburgh Steelers' No. 22 pick in 1953. Landrigan had been the Steelers' 19th pick in 1945 and Botsford the No. 26 pick of the Boston Yanks in 1946.

Several would be head coaches: Williams, a Bronze Star winner, with the Hawaii Marines in 1953 and 1954 and at Parris Island in 1955; Landrigan, a Silver Star and Bronze Star holder, at Parris Island in 1956; and Picton at Wilkes in 1957.

And Williams and Landrigan would attain the rank of colonel before retiring.

What goes up, must come down.

Agganis, who reported to Lejeune in time for the 1950 season, was discharged for dependency reasons to return to Boston University in time for the 1951 season opener against William & Mary. And, of course, who does Lejeune play that season? Boston University, a 16-0 winner as the Marines fumbled twice within the 1 and had two TD's called back on penalties.

Agganis would complete 104 of 185 passes that season for 1,402 yards and 14 TD's. As a senior, he would connect on 67 of 125 passes for 766 yards and 5 TD's and be named the Senior Bowl MVP.

But baseball was his love. He signed with the Boston Red Sox for a $60,000 bonus and played in 157 major-league games and was hitting .313 in 1955 before he died from a blood clot after a bout with viral pneumonia. Some 30,000 people, many of whom had followed Agganis' heroics since his high-school days, filed past the altar.

Camp Lejeune played four other college teams during an unusual 6-5-1 season in which they were selected for two bowl games — and lost both.

In addition, they lost to North Carolina College, 26-13, in a scrimmage, but routed the Force Troop All-Stars, 67-0, in a pre-bowl exhibition.

The trip to Biloxi, Miss., for the Electronics Bowl was not as successful as in 1950 because Kessler Field (10-1) obtained revenge with a 13-0 victory.

Then it was off to Tampa for the Cigar Bowl and a 20-0 loss to the Brooke (Texas) Army Medical Center as the offense was contained again. Brooke (9-1) was coached by the father of NFL star Tommy Kramer.

The 1951 Lejeune team was light — the starting backfield averaged 175 — and lacked a Division I-type back to lead the attack, often relying on the defense for victory.

Still there were the 6-3-1 regular-season record and a No. 7 ranking by Touchdown Tips for the team coached by Maj. Joe Donahoe (Navy, Quantico). A 20-13 victory over Quantico was a highlight. George Greco scored twice and Picton once.

And the Marines tied Xavier, which won nine and tied one, 7-7. They beat the other college opponents: Youngstown, St. Bonaventure and Morris-Harvey.

Picton was All-Marine, as were 6-2, 265-pound guard Frank Letteri (Geneva) and end Paul Sweezy (2 seasons at Parris Island), who caught 17 passes for 292 yards and scored 43 points prior to the Brooke game. Picton succeeded Agganis at quarterback and completed 39 of 94 passes for 685 yards prior to the Brooke game.

Back Jack Kroll was a first-team Armed Forces Press Service selection.

Ed Romankowski (2 seasons at Quantico) had six interceptions and was second-team All-Marine. The versatile back also caught 7 passes, handled 12 punt returns and 4 kickoffs and rushed for 142 yards prior to the Brooke game. Veteran guard Wit Bacauskas (Columbia, Quantico) also was second-team All-Marine.

Picton and 11 others had returned from the 1950 team.

The Marines also were bolstered by 220-pound end Ralph Everist (Northwestern), 225-pound tackle Bert Gigli (China, Lejeune and 2 seasons at Quantico), 230-pound tackle Bill Prather (Southwestern Louisiana, 2 seasons at Parris Island), 225-pound tackle Gus Yahn (Youngstown), 6-6, 215-pound tackle Dave McConnell (Columbia), 245-pound guard George Antoine, guard Al Viola, 210-pound guard Bernie Norem (3 seasons at Quantico), Greco (3 seasons at Quantico); back Bob Gault (2 seasons at Lejeune), home from combat in Korea, and back Jack Seiferling (Utah State, Colorado College, Fresno State). Greco was the leading rusher with 385 yards prior to the Brooke game.

Capt. Bill Milner (Wake Forest, Duke, FMF Pacific, Chicago Bears, New York Giants) served as line coach and as a 6-3, 230-pound linebacker. Lt. Gaspar Urban (Notre Dame, Camp Lejeune, FMF Pacific, Chicago Rockets) was another assistant. Both were reservists who had been mobilized.

1950

Record: 41-7 Eglin AFB, 7-13 Tampa, 0-0 Cherry Point, 87-0 Turner AFB, 55-7 Bolling AFB, 27-13 Ft. Jackson, 7-42 Quantico, 26-0 Shepherd, 33-14 Parris Island, 48-0 Little Creek, 32-7 Kessler Field (Electronics Bowl). (8-2-1). Ranked No. 3 among service teams by Williamson Rating System. Games with Atlantic Christian, Ft. Bragg and Warner Robins AFB canceled. Agganis second team All-Marine.

Coach: Maj. Bruno Andruska (Iowa)

Assistants: Lt. Harry Botsford (Boston University), Lt. Jim Landrigan (Holy Cross-Dartmouth), Maj. Dick Opp (Northeastern-Navy), Capt. Wally Williams (Boston University) (El Toro 1945)

Ends: Botsford (p-c), Ed Bracy, Jim Childs, Bill Dantschisich, Lou Darnell (North Carolina) (Pearl Harbor Marines 1946-48), Russ Godwin, Al Greenfield (Penn), John Haffley, John Hoey, Tom Lavery (Boston University), George Litchett, Felix Malevich, Joe Mathis (Richmond), Ray Potts, Tom Ruddy, John Schuetzner (Pacific Fleet, Great Lakes) (South Carolina), Francis Scruggs, Senecal, Bill Teefey (Richmond) (1st MarDiv 1944) (North Carolina), Duane Tiggers

Tackles: Dick Allison, John Dempsey (Maryland), Bob Donley, George Ladeau (Springfield), Landrigan (p-c), Jim Leary, Frank Letteri (Geneva), Angelo Marchi, Les Molnar, Ed O'Connor (Maryland) (Quantico 1946-47), Harry Paterson, Dick Pickett, Tom Ruddy, Charles Sanders, Don Smith, Rufus Williams

Guards: Charles Andris, Byron Bakewell (Penn State), Dick Boss, Charles Boyer, Don Brawn (Maine), Brost, Jerome Combs (Holy Cross), Stan Ellis, Tony Giancurso (Camp Pendleton 1947), Bob Herson (Rhode Island), J.W. Janes, Kelly, Henry Lay, Frank Letteri (Geneva), Fred McClintock (Auburn), Jim Pharr (Richmond), Lou Pichon, Tom Reeves (Shaw), Jim Regan (Villanova) (Camp Pendleton 1946), Gene Schwartz (Purdue), Wayne Steele (Syracuse-Bucknell), Thomas, Bruce Turner

Centers: Charles Baker, Paul Barrow, Roswell Bridger, Belos Hibner, Clarence McCullough, Jim O'Connell (Holy Cross), Tony Scaperotta, Ken Schoff (Baldwin-Wallace), Ken Sharpe, Roy Stephan (York), Fred Tullai (Temple-Maryland) (Parris Island 1948), Ernest Wegner

Backs: Harry "Golden Greek" Agganis (Boston University), Ed Ahonen, Phil Bailey, Martin Barnes, Roger Beattie, Boller, Dave Bostian, John Callahan, Art Calogero (Catholic), Cal Clark, Joe Cordery (Penn State), Erskine Crews, Val Criado, Lou DeLuccrezia (Ewa 1947), Devine, Gonzales, Goodwin, Haines, Tom Hodson (Drexel), John Kitabjian, Jack Kroll, Joe Kuzar, Dave Lasowitz, Gene MacDonald (New York Tech), Mack, Al Mahoney (John Carroll) (Corpus Christi 1945), Grover Martin (William & Mary), Gerald McGraw, Bill McProuty, Guy Merkel, Larry Miller, Bill Minahan, Moore, Bill Moran, Tony Palazzo, Ed Pawloski, Jack Picton (Temple-Wilkes) (Parris Island 1947-49), Jack Place (William & Mary) (Quantico 1947), Riley, Art Stackhouse, Bob Wagner (Nebraska) (Great Lakes, Del Mar Marines), Walsh, Werner, Bob Wiemer, Williams (p-c), Steve Zakula

1951

Record: 7-34 Ft. Jackson, 19-6 Youngstown, 7-7 Xavier of Ohio, 0-16 Boston University, 69-7 Cherry Point, 20-0 Eglin AFB, 20-13 Quantico, 20-10 St. Bonaventure, 21-7 Morris-Harvey, 13-24 Parris Island, 0-13 Kessler Field (Electronics Bowl), 0-20 Brooke AMC (Cigar Bowl). (6-5-1). (Lost to North Carolina College, 26-13, in a preseason exhibition, and beat Force Troops, 67-0, prior to the bowls.) Was ranked No. 7 by Touchdown Tips. Xavier posted a 9-0-1 record. Letteri, Picton and Sweezey were All-Marine, Bacauskas and Romankowski second team.)

Coach: Maj. Joe donahoe (Navy) (Quantico 1947-48, assistant 1949-50)

Assistants: Lt. Fritz Jackson (Maryland-Colgate), Capt. Clark King (Nebraska State Teachers), Lt. George Knezevich (Western Michigan), Capt. Chuck Milner (South Carolina-Duke) (Hawaii Marines 1945), Lt. Bill O'Brien (Southern Illinois), Lt. Dick Piskoty (Miami of Ohio), Lt. Bill Russell (Penn State-Villanova), Lt. Gaspar Urban (Notre Dame) (Hawaii Marines 1945)

Ends: Charles Davidson, Gene Foxworth, Pat Gibbons (Omaha), Bob Goodfellow (Arizona State), Jas Miller (NE Mississippi JC), John Schuetzner (Pacific Fleet, Great Lakes) (South Carolina), Roy Stephens (York), Paul Sweezey (South Carolina), Bob Williams

Tackles: Charles Bittner, Harold Brooks (Washington & Lee), Bert Gigli (China Marines 1947, Quantico 1949-50), Bernard Hoffman (Eau Claire), Frank Letteri (Geneva), Dave McConnell (Columbia), Bill Prather (Southwestern Louisiana) (Parris Island 1948-49), Ken Schiweck (Navy) (Quantico 1949)

Guards: George Antoine. Wit Bacauskas (Columbia) (Quantico 1950), Byron Bakewell (Penn State), Jerome Combs (Holy Cross), Frank Glennon, Milner (p-c), Bernie Norem (Quantico 1947-49), Lou Pichon, Carl Plantholt (Eastern Kentucky), Tom Reeves (Shaw), Al Viola (Georgia-Northwestern), Gus Yahn (Youngstown)

Centers: John Dempsey (Maryland), John Griffin, Don Kelly, Jack Kelly (Wisconsin), Jack Rayburn (Arkansas State), Jim Ruehl (Ohio State), Ken Schoff (Baldwin-Wallace)

Backs: Jim Bond, York Eggleston, Dick Enzminger (Miami of Ohio), Ralph Everist (Northwestern), Bob Gault (Illinois), George Greco (Quantico 1948-50), John Herbst (Baker), Ed Johnson (Quantico 1949-50), Bill Kelly, Jack Kroll, Dave Lechnir (Pearl Harbor Marines), James LeVoy (Quantico 1950), Vince Milano (Connecticut), Bill Minahan, Jim Northcote, Bob Penner, Russ Picton (Temple-Wilkes), Eddie Price, Ed Romankowski (Quantico 1949-50), John Seiferling (Utah State-Colorado College-Fresno State), Bob Snell, Elmer Tolbert, Gene Wisniewski (Duquesne), Paul Woodard (Shaw)

Back-to-back Success

Camp Lejeune was on a roll, posting a 7-3 record in 1952 for its fifth straight winning season and a No. 8 ranking by the Williamson Rating Service.

Assignments to the Far East and the release of some reservists meant the loss of the nucleus of the 1951 team. But the coach, Maj. Joe Donahoe (Navy), hauled in players from a variety of places and Marines also returned from the Far East.

And there was muscle: nine weighed in at 225 or heavier.

The Leathernecks shot to a 7-1 start, including Catawba, Xavier, Dayton and Baldwin-Wallace among their victims.

Wrote a Dayton paper:

"At the end of the first quarter, and again at the end of the first half, the scoreboard in U.D. stadium showed: Dayton 19, Camp Lejeune 0. The university's first Dad's Day was a tremendous success.

"Oh, yeah! You can tell that to the Marines.

"Tell it to the Lejeune Marines especially. ... At the end of the fourth quarter, which is the one that counts, the scoreboard showed Dayton 19 (still), Camp Lejeune 23.

"What a comeback it had been! And what a climax! The winning TD scored on an 81-yard pass play" in the final period from Bill Weeks (Iowa State) to Frank Nastro (South Carolina).

Lejeune also thrashed Quantico (8-3), 25-2. It lost to Ft. Jackson, 13-6, but rolled over Ft. Eustis (9-2), 18-0.

Lejeune lost in the mud to Bolling Field, 7-6, which in the final poll would be the nation's No. 1 service team. Bolling (11-1) scored in the first quarter, Lejeune in the final minutes as John O'Loughlin (St. Bonaventure) connected with Paul Rapp (Duquesne) on a 78-yard pass play. But Jim Howe's extra-point attempt was unsuccessful.

Lejeune had steamrollered Cherry Point, 62-14, setting up a climactic Thanksgiving Day meeting with Parris Island for the East Coast Marine title. But the game was the turkey as Lejeune, apparently unable to recover from the loss to Bolling, went down by a 54-20 score before PI (9-3-1).

Seven players from the 1951 Quantico team were assigned to Lejeune: ends Stan Lewza (St. Bonaventure) and Dick Shanor (Wyoming); guard Bob Langan; and backs Bill Hawkins (VMI, Navy), Joe Krulock (Scranton), O'Loughlin and "Wingin' Willie" Weeks.

Eleven returned from the 1951 Lejeune team. End Harrison Frasier (Navy, Quantico) reported. So did Rapp, a 14th-round draft choice of the New York Yanks in 1951; 6-4, 249-pound tackle Don Owens (Parris Island) and 218-pound guard Paul Stephenson (3 seasons at Quantico). Owens later would be a Little All-American at Southern Mississippi and play seven seasons in the NFL.

There were young but talented players checking in such as tackle Lew Golic, to play seven seasons in the Canadian Football League and have three sons star at Notre Dame in the 1970s and '80s and two of them (Bob and Mike) in the NFL; 212-pound tackle John Maultsby, to play at North Carolina in 1954 and '55 and later in Canada; 230-pound tackle Tony Anton and back Al Hoisington, to play two seasons in the AFL.

But the bonus was the addition of more black players. Guard Tom Reeves and back Paul Woodard, both from Shaw, were among Lejeune's first in 1951. They were joined in 1952 by, among others, 237-pound guard Bob Brown (Florida A&M), 225-pound tackle Art Davis (Alabama State), to play with the Chicago Bears a year later, and 230-pound tackle Willie McClung (Florida A&M), to play seven seasons in the NFL and one in Canada.

Davis, Frasier, guard Carl Plantholt (Eastern Kentucky), guard Al Viola and back Orville Williams (Butler) were All-Marine selections by Leatherneck.

Weeks had been an 18th-round pick of the Philadelphia Eagles in 1951. Maultsby would be a 12th-round pick of the Los Angeles Rams in 1954, Owens a No. 3 pick by the Pittsburgh Steelers in 1957 and Viola a 23rd-round selection that year by the Washington Redskins.

It was a well-rounded group.

Weeks would coach at New Mexico from 1960-67; back Vern Gale (Wyoming) would coach four seasons at Valley City (N.D.) and seven at Wayne (Mich.). ■

And the beat went on into a sixth season, as Camp Lejeune — bolstered by players from other Marine bases — posted another winning record (8-3-1) and tied Quantico and Cherry Point for the 1953 East Coast Marine title.

With a nickname "Biff," Maj. John Crawley (Kansas State) seemed ideally cast as the Marine head coach. He had been line coach at Kansas State in 1948 and Camp Pendleton in 1949 and was head coach when Pendleton canceled the program in 1950.

Ten players returned from Lejeune's 7-3 team of 1952, but the Parris Island connection made the difference.

Assigned to Lejeune were ends Walt Bielich (Pittsburgh, 2 seasons at PI) and Terry Fails (Vanderbilt); 6-3, 245-pound tackle Rex Boggan (Mississippi, 2 seasons at PI), guards Charles Bossolina (Furman), Frank Rindoni (Tennessee, 2 seasons at PI), Dick Steber (Auburn) and Bill Stovall (Mississippi State, 2 seasons at PI); center Glen Graham (Florence Teachers, Camp Pendleton); and back Billy Hayes (North Carolina, 2 seasons at Parris Island).

And Parris Island had posted a 9-2 record in 1951 and 9-3-1 in 1952.

Quantico's 1952 team contributed end Joe Rilo (Villanova), 6-2, 238-pound tackle Ken Barfield (Mississippi), quarterback Joe Caprara (Notre Dame) and back Howard Hostetler (Oregon).

In addition, Crawley inherited ends John Dietz (Bloomsburg, Camp Fisher) and Bill Samer (Pittsburgh, Quantico); guard Charles Scott (2 seasons at Camp Pendleton); and backs Jerry Fouts (Oklahoma, 2 seasons at Camp Pendleton), Don Scardami (Pendleton) and Ray Gene Smith (Cameron, Midwestern, 2 seasons at Pendleton).

The defense, anchored by Boggan, Barfield and Golic, among others, was such that only nationally ranked Bolling AFB (8-3) scored more than two touchdowns. Lejeune held nine opponents to six points or less and two others to two touchdowns.

As in 1952, the 27-23 loss to Bolling was tough to swallow. But Lejeune recovered this time to roll over Cherry Point, 41-0, to tie for the East Coast title; Parris Island, 16-0, and NAS Pensacola (8-2) in the Charity Bowl at Key West, Fla. The other losses were to Ft. Lee (6-3-1), 13-7, and Quantico, 3-0, and the tie, 6-6, against Ft. Jackson (8-1-1).

Quantico (10-3) lost to Ft. Ord, 55-19, in the Poinsetta Bowl for the all-service title. The Virginia team had been upset by Cherry Point, 9-6, in the opener, setting up the East Coast title tie.

Boggan, to be an All-America selection in 1954 and a New York Giants tackle in 1955, and Graham were first-team All-Marine selections by Leatherneck.

Back Reggie Lee, Maultsby and Smith were second-team All-Marine choices.

Fails returned to Vanderbilt for the 1954 season, Fouts would play at Midwestern and Lee would enter Organized Baseball.

Crawley would coach MCRD San Diego in 1954 and Caprara the 1965 Quantico team.

Barfield, a 23-round draft choice in 1952, would play for the Redskins in 1954. Smith would intercept nine passes as a Chicago Bear from 1954-57; Fails would be a 19th-round draft choice of the Eagles in 1955 and Fouts a 22nd-round selection of the Rams in 1956.

Center Harold Brinson (Magnolia A&M, Tulane) would become president of Southern Arkansas University in 1976.

Even the Globe writer, Sgt. Steve Gerstel, would go on to sportswriting renown with United Press International.

1952

Record: 56-7 Catawba, 34-21 Xavier of Ohio, 6-13 Ft. Jackson, 23-19 Dayton, 18-0 Ft. Eustis, 25-2 Quantico, 62-14 Cherry Point, 32-7 Baldwuin-Wallace, 6-7 Bolling AFB, 20-54 Parris Island. (7-3). Ranked No. 8 by Williamson. Davis, Frasier, Plantholt, Viola and Willians named All-Marine.

Coach: Joe Donahoe (Navy) (Quantico 1947-48, assistant 1949-50)

Assistants: CWO Harry Hanson, Capt. George Knezevich (Western Michigan), Capt. Bill Russell (Penn State-Villanova), Capt. John Scarborough

Ends: Harrison Frasier (Navy) (Quantico 1950), Dick Layne (Ohio State-USC), Stan Lewza (St. Bonaventure) (Quantico 1951), Gerald McDermed, Charles Rapp (Duquesne), Dick Shanor (Wyoming) (Quantico 1951), Frank Stupar (Tennessee), Mel Yeshnick

Tackles: Tony Anton (Akron), Bob Brown (Florida A&M), Art Davis (Alabama State), Lew Golic (Indiana), Bernie Hoffman (Eau Claire), Fred Lippard (Appalachian), John Maultsby (North Carolina), Bill McClung (Florida A&M), Don Owens (Mississippi Southern) (Parris Island 1950), Bill Sutherland, Mert Vaserberg

Guards: Bob Berg, Bob Langan (Quantico 1951), Carl Plantholt (Eastern Kentucky), Tom Reeves (Shaw), Paul Stephenson (Quantico 1948-50), Al Viola (Georgia-Northwestern), John Wynne (Michigan State)

Centers: Harold Brinson (Magnolia A&M-Tulane), John Clark, Don Kelly, Steve Lazarus (Wayne), Jim Sutton

Backs: Phil Delpierre (Parsons), York Eggleston, Bob Gault (Illinois), Vern Gale (Wyoming), Bill Hawkins (VMI-Navy) (Quantico 1950-51), John Herbst (Baker), Al Hoisington (Pasadena JC), Bob Howe (Cincinnati), Frank Kreutzberg (Muhlenburg), Joe Krulock (Scranton) (Quantico 1951), Ray Lane (Northwestern), Al Nicholas (Wilkes), Frank Nastro (South Carolina), John O'Loughlin (St. Lawrence) (Quantico 1951), Owen Scanlon (Syracuse), Roy Stephens (York), Bill Weeks (Iowa State) (Quantico 1951), Orville Williams (Butler), Gene Wisniewski (Duquesne), Paul Woodard (Shaw)

1953

Record: 32-6 Baldwin-Wallace, 20-6 Ft. Monmouth, 7-13 Ft. Lee, 6-6 Ft. Jackson, 27-0 Kessler AFB, 27-0 Ft. Eustis, 0-3 Quantico, 7-2 Cherry Point, 23-27 Bolling AFB, 41-0 Cherry Point, 16-0 Parris Island, 13-12 Pensacola (Charity Bowl at Key West). (8-3-1). Was ranked No. 8 by Williamson on Nov. 6. and Smith second team.

Coach: Maj. John "Biff" Crawley (Kansas State)

Assistants: CWO Harry Henson, Capt. Bill Jones (Mississippi College), Capt. Cal Killeen (Bucknell-Navy) (Quantico 1949, Parris Island 1950, assistant 1951)

Ends: Walt Bielich (Pitt) (Parris Island 1951-52), John Dietz (Bloomsburg) (Camp Fisher 1953), Carl Dolan, Terry Fails (Vanderbilt) (Parris Island 1952), Dick Layne (Ohio State-USC), Joe Rilo (Villanova) (Quantico 1952), Bill Samer (Pitt) (Quantico 1951), Glen Sax, Mel Yeshnik

Tackles: Ken Barfield (Mississippi) (Quantico 1952), Rex Boggan (Mississippi) (Parris Island 1951-52), Lou Golic (Indiana), Fred Lippard (Appalachian), Jack Maultsby (North Carolina), Loyd Spencer, Bill Sutherland

Guards: Tony Anton (Akron), Charles Booth (South Carolina), Charles Bossolina (Furman) (Parris Island 1952), Henry Doak, Frank Rindoni (Tennessee) (Parris Island 1951-52), Charles Scott (Camp Pendleton (1952-53), Dick Steber (Auburn) (Parris Island 1952), Bill Stovall (East Mississippi JC-Mississippi State) (Parris Island 1951-52)

Centers: Ben Davis (Furman), Glen Graham (Florence Teachers) (Camp Pendleton 1951-52, Parris Island 1952), Steve Lazarus (Wayne), Jerry Schropp (Coe)

Backs: Bob Bechtel, Ron Byrd (Mississippi), Joe Caprara (Notre Dame) (Quantico 1952), John Connor, Jerry Fouts (Oklahoma-Midwestern) (Camp Pendleton 1951-52), Tom Gilson (Penn), Bill Hawkins (VMI-Navy) (Quantico 1950-51), Bill Hayes (North Carolina) (Parris Island 1951-52), Howard Hostetler (Oregon) Quantico 1951-52, Reggie Lee, Frank Nastro (South Carolina), Leon Robertson (Voorhees JC), Hugo Rosell, Don Scardami (Camp Pendleton 1952), Ray Gene Smith (Cameron-Oklahoma-Midwestern) (Camp Pendleton 1951-52)

Tackle Chuck Huneke had played at three colleges before joining the Marine Corps. He starred on the 1944 and '45 El Toro teams, then played three seasons of pro ball

Recovering in '55, '56

Camp Lejeune had its first losing season in 1954, but it wasn't a good year for East Coast Marine teams.

True, Quantico was (its usual) 10-2 self. But Parris Island went 6-5 and Cherry Point 1-9.

One reason: the Korean War was over, but a lot of good Marines — and football players — still were stationed in Korea and Japan, just in case.

The 1st Division team in Korea won eight and lost one; the 3rd Division in Japan had regimental play among the 3rd, 4th, 9th and 12th Marines, and the division all-stars competed in the Rice Bowl.

And the West Coast, for many of the same reasons, was strong, too: MCRD San Diego was 8-3 and Camp Pendleton 7-3. (El Toro had dropped football.)

Incredibly, Lejeune had only two players return from the 1953 team, part of the reason for a 2-9 finish.

Capt. Bill Jones (Mississippi College), who played in the 1940 North-South Game and was a Lejeune assistant in 1953, took over as head coach but didn't have too many horses.

Some help arrived from Quantico in the form of guard Gene Watto (Fordham), center Bob Loving (McMurry), 210-pound center Jerry Wenzel (St. Joseph's) and back Bob Meyers (Stanford, San Francisco 49ers). But much of Quantico's 1953 all-service runner-up team was assigned to Japan or Korea.

Guard Bob Brown (Florida A&M), 256, returned from the 1952 team. Tackle Art Hargrove (205) had played three seasons at Parris Island and two at Quantico. Guard Frank Durrer (Southeast Missouri), 205, had service experience at NAS Pensacola and NAS Memphis. Back Sam Saxton (205) put in four seasons at Cherry Point.

Reporting with major-college experience were ends Joe Hands (Duke) and Bill Owens (Colgate), both 205; tackles Bill "Moose" Connolly (Massachusetts), 205, and Charles Conaway (Penn), 215; guard Joe Kwiatkowski (Dayton) and backs Bill Lyons (Bowling Green) and Eldon Cadenasso (California), 215.

But one player with pro experience wasn't enough in the competitive service-football world. The victories were 13-0 over Cherry Point and a 10-8 upset of Pensacola (8-3).

Lejeune, in Marine competition, lost to Quantico, 26-19, and Parris Island, 27-0.

Meyers was virtually a one-man team, scoring 39 points, kicking a field goal to beat Pensacola and leading in every statistical department but ticket sales. He was a first-team Armed Forces Press Service selection and accorded All-Marine honors, as was Wenzel. Watto was a second-team selection.

The lack of returning personnel did give younger Marines a chance to develop. Tackle Dick "Tiny" Reynolds, at 6-6, 290, would play at Lejeune in 1955, Parris Island in 1956, North Carolina State from 1958-60 and be drafted by the Houston Oilers in the 7th round and Baltimore Colts in the 12th round.

Connolly would return to Massachusetts for the 1956 season, and Bill Lyons to Bowling Green for the 1956 and '57 seasons.

Meyers, a 16th-round draft selection of the 49ers in 1952, would play for Calgary (CFL) in 1955. Wenzel would try out with the Washington Redskins in 1955. Back John Lee, drafted by the Baltimore Colts in the 14th round in 1955, would play for Lejeune in 1955 and MCRD San Diego in 1960 and '61.

■

You could tell Camp Lejeune meant business in 1955 just by looking at the coaching staff.

The head coach, Maj. Charles Walker (Wabash), had coached MCRD San Diego to 8-2 and 11-0 records and Quantico to 8-3 and 10-3 seasons.

The assistants, Capt. Rudy Flores (Southwestern of Texas), Capt. Bill Jesse (Navy), Capt. Bernie Kaasmann, and Maj. Jim Mariades (Penn State) had combat experience and service-football backgrounds. All five had been part of Quantico's (13-0) All-Navy champion in 1948.

But it still took a 6-0 victory over Parris Island to post a winning 6-5 record.

Opportunistic early in the season, the Marines won four games by six points or fewer but lost to Bolling AFB, 14-13, and Ft. Eustis, 7-6, late in the year.

But the Bolling Generals (9-1-1) were the nation's No. 2 service team; Jackson finished with a 7-3-1 record.

The Marines also defeated Little Creek, Ft. Lee, Pensacola, Ft. Belvoir and Ft. Monroe. The other losses were to Ft. Monmouth, Ft. Jackson and Quantico, 27-7.

Although 10 players returned from the 1954 team, new faces led the way. Back Don Bingham (Sul Ross, Quantico) and 210-pound end Howie Pitt (Duke, Quantico) were All-Marine. Tackle Lou Florio (Boston College, Quantico), 235, and back Bill Roberts (Dartmouth, Quantico, Canada) were second-team choices of Leatherneck.

Bingham also was a first-team Navy Times selection.

Reporting also from Quantico were 220-pound tackle Joe Wojtys (Purdue), quarterback Pat Ryan (Holy Cross) and fullback Bill Tate (Illinois), Player of the Game in the 1952 Rose Bowl.

But the Parris Island connection — so badly lacking in 1954 — was the difference: end Ted Bates (Western Reserve), tackles Paul Mucke (220), Ed Tokus (220) and Bernie Zickefoose (220); guard Dick Bobo, centers Glenn Derr (240) and Bob Schuler; and backs Joe Merli (Scranton), Jim Ray (Vanderbilt) and Bob Rosabaugh. All but Schuler had spent two seasons with recruit depot teams.

End George Cordle, with eight seasons of service ball, reported, as did guard Al Neveu, with three seasons at PI and Quantico, and back Carroll Zaruba (Doane, 1st MarDiv).

The massive Tiny Reynolds returned, and help from the college front included 205-pound end John McKee (Mississippi State) and backs Al Androlewicz (St. Louis) and Ralph Troillet (Arkansas).

Bingham would join the Chicago Bears after Lejeune's 1955 season and in 1956 handle 13 punts and 17 kickoffs for the NFL Western

Conference champion. He had been a seventh-round pick by the Bears in 1953.

Florio would try out with the Bears in 1956 and Calgary in 1957. Zaruba would play with the Dallas Texans in 1960. Pitt had been drafted by the Chicago Cardinals in the 12th round in 1954. Tokus, who had played freshman ball at Georgia and been an All-Marine selection at PI in 1954, would be drafted by the Cleveland Browns in the 28th round in 1955.

Tate would coach Wake Forest from 1964-68, and 215-pound tackle Ralph Starenko (Valparaiso) would coach Concordia (Nebr.) from 1959-63, Augustana (Ill.) from 1964-68 and Augustana (S.D.) from 1969-76.

Guard Don Gautreaux would letter at Boston College in 1958 and 1960, Ray at Vanderbilt in 1956 and '57 and Zaruba at Nebraska from 1957-59.

■

After a losing season and an average year, Lejeune roared back. To some, the 1956 East Coast champion — big and deep and the nation's No. 3 service team — might have been Lejeune's best.

The Marines won eight and lost only to Bolling AFB, 21-6, and Ft. Jackson, 21-9.

Bolling (10-0) was the nation's No. 1 service team and Ft. Jackson (8-2) ranked No. 2.

Lejeune rolled over the last Parris Island team, 48-12, and Quantico, 9-6. (Cherry Point gave up varsity ball after the 1954 season.)

Other victories were over Little Creek, 27-13; Ft. Lee, 22-0; Ft. Belvoir, 21-12; Ft. Monmouth, 49-0; Ft. Eustis, 21-7; and Pensacola, 27-13.

Jesse, a center who was the only five-time All-Marine selection, moved up from an assistant in 1955 to the head position and had seven players back, including Gautreaux, who would be an All-Marine selection.

He inherited a gold mine from the 1955 Quantico team: ends Tom Hague (Ohio State), 210, and Tom Izbicki (Boston College); 285-pound tackle Frank Morze (Boston College); guards Willis Conatser (Cincinnati), Ed Patterson (North Carolina), 210, and Don Tate (Illinois); center Dick Frasor (Notre Dame); and backs Don Daly (Eastern Kentucky) and John Dixon (205), Glenn "Buzz" Wilson and Jerry Witt (210), all of Wisconsin. It might have been the best collection of players the Virginia base ever sent.

Daly and Morze were All-Marine selections; Frasor and Tate were second-team choices. Morze was a second-team AFPS selection.

End Dave Culmer, a veteran of four service seasons, reported, along with end Bob Warren (Arkansas, MCRD San Diego); 260-pound tackle Dave Powers (2 seasons at PI), center John Freeland (Shippensburg, 2 seasons at PI); quarterback Ernie Brown (Kansas State, 2 seasons at Pensacola); and backs John Auer (Ohio State, 2 seasons at PI) and 205-pound Dick Watkins (Panzer, 2 seasons at Quonset Point).

Brown was an All-Marine selection and Warren a second-team choice.

And if that wasn't enough, the college ranks provided end Bill Klaess (Brown), tackles Karl Bays (Eastern Kentucky), 222, Bob Higley (Northwestern), 225, and John Honse (Navy), 205; and backs Tom Bailes (Houston), 205, Lemon McHenry (Southern Mississippi) and John Williams (Colgate).

Flores and Kaasmann returned as assistants and were joined by Tom Parsons (Navy), a 1949 teammate at Quantico.

Morze, a No. 2 pick of the 49ers in 1955, would play for the 49ers from 1957-61, the Browns in 1962-63 and return to the 49ers in 1964.

Daly, a 17th-round draft choice of Detroit in 1955, would try out with the Lions in 1957. Joe Fowlkes, then an 18-year-old, 215-pound end, would try out with the Pittsburgh Steelers in 1960. Bailes had been drafted by the Philadelphia Eagles in the 20th round in 1954 and Witt by the Redskins in the 19th round that year.

1954

Record: 6-14 Little Creek, 7-19 Ft. Jackson, 14-33 Ft. Lee, 10-8 Pensacola, 7-43 Bolling AFB, 0-6 Georgia Tech JV, 19-26 Quantico, 13-0 Cherry Point, 2-7 Ft. Monmouth, 0-27 Parris Island, 0-26 Ft. Eustis. (2-9). Meyers and Wenzel All-Marine.; Watto second team. Ranked 21st by Williamson.
Coach: Capt. Bill Jones (Mississippi College)
Assistants: Lt. Jack Daut (Notre Dame), Lt. Bennie Davis (Furman), T/Sgt. Ted "Babe" Garcia (MCB San Diego 1939, Pearl Harbor Marines 1948-49, Treasure Island 1950), Lt. Grover Walser
Ends: Andy Balke (Delmar JC), Bob Benson (Notre Dame), John Gilligan (NYU), Joe Hands (Duke), Tom Lynch (Kent State), Joe O'Brien (North Carolina), Bill Owens (Colgate), Linwood Pledger, George Russell (Furman), Lou Scott (Indiana State), Ray Scott
Tackles: C. Babikian (Wagner), Bill "Moose" Connolly (Massachusetts), Charles Conoway (Penn), Charles Hall (Illinois), Art Hargrove (South Carolina) (Parris Island 1948-50, Quantico 1951-52), John Meehan (Marquette), Max Price (Purdue), Dick Reynolds (North Carolina State), J. Vanderwende (Muir JC)
Guards: Charles Booth (South Carolina), Bob Brown (Florida A&M), John Creamer (Dartmouth), Don Debella (Arnold), Frank Durrer (Southeast Missouri) (Pensacola, Memphis NAS), Bill Koozer (Chadron), Joe Kwiatkowski (Dayton), Jerry Schropp (Coe), Elmer Schweiss (St. Louis), Gene Watto (Fordham) (Quantico 1953)
Centers: Bob Loving (McMurry) (Quantico 1953), Bob Pophal (Stout), Tony Teresi (Buffalo), Jerry Wenzel (Indiana-St. Joseph's) (Quantico 1953)
Backs: Joe Ahern (Boston University), John Cadenasso (Cal), Don Cebulski (Southern Illinois), Frank DeAgostine, Dave Ficca (Fordham), Floyd Fraley (Kenyon), Dale Henner (Northeast Teachers), Ted Hughes (Texas Christian), Bob Jones (Western Illinois), Don Kilgore (SMU), John Lee (Georgia Tech), Bill Lyons (Bowling Green), Roy Madsen, Joe Marra (Oregon), Bob Meyers (Stanford) (Quantico 1953), Joe Robertson (Gardner-Webb), Leon Robertson (Voorhees JC), Bob Savacool (Vanderbilt), Sam Saxton (Cherry Point 1949-52), Frank Simas (St. Michael's), Brindley Thomas (Heidelberg)

1955

Record: 7-6 Little Creek, 40-6 Ft. Lee, 12-21 Ft. Monmouth, 12-6 Pensacola, 14-12 Ft. Belvoir, 7-27 Quantico, 6-14 Ft. Jackson, 53-0 Ft. Monroe, 13-14 Bolling AFB, 6-7 Ft. Eustis, 6-0 Parris Island. (6-5). Nine had played for Parris Island in 1953-54. Bingham and Pitt All-Marine; Florio and Roberts second team.
Coach: Maj. Charles Walker (Wabash) (Quantico 1947, assistant 1948, coach MCRD San Diego 1949-50, Quantico 1952-53)
Assistants: Capt. Rudy Flores (Southwestern of Texas-Texas) (Quantico 1947-49, San Diego 1950-51), Capt. Bill Jesse (Montana-Navy) (Quantico 1947-49, MCRD San Diego 1950-51, asst. Pearl Harbor Marines 1953-54), Capt. Bernie Kaasmann (Quantico 1948-50), Maj. Jim Mariades (Pitt-Penn State) (Quantico 1946-48)
Ends: Andy Balke (Delmar JC), Ted Bates (Western Reserve) (Parris Island 1953-54), George Cordle (Camp Pendleton 1947, Pensacola 1948, Quantico 1949-51, Pearl Harbor Marines 1953-54), Gene Dilhoff (Cincinnati), Joe Hands (Duke), John Lee (Georgia Tech), John McKee (Mississippi State), George Murphy (Fordham) (Quantico 1955), Howie Pitt (Duke) (Quantico 1954), Jay Reedy (St. Michael's)

210

Tackles: Lou Florio (Boston College) (Quantico 1954), Paul Mucke (Parris Island 1953-54), Dick Reynolds (North Carolina State), Ralph Starenko (Valpraiso), Blair Todino (Maryland), Ed Tokus (Georgia) (Parris Island 1953-54), Joe Wojtys (Purdue) (Quantico 1954), Bernie Zickefoose (Virginia) (Parris Island 1953-54)

Guards: Ted Bacote (Connecticut), Dick Bobo (Penn State) (Parris Island 1953-54), Cliff Camp (North Texas), Bill "Moose" Connolly (Massachusetts), Joe DeGregorio (Alabama), Frank Durrer (Southeast Missouri) (Pensacola, Memphis NAS), Don Gautreau (Boston College), Harold Himi (Southern State), Al Neveu (Parris Island 1949-50, Quantico 1951), Will Rice (Vanderbilt)

Centers: Glenn Derr (Dartmouth) (Parris Island 1953-54), Gene Hoefling (Tulsa), Jesse (p-c), Bob Schuler (Colorado A&M), (Parris Island 1954), Sam Williams

Backs: Al Androlowicz (St. Louis-Missouri), Joe Arahill, Don Bingham (Sul Ross) (Quantico 1954), Flores (p-c), Bob Hill, Ted Hughes (TCU), Al Jeris (Buffalo), Don Kilgore (SMU), Bill Lyons (Bowling Green), Joe Marra (Oregon), Joe Merli (Scranton) (Parris Island 1953-54), Jim Ray (Vanderbilt) (Parris Island 1953-54), Bill Roberts (Dartmouth) (Quantico 1954), Bob Rosabaugh (Penn State) (Parris Island 1953-54), Pat Ryan (Holy Cross) (Quantico 1954), Bill Tate (Illinois) (Quantico 1954), Ralph Troillet (Little Rock JC-Arkansas), Carroll Zaruba (Doane-Nebraska) (1st MarDiv 1954)

1956

Record: 27-13 Little Creek, 22-0 Ft. Lee, 48-12 Parris Island, 21-12 Ft. Belvoir, 49-0 Ft. Monmouth, 6-21 Bolling AFB, 21-7 Ft. Eustis, 9-6 Quantico, 9-21 Ft. Jackson, 27-13 Pensacola. (8-2). East Coast Marine champion. Brown, Daly, Gautreau and Morze All-Marine; Frasor, Tate and Warren second team.

Coach: Bill Jesse (Montana-Navy) (Quantico 1947-49, MCRD San Diego 1950-51, asst. Pearl Harbor Marines 1953-54)

Assistants: George Cordle (Camp Pendleton 1947, Pensacola 1948, Quantico 1949-51, Pearl Harbor Marines 1953-54), Capt. Rudy Flores (Southwestern of Texas-Texas) (Quantico 1947-49, San Diego 1950-51), Capt. Bernie Kaasmann (Quantico 1948-50), Capt. Tom Parsons (Navy) (Quantico 1949-50, asst. Pearl Harbor Marines 1953)

Ends: Ray Armstead, Dave Culmer (El Toro 1950-52), Joe Fowlkes, Tom Hague (Ohio State) (Quantico 1955), Tom Izbicki (Boston College) (Quantico 1955), Bill Klaess (Brown), Charles Pitzen (Toledo), Charles Rogers, Bob Warren (Arkansas) (MCRD San Diego)

Tackles: Karl Bays (Eastern Kentucky), Bob Higley (Northwestern), John Honse (Navy), Frank Morze (Boston College) (Quantico 1955), Paul Mucke (Parris Island 1953-54), Dave Powers (Georgia Tech) (Parris Island 1954-55), Blair Todino (Maryland), Sam Williams

Guards: Willis Conatser (Cincinnati) (Quantico 1955), Don Gautreau (Boston College), Al Neveu (Parris Island 1949-50, Quantico 1951), Ed Patterson (North Carolina) (Quantico 1955), Jim Peal (Virginia State), Don Seedor, Don Tate (Illinois) (Quantico 1955)

Centers: Bill Belcher (San Angelo JC), Joe DeGregorio (Alabama), Dick Frasor (Notre Dame) (Quantico 1955), John Freeland (Shippensburg) (Parris Island 1954-55), Oran Zaebst (Sewanee)

Backs: Pasquale Altieri (Brown), Joe Arahill, John Auer (Ohio State) (Parris Island 1954-55), Tom Bailes (Houston), Ernie Brown (Kansas State) (Pensacola 1954-55), Don Daly (Eastern Kentucky) (Quantico 1955), John Dixon (Wisconsin) (Quantico 1955), Cliff Hoppe (Missouri Valley), Leemon McHenry (Mississippi Southern), Billy Riley, Norm Shaw, Jim Strange, Dick Watkins (Panzer) (Quonset Point NAS), John Williams (Colgate), Glen "Buzz" Wilson (Wisconsin) (Quantico 1955), Jerry Witt (Wisconsin) (Quantico 1955)

New River Fields Team

A varsity team at MCAS in New River, N.C., was one of the few the Marines fielded after Quantico dropped football in late 1972.

Coached by Capt. Mike Gambino, New River won six and lost four. The record:

0-34 Ft. Bragg, 0-63 Dayton JV, 20-14 Charlotte Police Academy, 6-26 William & Mary JV, 20-0 North Carolina-Wilmington, 12-6 North Carolina (club), 6-36 The Citadel JV, 27-0 Raleigh Raiders, 20-6 Eastern North Carolina All-Stars, 26-12 Little Creek.

Title Bid in '58

The 1957 season was two-sided for Camp Lejeune: a 1-4 start but a 3-0-1 finish.

Capt. Wil Overgaard, who as a teen-ager fought with the Marines in the South Pacific, had a rocky start as head coach but finished strong and also laid the groundwork for the 7-3-1 season of 1958.

Overgaard, a tackle, returned to active duty for the Korean War, winning a Bronze Star, and played at Quantico in 1951 and Parris Island in 1953. He was an assistant at PI in 1954 and at Little Creek in 1955 and the head coach at Little Creek in 1956, posting a base-record 9-2-1 record.

Nine players returned from the 1956 team, including guard Don Tate (Illinois, Quantico), a 1957 All-Marine selection. Player-coach Ernie Brown (Kansas State, NAS Pensacola), another returnee, was a second-team All-Marine selection in '57.

Players with service experience included end Howard George (2 seasons, Hawaii Marines), 215-pound guard Charles Gill (Parris Island), 204-pound center Mike Cwayna (Wisconsin, Quantico), 207-pound center Lou Hallow (East Carolina, MCRD San Diego), back Bob Boyer (Bethany, Pensacola), back Emidio Petrarca (Boston College, Quantico) and back Ray Wrabley (St. Vincent's, Quantico). But there wasn't a player from Quantico's 1956 edition.

And the team was light (two players over 220) and had no Division I-type players reporting. Overgaard had to rely on small-college players and enlisted just out of high school against big-time service teams.

Bolling Field (11-0 and the nation's top service team), for example, started three players from Notre Dame, and one each from Oklahoma A&M, Tulane, Pennsylvania, Pittsburgh, Indiana, Army, Southern Methodist and Kansas State in its 26-0 victory at Lejeune. It had 22 players 200 or heavier on the roster.

Against Bolling, Lejeune started 198-pound Henry Bolin (Hobart) and 207-pound Joe Fowlkes at ends, 217-pound Roger Beckley (Buffalo) and 205-pound Jim Peal (Virginia State) at tackles, Tate (200) and 197-pound Bob Callahan (Trenton) at guards, Hallow at center, Brown (193) at quarterback, Don King (177) and 198-pound Dick Watkins (Panzer) at the halves and 195-pound John Williams (Colgate) at fullback.

Lejeune also lost to Little Creek, Eglin AFB and Shaw AFB, but defeated Ft. Eustis, Lockbourne AFB, Pensacola and Ft. Stewart, and tied Quantico, 26-26.

"East Coast Marines looked on the Quantico-Lejeune game as similar to the Army-Navy game," said assistant Bernie Kaasmann, a Bronze Star holder. "No matter how loaded either team was, it was always a battle to the bitter end."

Kaasman, ironically, would be an assistant at Quantico in 1960 and '61.

212

The 1957 efforts might have marked the best coaching job by Overgaard, who also would direct Quantico to 11-0, 9-2 and 9-4 records from 1959-61.

Marring the season, however, was Watkins, a staff sergeant, being shot to death in nearby Jacksonville.

"He was a great person on and off the field," Kaasmann said, "a great athlete, and admired by all who knew him."

Hallow, a former Little All-American, also was an All-Marine choice; Beckley, Callahan and 212-pound back Willis Fjerstad were second-team picks.

Tackle Don Christman (215) would play for Richmond from 1959-61. He would be drafted by the Boston Patriots on the 24th round and have a 1962 tryout. Hallow, a 26th-round pick of the Los Angeles Rams in 1955, would try out with the Patriots in 1961. Fjerstad would be drafted by the Pittsburgh Steelers in 1959 on the 30th round. King would play for Syracuse from 1960-62 and try out with the Detroit Lions in 1963. Petrarca, drafted by the Lions on the 18th round in 1956, would try out with Ottawa (CFL).

■

But 1958 was a different story as Lejeune, with the help of 13 former Quantico players, defeated Quantico, 13-6, and traveled 3,000 miles to face MCRD San Diego for the All-Marine title.

Overgaard had one of the finest end corps of any Marine team: Ron Beagle, a former Navy All-American, Maxwell Trophy winner and All-Marine selection at Quantico and on Okinawa; Fowlkes, George, 206-pound Conrad Hitchler (Hawaii Marines) and Jim Mora (Occidental, Quantico).

Beagle, 211-pound guard Ron Botchan (Occidental, Quantico), center Homer Hobgood (Elon), Mora, back Herb Naaken (Utah, Quantico) and quarterback Marshall Newman (North Carolina) were All-Marine selections.

Beagle was a first-team Armed Forces Press Service pick; Botchan and Newman were second-team.

Newman completed 64 of 126 passes for 1,123 yards and 12 TD's. Beagle, a future selection to the College Football Hall of Fame, caught 18 for 315 yards and four TD's, and Mora 18 for 251 and two scores.

Carey "Choo Choo" Henley (Chattanooga) was Mr. Do It All. The 5-10, 190-pound all-purpose back averaged 4.1 yards a carry, 20 yards on punt returns and 19.3 on kickoff returns, caught 6 passes for 181 yards and scored 37 points.

Tackle Dick Guy (Ohio State, Quantico), 205-pound guard Jim Schwartz (Xavier, Quantico) and backs Fred Beasley (Duke) and Henley were second-team All-Marine choices.

Tackle Dave Six (Parris Island), 220; and backs Don Swanson (Minnesota, Quantico), Y.C. McNeese and Art Wilson (Columbia), among others, also received some starting assignments.

The season highlight was the victory over Quantico.

"Harry Jefferson and Quantico were upset by a Cinderella Camp Lejeune eleven," reported the Globe base paper, "as the locals scored a smashing win over the conquerors of Rutgers and Villanova. Playing before 1,500 fans Thanksgiving Day morning, Lejeune swept past the host team to take the East Coast championship."

But for the US Air Force, it would have been quite a season. Bolling AFB (8-1-1) posted a 33-14 victory over Lejeune. Eglin AFB (10-0-1), the nation's top service team, won, 20-8.

Lejeune also defeated Ft. Lee, the 82nd Airborne, Ft. Bragg, Pensacola, Lockbourne AFB (on tackle Bob Williams' field goal with 33 seconds left) and Ft. Dix, and tied the Norfolk Tars.

But the game they can't wipe off the record was a 62-22 loss to San Diego on Dec. 14 before 18,000 in the inaugural Leatherneck Bowl.

In a 1989 interview, Maj. Gen. James P. Riseley, Lejeune's commanding general in 1958, still maintained that the referees permitted San Diego to move before the ball was snapped throughout the game.

San Diego had taken a 48-0 lead only to have Lejeune score three times in the third period, two of the TD's on Newman passes. The hosts "pushed over another pair of touchdowns to ice the game and win the 'mythical' Marine Corps championship," Leatherneck reported.

But this wasn't just any San Diego team. The recruit depot had won nine and lost two prior to meeting Lejeune. And it had 20 players, including future coach Darryl Rogers, from its 10-1 team of 1957.

As for the Lejeune ends, Hitchler, to play at Missouri from 1960-62 and receive All-America honors as a senior, would be with Calgary (CFL) from 1963-65. Mora would coach his alma mater three seasons, the Baltimore and Philadelphia Stars to two USFL titles and take over the New Orleans Saints in 1986. Beagle, a 17th-round pick of the Chicago Cardinals in 1956, would try out with the Oakland Raiders in 1960.

Botchan, to play with the Los Angeles Chargers in 1960 and Houston Oilers in 1962, would become an NFL game official.

Henley would play at Chattanooga from 1959-61, be drafted by Buffalo in the 21st round and play for the Bills in 1962.

Naaken had been a fifth-round choice of the Rams in 1956 and tried out before reporting to Quantico. Tackle Vern Ellison (235) had been a 12th-round pick of the Steelers in 1957. He would coach Quantico in 1964. Guy had been an 18th-round selection of the San Francisco 49ers in 1957.

■

You have 12 players back from a 7-3-1 team, including a standout passing combination. You add four from Quantico, including All-America and All-Marine linebacker Sam Valentine (Penn State). You're a lock for a banner season. Right?

Wrong, in the case of the 1959 Lejeune team, which finished below .500 with four victories and seven loses.

Maj. Jim Quinn (Fordham), a Bronze Star holder, took over as head coach after four seasons as an assistant at Parris Island, Quantico and Lejeune.

In retrospect, the team wasn't as good as it appeared on paper. The bottom line was that only one player was drafted by NFL or AFL teams, and he (Beagle) was injured against Pensacola and missed most of the season.

The 1955 team had six players drafted, the '56 team had four, the '57 team had five and the '58 team had six. The talent flow that had marked the 1950s was slowing, although it wasn't obvious yet.

And 210-pound center Rex Tatum (Memphis State) was the lone new Division I type player.

Still, the 1959 team was exciting. Newman completed 114 of 223 passes for 1,436 yards and 13 TD's. Mora had 47 receptions for 529 yards.

And the team won three of its last four, the loss to Quantico, 22-21. A Lejeune victory might have been ranked as one of the great upsets of Marine football. Quantico went 11-0, including a 90-0 bowl victory.

Botchan (now at 230), Mora, Newman and Valentine (205), along with newcomer Mel Anderson in the backfield, were All-Marine selections.

Botchan also was a first-team Armed Forces Press Service choice, and Newman and Valentine second-team.

September and October had been forgettable, as Lejeune beat Ft. Lee but lost to North Carolina A&T, the Norfolk Tars, Pensacola, Ft. Campbell, Bolling AFB (its last season) and Mitchell AFB. Then Lejeune routed Ft. Gordon, 86-8; and edged Ft. Bragg, 17-12, and Ft. Dix, 8-0.

Anderson, a late starter, scored five TD's and rushed for 227 yards in 48 carries and caught 11 passes for 227 yards. He would play for Lejeune in 1960-61 and try out with Ottawa in 1962.

Quinn's team did have some bulk, although not necessarily on the first team or in the 235-pound range. He also could call on ends Lincoln Evans (208) and Frank Stankunas (205); tackles William Keck (Tulsa), 220, Rudy Kasarda (210), Charles Connor (220), Frank Yanosky (225) and Ed Walsh (Penn), (225); guards Gary Byrd (220), and Leo Garcia (220) and center Don Feldman (209).

Back Bob Fearnside would play for Bowling Green from 1960-62.

1957

Record: 10-14 Little Creek, 0-26 Bolling AFB, 14-19 Eglin AFB, 21-10 Ft. Eustis, 21-26 Shaw AFB, 23-13 Lockbourne AFB, 26-26 Quantico, 7-6 Pensacola, 36-0 Ft. Stewart. (4-4-1). Hallow and Tate All-Marine; Beckley, Brown, Callahan and Fjerstad second team.

Coach: Capt. Wil Overgaard (Idaho) (Quantico 1951, Parris Island 1953, assistant 1954, Little Creek 1955, coach Little Creek 1956)

Assistants: Lt. Ernie Brown (Kansas State) (Pensacola 54-55), T/Sgt. George Cordle (Camp Pendleton 1947, Pensacola 1948, Quantico 1949-51, Pearl Harbor Marines 1953-54), Capt. Bernie Kaasmann (Quantico 1948-50), Lt. John Williams (Colgate)

Ends: Henry Bolin (Hobart), Bill Crozier (West Chester), Joe Fowlkes, Howard George (Pearl Harbor Marines 1954-55), Mike Minutelli (Ohio State), Mike Newbold (Penn State), Don Smith, Roger Smyth (Kenyon), B. Yelvington (Arizona)

Tackles: Roger Beckley (Buffalo), Don Christman (Richmond), Mike Friedberg (Millersville), Bill Hall, Jim Kunsman (The Citadel), Henry Kwiatkowski (Buffalo), Jim Peal (Virginia State), Bob Schlatzer (William & Mary)

Guards: Bill Beyer (Baldwin-Wallace), Bob Callahan (Trenton), Fran Cornelius (Lock Haven), Tom Davis (South Carolina), Charles Gill (Florida) (Parris Island 1956), Nick Kobak, Bill Motley (Morehead), Don Tate (Illinois) (Quantico 1955)

Centers: Mike Cwayna (Wisconsin) (Quantico 1955), Lou Hallow (East Carolina) (MCRD San Diego 1956), Ron Hicks (South Carolina)

Backs: Francis Allen (The Citadel), Pasquale Altieri (Brown), Tom Bailes (Houston), Bob Boyer (Bethany) (Pensacola 1956), Edgar Brannon (Florida State) Brown (p-c), Ed Cantine (Vermont), Willis Fjerstad, Jim Glowack (Minnesota), Don King (Syracuse), J.C. McNease, Ellsworth Morgan (Yale), Emidio Petrarca (Boston College) (Quantico 1956), Bill Riley, Dick Watkins (Panzer) (Quonset Point NAS) (killed in mid-season), Williams p-c, Ray Wrabley (St. Vincent's) (Quantico 1955)

1958

Record: 13-13 Norfolk Tars, 27-6 Ft. Lee, 8-20 Eglin AFB, 14-6 82nd Airborne, 14-33 Bolling AFB, 50-0 Ft. Bragg, 8-6 Pensacola, 9-6 Lockbourne AFB, 34-12 Ft. Dix, 13-6 quantico, 22-62 MCRD San Diego (All-Marine title). (7-3-1). Marshall Newman completed 64 of 126 passes for 1,123 yards and 12 TDs. Beagle, Botchan, Hobgood, Mora, Naaken and Newman were All-Marine; Beasley, Guy, Henley and Schwartz second team.

Coach: Capt. Wil Overgaard (Idaho) (Quantico 1951, Parris Island 1953, assistant 1954, Little Creek 1955, coach Little Creek 1956)

Assistants: Lt. Fred Campbell (Duke) (Quantico 1956), T/Sgt. George Cordle (Camp Pendleton 1947, Pensacola 1948, Quantico 1949-51, Pearl Harbor Marines 1953-54), Capt. Jim Quinn (Fordham) (assistant Parris Island 1952, Quantico 1954-55)

Ends: Dave Ardapple (Iowa), Ron Beagle (Navy) (Quantico 1956, Okinawa 1957), Joe Fowlkes, Howard George (Hawaii Marines 1954-55), Conrad Hitchler (Hawaii 57) (Missouri), Jim Mora (Occidental) (Quantico 1957), Mike Newbold (Penn State), Charles Underwood

Tackles: John Bietendueffel (Slippery Rock), Jim Clark (Purdue), Charles Connor (Notre Dame), Vern Ellison (Oregon State) (Quantico 1957), J.R. Grabski, Dick Guy (Ohio State) (Quantico 1957), Art Hargrove (South Carolina) (Parris Island 1948-50, Quantico 1951-52), Joe Kubala, Jim Kunsman (The Citadel), Brian McNeely (Michigan State), Joe Murphy (Holy Cross) (Quantico 1957), Milt Oliver, Bob Owens, Dave Six (Cincinnati) (Parris Island 1956), Ed Walsh (Penn)

Guards: Nick Angele (Denver), Bill Beyer (Baldwin-Wallace), Frank Black (Kansas) (Quantico 1957), Ron Botchan (Occidental) (Quantico 1957), Charles Gill (Florida) (Parris Island 1956), Clarence Holland (Virginia State), J.A. Kozakiewicz, Jim Schwartz (Xavier of Ohio) (Quantico 1957, Camp Pendleton 1958), Joe Stranger, Jack Wilson (Okinawa 1957)

Centers: Dick Brittain, Homer Hobgood (Elon), Mike Minutelli (Ohio State), Jim Smiley (Oklahoma) (Quantico 1957)

Backs: Francis Allen (The Citadel), Pasquale Altieri (Brown), Fred Beasley (Duke), Dick Broderick (Fordham-Michigan State) (Quantico 1957), Jim Click (Denison), John Ferrari (Notre Dame), Willis Fjerstad, Joe Grindrod (West Chester), Carey "Choo Choo" Henley (Chattanooga), O.D. Jones (Sul Ross), Y.C. McNease, J.H. Mugford (Notre Dame), Herb Naaken (Utah) (Quantico 1957), Marshall Newman (North Carolina), Phil Senich (Kent State), Don Swanson (Minnesota) (Quantico 1957), Al Terry, Art Wilson (Columbia) (Quantico 1957)

1959

Record: 6-26 North Carolina A&T, 12-13 Norfolk Tars, 0-19 Pensacola, 13-36 Ft. Campbell, 31-8 Ft. Lee, 6-18 Bolling AFB, 6-12 Mitchell AFB, 86-8 Ft. Gordon, 17-12 Ft. Bragg, 8-0 Ft. Dix, 21-22 Quantico. (4-7). Marshall Newman completed 114 of 223 passes for 1,436 yards, 13 TDs. Jim Mora had 47 receptions for 529 yards. Anderson, Botchan, Mora, Newman and Valentine All-Marine.

Coach: Capt. Jim Quinn (Fordham) (assistant Parris Island 1952, Quantico 1954-55)

Assistants: George Cordle (Camp Pendleton 1947, Pensacola 1948, Quantico 1949-51, Pearl Harbor Marines 1953-54), Lt. Jim Schwartz (Xavier of Ohio) (Quantico 1957, Camp Pendleton 1958), Lt. Don Swanson (Minnesota) (Quantico 1957)

Ends: Ron Beagle (Navy) (Quantico 1956, Okinawa 1957), Lincoln Evans, Howard George (Pearl Harbor Marines 1954-55), Jim Mora (Occidental) (Quantico 1957), Frank Stankunas, Don Waits (Pearl River JC-Mississippi Southern), Bob Ware

Tackles: Al Brennan (Denver-Tampa), Charles Connor (Notre Dame), Rudy Kasarda, Bill Keck (Tulsa), Paul Sharp (Southeastern Louisiana), Sam Thornton, Ed Walsh (Penn) (Quantico 1957), Frank Yanosky (The Citadel)

Guards: Ron Botchan (Occidental) (Quantico 1957), Gary Byrd, Bob Cupit (Upsala), Tony DeMatteo (Elon), Walt Fronzaglio, Leo Garcia (Palomar JC), Norm Hofler, Milt Oliver, Don Tennant, Sam Valentine (Penn State) (Quantico 1957-58), Jim Winebrake (Wilkes)

Centers: Don Feldman, Homer Hobgood (Elon), Cavel Raglio (Chattanooga), Rex Tatum (Memphis State)

Backs: Mel Anderson, Ken Easley (Virginia State), Vince Cesare, Bob Fearnside (Bowling Green), John Ferrari (Notre Dame), Joe Grindrod (West Chester), Jim Jeter (Hawaii Marines), Martin Klein, Jack Mossburg (Kentucky), John Mugford (Notre Dame), Marshall Newman (North Carolina), Tom Sacramone (New Haven) (Quantico 1958), Carlton Smith (Okinawa 1958), Ralph Tropeano (Ithaca), Keith wilson (Kansas State), John Wuenschel (Stetson) (Quantico 1958)

Lejeune's Last Teams

Who could have foretold in 1960 that the decade arguably would be the most tumultuous of the century and that Lejeune would give up football in five years?

The decade started auspiciously, with Lejeune posting a 7-3 record in 1960 and an 8-1 mark in 1961.

Denis Horn (Ithaca) was head coach in 1960 and between holdovers from 1959 and three reinforcements from Quantico's (11-0) team of '59 fashioned a three-team concept.

It was good enough to defeat the Norfolk Tars, Ft. Campbell, Ft. Lee, Ft. Belvoir, Mitchell AFB, Ft. Dix and Ft. Eustis as Lejeune literally had the Army sign on opponents. The losses were within the Department of the Navy: to NAS Pensacola, MCRD San Diego and Quantico.

End Joe Losack (Texas, Quantico) and guard Jim Winebrake (Wilkes) were named All-Marine by Leatherneck magazine.

The three Quantico hands reporting were player-coach Dave Stecchi (Holy Cross), tackle Ron Cherubini (Villanova) and back Dennis Pardee (Case, Pensacola).

Cherubini, to receive the Bronze Star in Vietnam, would coach the Lejeune team in 1965 and Quantico in 1966.

■

Seven points separated Lejeune from the base's only unbeaten season in 1961.

The Marines defeated Ft. Benning, Pensacola, Ft. Belvoir, Eglin AFB, Ft. Campbell, Ft. Lee, Ft. Dix and Quantico and tied for second in the East Coast Interservice Conference. The 19-0 victory over Quantico, before 10,000 at Lejeune, broke a 21-game winning streak by the Virginia base against service opponents.

The team's .889 winning percentage was the best in base history.

But no apology was needed for the 12-6 loss to Ft. Eustis. The Army base posted a 9-2 record as the national service champion.

Phil Monahan, captain of Navy's 1955 Sugar Bowl winner and a former assistant at Quantico and Navy, emphasized defense as head coach. Lejeune shut out three teams, allowed but a touchdown in three games and, overall, permitted 60 points in nine games.

Monahan, to be awarded two Bronze Stars in Vietnam, would be selected as a general.

Backs Mel Anderson and John Parrinello (Rochester, Quantico) were All-Marine selections as the offense, too, was heard from. Lejeune scored 27 or more points in five of the nine games. Monahan was deep in the backfield, with Dan Droze (North Carolina, Quantico, Far East), Chuck Latting (Iowa State, Pensacola, Quantico), Bob Miller (Lenoir-Rhyne, Quantico) and quarterback Bob Schwarze (The Citadel, Quantico) complementing Anderson and Parrinello.

Parrinello, the team's Most Valuable Player, scored 44 points and rushed for 437 yards on 84 carries. Latting scored 41 points and Anderson rushed for 440 yards on 75 carries.

Tackle Larry Wagner (Vanderbilt, Quantico) had been drafted by the Boston Patriots and tried out with the New York Titans in 1960 before reporting to active duty.

One Lejeune player was heard from in another sport. End Percy Price, as a boxer, had decisioned Muhammad Ali in the 1960 Olympic Trials (Ali's only loss until 1971) and would fight 400-plus bouts as a Marine, winning three All-Marine heavyweight titles and two interservice titles (including a decision over Duane Bobick).

Droze would be a businessman and longtime assistant coach at Catholic and Georgetown.

Assistant Mike Dau (Lake Forest, Far East) would become the coach at his alma mater in 1966.

A look at other seasons:

1962 (2-3): The Ft. Eustis game and the remainder of the schedule, including the Quantico game, were cancelled because of the national emergency.

Monahan, at the helm again, saw his team beat Ft. Belvoir and Ft. Devens but lose to Ft. Benning, Pensacola and Ft. Campbell.

Players included end Frank Weber (Lenoir-Rhyne, Quantico), tackles Wagner and Art Whittier (Virginia Tech, Quantico), guard Charles Gill (Parris Island, Lejeune 1957-58), and backs Droze, Darrell Fitts (Quantico), Ralph Kincaid (a Little All-American at William Jewell; Quantico) and Art Redden (Arkansas AM&N), another top Marine boxer.

1963 (4-5): The assassination of President Kennedy resulted in the cancellation of the final two games, including the traditional Quantico contest. Lejeune, coached by Alan Fiers, had beaten Ft. Belvoir, Ft. Dix (twice) and Ft. Lee, but lost to Ft. Benning, Pensacola, Ft. Campbell, Ft. Eustis and Ft. Bragg.

End Charles Heard and Redden received All-Marine honors.

Players included tackles Frank Butsko (Navy, Quantico) and Whittier, and back Paul Terhes (Bucknell, Quantico). Terhes had been drafted in the seventh round by the Patriots and the eighth round by the Baltimore Colts. He was at the Patriots' 1961 camp before reporting to Quantico.

1964 (0-8-1): There wasn't much to write home about as Lejeune, coached by Lt. Col. Ray "Stormy" Davis (Hardin-Simmons), lost eight and tied Ft. Lee. The losses were to Ft. Benning, Pensacola, Elon, Ft. Campbell, Ft. Eustis, Ft. Bragg, Quantico (28-0) and Ft. Hood.

The Quantico game was the first between the rivals since 1961.

Center Ron Case and back Jim Ross (Quantico) were All-Marine selections.

Another boxer turned to the gridiron: end Ken Norton (Northeast Missouri). He would be recognized as the WBC heavyweight champion in 1978 but lost the title to Larry Holmes.

Players included 204-pound tackle Phil Lombardo (Boston University, Quantico), guards Bob Everett (Arkansas State, Quantico), 215, and Pete Optekar (Navy, Quantico), and Redden.

Kicker Clark Blake would letter at Northeast Louisiana from 1966-69 and be the school's career scoring leader with 154 points on 24 field goals, 76 extra points and a touchdown.

Case would be the football coach at Carson-Newman in 1978-79 and an assistant at Richmond, Carson-Newman, Maryville, West Texas and Mississippi.

1965 (5-3): Cherubini, a former Lejeune player, took over as head coach for what would be the base's last varsity season.

The Marines, behind a winged-T attack, posted a 5-3 record, beating Elon, North Carolina A&T, Huntsville Rockets, DePauw and Pensacola, and losing to Pensacola and Quantico (twice).

Ends Don Bertolazzi and Woody Wilson, tackles Ned Chappell, Phil Gehringer (225) and Darrell Lasater (MCRD San Diego); Optekar, center Ed Craig, and backs Bob Johnson (Wagner), Ron Nay (Westminster) and Blake were All-Marine selections. Other players included 205-pound end Garland Jones (Austin Peay, Howard, Quantico) and center Marc Glasgow (Ohio University, Quantico).

1966: Dropped football

1960

Record: 31-8 Norfolk Tars, 0-32 Pensacola NAS, 16-0 Ft. Campbell, 47-0 Ft. Lee, 8-28 MCRD San Diego, 55-12 Ft. Belvoir, 23-6 Mitchell AFB, 20-6 Ft. Dix, 15-36 Quantico, 15-14 Ft. Eustis (7-3).

Coach: Denis Horn (Ithaca)

Assistants: Brian Moore (Michigan State), Ike Schneider (New Hampshire) (Pensacola NAS), Dave Stecchi (Fordham-Holy Cross) (Quantico 1959), Charles Zielinski (Northeastern-Boston College)

Ends: Ed Long (Marquette), Joe Losack (Wharton JC-Texas) (Quantico 1957-58), Charles Rix (Rhode Island) (Parris Island 1953, Norfolk), Lee Russ, Stecchi (p-c), Bob Ware.

Tackles: Ron Cherubini (Villanova) (Quantico 1958-59) (Bronze Star), Ben Chitko (China Lake 1952-53), Joe Ernest, Jim Shorter, Sam Thornton.

Guards: Norm Hofler, Marv Lassiter, Milt Oliver, Jerry Smythe (Idaho), Jim Winebrake (Wilkes).

Centers: Ed Craig (Wingate JC), Barrie Delp (Purdue) (Quantico 1958)

Backs: Mel Anderson, Vince Cesare, Bob Cooke, Bob Fennessy, John Ferrari (Notre Dame), Martin Klein, Jim Lipscomb, Jack Mossburg (Kentucky), Dennis Pardee (Case) (Pensacola NAS 1957, Quantico 1958-59), Tom Sacramone (Southern Connecticut) (Quantico 1958), Keith Wilson (Kansas St.)

(INCOMPLETE)

1961

Record: 27-7 Ft. Benning, 17-15 Pensacola NAS, 39-8 Ft. Belvoir, 40-6 Eglin AFB, 6-0 Ft. Campbell, 6-12 Ft. Eustis, 27-0 Ft. Lee, 28-12 Ft. Dix, 19-0 Quantico (8-1).

Coach: John Phil Monahan (Navy) (asst. Quantico 1956) (2 Bronze Stars) (generals)

Assistants: Mike Dau (Lake Forest) (Far East 1959, asst. Far East 1960), Joe Dimincantonio (Springfield), Jim Hardin (Western Kentucky) (Quantico 1959-60), Joe Losack (Wharton JC-Texas) (Quantico 1957-58)

Ends: Percy Price (Hawaii Marines 1958, Quantico 1959-60), Lee Russ, Bill Wilson

Tackles: Ben Chitko (China Lake 1952-53), Ulysses Frier, Tom Montgomery, Jim Shorter, Larry Wagner (Vanderbilt) (Quantico 1960)

Guards: Jack Ebbitt, Tom Harwell (Jacksonville St.), Norm Hofler, Marv Lassiter

Centers: Ed Craig (Wingate JC)

Backs: Mel Anderson, Vince Cesare, Dan Droze (North Carolina) (Quantico 1959, Far East 1960), Harvey Eggleston, Dave Holtsclaw, Chuck Latting (Iowa St.) (Pensacola 1959, Quantico 1960), Frank Long, Bob Miller (Lenoir-Rhyne) (Quantico 1960), John Parrinello (Rochester) (Quantico 1960), Bob Schwarze (The Citadel) (Quantico 1959-60), Jerry Sylvara, Bill Tasker

(INCOMPLETE)

1962

Record: 14-21 Ft. Benning, 0-19 Pensacola NAS, 42-0 Ft. Belvoir, 35-0 Ft. Devens, 0-17 Ft. Campbell. Ft. Eustis game and remainder of schedule cancelled because of a national emergency. (2-3)

Coach: Capt. John Phil Monahan (Navy) (asst. Quantico 1956) (2 Bronze Stars) (generals)

Assistants: Joe Dimincantonio (Springfield), Joe Losack (Wharton JC-Texas) (Quantico 1957-58), Larry Tucker (Mississippi College)

Ends: Hal Krause, Frank Long, Lawson Manous, Chuck Rix (Rhode Island) (Parris Island 1953, Norfolk), Frank Weber (Lenoir-Rhyne) (Quantico 1961), Ken Williams

Tackles: Bill Hatcher (Parris Island), Tom Montgomery, Larry Wagner (Vanderbilt) (Quantico 1960), Art Whittier (Virginia Tech) (Quantico 1961)

Guards: Jack Ebbitt, Charles Gill (Florida) (Parris Island 1956), Tom Harwell (Jacksonville St.), Norm Hofler

Centers: Frank Janes (Auburn), Marv Lassiter, Dallas Zieber.

Backs: J. Beck, Vince Cesare, Dan Droze (North Carolina) (Quantico 1959, Far East 1960), Mike Dunn, Harvey Eggleston, Darrell Fitts (Alabama) (Quantico 1961), Tony Harris, Eddie Hatchett, Dave Holtsclaw, Ralph Kincaid (William Jewell) (Quantico 1961), Art Redden (Arkansas AM&N), Jerry Sylvara, Bill Tasker
(INCOMPLETE)

1963

Record: 0-17 Ft. Benning, 0-20 Pensacola NAS, 21-0 Ft. Belvoir, 35-8 Ft. Dix, 23-31 Ft. Campbell, 7-13 Ft. Eustis, 14-3 Ft. Lee, 36-24 Ft. Dix, 9-27 Ft. Bragg. Remainder of schedule, including Quantico game, cancelled because of the death of President Kennedy. (4-5)

Coach: Alan Fiers (Ohio State)

Assistants: Dave Beinner (Delaware), Tom Grantham (Wisconsin), Bob Niessner (Wagner), Larry Tucker (Mississippi College), Frank Weber (Lenoir-Rhyne) (Quantico 1961-62)

Ends: Charles Heard (Arizona), Hal Krause, W. Wilson

Tackles: Frank Butsko (Navy) (Quantico 1961-62), Art Whittier (Virginia Tech) (Quantico 1961)

Guards: R. Duprell, J. Griesbaum, D. Lund

Centers: R. Estler

Backs: G. Barnes, J. Beck, Mike Dunn, F. Harding, Tony Harris, Eddie Hatchett, Frank Long, Art Redden (Arkansas AM&N), Paul Terhes (Bucknell) (Quantico 1961-62)
(INCOMPLETE)

1964

Record: 0-39 Ft. Benning, 3-7 Pensacola, 7-9 Elon, 3-7 Ft. Campbell, 0-44 Ft. Eustis, 13-13 Ft. Lee, 20-27 Ft. Bragg, 0-28 Quantico, 7-27 Ft. Hood (0-8-1)

Coach: Lt. Col. Ray "Stormy" Davis (Hardin-Simmons) (asst. Quantico 1952-53, asst. Hawaii Marines 1955-56)

Assistants: Herman Brauch (Colgate) (Quantico 1962-63), Jim Davis (Oklahoma) (Quantico 1962-63), Dick Lucas

Ends: Jim Griffin, Charles Heard (Arizona), Eli Knighten, Walt Morse, Ken Norton (Northeast Missouri) (boxing), John Tomasweski (Kent St.)

Tackles: Phil Gehringer, Charles Hayes, George Lombardo (Michigan St.-Boston Univ.) (Quantico 1963), Paul Lund, Jim Merritt (Itawamba JC), Pat Strano

Guards: Bob Everett (Arkansas St.) (Quantico 1962-63), Paul Fedor (North Carolina), Jerry Miller, Pete Optekar (Navy) (Quantico 1963), Lovell Patterson, Dick Serman (Geneva), John Westmoreland

Centers: Larry Ake, Ron Case, George Taliaferro

Backs: Johnnie Blount, John Boyl (Cal), Joe Carter, Tony Conzo, Phil Hill, Larry Humphries, Billy Johnson, Bob Johnson (Wagner), Jim Laurent (Waynesburg), Bill Leedy, Jeff Mair, Leo Myzick, Ron Nay (Westminster), Art Redden (Arkansas AM&N), Jim Ross (Quantico 1960-63), Davis Sanders, Jim Stewart

Kicker: Clark Blake (Northeast Louisiana)

1965

Record: 6-3 Elon, 17-14 North Carolina A&T, 14-7 Huntsville Rockets, 0-35 Pensacola NAS, 30-14 DePauw, 12-36 Quantico, 7-14 Quantico, 25-14 Pensacola (5-3)

Coach: Ron Cherubini (Villanova) (Quantico 1958-59) (Bronze Star)

Assistants: J.A. Kellogg (DePauw), Brian Morse (Principia), J. Shulte (Marquette)

Ends: Don Bartolazzi, Herb Brooks, Garland Jones (Austin Peay-Howard) (Quantico 1964), Woody Wilson

Tackles: Ned Chappell, Phil Gehringer, Darrell Lasater (San Diego CC), Pat Strano

Guards: Pete Optekar (Navy) (Quantico 1963)

Centers: Ed Craig, Marc Glasgow (Ohio Univ.)

Backs: Brian Biggs (Washington), Bill Daugherty, Bob Johnson (Wagner), Jim Laurent (Waynesburg), Ron Nay (Westminster)

Kicker: Clark Blake (Northeast Louisiana)
(INCOMPLETE)

PI: Points Galore

The Parris Island team made its point in 1951 and 1952 — actually 399 of them in one season and 505 in the other.

There was nothing to be defensive about during that Korean War period as PI grabbed off the best of the volunteers and draftees passing through the famed boot camp and kept enough of them around to win 18, lose 5 and tie 1 in the two-year period under Coach J.T. Hill.

Only one other Marine team (San Diego with 524 in 1950) scored more points in a season than the Parris Island Marines (their team nickname) in that 1952 season.

Team statisticians had difficulty keeping up with the blizzard of points:

- Eglin (Fla.) Air Force Base fell, 87-0, as 11 players scored touchdowns.
- The Jacksonville (Fla.) Naval Air Station was a 74-0 victim.
- The Cherry Point Flyers went down, 59-0.
- Stetson University was a 54-13 loser.
- Camp Lejeune took a 54-20 thumping.

The East Coast Marine champions also defeated Quantico and the Army's Indiantown Gap, tied Villanova, but lost to Ft. Eustis, Ft. Jackson and MCRD San Diego, 21-12, in the Boot Bowl that, in effect, decided the All-Marine title. The Boot Bowl, played in Savannah, Ga., on, appropriately, Nov. 10 and televised nationally by CBS, was replete with a rotating trophy of a boondocker.

And, to top it off, PI — which boasted 11 All-Marine and three All-Service players — won two postseason games, defeating Ft. Jackson, 19-7, in the Legion Bowl, and Special Troops of Ft. Benning, 49-0, in the Christmas Bowl, for a 9-3-1 record.

The highlight of the season, of course, was a 20-20 tie with Villanova, at the time the No. 10 team in The Associated Press poll.

And this followed Hill's 1951 team that won the All-Marine title, posted a 9-2 record, and scored more than 60 points three times.

The teams were nationally recognized, too, despite playing under the scorching Carolina sun and in the oppressive humidity. The Williamson Rating Service in early November had the 1951 team ranked fourth among service teams, and at a comparable period the 1952 team was fifth.

Besides Hill, a former guard at Navy and line coach at Quantico, the glue holding the two teams together was an old pro quarterback, Sam Vacanti, who called not only Iowa but also Purdue and Nebraska home and put in three seasons in the All-America Football Conference.

The only officer to play on the '51 club, Vacanti, 29, later an Omaha city councilman, helped mold a squad of teen-agers, college sophomores, a few college graduates and a sprinkling of pro prospects and future coaches into one of the Corps' most exciting teams — ever. He threw TD passes, ran for scores when necessary, and kicked extra points and field goals.

Vacanti, who was 5-11 and 210, had been around. A quarterback at Iowa in 1942, he played as a Marine V-12 trainee at Purdue in 1943 when the Boilermakers were fifth-ranked nationally, and came back from World War II to wrap up his college career in 1946 at Nebraska.

Then came the 1947 season with the Chicago Rockets, a split year in '48 with the Rockets and Baltimore Colts and a final season (and the AAFC's final year, too) with the Colts in '49 before being recalled to active duty during the Korean War.

Vacanti — who wore No. 33 in 1951 and No. 67 in 1952 — obviously had some help, such as:

1951 season

■ End Bob Schnelker (Bowling Green), later to play with the Eagles in 1953, the Giants from 1954-60 and the Vikings and Steelers in 1961, and be an assistant coach for seven NFL teams.

■ Tackle Rex Boggan, 225, who would be an All-American at Mississippi in 1954 and play for the Giants in 1955.

■ Guard Don King, 235 (Kentucky), later to be with the Browns in 1954, the Eagles and Packers in 1956 and the Broncos in 1960.

■ Guard Jim Niblack (Florida), who would coach at two universities and in the World Football League, the National Football League and the United States Football League.

■ Back Leo Elter (Villanova-Duquesne), later to perform for the Steelers in 1953-54, the Redskins from 1955-57 and the Steelers from 1958-59.

■ Back Billy Mixon (Georgia), who would join the 49ers for the 1953 and 1954 seasons.

■ Guard Ray Suchy, 225 (Wisconsin-Nevada), and tackle Ted Ghleman, 225 (William & Mary), to add needed size.

1952 season

Helping the Marines on the points binge, besides Schnelker (who was All-Service), Boggan, King, Niblack, Elter, Idzik and Mixon, were:

■ Ken MacAfee (Alabama), later to star with the Giants from 1954-58, and the Eagles and Redskins in 1959, and whose son made headlines as a tight end at Notre Dame and with the 49ers in the late 1970s.

■ Tackle Roscoe Hansen (Georgia), who had been a rookie with the Eagles in 1951.

■ All-Service Center George Radosevich (Pitt), who would be with the Steelers in 1953 and the Colts from 1954-56.

■ Back John Idzik, later the coach at the University of Detroit and an assistant at four colleges and with five pro teams.

■ Back George Kinek, a No. 4 draft pick of the Rams who played for the Cardinals in 1954.

■ Back Billy Hayes (North Carolina), who was All-Marine both seasons and All-Service in 1952.

A number of players on the 1951 and '52 teams had completed their freshman and/or sophomore years but had to leave college just ahead of the draft or because of it. And some of them would return to college and to football after their hitches.

222

The teams had a Southern college flavor. In 1951, for example, there were six players from Florida, five from Ole Miss, and four each from Wake Forest and William & Mary.

But the traditional Marine recruiting territory in Pennsylvania was not forgotten. Thirteen members of the 1952 team hailed from the Keystone State. And some of those 13 still lived in Pennsylvania in the 1980s.

1951

Record: 20-33 Wofford, 13-21 Ft. Jackson, 20-14 Quantico, 41-0 Little Creek, 63-13 Jacksonville NAS, 62-13 Ft. Lee, 48-0 Miami (Fla.). JV, 16-9 MCRD San Diego (Boot Bowl), 62-7 Cherry Point, 24-13 Camp Lejeune, 30-13 MCRD San Diego (All-Marine title). (9-2). Shaw Field game canceled. Hayes and Mixon All-Marine; Hunter, Riggins and Vacanti second team.

Coach: Maj. J.T. Hill (Navy) (asst. Quantico 1949-50)

Assistants: Capt. Al Denham, (Howard), Cal Killeen (Bucknell-Navy) (Quantico 1949), Capt. Bill McLain (North Carolina), Capt. Ralph Noble (Rice-Southwestern Louisiana), Capt. Art Ramage (Coffeyville JC-Tulsa)

Ends: Walt Bielich (Pitt), Joe Connors (William & Mary), Tom Edwards (Auburn), Lee Goodlow (William & Mary), Billy Granger (South Carolina), Hiner, Brooker Kelly (Florida), Joe Raich, Bob Schnelker (Bowling Green), John Sherwood (Brigham Young)

Tackles: Rex Boggan (Mississippi), Bob Dockery (South Carolina), Ted Ghelmann (William & Mary), Hansen, Neil Huffman (Pitt), Dan Hunter (Florida), Frank Rindoni (Tennessee), Wanny Truman (Morris-Harvey), Bill Walters (Mississippi)

Guards: Chris Carpenter (North Carolina), Henry Carson (Wake Forest), Bill King (North Carolina State), Don King (Kentucky), Jim Niblack (Florida), Percey Steele (Wake Forest), Bill Stovall (East Mississippi JC-Mississippi State), Ray Suchy (Wisconsin-Nevada), Ed Warnet (Pitt)

Centers: Roy Delaney (Boston College), Paul Gonsalves (Wentworth), Ed Kercher (Florida), Benny Rice (Tulane), Billy Riggins (Memphis State), Ned Suttle (Mississippi)

Backs: Ervin Bales (Florida), Bill Bately (Mississippi), Bill "Whitey" Campbell (Corpus Christi), Tom Casey, Leo Elter (Villanova-Duquesne), Bill Hayes (North Carolina), Ed Holoka (Nevada), Arch Johnson (Belmont-Abbey), Bill Krohto (Albright), Ed Lair, Ted Majewski (Bowling Green), Maurice Mantz (Wake Forest), Bill Martin (William & Mary), Bill McKinney (Miami), Billy Mixon (Georgia), Keith Munyan (Ohio University-William Carey-Louisiana College), Peter Procops (Cortland), Joe Robbins (Mississippi), Bill Sichko (Pitt), Dick Travagline (Wake Forest), Sam Vacanti (Iowa-Purdue-Nebraska), Charles Wagely, Walters, Bill Watson (Florida).

1952

Record: 13-20 Ft. Eustis, 74-0 Jacksonville NAS, 22-7 Quantico, 21-13 Indiantown Gap, 59-0 Cherry Point, 54-13 Stetson, 20-20 Villanova, 12-21 MCRD San Diego (Boot Bowl), 87-0 Eglin AFB, 21-31 Ft. Jackson, 54-20 Camp Lejeune, 19-7 Ft. Jackson (Legion Bowl). (9-3-1). Boggan, Bucci, Elliott, Hansen, Hayes, Idzik, Lashley, Mixon, Radosevich, Schnelker and Vacanti All-Marine.

Coach: Lt. Col. J.T. Hill (Navy) (asst. Quantico 1949-50)

Assistants: Jim Quinn (Fordham), Capt. Art Ramage (Coffeyville JC-Tulsa)

Ends: Walt Bielich (Pitt), Nick DeRosa (Pitt), Jerry Elliott (Auburn), Terry Fails (Vanderbilt), Ed Filipovitz (Georgia), Billy Granger (South Carolina), Ken MacAfee (Alabama), Bob Schnelker (Bowling Green)

Tackles: Rex Boggan (Mississippi), Erin Fox (Boston University), Lou Harrelson (South Carolina), Roscoe Hansen (North Carolina), John Ilari (Kentucky), Don King (Kentucky), Jim Niblack (Florida), Ed Taffer (Furman)

Guards: Jerry Angel (George Washington), Charles Bossolina (Furman), Gil Bucci (Pitt), Bill King (North Carolina State), Dick Lashley (Florida), Frank Rindoni (Tennessee), Tobias Sherrill (Duke), Percey Steele (Wake Forest), Dick Steber (Auburn), Bill Stovall (East Mississippi JC-Mississippi State)

Centers: Glenn Graham (Florence Teachers) (Camp Pendleton 1951-52), Ed Kercher (Florida), George Radosevich (Pitt), Bernard Rice (Tulane), John Wagner (Columbia)

Backs: Paul Anders (Penn State), Ervin Bales (Florida), Ed Brandenburg (Mississippi), Jim Brigman (Clemson), Dick Czaplinski (Miami of Fla.), Tom Danforth (Belmont-Abbey), Roy Delaney (Boston College), Phil Dettore (Penn), Leo Elter (Villanova-Duquesne), Billy Hayes (North Carolina), Ed Holoka (Nevada), John Idzik (Maryland), George Kinek (Tulane), Billy Mixon (Georgia), Dick Travagline (Wake Forest), Sam Vacanti (Iowa-Purdue-Nebraska)

That Base In S.C.

You've seen the auto-license lament "So Many Men, So Little Time" on a flashy car driven by a beautiful woman.

That, oddly, has been the problem at Parris Island through the years — for recruit training as well as football.

Collectively, more football players have passed through PI than Quantico, the Marine Corps' football bastion.

But, of course, there have been other things to do at the hard-nosed South Carolina base where, through the years, recruit training has been speeded up or slowed down, depending on the world situation.

Such training started at the base in 1911 and more than 200,000 recruits alone were trained during World War II. But the number of battalions fell from 13 to two after the rapid demobilization, only to swell again during the Korean War.

And when boot camp was completed, amid the sandfleas, heat, humidity and isolation, the PI-trained Marines generally headed off to other bases, some of them even to come back and haunt their "alma mater" when competing for Quantico, Camp Lejeune or Cherry Point teams.

The PI stories, of course, are legion.

The late quarterback Paul Governali (Columbia), a member of the College Hall of Fame and a key in El Toro's success in 1944-45, recalled his introduction.

"How can anyone forget their DI?" he asked when addressing the Islanders' 1955 football banquet. "We (arrived and) headed out over a swamp and the sole came loose on my shoe. We were walking so fast and were so crowded that I couldn't bend down and take my shoe off.

"Finally, I just kicked that shoe off and went the rest of the way with one shoe. *That* is my most vivid memory of Parris Island."

The biggest concentration of football talent no doubt took place in late 1943 and early 1944 when thousands of V-12 trainees poured in. They had attended college as Marine Reserves until summoned Nov. 1 for boot camp.

Cpl. Robert B. Van Atta, in a dispatch carried by the Charleston (S.C.) News & Courier, wrote:

"Football All-Americans are the most predominate, with such personalities as Angelo Bertelli of Notre Dame, the Springfield (Mass.) 'Rifle;' Tony Butkovich, Purdue fullback who led the Big Ten in scoring in 1943 although he played in only six games; Alex Agase, who won the distinction of being named All-American at two different institutions of higher learning (Illinois in '42 and Purdue in '43) at his guard position; Ralph Heywood, vicious USC end; Pat Preston, powerful Duke tackle; John "Modesto" Podesto, offensive backbone on Amos Alonzo Stagg's College of the Pacific eleven, and Leon "Mickey" McCardle, diminutive USC quarterback."

Bertelli only had won the Heisman Trophy.

But that wasn't all.

"Outstanding sectional headliners also carve a niche in personnel," Van Atta wrote, "as represented by All-Eastern aces Mike Micka, Colgate fullback; George Sutch, University of Rochester plunging back; Elmer Jones, Franklin & Marshall guard; and Bert Gianelli, All-Coast College of the Pacific tackle; All-Southern Tommy Davis and Leo Long, from Duke's backfield; Baylor's fullback, (Tuffy) McCormick, and a host of others. ..."

But there was more:

"The participants in the Rose Bowl game find their teams weakened by the loss of veterans who are stationed here," Van Atta wrote. "In addition to Heywood and McCardle, Jeff Cravath, USC mentor, bemoans the absence of Howard Callanan, meteoric All-Coast halfback; and Pete McPhail, his other starting terminal.

"Washington's Huskies are minus top Pacific Coast scorer Jacob Stoves, a halfback who recorded nearly 50 points in four games."

A nationally circulated Marine Corps photo showed Davis, Micka, Gianelli, Jones, Agase, Preston, Heywood, Bertelli, Podesto, Butkovich and McCardle, "wearing the uniforms of U.S. Marines in boot training" at Parris Island.

There had been 25 players selected first-team All-American in 1943; six of them were in the photo.

And there were many others with football reputations at the base at the time.

But with training the reason for PI's being it had to be downhill from that point.

Actually, the base, which had teams as early as 1909 and from 1921-27 and 1931-32, did not field one from 1933 through 1946.

Capt. John Paul was at the helm in 1947 when PI resumed varsity football, winning three while losing six with a team that had a lot of dedication, some talent and apparently no college experience. (Several players did play college ball later on the GI Bill.)

The victories were over the Green Cove Springs (Fla.) Navy, Cherry Point and Ft. Jackson. It was a beginning.

Back Bayard "Rebel" Pickett was selected All-Marine by Leatherneck magazine, and end Paul Sweezy second team.

Other teams and highlights:

■ **1948 (5-4 record):** Lt. Col. George Stallings, a Bronze Star holder, had nine holdovers to build on and grabbed a few recruits with college experience before they got out the gates.

Two losses were to Marine teams: Quantico (a 13-0 record), 51-7, and Camp Lejeune, 33-6. But there were victories over Ft. Jackson, Ft. Benning, Greenville AFB, Brooke Medical Center and Cherry Point.

Guard Bill Eysenbach was an All-Marine choice and back Russ Picton a second-team selection.

Backs, in particular, would be heard from later. John Huzvar turned up at North Carolina State, Pitt and Georgia and played for the Philadelphia Eagles and Baltimore Colts. Picton would be a college coach at Wilkes and Hugh "Red" Kreiver would become a Florida schools superintendent.

■ **1949 (7-2):** Lt. Ted Stawicki (American Univ.-Morningside), another Bronze Star holder who also would coach Camp Pendleton, 9th Marines and Hawaii Marines teams, made his debut after three seasons as a Quantico lineman.

He pulled what strings he had to, retaining 17 with PI experience and adding top recruit graduates. The result: The Islanders challenged Lejeune for the 6th Naval District title before losing, 7-0. The other loss was to Ft. Bragg, 24-13.

And the highlight of the season was a 19-13 victory over MCRD San Diego in the first Boot Bowl.

Guard John Leroy Jr. and Picton were All-Marine selections, and center Tony Beatrice was second-team.

But, significantly, the Islanders started to lay the groundwork for some of their fearsome lines.

Tackle Bill Prather (Southwestern Louisiana), at 6-4, 240, was back for a second season. Tackle John Stewart stood 6-7 and weighed 245.

■ **1950 (4-5):** The Korean War had just started, and the focus had to be on recruit training. Amazingly, PI posted a 4-5 record behind All-Marine selection Bob Scott, a guard, and end Bob Smith (Navy) and back Whitey Campbell (Corpus Christi Univ.), both second-team choices. (Smith, an aviator, would be an MIA in Vietnam, later classified as PFOD — presumed finding of death.)

It was Stawicki's only losing season as a coach.

Marring the season was a 57-18 loss to San Diego in the Boot Bowl. But San Diego won all 11 games and had run up scores of 100-0 and 75-0 during the season.

PI opponents, though, had to work for victory. Stewart was back, and joined by tackles Don King (6-2, 240), Don Owens (6-6, 245) and Dan Hunter (Florida). King would play in the NFL and AFL and Owens for Southern Mississippi and seven years as a pro after signing with both the Canadian League and the NFL as a rookie.

Back Cal Killeen (Bucknell-Navy) would don general's stars.

■ **1951 (9-2) and 1952 (9-3-1):** see separate chapter

■ **1953 (1-8-1):** The cupboard was bare for Lt. Col. Bruno Andruska (Iowa), with the victory over the Atlanta General Supply Depot and the tie against MCAS Miami. Andruska had coached Lejeune in 1949-50 and been a U.N. observer in Palestine.

Guard Gil Bucci, one of only two holdovers from 1952, was second-team All-Marine.

Back Leroy Labat (LSU), the "Black Stallion of the Bayous," had led the Tigers in rushing in 1951, played in the Blue-Gray Game and was drafted by the Colts.

Tackle Wil Overgaard (Idaho), a Bronze Star winner, would be heard from more as a coach, posting a 40-13-2 record in five seasons at Lejeune and Quantico.

■ **1954 (6-5):** There was some life left, as Andruska retained 14 veterans and was reinforced by players with college and freshman experience. Many of them had enlisted to avoid a draft seeking to replace the many Korean veterans being released.

The Islanders gave Quantico a battle before losing, 39-21, and defeated Camp Lejeune, 27-0.

Tackle Ed Tokus was All-Marine and fullback Jim Ray (Vanderbilt) second-team.

Quarterback Fred Pancoast (Tampa) would go on to head-coaching jobs at Tampa, Memphis State and Vanderbilt.

■ **1955 (4-6):** Maj. Wally Williams, a Bronze Star holder fresh from coaching the Hawaii Marines in 1953-54, took over. An 11-letter winner at Boston University and former drill instructor, he had played for the Chicago Rockets and Boston Yanks and been recalled in 1950 in time to be a Lejeune player-coach under Andruska.

Guard Vic Rimkus (Holy Cross) was All-Marine and guard Carl "Moose" Valletto second-team. Valletto would letter at Alabama in 1957-58 and 1960 and receive a tryout with the Pittsburgh Steelers.

But the season perhaps is best remembered for the presence of an assistant coach. Lt. Vince Dooley (Auburn) would become one of the country's best-known and most-successful coaches at Georgia.

■ **1956 (0-9):** It fell to Maj. "Big Jim" Landrigan to try and field a team amid training restrictions imposed after publicized recruit deaths stemming from a forced march and the subsequent court-martial proceedings. And it was next to impossible.

Landrigan had the qualifications from both Marine Corps and athletic points of view. He had played at Holy Cross and Dartmouth and with the Colts; been a player-coach for Andruska at Lejeune and an assistant at PI; and been awarded the Silver Star and Bronze Star.

The Islanders, gutty but thin in numbers, were shut out only once but couldn't hold opponents to under 26 points in a game. Some losses were one-sided.

Recalls center Bill Boyle (Massachusetts-Coast Guard Academy): "All the players except the player-coaches were enlisted men," a condition after the recruit deaths.

Another condition was a training restriction. "Because of that, myself and two other players could not join the team until after the Lejeune game in October," Boyle said.

Back Ed Post (Duke) was second-team All-Marine.

One of the tackles was a big, raw kid, Dick "Tiny" Reynolds, who had played two seasons at Lejeune. He would perform at North Carolina State from 1958-60 and be drafted by the Colts and Houston Oilers.

But there weren't enough Reynoldses. Parris Island would drop varsity football in 1957.

1947

Record: 13-27 Jacksonville NAS, 0-20 Ft. Benning, 13-28 Ft. Bragg, 0-20 Presbyterian, 46-0 Green Cove Springs Navy, 6-16 Norfolk NAS, 20-0 Cherry Point, 13-27 Quantico, 57-0 Ft. Jackson. (3-6). Pickett All-Marine, Sweezey second team.

Coach: Capt. John Paul **Assistants:** NA

Ends: M.W. Dittman, Pierre Dumont, J.H. Etter, Joe Hess, C.E. Lindsey, D. Mulvaney, Paul Sweezey (South Carolina), G.W. Wiseman

Tackles: G.L. Benoit, Bob Keller, A.J. Lankas, D.R. Weinacht, Frank Winn

Guards: C.J. Baudhuin, G.F. Fabian, Myron Kraemer, John Leroy, J.J. Worst

Centers: Tony Beatrice, J.N. Harbin, D.W. Lawson, J.L. Southern

Backs: A.R. Baldwin, Ed Bolton, D.C. Chancey, Art Dunkerton, H.E. Haile, Art Husband (Wake Forest), John McMahon, Bayard "Rebel" Pickett (South Carolina) (asst. Pendleton 1953), Russ Picton (Temple-Wilkes), Jay Thames (Auburn)

1948

Record: 20-0 Ft. Jackson, 12-0 Ft. Benning, 21-6 Greenvuille AFB, 0-7 Jacksonville NAS, 37-0 Brooke Medical, 26-6 Cherry Point, 13-20 Ft. Bragg, 7-51 Quantico, 6-33 Camp Lejeune. (5-4). Second Greenville AFB game canceled. Eysenbach All-Marine, Picton second team.

Coach: Lt. Col. George stallings

Assistants: Capt. Hal Lindfelt (Iowa-Augustana of Ill.) (MCB San Diego 1936-38), Lt. R.E. Martin

Ends: Joe Hammond, Joe Hess, P.P. Moretti, W.N. Pruitt, Clark Rowe, C.R. Smith, Dick Wronek

Tackles: R.E. Boss, Art Hargrove (South Carolina), Bob Keller, A.J. Lankas, L.J. Michaels, Bill Prather (Southwestern Louisiana), Don Stevens, Fred Tullai (Temple-Maryland), D.R. Weinacht, P.T. Young

Guards: Bill Eysenbach, John Leroy, Bob Scott

Centers: Al Ansani, Tony Beatrice, N.F. Sponcey, J.H. Thomas

Backs: Len Aloy (Nevada), M. Corpolongo, Art Dunkerton, Art Husband (Wake Forest), John Huzvar (North Carolina State-Pitt-Georgia), Bob Kaiser, T.J. Kearns, Paul Kelly, Hugh Kriever (Louisville), G.W.A. Lobb, Ed Petrevich, Russ Picton (Temple-Wilkes), Tom Reese, Billy Sanders

1949

Record: 13-12 Memphis NATTC, 6-0 Ft. Jackson, 12-0 Cherry Point, 15-7 Jacksonville NAS, 37-0 Chatham AFB, 13-24 Ft. Bragg, 41-14 Ft. Benning, 0-7 Camp Lejeune, 19-13 MCRD San Diego (Boot Bowl). (7-2). Leroy and Picton were All-Marine, Beatrice second team.

Coach: Lt. Ted Stawicki (American-Morningside) (Quantico 1946-48)

Assistants: Hal McKenna (Quantico 1947-48), Hal Lindfelt (Iowa-Augustana of Ill.) (MCB San Diego 1936-38), Tony Messina (Cal-Pacific) (Quantico 1947-48)

Ends: Lamar Benford, Bill Campbell, G.J. Driscoll, Joe Hammond, Joe Hess, J.F. MacKay, McCartney, W.A. Nair, John Pomarica, Joe Raich, Clark Rowe, Paul Sweezey (South Carolina)

Tackles: Art Hargrove (South Carolina), J.P. Jerabek, Bob Keller, Bill Kelley, Bill Prather (Southwest Louisiana), N.E. Ritter, Robinson, Don Stevens, John Stewart

Guards: Avaloz, R.E. Boss, Bill Harris, Myron Kraemer, John Leroy, Bob MacKewen, Al Neveu, D.L. Proctor, Gordon Sanders, Bob Scott, Weisner.

Centers: Tony Beatrice, Gary Curtiss, Bob Elder, Omrod, Norm Sponcey, M.L. Travis

Backs: J.H. Allen, Len Aloy (Nevada), Whitey Campbell (Corpus Christi), M. Illitch, Bob Kaiser, George Kessler, Hugh Kriever (Louisville), Ed Lair, G.H. Lightfoot, J.J. Lynch, Arch Martin, Russ Mavis, George Mears, Lenny Meckalavage (Indiana), Ed Petrevich, Russ Picton (Temple-Wilkes), Rich Santos, Earl Weed, B.J. Wolfenbarger

1950

Record: 0-56 Citadel, 6-20 Cherry Point, 40-0 Ft. Lee, 40-20 Jacksonville NAS, 25-0 Camp Stewart, 13-6 Little Creek, 18-57 MCRD San Diego (Boot Bowl), 14-33 Camp Lejeune, 19-33 Ft. Jackson. (4-5). Scott All-Marine, Whitey Campbell and Smith second team.

Coach: Ted Stawicki (American-Morningside) (Quantico 1946-48)

Assistants: Capt. Hal Lindfelt (Iowa-Augustana of Ill.) (MCB San Diego 1936-38), T/Sgt. Hal McKenna (Quantico 1947-48), Lt. Tony Messina (Cal-Pacific) (Quantico 1947-48)

Ends: Lamar Benford, Ron Beyler, Bill Campbell, Ed Dobrowolski, Mike Kelley, Joe Raich, Clark Rowe, Bob Smith (Navy) (Quantico 1948-49) (KIA)

Tackles: Dan Bendokas, Boyle, John Byrne, Bob Dockery (South Carolina), Art Hargrove (South Carolina), Dan Hunter (Florida), Eddie Johns, Don King (Kentucky), Don Owens (Mississippi Southern), Joe Peterson, Don Stevens, John Stewart

Guards: Autrey, Don Knapp, Myron Kraemer, Bob MacKewen, Al Neveu, Herb Roberts, Gordon Sanders, Bob Scott, Gerald Streetman

Centers: Tony Beatrice, Gary Curtiss, Bob Neiman, Mike Settle

Backs: Dick Ambrogi (Penn-Navy) (Quantico 1948-49), Ervin Bales (Florida), Len Billock, John Bonacorte, Whitey Campbell (Corpus Christi), Bob Chapman, Marion Edison, George Gallo, Arch Johnson (Belmont-Abbey), Bob Kaiser, George Kessler, Cal Killeen (Bucknell-Navy) (Quantico 1949), Ed Lair, Arch Martin, George Mears, Rich Santos, Andy Thain, Dick Travagline (Wake Forest), Charles Wageley, Earl Weed, Bob Weddle.

1953

Record: 0-40 Southern Mississippi, 6-19 Wofford, 7-32 Ft. Monmouth, 0-19 Cherry Point, 0-35 Quantico, 7-28 Little Creek, 28-28 MCAS Miami, 0-28 Ft. Jackson, 0-16 Camp Lejeune, 59-12 Atlanta General Supply Depot. (1-8-1). Bucci second team All-Marine.

Coach: Lt. Col. Bruno Andruska (Iowa) (coach Lejeune 1949-50)

Assistants: Capt. Wendell Beard (New Mexico-California) (Quantico 1949, Pendleton 1951), Capt. Joe Brady (Columbia-Dartmouth), Capt. Cas Ksycewski (Catholic) (Quantico 49-50, assistant 1951), Capt. Bob Maiden (Colorado State Teachers) (Quantico 1949)

Ends: Ted Bates (Western Reserve), Bill Dunderdale, Tom Edwards (Auburn), John Knight, Bob Lewis (Elon), Charles Rix (Rhode Island), Dave Scofield, Joe Wasilewski (Dickinson of Pa.), Ben Wright (Catawba)

Tackles: Dave Arnold (Clemson), Dick Cassels (Muhlenburg-Catawba), Fred Critz, Roger Dalehite (North Carolina), Lou Harrelson (South Carolina), Bill Keepper (Ill. Wesleyan), Paul Mucke, Wil Overgaard (Idaho) (Quantico 1951), Jim Stoeker, Ed Tokus (Georgia), Bernard Zickefoose (Virginia)

Guards: Dick Bobo (Penn State), Bob Brown (Marietta), Gil Bucci (Pitt), George Carmody (Marquette-Utah State), Howard Devoid, John Ilari (Kentucky), Bob Jordan (Jacksonville of Ala.), Don McLaughlin, Jim Sadie (West Virginia), Ray Snyder, Dick Valentine (Westminster of Pa.)

Centers: George Boemerman (North Carolina State), Glenn Derr (Dartmouth), Charles Miller (Davidson), John Rooney

Backs: Oliver Ackerman (West Georgia), Sam Angotti, Jim Brigman (Clemson), Frank Dillon (Villanova), Jim Finn (Penn State-Arkansas), Fred Girgis, Boyce Jarrett (Morris-Harvey), Rod Lash (Bowling Green), LeRoy Labat (LSU), George Lunn (Middle Tennessee), Maiden (p-c), Rocco Marzzarella (Michigan State), Joe Merli (Scranton), Keith Munyan (Ohio University-William Carey-Louisiana College), Colie Peake (South Carolina), Herb Price, Jim Ray (Vanderbilt), Allen Rizer (Notre dame-Dayton) (El Toro 1952-53), Bob Rosbaugh (Penn State), Stan Sterger (Indiana) (Quantico 1953), Gene Wisniewski (Duquesne) (Camp Lejeune (1951-52), Harlan Young. **Others:** Al Sigman

1954

Record: 46-0 Charleston AFB, 6-7 Little Creek, 33-0 Cherry Point, 13-37 Ft. Jackson, 20-13 Ft. Monmouth, 13-21 Pensacola, 50-0 Kindley AFB, 21-39 Quantico, 26-0 Norfolk NAS, 13-18 Shaw AFB, 27-0 Camp Lejeune. (6-5). Ranked No. 16 by Williamson Rating Service. Tokus named All-Marine, Ray second team.

Coach: Lt. Col. Bruno Andruska (Iowa) (coach Lejeune 1949-50)

Assistants: Capt. Joe Brady (Columbia-Dartmouth), Capt. Carl Cooper (Howard of Ala.), Capt. McCoy "Hoss" Hewlett (Auburn-Duke), Wil Overgaard (Idaho) (Quantico 1951)

Ends: Billy Allen (Virginia Tech), Ted Bates (Western Reserve), Jerry Bishop (Wake Forest), Hezekiah Braxton (Virginia-Virginia Union), Glenn Derr (Dartmouth), Joe LaFrance (Connecticut), John McNulty (Indiana), Bill Southworth (Illinois), Andy Zenuch (Fordham)

Tackles: Dave Arnold (Clemson), Francis Branagan (Penn), Dick Cassels (Muhlenburg-Catawba), Roland Douglas (Georgia Tech), Tom McDevitt (Georgia Tech), Paul Mucke, David Powers (Georgia Tech), Ed Tokus (Georgia), Bernard Zickefoose (Virginia)

Guards: Dave Abram, Dick Bobo (Penn State), Roy Colquitt (Idaho) (Quantico 1953), Walt Connolly (Yale), Bob Glenn (Sewanee), Tom Jones (Florida), Emil Marquardt (Hawaii), Mickey Oates (Fordham), Pat O'Callaghan (Michigan), Joe Sims (Oklahoma A&M), Ray Snyder

Centers: Leo Bland (Akron), Jim Ray (Vanderbilt), Bob Schuler (Colorado A&M), Al St. Peter (Mississippi State)

Backs: Sam Angotti, John Auer (Ohio State), Jack Bass (Mississippi College), Joe Beilman (Georgia), Matt Boyle (Boston University), Bob Brozina (Maryland), C.D. Cureton (Wayne of Mich.), Earl Dukes (Georgia Tech-Chattanooga), Jim Finn (Penn State-Arkansas), John Freeland (Shippensburg), Wayne Guy (Indiana State), Bob Jennings (Penn State), O.E. Korell (Amherst), Dom Massella (Boston University), John Martin (Akron), John Matkowsky (Potomac JC-Chattanooga), Joe Merli (Scranton), Bob Miller, Fred Pancoast (Tampa), Francis Penn, Bob Rosbaugh (Penn State), Lou Walker (Mississippi Southern). **Kicker:** Don Decker (Maryland)

1955

Record: 25-0 Little Creek, 0-21 Quantico, 25-6 Ft. Benning, 6-28 Shaw AFB, 6-36 Pensacola, 27-16 Norfolk Tars, 13-26 Chattanooga, 0-20 Ft. Jackson, 0-6 Camp Lejeune, 13-7 Ft. Lee. (4-6). Scrimmaged the Citadel. Ranked No. 16 by Williamson Rating Service. Rimkus All-Marine, Valletto second team

Coach: Maj. Wally Williams (Boston University) (El Toro 45, Camp Lejeune 1950, asst. Quantico 1952, coach Hawaii Marines 1953-54)

Assistants: Lt. Vince Dooley (Auburn) (Quantico 1954), Capt. McCoy "Hoss" Hewlett (Auburn-Duke), Capt. "Big Jim" Landrigan (Holy Cross-Dartmouth) (Camp Lejeune 1950)

Ends: Jube Belcher (San Angelo JC-Trinity of Texas), Charles Gookin (Tennessee), Joe Harrington (Holy Cross) (Quantico 1954), Joe La France (Connecticut), Len La Pierre (Rhode Island), Mickey Oates (Fordham), Al St. Peter (Mississippi State), Bill Smith (Miami of Florida), Bill Southworth (Ill.)

Tackles: Hal Devine (Memphis State), Joe DiGrazio (Villanova), Jack Grabski, Emil Marquardt (Hawaii), D.E. Metzler, Dave Powers (Georgia Tech), Glen Tribett, Carl Valletto (Alabama) (Camp Pendleton-1st Marine Division 1954)

Guards: Mack Rogers (Georgia), Ruby McMahon (Maryland), Dave McInturff (Tennessee) (1st Marine Division 1954), Pete Pichon, Vic Rimkus (Holy Cross) (Quantico 1954), Gene Uccellini (Pitt)

Centers: Jerry Bishop (Wake Forest), Joe Cindrich (Pitt), Tony DiPaolo (Bloomsburg) (Quantico 1954), Ed Lynch

Backs: John Auer (Ohio State), Bill Banks, Jim Barton (Murray State), Joe Beilman (Georgia), Lou Biacchi (Fordham) (Cherry Point 1954), C.D. Cureton (Wayne of Mich.), John Freeland (Shippensburg), Gene Hall (East Tennessee), Nat Lee (Adelphi), Russ Lutz (William & Mary) (3rd Marine Division 1954), John Martin (Akron), Bob McCrary (Mississippi Southern), Ed Mershad (Dayton), Bob Miller (The Citadel), Hal Norton, Lou Walker (Mississippi Southern), Dick Zotti (Boston College) (Quantico 1954). **Kickers:** Don Decker (Maryland), coach Williams

1956

Record: 14-27 Ft. Benning, 7-26 Ft. Jackson, 12-48 Camp Lejeune, 17-33 Norfolk Tars, 6-40 Quantico, 12-48 Shaw AFB, 0-36 Ft. Lee, 20-34 Eglin AFB, 7-26 Little Creek. (0-9). Training restrictions in the wake of the death of recruits and the McKeon court-martial limited football participation. Post was second team All-Marine.

Coach: Maj. Jim Landrigan (Holy Cross-Dartmouth) (Camp Lejeune 1950)

Assistant: Capt. Bayard Pickett (South Carolina) (Camp Pendleton 1953)

Ends: Blodgett, Lump Lombardo, Dusty Negron, Al St. Peter (Mississippi State), Jim Schemote

Tackles: Bartholomew, Blanchard, Manny Congedo (Villanova-Colorado), Fish, Dick "Tiny" Reynolds (North Carolina State) (Camp Lejeune 1954), Bob Williams (South Carolina State)

Guards: Hicks, Dave Six (Cincinnati), Felix Kwiatkowski, David Slaughter (Lincoln of Pa.), Roger Smythe

Centers: Autrey (Wofford), Bill Boyle (Massachusetts-Coast Guard Academy), Len La Pierre (Rhode Island)

Backs: Able, Jube Belcher (San Angelo JC-Trinity of Texas), Don Brown (Rhode Island), Joe Counts USN (Presbyterian), Lee, Ed Post (Duke), Fred Schnable, Bill Smith (Miami of Fla.), Charlie Walker

1957

Football discontinued.

Bob Schnelker (Bowling Green), an All-Marine end at Parris Island in 1952, played pro ball nine seasons and was an NFL assistant with seven teams.

Pendleton Beats 'USC'

Yes, Virginia, there is a Santa Claus. And, yes, the Camp Pendleton Marines once defeated USC.

The year was 1951, the date Sept. 29, the place the Los Angeles Coliseum, and the score 27-17. But you won't find the contest listed in University of Southern California media guides even though the National Collegiate Athletic Association certified it as a victory and the score was listed as such in the 1952 Official NCAA Football Guide.

The mighty Trojans (7 victories, 3 other defeats) were playing a doubleheader that day, against San Diego Navy (a 41-7 triumph) and Pendleton. They naturally counted the San Diego victory.

Admittedly, USC used some second- and third-stringers, although the defense, according to the game program, could call on the likes of backs Frank Gifford, Jim Sears and Rudy Bukich, tackle Charles Ane, guard Elmer Willhoite and linebacker Pat Cannamela.

Charlie Harris scored three touchdowns to lead the Leathernecks.

USC protested loudly — quite loudly — but the NCAA, as it is wont to do, held fast and said that, indeed, the scarlet and gold won although the purpose of the game basically was to exercise the non-regulars.

As they say, you can look it up.

And the Marines aren't about to waive a victory over one of the nation's foremost football powers.

Actually, it was that kind of a year for Camp Pendleton, which faced one of the toughest schedules any Marine team *ever* faced. Besides USC, Pendleton went against the NFL Los Angeles Rams tor one quarter before 18,000 in a preseason San Diego benefit game, and lost, 26-0, to the University of San Francisco as Hall of Famer Ollie Matson scored twice.

The undefeated Dons, coached by Joe Kuharich, only happened to be one of the finest teams ever assembled. They also boasted of back Scooter Scudero, quarterback Ed Brown, end Bob St. Clair, tackles Gino Marchetti and Lou Stephens, and center Burl Toler, and won all nine games. The publicist? A student named Pete Rozelle.

(Brown would quarterback MCRD San Diego in 1952 and Camp Pendleton in 1953 before embarking on a 12-year pro career with the Bears, Steelers and Colts.)

Camp Pendleton, a sprawling San Diego County base, had not fielded a team in 1950, and the '51 season was to be one of extremes.

Because of the recall of Marine reservists, there was enough talent on hand in the late spring and summer to have played the Rams for at least a half, not just a quarter.

For example, Pendleton had defeated MCRD San Diego, 18-6, to close spring football, and San Diego was coming off an 11-0 season in 1950 when it scored a Marine-record 524 points.

And nine Pendleton players had been drafted by the pros.

But by by the end of the season, the squad was down to 27 because of orders to Korea, injuries and civilian separations, and some players had to play both offense and defense in the new two-platoon era.

Three players — backs Joe Ferem and Joe Bartos (Navy) and All-America end Herb Hein in particular — were gone by late August.

It truly became a unit of a few good men.

When mentioning 1951, one name comes to mind: end Cloyce Box, an end with the Detroit Lions in 1950, All-Service with the Pendleton Leathernecks in 1951, and an All-Pro in 1952 back with the Lions. He twice was selected for the Pro Bowl. Box and brother Cloyce had performed for Cheesie Neil's Boat Basin team at Pendleton in 1945, then both played for West Texas.

Neil, later with the San Diego State athletic department, kept in touch with rancher Box on football trips to the Lone Star State.

"He must have owned all of west Texas," Neil would maintain.

Box hit it big in the energy business and in Texas, at 6-4, 220 pounds, was looked up to in more ways than one.

The National Inquirer in a 1986 feature on televison's "Dallas" told of Box's influence on filming one episode.

"In the early days of filming, when 'Dallas' was shot at a Frisco, Texas, ranch owned by Mr. and Mrs. Cloyce Box, Sue Ellen was scheduled to play a scene on horseback, and the production crew had dutifully provided a local horse."

But Box told producer Leonard Katzman that a "woman of Sue Ellen's financial position should be riding a better quality horse."

And he quickly trotted out "his own $250,000 quarter horse as a loan. The scene went without a hitch. Sue Ellen looked grand, Box endeared himself to Katzman forever, and the crew learned the lesson of properly casting livestock," wrote the inquirer's Suzy Kalter.

Box joined the Lions in 1949 as a halfback and enjoyed only moderate success, carrying 30 times for 62 yards, catching 15 passes for 276 yards and four TDs, and returning three kickoffs.

But new coach Buddy Parker switched him to end in 1950 — and the results were awesome. Box caught 50 passes for 1,009 yards and 11 TDs. The yardage was second only to that of Hall of Famer Tom Fears of the Rams. Against the Colts on Dec. 3, 1950, Box's yardage on 13 receptions totaled 302, a total still among the 10 best in pro annals.

Box returned to the Lions in 1952, catching 42 passes for 924 yards and 15 TDS, and closed out his NFL career with the Lions in 1953-54 before making his mark in the business world.

It was a wily, veteran, talented, somewhat unhappy team at Pendleton that '51 season because, for many, their civilian lives had been interrupted by war for a second time. If there was a silver lining, it was that younger men were in greater demand to fight in Korea.

Twenty-three of the players, probably more, had been recalled to active duty from civilian status.

The senior partner was tackle Walt Szot, 31, a 6-1, 225-pound All-Marine tackle, who had played for the Chicago Cardinals from 1946-48 and the Pittsburgh Steelers in 1949-1950.

If there was a common denominator, it was that many had played college ball in 1943 and/or 1944 as Marine V-12 trainees, often at a school other than their alma mater.

There were Hein, tackle Chuck Dellago and back Jerry Carle, all of whom played at Minnesota in 1942 but for Northwestern in 1943.

(Carle, the Pendleton coach in 1952, coached Colorado College from 1957-8.9.)

Center Jim Cloud (Southern Methodist), Thurman "Jesse" Owens (Tulane) and back Billy Willard (Rice) all were members of a 1943 Southwestern Louisiana team that should have been ranked in the Top 10.

(Owens, who was selected as a regular officer after starring and graduating at Cincinnati, became a general and twice was awarded the Legion of Merit as well as a Bronze Star.)

End Jack Hussey played at North Carolina in that '43 season, Szot at Bucknell, guard Bob Mirth (Moravian) at Muhlenburg, guard Rex Wells (Idaho State) at Michigan, Ferem (St. Mary's) at Pacific, back Pete Glick at Princeton and quarterback Mickey McCardle at USC.

Owens, 6-3, 230-pound tackle Bob Buel (Franklin & Marshall) and tackle Don O'Neil (Denison) played as Marine V-12 trainees in 1944. Buel was a former Wisconsin lineman.

McCardle, who lettered at USC in 1942-43 and 1946-47 and quarterbacked the famed El Toro Marines in 1944-45, tried out for the Pendleton team but soon quit, saying, "I've been away too long."

(McCardle had dubbed for actor John Hodiak in the movie "Saturday's Hero.")

And there was a solid pro background, too. Besides Box and Szot, there were Bartos (Redskins, 1950) and guard Lloyd Baxter (Packers, 1948). In addition, tackle Wendel Beard, Buel, Dellago, Mirth and end Harry Sortal received pro tryouts.

Back Ray Gene Smith would intercept nine passes for the Chicago Bears from 1954-57, and Harris, after a tryout with the Cleveland Browns in 1957, would hook on with the new Los Angeles Chargers in 1960.

And the Leathernecks weren't small, either. Other heavyweights, besides Box, Buel and Szot, were tackle Joe Scott (6-2, 271), Beard (6-2, 250), tackle Angus Alford (6-1, 240), guard Bob Emery (6-0, 230) and tackle Guy Way (6-0, 230).

Thirteen players were 25 or older and, according to one game program, only seven were under 20.

But a number returned to college ball after their tours were up: end Jerry Fouts to Midwestern, guard George Oliver to LSU, center Tony Karakas to Missouri, and backs Harris to Georgia, Fred Rippel to Iowa State, Jack Wages to North Texas and Don "Skip" White to Fresno State, among others.

Trying to preside over a team distracted by the war, and the families and businesses they left behind, was Maj. Ralph Cormany, who was a top guard at Loras (Iowa) and coached in 1949-50 at Rockhurst College. Not coincidentally, as a lieutenant he had been Officer in Charge of the Gustavus-Adolphus (Minn.) Marine V-12 unit in 1943 and also was assistant coach of the football team.

His '51 Pendleton Leathernecks, besides surprising USC, defeated the Coronado Amphibs, Ft. Ord, SubPac, El Toro and the University of Hawaii. Sandwiched in between were losses to AirPac, to USF, MCRD San Diego (for the West Coast Marine title), San Diego Naval Training Center and Ft. Ord.

In 1933, the Marine Corps base at San Diego came within a whisker — an an asterisk — of the record books in a 14-13 setback to California, Southern Branch. The asterisk applies because today the school, of course, is known as UCLA.

So, whatever the circumstances, a Marine team can boast of a victory over USC. Call it one for the book — the record book.

Record: 27-28 AirPac, 26-10 NAB Coronado, 27-17 Southern California, 0-26 Univ. of San Francisco, 21-6 Ft. Ord, 26-21 SubPac, 0-12 MCRD San Digo, 0-21 San Diego NTC, 31-0 MCAS El Toro, 7-21 Ft. Ord, 31-26 Univ. of Hawaii. (6-5). Listing includes players who briefly were with team (Ferem, Hein, Bartos). Szot was All-Marine; Pfeifer was on second team

Coach: Maj. Ralph Cormany (Loras)

Assistants: Bob Breitbard (civilian), Lt. Lorenzo "Dick" Howard (Utah State), Capt. Bill "Potch" Pottenger (Springfield, Mo., Teachers) (Camp Lejeune 1944)

Ends: Jim Baxter (Marin JC), Cloyce Box (West Texas), Jerry Fouts (Oklahoma-Midwestern), Herb Hein (Minnesota-Northwestern) (PH Marines 1945), Jack Hussey (North Carolina), Holly Murdoch, Don O'Neil (Denison-Missouri Valley), Thurman "Jesse" Owens (Tulane-Southwestern Louisiana-Cincinnati), Ray Pfeifer (Rice) (Camp Lejeune; Quantico 1948), John Scott (Tennessee State), Harry Sortal (St. Louis)

Tackles: Angus Alford (Wharton JC), Wendel Beard (New Mexico-California) (Quantico 1949), Bob Buel (Wisconsin-Franklin & Marshall), Chuck Dellago (Minnesota-Northwestern) (Camp Lejeune 1944), Ray Hill, Indian Joe Scott (Oklahoma A&M-Fort Lewis JC), Dick Self (Texas A&M), Tom Sweetland (Compton JC), Walt Szot (Bucknell), Clarence Underhill, Guy Way (UCLA) (El Toro 1944, Great Lakes 1946)

Guards: Lloyd Baxter (SMU), Ernest Cunningham (Midwestern), Bob Emery (Hope), Bob King (Los Angeles CC) (11th Naval District 1947), Bob Mirth (Moravian-Muhlenburg), George Oliver (LSU), Frank Snyder, Billy Valentine (Rice-Midwestern), Rex Wells (Idaho State-Michigan), Dean Westgaard

Centers: Jim Cloud (Southern Methodist-Southwestern Louisiana), Joe Cribari (Denver), Henry Fitzgibbons (Arkansas), Glen Graham (Florence Teachers), Tony Karakas (Missouri)

Backs: Joe Bartos (Navy) (Quantico 1947-48), Doug Brooks (Minnesota-Nebraska), Jerry Carle (Minnesota-Northwestern), Lew Cook, John Duke (Rice-Austin), Joe Ferem (St. Mary's-Pacific) (Camp Lejeune 1944, PH Marines 1945), Pete Glick (Princeton), Charlie Harris (Georgia), Bob Hodal (Great Lakes 1946-48), Don Klingler (North Carolina State), Mickey McCardle (USC) (El Toro 1944-45), Jiggs McVay (Louisiana State), Don Morrison, Dick Nave (Marin JC), Fred Rippel (Bradley-Iowa State), Jack Robertson (Austin), Fred Simmons, Ray Gene Smith (Cameron-Oklahoma-Midwestern), Robert Taylor, Jack Wages (Abilene Christian-North Texas), Earl Ward (Texas Christian), Don "Skip" White (Fresno State) (MCRD San Diego 1948), Billy Willard (Rice-Southwestern Louisiana), Keith Woods

---

Spring training: 18-6 MCRD San Diego

Coach: Pottenger

Ends: Baxter, Box, Ellery, Owens, Pfeifer. **Tackles:** Dellago, Hill, McMurray, Lyle Nelson (California), Bill Rush (Cal), Szot. **Guards:** Emery, Paul McMahon (Navy-Washburn), Mirth, Oliver, Dave Ridderhof (Navy) (Quantico 1950), Valentine. **Centers:** Graham, Karakas. **Backs:** Cook, Charles Dunne (USC), Ferem, Harris, Hodal, Roger Hyatt, Paul Mareks (Long Beach CC), McVay, John O'Brien, Earl Roth (Maryland) (Quantico 1950), Russell, Simmons. Ward

Hackman At Pendleton

Camp Pendleton had a good football team in 1949 and the Camp Pendleton scout a good sports staff to cover it that season.

As the team posted a 10-1-1 record and lost to Quantico by a point for the All-Navy title, the paper ran feature stories on various players. By late November and early December, the staff was down to interviewing substitutes.

A researcher scanning microfilm came to page 6 of the Dec. 2 issue and remarked, "Gee, that looks like (actor) Gene Hackman."

Under the photo, it said: "Pfc. Gene Hackman."

The story noted that the 6-0, 189-pound, 19-year-old Hackman graduated from Plainville (Ill.) High and had served in China.

Football and the Marine Corps were a springboard also for others into the entertainment field, including:

Ed Arnold (El Toro 1959-60), Los Angeles TV/radio announcer; spokesman for "Hour of Power"

Pervis Atkins (San Francisco St., Santa Ana JC, Camp Pendleton 1956, New Mexico State All-American), film/TV actor

Brian Dennehy (Columbia), film/TV actor

Vince Dooley (Auburn, Quantico 1954, Parris Island assistant 1955, coach at Georgia 25 seasons; Georgia athletic director), ESPN football commentator

Abe Gibron (Purdue, 11 seasons in NFL, coach of Chicago Bears, Chicago Wind), played himself in TV movie "Brian's Song"

Jack Ging (Oklahoma, CFL, Quantico 1955), character actor in movies, TV

Bob Herwig (Cal, College Football Hall of Fame), was married to Kathleen Winsor, author of "Forever amber" (Navy Cross)

Elroy Hirsch (Wisconsin, Michigan, Camp Lejeune 1944, El Toro 1945, College and Pro Football Halls of Fame; pro executive, Wisconsin athletic director), actor; "Crazylegs;" "Unchained Melody"

Keith Jackson, commentator, writer, producer, ABC/TV sports

Jock Mahoney (Iowa, El Toro 1945), movie actor; TV series "Yancy Derringer"

Bob Mathias (Stanford, two-time Olympic decathlon champion), movie/TV actor

Mickey McCardle (USC, El Toro 1944-45), stand-in for John Hodiak in "Saturday's Hero"

Fred "Curly" Morrison (Ohio State, seven seasons in NFL, pro executive), one of first NFL players to serve as a CBS/TV football commentator; also narrated half-hour show for syndication

Conrad A. Schultz (Oregon), opera singer; Capitol records; radio, TV and film appearances (Navy Cross)

Dennis Swanson, president of ABC Sports

And there were those who brought skills to the Corps:

Charles Erb (Cal, coach at Nevada, Idaho), LA radio announcer in early 1940s (WWI)

Ben Finney (El Toro business manager 1944-45) (see separate chapter on El Toro)

Gordon Marston, specialized in sports for Yankee Network

Hal Wolf, a 1940s West Coast sportscaster, broadcaster

Also: Donn Bernstein, ABC Sports/TV; Ernie Harwell, formerly announced Colts and Giants games; Bob Murphy, announced Oklahoma, Oklahoma A&M, Florida St. games (Jack's brother); Bill O'Donnell, broadcast Colts games and handled NBC assignments; Bum Phillips, Houston Oilers' network; Red Pitcher, voice of East Tennessee University athletics and formerly announced Xavier and Univ. of Cincinnati games; Sam Rutigliano, former football analyst, NBC, ESPN

A Mixed Bag

You'd think that Camp Pendleton, with its infantry connections, beautiful beaches, rolling hills and moderate climate, would have been the Corps' prime football territory.

But such, of course, was not the case.

From the first team in 1945 until the last in 1958 (there were no varsity programs in 1946, 1950 or 1957), the base did not field a losing team but only twice reached the All-Navy or All-Marine finals and was not a regular factor in deciding championships. Moreover, its record against the San Diego Marines was 2-5-1.

There were reasons, of course: wars to be fought, training commitments, division movements, commanders not interested in athletics.

"Name" players passed through but, in many cases, were headed overseas or returning to the States for release to civilian status. (A number of them did play for the Pacific Coast Football League's San Diego Bombers at a time Pendleton did not field teams.)

Still, other bases faced problems, too.

Especially ironic were circumstances surrounding the first team. Marine custom normally would dictate that a "grunts" base field the nationally ranked team. But, instead, the honor went to, of all things, an air station (El Toro).

Coach R. Jean "Cheesie" Neil, one of the Marines' top all-around athletes, recalls his Pendleton team being invited up to play the El Toro "second string" in 1945.

Out trotted All-Pro tackle Wilbur "Wee Willie Wilkin," Hall of Fame back Elroy "Crazylegs" Hirsch, Hall of Fame quarterback Paul Governali, Knute Rockne Trophy winner Bob Dove, Olympic wrestler Vern Gagne, and other pro and college standouts for El Toro.

The score, as might be expected, was 61-0.

"On my return," said Neil, a career Marine, "Gen. H.M. Smith held up the newspaper and gave me the worst chewing out I ever got. And I've had some."

To many, H.M. stood for Howling Mad.

Smith also decreed that Pendleton no longer would furnish El Toro with players the caliber of Hirsch.

The Sept. 7, 1945 base paper at El Toro had noted that "Lt. Hirsch has been 'visiting' at the base the past week, watching the local grid squad work out. He is stationed at Camp Pendleton."

Maj. Ben Finney, the El Toro business manager, morale officer, showman, team spokesman, ticket seller, etc., said: "When I learned that Hirsch (and another player) were in San Diego waiting to board a transport for overseas duty, I flew to Washington to have their orders changed. What the hell, the war was over. I'm not at all certain they ever knew just what had happened."

And while the Flying Marines would challenge the Fleet City Bluejackets in a Los Angeles Coliseum game that had a nationwide following, the Pendleton team (Amphibious Boat Basin) would disband. A December game with Colorado College had to be canceled because 24 of the 33 Pendleton players were transferred or discharged.

Still, Pendleton won three games and boasted of such players as Mike Kasap (Illinois, Purdue, Baltimore Colts, Buffalo Bills), end Cloyce Box, to star at West Texas and be an All-Pro for the Detroit Lions, and back Otto Kofler, to be a college coach and father of Matt, a quarterback at San Diego State and in the NFL.

There was no base team in 1946, although the Del Mar Marines in late fall fielded the first of their two teams.

Big things were expected in 1947, so big that initial plans called for both base and 1st Marine Division teams. But they finally settled on one team, nicknamed simply the Marines and coached by Maj. Dick Strickler (Virginia Military), a decorated officer who had played for MCB San Diego in 1940.

And Pendleton (6-3) got off to a fast start, winning five, before losing three times, one a 20-7 defeat by North Island NAS before 40,000 at a Navy Day game. Tackle Charles Milam and end Ray Pfeifer received All-Marine honors, with guard Ted Bertagni and back Wes Barrette selected on the second team.

There was little complaining about the end play. Besides Pfeifer, Pendleton had Bill Flynn, who would return to Notre Dame's unbeaten 1948 and 1949 teams, and Bill Marker, who would play for West Virginia and receive a tryout with the Washington Redskins.

Other teams and highlights:

■ **1948 (6-4):** With the '47 program to build on, Pendleton expanded the schedule to 10 games, added back John Beckett (Navy) and suffered narrow losses (18-13, 22-13 and 12-7) plus a 37-19 setback as 40,000 watched the Navy Day game against DesPac at the Rose Bowl in Pasadena.

Tackle Bob Fierke was All-Marine, and center Don Gray, Marker and back Joe Sabol second-team on a young squad coached by Maj. Jim Breen.

■ **1949 (10-1-1):** This was arguably Pendleton's best team, being ranked No. 1 in the country among service teams part of the season by the Williamson Rating Service and reaching the All-Navy finals.

The loss, 14-13, to Quantico, was on a chilly, overcast day at the Los Angeles Coliseum as Pendleton missed a field goal as time ran out.

Pendleton and MCRD San Diego, which did not meet, tied with 4-1 records for the West Coast Navy League title. The league, by a 4-1 vote, selected Pendleton for the playoffs, partly because San Diego had been a finalist in the 1948 All-Navy title game. Any hard feelings were short-lived; 16 players, mostly from San Diego, bolstered Pendleton (technically the 11th Naval District team) for the Quantico game.

The coach, Lt. Col. Hal Roise (Idaho), had played for the San Diego Marines in 1940 and in two wars would collect two Navy Crosses, a Legion of Merit and a Bronze Star. He knew his way around a football field, too: He'd been a 10th-round draft choice of the Chicago Bears in 1939.

The squad was deeper than in 1947 and 1948 and finally had a superstar, back Joe Bartos (Navy), who scored 15 TDs in leading

Quantico to a 12-1 record in 1947 and had 86 points in 1948 on Quantico's way to a 13-0 record. Bartos, perhaps one of the finest Marine backs ever to suit up, was All-Marine for a third season as he scored 80 points for Pendleton. End Art Specht also was all-Marine, and backs Chuck Henry and Gene Moore, who was wounded at Peleliu and Okinawa, and guard Bob Hunemiller were second-team.

■ **1951 (6-5):** see separate chapter.

■ **1952 (6-4):** In one of the greatest performances by a Marine back of any era, Charlie Harris scored 120 points. Incredibly, he was not selected All-Marine. But neither was any Pendleton player in an embarrassing oversight.

Harris returned to Georgia for two seasons and would have tryouts in the NFL and the new American Football League.

A name at end didn't merit much attention at the time, but Eugene "Big Daddy" Lipscomb would be heard from. Remarkably, the 6-6, 265-pounder and future Pro Hall of Famer played end on offense as well as tackle on defense.

Back Ray Gene Smith went on to four seasons in the NFL.

Coach Jerry Carle (Minnesota and Northwestern), who began coaching at Colorado College in 1957, still was coaching at the Rocky Mountain school in 1989.

■ **1953 (5-3-1):** A "sleeper" team captured the West Coast Marine title but fell to Quantico, 21-14, for the All-Marine title, partly because of the loss of Lipscomb and tackle Harold Bradley (Iowa) to the NFL and the 1st MarDiv to Korea.

Guard Ray Suchy was an All-Marine selection, and quarterback Ed Brown (Univ. of San Francisco), tackle Ken Huxhold (Wisconsin) and end Willie Roberts (Tulsa) were second-team.

Brown went on to be a 12-season quarterback with the Bears and Pittsburgh Steelers, Roberts would head to the Canadian Football League and Huxhold would play for the Philadelphia Eagles.

Other future pros would be linebacker Bob Griffin (Arkansas), who also would be a longtime NFL assistant, and back John Mazur (Notre Dame), who would play in the CFL and coach the New England Patriots.

The coach, Maj. Ted Stawicki (American and Morningside), had a career 38-15-3 record, which placed him seventh all-time in victories among Marine coaches.

■ **1954 (7-3):** There was a college atmosphere again as Utah State, North Texas, Vanderbilt, Princeton, Tulsa, Northwestern, Iowa, Purdue, Notre Dame, Idaho State, Mississippi State, Colgate, Denver, California and Villanova were represented.

Pendleton lost to MCRD San Diego, 20-0, in the regular season but tied the depot for the 11th ND title — only to lose in a playoff, 26-19.

When the Marines were good, they were very, very good, winning 78-0, 55-6, 53-6 and 78-0. The other loss was to Ft. Ord (10-3-1), 48-14.

All-America end Frank McPhee (Princeton) was All-Marine; back John Callard (Long Beach CC-Denver), Roberts and tackle Walt Vellieu (Purdue) were second-team.

■ **1955 (5-2):** The Marines defeated the San Diego Marines for the first time, 34-14, and won West Coast Marine and 11th Naval District titles.

Center Dick Petty (USC) was named the Most Valuable Player in the naval district as well as being All-Marine.

But the Marines fell to Ft. Ord (11-2), 40-7, for the fifth straight time, and to Hamilton AFB. On the other hand, the Eagle Rock AC came the closest of any victims (20 points).

The coach was Al Thomas, who had played for the Maui Marines in 1944 and Northwestern, including a 1949 Rose Bowl appearance; was awarded three Silver Stars and a Legion of Merit; and rose to the rank of colonel. An assistant was Jim Erkenbeck (San Diego State), who would have a long career as a college and pro assistant.

End Sam Ward (Rice) and back Charles Wyss also were All-Marine selections, and back Bob Miller second-team. Overlooked was back Alex Bravo (Cal Poly San Luis Obispo), who would play four seasons for the Los Angeles Rams and Oakland Raiders and one in the CFL.

■ **1956 (8-1):** Arguably, the team was as good as the 1949 Marines, losing only to Don Coryell's (10-1) Ft. Ord team, 26-7. Some of the victories were lopsided: 38-0, 63-14, 52-20 and 78-6.

Maj. Joe Stribling, from the "Old Corps" and a prewar player at Hardin-Simmons, guided the Marines to the 11th Naval District title.

A highlight, of course, was the 52-20 drubbing of MCRD San Diego that turned into a track meet. Fred Magett scored TDs on runs of 58, 70 and 64 yards; Dick Washington (Notre Dame) on 40- and 61-yard runs; and Wayne Buchert (Whitworth) on an 80-yard punt return.

Gen. Thomas Wornham was the San Diego CG and brought an entourage to support the team.

"It was the Marine Corps birthday," recalled Pendleton tackle George Lefferts (Idaho). "The 'Marine Corps Hymn' is synonymous with a college fight song and was played every time we scored a TD. Our band played 'Semper Fidelis' when MCRD scored.

"Naturally, Marines stand at attention when the 'Marine Hymn' is played, so all the Marines from San Diego had to stand after we scored, which was eight times that day, and I heard that Gen. Wornham was furious."

(He didn't stay furious for long, however. Lefferts, Lewis and Johns were transferred to San Diego in 1957. "I suspect that Gen. Wornham had something to do with that," Lefferts said. "He was a magnificent man and was helpful in getting my family established in the San Diego community.")

Again, college experience was telling in Pendleton's '56 success. Represented were North Carolina, San Jose State, Idaho, Arizona, USC, California, San Diego State, Wisconsin, Duke, Tulsa and Notre Dame.

And Pendleton received a contingent of Quantico veterans: end John Rushing (Redlands), tackle John Hamber (San Jose State), Lefferts, tackle Ernie Lewis (Arizona), tackle Frank Pavich (USC), guard Mike Giddings (California), center John Palmer (Duke) and Buchert.

In addition, Stribling inherited seven players from Pendleton's '55 team and transfers brought in tackle Walt Beddeo, quarterback Bob Bohn (Tulsa), and Magett and Washington from San Diego.

Buchert had been an NAIA Little All-American, as had center Mel Loncaric of Northeast Missouri.

Another trait was the talent of the young, enlisted Marines. Beddeo went on to letter at Denver, center .Dick Loncar at Northeast Louisiana (and get a tryout with the Steelers), back David Kurtz at Purdue and back Bob Miller at Denver. But the biggest headlines would go to All-American Pervis Atkins at New Mexico State, who would return kicks six years in the NFL before turning to an acting career.

Washington would play in the CFL, and Giddings would be head coach at Glendale JC, Utah and Hawaii (WFL) and an assistant at USC and with the San Francisco 49ers and Denver Broncos before operating a pro scouting service in Newport Beach, Cal.

Again, Leatherneck overlooked Pendleton's accomplishments. Rushing was the lone All-Marine selection. Hamber and Eddie Johns (San Diego State) were second-team.

■ **1957 (no varsity team).** A schedule of 11-man regimental games was established. One of the players was the well-traveled Mike Mercer of the 5th Marines, who kicked at Minnesota, Florida State, Hardin-Simmons and Northern Arizona; for the Minnesota Vikings, Raiders, Kansas City Chiefs, Buffalo Bills, Green Bay Packers and San Diego Chargers; and in Super Bowl I.

■ **1958 (4-3-1):** Stawicki returned for the base's final varsity season and had a coaching staff almost as tough as the team: Wendell Beard (New Mexico, California, a pro tryout, Quantico, Pendleton, two Bronze Stars); Bob Loughridge, a tri-captain at Oklahoma; and George Smith, a future general.

The base again profited from transfers, adding eight players from Quantico's 1957 team: ends Bob Morman (Northwestern), Walt Nadzak (Denison) and Darrell Sorrell (Duke), guard John Dekleva (Colorado A&M), center Don Karnoscak (Colorado), back Frank Jeske (Northwestern), back Jim Schwartz (Xavier) and back Jack Wolff (Colorado A&M).

Nadzak would coach at Juniata (Pa.) and Connecticut and become athletic director at The Citadel. Karnoscak and Wolff would get tryouts with the Broncos.

Dekleva and Karnoscak were second-team all-Marine in a season in which some victories came easily: 64-0, 89-6 and 87-0.

■

The Bobb McKittricks and Roger Theders would follow, but Pendleton returned to regimental play. Both went on to long college and pro coaching careers.

1945 (Boat Basin)

Record: 46-0 Fallbrook NAD, 0-61 MCAS El Toro, 13-6 Stockton AAB 13-6, 39-0 California-American Institute. (3-1). A game was scheduled Nov. 9 with the Mitchell Convalescent Hospital. A December game with Colorado College was cancelled because 24 of the 33 Pendleton players had been transferred or discharged. The team scrimmaged San Diego State.

Coaches: Capt. Jean "Cheesie" Neil (MCB San Diego 1930-34, coach PH Marines 1936), Capt. Bob Rann (Michigan State) (MCB San Diego 1940). **Assistants:** NA

Ends: Boyce Box (North Carolina-West Texas), Cloyce Box (West Texas), Clark, Dingfelder (Bucknell), John Machado (Loyola of LA-Flagstaff Teachers), McNut, Art Pollock (Syracuse-Colgate)

Tackles: Anthony, Ed Bush (Minnesota-Northwestern-Penn State), Hintze, Herman Jones (Mississippi), Mike Kasap (Illinois-Purdue), Bruce Meyers (Washington), Reed (Colorado), Schwarts, Wagnon (Colorado)

Guards: Baker, Brockman, Brown, Dawn, Hochman (MCB San Diego), Frank Lauterbur (Oberlin-Mt. Union), George Meyers (Washington) (Camp Lejeune 1944), Michaelkiviczy, Miller
Centers: Bill Goodnight (Colorado College), Ricord, R. Scott (Pasadena JC)
Backs: Anderson (California), Angele, Burroughs, Larry Declusin (St. Mary's) (San Diego Marines 1943), Fagan, Fester, Glasgow, Gott (Pacific), Al or Marv Grubaugh (Nebraska-Northwestern), John Haggin (Colorado College), Hanlon, Haskett, Art Honegger (Cal) (Camp Lejeune 1944), Fred Klemenok (USF-Pacific), Otto Kofler (Washington State), Mattson (New Mexico), Bill Patapoff (Santa Clara-USC), Joyce Pipkin (Arkansas), Pyfer (Washington), Rann (p-c), Shaw, Shirley, Smith, Tipton, George Vercelli (Loyola of LA-Flagstaff Teachers), Wilson, Bob Winship (Loyola of LA-Flagstaff Teachers-Southwestern Louisiana), John Zeigler (Colorado-College College). **Kicker:** Miller

1946 (Del Mar Marines)

Record: 0-0 San Diego Tolltecs, 21-6 SD Tolltecs.
Coach: MTsgt. Charles earnest. **Assistant:** WO Buster.
End: Bill Flynn (Notre Dame). **Line:** Boudreeau, Egli, Marr, McDonald, Moore (UCLA), Peterson (USC), Jim Regan (Villanova). **Backs:** Warren "Brud" Davis (Colgate) Bill Emmett, Wally Harrison (Illinois), Lew Ragone (Texas), Williams

1947

Record: 19-0 DesPac, 28-6 Ream Field, 20-0 Terminal Island, 43-0 SubForce, 58-0 San Diego Naval Station, 7-20 North Island NAS, 6-19 Washington Frosh, 13-46 El Toro, 20-0 San Diego NTC. (6-3). Plans were abandoned to field both base and 1st Marine Division teams. Pendleton scrimmaged Pepperdine. Record crowd of 40,000 saw Navy Day game with North Island. Milam and Pfeifer All-Marine; Barrette and Bertagni second team.
Coach: Maj. R.D. Strickler (VMI) (MCB San Diego 1940)
Assistants: Lt. D.E. Ezell (TCU-North Texas Agriculture) (El Toro 1945), Lt. J.A. Grant, T/Sgt. Clarence Klinck (MCB San Diego 1937-40), Lt. R.C. Knauf, M/Sgt. E.B. Vassar (11th Cavalry 1930, West Coast Army 1931, MCB San Diego 1940)
Ends: George Cordle, Bill Flynn (Notre Dame), Felix Malewich, Bill Marker (West Virginia), Ray Pfeifer (Rice), John Ruhwedel
Tackles: Dick Almes, Galdouckas, Bill Gribble, Joe Lucchici, Charles Milam (Arkansas), Calvin Roberts
Guards: Ted Bertagni (Wyoming), Briggs, Tony Giancurso, Pat Henry, Al Kuehner, Ray Roy, Vargas
Centers: Don Gray, J.M. King (Notre Dame), Frank Schneider (China 1946)
Backs: Wes Barrette, John Buckley, Warren "Brud" Davis (CVolgate), Ed Fedosky, Glenn Handleton, Wally Harrison (Illinois), Hashman, A.H. Hurley, Mel Jorgensen, Tom Ragucci, Joe Stringfellow, Elwood Theis, Bill Thomas, Wayne Ubben (Wichita) (PH Marines 1946), Will Zaudtke (Macalester-Gustavus Adolphus-Bowling Green)
Also: Anderson, Barsotti, Bennett, Burrows, Chambers, Conrick, Hamilton, Maher, Mandeville, McGinn, Sarros, Sharp, J. Wieczorek

1947 Del Mar Marines)

Record: 7-13 San Diego NTC, 6-45 North Island NAS, 0-19 SubForce, 0-40 MCB San Diego, 0-22 Oceanside JC. Game with San Diego NS on Nov. 27.
Coach, assistants: NA.
Ends: Jensen, Clement. **Tackles:** Deveas, Wilson. **Guards:** McCauley, Oats. **Center:** Downs.
Backs: Gorham, Kwiecinski, Ted Leaman, O'Toole, Sperin, Joe Zakula. **Kicker:** Kern.

1948

Record: 62-0 Tongue Point NAS, 13-18 North Island NAS, 13-22 San Diego NTC, 19-6 Camp Stoneman, 19-37 DesPac, 14-0 El Toro, 31-0 Terminal Island, 7-12 PhibPac, 33-0 NAS Seattle, 19-13 Oceanside JC. (6-4). Crowd of 40,000 Saw Navy Day game with DesPac at Rose Bowl. JV team played Fallbrook Legion. Fierke was all-Marine; Gray, Marker and Sabol were second team; Beckett, Gray, Koehler and Marker were named to All-FMF Pacific team.
Coach: Maj. Jim Breen (Newark Bears)
Assistants: Lt. Jim Grant, T/Sgt. Clarence Klinck (MCB San Diego 1937-40), M/Sgt. E.B. Vassar (11th Cavalry 1930, West Coast Army 1931, MCB San Diego 1940
Ends: Don Hebert, Felix Malevich, Bill Marker (West Virginia), John Ruscilti
Tackles: Dick Almes, Bob Fierke, Bill Gribble, Joe Luchiccia, Hank Spahn
Guards: Pat Henry, Herman Jelinik, Walt Moore (Los Angeles CC), George Rader, Ray Roy, Trombetta

Centers: Marshall George (Rice-Southwestern of Texas), Don Gray, Max Maxwell, Tex Vaughn

Backs: John Beckett (Navy) (Pensacola 1946, Jacksonville NAS 1947), Argyll Conner, Darrell Gentry, Charles Hall, George Harrison, Charles Henry (Central Oklahoma), Bill Holloway, Bob Koehler (China 1946-47), Bob McKenzie, Bob Penner, Walt Perko, Tom Ragucci, Joe Sabol, Lindy Scialla, Bob Suster, Wayne Ubben (Wichita) (PH Marines 1946), Watson, Will Zaudtke (Macalester-Gustavus Adolphus-Bowling Green)

1949

Record: 33-0 North Island NAS, 14-14 Cal Ramblers, 28-0 SubPac, 1-0 Whidby Island NAS (forfeit), 35-0 Treasure Island, 19-13 DesPac, 33-6 PhibPac, 54-0 MCAS El Toro, 32-13 San Diego NTC, 32-14 DesPac (playoff), 68-0 Hawaii All-Stars (playoff), 13-14 Quantico (All-Marine title). (10-1-1). Ranked No. 1 by Williamson for part of season. Augmented by 18 players from MCRD San Diego for playoffs. Bartos and Specht All-Marine; Henry, Hunemiller and Moore second team. Specht, Almes, Gobeli and Bartos named to All-FMF Pacific team.

Coach: Lt. Col. Hal Roise (Idaho) (MCB San Diego 1940)

Assistants: Bob Breitbard (civilian), Capt. John "Biff" Crawley (Kansas State), M/Sgt. James Stevens (MCB San Diego), Robert "Bull" Trometter (St. Mary's) (MCB San Diego 1936-40, coach MCB and MCRD San Diego 1947-48)

Ends: Ed Carney (Bradley), Bob Carson (Kansas-Navy), Tom Ellery, Gene Hackman, Jim Hodgin, Charles McPherson, Bobby Miller, Charles Shepherd, Art Specht

Tackles: Dick Almes, Henry Cooks, Joe Farrell, Bob Fierke, Vern Maline, Alex Marusich, Rader, Oliver Shemayne, Henry Spahn, Charles Wymss

Guards: Boyce Ford, Bob Gobeli, Bob Hunemiller (Guam 1947-48), Mike Melonas (Guam 1948), Bob Moon (Great Lakes 1948), Tom Sanders (Oklahoma), Jack Sharkey, Joe Stranger, Earl Weidenbach, Elra Young (Centenary)

Centers: Travis Atkins, Jim Cox, Lew Niemann, Charles Stephenson (St. Lawrence-Holy Cross), John Williams (Citadel) (Quantico 1948)

Backs: Joe Bartos (Navy) (Quantico 1947-48), Bill Bender, Ken Collier, Argyll Conner, Lou Cook, Cy Degulis (Cornell) (Quantico 1948), Curtis DeRoche, Darrel Gentry, Frank Guidone, Charles Henry (Central Oklahoma), Bob Hodal (Great Lakes 1946-48), Art Leary, Gene Moore (East-Central Oklahoma) (MCB and MCRD San Diego 1947-48), Bob Penner, Walt Perko, Milford Pritchard, Mark Rainer (Auburn-Duke) (NAB Coronado; MCB San Diego 1947), Billy Sanders (Parris Island 1948), Ed Walsh, Earl Ward (TCU), Wilson

Kicker: Trometter

1950

No base team because of the Korean War. Maj. John "Biff" Crawley (Kansas State) was to have been head coach.

1952

Record: 19-39 Ft. Ord, 29-11 Camp Cooke, 40-20 Luke AFB, 56-13 Barstow Marines, 27-6 Lowry AFB, 33-42 MCRD San Diego, 41-13 MCAS El Toro, 15-56 San Diego NTS, 0-34 PhibPac, 27-12 North Island NAS. (6-4). Charlie Harris scored 120 points.

Coach: Jerry Carle (Minnesota-Northwestern)

Assistants: Capt. Henry Armstrong (Rice-Southwestern Louisiana) (PH Marines 1945), Capt. J.E. Cloud (SMU-Southwestern Louisiana), Joe Cribari (Denver), Frank McDonald

Ends: Ron Broward, Joe Connors (William & Mary) (Parris Island 1951), Jerry Fouts (Oklahoma-Midwestern), "Big Daddy" Lipscomb, Len Zelinka (Los Angeles CC-Santa Ana JC)

Tackles: Jack Adams, Angus Alford (Wharton JC), Jim Hanker (Oregon State) (Quantico 1951), Charles Keese, John Linnemanstons (Marquette), John Tillo (Iowa State) (Quantico 1951)

Guards: Ray Bakker (Yakima JC), Mike Bazzy (Michigan State), Bill Brazil, Manny Corsil (Colorado), Fred Doty, John McGrady, Earl Riley (St. Ambrose), Charles Scott, Floyd Shillings (Arizona), Ray Suchy (Wisconsin-Nevada) (Parris Island 1951), Bill Webb

Centers: Glenn Graham (Florence Tch.) (Parris Island 1952), Lou Gregory, Bill Pierce, Dean Westgaard

Backs: Don Bonaparte, Sam Boone, Ken Bracken, Bill Crowe (Indiana Central), John Dias (San Diego State), Larry Gast, Gordon Gotts (Nortrhwestern), Ed Grimes, Charles Harris (Georgia), Sam Kahalewai (Hawaii), Pat Kendlep (Stockton JC), Chuck Oertel, Ed Reagin, Fred Rippel (Bradley-Iowa State), Laverne Rohlfson, Don Scardami, Ray Gene Smith (Cameron-Oklahoma-Midwestern), Lacy Thomas, Earl Tieppo, Elmer Tolbert, Towns, Jack Wages (Abilene Christian-North Texas), Gus Zavaletta (Monterrey Tech). **Kicker:** Art Robinson

1953

Record: 34-7 MCAS El Toro, 0-40 Ft. Ord, 40-18 Barstow Marines, 13-13 MCRD San Diego, 22-14 North Island NAS, 7-21 San Diego NTC, 19-13 PhibPac, 26-19 Ft. Lewis, 14-21 Quantico (All-Marine title). (5-3-1). Suchy All-Marine; Brown, Huxhold and Roberts second team. Nine played on Navy-Marine All-Stars, who lost to Rams, 72-19, in preseason Navy Relief game. Lipscomb and Bradley were released early in season. Team also lost 1st MarDiv players but was West Coast champion.

Coach: Ted Stawicki (American-Morningside) (Quantico 1946-48; coach Parris Island 1949-50)

Assistants: Capt. Allen "Scotty" Harris (Ohio State), Lt. Lee Haslinger (Cincinnati), Lt. Bob O'Malley (Detroit)

Ends: Bob Bell (MCRD San Diego 1948-52), "Big Daddy" Lipscomb, Howard Powell (Tennessee State), Willie Roberts (Tulsa), George Taylor (NE Mississippi JC), Harold Turner (Tennessee State) (MCRD San Diego 1952), Len Zelinka (Los Angeles CC-Santa Ana JC)

Tackles: Harold Bradley (Iowa) (MCRD San Diego 1951-52), Pat Flanagan (Marquette) (MCRD San Diego 1951) Don Hale, Tom Hill (Oregon College), Ken Huxhold (Wisconsin) (Quantico 1952), Arnold Johnson (Stockton JC), Willie Moore, Bill Webb (Camp Fisher 1953)

Guards: Ray Bakker (Yakima JC), Bob Conklin (San Diego State), MCRD San Diego 1952; El Toro 1953), Fred Doty, Harold Eggleston, Bob Griffin (Arkansas) (MCRD San Diego 1952), Bob Holt (Hastings), Tom Reeves (Shaw) (Camp Lejeune 1950-52), Earl Riley (St. Ambrose), Charles Scott (Camp Lejeune 1953), Floyd Shillings (Arizona), Len Stewart (Fresno State) (Quantico 1952), Ray Suchy (Wisconsin-Nevada) (Parris Island 1951)

Centers: Mike Bazzy (Michigan State), John Hendon (San Francisco CC), Bill Moore (Loras), Chuck Pierce, Bruce Rehn (Washington) (Quantico 1951)

Backs: Ed Brown (Univ. of San Francisco) (MCRD San Diego 1952), Jim Bujol, John Carlile, Tom Carodine (Boys Town-Loyola LA-Nebraska) (MCRD San Diego 1952), Dave Daggett, Rick Ellis (San Francisco State) (MCRD San Diego 1952), Larry Gast, Bob Gault (Illinois) (Camp Lejeune 1948-49, 1951), Dick Gonzales, Gordon Gotts (Northwestern), George Granger (Barstow Marines 1951-52), Bob Harrison (South Georgia) (Cherry Point 1952), Herb Hunter (Tennessee State) (MCRD San Diego 1952), Pat Kendlep (Stockton JC), Jim Lester, Billy Martin (Paris JC), John Mazur (Notre Dame) (Quantico 1952), Bob Montgomery (Drake), Gerald Nesbitt, Brad Ogden (USC), Gary Pickens (Oregon), Bayard Pickett (South Carolina) (Parris Island 1947), Charles Reid (Texas College), Mike Ryan (Minnesota) (MCRD San Diego 1952), Lacy Thomas, Ray Thompson, Bob Tougas (Providence) (Quantico 1951), Towns, Gus Zavaletta (Monterrey Tech)

1954

Record: 11-7 Hamilton AFB, 27-21 Eagle Rock AC, 78-0 Edwards AFB, 14-48 Ft. Ord, 0-20 MCRD San Diego, 55-6 Barstow Marines, 53-6 North Island NAS, 27-7 PhibPac, 78-0 San Diego NTC, 19-26 MCRD San Diego (playoff for 11th Naval District title). (7-3). Ranked No. 20 by Williamson. Six played on Navy-Marine All-Stars team that lost in preseason benefit to Redskins, 52-0. McPhee All-Marine; Callard, Roberts and Viellieu second team.

Coach: Bill Sigler (North Carolina-Michigan) (p-c Quantico 1946, asst. Quantico 1947, MCRD San Diego 1949, Quantico 1952-53)

Assistants: Jim Delaney (MCRD San Diego 1948-50, asst. San Diego 1953), Charles George (Furman), Allen "Scotty" Harris (Ohio State), Jim Parker (Baylor) (Quantico 1953), Al Thomas (Northwestern) (Maui Marines 1944, asst. Quantico 1953)

Ends: Larry Cooley (Utah State) (MCRD San Diego 1953), Larry Foster (Illinois), Bob Gandy (North Texas), Bob Hines (Vanderbilt), John Kammerman (Utah State) (MCRD San Diego 1953), John Manaco, Frank McPhee (Princeton) (Quantico 1953), Willie Roberts (Tulsa)

Tackles: Sam Craig (MCRD San Diego 1953), Jack Davis (Oklahoma) (MCRD San Diego 1953), Ezra Gordon (Victoria JC) (MCRD San Diego 1953), Jim Howe (Northwestern) (Camp Fisher 1953), Dale Lewis (Marquette), George Palmer (Iowa-Fresno State) (MCRD San Diego 1954), Mel Ratkowich, Tom Robinson (Vanderbilt), Bill Scales (Monterey JC), Carl Valletto (Alabama) (1st MarDiv 1954), Walt Viellieu (Purdue) (Quantico 1953), Jim Weithmann (Notre Dame)

Guards: Otis Bealmear (Oklahoma) (MCRD San Diego 1953), John Campo (Detroit), Percy Christensen (Idaho State), Bill Donaldson, Tom Keegan (Michigan State), Joe Logan (Mississippi State) (MCRD San Diego 1953-54), Jim Myers (Santa Rosa JC), Bill O'Hara (Vanport CC-Lewis & Clark), Julius Sandras (LSU)

Centers: Les Akeo, Bob Banaga (San Diego CC) (MCRD San Diego 1953), Ed Johnson, Don Main (Colgate), Clare McCullough

Backs: John Callard (Long Beach CC-Denver), Bob Harrison (South Georgia) (Cherry Point 1952), Dick Harvey (San Angelo JC-North Texas), Bob Holliday (Sam Houston) (MCRD San Diego 1953), Jim Lester, Jim Marinos (Cal) (MCRD San Diego 1953), Denny Moore (Minnesota), Charles McNeill (Tyler JC-North Texas), Chuck Reid, Jim Smith, Ron Steel, George Stephenson (UCLA) (MCRD San Diego 1953), Ray Thompson, Joe Till (Villanova), Bill Tryon (Princeton), Bobby Wilson (Oklahoma A&M), Chuck Wyss

1955

Record: 89-0 Point Mugu NAS, 53-0 San Diego NTC, 20-0 Eagle Rock AC, 7-40 Ft. Ord, 0-35 Hamilton AFB, 34-14 MCRD San Diego, 33-7 North Island NAS. (5-2). Petty, Ward and Wyss All-Marine; Miller second team. Petty 11th Naval District Player of the Year.

Coach: Al Thomas (Northwestern) (Maui Marines 1944, asst. Quantico 1953)

Assistants: Pat Cacace (Boston College) (Quantico 1954), Charles George (Furman), Jim Erkenbeck (San Diego State) (Quantico 1953) (p-c 1st MarDiv 1954), Don Penza (Notre Dame) (Quantico 1954), Joe Till (Villanova)

Ends: Ray Bates, Robbie Bessent (Pasadena JC), Hal Byrd, Paul Crowley (Harvard) (Quantico 1954), Larry Foster (Illinois), Bob Hardie (North Texas), Ed Peasley (Washington), Fred Voss (Carleton) (Quantico 1954), Sam Ward (Rice), George Wood, Stan Wyatt

Tackles: Elmer Brooks (3rd MarDiv 1954), George Burcher (New Mexico), Sam Craig (MCRD San Diego 1954), Jesus Esparza (New Mexico) (Quantico 1954), Martin Hurd (Vallejo JC), Dale Lewis (Marquette), Del Scales (Monterey JC), Elmer Sewell, Lon Ussell (1st MarDiv 1954)

Guards: Joe Bessent, Don Branson, Ron Carney (1st MarDiv 1954), Art Debetaz (Notre Dame-Southeastern Louisiana), Earnest Delco, Carlos Gonzales, Laural Bobick, Dan Laidman, Joe Massey, Jim Meenan, Cal Patch, Jules Sandras (LSU), Lloyd Vickery (San Jose State), Bud Walls

Centers: Ben Koeneman, Mark Loncar (Notre Dame-Northeast Louisiana), Charles Paxton, Dick Petty (USC) (Quantico 1954)

Backs: Alex Bravo (Cal Poly SLO) (Quantico 1954), Jack Burrell (3rd MarDiv), John Carlile (1st MarDiv 1954), Ross Carlson (Valparaiso), Red Donaldson (Baylor) (Quantico), George Graham (Nevada), Bob Hammond (Nebraska), Jerry Harris, Ed Joseph, Jim Meadows (Los Angeles CC), Bob Miller (Alabama-Denver), Denny Moore (Minnesota), Don Moore, Ray Phillips, Ray Powell (Oklahoma) (Quantico 1954), Bill Rigsbee, Bill Tryon (Princeton), Willie Wills (Southern Illinois), Charles Wyss

1956

Record: 32-14 Hamilton AFB, 21-9 Eagle Rock AC, 18-14 Ft. Bliss, 7-26 Ft. Ord, 38-0 Camp Carson, 21-14 San Diego NTC, 63-14 North Island NAS, 52-20 MCRD San Diego, 78-6 Compton JV. (8-1). Won 11th Naval District title. Joined San Diego NTC and Ft. Ord to play Rams in preseason benefit game in Long Beach. Scrimmaged San Diego State, Palomar JC. Rushing All-Marine; Hamber and Johns second team.

Coach: Maj. Joe Stribling (Hardin-Simmons) (asst. MCRD San Diego 1952)

Assistants: Lt. Pat Cacace (Boston College) (Quantico 1954), Lt. Ron Keifer, Capt. Ken Schieweck (Northwestern-Navy) (Quantico 1949, Camp Lejeune 1951, asst. MCRD San Diego 1954), Lt. Joe Till (Villanova)

Ends: Earl Allen (Arizona State at Flagstaff), Hal Byrd, James Cook, Dick Kocornick (North Carolina), R.J. Marchewka (Illinois), John Rushing (Redlands) (Quantico 1955), Kay Schulz (Sacramento JC), C.F. Snyder (Chico State) (MCRD San Diego 1955), Jess Vallez, Gerald Woods

Tackles: Walt Beddeo (Nebraska-Denver) (MCRD San Diego 1955), Elmer Brooks, John Hamber (San Jose State) (Quantico 1954-55), George Lefferts (Idaho) (Quantico 1955), Ernie Lewis (Arizona) (Quantico 1955), Bob Merrill (Menlo JC), Frank Pavich (USC) (Quantico 1955), Glenn Rohde (Kearney), Delmer Sewell (Texas)

Guards: H.M. Collins (St. Benedict), M.W. Connors (Lewis), Ernest Delco, Mike Giddings (Cal) (Quantico 1955), Gerald Hawley (Huron), Eddie Johns (San Diego State), J.A. Pack (Morris-Harvey), G.F. Walsdorf (Wisconsin), James Welch (Chattanooga)

Centers: P.J. Hunt, Dick Loncar (Notre Dame-Northeastern Louisiana), Mel Loncaric (Northeast Missouri), John Palmer (Duke) (Quantico 1955), J.J. Palumbo (Ohio State)

Backs: Pervis Atkins (San Francisco State-Santa Ana JC-New Mexico State), Bob Bohn (Tulsa) (MCRD San Diego 1954-55), Luther Bryson, Wayne Buchert (Whitworth) (Quantico 1955), Bill Coleman, Van Crooms (Los Angeles CC), John Danley, Don Doty, George Graham (Nevada), Bob Hammond (Nebraska), David Kurtz (Purdue), Fred Maggett (Michigan State) (MCRD San Diego 1954-55), Bob Miller (Alabama-Denver), J.A. Millett (Cortland), Don Moore, Rayford Phillips, chuck Prater, Ralph See, Dick Washington (Notre Dame) (MCRD San Diego 1954-55), William Williams (Michigan State)

1957

Record: 6-45 Cal Poly Pomona, 0-54 Univ. of San Diego (only scores available). A check of the base paper and Oceanside Blade-Tribune could not confirm these scores, which are listed in the 1958 NCAA Guide.

Coach: NA. **Assistants:** NA. **Roster:** NA

A schedule of 11-man regimental ball was established.

Backs Cliff Burkhalter and Lew Erber (Montclair) and kicker Mike Mercer (Minnesota-Florida State-Hardin-Simmons and Northern Arizona) played for the 5th Marines.

Players for the 7th Marines included backs Wayne Buchert (Whitworth) and Van Crooms (Los Angeles CC).

Don Roberts (Gustavus-Adolphus) was the coach of the 11th Marines. Assistants were Lt. Dick Comer (Indiana State) and Lt. Mort Chute (Princeton). Players included back Bill Bivens and Bobby Loving and end Joe Marchewka (Illinois).

Back Bob Soltis (Northern Illinois) performed for the Division Service Battalion.

1958

Record: 12-6 Cal Poly Pomona, 7-7 Eagle Rock AC, 64-0 Venice AC, 6-47 Hamilton AFB, 89-6 Torrance Steelers, 6-14 Montebello Rams, 6-34 MCRD San Diego, 87-0 McClellan AFB. (4-3-1). Scrimmaged San Diego State and San Diego CC. Dekleva and Karnoscak second-team All-Marine.

Coach: Ted Stawicki (American-Morningside) (Quantico 1946-48; coach Parris Island 1949-50, 3rd MarDiv All-Stars 1954, Hawaii Marines 1955-56)

Assistants: Wendel Beard (New Mexico-Cal) (Quantico 1949, asst. Parris Island 1953), Lt. Bob Loughridge (Oklahoma), Capt. George Smith (Dickinson of Pa.)

Ends: R.F. Donahue, W.C. Jones, Hal Krause, Bob Marchewka (Illinois), Bob Morman (Northwestern) (Quantico 1957), Walt Nadzak (Denison) (Quantico 1957), R.Y. Ortiz, B.R. Smith, W. Smith, Darrell Sorrell (Duke) (Quantico 1957)

Tackles: Beard (p-c), Mike Brown, J.R. Byars, C.O. Caldwell, A.A. Cheney, G. Finnefrock, Ray Gilstrap, Ed Wawrzynak

Guards: T.G. Boller, John Dekleva (Colorado A&M) (Quantico 1957), M.A. Faust, H.D. Friedrichs, J.L. Griffith, Ernie Kaii, T.A. Quinn, K.R. Ritchey, George Stevens

Centers: M.T. Belvin, Don Karnoscak (Colorado) (Quantico 1957), J.F. O'Rourke, S.W. Siskovic, W.H. Towe

Backs: R.W. Allen, S. Azzinarro, Bill Bivens, Cliff Burkhalter, Bobby Crick, M.D. Farrier, George Gallagher, George Guidry (MCRD San Diego 1956-57), D. Hibbs, Frank Jeske (Northwestern) (Quantico 1957), R.L. McLean, Jim Schwartz (Xavier of Ohio) (Quantico 1957, Camp Lejeune 1958), Vince Smith, Willie Smith, Bob Soltis (Northern Illinois), Larry Williams (MCRD San Diego 1956), Jack Wolff (Colorado A&M) (Quantico 1957), J.C. Yearout

1959

Dropped varsity football, resumed regimental ball. The 11th Marines were led by Lt. Bobb McKittrick (Oregon State). The coach was Lt. Robert Black (Montana State), the assistants Lts. J.D. Smith (Iowa), Jerry Clayton (Duke) and Jack Smith. Scrimmaged Cal Western. Played Twentynine Palms in Cannoncocker Bowl in Twentynine Palms.

Other El Toro Teams

What do you do for an encore after returning only the coach from arguably the greatest football team in Marine Corps history?

At El Toro, player-coach Jack Lee (Carnegie Tech, Georgia Pre-Flight, Pittsburgh Steelers) and his staff regrouped and made what economists today might call a soft landing.

The Flying Bulls with a combination of youth and experience won four, lost five and were ranked 20th among service teams by the Williamson Rating Service. The four victories were over Navy teams.

Lt. Lee, a pilot, even flew one of the two planes taking the team to away games.

Another aviator, 220-pound tackle Charles Abrahams (Simpson), also helped the Flying Bulls get off the ground that season. Abrahams would play at El Toro in 1947, at Quantico in 1948 and 1949 and coach the Cherry Point team in 1953. He would receive a DFC and four Air Medals in Korea.

End Ernie Moersch was a first-team All-West Coast Navy selection and back Gerald Swindler was on the second team.

Back Denzil Eaton, with freshman experience at Oklahoma A&M, was a workhorse on offense. Guard Jim Keesling (Duke) gave his best at age 32.

Guard Bill Kopas, 206, had played at Quantico in 1940 and '41 and received a DFC in WWII.

Assistant coach Ed Berry (Scranton), a 210-pound center, was awarded a DFC in WWII and would be killed in Korea.

■

One man helped bring back the excitement in 1947.

Teen-ager Al "Hoagy" Carmichael, who had attended Gardena High School in an adjoining county, scored five touchdowns against NAS Whidby Island and nine overall as the Flying Bulls went 6-3 and won three of their last four.

End Bob Logel, who had played at MCAS Miramar in 1946, and guard Neil Franklin, who would letter at SMU in 1948-50, were selected All-Marine by Leatherneck. Abrahams was a second-team choice.

Back Bill Ziemek was a first-team All-West Coast Navy selection, while tackle Howard Johnson was a first-team and Kopas a second-team All-Marine choice of the Parris Island "Boot."

The end corps, with Moersch; Logel, who had no college experience but who would play with the Buffalo Bills in 1949; Ralph McLeod, to play at LSU from 1950-52; Bill Miller (Minnesota), 210-pound Bob Richter (Oklahoma), basketball standout John Sullivan (Niagara) and Forrest "Frosty" Westering, to play at Omaha and become one of the nation's top small-college coaches, was top-drawer.

With Capt. Ed Cornwell, the 1946 Ewa Marines coach, at the helm and bolstered by much of the 1946 Miramar team, El Toro scored 38 or more points in four games. It crushed Whidby Island, 71-0, and NTS San Diego, 73-0, as Carmichael scored twice, and was runner-up in the

11th Naval District race and third in the West Coast Naval Aviation Conference.

Carmichael also scored twice as El Toro defeated Camp Pendleton's first varsity team, 46-13.

At guard was Joe Polidori, another Miramar alumnus. He would play at El Toro from 1948-50, with Camp Fisher in 1953, and coach the 1st Division team in 1954 and MCRD San Diego in 1956. He would be awarded the Bronze Star in Vietnam.

Back Bill Chesak (Miramar), to play at Texas Western in 1949, and George Pillon (Detroit, St. Mary's Pre-Flight, DFC in WWII, Miramar) also helped with the attack, but Eaton missed most of the season because of an injury.

Carmichael would play for El Toro in 1948, score 19 TD's and lead Santa Ana JC to the Little Rose Bowl in 1949 and star at USC from 1950-52, playing in the big Rose Bowl game against Wisconsin in 1953. He would be a No. 1 draft pick of the Green Bay Packers.

In all, Carmichael, one of pro football's top all-time kick returners, would handle 191 kickoffs for 4,798 yards and 122 punts for 912 yards, plus catch 112 passes for 1,633 yards and rush 222 times for 947 yards. That would total 8,290 all-purpose yards. He would score 84 points in eight NFL and AAFC seasons and still is co-holder of the kickoff-return record for his 1956 runback of 106 yards against the Chicago Bears.

Westering would post a 171-60-4 coaching record in 24 seasons (through 1987) at Parsons, Lea (Minn.) and Pacific Lutheran. His Tacoma, Wash., teams would win the NAIA Division II title in 1980 and share it in 1987 and be the runner-up in 1983 and 1985.

Back Bob Hunter would letter at LSU in 1950.

Other seasons:

■ **1948 (5-7):** An injury to Carmichael hurt the Flying Bulls' chances in a marathon season. A 13th game, against MCRD, was cancelled.

He scored two TD's and rushed for 156 yards in a 27-0 victory over March AFB but was injured on the first play against Fairfield AFB. He missed the NAS Alameda game, and, limping, entered the fourth quarter and returned a kickoff 90 yards for a score against Colorado Mines. He reinjured the ankle against Ft. Bliss. Later, he fractured the ankle in practice and was out for the season.

Richter was second-team All-Marine, and Carmichael (despite being in parts of only five games), Eaton and guard Fred Owens (Ewa Marines) were on an honorary All-FMF Pacific team. Carmichael and 212-pound tackle Reggie Royer were second-team All-West Coast Navy selections.

Back Ed Tillman (2 seasons at Cherry Point, Ewa Marines) also was a standout on offense.

Keesling was still going all-out at age 34.

Owens would play at Orange Coast (Calif.) College in 1949-50. As Dr. Owens, he would become director of business services at Golden West (Calif.) College.

At least five players: ends Jim Berault and Bill Weatherred, tackle Cliff Leonard, center Bob Swenson and kicker Floyd Strain, would join Carmichael at Santa Ana College to help post a 9-1 record in 1949.

■ **1949 (4-5):** Capt. Al James (LSU) took over the coaching reins, and the small and light team posted a 4-3 mark before running out of steam the last two games, losing to Camp Pendleton, 54-0, and MCRD, 47-0.

Owens and back Jim Estergall were named to an All-FMC Pacific team.

Keesling, now 35, would be at center again.

Another veteran was end Elmore Ravensburg (Xavier), who had played with Georgia Pre-Flight in 1943, St. Mary's Pre-Flight in 1944 and the Ewa Marines in 1946. He would be awarded the DFC and an Air Medal in Korea.

But the main man was 9.8 sprinter Chuck Swinden, who would play also for El Toro in 1950 and '51 and Santa Ana College in 1952.

He also would be in the news for courting and marrying heiress Joan Irvine (Smith), whose wealth in the late 1980s was estimated from $180 million to in excess of $300 million. They had one child but were divorced after two years of marriage. She would marry three other times.

A 1987 news report referred thusly to the then 53-year-old Smith: "... Once a social gadabout, increasingly tagged as a reclusive eccentric until she emerged two years ago to launch a high-profile horse-jumping derby in San Juan Capistrano. An an energetic heiress, she's rattled corporate cages, changed federal laws and wrestled giants like Mobil Oil Corp. in her 28-year battle with various company managements over her inheritance."

The season marked the first at El Toro for MSgt. Mike Cervin, the assistant coach, who had played at Cherry Point in 1944 and been an assistant with the N.C. team in 1945-48. He would be an assistant at El Toro again in 1950 and '53.

James would coach the MCAS Miami team in 1953. Guard Frank Watkins would letter at Washington State in 1954.

■ **1950 (3-6):** Cornwell returned as head coach, and his Flying Bulls were streaky, losing four, winning three and losing two.

Setting the program back was cancellation of spring football. And now, as at other Marine bases, football took a back seat to a new war.

As was the case in 1949, the team was light and had only a handful of players with college-varsity experience. Hardly a time to challenge an MCRD-caliber team.

Tillman was a first-team 11th Naval District selection and second-team All-West Coast Navy. Bob Becker scored eight times, and end Dave Culmer (Lejeune), Moersch, Polidori, guard Gene Thompson (Cherry Point), Watkins, back Doug Arndt (St. Cloud and Minnesota) and Swinden, among others, were standouts.

■ **1951 (3-7):** Two reservists recalled for the Korean War picked up the coaching reins, with Charles Getchell (Temple, Lejeune), who also played pro basketball, at the helm, and Lt. Don Lehmkuhl (Iowa, Purdue, FMF Pacific) an assistant.

The war effort naturally had priority, and in November there were fewer than 25 players because of injuries, transfers or discharges. The squad hardly had enough to scrimmage. As might be expected, North

Island won by 49, USC Spartans by 22, MCRD by 53, NAB Coronado by 27, SubPac by 66 and Pendleton by 31.

Standing out amid the wreckage was 214-pound guard John Idoux (Kansas), a second-team All-Marine selection.

Swinden, a second-team All-West Coast Navy selection, was virtually a one-man show on offense, carrying 130 times for 599 yards, catching 10 passes, returning 15 kickoffs for 303 yards and scoring 30 points. The second-leading rusher, Art Atterbury (New Mexico A&M), was in just three games.

Culmer, end Jesse Hodges (Butler, 4 seasons at MCRD), 215-pound tackle Les Cates, Watkins and Arndt were among the standouts. Cates would play for Santa Ana JC in 1954 and UCLA in 1956.

■ **1952 (2-6-1):** Don Davis (Central of Iowa) tried his hand as coach. With a thin, light squad, the results were predictable: MCRD won by 60, Coronado by 53 and Pendleton by 28. At least 14 players were lost to injuries, transfers or discharges.

There was college experience for a change: end Darrell Riggs (UCLA), guard Dan Labat (LSU), back Cheney Close (William Jewell, 2 seasons at MCRD), back Phil Haas (Lawrence, MCRD) and back Allen Rizer (Dayton), to go with Culmer, Cates and back Phil Brown (Memphis NAS, Parris Island).

Riggs was a second-team All-West Coast Navy selection.

Back Gene Fodge would post a 1-1 record as a pitcher for the Chicago Cubs in 1958.

■ **1953 (2-6):** At last, Davis had a player who could have started for the great El Toro teams of 1944 and '45 in 6-3, 225-pound back-linebacker Rob Goode (Texas A&M, MCRD). He was an All-Marine selection and third-team All-Service choice who scored twice and passed for six TD's.

Goode, a No. 1 draft pick, had played with the Washington Redskins from 1949-51 and would return to the 'Skins for the 1954 and '55 seasons and close out his pro career with the Philadelphia Eagles in 1955.

Davis would coach at Santa Ana JC in 1955 and '56.

Cates, Labat, 210-pound tackle Dick "Rusty" McKee (Hutchinson JC, Missouri), guard Bob Conklin (MCRD, Pensacola), and backs Bob Carew (Hamline, MCRD), Fodge, Herb Price (Lincoln), Rizer, Ivan Storer (Pensacola) and Dean Westgaard (2 seasons at Pendleton) were among the stalwarts.

■ **1954-56:** no teams

■ **1957:** Six base teams competed: MWSG-37, MAG-15, MAG-33, MAG-36, Station Razorbacks and AirPac. In outside competition, the MAG-15 Rams defeated La Verne, 14-12, but the Station Razorbacks lost to Barstow, 23-6.

■ **1958 (6-3):** Competing as the MCAF Bulldogs, they lost to three college teams: Claremont-Mudd, 16-6 and 18-14, and La Verne, 41-18. They also scrimmaged two junior-college teams. The victories were over a Navy team (twice), three Marine teams and a prison squad.

The coach was Lt. Dick Irrgang (Drexel), with standouts including reservist Mike Giddings (California, Quantico, Camp Pendleton), later to be one of pro football's top talent scouts, and back Carroll Matthews, who scored on 95- and 72-yard runs.

■ **1959 (2-9):** MCAF, coached by Irrgang and later Lt. Bill Casanova (Marquette), played a junior college-military-semipro-civilian schedule. But there were only 20 players on hand late in the season.

Also fielding a team was MAG-15, which beat $\overline{MCAF}$, 12-6, but lost to Memphis NAS, 12-0. A tackle was Ed Arnold, to play at Santa Ana JC in 1961 and become a leading Southern California radio and TV sports and news commentator, a spokesman for Dr. Robert Schuller's "Hour of Power," a popular banquet emcee and a recipient of various civic awards.

"I feel an obligation to do what I can for other people," Arnold told a Los Angeles reporter. "I feel I owe it to the community."

■ **1960:** Maj. E.M. Oster was at the helm of the 3rd Marine Air Wing team, and Culmer, a track and field standout, reported for his sixth season of service football. Arnold was a tackle.

"Joining the Marines (at 17) was the smartest thing I've ever done," Arnold told the interviewer. "It may sound trite, but I went in a young boy and came out a man."

The big news that season was the reporting of two young players, Gary Larsen and back Dunn Marteen.

Larsen after leaving the Corps and graduating from Concordia (Minn.), would play a season with the Los Angeles Rams and 10 with the Minnesota Vikings, appearing in three Super Bowls. The 6-5, 256-pound Larsen, a key part of the famed "Purple People Eaters," would be selected twice for the Pro Bowl.

Marteen, to play for the same coach at Santa Ana JC in 1961 and '62 and at Los Angeles State in 1963 and '64, would be with Ottawa (CFL) in 1965 and Montreal (Continental) in 1966 and '67. He would complete 90 of 187 passes for 1,484 yards and 14 TD's and run for 327 yards in 1966.

■ **1961 (6-2):** Larsen and Marteen were gone, but Howard Kindig, another future pro standout, reported. Already 6-6 and 245, Kindig would compete for LA State and be a draft pick of the Eagles and San Diego Chargers in 1964, play for the Chargers from 1965-67, Buffalo Bills from 1967-71, Miami Dolphins from 1972-73 and New York Jets in 1974. He would be on the Dolphins' 1973 Super Bowl team and play two seasons in the World Football League.

■ **1962-81:** No varsity teams

■ **1982 (5-5):** The base fielded the start of perhaps the last of the Marine varsity teams, posting a 5-5 record under Lt. Col. John Grant against primarily a junior-college schedule.

■ **1983 (0-7):** Grant's charges went up again against a JC schedule but not with as much success.

"We want to send that one guy to school, just give him an opportunity," Grant said in an interview.

Added Cmdr. Tom Chiomento, an assistant, "Recreation, sure. But our intent also is to take some young Marines who couldn't afford to go to college, let them show their potential on the college level and get them looked at."

It was not known how successful the attempt was.

The game had come a long way from Hanley's forces of 1944 and '45. Of 63 players on a program for a Dixie JC game, 35 weighed 200 or more. Tackle Tommy Pillows was 275 and linebacker William Dallas 250.

- ■ **1984:** Apparently no varsity team
- ■ **1985:** The base played one or more JC teams.

1946 (Flying Bulls)
Record: 0-18 Pacific JV, 6-31 North Island NAS, 21-0 USS Sperry, 32-0 Sand Pointe NAS, 12-0 Alameda NAS, 32-0 Sand Pointe NAS, 0-26 Cal Poly San Luis Obispo, 6-19 MCAS Miramar, 0-20 Ft. Lewis. (4-5). Ranked No. 20 by Williamson.

Coach — Lt. Jack Lee (See El Toro 1945) (As a pilot, he flew one of the two planes taking team on road games.)

Assistants — Capt. Ed Berry (Scranton) (KIA), Capt. Jack Little (San Jose State), Lt. Al Montrief (MCB San Diego 1938-40)

Ends — Don Edgerly, Ewing, Glen Jennings, Harold Lollar, Joe Lynch (Hamline) (Iowa Pre-Flight), John McCloskey (Utah), Bill Miller (Minnesota), Ernie Moersch, Tom Orr (Arkansas), Bob Richter (Oklahoma), John Sullivan (Niagara) (athletic officer at MCAS, Miami 1955)

Tackles — Chas. Abrahams (Simpson) (Quantico 1948-49, coach Cherry Point 1952-53), Tony Aguilar, Bob Allen (San Diego NTC), R. Boyer, Don Cox, John Hudspeth, John Killam (Mississippi), Marion McCauley, Reg Royer, Bill Scoggins (Memphis State), Walter Tuz, Ed Woudenberg (UCLA)

Guards — Berry (p-c), Ed Castle (Maryville Teachers), Joe Inman, George Kew, Bill Kopas (Quantico 1940-41), Ernie Lenzen, Bill Maynard, Stressler O'Daye, Tom Schmidt (Kenosha Packers)

Centers — Jim Keesling (Duke) (age 32), Perry Ramesch (Pacific), Paul Rushing

Backs — Dwayne Adams (Kansas), Don Bellinger (Oregon State), Bill Burrows, Jason Cannon, Nick Camola, Denzil Eaton (Oklahoma A&M), Bill Ewing, Ken Fiegener (Southwest Oklahoma) (St. Mary's Pre-Flight), Joe Frazier, Don Hamacher, Jim Kennon, Lasser, Lee (p-c), Cliff Leonard (Santa Ana JC), Henry Little (MCAS Santa Barbara 1945), John Parsons, Jerome Peralta, Dick Rash (San Diego State), John Schels, Art Schmagel (Maryville Teachers) (Quantico 1946), Bill Skeka (Quantico 1940-41), Jerry Swindler, Stan Starnowski, Tom Turner (Texas Christian), Lloyd Walsh (Winona)

1947
Record: 19-0 Terminal Island, 7-14 North Island NAS, 18-6 San Diego NTC, 71-0 Whidby Island NAS, 6-17 Alameda NAS, 73-0 San Diego NS, 0-21 DesPac, 46-13 Camp Pendleton, 38-19 Ft. Bliss. (6-3). Al Carmichael scored 5 TDS against Whidby and led service scorers in U.S. Bob Logel and Neil Franklin were All-Marine, Abrahams 2nd team.

Coach — Ed Cornwell (Santa Ana JC-San Francisco-USC) (Corpus Christi 1942) (Coach MCAS Ewa 1946)

Assistants — Jim Johnson (Missouri) (North Island 1946) (p-c), MSgt. John Wood (Missouri) (coach Bremerton NB 1946)

Ends — Bob Hunter (Louisiana State), Bob Logel (MCAS Miramar 1946) (pros), Ralph McLeod (Louisiana State), Bill Miller (Minnesota), Ernie Moersch, Bob Richter (Oklahoma), John Sullivan (Niagara) (athletic officer at MCAS, Miami 1955), Forrest Westering (Drake-Omaha)

Tackles — Charles Abrahams (See El Toro 1946), Don Cox, Howard Johnson (MCAS Miramar 1946), Reg Royer, Gene Tetrick, Troup

Guards — Neil Franklin (MCAS Miramar 1946) (Southern Methodist), Fred Kuhlman (Iowa Pre-Flight), Bill Kopas (Quantico 1940-41), Geo. Poff (MCAS Miramar 1946), Joe Polidori (MCAS Miramar 1946, Camp Fisher 1953, coach 1st MarDiv 1954, asst. MCRD SD 1955, coach MCRD 1956)

Centers — Andy Roland, John Shoden (Long Beach CC), Murph Wieczorek (South Dakota)

Backs — Doug Arndt (St. Cloud and Minnesota), Bob Barnes, Bowman, Al "Hoagy" Carmichael (Santa Ana JC, USC) (pros), Bill Chesak (Wisconsin-Texas Western) (MCAS Miramar 1946), Chuck Dove (Maryland), Denzil Eaton (Oklahoma A&M), Bill Ewing, Dick Jarrett, Don Jensen (MCAS Ewa 1946), King, Larmon, Cliff Leonard (Santa Ana JC), Ott, George Pillon (Detroit) (St. Mary's Pre-Flight, MCAS Miramar 1946), Schels, Valentine, Hank Wheeler, Bill Ziemek

Kicker — Stressler O'Daye

Also — Adams, Baker, Brayton, Buechler, Chaudet, Edwards, Harmon, Hudson, Hungerford, Jones, Olson, Sage, Siefried, Terrel

1948
Record: 27-0 March Field, 18-6 Ft. Riley, 46-0 Fairfield AAB, 0-17 Alameda NAS, 7-18 Colorado Mines, 20-12 Ft. Bliss, 7-46 Navy JV, 0-14 Camp Pendleton, 6-25 North Island NAS, 6-27 DesPac, 0-6 LA Marine Reserves, 38-20 Whidby Island NAS. (5-7). Canceled MCRD San Diego game. Al

Carmichael was injured part of season. Bob Richter 2nd team All-Marine. Named to All-FMF Pacific team were Carmichael, Denzil Eaton and Fred Owens.

Coach — Capt. Ed Cornwell (See El Toro 1947)

Assistants — Capt. Al James (Louisiana State), Maj. Jim Johnson (See El Toro 1947), MSgt. John Wood (See El Toro 1947)

Ends — Jim Berault (Santa Ana JC), Dick Brauner, Don Cox, Sid Fis(c)her (Colorado College), Jack Kennevick, Ralph McLeod (Louisiana State), Martin Mechler, Ernie Moersch, Bob Richter (Oklahoma), Bill Weatherred (Santa Ana JC), Bill Wachsler (Navy)

Tackles — Walt Croas, Lou Hubert, Fred Kuhlman (Iowa Pre-Flight), Cliff Leonard (Santa Ana JC), Reg Royer, Ralph Tetrick

Guards — Bill Bush, Bob Harper, Howard Johnson (MCAS Miramar 1946), Bill Kopas (Quantico 1940-41), Bob Nesmith, Fred Owens (MCAS Ewa 1947) (Orange Coast College), George Poff (MCAS Miramar 1946), Joe Polidori (See El Toro 1947)

Centers — Jim Keesling (Duke), Kennedy, Bob Laing (Navy), Dan Montesaro (MCAS Ewa 1947), Bob Swenson (Santa Ana JC), Clyde Watson

Backs — Howard Bowling, Al "Hoagy" Carmichael (Santa Ana JC-USC) (pros), Denzil Eaton (Oklahoma A&M), Jim Estergall   John Homan, Bob Hunter (Louisiana State), Don Jensen (MCAS Ewa 1946), Bob Lee, Tom McAuliffe (MCAS Ewa 1946), Jim Powers, Charles Robinson, Bob Scott, Ed Tillman (Cherry Point 1945-46, MCAS Ewa 1947), Hal Ubernosky, Woser

Kicker — Floyd Strain (Santa Ana JC)

1949

Record: 13-7 PhibPac, 0-36 Cal Ramblers, 18-6 Bremerton Navy, 13-12 North Island NAS, 2-25 San Diego NTC, 28-0 Fairfield AAB, 25-29 Terminal Island, 0-54 Camp Pendleton, 0-47 MCRD San Diego. (4-5). Fred Owens and Jim Estergall were named to All-FMF Pacific team.

Coach — Capt. Al James (LSU)

Assistant — MSgt. Mike Cervin (St. Ambrose-Mississippi) (Cherry Point 1944, asst. 1945-48)

Ends — Jim Berault (Santa Ana JC), Floyd Bos, Chuck Emery (Southern State), Arnold Falk, George Gray, Jack Kennevick, Elmore Ravensburg (Xavier) (Georgia Pre-Flight 1943, St. Mary's Pre-Flight 1944, MCAS Ewa 1946), Bob Richter (Oklahoma), Martin Terrell, Bill West

Tackles — Mac "Red" Corwin, Jim Hays, Art Katen, Jose Rodriguez, Jim Thomas

Guards — Charles Arnold, Lewis Humphrey (MCRD San Diego), Kermit Isaacson, Jim Mann, Fred Owens (Orange Coast College), Joe Polidori (See El Toro 1948), Frank Watkins (Washington State)

Centers — Jim Keesling (Duke), Tom Kennedy, Bob Miller, Len Smith

Backs — Jim Amos, Bob Becker, Howard Bowling, John De Forest, Walt Domina (Norwich), Lou Elder, Jim Estergall   Len Farrell, Jim Fisher, Vern Guric (MCRD San Diego), Tom Hathaway, Don Jensen, George Kaiffer, Dick Peterson, Chuck Robinson, Clyde Shaw, Chuck Swinden (Santa Ana JC), Hal Ubernosky, Elmer Winn

1950

Record: 0-12 AirPac, 19-32 Santa Ana JC, 14-26 Los Angeles CC, 0-14 San Diego NTC, 38-6 Long Beach NS, 50-6 TraPac, 32-0 North Island NAS, 6-13 SubPac, 7-41 MCRD San Diego. (3-6). Spring training was canceled. Al James was to be the coach but was transferred. Assistants were to be Cervin, Lt. Sid Fischer (Colorado College), Capt. Warren Watson

Coach — Ed Cornwell (See El Toro 1948)

Assistants — M/Sgt. Mike Cervin (See El Toro 1949), Capt. Pete Janssen (Drew) (coach 1st MAW in China 1947), TSgt. Pete Ulin

Ends — Dave Culmer (Camp Lejeune 1949), Dennis, Bob Fisher, Ed Goss, Chuck Koehler, Doug Maijala, Ernie Moersch, Pannell, Martin Terrell, Wayne Vose

Tackles — Carl Boe, Bob Calkins, John Cisek, Glenn Hadley, Tom Hardy, Shul Joseph, Paige Larsen, Matt Pepe, W. Stephens, Jim Wimberg

Guards — Brennan, Phil Carter, Rene Duzac, Boyce Ford (Camp Pendleton 1949), Jim Ludlow, Joe Polidori (See El Toro 1949), Art Robinson, Bob Sage, Bob Silver, Gene Thompson (Cherry Point 1946), Ed Tillman (See El Toro 1948), Mike Tinney, Frank Watkins (Washington State), Alan Weinstein

Centers — Bill Clay, Moe McGee, Jack Pevehouse (SMU) (recalled)

Backs — Jim Amos, John Anderson, Doug Arndt (St. Cloud and Minnesota) (recalled), Art Atterbury (New Mexico A&M), Bob Becker, Rusty Burgess, Buster, Cerum, Bill Cornelli, John De Forest, Ed Gallick, Ed Greer, Jim Fisher, Harold Glass, Joe Gragnano (Lafayette), John Jank, Bob Jones, Lou Moad, Art Pannell, Jack Reynolds, Rogers, Clyde Shaw, Chuck Swinden (Santa Ana JC), Hal Ubernosky, Dick Williams, John Wolcott (LSU)

1951

Record: 7-56 North Island NAS, 19-16 Santa Ana JC, 13-35 USC Spartans, 0-53 MCRD San Diego, 0-27 NAB Coronado, 14-30 TraPac, 16-6 Barstow Marines, 0-66 SubPac, 26-13 Terminal

252

Island, 0-31 Camp Pendleton. (3-7). Fewer than 25 players were available in November because of injuries, transfers and releases of recalled reservists. Team could hardly scrimmage. John Idoux was 2nd team All-Marine.

Coach — Chas. Getchell (Temple) (Camp Lejeune 1944) (pro football and basketball) (recalled)

Assistants — Lt. Ed Boissy (Toledo) (Iowa Pre-Flight), Lt. Don Lehmkuhl (Iowa-Purdue) (Pearl Harbor 1945) (recalled)

Ends — Cannon, Dave Culmer (Camp Lejeune 1949), Arnold Falk, Jim Falk, Bob Fisher, Gene Furan, Ed Goss, Jim Gulley, Jesse Hodges (Butler) (MCRD San Diego 1948-51), Baxter Jimmerson, Marlie Richardson, Art Smith, Jim Sousa

Tackles — George Ackerman, Jack Bates, Les Cates (Santa Ana JC-UCLA), Tom Hardy, Dutch Hollen, Paige Larsen, Marvil Morgan, Henry Sadorus, Frank Wolverton

Guards — Igantius Brown, Rene Duzac, Cliff Frazier, Lou Harris, John Idoux (Kansas), Kermit Isaacson, Russ Kelly, Don Korzak, Paul Pfister, Frank Watkins (Washington State)

Centers — Rulan Arrigona, Alex Groswerd, Bob Miller

Backs — Jim Amos, John Anderson, Doug Arndt (St. Cloud and Minnesota) (recalled), Art Atterbury (New Mexico A&M), Bob Becker, Bill Clay, Herb Glass, Joe Gragnano (Lafayette), Paul Jones, Don Mohn, Nick Monti, Dan Morrison, Tom Pahl, Hal Pettit, Jack Reynolds, Nick Rozak, Don Seaman, John Spurr, Ray Studer, Chuck Swinden (Santa Ana JC), Roy Tettleton

1952

Record: 6-66 MCRD San Diego, 0-53 NAB Coronado, 0-18 Barstow Marines, 13-0 TraPac, 0-19 Fullerton JC, 13-41 Camp Pendleton, 46-0 China Lake, 7-7 North Island NAS, 14-19 Terminal Island (2-6-1).

Coach — Don Davis (Central of Iowa)

Assistants — Pfc. Al Gebbert (Notre Dame) (p-c), Capt. Chas. Getchell (See El Toro 1951), Lt. Larry Parr (Simpson), Lt. John Richards (Santa Ana JC-Pacific-UC Santa Barbara), Maj. Jack Sloan (Cal) (asst. Cherry Point 1944-45, coach 1948, 1950)

Ends — Dave Culmer (Camp Lejeune 1949), Tom Larson, Olin Painter, Darrell Riggs (UCLA), Jerry Sullivan, George Wright (Western State)

Tackles — Bob Amland (Carleton), Les Cates (Santa Ana JC-UCLA), Joe Heckle (Northwestern), John Meehan (Mississippi State), John Savino

Guards — Ignatius Brown, Henry Gowen (Houston), Dan Labat (LSU), Jim Ludlow

Centers — Rod Hurich (Santa Ana JC), Tom Steward, Bob Vanderlinen (Central of Iowa)

Backs — Phil Brown (Memphis NAS), Parris Island), Cheney Close (William Jewell) (MCRD San Diego 1950-51), Gene Fodge (baseball), Phil Haas (Lawrence) (MCRD San Diego 1951), Russ Linnell (Utah State), Glenn Oelke (La Crosse Teachers), Allen Rizer (Notre Dame-Dayton), Al Rowe (Tennessee State), Al Sigman, John Silva (Santa Clara), Art Smith, Carl Takocs (San Francisco), Dick Zielinski

1953

Record: 19-32 Ft. Lewis, 6-13 Eagle Rock AC, 0-27 PhibPac, 18-7 Barstow Marines, 16-21 MCRD San Diego, 7-34 Camp Pendleton, 26-7 Long Beach NS, 2-33 North Island NAS. (2-6). China Lake game canceled. Rob Goode was All-Marine.

Coach — Don Davis (Central of Iowa)

Assistants — Lt. Mike Cervin (See El Toro 1950), Al Gebbert (Notre Dame), Rob Goode (Texas A&M) (pros) (MCRD San Diego 1952), Capt. Dick Watson (Washington)

Ends — Kaye Andrews, Buster Chancey, Raphael Cooke (Nebraska), Norm Cudney, Wallace Daley, Jim Davis, George Gray, Garry Harvey (Cherry Point 1952), Jerry Kearney, R.A. Morrow, Larry Pieper, Jack Rollins, Gerald Sullivan

Tackles — Les Cates (Santa Ana JC-UCLA), Bob Denton, Ed Galuski, Don Jasinski, Fred Kuhl (Santa Ana JC), Dan Labat (LSU), Dick "Rusty" McKee (Hutchinson JC-Missouri) (MCRD San Diego 1952), Larry Mylet, George Murray (Bowdoin), Walt Riebeling, Tom Steward, Frank Strocchia (Santa Ana JC)

Guards — M. Aslin, Bob Conklin (MCRD San Diego 1952, Pensacola 1953), Dan Fortenberry, Bill Gebhard, Don Jordan (Santa Ana JC), Tom Larson, Jim Ludlow, Jim Meza, Charles Ramsey, R.L. Watson

Centers — Billy Baker, Joe Barbagello (Boston College), Rod Hurich (Santa Ana JC)

Backs — Sam Brown, Bob Carew (Hamline) (MCRD San Diego 1952), Ed de Harne, Gene Fodge (baseball), Goode p-c, John Hilton, Sam Kahalewai (Hawaii) (Camp Pendleton 1952), A.H. Lee, Joe Lindsey, Jerry Matney, Herb Price (Lincoln), A V Peal, Allen Rizer (Notre Dame-Dayton), Al Sigman, Scipio Spann (Compton JC), Ivan Storer (Pensacola 1952), Bob Wofford, Dean Westgaard (Camp Pendleton 1951-52)

1954-55-56 (No Teams)

1957

Record: Six base teams competed. MAG-15 defeated University of La Verne, 14-12. Players included end Fritz Shunke, backs Pat DeMarchi, Dave Peasback, Jerry Reinecker. Station Razorbacks lost to Barstow Marines, 23-6. Players included backs Ron Coleman, Tom Gandziarski, Bill "Dixie" Walker and kicker Juck.

1958 (MCAF Bulldogs)

Record: 45-0 Seal Beach NAD, 13-0 7th Marines, 6-16 Claremont-Mudd, 18-42 La Verne, 14-18 Claremont-Mudd, 66-0 Seal Beach NAD, 19-7 1st Div Hq Bn. (6-3). Missing Chino Prison, Twentynine Palms games. Team scrimmaged Orange Coast College, Santa Ana JC.
Coach — Lt. Dick Irrgang (Drexel) **Assistants** — NA
Ends — Johnson, Kupchuk (Penn), O'Banion, Jim Pappas, Roger Schaeffer, Jim Turner
Tackles — Bradford, Charles Carter, Allen Lane, Jack Scott
Guards — Joe Garcia, Bill Richards
Centers — Mike Giddings (Cal) (Quantico 1955, Camp Pendleton 1956)
Backs — Jack Finnell, Andy Griffin (Corpus Christi), Jividen, Ron Ledoucher, Carroll Matthews, John Palasoutas, Bob Williams

1959 (MCAF Bulldogs)

Record: 7-19 San Gabriel Vikings, 0-30 Santa Ana JC, 6-12 MAG-15, 6-64 Chino Prison, 35-0 Air Pac El Toro, 20-14 AirPac El Toro, 0-33 Venice AC, 0-28 Twentynine Palms, 0-32 Twentynine Palms, 0-54 Hamilton AFB. Lost to Seal Beach NAD. (2-9).
Coach — Dick Irrgang (Drexel), succeeded by Lt. Bill Casanova (Marquette)
Assistants — TSgt. Vic Durand, player-coach Lt. Bill Miggs (Harvard), player-coach Lt. Bill Sweeney (West Virginia)
Ends — Roger Schaeffer, Solomon
Tackles — Capt. Dennis Anderson, Charles Carter, Bob Fleetwood, Alan Lane
Guards — Lyle Dixon, Lon Homalka **Centers** — NA
Backs — John Birge, Bob Boyer, Casanova, Johnny Johnson, Red Miner, Bill Price, Chuck Simmons
MAG-15: 12-6 MCAF, 0-12 Memphis NAS. **T** Ed Arnold (Santa Ana JC)
AIR PAC: 0-35 MCAF, 14-20 MCAF, 7-20 1st FSR
The San Diego Chevron listed 2 games: 0-36, 0-55 Eagle Rock AC by an El Toro team

1960 (3rd MAW)

Record: 8-45 Hamilton AFB, 14-0 China Lake, 20-27 Cal Ramblers, 7-37 Santa Clara, 6-14 Memphis Navy (at Hot Springs, Ark.), 10-6 Los Angeles State JV, 6-26 USC Freshmen, 36-14 China Lake, 14-24 1st MarDiv All-Stars. (3-6).
Coach — Maj. E.M. Oster
Assistants — Player-coach Lt. Jim Hagen (Oklahoma), SSgt. T.R. Hyatt, player-coach Lt. W.A. Sawyer
Ends — Dave Culmer (Camp Lejeune 1949, El Toro 1950-52, Camp Lejeune 1956), Rudy Kimbers, Allen Martin, Harry McCabe, John Shaver, Tom Singleton
Tackles — John Abram, Ed Arnold (Santa Ana JC), Allen Hardesty, Willie Jackson, Fred McLean (Ottawa) (MCRD San Diego, Pensacola), Randy Pepper, Pete Petras, Dave Salum (Whittier)
Guards — Carl Anderson, Gary Larsen (Concordia of Minn.) (pros), Nick Kamar, Charles Summers
Centers — Dave Bailey, Jim Barnes, Jim Brooks
Backs — Chuck Benys, Darrell Cook, Paul Davin, Ray Del Rio, Jim Hagen (p-c), Gene Honerlew (Kentucky), Dunn Marteen (Santa Ana JC, Los Angeles State) (pros), Jim Sanders, Dennis Schumm

1961

Record: 27-20 Claremont-Mudd, 26-6 Cal Poly San Luis Obispo JV, 12-8 LA Pacific College, 0-21 Cal Frosh, 15-0 Chino Wolves, 8-27 USC Frosh, 42-0 Southern California College, 18-12 UC Riverside. (6-2). Scrimmaged Orange Coast College.
Coach — Jim Hagan (Oklahoma)
Assistants — Bill Halterman, Joe Loo, Jim McClure, Al Ranson
Ends — Norm Burroughs (Rice) (Memphis NAS), F. Jones, George O'Connor, H. Richardson, Don Roberts, Gil Tindley
Tackles — Frank Blanco (New Mexico Highlands), R. Chambers, L. Culbreath, Willie Jackson, Howard Kindig (Los Angeles State) (pros), G. Peterson, R. Reed, Walt Piusz (Slippery Rock) (Glenview NAS), Dave Salum (Whittier)
Guards — Tom Bland, J. Burke, Larry Gregg, S. Reynolds, R. Severin
Centers — H. Davidson, G. Hartsock, Fred McLean

Backs — John Birge, Ray Brown, Jim Casey, R. Fowler, Jim Hicks, Gene Honerlew (Kentucky), T. Hopkins, Jerry Hunter, H. Hutchengs, Rudy Kimbers, D. Lambrecht, Kack LaMountain, M. Lawson, Martin Levy (Tulane), Benny Madrid (Mexico City), Fred McLean (Ottawa) (MCRD San Diego, Pensacola), T. Moss, J. Parker, Dennis Schumm, T. Sterling

1962-80 (No Teams)

1981 (Base Teams)
Played teams from Camp Pendleton-Twentynine Palms, Camp Lejeune
Lt. Col. John Grant coached one base team to 8-0 regular-season record
Assistants, players — NA

1982 (Bulls)
Record: 33-6 Desert JC, 0-44 Taft JC, 0-34 Arizona Western JC, 7-14 Ontario Crushers, 24-6 Western California Institute, 8-14 Western California Institute, 0-29 Glendale (Ariz.) CC, 23-16 Alameda NAS, 27-19 Western California Institute (5-5). Played Edwards AFB, scrimmaged Mt. San Jacinto JC.
Coach — Lt. Col. John Grant. **Assistants** — NA
Ends — Benny Mitchell, Joe Oliver, Keith Williams
Linebackers — Bear Alderson, Larry Morgan
Backs — Jay Ayers, Grant Bullock, Caito, Tyrone Dobbs, Joe Hodge, John or Eddie Scott, Wes Smith, Washington
Kicker — Abel Rasmussen

1983
Record: 0-19 Pasadena JC, 0-31 Desert JC, 0-40 Scottsdale JC, 0-24 Long Beach CC, 6-10 Arizona Western JC, 21-41 Glendale (Ariz.) JC, 6-55 Dixie JC (incomplete). Canceled UC Santa Barbara
Coach — Lt. Col. John Grant. **Assistant** — Cmdr. Tom Chiomento
Ends — Brian Blevins, M. Braxton, Vince Corbett, Clyde Green, Lamar Jackson, D. Jacobsen, G. Jones, T. Jones, Oliver Joseph, Ken King, T.R. Robinson, J. Smith
Tackles — U.O. Anosik, D.L. Bodell, Mike Chrysler, Richard Ellis, Nathan Newell, Tommy Pillows, Dan Schroeder, Talton Tait, James Warren, Dave Weimer
Guards — S. Austin, Luigi Berge, Henry Blackwell, Dwayne Carroll, William Dallas, Mark Easton, Willie Edmonson, Mike Frehauff, W. Howard, Alan Ienn, Glenn Jones, Walt May, Tony Ortiz, D.D. Smith, K. Sutting, Eric Wheeler
Centers — John Higgins, John Hittle, Bob Lehmann
Backs — Charles Bellamy, Willie Bennett, Gordon Boss, Kraig Bougher, Adam Bryant, Gaynor Bullock, Grant Bullock, Tyrone Dabbs, Nate Debose, A. Grant, Steve Hibbler, Bob Hurst, Searcy Jackson, Rickey Jordan, Alan McGee, Vinnie Mitchell, Kevin Perry, John Reed, A.M. Sagiao, Geo. Slappy, Darin Thomas, Kyle Toomer, Len Ware. **Kicker** — C. Taylor

1984 (Apparently No Team)

1985
6-42 Los Angeles Valley CC (incomplete)
3rd MAW Wild Bunch lost, 22-7, to Los Angeles Police Department Centurions on 3-22-86 at East Los Angeles College in charity game.
Assistant — Lloyd Handy. **LB**: Willie Howard (MAG-11)

El Toro/1991
Record: 34-0 Caltech (Toy Bowl), 20-9 Orange County Cowboys (incomplete)
Coach: NA. Players: NA

Q-U-A-N-T-I-C-O (slow) (sing)
Q-U-A-N-T-I-C-O (slow) (sing)
Q-U-A-N-T-I-C-O (slow) (sing)
Q-U-A-N-T-I-C-O (fast) (yell)
Devildogs! Devildogs! Devildogs!

A Quantico cheer

Long Way From Home

It was not your typical postseason game, a Notre Dame versus Alabama matchup.

Rather, on Jan. 1, 1948, the officers of the Snake Pit went against officers of the Goats Nest.

The site: the Tsingtao, China, Race Course.

The Snake Pit won, 13-0, on two passes from Melvin to Beverly.

SNAKE PIT
Coach: Capt. John Lindsay
Ends: Larsen, Leitholt. Tackles: Gilmore, Ronzone. Guards: Lindsay, Reece. Center: Shepherd.
Backs: Beverly, Melvin, Miller, Radics.

GOATS NEST
Coach: NA. Ends: Marsh, Tice. Tackles: Debelle, Tobin. Guards: Armstrong, Fielder. Center: Paetow. Backs: Capraro, Connors, Griffin, Rollins, Wood

---

With the turmoil in China, the games were a welcome distraction.

But they also were taken seriously.

Recalls Maj. E.W. Rothenburger (ret.) of Newport Beach, Cal.: Col. George McHenry (himself a football standout) was CO, 1st Marines and went through the jackets of his officers.

"He called me in and asked if I knew a league was being formed. I said I would be happy to coach the ends. He advised me he already had a coach and that I was scheduled to play.

"I replied I was 30, hadn't played since college, and, besides, my wife and son were on their way from the States.

"The day my family arrived, a game was scheduled. Col. McHenry told me not to be concerned - he would send his staff car to the airfield to pick them up and bring them to the football field since the game would already be in progress."

1947 ALL-TSINGTAO TEAM (Marines listed)
E A.J. Halliwell (1st Marines), T R.H. Patton (12th Service Bn), C C.R. Stephens (1st Marines), T T.D. Leahy (H&S Bn), B M.J. Stolarz (H&S Bn), B W.C. Bell (12th Service Bn)

SECOND TEAM
E G.J. Tice (H&S Bn), T U. Gigli (1st Marines), G J.A. Lindsay (H&S Bn), C G.C. Stringer (12th Service Bn), T E.S. Angeli (3rd Marines), QB R.B. Morgan (12th Service Bn), HB W.D. Tyson (Marine Air), HB A.T. Frederico (Marine Air), FB A.C. Beverly (H&S Bn).

1ST MARINES
Record: 6-1-1 (league champion)
Coach: Lt. Bill Hickman
Players: Emil Radics, Rhodes, Jerome Tharpe (captain) (incomplete)

3RD MARINES
Players: E.J. Miller

RESULTS: H&S Bn 12, Army 6; 1st Marines 20, H&S Bn 19, Marine Air 6 3rd Marines 0 (incomplete

China — 1946

Undefeated Army 11th Airborne Division Angels, champion of Japan, defeated Marine-Navy All-Stars, 12-0, on Jan. 1, 1947, in second China Bowl game at Shanghai.

All-Stars: **Line:** Brown, Ryan. **Backs:** Andreason, Claude Hipps (Georgia), Maxson, Meyers, Moore, Sullivan (not necessarily all Marines)

Pioneer Battalion had defeated 2nd Battalion, 5th Marines, 12-6, and 1st Marine Air Wing, 6-0, for the North China title.

Pioneer Bn.: **Coaches:** Maj. Nat Morgenthal and Lt. Rudy Radick. **Line:** Dostal, Kenworthy, Kinarien, Bob Koehler, Radick (p-c), Seltzer, Smith, Whitlow. **Backs:** R.A. Beauceliel, John Curtis, Harold Dees, Claude Hipps (Georgia), Frances Hipps, John Monroe. **Also:** Joe Mongioui, E.F. Sexton

Air Wing: Bocanegra, Ewbank, Majewski.

Frank Schneider played for one of the teams.

China — 1947

Marines (Guam) beat China All-Stars, 45-0, in a bowl game at Shanghai

Tackles: Umberto Gigli, Bob Patton (Clemson). **Backs:** Claude Hipps (Georgia), Bob Koehler

The 1st Marine Air Wing had been runner-up in the North China League with a 14-1 record.

Coach: Robert Janssen (Drew). **Tackle:** Leroy Johnson

1st Marine Brigade, Guam — 1947

Was the Marianas champion. Lost to NAS Ford Island, 20-6, in All-Navy playoffs in Hawaii (incomplete)

A Guam team beat the China All-Stars, 45-0, in a bowl game at Shanghai

Coach: Capt. Cummings. **Assistant:** Lt. Blaha (Navy) **Players:** guard Charles Hunemiller, back George Greco, plus Ted Bly, John Craig

1st Marines, China — 1948

Record: 7-0 3rd Marines, 12-6 H&S Bn., 14-0 USS Estes, 19-6 Port Facilities, 0-0 AirFMFWestPac, 20-0 USS Roosevelt, 26-0 USS Repose, 2-0 Guam (playoffs), 40-6 ComNavPhil (playoffs) (8-0-1) No transportation was available for All-Navy playoffs in Hawaii.

Coach: Lt. William Hickman, Maj. Stimson

Assistants: Lt. League, Lt. Stephenson

Players: Anderson, Argsy, Barton, Brown (possibly 2 or 3 by that name), Chimer, Commers, Compton, Cooke, Dierkson, Diets (c-c), Durfey, Eggers, Fowler, Giacalare, Goezzer, Halliwell, Helminger, Helmlock, Jones, Kornegger, Lanehart, Maille, McCandless, McMorris, Minichelle, Passi, Pichon (c-c), Raum, Rhodes, Roberts, Sharp, Spencer, Zine

1st Marine Brigade, Guam — 1948

Record: 5-5-3 (lost, 2-0, to 1st Marines of China in a playoff) (incomplete)

Coach, assistant: not available

Players: Tackles Leroy Johnson and Ed Ortnak, guard Chas. Hunemiller. Guard Mike Melonas played for one of the teams.

Thomas Riley (VMI) (asst. Norfolk Marines 1936) (generals) either coached this team or another Guam team.

Ortnak (MAG-24), Johnson (Brigade) and Hunemiller (Brigade) were named to All-FMF Pacific team.

Guam — 1949

End Bob Moore, center Vince Improto and end Ed Rush, all of FMF Guam, and John Stephens of 5th Base Depot, were named to All-FMF Pacific team.

One Magic Moment

Like a meteor, the Camp Fisher football team had a moment of brilliance in 1953 and, almost as quickly, faded from sight.

But the view was spectacular while it lasted for the base in Japan that housed the 1st Provisional Casual Center and at one point only 250 officers and enlisted personnel. Even the commandant followed its football fortunes as did Marine commands worldwide.

It had been a far different story, however, earlier in the season when only a handful of players reported to the coach, Lt. John Mitchell (Erskine), and Camp Fisher was embarrassed in an exhibition loss to an Air Force outfit that had nine Marines of the 1st Air Wing as starters.

Camp Fisher split two games before being routed, 46-6, by the 187th Airborne Regiment.

"But the defeat helped the Marines more than they knew as they staggered off the playing field," the Leatherneck said. "Gen. (Robert H.) Pepper had been in the stands watching the Marines wage the losing battle. He followed the team into the dressing room and told Mitchell: 'You and your boys have got a lot of spirit, but not enough horses.' "

What came next resembled Belmont or Pimlico.

Camp Fisher added experienced players, and Maj. Gen. Pepper, the commanding general, decided to augment with personnel from his 3rd Marine Division.

Starting a "new" season about the time of the Marine Corps birthday, the Bulldogs rolled to five straight victories, including a playoff for the championship of the Southwest Command plus Sukiyaki Bowl and Rice Bowl triumphs. It was the first time the Marines had played in the Rice Bowl.

Said the Leatherneck: "To Col. Herbert R. Nusbaum (the base CO), the victory was the climax to a hope nurtured through five months of headaches and disappointments and a few pleasant surprises. The little team from an almost unknown Marine base had started the season with a squad of messcooks, off-duty MPs and anyone able to get into a football uniform. Now it was a first-rate team capable of reckoning with the best the other services had to offer. It hadn't come easy."

This was just not *any* team, however. It had a nucleus of the 1952 Quantico team: coach Jack Nix (USC, San Francisco 49ers), 210-pound end Jim Mutscheller (Notre Dame), 205-pound guard Ben Amsler (South Carolina), back Leon "Bud" Carson (North Carolina) and quarterback Bill DeChard (Holy Cross).

And throw in 215-pound tackle Jim Howe (Northwestern), 210-pound center Bobby Kelley (West Texas), 225-pound guard Toby Sherrill (Duke, Parris Island) and 225-pound tackle Ernie Cheatham (Loyola of Los Angeles).

DeChard was an 11th-round draft pick of the Washington Redskins in 1951. Mutscheller would star for the Baltimore Colts from 1954-61, Cheatham would be a linebacker for the Pittsburgh Steelers and Colts in 1954, Kelley would play for the Philadelphia Eagles in 1955-56 and tackle John Linnemanstons, after returning to Marquette, would try out with the Redskins in 1956. Carson would become a successful college and pro coach.

The night before the Sukiyaki Bowl, the Marines of the base "had held a regular old collegiate rally, complete with bonfire," the Leatherneck said.

Camp Fisher, picked as the underdog by Stars & Stripes, then stunned the Camp Tokyo Bulldogs, 53-6, before 5,000 at Kyoto. According to one account, they "romped over, around and through the Army eleven." The losers scored with a minute remaining.

A crowd of 37,000, including Gen. Pepper and the 65-piece division band, was on hand for the seventh annual Rice Bowl on Jan. 1, 1954 at Tokyo's Meiji Stadium. The Marines beat the Nagoya Comets, 19-13, to capture the Japan interservice championship and hand the Air Force team its first loss in 14 games.

Halfback Horace Rankin broke a 13-13, fourth-quarter tie with a 4-yard scoring run. He had intercepted the ball on the Camp Fisher 35 and returned it to the Nagoya 16 to set up the touchdown.

Earlier, Carson had scored from the 5 and Rankin from the 7.

Said one account: Camp Fisher "went into the Rice Bowl game knowing that, win, lose or draw, it had put the little-known Marine post on the football map."

A dispatch from Gen. Pepper said: "To all persons responsible for the outstanding performance of the 1954 Rice Bowl champions and, in particular, to Coaches Nix, Mitchell, (Billy Joe) Harper and co-captains DeChard and Mutscheller, my heartiest congratulations. The clean and sportsmanlike conduct displayed on the field is a tribute to and maintains the true spirit of the United States Marines Corps when competing in contests requiring skill, determination and strength. Well done to all hands."

Within months, tne team had disbanded.

Record: 0-7 Camp Kobe Army, def. Nara Army, 6-46 187th Airborne Regiment, 13-12 Camp Otsu Army, 27-7 Osaka Army, 35-7 Camp Otsu (playoff), 53-6 Camp Tokyo Army (Sukiyaki Bowl), 19-13 Nagoya Air Force Comets (Rice Bowl) (6-2) Scrimmaged Itami Air Force.

Coach: Lt. Jack Nix (USC, Quantico 1952)

Assistants: Lt. Billy Joe Harper (Tulane, Quantico 1952), Lt. John Mitchell (Erskine, Quantico 1952)

Ends: Ron Barry, Ed Clark, John Dietz (Bloomsburg, Camp Lejeune 1953), Virgil Franklin, Jim Mutscheller (Notre Dame, Quantico 1952), Bob Wilson

Tackles: Floyd Cavin, Ernie Cheatham (Loyola of Los Angeles), Finn, Jim Howe (Northwestern), John Linnemanstons (Marquette, Camp Pendleton 1952), Picarello, Walt Warren, Bill Webb (Camp Pendleton 1952-53)

Guards: Ben Amsler (South Carolina, Quantico 1952), Bob Dolmetsch, Herey, Joe Polidori (MCAS Miramar 1946, MCAS El Toro 1947-50), Toby Sherrill (Duke, Parris Island 1952), Glenn Smith (Oklahoma A&M), Jim Weckel, Willis

Centers: Randy Barrett, Ed Bosch, D'alesanero, Tim Gildea, Bobby Kelley (West Texas)

Backs: Bill Bell, Bud Carson (North Carolina, Quantico 1952), Bill DeChard (Holy Cross, Quantico 1952), Dumas, Art Jolly, Kabana, Ray Melton, Bobby Moore, Horace Rankin, Taylor, Ed Ward (Mt. St. Mary's), John Williams

Rice Bowl Loss

If at first you succeed, try, try again.

And the Marines did try, defeating the Army All-Stars in the Sukiyaka Bowl and shooting for a second Rice Bowl victory on Jan. 1, 1955 in the Meiji Stadium in Tokyo where in 1954 they had beaten an Air Force team for the Japan interservice title.

But back John Hayden Fry (Baylor) was injured on the first defensive play, a possible omen as the 3rd Division All-Stars lost to the Air Force All-Stars, 21-14.

The Marines this time utilized players from their teams in the 1954 Southwest Command A League (principally the 3rd, 4th, 9th and 12th Marines) because the Rice Bowl reverted to an all-star format.

And tackle Sam Duca (Arizona State) and center Don Agler had played for the 1953 Cherry Point team that upset Quantico, 9-6.

Coaching the All-Stars was Capt. Ted Stawicki (American, Morningside), a veteran Marine player and coach who brought 16 players from his 9th Marines (6-0) to the All-Stars. The All-Star team was not as big, experienced or explosive as Camp Fisher's. Duca and Kramer were the only Division I-type players over 210. And the all-star format did not lend itself to the cohesiveness and excitement of a season such as Camp Fisher had enjoyed.

Still, just being in the Rice Bowl again was an achievement. A year earlier, Leatherneck commented that the "Marines had not tried to enter a team in competition (prior to 1953) and with good reason, there weren't enough good Marines concentrated in any one area to muster a set of doubles for ping pong — let alone a 35-man football squad."

Stawicki, in seven seasons at Parris Island, Camp Pendleton, Hawaii and in Japan, coached teams to 38 victories against 15 losses and 3 ties.

Just as Camp Fisher in 1953 drew on the 1952 Quantico team, so the 1954 all-star aggregation benefitted from Quantico's 1953 all-service runner-up: backs Fry, John Mounie (Duke) and John Pettibon (Notre Dame, Dallas Texans), end Bob Trout (Baylor) and tackle Tony Kramer (Dayton), among others.

Fry, of course, went on to a highly visible coaching career at SMU, North Texas and Iowa. Pettibon, a seventh-round round pick by Dallas in 1952, would play for the Cleveland Browns in 1955-56 and the Green Bay Packers in 1957. Trout was a 27th-round draft choice of the Detroit Lions in 1952.

Coach: Capt. Ted Stawicki (American, Morningside, Quantico 1946-48, coach Parris Island 1949-50, coach Camp Pendleton 1953)

Assistants: Capt. Ralph Heywood (USC, El Toro 1945, player-coach Quantico 1952), Capt. Jim Robinson

Ends: Clarence Cook, John Hekker, J.E. Sende (UCLA), Bob Trout (Baylor, Quantico 1953), Bob Wilson (Camp Fisher (1953)

Tackles: Yhinio Arreguy, Elmer Brooks, Floyd Cavin (Camp Fisher 1953), Sam Duca (Arizona State, MCRD San Diego 1952, Cherry Point 1953), Bob Eitel, Tony Kramer (Dayton, Quantico 1953)

Guards: Howard Devoid, Hitower Hammac, Ron McNeil, Jim Norman, John Tronoski, Dan Wagner
Centers: Don Agler (Cherry Point 1953), Howard Jackson, Charles Paxton
Backs: Glenn Anderson, Jack Burrell, Dick Collins, John Hayden Fry (Baylor, Quantico 1953), Jerry Haskins (Oklahoma), Harold Heier, Jackson King (Colgate, Quantico 1953), Harry Kon, Russ Lutz, John Markowitz, John Mounie (Duke, Quantico 1953), John O'Shea, John Pettibon (Notre Dame, Quantico 1953), John Shackleford, Russ Smale (Quantico 1953)

3rd Marines

Record: 0-32 1st MarDiv, lost twice to 4th Marines (incomplete)
Heywood*, Brooks*, Haskins*, Heier*.

4th Marines

Record: beat 12th Marines twice, beat 3rd Marines twice, beat NAS Iwakuni (5-4) (incomplete)
Coach: Paul Lentz (Guilford) (Mosquito Bowl; asst. Quantico 1953)
Assistant: Lt. Dan Wagner*
Players: Paul Ancira, Gene Arreguy*, Lonnie Brown, Dom Cappachione, Don Cook, Jerome Ebert, Robert Eitel*, Roger Ferguson, Frank Gilbert, Ellis Harris, Winfred Harris, Fred Hines, David Hood, Joe Janssens, Charles Koani, Harry Kon*, Miles Lund, Jack Macko, Joe McAnerney, Miles McAtee, Joe McFadden, Robert Miller (USN), Ernest Odenburgh, Charles Paxton*, Marty Renzhofer, William Rigsbee, Phil Robinson, Greg Sarkisian, Larry Schweinfurt, Russ Smale*, Tom Souza, Robert Spreew, Don Turner, Jack Williams

9th Marines

Record: 6-0 (scores not available)
Coach: Stawicki*. **Assistants:** not available
Ends: Cook*, Hekker*, McWitty, Roderick, Trout*, Wilson*
Tackles: Cavin*, Holliday, T. Johnson, Kramer*, Paul Stephens (South Carolina, Quantico 1953), F.T. Zeh
Guards: Duca*, Hammac*, J. Harrell, R.C. Hughes, J.R. Keller, Norman*
Centers: Agler*, Jackson*, S.G. Qualey
Backs: J.L. Abney, G.E. Fowler, Fry*, Laverne Hall, B.G. Harris, R.E. Hill, B. Holman, King*, J. McAlpine, Mounie*, Dick Neveux (Detroit, Quantico 1953), O'Shea*, Pettibon*, L.E. Plaster, R.D. Rodgers

12th Marines

Record: 7-6 Navy Flyers, lost twice to 4th Marines (incomplete)
Coach: Robinson*. **Assistant:** Ray Terrell (Mississipi, NAS Jacksonville 1942, Camp Lejeune 1943, Quantico 1949-50, asst. Quantico 1951)
Ends: Loren Comstock, Joe Edwards, Bob McDuffie, Pete May, Mel Nonaka, Garnett Weeks, Phil Wilson
Tackles: Tom Barger, Fred Hardy, Bill Luoma, DeWayne Manuel, John McGrath, Curvin Snyder, Dick Younis
Guards: Pat Collins, Jerry Howard, Ron Hunter, McNeil*, Dick Paxson, Joe Radicia, Tronoski*
Centers: Chuck Fuellgraf, Howard Lowe, Dale Powers
Backs: Dusty Baugh, Tom Bickford, Burrell*, Bill Carter, Collins*, John Gilbreath, Ron Graigmiles, Bob Harvey, Lowell Hoff, Enoch Huff, Stu Hollins, Lutz*, Jerry Martin, Frank Parker, Shackleford*, Rick Yacone
* Member of division all-star team

MAG-11

Anderson*, Markowitz*, Sende*

Service Regiment

Devoid*

MCAS Iwakuni/1955

Record: not available
Coach: not available
Backs: Ed Mioduszewski (William & Mary, Quantico 1954), who played for Navy All-Stars in Rice Bowl playoffs

Far East/1955

Record: not available
Coach: not available
Centers: Ed Johnson (Pittsburgh)
(incomplete)

NAS Atsugi (Navy-Marine Stars)/1957

Record: 31-0 Yokohama Port Clippers, 20-31 Fuchu AF Tornadoes (incomplete)
Coach: not available
Ends: Fred Walton
Backs: Bob Cullom, Dave Lurts, Jim Ogelsby, Billy/Joe Todd, Dick Wahl, John Wiren
(not all necessarily Marines)
(incomplete)

MCAS Iwakuni/1957

Record: not available
Coach: not available
Kicker: Tad Weed (Ohio St., Quantico 1956)
(incomplete)

Far East/1959

Record: not available
Coach: not available
Tackles: Mike Dau (Lake Forest)
(incomplete)

Far East/1960

Record: not available
Coach: not available
Assistant: Mike Dau (Lake Forest)
Backs: Dan Droze (North Carolina, Quantico 1959); All-Far East selection

Chalmers "Bump" Elliott played with Purdue, Fleet Marine Force Pacific and Michigan; coached at Michigan, and was athletic director at Iowa.

Korean Juggernaut

The First Marine Division football team in 1954 was big, it was smart, it was good.

Guard Tom Roggeman (Purdue) weighed in at 240, tackles Lon Unsell and Carl Valletto at 235, tackle Don Deskins (Adelphi) at 230, and tackles Tom Roche (Northwestern) and Joe Ditta at 225. Thirteen others were 200 or more.

As for brains, Roggeman, the team captain, would be a longtime assistant coach at Purdue, Arizona and USC. Center Jim Erkenbeck (San Diego State) would be an assistant at his alma mater, at Utah State, Washington State and California, in Canada, in the USFL and with the New Orleans Saints, Dallas Cowboys and Kansas City Chiefs. Center Bob Peck (Stetson) would become athletic director at Williams. Deskins would receive his M.A. and Ph.D. at Michigan and become a professor of geography and sociology at the Ann Arbor, Mich., university.

As for ability, Coach Joe Polidori's Marines won eight and lost only to the Seoul Military Post, 16-14, as they captured the 8th Army championship. In the loss, the Army scored on two blocked punts and a safety and the Marines were penalized 120 yards. The division team outrushed Seoul, 135 yards to 35, and outpassed the soldiers, 68 to 20.

Along the way, however, the Marines won by 32, 46, 16, 47, 14, 12 and 32 points. The 8th Army headquarters said a playoff between the Seoul team, the league's second-half winner, and the 1st Division, the first-half winner, was not feasible because of anticipated cold weather.

Roggeman, end Merrill Jacobs (St. Mary's, San Francisco State), Roche, guard Jim Pozza (Marquette) and quarterback John Cahill (Boston Univ.) received all-league honors.

The 1st Division, like 3rd Division teams in Japan, was the beneficiary of players from Quantico's 1953 service runner-up: Jacobs, Roche, Roggeman, Peck, Erkenbeck and back John Amberg (Kansas and two seasons with the New York Giants).

Some players also had college, pro and service football ahead of them. Deskins would letter at Michigan in 1958 and 1959 and play with the new Oakland Raiders in 1960. Valletto would letter at Alabama in 1957, 1958 and 1960 and try out with the Pittsburgh Steelers in 1961. (A son, David, would letter at Tennessee-Martin and Alabama in the '80s.) Center Bobby Kelley (West Texas) would play with the Philadelphia Eagles in 1955 and 1956. Back Carroll Zaruba (Doane) would letter at Nebrasaka in 1957, 1958 and 1959 and play with the Dallas Texans in 1960. Jacobs would be with the Hawaii Marines in 1955 and 1956 and MCRD San Diego in 1957.

And, incredibly, more than a decade later, Herb Travenio would score 110 points as the San Diego Chargers' placekicker in 1964 and 1965 after playing at MCRD San Diego in 1962 and 1963.

Record: 32-0 3rd Marines, 46-0 Seoul Military Post, 23-7 7th Infantry Division, 47-0 I Corps Headquarters, 21-7 24th Infantry Division, 14-16 Seoul Military Post, 19-7 1st Infantry Division, 39-7 I Corps Headquarters, 1-0 24th Infantry Division (8-1)

Coach: Joe Polidori (MCAS Miramar 1946, MCAS El Toro 1947-50, Camp Fisher 1953)

Assistants: John Amberg (Kansas, Quantico 1953), Walt Cook (William Jewell), Bob Peck (Stetson, Quantico 1953)

Ends: George Abrams, John Flippin (Wyoming, MCRD San Diego 1953), Gene Goodvich, Merrill Jacobs (St. Mary's, San Francisco State, Quantico 1953), Chuck Manning, John McLoughlin (Fordham), Fred Sharp, Don Taylor (MCRD San Diego 1952-53), Hal Williams

Tackles: Don Deskins (Adelphi), Joe Ditta (Tulane), Kelly McGill, Dave McInturff (Tennessee), Jim Parish, Tom Roche (Northwestern) (Quantico 1953), Lon Unsell, Carl Valletto (Camp Pendleton) (later at Alabama)

Guards: Ron Carney, Paul Feagan (Washburn), John Haita, J.L. Massey, Jim Pozza (Marquette), Tom Roggeman (Purdue, Quantico 1953), Dick Williams, Willis Zumwalt

Centers: Jim Erkenbeck (San Diego State, Quantico 1953), Bob Kelley (West Texas, Camp Fisher 1953), Peck

Backs: Amberg, John Cahill (Boston Univ.), John Carlile (Camp Pendleton 1953), Cook, Dave Daggett (Camp Pendleton 1953), Lucious Daley (Adams State), Chuck Desadier (Northwest Louisiana), Frank Drougel, Hank Fry, Lou Koval, Rocco Marzzarella (Michigan State, Parris Island 1953), Lincoln Moneace, Don Moore, Rayford Phillips, Radford, Fred Sorrenti, Herb Travenio (Texas College), Carroll Zaruba (Doane)

Boot Bowl Rivalry

I t was a natural rivalry if there ever was one: the recruit depots of San Diego and Parris Island challenging each other for Boot Bowl honors.

And, as might be expected, the competition was fierce and neither team was dominant. They alternated game sites between the two coasts and San Diego's staff NCO's presented a rotating trophy to the winner. San Diego won two games; so did Parris Island.

A 1951 game program said "alumni of the two recruit depots anxiously await the outcome of the contest."

Host Parris Island won the first matchup, 19-13, in 1949, as Len Aloy, Bob Kaiser and Russ Picton scored TD's. Ed Petrovich had a 95-yard kickoff return nullified by a penalty.

But host San Diego crushed PI, 57-18, in 1950 on its way to an 11-0 season. Volney "Skeet" Quinlan scored four TD's (including one of 90 yards), and Paul Marinelli, Don Brand, Bob Collins and Mike Michon one each. PI's Dick Travagline returned an interception 95 yards for a TD.

Parris Island obtained revenge in 1951 with a 16-9 victory at Savannah, Ga., as Billy Mixon and Billy Hayes scored touchdowns and Sam Vacanti kicked a field goal.

The game program noted that "Marine Corps officials decided to switch the game to Savannah to enable civilians a chance to see the military classic."

Host San Diego evened the series in 1952 with a 21-12 triumph on national television.

Over There

There were some good football teams on Okinawa. The problem is that not many people knew about them and not many records are available to publicize the competition and successes.

From about the mid-'50s to the early '70s, Marine teams fought each other as well as Army and Air Force rivals. There were league games, playoffs, bowl games and occasional contests in Japan.

Players and coaches such as Ron Beagle, Mike Sweatman, Walt Nadzak, King Dixon, Jim Royer, Ron Brown, Ed Heuring and Steve Bernstein, and team names such as the Royals, Strikers, Leathernecks and Devil Dogs marked the era.

3rd Division (Camp McGill)-1955

Record: not available
Coach: not available
Ends: Red Warren
Backs: Bob Black, who was MVP against the Army in the Torii Bowl

9th Marines/1955

Record: Team played in Typhoon Bowl on Okinawa (incomplete)
Coach: not available
Backs: Bob Ortman
(incomplete)

3rd Division (Camp McGill)-1956

Record: Played Air Force All-Stars in Sukiyaki Bowl (incomplete)
Coach: Morgan Murphy
Roster: not available

1956 teams

Records: not available; **Coaches:** not available
Backs: Lester Campbell
(incomplete)

1957 teams

Records: Camp Sukiran 14 Streaks, Yokota AF Raiders 7; Yokosuka Seahawks 31, Camp Courtney 0; Johnson AFB 6, Camp Sukiran 0 (Rice Bowl, Tokyo) (incomplete)
Coaches: not available
Ends: Ron Beagle (Navy, Quantico 1956), Camp Sukiran
Tackles: Howard Long (Tulane, Arkansas St., Arkansas Tech), Streaks
Backs: Dick Graf, Streaks; Rod Stephen, Streaks; Don "Hub" Wilson (Rice, Quantico 1956), Streaks
Kicker: Roger Gaillard, Streaks
(incomplete)

1958 teams

Records: Air Force All-Stars 60, Marine All-Stars 0 (Okinawa Shuri Bowl)
Coaches: Jim Royer (Navy, Quantico 1957)
(Interservice first team)
Ends: Don Williams, Streaks; Joel Blodgett, Royals.
Tackles: Roger Beckley (Buffalo, Camp Lejeune 1956), Streaks

Backs: Tom Myrick, Streaks; Fred Parisi, Royals
Also: Carlton Smith
(incomplete)

1959-60 teams

No records available

1961 teams

Strikers

Record: not available
Coach: King Dixon (South Carolina, Quantico 1959-60)
Roster: not available

1962 teams

Strikers

Record: The island Interservice and mythical Far East champions. Defeated Army's 7th Infantry Division Bayonets in Sukiyaki Bowl before 9,000 at Camp Sukiran (score NA). (10-1) (incomplete)
Coach: Hank Freese
Linemen: Billie Hook, Gampy Pelligrini
Backs: Hugh Oldham
(incomplete)

Royals

Record: not available
Coach: Ron Brown (Los Angeles Valley CC, Montana St.) (KIA)
Roster: not available

Others

Glenn Kirk (Austin, Quantico 1961), not clear which team
Hugh Oldham, not clear which team
Erroll Yeager (Murray St.), not clear which team

1963 teams

Streaks

Record: not available
Coach: Mike Giacinto (Notre Dame, Quantico 1962)
Assistant: Bill Collins (The Citadel)
Ends: Charlie Abbott, Earl Allen (Arizona St. at Flagstaff, Camp Pendleton 1956, MCRD San Diego 1960-62), Larry Barry (Michigan), John Bruce, Amos Coleman, Larry Mosley, Lynn Oxenreider (Princeton, Quantico 1961-62)
Tackles: James Breckenridge (Arizona St.), Jim Curtis, Lawrence Jimmerson (Arizona St.), Ron Nadonly
Guards: Les Berggren, Joseph Day, Leo Francisco (Compton CC), Doug Graham, Dick Hunt, Charles McCloud (Houston), John Seward, Larry Small, Ernest Vetkoeher, Howard Young
Centers: Tom Badillo (Southwestern CC), Boyd Cox, Charles Paxton
Quarterback: Eddie Parham, Joe Schulte (Marquette), Gerald Stevens
Backs: Ray Bolden, Jerry Bowerman, John Frieman (Wisconsin), Slick Gardner, Jerry Griffith, Willie Jones, Elwyn McRoy, Bill Nicholson, Charles Pehy, Al Richman, Ieon Thomas, Jerald Thomas, David Thompkins (Grand Rapids JC), Douglas Warner

Royals

Record: not available
Coach: T.E. Race
Assistants: J.L. Lanzvecchia, A.F. Myers
Ends: R.R. Christian, D.J. Counsell, W.G. Powers, J.E. Riles, M.A. Tuinstra
Tackles: Terry Conley (Indiana, MCRD San Diego 1962), S. Nelson, C. Phillips, J.R. Shirripa, B.E. Walker
Guards: L.F. Crawford, K.M. Damm, D. Tate, J.R. Zeiber
Linebackers: J.K. Bean, F.E. Blanco, Bob Federspiel (Columbia, Quantico 1962), R.H. Welch,
Centers: W. Jefferson
Quarterbacks: T.P. Bair, L. Kislowski

Backs: L.S. Ake, L.W. Bauer, J.E. Brown, T.R. Drake, K. Jones, H.E. Keller, J.W. Mann, C.W. Milner, A. Reeves, G.D. Rickett, J.T. Shamburg, J.W. Stzmbribge, J.S. Walter, B. Wilson, J.N. Wright

Also: Bill Cervanek (Iowa St., Quantico 1962), Lucas

Others

Record: 5-3 (incomplete)
Coach: Howard Long (Tulane, Arkansas St., Arkansas Tech, Quantico assistant 1962)
Players: not available

1964 teams

Records: 3rd MarDiv defeated 7th Infantry Division Bayonets, 27-14, for Far East championship (incomplete)
Coaches: not available
Backs: John Dixon (Central St. of Ohio), Jack Wallace (Ohio St., Quantico 1963)
(not clear whether they played for the division or other teams)
(incomplete)

1965-67 teams

No records available

1968 teams

Records: not available
Coaches: Cliff Yoshida (Cal Poly Pomona, Quantico 1966)
Assistants: Steve Bernstein (Cerritos CC, Occidental, Quantico 1967), Gene Miller, John Turner (VMI)
Players: Jim Johnson (Sequoias CC)
(incomplete)

1969 teams

No records available

1970 teams

Devil Dogs

Record: (10-1) and a title (incomplete)
Coach: Mike Sweatman (Kansas, Quantico 1969)
Assistants: Ev Keene (Boise JC, Rhode Island, Quantico 1969), Mike Zoffuto (West Texas)
Ends: Dennis Blake; **guards:** Mike Zizzo (Villanova)
Also: Zoffutto
(incomplete)

Leathernecks

Record: not available
Coach: not available
Assistants: Thom Park (Brown, West Chester)
Tackles: Seton Siff (DePauw); **guards:** Greg Sundy (Augustana of S.D.); **backs:** Bob Sweat (Richmond)
(incomplete)

1971 teams

Devil Dogs

Record: 58-14 COMUSNAVPHIL Admirals (incomplete)
Coach: Bob Peterson
Players: Burrell Godbold (INCOMPLETE)

1972 teams

Records: not available but won the Army championship. Hare's teams posted a 16-1-1 record in two seasons.
Coaches: Dave Hare (Spokane CC)
Rosters: not available

1973 teams

Leathernecks

Record: 6-13 COMUSNAVPHIL Admirals, 13-20 COMUSNAVPHIL Admirals (incomplete)
Coach: NA
Tight ends: R. Harris, L. Mallory. **Wide receivers:** W. Byrd, L. Ewing, J. Pamer. **Guards:** T. Gutierrez, Kenner, M. Matthews, E. Palmer, A. Prosser, R. Reavis, A. Rouis. **Centers:** F. Aguilar. **Quarterbacks:** J. Blackstock, W. Holloway. **Running backs:** J. Cowan, R. Dunlap, D. Edwards, L. Ervin, T. Fagan, K. Garza, K. Smith. **Linebackers:** R. Fauste, C. Gibson, A. Henderson, R. Lewis, O. McKee, M. Neal, W. Songer, R. Walsh. **Tackles:** M. Crenshaw, R. Dingle, S. Graves III, D. Moore, M. Navage, J. Villalobos. **Defensive end:** J. Williams. **Defensive backs:** K. Crowder, D. Desmarias, M. Grages, G. Guy, K. Lawson, R. Simmons, R. Trotter. **Safety:** C. Young. **Kicker:** W. Nickels

Devil Dogs

Record: 6-21 COMUSNAVPHIL Admirals, 0-16 COMUSNAVPHIL Admirals (incomplete)
Coach: NA. **Players:** NA

Other coaches, players (years not available)

Ron Case, Coach Allen "Scotty" Harris, Coach Ed Heuring (Maryland, Quantico 1961), Ben Lett, Walt Nadzak (Denison, Quantico 1957, Camp Pendleton 1958), Bob Ortman (Quantico 1956), John Proctor (San Diego CC), Troy Perkins (Arkansas Baptist), Bob Roche, Carlton Smith

---

Quantico Wins 13 in '48

Quantico's 13 victories in the 1948 season are the most by a Marine team.

In the process, the Virginia team scored 419 points and defeated Ft. Belvoir, Camp Lejeune, Wayne (Mich.), Bolling Field, Ft. Benning, NAS Patuxent, Xavier, St. Francis (Pa.), Parris Island, Navy Prep School, Little Creek, MCRD San Diego (All-Navy title) and Ft. Bragg (all-service title).

The 1947 Quantico and 1963 San Diego teams each won 12. Quantico rang up 444 points and San Diego 429.

Eleven-game winners were San Diego (1939), Quantico (1949), San Diego (1950) and Quantico (1959).

Ten-game winners were Mare Island (1918), Parris Island (1926), All-Marines (1926 and 1927), Camp Lejeune (1949), Camp Pendleton (1949), Quantico (1953 and 1954), San Diego (1957, 1958 and 1959), Quantico (1963) and San Diego (1964).

Football in Morocco

Morocco, too, is part of the Marine football tradition.

The Marine Barracks at Port Lyautey in 1957 defeated the 316th Air Division's Site 11, 13-6.

Leading the victory were backs Bill Jones, Don Mitchner and Gil Smith (Morgan State) and kicker Joe Looney.

Hardly Off Ground

Football teams at MCAS, Miami, never really got off the ground.

The Korean War was being fought, and the more established air stations at Cherry Point and El Toro even found the gridiron going difficult.

End Jerry Elliott (Auburn) perhaps was the top Miami player in that 1951-53 era, having received All-Marine honors at Parris Island in 1952.

The Barracudas defeated NAS Jacksonville in 1952 and 1953 and tied Parris Island in '53.

1951

Record: 6-14 Miami JV, 59-0 Miami Trojans, 7-16 Cherry Point (incomplete)
Coach: not available. **Assistants:** not available. Players: not available.

1952

Record: 7-31 Pensacola, 0-21 508th Airborne Infantry Regiment (Ft. Benning), 26-13 NAS Jacksonville, 12-6 Sewart AFB, 20-6 Miami Trojans (incomplete) (4-4)
Coach: not available. **Assistants:** not available. **Players:** not available.

1953

Record: 28-28 Parris Island, 0-39 Pensacola, 6-46 Cherry Point, 0-65 Ft. Jackson, 13-7 NAS Jacksonville, 0-15 Eglin AFB, 0-32 Miami B team, 27-0 Alexandria AFB, 27-7 Camp Polk (3-5-1)
Coach: Al James (LSU, coach El Toro 1949). **Assistant:** William R. Marshall
Ends: Bob Beckley, Ernest Dodson, Jerry Elliott (Auburn, Parris Island 1952), Cornelius Scott, Paul Woodard
Tackles: Owen Boland, Bill Chambers, Angelo Paternostro, Karl Perryman, Delbert Roy, Doug Tiffany
Guards: Robert Adams, John Coolahan, C. Gulbrondsen, Ottice Hicks, Charles Manchac, Jim Neese, George Rue, Bill Unger
Centers: Herb Daly, Edward Kercher, Dick Polak
Backs: Paul Attaya, John Attix, George Donaldson, Don Donovan, Joe Dorsey, Jim Fanelli, Bartley Fitzgerald, John Gasperic, Cliff King, Donald Lewis, Harry Mackey, Ted McQuade, Jay Mercer (Monmouth-Illinois Wesleyan), L. Roberts, Charles Scoville, Carl Sherwin, Ed Standa
Others: Frank Merriwell

Lousma A Wolverine

Astronaut Jack Lousma lettered with the Michigan football team in 1956.

Lousma was pilot in 1973 for Skylab-3 on a $59\frac{1}{2}$-day flight that set a single-mission record. He was the backup docking-module pilot for the Apollo-Soyuz Test Project in 1975 and commanded the third flight of the Space Shuttle Columbia, an eight-day mission in 1982.

He received NASA's Distinguished Service Medal in 1973, the Navy's Distinguished Service Medal in 1974; the Collier Trophy in 1973; the MCAA Exceptional Achievement Award in 1974, the Goddard Trophy in 1975 and the Chanute Award in 1975.

Barstow's Hot Teams

Unless you're a "desert rat," Barstow probably isn't for you.

Especially in the early 1950s, before air-conditioning was as widespread as today and before thousands of people started settling in the California desert and easing some of the loneliness. Some Marines saw assignment to Barstow as punishment.

Nevertheless, the base produced competitive football teams from 1951 through 1957 — with but one losing season — against service, college and semi-pro opposition. It lost its three games with Camp Pendleton, its only contest with the San Diego Marines and was 1-2 against El Toro.

By today's terms, the Barstow teams were of Division II or Division III quality.

There were exceptions, however.

Jim Weatherall had been the Outland Trophy winner at Oklahoma in 1951 and a standout tackle at Quantico in 1952. The 6-1, 230-pound Weatherall was a player-coach as Barstow posted a 5-4 record in 1953. Weatherall received All-Service honors and was a second-team All-Marine selection at Barstow.

After Marine service, he played for the Philadelphia Eagles from 1955 to 1957, the Washington Redskins in 1958 and the Detroit Lions in 1959 and '60. A second-round Eagles draft choice in 1952, he was selected for two Pro Bowls.

Coach Pat Ryan (Holy Cross), after seasons at Quantico in 1954 and Camp Lejeune in 1955, quarterbacked the Bulldogs to 5-4 and 7-3 records in 1956 and 1957, the base's last two varsity teams. In 1956, Barstow lost to George Allen-coached Whittier, 7-6.

Ryan completed 126 of 146 passes for 2,022 yards and 20 TDs (he ran for nine TDs) in 1956 and was 101 of 201 for 1,509 yards and 12 TDs in 1957. He was second-team All-Sea Service in 1956 and 1957 and All-Marine in '57. He was a player-coach with the Hawaii Marines in 1958 and received a tryout with the Green Bay Packers in 1959.

1950

Schedule cancelled because of Korean War commitments.

1951

Record: 18-0 Redlands, 19-13 NAB Coronado, 6-16 El Toro, 13-6 Terminal Island, 48-6 TraPac, 26-7 Pt. Mugu, 50-7 Nellis AFB. Defeated Inyokern, def. Los Angeles St. JV. (8-1; possibly incomplete)
Coach: Not available. **Assistants:** not available.
Ends: Stan Diemler, Ed West
Tackles: Hannah, Nicochea
Guards: Eckles, Walker
Centers: Farrell
Backs: Atwood DeVaughn (Bishop), Geo. Granger, Jim Greene, Lipscomb, Don Penaflor (INCOMPLETE)

1952

Record: 19-6 TraPac, 28-6 George AFB, 27-7 TraPac, 18-0 El Toro, 13-56 Camp Pendleton, 46-7 Ft. MacArthur, 32-6 NOTS Inyokern, 6-7 Pt. Mugu, 0-53 NAB Coronado, 7-12 Alameda NAS, 20-16 NS Long Beach, 12-9 Edwards AFB (Desert Bowl) (8-4)
Coach: Not available. **Assistants:** not available
Ends: R. Pogacnik, Ed West
Tackles: B. Myers, W. Walker
Guards: Ernie Cunningham,, Bob Hamby, Upton Henderson, S. Lane, Bob Salvidio
Centers: Paul Miller, Alan Nelson, Cal Randle (Eastern Washington)
Backs: Atwood DeVaughn (Bishop), Larry English, Geo. Granger, Ed Hicks, Ed McKechnie, A. Proyle
(INCOMPLETE)

1953

Record: 20-0 NAS Alameda, 7-18 El Toro, 26-6 Edwards AFB, 37-0 China Lake, 18-40 Camp Pendleton, 19-7 NS Long Beach, 12-14 Treasure Island, 6-19 Pt. Mugu, 43-0 NAD Hawthorne (5-4)
Coach: N. "Tex" Lisman
Assistants: Charles Brown, Jim Weatherall (Oklahoma) (Quantico 1952)
Ends: Tom Ellery, Lloyd Longino, Herb Mundy, Stan Reed
Tackles: Cliff Brookshier, Geo. Matulich, Pete Salopek, Frank Turner (Quantico 1951-52), Weatherall (p-c), Tony Wozniak
Guards: Lynell Clubine, Ernest Cunningham, Howard Evans, Upton Henderson, Bob Salvidio
Centers: John Ferguson, Allen Nelson, Peter Omer
Backs: Arch Brooks, Brown (p-c), Avery Burton, Charles Cannia, Roy Craig, David English, Bob Hessler, Ed Hicks, John Kabeiseman, Dorsey Lightner, Ed McKechnie, Geo. Pang, Cal Randle (Eastern Washington), Mike Serna (Compton JC-Cal Poly) (MCRD San Diego 1952), Leo Steele, Don Town, Umberto Vega, Jack Wages (Abilene Christian, North Texas) (Camp Pendleton 1951-52)
Also: Tony Bernitsky, David Wein

1954

Record: 7-7 Bay Cities AC, 0-40 MCRD San Diego, 6-55 Camp Pendleton, 13-20 NS Long Beach, 0-37 Eagle Rock AC, 0-21 NAS North Island, 8-14 Chino Prison, 27-20 Pt. Mugu, 25-0 Edwards AFB, 38-7 Twentynine Palms (3-6-1)
Coach: Jim Olsen. **Assistants:** Not available
Ends: Carl Duebner (Marquette), Gil Hawkins
Tackles: Ken Aldridge (Murray Agri.), Reggie Fernandez, Bob Van Sickle
Guards: Howard Evans, Tom Schwalbach (Northern Michigan), Gene Thomas
Centers: Richard Boring
Backs: Bill Davis (SMU), Geo. Douglas (Contra Costa JC), John Gill, Charles Thornhill
(INCOMPLETE)

1955

Record: 20-20 Redlands, 27-0 Mira Costa JC, 13-0 Ft. Huachuca, 27-6 Chino Prison, 14-0 Pt. Mugu, 28-19 Bay Cities AC, 0-19 Edwards AFB, 20-13 Edwards AFB, 0-25 Terminal Island (6-2-1)
Coach: Not available. **Assistants:** Not available.
Ends: George Murray
Tackles: Reggie Fernandez, Valento
Guards: Jim Reed (Southwest Missouri)
Centers: Crawford
Backs: Tom Reynolds (Iowa St. Teachers), Tom Schwalbach (Northern Michigan)
(INCOMPLETE)

1956

Record: 39-25 Caltech, 31-16 Pomona-Claremont, 6-7 Whittier, 12-27 Occidental, 19-21 Cal Poly Pomona, 19-21 Redlands, 46-32 Compton JC JV, 47-13 Edwards AFB, 33-6 Ft. Huachuca (Sight Bowl) (5-4). Scrimmaged Pepperdine
Coach: Pat Ryan (Holy Cross) (Quantico 1954, Camp Lejeune 1955)
Assistants: George Murphy (Fordham) (Quantico-Camp Lejeune 1955), George Murray, Harvey Warren (3rd MarDiv 1955)
Ends: Harold Hansen, Murphy (p-c), J.C. Nowlin, Warren (p-c), Norm Wilson
Tackles: Reggie Fernandez, Pat Fonseca, Foss, Ron Hadsall, L.P. Hanaway, Paul Lockhart, Andy Yosurek

Guards: Mark Angeli, L.J. Bertrand, Henry Carmichael, Garry Foss, H.E. Johnson, Henry Kaikuana, Eric Kama, Arch Mahaulau, Tom Stewart, E.D. Thomason

Centers: Leo Bricker, Jim Dowling, A.H. Wolz

Backs: Grover Carey, Charles DeSadiers (1st MarDiv 1954, Hawaii Marines 1955), Ed Hicks, Bob Kanae, Kirkie, Jim Ragan, Ryan (p-c), Charles Spears

1957

Record: 20-34 Cal Poly Pomona, 19-0 Occidental, 25-20 Pomona, 27-12 Redlands, 13-20 Univ. of San Diego, 0-51 Whittier, 66-6 Compton JC JV, 23-6 El Toro Razorbacks, 33-6 Twentynine Palms, 47-32 Twentynine Palms (7-3)

Coach: Pat Ryan (Holy Cross) (Quantico 1954, Camp Lejeune 1955)

Assistants: Pat Fonseca, Hans Jacobsen (Drake) (MCRD San Diego 1948-51, asst. 1953-54)

Ends: Bob Brunk, Tom Clark, Gerald Freeman, Jim Galvin (Notre Dame), Jim Glynn, Jerry Heidorn, Stan Jasinowski, Jim Sieg, Sam Smith, Norm Wilson

Tackles: Jim Fernandez, Tom Love, Jack Mendenhall, Bill Sottoriva, Marv Wietz

Guards: Henry Carmichael, Mike Carter, Ernie Delco (Camp Pendleton 1955-56), Arch Mahualua, Sam Robertson

Centers: Conrad Aquayo, Jacobsen (p-c), Joe Kua, A.H. Wolz, Bill Worrell

Backs: Welles "Butch" Bacon, Dick Boring, Don Brinkman (Montana St.), Jimmy Gregor, Ed Hicks, Al Knighten, Bob Owens, Jim Regan, Ryan (p-c), Jerome Slewinski, Charles Spears, Duck Sulik, Thurston Thompson, Paul Yoakum

(Had lost to MCRD San Diego, 42-12, in an Armed Forces Day game.)

1958

Dropped varsity football

Mike Giddings heads up Proscout Inc. of Newport Beach, Cal., which looks over prospects for the Bills, Bengals, Cowboys, Broncos, Oilers, Chiefs, Dolphins, Vikings, Saints, Eagles and Buccaneers. He played with California, Quantico, Camp Pendleton and MCAF, Tustin

Pigskin Paradise

F our postwar Marine teams in Hawaii came within a victory of an undefeated season.

Ted Stawicki's 1956 edition finally went unbeaten, winning all seven games and capturing the University-Armed Forces Conference title.

Second-team All-Marine selection Al Daniels and Ken Wedemeyer (Herman's brother) led an offense that averaged 31 points a game. The team had size (20 players at 200 or more), depth and a balanced officer-enlisted mix.

Stawicki (American, Morningside, Quantico) had coached the Parris Island teams in 1949 and 1950, Camp Pendleton in 1953 and the 3rd Division All-Stars in 1954. His 1955 Hawaii Marines finished with a 4-1-1 record, the loss to the University of Hawaii, 20-19.

Eleven players returned for the 1956 season. Stawicki also picked up backs Vince Jazwinski (Brown) and Jim Milne (Missouri) from Quantico and Marv Fiorini from MCRD San Diego, and linemen Howard Conrad and John Wynne (210) from San Diego; Emil Marquardt (225) from Parris Island and John Glover (210) from Camp McGill.

Daniels would play for South Dakota in 1958 and 1959 and Gates for the University of San Diego and Oregon State and in the Canadian Football League.

The 1946 Camp Catlin team (8-1), 1953 Pearl Harbor Marines (5-1-1) and 1954 Hawaii Marines (7-1) were other standout teams in the 1946-58 period, several years of which found minimal Marine varsity participation. A look at the seasons:

■ **1946:** Camp Catlin, runner-up in the Hawaiian Service League, was coached by (Navy) Lt. Les Horvath (Ohio State), the 1944 Heisman Trophy winner.

The Ewa Marines (6-3), coached by Charles Cornwell, later to direct the 1947, 1948 and 1950 El Toro teams, featured end Elmore Ravensburg (Xavier, Georgia Pre-Flight, St. Mary's Pre-Flight) and player-coach Frank Boyd (Oregon, El Toro).

The Pearl Harbor Marines, coached by Lts. Nick Canzona and D.E. Spencer, featured end Lou Darnell (later of North Carolina) and back Wayne Ubben (later of Wichita State).

In a 1988 letter to Leatherneck magazine, 1stSgt John Thompson Jr. (ret.) of Citrus Heights, Cal., recalled when Ewa defeated the Marine Barracks, 46-6.

"Col. Lewis Puller was tormented by the fact that a group of 'airedales' were trouncing his men," Thompson wrote.

■ **1953:** The Pearl Harbor Marines, coached by Wally Williams (Boston University, El Toro, Camp Lejeune) lost only to the Hawaii 49ers, 28-16, and were runner-up in the University-Armed Forces Conference.

Standouts included tackles Joe Matesic (Indiana, Arizona State) and Willie McClung (Florida A&M, Camp Lejeune), and backs Skippy

Dyer and Mike Michon (Rice, MCRD San Diego).

McClung would play seven seasons in the NFL and one in Canada. Dyer later played for the University of Hawaii and went into Organized Baseball. Michon would letter at Houston in 1956-57.

Kaneohe Bay (2-3), coached by Lt. Col. George Stallings, featured end Joe Connors (William & Mary, Parris Island, Camp Pendleton) and back Bill Jensen (Iowa State). Jensen returned to the Ames, Iowa, school for the 1955 and 1956 seasons.

Marines in 1951 and 1952 had participated in a six-man interservice football league.

Tom Parsons (Navy, Quantico), a Pearl Harbor assistant in 1953, recalled that "television had not made it to the islands and sports drew big crowds."

There were "big turnouts at the Naval Base, where we played our games," Parsons said. "A riot nearly started one afternoon as we were winning, and a very loud Marine spectator stood up and announced, 'After the game, we're all gonna rent a glass-bottom boat and go inspect the fleet.'"

■ **1954:** The Pearl Harbor Marines and Kaneohe Bay combined, and Dyer was All-Marine as Williams' Hawaii Marines lost only to the University of Hawaii, 45-13, and captured the University-Armed Forces Conference title.

The team had 10 players from the two 1953 Hawaii elevens and received six players from MCRD San Diego: ends Max Hawkins and Ron Hoenisch (Wisconsin), tackle Bill Lammes (West Texas), guards Don Davis and Phil Muscarello (Southern Mississippi) and back Arnie Burwitz (Arizona).

■ **1955:** Stawicki's team, despite the loss to Hawaii and 7-7 tie with the Hawaiian Rams, arguably was the best of the postwar teams.

Hawaii, for example, had 11 members of the 1954 MCRD San Diego team plus 11 with other service experience.

Tackle Don Deskins (Adelphi, 1st Marine Division), an All-Marine and All-Sea Service selection at 220 pounds, would play for Quantico in 1956, Michigan in 1958 and 1959 and the Oakland Raiders in 1960.

At the ends, Joe Hubby (MCRD) would play for USC in 1956 and 1957, Merrill Jacobs (St. Mary's, San Francisco State, Quantico, 1st Marine Division) for the Hawaii Marines in 1956 and MCRD in 1957, and Joe Young (St. Benedict's, Marquette, MCRD) at Arizona in 1956 and 1957, briefly in Canada and with the Denver Broncos in 1960-61. Bob Kirkpatrick (Tennessee) had played two seasons at MCRD San Diego.

Also at tackles, 210-pound Dewey Wade (Kansas State, MCRD), would try out with the San Francisco 49ers in 1956 and Joe Ditta (1st Marine Division, Tulane) weighed 231.

At the guards, Howard Evans had two seasons with the Barstow Marines and Joe Logan (Mississippi State, MCRD, Camp Pendleton) would return to Mississippi State for the 1956-58 seasons.

At center were Fred Martin (Arizona, MCRD) and Larry Yonkee (MCRD), who would letter at Wyoming in 1957.

Backs included Gates, John Giangiorgi (Loras, MCRD), who would letter at Bradley in 1956; Carl Gunn (Arkansas, MCRD), Harold Jackson (Southern, 2 seasons with MCRD) and Bob Moneymaker (Santa Barbara State, MCRD), who would letter at San Diego State in 1956.

Deskins, Gates, Jackson, Wade and Young were drafted by NFL teams.

■ **1957:** Maj. Marv "Hoss" Hewlett (Auburn, Duke) coached the Hawaii Marines to a 3-2-1 (or 2-3-1) record, as 210-pound guard Joe D'Agostino (Florida), Daniels, end Dick Gagliardi (Boston College, Quantico), tackle Glover and Wedemeyer (BYU) were All-Marine. Guard Mike Collins, 247-pound tackle Manny Congedo (Parris Island), back Fred Franco (Navy, Quantico), Jazwinski (210), back John Nisbet (Rice, Quantico) and guard Bobby White (Northeastern Oklahoma) were second team.

An assistant coach was Capt. (later general) Charles Cooper (Mississippi, Navy, Quantico).

Conrad Hitchler would play for Camp Lejeune in 1958, and Missouri from 1960-62 — receiving All-America honors his senior year — and three seasons in Canada.

Tackle Bill Frank (MCRD San Diego), a 240-pounder, would letter at Colorado in 1961-62 and play for British Columbia in 1963, the Dallas Cowboys in 1964, Toronto 1965-68 and Winnipeg 1970-76. Glover would star for MCRD San Diego in 1958 and 1959.

End Wilson Allison (Baylor), a 220-pounder; Congedo, D'Agostino, Frank and Gates were NFL draft choices.

■ **1958:** Allen "Scotty" Harris coached the Hawaii Marines to a 4-4 record in their final season of varsity competition.

Congedo was All-Marine, and Collins, end Frank Gallagher and back Harldon Willman (North Dakota State) second team.

End Herb Grenke would play for Wisconsin-Milwaukee in 1961-62 and go into college coaching. At Northern Michigan, he posted a 35-16 record from 1983-87.

Another end, 210-pound Percy Price, would play at Quantico in 1959-60 but be better known for his boxing prowess. He decisioned Muhammad Ali in the 1960 Olympic Trials (Ali's only loss until 1971); and fought 400-plus bouts as a Marine, winning three All-Marine heavyweight titles and two interservice titles (including a decision over Duane Bobick).

Player-coach Pat Ryan (Holy Cross) had quarterbacked Quantico, Camp Lejeune and Barstow and tried out with the Green Bay Packers in 1959.

■ **1959:** Football dropped.

Ewa Marines 1946

Record: 0-6 Schofield Barracks, 46-6 Marine Barracks. (6-3) (incomplete)
Coach: Charles Cornwell (Santa Ana JC- Univ. of San Francisco-USC)
Assistants: Capt. Frank Boyd (Riverside JC-Oregon) (El Toro 1945), Capt. E. Pope
Ends: N.J. Anderson, R.W. Atwater, B.L. DeMuth, R.G. Miller, R.E. Mitchell, Elmore Ravensburg (Xavier of Ohio) (Ga. Pre-Flight 1943, St. Mary's Pre-Flight 1944), P.M. Reynolds, A.W. Rose, D.M. Smith, L. Spandle, W.J. Speisel (Jacksonville NAS), Weise.
Tackles: B.C. Grisson, H.E. Knight, C.R. Kozel, R.H. Lindsay, R.H. Mitchell, J.M. Worthington

Guards: W.P. D'Antonio (Hinds JC), W.B. Bass (Abilene Christian), L.C. Clark, Gobles, L.L. Greenberg, J.S. Hobbs, J.C. Jones, Pope (p-c), R. Rolles, J.J. Schott.
Centers: R.F. Bordelon, V.J. Johnson, F.J. Jones, J.R. Lock
Backs: Boyd (p-c), Cornwell (p-c), L.G. Hubbard, D.J. Jensen, S.G. Jones, G. Lloyd, Tom McAuliffe, D.F. Moore, H.L. Murphy, Eraine Patrias (St. John's of Minn.), S.J. Posluszny (Northeastern), K.B. Scott, D.R. Staley, G.L. Wilson

Pearl Harbor Marines 1946

Record: 6-46 Ewa Marines (incomplete)
Coaches: Lt. Nick Canzona (St. Mary's of Minn.-Notre Dame-Cornell), Lt. D.E. Spencer
Ends: Lou Darnell (later of North Carolina), Poole, Schuetz, Verra
Tackles: Healy, Lowry, Pike, Schweikert, Winters
Guards: Culverhouse, Fayo, Hyde, McGowan, Rathburn, Scarpelli, Schinker, Secrease, Spencer (p-c), Young
Centers: Cochrane, Sewell, Swezozough
Backs: Canzona (p-c), Carlson, Chaplin, Henderson, Slater, Wayne Ubben (later of Wichita St.)

Camp Catlin 1946

Record: 8-14 Ford Island. (8-1) (incomplete). Won Marine title, was runner-up in Hawaiian Service League
Coach: Col. H.L. Brown
Assistants: Navy Lt. (jg.) Les Horvath (Ohio St.) (Heisman Trophy winner 1944), Lt. Tom McKee
Ends: Campbell, Colin Hughes, Don Johansen, Bob Kieffer, John Lopeman (San Francisco CC), Dick Richardson, Jim Turley, Dick Wakeman
Tackles: Dan Bendokas, Don Clark, Chet Kroliowski, Charles Larsen, Clarence Stodghill
Guards: James Barr (Norwich-Cornell), Walter Buetikoffer, Charles Foran, Luther Hodapp, Samson Martin, Jack Moser
Centers: Stan Benson, Ralph Johnson, Garth Sturdevan
Backs: Bob Acree, Bob Bille, Ralph Brown, Warren Flournoy, Martin Gagliano, Marian Gonzales, Horvath (p-c), Ray Isham, Tim Kearns (De Kalb Tch.), Alex Konoff, Maurice Lisman (Elon), Perry Pullins, Angelo Roberto, Marvin Smith, Ralph Wood.

Hawaii Marines 1947

Record: not available. **Coach:** not available.
Roster: end Lou Darnell (later of North Carolina) (played for Hawaiian All-Stars in Navy playoffs)
(incomplete)

Ewa Flying Marines 1947

Record: 0-10 Ford Island. (incomplete) **Coach:** not available.
Roster: back Ed Tillman (Cherry Point 1945-46)
(incomplete)

Kaneohe Bay Marines 1948

Record: 12-33 Ford Island (incomplete)
Coach: not available
Ends: Lou Darnell (later of North Carolina); **tackles:** Babe Garcia (San Diego in the '30s); **guards:** Maury Gilbert.
Darnell named to All-FMF Pacific team.
(incomplete)

Hawaii Marines 1949

Record: not available.
Coach: not available.
Roster: tackle Babe Garcia (San Diego in the '30s); **guards:** Maury Gilbert
(incomplete)
Pearl Harbor Packers defeated Marine Forces, 26-6, 26-7 (not known if Garcia and Gilbert played for Marine Forces.)

Marine teams 1950-52

Records not available

Kaneohe Bay 1953

Record: 13-6 Barber's Point, 19-13 USARPAC, 7-19 Pearl Harbor Marines, 13-40 Pearl Harbor Navy, 0-27 Hawaii 49ers. (2-3)

Coach: Lt. Col. George Stallings (coach Parris Island 1948)
Assistants: Maj. Merle Kime, Maj. Mitch Sadler (Rice) (Camp Lejeune 1948)
Ends: Joe Connors (William & Mary) (Parris Island 1951, Camp Pendleton 1952), John Renshaw, George Smith
Tackles: Jack Adams (Camp Pendleton 1952), Al Hackney (later of Santa Ana JC), John Madden, Myron Wolens
Guards: George Lockett (San Diego 1952), Bob Nichols
Centers: Herb Young
Backs: Ernie Billinovic, Harold Hufford, Bill Jensen (Iowa St.), Stan Kaluahine (Hawaii), Fred Lindy, Lionel "Scooter" Miles, Bob Radford, Howard Seward. **Also:** Hal Berry, R. Hawk
(incomplete)

Pearl Harbor Marines 1953

Record: 13-7 Barber's Point, 7-7 USARPAC, 19-7 Kaneohe Bay, 27-7 Univ. of Hawaii, 16-28 Hawaii 49ers, 47-12 Islanders, 28-6 Pearl Harbor Navy. (5-1-1). Runner-up in University-Armed Forces Conference
Coach: Wally Williams (Boston Univ.) (El Toro 1945, player-coach Camp Lejeune 1950, asst. Quantico 1952)
Assistants: R. Gunderson, Bill Jesse (Montana-Navy) (Quantico 1947-49, San Diego 1950-51), Tom Parsons (Navy) (Quantico 1949-50)
Ends: Doug Andreason, Oscar Bly, George Cordle (Camp Lejeune 1946, Camp Pendleton 1947, Pensacola 1948, Quantico 1949-51), Jim Hull, Ken Oberlin, Nick Phillips, Don Scott
Tackles: Alvin Banta, Ed Buckingham (later of Minnesota), Virgil Humphrey, Tom Krupa, Joe Matesic (Indiana), Willie McClung (Florida A&M) (Camp Lejeune 1952), Charles Nangle
Guards: Leland Chandler, Floyd Guillotte, Tom Lyons, Tom O'Connor, Ed Stanton
Centers: Bill Costello, Bill Davis, Mel Faust, Bill Ward
Backs: Pete Ballaban, Dennis Behunick, Bob Berg, Bob Bonapart, Bernal Crow, Dick Denham, Skippy Dyer (later of Univ. of Hawaii), Earl Jackson, Mike Michon (Rice) (San Diego 1950-52) (later of Univ. of Houston), Bob Miller, Owen Scanlon (Syracuse) (Camp Lejeune 1952), Andy Thrain
(incomplete)

Hawaii Marines 1954

Record: 13-45 Univ. of Hawaii, 19-13 Pearl Harbor Navy, 14-7 Hawaii Rams, 40-6 Army Pacific, 53-0 Honolulu Town Team, 37-7 Pearl Harbor Navy. (7-1) (incomplete) Champion of University-Armed Forces Conference. Andreason, Billovic, Dyer (MVP), Michon, Muscarello and one other played for host team in Hula Bowl.
Coach: Maj. Wally Williams (Boston Univ.) (El Toro 1945, player-coach Camp Lejeune 1950, asst. Quantico 1952)
Assistants: Capt. Bill Jesse (Montana-Navy) (Quantico 1947-49, San Diego 1950-51), Lt. Bill Rowe (Colgate)
Ends: Telly Green, Max Hawkins (San Diego 1953), Ron Hoenisch (Wisconsin) (San Diego 1952-53), Wallace Kim, Jim O'Connor, Nat O'Neal, Lew Sanders
Tackles: Ed Buckingham (later of Minn.), Bob Denton, Al Hackney (later of Santa Ana JC), Hunn, Bill Lammes (West Texas) (San Diego 1952-53), Stan Parr, Bill Robitaille
Guards: Doug Andreason, Chuck Carpenter, Don Davis (San Diego 1953), Phil Muscarello (Southern Mississippi) (San Diego 1953), Rowe (p-c), Charles Williams
Centers: Dick Cook, Bill Ward, John Wynne (Michigan St.) (Camp Lejeune 1952)
Backs: Ernie Billinovic, Carl Bryant, Al Bulano, Arnie Burwitz (Arizona) (San Diego 1952-53), Sam Coppola, Skippy Dyer (later of Univ. of Hawaii), Larry Henderson, Bill Jensen (Iowa St.), Fred Lindy, Mike Michon (Rice) (San Diego 1950-52) (later of Univ. of Houston), Lionel "Scooter" Miles, Don Sutton, Bill Thiry, Al Umstead.
Also: Adams, Brooks, Jim DiBernardo, Heizer, Lyons, Mendiola, Pederson, Price, Ramage, Raphalides, Wade

Hawaii Marines 1955

Record: 7-7 Rams, 38-7 Pearl Harbor Navy, 19-20 Univ. of Hawaii, 27-2 Navy, 1-0 Univ. of Hawaii (forfeit), 34-6 Rams. (4-1-1) Deskins, Evans, Jacobs, Logan, Martin and Wade joined Hawaii All-Stars for Jan. 1 Hula Bowl game.
Coach: Maj. Ted Stawicki (American-Morningside) (Quantico 1946-48, coach Parris Island 1949-50, Camp Pendleton 1953, 3rd MarDiv All-Stars 1954)
Assistants: Ray Davis (Hardin-Simmons) (asst. Quantico 1952-53), Lt. John Karski, Hal Lindfeld (Iowa-Augustana of Ill.) (San Diego 1936-38, asst. Parris Island 1948-50), John Madden

Ends: Joe Hubby (USC) (San Diego 1954), Merrill Jacobs (St. Mary's-San Francisco St.) (Quantico 1953, 1st MarDiv 1954), Wally Kim, Bob Kirkpatrick (Tennessee) (San Diego 1953-54), Jim Smith, Charles Stewart, Joe Young (St. Benedict's-Marquette) (San Diego 1953-54) (later of Arizona)

Tackles: Les Akeo, Gene Arreguy, Bill Clarke (Willamette), Don Deskins (Adelphi) (1st MarDiv 1954) (later of Michigan), Jack Dick, Joe Ditta (Tulane) (1st MarDiv 1954), Dewey Wade (Kansas St.) (San Diego 1953), Clark Wasson

Guards: Joe Bruton, Dick Carpenter, Bill DeBell, Howard Evans (Barstow 1953-54), Corky Gaines, Joe Logan (Mississippi St.) (San Diego 1953-54, Camp Pendleton 1954), Bob Reis (Miami) (San Diego 1954), Dave Sheehan

Centers: Howard Jackson, Fred Martin (Arizona) (San Diego 1954), Al Stashis, Larry Yonkee (Wyoming) (San Diego 1954)

Backs: Ben Addlego, Paul Ancira, Gus Bernard, Bucky Buiano, Elbert Butler, Jim Chavis, Charles DeSadier (1st MarDiv 1954), Jim Donovan, Tom Gates (Oceanside JC-San Bernardino JC, later of Univ. of San Diego and Oregon St.), John Giangiorgi (Loras) (San Diego 1953-54) (later of Bradley), Carl Gunn (Arkansas) (San Diego 1954), Laverne Hall (9th Marines 1954), Jerry Haskins (Oklahoma) (3rd MarDiv 1954), Harold Jackson (Southern) (San Diego 1953-54), Wayne Jett, Tom Kelly, Harry Kon (4th Marines 1954), Joe McNamara, Bob Moneymaker (El Camino JC-Santa Barbara St.) (San Diego 1954), Bob Trader (Virginia)

Hawaii Marines 1956

Record: 13-0 Pearl Harbor Navy, 46-14 Hawaii Rams, 29-0 Pearl Harbor Navy, 19-0 Hawaii Rams, 7-2 Univ. of Hawaii, 6-0 Hawaii Rams, 46-0 Pearl Harbor Navy. (7-0).

Coach: Maj. Ted Stawicki (American-Morningside) (Quantico 1946-48, coach Parris Island 1949-50, Camp Pendleton 1953, 3rd MarDiv All-Stars 1954)

Assistants: Ray Davis (Hardin-Simmons) (asst. Quantico 1952-53), Lt. John Karski, Hal Lindfeld (Iowa-Augustana of Ill.) (San Diego 1936-38, asst. Parris Island 1948-50), Bob Maiden (Colorado St. Tch.) (Quantico 1949, asst. Parris Island 1953)

Linemen: Frank Abernathy (Furman), Angelo Aguiar (San Mateo JC), Mike Arnstein (Stanford), La Monte Baker (Mt. San Antonio JC) (Navy's Iwakuni Toriis 1955), Larry Brown, Dick Carpenter, Bill Clarke (Willamette), Jere Cochrane, Howard Conrad (St. Mary's-USC) (Ft. Ord, Ft. Bragg, San Diego 1955), Darrel Downing (Iowa), John Glover (Camp McGill 1955), Dick Greatorex, Roger Haire (Moorhead), Ron Huston (Drake), Merrill Jacobs (St. Mary's-San Francisco St.) (Quantico 1953, 1st MarDiv 1954), Markel Jones, Bob Marcus, Emil Marquardt (Univ. of Hawaii) (Parris Island 1954-55), Ray Ortiz (San Diego JC), Joe Perry (Syracuse), George Salazar (Pacific) (San Diego 1950), Jim Smith, Don Tippit, Leroy Wenzel (Jacksonville NAS 1953), Jim Wynne (Michigan St.) (Camp Lejeune 1952, San Diego 1955), Joe Young (Connors JC)

Backs: Elbert Butler, Jim Chavis, Al Daniels (later of South Dakota), Marv Fiorini (Cal) (San Diego 1955), Tom Gates (Oceanside JC-San Bernardino JC, later of Univ. of San Diego and Oregon St.), Wayne Glover, Jim Hall, Laverne Hall (9th Marines 1954), Bob Hamma, Jerry Haskins (Oklahoma) (3rd MarDiv 1954), Vince Jazwinski (Brown) (Quantico 1954), Dave Kline (Detroit), Harry Kon (4th Marines 1954), Jim Milne (Missouri) (Quantico 1955), Mike Ricketts (Monterey JC), Joe Rodriguez (New Mexico Highlands), Carl Rohnke, Bob Tafoya, Bob Trader (Virginia), Ken Wedemeyer (BYU)

Hawaii Marines 1957

Record: 7-7 Univ. of Hawaii, 25-0 San Diego St., 7-32 MCRD San Diego, 13-20 MCRD San Diego, 12-14 Rams, 33-0 Rams. (3-2-1 or 2-3-1).

Coach: Maj. Marv Hewlett (Auburn-Duke) (asst. Parris Island 1954-55)

Assistants: Capt. Charles Cooper (Mississippi-Navy) (asst. Quantico 1950), Maj. Hal Lindfeld (Iowa-Augustana of Ill.) (San Diego 1936-38, asst. Parris Island 1948-50), Lt. John Miller (USC) (Quantico 1956)

Ends: Wilson Allison (Baylor) (San Diego 1955-56), Charles Atwater, Ernest Brooks, Dick Gagliardi (Boston College) (Quantico 1955-56), Roger Haire (Moorhead), Conrad Hitchler (later an All-American at Missouri), Wayne Lee, Lump Lombardo (Parris Island 1956), Ray Ortiz (San Diego CC), Lim Salser (San Diego 1956)

Tackles: Manny "Moose" Congedo (Villanova) (Parris Island 1956) (later at Colorado), DeWayne Flannery, Bill Frank (San Diego 1955-56) (later at San Diego CC, Colorado), John Glover (Camp McGill 1955), Ron Ruston (Drake), Harvey Semler, Lou Summerford (Chattanooga) (Parris Island)

Guards: Marion Bundy, Mike Collins (St. Benedict's) (Camp Pendleton 1956), Joe D'Agostino (Florida), Bill Julian, Emil Marquardt (Univ. of Hawaii) (Parris Island 1954-55), Joe Schloderer (East Los Angeles CC-UCLA) (San Diego 1955-56), Bobby White (Northeastern St.)

Centers: Wyllis Fisher (San Diego 1956), Vince Jazwinski (Brown) (Quantico 1955), Dick McNally (Boston Univ.), Joe Petruska

278

Backs: Charles Armstrong (Miami of Ohio), Al Daniels (later of South Dakota), Fred Franco (Brown-Navy) (Quantico 1954-55), Tom Gates (Oceanside JC-San Bernardino JC, later of Univ. of San Diego and Oregon St.), Dick Hedrick, Dave Kline (Detroit), Dave Michael (Vermont), Jim Milne (Missouri) (Quantico 1955), John Nisbet (Rice) (Quantico 1956), Larry Patzer (Purdue), Ed Post (Duke) (Parris Island 1956), Larry Wedemeyer (BYU), Harldon "Jug" Willman (North Dakota St.) (San Diego 1955-56)

Hawaii Marines 1958

Record: 28-23 Univ. of Hawaii, 8-12 Univ. of Hawaii, 0-6 Hawaii Rams, 52-0 Maui National Guard, 6-19 MCRD San Diego, 23-6 Hawaii Rams, 12-14 Hawaii Rams, 64-2 25th Infantry. (4-4)
Coach: Capt. Allen "Scotty" Harris (Ohio St.) (asst. Camp Lejeune, Camp Pendleton 1953-54, coach Okinawa's Sukiran Streaks)
Assistants: Lt. Mike Collins (St. Benedict's) (Camp Pendleton 1956), Lt. Pat Ryan (Holy Cross) (Quantico 1954, Camp Lejeune 1955, coach Barstow 1956-57)
Ends: Frank Gallagher, Herb Grenke (Wartburg; later of Wisc.-Milwaukee), Don Lehman, Carroll Miller, Jimmie Price (Atsugi Navy-Marine Flyers 1957), Percy Price, Fred Sauer (Grand Rapids JC), Len Shafley (Twentynine Palms 1956), Lou Summerford (Chattanooga) (Parris Island)
Tackles: Jim Cavanaugh, Manny "Moose" Congedo (Villanova) (Parris Island 1956) (later of Colorado), Eddie Ervin, DeWayne Flannery, Bill Frank (San Diego 1955-56) (later of San Diego CC, Colorado), Bill Julian, Eddie McCourt (Barstow 1957), Maurice Schoors (Camp Pendleton), Hal Shawver
Guards: Dave Akers (Barstow), Charles Atwater, Collins (p-c), J.A. Haertsch, Clois McClure (College of the Sequoias CC), P.J. Puglise (Miami of Fla.), Joe Schloderer (East Los Angeles CC-UCLA) (San Diego 1955-56), Fred Wiese
Centers: Dick Haggard (William Jewell), James Westmoreland (NW Mississippi JC-Arkansas St.)
Backs: Welles "Butch" Bacon (Barstow 1957), Roger Beattie (Camp Lejeune 1950, Quantico 1955), Rocco Dianno (Temple), Ken Faulkner, Stewart Flythe (St. Paul's of Va.), Phil Harris, Fred Johnson, John Lewis (Shaw) (Okinawa), Don Long (Alabama), Ed Post (Duke) (Parris Island 1956), Ryan (p-c), Warren Sheehan (Northeastern), Bruno Stanistawski (West Virginia), Henry Talamantez (Baylor) (Quantico 1956, Okinawa), Mike Tassian (Nebraska), Harldon "Jug" Willman (North Dakota St.) (San Diego 1955-56)

Hawaii Marines 1959

Dropped football

Ken Norton, the WBC heavyweight champion in 1978 who lost the title to Larry Holmes, played football at Camp Lèjeune

Not Outfought

The teams at Cherry Point might not have set any records but they did establish character.

Generally outweighed and outnumbered, the Flyers had only four winning seasons from 1943 through 1954, when the sport was dropped. And they never did defeat rival Camp Lejeune in seven games (one was a tie). Against Parris Island, the record was 2-6 and against Quantico, 2-4. But few opponents questioned the players' manhood. And some lessons learned on the playing field no doubt were remembered in combat.

Like El Toro, Cherry Point didn't have many college stars or the 6-3, 240-pound growing boys on its side. Instead, the Flyers fielded the mechanics, the clerks, the support people. Seldom were the aviators, top players in their own right, available.

Still, the eastern North Carolina base had its moments.

The 9-6 opening victory over Quantico, the eventual All-Marine champion in 1953, ranks among the Corps' major upsets.

The 1943 team boasted teen-agers Leo Nomellini and Ernie Stautner, both destined for the Pro Hall of Fame (see separate chapter).

The 1948-49-50 teams posted 7-5, 6-5-1 and 6-2-1 records, respectively.

The 1954 team featured All-Service linebacker Chuck Weber (West Chester), who would play and coach in the NFL.

A look at the teams:

■ **1944 (3-7 record):** The schedule and coaching staff were top-drawer. The Flyers played such powers as North Carolina Pre-Flight, Camp Peary, Georgia Pre-Flight, the University of North Carolina, Morris Field (3rd Air Force) and unbeaten Bainbridge Naval Training Center.

The coach was T/Sgt. "Big Jim" MacMurdo from the University of Pittsburgh, who had played four seasons with the Philadelphia Eagles. The associate head coach was the legendary Maurice "Clipper" Smith, who had been George Gipp's center at Notre Dame and had coached at Gonzaga, Santa Clara and Villanova. He joined up at age 45 to take part in the action. After the war, he'd coach the University of San Francisco, the NFL Boston Yanks and Lafayette.

A guard was Maj. Lou Conti (Cornell), to be a '53 assistant and later a general.

■ **1945 (2-8 record):** The team, coached by Capt. Bernard Nygren (San Jose State, the Los Angeles Dons and the Brooklyn Dodgers), can say it scrimmaged the Washington Redskins twice. A back was Joe Geri, later to star at Georgia and with the Pittsburgh Steelers. But the return of players — and Nygren — to civilian life overshadowed the season.

■ **1946 (3-7-1):** M/Sgt. Don Plato, who in service ball had been a player and coach, took over a young and inexperienced team. Only about half a dozen players had college experience. But the Flyers defeated Quantico's first postwar team, 13-7. Tackle John Kreamcheck started on a path that would take him to William & Mary and the Chicago Bears.

■ **1947 (2-6 record):** Kreamchek was among the few bright spots for Coach Ed Berry (Scranton), who would be killed in Korea. For the first time since 1943, the schedule was wholly against service teams.

■ **1948 (7-5 record):** Capt. Jack Sloan, a World War II and Korean aviator, got the most out of the available talent. Led by Kreamchek and center George Vavrek, the Flyers posted their first winning record since '43.

■ **1949 (6-5-1 record):** Jim Tuma, a top Corps basketball coach, lost Kreamchek but added second-team All-Marine tackle Sam Saxton and kept Vavrek and several holdovers, as the Flyers again tackled a 12-game schedule.

■ **1950 (6-2-1 record):** Sloan returned as did 10 players from the '49 team, including Saxton. Reservists called up in August helped. Tom Dockery, a guard, and back Tom Shepherd were second-team All-Marine selections.

■ **1951 (0-8-1 record):** Capt. Jack "Whitey" Lee (Carnegie Tech), who had played for the Steelers and El Toro's 1945 juggernaut, found the cupboard bare as Korean War commitments siphoned off the player pool. The Flyers could tie only a weak Norfolk NAS team, 0-0. Back Tony Kapilewski was second-team All-Marine.

■ **1952 (3-7 record):** Capt. Chuck Abrahams (Simpson), a decorated aviator who had played four seasons at El Toro and Quantico, had better fortune, defeating MCAS, Miami; Norfolk NAS and Patuxent River NAS. By any comparison, however, it was easier than his being rescued 60 miles behind enemy lines in Korea after being shot down.

■ **1953 (6-6):** Besides defeating Quantico, the Flyers downed Parris Island, Norfolk NAS; MCAS, Miami; Ft. Benning and Lawson (Ga.) AFB, for one of their last hurrahs. A 7-2 loss to Lejeune cost them the East Coast Marine championship. End Nick DeRosa (Pittsburgh), tackle Sam Duca (Arizona State) and back Ed Brandenburg were All-Marine. Back George Kinek (Tulane) and tackle J.T. Seaholm (Texas) were NFL draftees as the Flyers finally got some players from PI, MCRD San Diego and Quantico teams.

■ **1954 (1-9 record):** Capt. Robert "Chick" Whalen's was at the helm, and one can imagine how bad it would have been but for Weber and Seaholm. Quarterback Lou Biacchi was second-team All-Marine. The victory was over the Norfolk Navy, 6-0.

■

Talk about upsets: Cherry Point's 1953 victory over Quantico has to be one of the biggest in Marine annals.

Quantico was loaded with college stars, and the offense featured backs such as John Amberg (Kansas), John Hayden Fry (Baylor) and John Pettibon (Notre Dame) and ends Ken MacAfee (Alabama), Frank McPhee (Princeton) and Bob Trout (Baylor). The Virginia team would post a 10-2 record before losing to Ft. Ord and Ollie Matson, 55-19, for the national service title.

Cherry Point had beaten Quantico only once and a number of its losses were lopsided.

So Coach Charles Abrahams and his Flyers surprised Quantico, 9-6, in the season-opener on Angelo Lombardo's touchdown, Paul Russel's extra point and a safety.

The Flyers, despite an influx of players from the 1952 Quantico, Parris Island and San Diego teams, lost five of their next six before finishing with a 6-6 record.

■

The fact that I went out for the 1954 Cherry Point team might tell how bad it was.

The nucleus of the 1953 team was back in civilian life and the Marine Corps hadn't sent much to replace it. El Toro and Miami, other Marine air stations, gave up their programs, and Cherry Point probably should have.

Losses such as 46-13, 33-0, 44-14 and 60-15 were offset only by a 6-0 victory over the Norfolk Navy, hardly a powerhouse.

But one can only ponder how embarrassing the record would have been without tackle Chuck Weber, a virtual one-man team.

How good was he? He was so good he was chosen All-Marine and All-Navy although performing for a team with a 1-9 record that surrendered 267 points.

He was, in a word, awesome.

But he arrived virtually an unknown, although earning Little All-America honors at West Chester (Pa.). He hadn't played for Quantico, where Marine reputations were made.

And instead of commanding a crack platoon in the 2nd Marine Division at Camp Lejeune, he was among a group assigned as, of all things, air intelligence officers to the 2nd Marine Air Wing. This was a long-range move designed to beef up the Corps' G-2 capability after intelligence shortcomings in Korea.

Cherry Point obviously did not mark the end of Weber's football career. He was a linebacker with the Cleveland Browns in 1955-56, the Chicago Cardinals from 1956-58 and the Philadelphia Eagles from 1959-61, which included their NFL title team in 1960. Weber also was an assistant coach for 22 years in the NFL and American Football League with the Patriots 1964-67, Chargers 1968-69, Bengals 1970-75, Cardinals 1976-77, Browns 1978-79, Colts 1980-81 and Chargers 1982-85.

And talk about a franchise player! With Weber in the NFL in 1955, Cherry Point gave up varsity football.

1944

Record: 14-27 N.C. Pre-Flight, 0-20 Camp Peary, 0-33 Georgia Pre-Flight, 14-20 North Carolina, 7-29 Morris Field, 6-0 Camp Lee, 0-33 Jacksonville NAS, 7-50 Bainbridge NTC, 35-0 Chatham Field, 13-0 Camp Lee. (3-7)

Coach: T/Sgt. "Big Jim" MacMurdo (Pitt)

Associate head coach: Maj. Maurice "Clipper" Smith (Notre Dame)

Assistants: WO Charles Glick, T/Sgt. Ed McGee (Columbia), Jack Sloan (Cal)

Ends: Dave Barker, Ed Birkin, Len Clerc, Dennis Gallagher, Francis Hurling (Southern Illinois), Lafayette King (Georgia) (El Toro 1945), Bill Mitchell, Jack Prell, Les Sanborn (Santa Clara), Al Sollay (LSU), Pete Wolkodoff (Buffalo), Alex Xenakis

Tackles: Joe Berkowitz, Art Burke, Mike Cervin (St. Ambrose, Mississippi) (asst. El Toro 1949-50, 1953), Bill Davies (Kent State), Elmer Gagosian, John Gorecynski (St. Louis), Ed Hardy (William & Mary) (El Toro 1945), Lou Mackey, Glenn Nickelsen (Utah State)

Guards: Joe Brazowsky (Keystone JC), Pat Cicala, Lou Conti (Cornell), Gerald Coushore (Bethany of Kansas), Remand David, Tow Dowling (Santa Clara), John Ferguson (Fordham), Leo Gerlach (Northwestern), Ted Hapanowicz (George Washington-Penn-Penn State-Cornell), John Hyle (Georgetown-Cornell) (El Toro 1945; MCAS Santa Barbara 1945), Bill Kennedy, R.E. Snyder, Jim Stone (Ball State), Ray Varanka

Centers: Bob Benham (Morris-Harvey), Sam Brazinsky (Villanova) (El Toro 1945), Larry Davis (Dayton-Penn State) (El Toro 1945), Ed Doucette, Dan Garfinkel, Tom Howes (Knox), George Patrick (North Carolina)

Backs: Don Ahearn, Johnny August (Alabama-North Carolina), Bob Baumann, R. Buchanan (Mississippi), Tom Clavin (Villanova), Bill Foley (Detroit), Charles Frenn, Ed Gallik (Duquesne), Wilford Guite, Walt "Mouse" Halsall (South Carolina) (El Toro 1945; MCAS Santa Barbara 1945), Don Hansen (Rollins), Bob Horton (Missouri), Earl Lambert (Manhattan-Dartmouth), Elwin Leet (Platteville), Hugo Marcolini (St. Bonaventure), Bob McDonald (Nassau JC), Pete Mitchell, Gil Purucker (Peru Teachers) (Camp Lejeune 1943), Ken Reese (Alabama) (El Toro 1945; MCAS Santa Barbara 1945); John Richter (Michigan), Jim Rodich, Don Sullivan, Bill Sweeney, Roy Ward (Tulsa) (San Diego 1943), John Wyckoff (Ohio University)

Also: Cappelle, Cook, Dugee, Socia, Valdetoro, J. Williams

1945

Record: 0-26 Jacksonville NAS, 6-0 Oak Grove Marines, 26-0 Camp Mackall, 0-20 3rd Air Force, 14-20 North Carolina, 0-27 Air Transport Command, 0-27 Camp Peary, 7-27 Camp Lee, 0-7 Camp Peary, 0-41 Kessler Field. (2-8). Game canceled with 1st Air Force. Scrimmaged Washington Redskins twice.

Coaches: Capt. Bernard Nygren (San Jose State), Capt. Charles Wiesenfeld (MIT)

Assistants: Andy Anderson (Nevada), Mike Cervin (St. Ambrose, Mississippi) (asst. El Toro 1949-50, 1953), George Gwinn, Jack Sloan (Cal)

Ends: Patsy Cicala, Herb Dennis (Southeastern Louisiana), Norm Ferrell, Hugh Jackson, Jim Jones (Kent State) (El Toro 1944), John Leitner (South Carolina), Bob Mott (LA Bulldogs), Joe Polce (Geneva, Indiana), W.H. Smith, Cal Steveson (Texas Tech), Carl Tipton

Tackles: George Alevizon (CCNY) (Camp Lejeune 1944), Bill Bloomer (Michigan Normal), Eli Broglio (Ohio State), Joe Cole (Idaho), Bill Davies (Kent State), Holley Heard (LSU-Southwestern Louisiana), Jim Highland (DePauw), Bob Morris, Bob Meyers (Pitt).

Guards: Leon Cartwright, Otis Chapman, Bob Coleman (Oregon State), Jim Dickey (Catawba-Duke), Truman Frazier, Owen Hale (Vanderbilt), J.D. Kelly, Clarence Lumpkin, Marvin Mims, William Ramoath, Bob Stuart, Bernie Watts (North Carolina State)

Centers: John Brown (Citadel), Earl Martin (Ohio State), Don Seaman

Backs: Dave Barbosa, Gene Chadwick (LSU), Joe Clavin (Norwich), Tom Clavin (Villanova), Gil Conner (Willamette), Harry Crocker, Alex Curry (Villanova), Joe Geri (Georgia) (Camp Lejeune 1944), John Grout (Yale) (Camp Lejeune 1944), Alvin Hall (Furmnan), Don Hansen (Rollins), Bob Horton (Missouri), Hardy Johnson, D.M. Kemp, Vince La Paglia (Klamath Falls 1944), Charles Manichia (Texas A&M), John McEvoy (Lawrence Tech), John Owens, James Rearic (Duquesne), Harry Russell, Stan Seneca, Chris Stefan (Ohio University), Bill Sunday (Texas), Ed Tillman, Wiesenfeld (p-c), Bob Williams (Auburn).

1946

Record: 7-29 Catawba, 12-14 Ft. Bragg, 13-7 Quantico, 0-21 Jacksonville NAS, 0-44 Ft. Benning, 12-13 Duke B, 39-0 Norfolk Marines, 0-25 Quantico, 13-6 Ft. Bragg, 0-39 Ft. Benning, 0-0 Norfolk NRS. (3-7-1). Ranked 18th among service teams by Williamson Rating Service.

Coach: M/Sgt. Don Plato (Colgate-St. Lawrence) (Quantico 1941, Jacksonville NAS 1942, coach Ward Island Marines 1943)

Assistants: Capt. George Carter (Bowling Green) (Iowa Pre-Flight), Mike Cervin (St. Ambrose-Mississippi) (asst. El Toro 1949-50, 1953), Shelton

Ends: Roy Bailey (Tulane), F. Berry, Boyd, H.F. Brady, John Flynn, Gonzales, A.J. Hargrove, George Jones, Rouche, B. Sears, Austin Shoemaker, Tom Whicard

Tackles: A. Anderson, James Barry, Joe Boni, Henry Borkowski, Couch, Follansbee, J.J. Hogan, John Kreamcheck (William & Mary), Kemper, John Minick, H.I. Minor, Rhinke, Boyd Sears

Guards: F.J. Clark, Ralph Darnell, M.R. Faith, S.O. Hall, Jack Hogan, Bruce Jamerson, George Lee, C.R. Lester, Frank Mareska, Charles Mongin, P.A. Patelle, G. Rheinbacher, Tom Russo, Bob Silk, J.D. Smith, George Stone, Bob Vollmer, Bill Whitney

Centers: J.R. Halstead, Henry Minor, Gene Thompson, Walter Young, Fred Zumath

Backs: Albanese, Earl Albertazzi, H.B. Ayers, R.E. Baker, Russ Beach, L.B. Branch, R.E. Campbell (Arizona), Carol Cox (Clemson), Jack Hall (Newberry), H.A. Hoerster, Bob Kersey (Purdue), Mallie (Georgia), Bill O'Neal, R. Quinn, R.L. Riggs, Len Robbins, Phil Secrist, Charles Springer, Dallas Stahr, Ben Stokes, B.D. Sweely, Ed Tillman, E.T. Ward

1947

Record: 0-2 Ft. Benning, 26-6 Norfolk NRS, 6-37 Jacksonville NAS, 13-6 Pensacola Hellcats, 7-14 Ft. Bragg, 0-20 Parris Island, 7-53 Ft. Benning, 0-47 Quantico. (2-6)

Coach: Ed Berry (Scranton) (El toro 1946) (KIA)
Assistants: M/Sgt. Mike cervin (St. ambrose-Mississippi) (asst. el toro 1949-50, 19530, Capt. Bob "Smokie" Hayes (Nebraska)
Ends: Bertram, Bill Buescher, John Flynn, George Jones, Chuck Kearns, Bill Kriswell, Emmons Maloney, McCaleb, Rouche
Tackles: John Kreamchek (William & Mary), Charles Reinke, Schillie, Bob Silk, Bernie Weakley, Jim Whitaker, Don Wilcox
Guards: Ralph Antoniello, Norm Boudreau, Frank Clark, Mariano DiPiazza, Howard Lowe, Andy Quasney, Vince Shearin, Ken Wells
Centers: Berry (p-c), Mel Dykes, Farmer, George Hooper, Bob Hospen, Oscar Vail, George Vavrek
Backs: Beauchamp, Al Bernard, Howard Eades, Herb Gholson, Bob Kersey (Purdue), Harold Law, Don Machan, Bill O'Neal, Eraine Patrias (Ewa 1946), George Ring, Phil Secrist, Talkington, Frank Wallington

1948

Record: 13-7 East Carolina, 19-0 Eglin AFB, 6-58 Ft. Bragg, 19-6 Oceana NAS, 38-7 Quonset Point NAS, 31-0 Philadelphia NB, 6-26 Parris Island, 6-26 Jacksonville NAS, 13-40 Camp Lejeune, 56-0 USS Coral Sea, 19-7 Barin Field (Pensacola), 13-19 Miami Frosh. (7-5)
Coach: Jack Sloan (Cal)
Assistant: Mike Cervin (St. Ambrose-Mississippi) (asst. El Toro 1949-50, 1953)
Ends: Paul Garrison; **Tackles:** Jim Couzens, John Kreamchek (William & Mary); **Guards:** NA; **Centers:** Jake Beckman, George Vavrek; **Backs:** Mel Arnold, Jack Christiansen, Al Cullen, Jim Delenge, Bob Kadow, Eraine Patrias (Ewa 1946), Tom Shepherd, Don Thompoulos; **Also:** Cecil Cleveland, Angelo Cosenzo, Diaz, Richard Erickson, Jim Falk, Earl Jackson, Ed Kolczynski, Puckett, Joe Speer, Stark, Ragan Stokes (INCOMPLETE)

1949

Record: 33-0 Edenton MCAF, 0-24 East Carolina, 6-21 Eglin AFB, 0-12 Parris Island, 13-13 Ft. Jackson, 14-0 Jacksonville NAS, 0-29 Camp Lejeune, 21-0 Great Lakes, 47-2 Philadelphia NB, 22-21 Ft. Bragg, 14-7 Little Creek, 13-19 Miami Frosh). (6-5-1). Saxton second team All-Marine.
Coach: Jim Tuma (asst. Miramar MCAS 1946)
Assistant: Lt. Bill Kopas (Quantico 1940-41, El Toro 1946-48), Art Schmagel (Maryville Teachers) (El Toro 1946, Quantico 1946-47, Hawaii A-S 1948)
Ends: C.E. Cleveland, W.E. Phillips; **Tackles:** Bill Leonix, Sam Saxton, Jess Thompson; **Guards:** John Davis, T.H. Dockery; **Center:** Vince Parenti; **Backs:** B.J. Bond, Jack Christiansen, Tony Kapelewski, Frank Michalski, J.B. Moore, Eraine Patrias (Ewa 1946), George Pillon (Detroit) (St. Mary's Pre-Flight, MCAS Miramar 1946, El Toro 1947), Tom Shepherd, Don Thompoulos (INCOMPLETE)

1950

Record: 14-0 Bolling field, 74-0 Aberdeen PG, 20-6 Parris Island, 27-2 Eglin AFB, 6-25 Miami Frosh, 0-0 Camp Lejeune, 12-20 East Carolina, 32-13 Ft. Jackson, 22-12 Little Creek. (6-2-1). Dockery and Shepherd second-team All-Marine.
Coach: Jack Sloan (cal)
Assistants: Lt. Bill Kopas (Quantico 19409-41, El Toro 1946-48), Lt. Eraine Patrias (Ewa 1946), Capt. Art Schmagel (Maryville Teachers) (El Toro 1946, Quantico 1946-47, Hawaii A-S 1948)
Ends: Erfert, Charles Ford, Gilmore, Tom Hoffman (Monmouth), Miller, Phillips, Scanlon
Tackles: Brown, Caplinger, Cook, Nepa, Payne, Sam Saxton, Seagraves, Zerby
Guards: Crossman, T.H. Dockery, Gregory, Chuck Lemire, Montonaro, Musto, Al Pacifico, Razcka, Dick Stanley
Centers: Aielo, Dravis, Middleton, Parente
Backs: Anderson, Bilek, Jack Christiansen, Cosenzo, Cullen, Erickson, Tony Kapelewski, Frank Michalski, Monty, Moran, Nelson, Pickern, George Pillon (Detroit) (St. Mary's Pre-Flight, MCAS Miramar 1946, El Toro 1947), Tom Shepherd, Don Thompoulos, Witkowski

1951

Record: 0-13 Patuxent NAS, 19-30 Bainbridge Navy, 7-69 Camp Lejeune, 14-46 Ft. Eustis, 0-65 Ft. Jackson, 0-45 East Carolina, 7-62 Parris Island, 0-0 Norfolk NAS. (0-8-1, missing result). Kapelewski second team All-Marine.
Coach: Capt. Jack "Whitey" Lee (Carnegie Tech) (North Carolina Pre-Flight 1942, El Toro 1945, coach El Toro 1946, coach Ford Island 1947, coach Edenton 1949)

Assistants: Capts. Irvin Barney, Henry Brandon, Doug Hollingsworth

Ends: Barranger, Brown, Coyne, Cummings, Erfert, Charles Ford, Gilmore, Al Padgett, Smith, Swanson, Winn

Tackles: Bob Buresh, Demalo, Gilbert, Jacoby, Kowalski, Musto, Oettinger, Al Pacifico, Scanlon, Stephens, Tobin

Guards: Cowan, Haas, Chuck Lemire, Martilotti, Megrue, Moretti, Rutnik, Sanders, Sam Saxton, Dick Stanley, Walsh, Wisdom, Zuccaro

Centers: Tony Beatrice (Parris Island 1947-50), Charles Brochu, Childers, Cobb

Backs: Ormand Anderson, Hank Bauer, Bilek, Collins, Collum, Curzon, Daniello, Elder, Erickson, Goodyear, Tony Kapelewski, Leho, Medina, J.B. Moore, Morelko, Rasor, Ken Reese (Alabama) (El Toro 1945, MCAS Santa Barbara 1945), Savage, Stuart, Woods.

1952

Record: 16-7 Miami MCAS, 0-28 Quantico, 0-28 Ft. Eustis, 0-64 Ft. Jackson, 0-59 Parris Island, 14-62 Camp Lejeune, 0-54 Bolling AFB, 0-14 or 0-26 Bainbridge Navy, 45-0 Norfolk NAS, 14-0 Patuxent River NAS. (3-7)

Coach: Capt. Charles abrahams (Simpson0, (El toro 1946-47, Quantico 1948-49)

Assistants: Capt. John Staples (Alabama-North Carolina), Lt. John Sullivan (Niagara) (El Toro 1946-47, athletic officer MCAS Miami 1955), Lt. Bill Sylvester (Butler)

Ends: Bill Best (Florida A&M), Harvey Gilmore, Gary Harvey, Joe Henderson, Chet Meternick, Leighton Nash, Sam Saxton.

Tackles: Dick Hunn, Ed Jedrzejek, Ed Knacksted, Harry Knight, Tony Lewandioski, George Nisbet, Jim Reilly, Dick Rincon, Dewey Shaleen, John Wathen, Jim Wheeler (St. Francis)

Guards: Art Bernardi (Thiel), Ken Bracy, Dick Coffey, Walt Dennison, Stan Drakalich, Tom Marino (Canisius), Chuck Raasch (Western Illinois), Tony Spera, Knox Thompson (Memphis State)

Centers: Charles Brochu, Jerry Brooks, Floyd Murphy, Bob Reed, Steve Vaghy (Iowa)

Backs: Ed Bailey, Lou Caporale, Horace Cooper, Tom Crawforth (Butler), Herald Crowson (Mississippi State), Lee Derrick, Ernest Fiore (Temple), Jim Gardner, John Green, Bob Harrison (South Georgia), Bill Holt, Earl Howell, Len Kubiak (Duquesne), Joe Morelli, Russ Murphy (Winston-Salem), Vince Nagy, Dave Newsome, Derriel Owens, Martin Patterson (Alabama), Charles Roundtree, Stan Rusin, Paul Russell, Roger Stuart, Stan Zuchowski

1953

Record: 9-6 Quantico, 7-8 Little Creek, 0-25 Ft. Jackson, 19-0 Parris Island, 6-33 Bainbridge Navy, 6-21 Ft. Lee, 2-7 Camp Lejeune, 24-6 Norfolk NAS, 0-32 Ft. Eustis, 46-6 Miami MCAS, 54-12 Ft. Benning, 50-12 Lawson AFB. (6-6). DeRosa, Duca and Brandenburg selected All-Marine.

Coach: Capt. Charles Abrahams (Simpson) (El Toro 1946-47, Quantico 1948-49)

Assistants: Guy Campo, Maj. Lou Conti (Cornell), Lt. James Cook, Sgt. Joe Johnson, Maj. Andy Kelly (Georgia Tech)

Ends: John Barnhardt, Bob Benson, Gene Brooks, Nick DeRosa (Pitt) (Parris Island 1952), Tom Healy, Joe Henderson

Tackles: Sam Duca (Arizona State) (MCRD San Diego 1952), George Foley (Holy Cross) (Quantico 1952), Bob Reed, J.T. "Tex" Seaholm (Texas) (MCRD San Diego 1952), Jim Wheeler (St. Francis)

Guards: Art Bernardi (Thiel), Dick Coffey, Hal Kaufman (Purdue), James Kriel, Frank Malack, John Roussos

Centers: Don Agler, John McKendrick, Dick Murphy (Holy Cross), Steve Vaghy (Iowa)

Backs: Ed Brandenburg (Mississippi) (Parris Island 1952), John Cullity (Holy Cross) (Quantico 1952), Joe Kelly, George Kinek (Tulane) (Parris Island 1952), Angelo Lombardo (Purdue), Pete McCord (Alabama), Russ Murphy (Winston-Salem), Martin Patterson (Alabama), Bill Pickett (Pitt)

1954

Record: 7-20 Ft. Lee, 6-0 Norfolk Navy, 14-44 Ft. Eustis, 0-33 Parris Island, 0-13 Bainbridge Navy, 13-46 Quantico, 7-20 Little Creek, 15-60 Bolling AFB, 0-18 Ft. Jackson, 0-13 Camp Lejeune. (1-9).

Coach: Capt. Robert 'Chick" Whalen

Assistants: Jim Craine (Wisconsin), Lt. Norm Goodman (DePauw), Lt. Jim Hays (Toledo)

Ends: Joe Angerio, Harold Bailey, Nate Dunson, Bill Peruskie (New Mexico), Harold Rackliff, Vince Vieten (Hofstra), Bill Wiggins (Auburn)

Tackles: Ken Elmore (Texas Tech-New Mexico), Don Gero, Hodges (Hampden-Sydney), J.T. "Tex" Seaholm (Texas) (MCRD San Diego 1952), Ed Treseler, Charles Weber (West Chester), Raymon Wynn (Texas College)

Guards: Joe Andrew (Southeast Louisiana), John Higgins, Jim Lofton (Vanderbilt), Glen Tribett, Elmer Turner (Arkansas), R.F. Schweigerdt (Mississippi Valley)

Centers: Jess Berry (South Carolina) (Quantico 1953), Jim Hill, Andy Kastak

Backs: Lou Biacchi (Fordham), Bob Craig (Lock Haven), Howard Finney (Harvard), Dick Foster (Vanderbilt), Ed Hicks (Cal), Dayton Lewis (Colorado A&M), Joe Meduri (Western Reserve), Dave Moore (Fairmont), Bill Pickett (Pitt), Norval Powell, Gene Robinson (Lenoir-Rhyne), Dick Scheall, Terrence Sweeney (Colgate), Joe Turman

1955

Football discontinued.

Center George "Socko" Vavrek turned in four seasons for Cherry Point and Quantico.

They Also Played

And there were the bases that might have played just one, or only a few seasons, or might have been in an out-of-the-way location and without a base paper or public information/affairs office to chart and publicize the results. Among these post-1941 teams were:

1958/Alameda Marines

Record: 28-6 Moffett Field, 0-22 McClelland Field, 14-13 Alameda NAS, 7-15 Alameda NAS (incomplete)
Coach: not available; **roster:** not available

1944/Eagle Mountain Lake (Texas) Rangers

Record: 0-6 Bryan AAF, 7-0 John Tarleton, 6-6 Beaumont Hospital, 19-6 Beaumont Hospital, 0-6 Ellington Field, 0-33 Ellington Field, 0-20 Blackland AAF (2-4-1)
Coach: not available. **Backs:** Roger Roggatz (Drake); **roster:** not available

1949/MCAF, Edenton (N.C.)

Record: 0-80 Elon, 0-67 East Carolina, 0-30 NAS Jacksonville, 0-33 Cherry Point (incomplete)
Coach: Jack Lee (Carnegie Tech, Georgia Pre-Flight 1942, El Toro 1945, El Toro coach 1946, Ford Island coach 1947)
Roster: not available

1954/Edenton
Record: not available; **player-coach:** Wit Bacauskas (Columbia, Quantico 1950, Camp Lejeune 1951, Pensacola 1952); **roster:** not available

MD Fallbrook/1944

Record: 2-53 NAB Coronado B team, 13-48 NAB Coronado B
Coach, assistant: not available
Players: B Kusner
(INCOMPLETE)

1947/Great Lakes Marines

Record: 14-0 Glenview NAS, 18-0 Chicago Torpedoes, 0-7 Elgin Torpedoes (incomplete)
Coach: not available; **ends:** Steponaitis, Weddington; **kicker:** Briggs; **backs:** Macomber, Nelson, Robertson, Wilson
(incomplete)

1948/Marine Barracks, NAD, Hawthorne (Nev.)

Record: 0-88 Lassen JC (incomplete)
Coach: not available; **roster:** not available

1952/Hawthorne
Record: 6-6 Lassen JC, 13-0 Lassen JC (incomplete)
Coach: not available; **roster:** not available

1953/Hawthorne
Record: 0-43 Barstow, 7-12 NOTS China Lake, 13-6 NOTS China Lake, 22-0 Lassen JC, 34-0 Lassen JC, 13-19 Mather AFB (3-3)
Coach: Charles Hall; **assistant:** not available.
Ends: Don Garner, Buddy Gettings, Andy Watson; **tackles:** Ed Fox, George Kinmouth, Charles Nyte, Paul Rodarte, Dick Schuler, Darryl Thurston; **guards:** Ray Brown, Kay McShane, Ken Roach, George Williams; **centers:** Francis Poole, Dick Temple, Jennings Warn; **backs:** John Barth, Larry Fields, Dick Heidebrink, George Lenston, W. McCormack, Levi Matthews, Bob Rippstein, Al Spriggs, John Tapscott

1944/New Orleans Officers Transportation School (Sea Raiders)

Record: 0-35 Tulane, 0-47 Arkansas A&M, 0-20 Louisiana Normal, 7-19 Gulfport Navy, 0-72 Louisiana Tech, 0-21 Algiers Navy, 18-0 LaGarde Hospital, 0-27 Gulfport AAF (1-7)
Coach: Al Pesacky; **assistant:** not available
Ends: Lineberry, Neil; **tackles:** Lincoln, Rogers; **guards:** D.C. Smith, F.W. Wright (Idaho St.); **centers:** J.W. Olson; **backs:** not available
(incomplete)

Norfolk Marines/1943

Record: 6-27 Apprentice School, 7-74 Richmond, 0-72 William & Mary, 0-40 Camp Lee, 6-55 Camp Lejeune, 0-20 Richmond AAB, 0-40 Richmond AAB, 0-18 Ft. Monroe, 6-44 Ft. Monroe (0-9)
Coach: not available
Ends: Bloomer (St. Joseph's), Elwood, Fee, Shelor, Smith, Swerock; **tackles:** Blythe, Hay, Knepper, Melonya, Nixon (Boston College); **guards:** Gaizunas, Pizza, Sullivan, Von Bergen; **centers:** Bartoshevich, Moharski; **backs:** Adams, Brooks, Fernadez, Gratton, Hill (Penn), Holieb, Lapp (Franklin & Marshall), Pledge, Elmer Sullivan, Wolf, Zeiders

Norfolk/1946

Record: 0-39 Cherry Point (incomplete)
Coach: not available; **roster:** not available

Norfolk/1948

Record: 0-42 Camp Lejeune (incomplete)
Coach: not available; **roster:** not available

Norfolk/1953

Record: 0-48 Ft. Belvoir, 17-35 Little Creek (incomplete)
Coach: not available; **roster:** not available

1945/Oak Grove (N.C.) Marines

Record: 0-20 Catawba, 0-6 Bogue Field, 0-6 Cherry Point, 10-6 MCAS Kinston, 7-0 Ft. Monroe, 0-0 NAS Oceana, 20-6 Camp Mackall (3-3-1)
Coach: Lt. E.W. Sackett; **assistant:** not available
Ends: Flynn, Tom O'Conner; **tackles:** Areas, Cecessa, Piel; **guards:** Archumbadit, Pete Grabareyak; **centers:** Woodall; **backs:** Ball, Morris, Popp, Shea, Woody Woodward
(incomplete)

1952/Department of Supply, Philadelphia

Record: 21-7 Dover AFB (incomplete)
Coach: not available; **roster:** not available

1953/Philadelphia

Record: 6-14 Cape May CG, 7-0 Southwest AC, 13-0 Williamston AC, 0-7 State Teachers College, 14-20 NAS Atlantic City, 20-20 Dover AFB, 13-26 Ashland Miners (2-4-1)
Coach: J. Morrell; **assistant:** K.B. Neal
Ends: E.C. Adams, E.W. Conrad, R.R. Gellette, W. Quinibar, B.G. Ramsey, R.R. Starr; **tackles:** J.S. Barshatsky, A.J. Florian, G.H. Ligaie, S. Long, R. Migliarese, J.M. Tharp; **guards:** V.C. Dutcher, J.N. Fletcher, H. Lauche, R.P. Perry, G.R. Tilghman, R.H. Wilson; **centers:** S. Cook, E.R. Davis, T.A.E. Thom; **backs:** L.A. Buynum, Dorrycott, J. Edwards, T.M. Forry, J. Glenn, Jack Goldsteen, H.R. Haves, Len Mengwasser, W. Payne, Stechishim, H.J. Vincent, R.L. Weidner

1953/Marine Barracks, Port Chicago (Cal.)
(might be 8-man)

Record: 6-40 USS Philippine Sea, 14-30 Moffett Field, 7-0 Western Sea Frontier, 0-21 NAS Oakland, 0-14 NSC Oakland, 14-7 San Francisco Marines, 21-12 Oakland Naval Hospital, 30-7 District Communications, 0-7 Mare Island Naval Shipbuilding, 30-28 Treasure Island, 6-32 NAS Alameda (5-6)

Coach: not available; **assistant:** not available
Ends: Richard Burns, Cedric Clayton, Goodrich; **tackles:** mot available; **guards:** not available; **centers:** Ed Kahaunaete, Sam Lofton; **backs:** Medeiros, Plaster, Rayner, Robinson, Sham, Vierra, Watson, Mel Wyer

1954/Twentynine Palms

Record: 6-47 Redlands, 7-38 Barstow, 0-6 Cal Baptist (incomplete)
Coach: not available; **roster:** not available

1957/Twentynine Palms
Record: 6-33 Barstow, 32-57 Barstow (incomplete)
Coach: not available; **roster:** not available

1959/Twentynine Palms
Record: 28-0 MCAF Tustin, 32-0 MCAF Tustin, was to play 11th Marines (Camp Pendleton) in Cannoncocker Bowl at Twentynine Palms on Thanksgiving (incomplete)
Coach: not available
Linebackers: Wells; **backs:** Bertram Brown, Tank Moore
(incomplete)

1984/Twentynine Palms
Record: cancelled game with Desert JC

Other scores

1942: El Centro JC 12, El Centro Marines 7
1949: Ft. Benning 74, Rome (Ga.) Marine Reserve 0
1950: Ft. Story 29, Marine Forwarding Depot 0
1953: Marine Forwarding Depot 20, NAS Chincoteague 6
503rd MP Battalion (Ft. Bragg) 20, 10th Marines (Camp Lejeune) 6
1955: Highland JC, St. Joseph (Mo.) Marines 0

Marines' Names Live On

The names of Marines live on through scholarships and awards.

The Byron H. Chase Memorial Trophy, for example, is "presented annually to the outstanding offensive and defensive linemen" at San Diego State.

Lt. Chase, a tackle at Quantico in 1951, was killed in action in Korea. He was awarded a Silver Star.

The Stephen D. Joyner Memorial Award is presented annually at Fullerton (Calif.) College to the "most inspirational athlete."

Lt. Joyner, a Grid-Wire JC All-America end at Fullerton, also played at San Diego State. He was killed in action in Vietnam.

The Eddie LeBaron Award has been presented annually since 1953 to an athlete at Pacific to honor "outstanding scholarship." One award winner was former Raiders coach Tom Flores. The award is made possible by a donation by Ralph Edwards of the "This Is Your Life" TV series.

Lt. LeBaron, who quarterbacked Quantico's 1950 team, was awarded the Bronze Star for heroism in Korea.

The Robert McCahill Award goes annually to a Marquette senior "who has shown outstanding leadership, scholarship and athletic ability."

Capt. McCahill was killed on Iwo Jima.

289

All-Marine Selections

All-Marine. The words conjure an image of toughness, of fitness, of strength, of honor.

And from 1947 through 1965 — with the exception of 1962 during the Cuban missile crisis — they also signified selection to a special fraternity of players: the best in the Marine Corps.

For some, it was a springboard to later success on the gridiron; for some, it was a stop between the college and the pro ranks; for others it was the pinnacle of their football careers.

"It may not satisfy all hands, but then all-star teams seldom do," the Leatherneck magazine wrote in announcing its first team.

Chosen by the sports staff of Leatherneck and/or coaches, the teams boasted such college stars as Harry Agganis (Boston University), Ron Beagle (Navy), King Dixon (South Carolina), Steve Eisenhauer (Navy), Worth Lutz (Duke), Frank McPhee (Princeton), John Pettibon (Notre Dame), J.D. Roberts (Oklahoma), Tom Singleton (Yale) and Sam Valentine (Penn State).

But perhaps it was in the pro arena that the All-Marines were most visible. For example, quarterback Ed Brown played 12 years in the National Football League, and quarterback Eddie LeBaron 11 years in the NFL and one in the Canadian Football League.

End Bob Dee put in 10 years in the NFL and the American Football League.

Guard Ted Karras and end Bob Schnelker each played in the NFL nine seasons.

Lasting eight years were tackle Frank Morze (NFL), end Jim Mutscheller (NFL), tackle Hank Schmidt (NFL, AFL) and center Bob Whitlow (NFL).

Other long-term pros were:

■ **Seven years:** tackle Jim Weatherall (CFL, NFL) and linebacker Chuck Weber (NFL).

■ **Six years:** back Gene Filipski (NFL, CFL), linebacker Bob Griffin (NFL, AFL), end Ken MacAfee (NFL) and back Billy Martin (NFL, CFL).

■ **Five years:** linebacker Rob Goode (NFL), guard Weldon Humble (AAFC, NFL), back Skeet Quinlan (NFL) and tackle Walt Szot (NFL).

And center Bill Jesse (Navy) was the only player selected five times, at Quantico 1947-48-49 and San Diego 1950-51.

"Jesse became the only gridder in Leatherneck's annals to earn a first-string nomination for five consecutive seasons," the magazine wrote in announcing his selection to the 1951 team. "At the end of the '51 season, Bill hung up his '41' and departed for the Korean hinterlands."

(Jesse left the Corps in the 1960s and ultimately became a dean at Allan Hancock College in Santa Maria, Cal. At age 60 he retained his athletic build and looked as though he could take the field again at any time.)

Selected four times was Quinlan (MCRD San Diego 1947-48-49-50).

Three-time first-team selections were back Joe Bartos, end Ron Beagle, back Alvin Hall, end Holly Hollingshead, guard-tackle Randy "Tex" Lawrence, guard Tony Stremic and center John Yohn.

Tackle John Glover, end Jim Mora and back Russ Picton were chosen twice on the first team, once on the second team. Guard Bill Butler, tackle John Hamber and back Gene Moore twice were chosen on the second team, once on the first team.

Players chosen on the first team received a statuette and a certificate.

But because of college rules changes, the size of the teams might vary. From 1947 through 1951, there was simply a first team and a second team.

In 1952, Leatherneck chose an offensive team and one for defense. Then from 1953 through 1956 it was back to first and second teams. In 1957 the magazine selected 22-man first and second teams. There was an 11-man 'A' squad plus an 11-man 'B' squad in 1958, and a 22-man Leatherneck squad in 1959. Leatherneck chose an 11-man team in 1960 and 1961, a 12-man team in 1963 (included a kicker), an 11-man team again in 1964, and offensive and defensive teams in 1965.

There were no all-Marine teams during World War II or the latter part of the Vietnam War. Thus, the likes of Bob Dove, Paul Governali, Crazylegs Hirsch, Les Steckel and Wee Willie Wilkin never were chosen.

Two players became generals: Ernie Cheatham, a former linebacker for NFL Steelers and Colts, and tackle John Hopkins, a standout at Navy.

And at least two died in combat: linebacker Bruce Capel (Illinois) and end Bob Smith (Navy).

The team was all-white in nature until 1952 when the first blacks, back Tom Carodine, tackle Art Davis and defensive back Orville Williams, broke the racial barrier. From then on, blacks were represented with regularity.

And Quantico, with its new second lieutenants fresh from the college ranks, and San Diego, with the pick of the new — and often mammoth — recruits, generally monopolized the selections.

The announcement of the honorees was accompanied by a review of the season, such as "Pendleton was the best in the West, and both Lejeune and Quantico earned Eastern plaudits" in 1956, and "Marine gridmen won two bowl titles," in 1959.

Or have a cliche-laced lead saved all season, such as "Imagine, if you can, the coach of a football team which has a Sherman tank at fullback, two battering rams at the halfbacks, a quarterback with the accuracy and range of the Polaris missile, and a line with the speed and durability of seven Ontoses," such as in 1964.

The selections:

Charles Abrahams T (El Toro 1947-2nd team, Quantico 1948, Quantico 1949-2nd), Bob Adelizzi C (Quantico 1958-2nd), Harry Agganis B (Camp Lejeune 1950-2nd), Ray Alberigi H (Quantico 1957-2nd, 1958-2nd), George Allen G (San Diego 1954, 1955-2nd), John Amberg B (Quantico 1953), Dick Ambrogi B (Quantico 1948-2nd), Granny Amos H (Quantico 1965), Art Anderson T (San Diego 1959, 1960), Mel Anderson H (Camp Lejeune 1959, 1961), Tony Anthony T (Quantico 1958).

Wit Bacauskas G (Camp Lejeune 1951-2nd), Dick Banky T (San Diego 1964), Wes Barrette B

(Camp Pendleton 1947-2nd), Glenn Barrington (USN) B (Quantico 1947), Don Bartolazzi E (Camp Lejeune 1965), Joe Bartos B (Quantico 1947, 1948, Camp Pendleton 1949), Don Bazemore G (Quantico 1947-2nd), Ron Beagle E (Quantico 1957, Okinawa 1957, Camp Lejeune 1958), Fred Beasley H (Camp Lejeune 1958-2nd), Tony Beatrice C (Parris Island 1949-2nd), Roger Beckley T (Camp Lejeune 1957-2nd, Okinawa 1958-2nd), John Bergamini C (San Diego 1953-2nd), Ted Bertagni G (Camp Pendleton 1947-2nd), Lou Biacchi B (Cherry Point 1954-2nd), Don Bingham B (Quantico 1954, Camp Lejeune 1955), Clark Blake F (Camp Lejeune 1965), Rex Boggan T (Parris Island 1952, Camp Lejeune 1953), Ron Botchan G-T (Quantico 1958, 1959), Pat Boyle G (Quantico 1947), Ed Brandenburg B (Cherry Point 1953), John Breiten T (Quantico 1965), Don Brinkman F (Barstow 1957-2nd), Dan Brogee E (San Diego 1950), Ernie Brooks E (San Diego 1959), Ed Brown B (Camp Pendleton 1953-2nd), Ed Brown G (San Diego 1951), Ernie Brown B-Q (Camp Lejeune 1956, Lejeune 1957-2nd), Fred Bucci G (Quantico 1956, 1957), Gil Bucci G (Parris Island 1952, PI 1953-2nd), Elbert Bullock G (San Diego 1958), Bill Butler G (San Diego 1949, SD 1949-2nd, SD 1950-2nd), Frank Butsko T (Quantico 1961).

Bob Callahan G (Camp Lejeune 1957-2nd), John Callard B (Camp Pendleton 1954-2nd), Doug Cameron B-F (Quantico 1956, 1957), Whitey Campbell B (Parris Island 1950-2nd), Bruce Capel LB (Quantico 1965) (KIA), Tom Carodine B (San Diego 1952), Donn Carswell G (San Diego 1960), Ron Case G (Camp Lejeune 1964), Jim Cauthron C (San Diego 1954-2nd), Al Chapman F (San Diego 1959), Ned Chappell T (Camp Lejeune 1965), Ernie Cheatham T (San Diego 1956), Ron Cherubini T (Quantico 1958-2nd), Mike Collins G (Hawaii 1957-2nd, 1958-2nd), Manny Congedo T (Hawaii 1957-2nd, 1958), Ed Conti LB (Quantico 1965), George Cordle E (Quantico 1949-2), Mike Cotten Q (Quantico 1965), Tom Cox E (Quantico 1965), Ed Craig C (Camp Lejeune 1965).

Joe D'Agostino G (Hawaii 1957), Don Daly B (Camp Lejeune 1956), Jack Damore C (Quantico 1955-2nd, 1956), Al Daniels H (Hawaii 1956-2nd, Hawaii 1957), Art Davis T (Camp Lejeune 1952), Jim Davis C (Quantico 1963), Tom Dawson E (Quantico 1947-2nd, Camp Lejeune 1948), Bob Dee E (Quantico 1955-2nd, 1956-2nd), John Dekleva G (Camp Pendleton 1958-2nd), Jim Delaney T (San Diego 1950-2nd), Nick DeRosa E (Cherry Point 1953), Don Deskins T (Hawaii 1955), King Dixon H (Quantico 1959, 1960), Tom Dockery G (Cherry Point 1950-2nd), Joe Donahue T (Quantico 1947-2nd), Bob Dove B (Quantico 1947-2nd), Sam Duca T (Cherry Point 1953), Phil Duplar F (Quantico 1959), Skippy Dyer B (Hawaii 1954).

Paul Ehrman G (San Diego 1964), Joe Eilers T (Quantico 1963), Steve Eisenhauer G (Quantico 1954, Pensacola 1955), Jerry Elliott E (Parris Island 1952), Bill Eysenbach G (Parris Island 1948).

Bob Farrell B (Quantico 1950-2nd), Bob Fierke T (Camp Pendleton 1948), Gene Filipski B (Quantico 1955-2nd), Frank Finizio F (San Diego 1964), Willis Fjerstad H (Camp Lejeune 1957-2nd), Rudy Flores Q (Quantico 1948, Quantico 1949-2nd), Lou Florio T (Camp Lejeune 1955-2nd), Fred Franco B (Quantico 1955, Hawaii 1957-2nd), Bill Franklin G (El Toro 1947), Chet Franklin G (Quantico 1958), Harrison Frasier E (Camp Lejeune 1952), Dick Frasor C (Camp Lejeune 1956-2nd), Don Fullam E (Quantico 1954-2nd).

Dick Gagliardi E (Hawaii 1957), Frank Gallagher E (Hawaii 1958-2nd), Edward Galloway C (San Diego 1947-2nd), Don Gautreau G (Camp Lejeune 1956), Phil Gehringer T (Camp Lejeune 1965), Nick Germanos E (Quantico 1958-2nd), Umberto Gigli T (Camp Lejeune 1948-2nd), Johnny Glover T (Hawaii 1957, San Diego 1958-2nd, 1959), Dennis Golden T (Quantico 1964), Rob Goode LB-B (San Diego 1952, El Toro 1953), Glen Graham C (Camp Lejeune 1953), Don Gray C (Camp Pendleton 1948-2nd), George Greco B (Quantico 1949-2nd), John Gregerson G (San Diego 1948-2nd), John Gremer G (San Diego 1957-2nd), Bob Griffin LB (San Diego 1952), Dick Guy T (Camp Lejeune 1958-2nd).

Tom Hague E (Quantico 1955-2nd), Alvin Hall H (San Diego 1957, 1958, 1959), Lou Hallow C (Camp Lejeune 1957), Jack Hamber T (Quantico 1954-2nd, Quantico 1955, Camp Pendleton 1956-2nd), Roscoe Hansen T (Parris Island 1952), Ernie Hargett E (Quantico 1948, Camp Lejeune 1949), Bob Havard T (San Diego 1949), Bill Hawkins B (Quantico 1950), Billy Hayes B (Parris Island 1951, 1952), Dave Hayes H (Quantico 1964), Charlie Heard E (Camp Lejeune 1963), Bob Heck E (Quantico 1950-2nd), Carey Henley H (Camp Lejeune 1958-2nd), Charles Henry B (Camp Pendleton 1949-2nd), Ed Heuring T (Quantico 1961), Claude Hipps B (Camp Lejeune 1948-2nd), Homer Hobgood C (Camp Lejeune 1958), Tim Holden LB (Quantico 1965), Marshall Hollingshead E (Quantico 1959, 1960, San Diego 1961), John Hopkins T (Quantico 1957), Jay Huffman G (Quantico 1963, 1964), Weldon Humble G (Quantico 1951), Bob Hunemiller G (Camp Pendleton 1949-2nd), Dan Hunter T (Parris Island 1951-2nd), Ken Huxhold T (Camp Pendleton 1953-2nd).

John Idoux G (El Toro 1951-2nd), John Idzik DB (Parris Island 1952).

Harold Jackson B (San Diego 1954-2nd), Jake Jacobs E (Hawaii 1957-2nd), Vince Jazwinski C (Hawaii 1957-2nd), Harry Jefferson B (Quantico 1958), Bill Jesse C (Quantico 1947, 1948, 1949, San Diego 1950, 1951), Eddie Johns G (Camp Pendleton 1956-2nd), Bob Johnson H (Camp Lejeune 1965), Cleveland Jones E (San Diego 1963, 1964).

Harry Kahuanui E (San Diego 1951), Tony Kapelewski B (Cherry Point 1951-2nd), Duke

292

Karnoscak C (Camp Pendleton 1958-2nd, San Diego 1959), Ted Karras G (San Diego 1957), Gordie Kellogg B (Quantico 1956-2nd), Carl Kilsgaard T (San Diego 1950), Al Knighten H (Barstow 1957-2nd), Cas Ksycewski T (Quantico 1950-2nd).

Don Laaksonen F (Quantico 1958), Dick Iashley G (Parris Island 1952), Darrell Lasater T (Camp Lejeune 1965), Randy Lawrence G-T (Quantico 1949, 1950, San Diego 1952), Steve Lawrence E (Quantico 1965), Eddie LeBaron B (Quantico 1950), Reggie Lee B (Camp Lejeune 1953-2nd), John Leroy G (Parris Island 1949), Frank Letteri T (Camp Lejeune 1951), Buddy Lewis T (San Diego 1957), Bob Logal E (El Toro 1947), Joe Losack E (Quantico 1958, Camp Lejeune 1960), Dick Lucas E (Quantico 1957), Worth Lutz B (Quantico 1955, 1956).

Ken Mac Afeee E (Quantico 1953-2nd), Larry Magilligan Q (Quantico 1958-2nd), Bill Marker E (Camp Pendleton 1948-2nd), Bob Marshall F (San Diego 1960), Billy Martin H (San Diego 1958, 1960), Russ Mather G (San Diego 1954-2nd), Tom Maudlin Q (Quantico 1960, San Diego 1961), John Maultsby G (Camp Lejeune 1953-2nd), Art McCaffray T (Quantico 1951-2nd), Bob McElroy E (Quantico 1949-2nd, 1950), John McGinley G (Quantico 1959), Jim McGowan DB (Quantico 1965), Frank McPhee E (Quantico 1953, Camp Pendleton 1954), Tom Meehan T (Quantico 1959), Ernie Merk H-F (San Diego 1957, 1958-2nd), Tony Messina B (Quantico 1947-2nd), Ron Meyer G (Quantico 1965), Bob Meyers (Quantico 1953-2nd, Camp Lejeune 1954), John Michon B (San Diego 1951-2nd), Charles Milam T (Camp Pendleton 1947), Bob Miller B (Camp Pendleton 1955-2nd), Billy Mixon B (Parris Island 1951, 1952), Gene Moore B (San Diego 1947-2nd, San Diego 1948), Jim Mora E (Quantico 1957-2nd, Camp Lejeune 1958, 1959), Morton Moriarity E (San Diego 1952-2nd), Frank Morze T (Camp Lejeune 1956), Jim Mutscheller E (Quantico 1952).

Herb Naaken H (Camp Lejeune 1958), Ron Nay DB (Camp Lejeune 1965), Marshall Newman Q (Camp Lejeune 1958, 1959), Pinky Nisbet Q (Hawaii 1957-2nd), Bernie Norem G (Quantico 1949).

Hugh Oldham H (San Diego 1963), Pete Optekar G (Quantico 1963, 1965).

John Parrinello F (Camp Lejeune 1961), Tom Parsons C (Quantico 1950-2nd), John Pettibon B (Quantico 1953), Dick Petty C (Camp Pendleton 1955), Ray Pfeifer E (Camp Pendleton 1947-2nd, 1951-2nd), Bayard Pickett B (Parris Island 1947), Dick Pickett B (San Diego 1956-2nd), Russ Picton B (Parris Island 1948-2nd, Parris Island 1949, Camp Lejeune 1951), Steve Piskach B (Quantico 1954), Howie Pitt E (Camp Lejeune 1955), Carl Plantholt G (Camp Lejeune 1952), Ed Post B (Parris Island 1956-2nd), Bob Prather T (Quantico 1948-2nd), Jimmy Pyles F (San Diego 1957, 1958)

Skeet Quinlan B (San Diego 1947, 1948, 1949, 1950).

George Radosevich C (Parris Island 1952), Jim Ray B (Parris Island 1954-2nd), Ed Rayburn T (Quantico 1956-2nd), Art Redden H (Camp Lejeune 1963), Tom Reis H (Quantico 1957-2nd), Bob Richter E (El Toro 1948-2nd), Billy Riggins C (Parris Island 1951-2nd), Vic Rimkus G (Parris Island 1955), Ted Ringer C (Quantico 1957-2nd), Bill Roberts B (Camp Lejeune 1955-2nd), Carrol Roberts E (San Diego 1959), Piggy Robinson E (San Diego 1957-2nd, 1958-2nd), J.D. Roberts G (Quantico 1955-2nd), Willie Roberts E (Camp Pendleton 1953-2nd, 1954-2nd), Hosea Rodgers B (Quantico 1950), Perry Rodrique F-H (San Diego 1963, 1964), Darryl Rogers B (San Diego 1958-2nd), Ed Romankowski B (Camp Lejeune 1951-2nd), Jim Ross E (Camp Lejeune 1964), Jim Royer T (Quantico 1957-2nd), John Rushing E (Camp Pendleton 1956), Pat Ryan Q (Barstow 1957).

Joe Sabol B (Camp Pendleton 1947-2nd), Tony Santaniello G (Quantico 1958-2nd), Sam Saxton T (Cherry Point 1949-2nd), Hank Schmidt T (San Diego 1957), Bob Schnelker E (Parris Island 1952), Jim Schwartz G (Camp Lejeune 1958-2nd), Bob Scott G (Parris Island 1950), Don Scott S (Quantico 1952), John Scott T (San Diego 1958), Don Seager H (Quantico 1958-2nd), Tom Shepherd B (Cherry Point 1950-2nd), Tom Singleton B (Quantico 1963, San Diego 1964), Bob Smith E (Parris Island 1950-2nd) (KIA), Ray Smith B (Camp Lejeune 1953-2nd), Art Specht E (Camp Pendleton 1949), Paul Stephenson G (Quantico 1950), Jack Stilwell E (San Diego 1957, 1958), Ed Strange C (San Diego 1957), Tony Stremic G (Quantico 1958, 1959, San Diego 1961), Ed Stuckrath LB (Quantico 1965), Ray Suchy G (Camp Pendleton 1953), Paul Sweezey E (Parris Island 1947-2nd, Camp Lejeune 1951), Steve Szabo DB (Quantico 1965), Walt Szot T (Camp Pendleton 1951).

Don Tate G (Camp Lejeune 1956-2nd, Lejeune 1957), Clem Thomas T (Quantico 1947), Dick Thomas B (Camp Lejeune 1949), Greg Thomasson T (Quantico 1958), Bob Timberlake E (Quantico 1958-2nd), Ed Tokus T (Parris Island 1954), Bob Tougas B (Camp Lejeune 1951), Herb Travenio K (San Diego 1963).

Sam Vacanti B (Parris Island 1951-2nd, 1952), Vern Valdez Q (San Diego 1958, 1959), Sam Valentine C-G (Quantico 1958, Camp Lejeune 1959), Carl Valletto T (Parris Island 1955-2nd), Stu Vaughn H (Quantico 1959), Walt Vellieu T (Camp Pendleton 1954-2nd), Al Viola G (Camp Lejeune 1952, Quantico 1953).

Art Wallace G (Quantico 1961), Pete Walski Q (San Diego 1957), Paul Ward T (San Diego 1960), Sam Ward E (Camp Pendleton 1955), Bob Warren E (Camp Lejeune 1956-2nd), Dick Washington B (San Diego 1955-2nd), Gene Watto G (Camp Lejeune 1954-2nd), Jim Weatherall T (Barstow 1953-2nd), Charles Weber T (Cherry Point 1954), Ken Wedemeyer H (Hawaii 1957), Marvin Weitz T

(Barstow 1957-2nd), Jerry Wenzel C (Camp Lejeune 1954), John Whalen T (Quantico 1963), Bobby White G (Hawaii 1957-2nd), Bob Whitlow G (San Diego 1959), Orville Williams DB (Camp Lejeune 1952), Jug Willman H (Hawaii 1958-2nd), Norm Wilson E (Barstow 1957-2nd), Woody Wilson E (Camp Lejeune 1965), James Wimberg T (Quantico 1948), Pete Winebrake G (Camp Lejeune 1960), Kelton Winston H (San Diego 1961), Chuck Wyss B (Camp Pendleton 1955).

John Yohn C (Quantico 1959, 1960, San Diego 1961), Joe Young E (San Diego 1954).

George Zadjeika E (Quantico 1961).

Lt. Eddie LeBaron, former quarterback at Pacific and Quantico, chows down with his troops in Korea. After the war, he went on to a standout NFL care

Interservice Honors

The Washington (D.C.) Touchdown Club four times named a Quantico Marine as Service Player of the Year.

Quarterback Eddie LeBaron (Pacific) was the choice in 1950 and guard Weldon Humble (Rice, Southwestern Louisiana) the 1951 selection.

Back John Amberg (Kansas) received the award in 1953 and back King Dixon (South Carolina) in 1959.

Other Marines receiving All-Service or inter-service mention included:

1917

John Beckett, Mare Island tackle; Walter Camp's All-Service team
Brick Mitchell, Mare Island end; second team, Walter Camp's All-Service team
Walter "Boots" Brown, Mare Island quarterback; and Hollis Huntington, Mare Island back; Walter Camp's all-sectional Service team
Eddie Mahan, League Island back; N.Y. Times' All-Service team

1918

Clarence Zimmerman, Mare Island end; Walter Camp's All-Service team
Jake Risley, Mare Island center; third team, Walter Camp's All-Service team
Benton Bangs, Mare Island back; and Bill Steers, Mare Island back; Walter Camp's All-Sectional Service team

1942

Joe Ruetz, St. Mary's Pre-Flight guard; Grantland Rice's All-Service team

1943

Pat Harder, Georgia Pre-Flight back, second team, All-Service team, AP, and first team, All-Southeast Service team, AP
Chuck Drulis, Camp Lejeune guard; Mid-Atlantic Service team, AP
Brad Ecklund, NAS Jacksonville center; John Hanzel, NAS Jacksonville guard, and Duke Iversen, NAS Jacksonville back; All-Southeast Service team, AP

1944

Pat Harder, Georgia Pre-Flight back, All-Southeast Service team, AP
Wilbur "Wee Willie" Wilkin, El Toro tackle, and Bob Dove, El Toro end, Coast All-Service team, United Press; Chuck Fenenbock, El Toro back, All-Coast team, Associated Press; Cliff Battles, El Toro back, second team, Coast All-Service, UP

1945

Paul Governali, first team, N.Y. Daily News All-Service team

FMF Pacific/1948

Ends: Lou Darnell, Pearl Harbor, and Bill Marker, Pendleton; **tackles:** Ed Ortnak, MAG-24, Guam, and Leroy Johnson, Brigade, Guam; **guards:** Bob Hunemiller, Brigade, Guam; and Fred Owens, El Toro; **center:** Don Gray, Pendleton; **backs:** John Beckett (Jr.), Pendleton; Denzil Eaton and Al Carmichael, El Toro; Bob Koehler, Pendleton

FMF Pacific/1949

Ends: Bob Moore, FMF Guam, and Art Specht, Pendleton; **tackles:** Fernand Autery, Camp Catlin, and Dick Almes, Pendleton; **guards:** Bob Goberli, Pendleton, and Fred Owens, El Toro; **center:** Vince Improto, FMF Guam; **backs:** Joe Bartos, Pendleton; Jim Estergall, El Toro; John Stephens, 5th Depot Base, Guam,; Ed Rush, FMF Guam

Williamson Rating Service/1953

(First team) T Jim Weatherall, Barstow; T Roscoe Hansen, Quantico; C Glen Graham, Lejeune; B John Pettibon, Quantico

(Second team) E Frank McPhee, Quantico; T Rex Boggan, Lejeune

(Third team) G Gil Bucci, PI; B George Kinek, Cherry Point; B Art Preston, San Diego

Navy-Marine All-Stars vs L.A. Rams/1953

Barstow: T Jim Weatherall (Oklahoma), QB Mike Serna (Cal Poly), HB Jack Wages (Abilene Christian)

Camp Pendleton: E Eugene "Big Daddy" Lipscomb, T Harold Bradley (Iowa), T John Feltch (Holy Cross), T Ken Huxhold (Wisconsin), G Ray Suchy (Wisconsin-Nevada), QB Ed Brown (Univ. of San Francisco), QB John Mazur (Notre Dame), HB Tom Carodine (Nebraska-Loyola of LA), FB Bob Tougas (Providence)

MCRD San Diego: T Rudy Trbovich (Purdue), C Phil Muscarello (Mississippi Southern), B A.T. DeVaughn (Bishop)

Korea/1954 (All-8th Army)

B John Cahill, E Merrill Jacobs, G Jim Pozza, T Jack Roche, G Tom Roggeman

1955

Fred Franco, Quantico back; MVP of Navy Times' All-Sea Service team

1957

Ted Karras, MCRD San Diego lineman; MVP runner-up of Navy Times' All-Sea Service team

The Navy Times also selected All-Sea Service teams of Navy and Marine players during the 1950s.

Readers helped elect their favorite players by casting votes, and the Navy Times carried weekly vote totals.

Among the Marine players honored were:

1952: (first team) T Jim Weatherall, Quantico; T Art Davis, Camp Lejeune; G Ray Suchy, Camp Pendleton; B Tom Carodine, MCRD San Diego; F Bill Hayes, Parris Island.

(second team) G Al Viola, Lejeune; G Randy Lawrence, San Diego; B Charles Harris, Pendleton; B Billy Mixon, PI; F Phil Delpierre, Lejeune

(third team) E Bob Schnelker; PI

1953: (first team) T Rex Boggan, Lejeune; G Al Viola, Quantico; C Glen Graham, Lejeune; B John Pettibon, Quantico

(second team) G Jack Lordo, San Diego; G John Bergamini, San Diego; B Ray Smith, Lejeune

(third team) E Frank McPhee, Quantico; T John Feltch, Pendleton; B Ed Brandenburg, Cherry Point; B Rob Goode, El Toro; B John Amberg, Quantico

1954 (first team) E Joe Young, San Diego; T Charles Weber, Cherry Point; T Ed Tokus, PI; G Steve Eisenhauer, Quantico; B Don Bingham, Quantico

(second team) G George Allen, San Diego; G Percy Christensen, Pendleton; C Jerry Wenzel, Lejeune; B Skippy Dyer, Hawaii; B John Callard, Pendleton

(third team) C Jim Cauthron, San Diego; B Steve Piskach, Quantico

1955: (first team) T John Hamber, Quantico; T Don Deskins, Hawaii; G Steve Eisenhauer, Pensacola; G Vic Rimkus, PI; C Dick Petty, Pendleton; B Don Bingham, Lejeune; F Fred Franco, Quantico

(second team) E Don Fullam, Pensacola; T Lou Florio, Lejeune; G Carl Valletto, PI; G George Allen, San Diego; G J.D. Roberts, Quantico; B Charles Wyss, Pendleton

(third team) E Howie Pitt, Lejeune; E Sam Ward, Pendleton; T Ernie Lewis, Quantico; B Joe Bellman, PI

Franco was the All-Sea Service MVP

1956: (first team) E Ron Beagle, Quantico; E John Rushing, Pendleton; C John Damore, Quantico

(second team) T Ernie Cheatham, San Diego; G David Slaughter, PI; C Dick Frasor, Lejeune; B Pat Ryan, Barstow; B Al Daniels, Hawaii

(third team) E Bob Warren, Lejeune; T Ernie Lewis, Pendleton; B Doug Cameron, Quantico; B Dick Washington, Pendleton

1957: (first team) T John Hopkins, Quantico; G Ted Karras, San Diego; C Lou Hallow, Lejeune
(second team) C Ed Strange, San Diego; Q Pat Ryan, Barstow; B Al Hall, San Diego
(third team) E Ron Beagle, Okinawa; E Norm Wilson, Barstow; G Fred Bucci, Quantico; G Mike Collins, Hawaii; Q Ernie Brown, Lejeune; B Hub Wilson, Okinawa
1958: (first team) E Ron Beagle, Lejeune; E Jim Robinson, San Diego; T Manny Congedo, Hawaii; C Sam Valentine, Quantico; B Harry Jefferson, Quantico
(second team) T Roger Beckley, Okinawa; G Ron Botchan, Lejeune; C Don Karnoscak, Pendleton; Q Marshall Newman, Lejeune; F Jim Pyles, San Diego
1959: (first team) T Ron Botchan, Lejeune; T Tom Meehan, Quantico; G Don Karnoscak, San Diego; Q Vern Valdez, San Diego; B King Dixon, Quantico; B Al Hall, San Diego
(second team) G Sam Valentine, Lejeune; Q Marshall Newman, Lejeune
1960 (first team) E Joe Losack, Lejeune; T Art Anderson, San Diego; C John Yohn, Quantico; Q Tom Maudlin, Quantico; B Billy Martin, San Diego; B Al Hall, San Diego; B King Dixon, Quantico
(second team) Marshall Hollingshead, Quantico; T Paul Ward, San Diego; B Mel Anderson, Lejeune; F Bob Marshall, Quantico

The Armed Forces Press Service also picked honor teams in the 1950s from among Army, Navy, Air Force, Coast Guard and Marine teams. Among the Marines selected were:

1951: (offense) E Cloyce Box, Camp Pendleton; G Weldon Humble, Quantico; B Dick Flowers, Quantico; B Billy Mixon, Parris Island
(defense) G Don King, PI, B Jack Kroll, Camp Lejeune
1952: (offense) C George Radosevich, PI; T Jim Weatherall, Quantico; E Jim Mutscheller, Quantico; B Bill Hayes, PI
(defense) E Bob Schnelker, PI; E Harrison Frasier, Lejeune
1953: (first team) E Frank McPhee, Quantico; G Gil Bucci, PI; B John Pettibon, Quantico
(second team) E Nick DeRosa, Cherry Point; T Eugene "Big Daddy" Lipscomb, Pendleton; B Bob Meyers, Quantico
1954: (first team) G Steve Eisenhauer, Quantico; E Frank McPhee, Pendleton; B Bob Meyers, Lejeune
(second team) B Gene Filipski, Quantico
1955: (first team) G Steve Eisenhauer, Pensacola; G J.D. Roberts, Quantico
(second team) B Fred Franco, Quantico; C Dick Petty, Pendleton; T Dewey Wade, Hawaii Marines; B Dick Zotti, PI
1956: (first team) E Ron Beagle, Quantico; E John Rushing, Pendleton
(second team) T Ernie Cheatham, MCRD San Diego; T Frank Morze, Lejeune
1957: (first team) G Ted Karras, San Diego
(incomplete)
1958: (first team) G Tony Stremic, Quantico; C Sam Valentine, Quantico; E Ron Beagle, Lejeune; B Harry Jefferson, Quantico
Jefferson was named the Outstanding Player

Box Still In Top 10

Sensational receiving in 1989 by wide receiver Willie "Flipper" Anderson of the Los Angeles Rams pushed former Marine Cloyce Box a notch down on the all-time list.

Anderson's 336 yards against the New Orleans Saints in a Nov. 26 game seen on ESPN game moved Box (West Texas) from No. 3 to No. 4 in single-game yardage with his 302 against the Baltimore Colts on Dec. 3, 1950. The previous leader had been Stephone Paige of the Kansas City Chiefs with 309 yards against the San Diego Chargers on Dec. 22, 1985.

A Pro Payoff

As Marines, they came in wave after wave to capture Pacific islands despite bitter fighting. As former Marines, they charged blocking and tackling dummies, teammates, opponents, referees and, occasionally, coaches and executives as they threw themselves into pro football, a growing sport that needed and welcomed them.

The All-America Football Conference made its debut in 1946 with teams in Brooklyn, Buffalo, Chicago, Cleveland, Los Angeles (the Dons), Miami, New York and San Francisco.

The established NFL, which had cut back during the war years, also moved a franchise, the Rams, to Los Angeles. As a result of two leagues, a bidding war — small by today's standards but one nevertheless — broke out. It lasted through the 1949 season, the AAFC's last.

The outbreak of the Korean War in 1950 meant the recall of some reservists and the enlistment of others. It also prepared a number of young Marines for pro ball after their duty tours.

And the establishment of the American Football League in 1960 again meant more jobs. Western teams, in particular, Denver, Los Angeles/San Diego and Oakland, had several Marines on their rosters.

■

But with the Vietnam war and Quantico giving up the sport (and a two-game series with Syracuse) after the 1972 season, the influx of Marines into pro football declined.

Oddly, this came at a time when former Marines such as Bill Arnsparger, Rick Forzano, Abe Gibron, John Mazur, John North, Bum Phillips, John Ralston, J.D. Roberts, Darryl Rogers, Les Steckel and Jim Mora were head NFL coaches.

Marine reinforcements for the NFL were few in the 1970s: back Willie Belton, back Moses Denson, back Glen Ellison, guard Cornelius Johnson, tackle-center Howard Kindig, back MacArthur Lane, guard-tackle Mike Montler and tackle Gary Larsen.

And there were few NFL players from the Corps in the 1980s.

Tight end Conrad Rucker closed a three-year pro career with the Tampa Bay Buccaneers and Rams in 1980. Cornerback John "Tony" Lowden had a 1984 tryout with the New England Patriots.

Kicker Steve Fehr (Navy) had a tryout in 1987 with the Cincinnati Bengals. Offensive guard Phil Pettey (Missouri) received a tryout with the Atlanta Falcons and was signed by the Washington Redskins in 1987. John Reed, 27, was declared ineligible because his college class had not graduated.

True, an Eddie Meyers (a Navy back) came along but military commitments and injuries nagged his career with the Falcons. He was on injured reserve in 1987 and cut at the 1988 training camp.

The principal impact player was nose tackle Tony Elliott (Wisconsin-Pratt CC-North Texas), a No. 5 draft pick who played for the New Orleans Saints from 1982-88.

There were other reminders, however.

The Baldingers (Brian, Rich and Gary), Bob and Mike Golic, Paul Hofer, Tony Karras, Matt Kofler, Pete Lazetich, Ken MacAfee Jr., Ken Norton Jr., Wade Phillips and Rick Venturi, among others, were in the pro arena. All are sons of former Marines.

■

Marines were being discharged from WWI service just as the NFL was being formed.

Benton "Biff" Bangs, Bert Baston (a Navy Cross winner), Dick Hanley, Tom Henry, Tut Imlay, Jack Meagher, Bob Peck and Johnny Scott, among others, played in the new league or, in 1926, the first (and one-year) American Football League.

One of the Corps' greatest players, Frank "The Great" Goettge, after wrenching consideration, turned down a lucrative contract with the New York Giants in the mid-1920s.

■

The Navy, through then-Capt. Tom Hamilton and its Pre-Flight program, grabbed many of the NFL players of the 1940, '41 and '42 seasons.

The Marine Corps did recruit among others, Ray Apolskis, Frank Balasz, Ed Beinor, Andy Chisick, Russ Cotton, Chuck Drulis, Dick Evans, Terry Fox, George Franck, Hugh Gallarneau (Bronze Star), Lew Hamity (DFC), Herman Hodges, Jim Lee Howell, Bill Lazetich, Don Miller, Jack Sanders, Paul Szakash, Si Titus (Silver Star), James Orville Tuttle and Wilbur "Wee Willie" Wilkin.

Jack Lummus, a 1941 New York Giant end, posthumously received the Medal of Honor for heroism on Iwo. Guard Howard "Smiley" Johnson, a Green Bay Packer in 1940 and '41, also was killed on Iwo. He received Silver Stars for heroism on Saipan and Iwo. End Chuck Behan (Lions), a Navy Cross winner, was killed on Okinawa.

A number of 30-and-overs from the pro wars also joined up in WWII: Hall of Fame back Cliff Battles, tackle Ben Boswell, guard Sam Knox, tackle "Big Jim" MacMurdo, end Charles Malone, center Tim Moynihan, Hall of Fame back Ernie Nevers, former rushing leader Jim Musick, tackle Claude "Cupe" Perry and tackle Jack "Tarzan" Riley, among others.

Much of the Marine impact on pro football in the 1950s, however, came either from a Cloyce Box, a Hardy "Thumper" Brown, a Don Doll, an Art Donovan, an Abe Gibron, a Jim Martin, a Thurman McGraw, a Leo Nomellini, an Ernie Stautner, who had served in WWII after graduating from high school, or a a Charlie Conerly, a Bob Dove, an Elroy "Crazylegs" Hirsch, a Pat Harder, a Darrell Palmer, who had played college ball before enlisting.

Guard Weldon Humble, center Len "Tuffy" McCormick, tackle Bill Milner, back Hosea Rodgers, guard Joe Signaigo, tackle Walt Szot and quarterback Sam Vacanti, among others, were recalled to active duty during the Korean War.

■

Younger Korean War Marines made their impact in the mid- and late 1950s: quarterback Ed Brown, linebacker Bob Griffin, quarterback Eddie LeBaron (Bronze Star), tackle Big Daddy

Lipscomb, end Ken MacAfee, guard Art Michalik, end Jim Mutscheller, tackle Don Owens, back Skeet Quinlan, end Bob Schnelker, tackle Volney Peters, tackle Jim Weatherall, linebacker Chuck Weber and center Ray Wietecha, among others.

And the march continued in the 1960s, as former Marines, primarily from Marine-base teams, ran, passed, kicked, blocked and tackled in the NFL and AFL. Those playing two or more seasons included:

T Art Anderson, B Pervis Atkins, T Ron Botchan, B Alex Bravo, E Hezekiah Braxton, B Al Carmichael, C Mike Connelly, E Bob Dee, B Bob Garner, B Alvin Hall, B Brad Hubbert, T Ted Karras, T John Klotz, E Dick Lucas, B Billy Martin, T Willie McClung, K Mike Mercer, T Paul Miller, T Frank Morze, E Phil Odle, T Hank Schmidt, T John Scott, T Orv Trask, K Herb Travenio, B Vern Valdez, T Paul Ward, C Bob Whitlow, B Kelton Winston, LB John Yohn and E Joe Young.

Players (NFL, AAFC, AFL)

Alex Agase G (Illinois-Purdue), Dons and Rockets (AAFC) 1947, Browns 1948-51 (AAFC/NFL), Colts 1953

Al Akins B (Washington St.-Washington), Browns 1946 (AAFC), Dodgers (AAFC) 1947-48, Bills (AAFC) 1948

Tom Alberghini G (Holy Cross), Steelers 1945

Vern Albery K (Muskingum), pre-season Cowboys 1969

John Amberg DB (Kansas), Giants 1951-52

Art Anderson T (Idaho), Bears 1961-62 and pre-season 1963, Steelers 1963 and pre-season 1964

Ray Apolskis G (Marquette), Chicago Cardinals 1941-42, 1945-50

Joe Arenas B (Omaha), 49ers 1951-57

Henry Armstrong T (Rice-Southwestern Louisiana), pre-season Cardinals 1948

Ron Aschbacher E (Oregon St.), pre-season 49ers 1955

Walt Ashcraft T-E (Long Beach CC-USC), pre-season Redskins 1953

Pervis Atkins HB-FL (San Francisco St.-Santa Ana JC-New Mexico St.), Rams 1961-63 and pre-season 1964, Redskins 1964-65, Raiders 1965-66 and pre-season 1967

Claude "Bo" Austin B (George Washington), pre-season Redskins 1957

Frank Balasz B (Iowa), Packers 1939-41, Chicago Cardinals 1941, 1945

Benton "Biff" Bangs B (Washington St.), Los Angeles Buccaneers 1926

Ken Barfield G (Mississippi), Redskins 1954

Solon Barnett T (Baylor-Southwestern of Texas), Packers 1945-46

Paul Barry B (Tulsa), Rams 1950, 1952, Redskins 1953, Chicago Cardinals 1954

Joe Bartos B (Navy), Redskins 1950

Bert Baston E (Minnesota), Hammond Pros 1919, Buffalo All-Americans 1920, Cleveland Panthers 1920, Cleveland Indians 1921

Cliff Battles B (West Virginia Wesleyan), Redskins 1932-37

Alf Bauman T (Northwestern), Rockets (AAFC) 1947, Eagles 1947, Bears 1948-50

Lloyd Baxter C (SMU), Packers 1948

Phil Bayer B (Columbia), signed with Eagles in 1942

Ron Beagle E (Navy), pre-season Raiders 1960

Wendell Beard T (New Mexico-Cal), pre-season Bears 1947, pre-season Redskins

Charles Behan E (De Kalb Teachers), Lions 1942 (killed in action on Okinawa)

Ed Beinor T (Notre Dame), Chicago Cardinals 1940-41, Redskins 1941-42

Jube Belcher E (San Angelo JC-Trinity of Texas), pre-season Texans 1960

Willie Belton B (Maryland St.), Falcons 1971-72, St. Louis Cardinals 1973-74, pre-season Bills

Ed Berrang E (Villanova), Redskins 1949-51, Lions 1951, Redskins 1952

Angelo Bertelli QB (Notre Dame), Dons (AAFC) 1946, Rockets (AAFC) 1947-48. (Heisman Trophy winner in 1943)

Don Bingham B (Sul Ross), Bears 1956

John T. "Blondy" Black B (Mississippi St.), pre-season NY Yankees 1946 (AAFC), Bisons (AAFC) 1946, Colts (AAFC) 1947

Bill Blackburn C (Rice-Southwestern Louisiana), Chicago Cardinals 1946-50
Lamar Blount E (Mississippi St.-Duke), Seahawks (AAFC) 1946, Bills (AAFC) 1947, Colts (AAFC) 1947
Wayne Bock T (Illinois), Chicago Cardinals 1957, Cardinals pre-season 1958 and 1959, Rams pre-season 1961
Fred Boensch G (Stanford-Cal), Redskins 1947-48 and pre-season 1949
Rex Boggan T (Mississipi), Giants 1955
Don Boll T (Nebraska), Redskins 1953-59, Giants 1960, pre-season Vikings 1961
Mendle Earl "Big John" Bond B (Texas Christian-North Texas Agri.), pre-season Boston Yanks 1947
Ben Boswell T (Texas Christian), Portsmouth Spartans 1933, Redskins 1934
Ron Botchan T (Occidental), Los Angeles Chargers 1960 and San Diego Chargers pre-season 1961, Oilers 1962
Cloyce Box E (West Texas-Louisiana Tech), Lions 1949-50, 1952-54
Harold Bradley G (Iowa), Browns 1954-56, Eagles 1958 and pre-season 1959
Alex Bravo B (Cal Poly SLO), Rams 1957-58, Raiders 1960-61 and pre-season 1962
Hezekiah Braxton E (Virginia Union), Chargers 1962, Bills 1963
Sam Brazinsky (Bray) C (Villanova), Bisons (AAFC) 1946
Marty Brill B (Penn-Notre Dame), pre-season Staten Island Stapletons 1931
Ed Brown QB (Univ. of San Francisco), Bears 1954-61, Steelers 1962-65, Colts 1965 and pre-season 1966
Hardy "Thumper" Brown LB (SMU-Tulsa), Dodgers (AAFC) 1948, Hornets (AAFC) 1949, Colts and Redskins 1950, 49ers 1951-56, Chicago Cardinals 1956, Broncos 1960
Gail Bruce E (Washington), 49ers (AAFC/NFL) 1948-51
Eddie Bryant E (Virginia-North Carolina), pre-season Boston Yanks 1945
Bob Buel T (Wisconsin-Franklin & Marshall), pre-season Bears 1947
George Bytsura T (Duquesne), signed with Eagles 1942
Ron Cahill B (Holy Cross), Chicago Cardinals 1943
Cleo Ralph Calcagni T (Penn-Cornell), Boston Yanks 1946, Steelers 1947-48
J.R. Callahan B (Texas), pre-season Lions 1947
Frank Callen G (St. Mary's), pre-season NY Yankees (AAFC) 1947
Gus Camarata B (Wartburg-Iowa St. Teachers-Western Michigan), pre-season Lions 1947
Jim Camp B (Randolph-Macon, Univ. of North Carolina), pre-season Chicago Cardinals 1948, Dodgers (AAFC) 1948
Al Carmichael B (Santa Ana JC-USC), Packers 1953-58 and pre-season 1959, Broncos 1960-61
Tom Carodine B (Boys Town-Loyola of LA-Nebraska), pre-season Browns 1954
Ken Casanega B (Santa Clara), 49ers (AAFC) 1946, 1948
Ernie Cheatham T (Loyola of LA), Colts and Steelers 1954
Andrew Chisick C (Villanova) Chicago Cardinals 1940-41
Don Christman E (Richmond), pre-season Patriots 1962
Gus Cifelli T (Notre Dame), Lions 1950-52, Packers 1953, Eagles and Steelers 1954
Wayne Clark E (Utah), Lions 1944-45
Walt Clay B (Colorado), Rockets (AAFC) 1946-47, Dons (AAFC) 1947-49
Jim Cody T (East Texas), pre-season Lions 1947
George Coleman C (San Diego St.), pre-season 49ers
William H. "Spot" Collins (Texas-Southwestern of Texas), Boston Yanks 1947
Charlie Conerly QB (Mississippi), Giants 1948-61
Mike Connelly C (Pasadena JC-Washington St.-Utah St.), Cowboys 1960-67, Steelers 1968
Earl Cook G (SMU), pre-season New York Yanks 1948, pre-season Redskins 1948, pre-season Colts 1949
Russ Cotton QB (Texas Mines), Dodgers 1941, Steelers 1942
Jim Cox G (Stanford-California), 49ers (AAFC) 1948
Bill Crass B (LSU), Chicago Cardinals 1937
Jim "Tank" Crawford G (Mississippi), pre-season Bears 1950
Billy Cromer B (Arkansas A&M-North Texas), pre-season Bears 1948
Jim Cullom G (Cal), NY Yanks 1951
Roland Dale E (Mississippi), Redskins 1950
Don Daly B (Eastern Kentucky), pre-season Lions 1957
John Damore C (Northwestern), Bears 1957, 1959 and pre-season 1960
Bob David G (Notre Dame-Villanova), Rams 1947-48, Rockets (AAFC) 1948
Art Davis T (Alabama St.), Bears 1953
Tom Dean T (SMU-Arkansas A&M), Boston Yanks 1946-47
Bob Dee E (Holy Cross), Redskins 1957-58 and pre-season 1959; Patriots 1960-67
Owen Dejanovich G (Northern Arizona), pre-season Oilers 1964

Chuck Dellago T (Minnesota-Northwestern), pre-season Eagles
Moses Denson B (Maryland St.), Redskins 1974-75
Don Deskins G (Adelphi-Michigan), Raiders 1960 and pre-season 1961
Jim Dickey E (Catawba-Duke), pre-season NY Yankees 1948
Don Doll B (USC), Lions 1949-52, Redskins 1953, Rams 1954
Charles Donley C (West Virginia Wesleyan), pre-season Eagles 1949
Art Donovan T (Boston College), Colts 1950, pre-season Browns 1951, NY Yanks 1951, Texans 1952, Colts 1953-61
Bob Dove E (Notre Dame), Rockets (AAFC) 1946-47, Chicago Cardinals 1948-53, Lions 1953-54
Mel Downey T (Holy Cross-Dartmouth-Villanova), pre-season Eagles 1947
Bert Dressler T (Marshall-North Carolina St.), pre-season Redskins 1947
Wally Dreyer B (Wisconsin-Michigan), Bears 1949, Packers 1950
Chuck Drulis G (Temple), pre-season Dodgers 1942, Bears 1942, 1945-49, Packers 1950
Bobby Dunlap B (Monmouth), offered contract by Eagles 1942 (Medal of Honor winner on Iwo Jima)
Brad Ecklund C (Oregon), NY Yankees (AAFC) and Yanks (NFL) 1949-51, Texans 1952, Colts 1953
Weldon Edwards T (TCU-North Texas Agri.) Redskins 1948
Chalmers "Bump" Elliott B (Purdue-Michigan), pre-season Lions 1947
Jim Ellis T (North Carolina-Duke), pre-season Rams 1947
Glenn Ellison B (Arkansas), Raiders 1971, pre-season Falcons
Leo Elter B (Villanova-Duquesne), Steelers 1953-54, Redskins 1955-57 and pre-season 1958, Steelers 1958-59
Bill Erickson G (Mississippi-North Carolina), Giants 1948, NY Yankees (AAFC) 1949
Jesus Esparza T (New Mexico A&M), pre-season Colts 1956
Dick Evans E (Iowa), Packers 1940, Chicago Cardinals 1941-42, Packers 1943
Jay Dale Evans B (Kansas St.), pre-season St. Louis Cardinals 1961, Broncos 1961
Gary Fallon B (Syracuse), pre-season Vikings 1962
Tom Farmer B (Iowa), Rams 1946, Redskins 1947-48
Chuck Fenenbock (UCLA), Lions 1943, 1945; Dons (AAFC) 1946-48, Rockets (AAFC) 1948
Steve Filipowicz B (Fordham), Giants 1945-46
Gene Filipski B (Army-Villanova), Giants 1956-57
Dick Fishel B (Syracuse), Dodgers 1933
Ray Fisher T (Eastern Illinois), Steelers 1959 and pre-season 1960, pre-season Cowboys 1961
Jack Flagerman C (St. Mary's), Dons (AAFC) 1948
Lou Florio T (Boston College), pre-season Bears 1956
Dick Flowers QB (Northwestern), Colts 1953
Dick Fouts T (Missouri), pre-season Rams 1956
Joe Fowlkes E, pre-season Steelers 1960
Terry Fox B (Miami of Fla.), Eagles 1941, 1945; Seahawks (AAFC) 1946
George Franck B (Minnesota), Giants 1941, 1945-47
Bill Frank T (San Diego CC-Colorado), Cowboys 1964 and pre-season 1965
John Fritsch T, pre-season Chiefs 1964, pre-season Chiefs 1965
Fred Fugazzi LB (Missouri Valley), pre-season Patriots 1965
Bernie Gallagher T (Penn-Princeton), Dons (AAFC) 1947, pre-season Colts (AAFC) 1948
Hugh Gallarneau B (Stanford), Bears 1941-42, 1945-47
Bob Garner B (Fresno St.), Los Angeles Chargers 1960 and pre-season 1961, Raiders 1961-63
John Genis G (Illinois-Purdue), signed with Colts in 1947, returned bonus to join FBI
Joe Geri B (Georgia), Steelers 1949-51, Chicago Cardinals 1952
Charles Getchell E (Temple), pre-season Phil-Pitt 1943, pre-season Dons (AAFC) 1946, Colts 1947
Lou Ghecas B (Georgetown), Eagles 1941
Ted Ghelmann T (William & Mary), pre-season Steelers 1951, pre-season Browns 1953
Abe Gibron T (Valparaiso-Purdue), Bills (AAFC) 1949, Browns 1950-56, Eagles 1956-57, Bears 1958-59
Sloko Gill G (Youngstown), Lions 1942
Dennis Golden DE (Holy Cross), pre-season Cowboys 1963, pre-season Patriots 1966
Rob Goode B (Texas A&M), Redskins 1949-51, 1954-55; Eagles 1955
Henry Goodman T (West Virginia), Lions 1942
Pete Gorgone B (Muhlenburg), Giants 1946
Henry Gotard G (Villanova), pre-season Broncos 1962
Paul Governali QB (Columbia), Boston Yanks 1946-47, Giants 1947-48
Bill Gray G (Oregon St.-USC), Redskins 1947-48
Nelson Green T (Tulsa), NY Yankees 1948

Bob Griffin G (Arkansas), Rams 1953-57 and pre-season 1958; pre-season Lions 1958, pre-season Cowboys 1960, Broncos 1961, St. Louis Cardinals 1961 and pre-season 1962

Don Griffin B (Illinois), Rockets (AAFC) 1946

George Grimes B (Virginia-North Carolina), pre-season Rams 1948, Lions 1948

Roger Grove B (Michigan St.), Packers 1931-35

Bill Hachten G (Stanford-Cal), Giants 1947 and pre-season 1948

Alvin Hall B, Rams 1961-63

Irving Hall B (Brown), Eagles 1942

Tom Hall B (Shurtleff), signed with Eagles 1942

Lou Hallow C (East Carolina), pre-season Patriots 1961

Lew Hamity B (Chicago), Bears 1941

Dick Handley C (Fresno St.-USC), Colts (AAFC) and 49ers (AAFC) 1947

Dick Hanley B (Washington St.), Racine Legion 1924

Roscoe Hansen T (North Carolina), Eagles 1951

Pat Harder B (Wisconsin), Chicago Cardinals 1946-50, Lions 1951-53

Charles Harris B (Georgia), pre-season Browns 1957, pre-season Los Angeles Chargers 1960

Dave Hayes B-LB (Penn St.), pre-season Patriots 1966

Jim Hays B (Toledo), pre-season Bears 1951

Ted Hazelwood T-G (North Carolina), pre-season Browns (AAFC) 1949, Hornets (AAFC) 1949, Redskins 1953

Bob Heck E (Purdue), pre-season 49ers (AAFC) 1949, Hornets (AAFC) 1949

Bob Hein E (Kent State), Dodgers (AAFC) 1947

Carey "Choo Choo" Henley B (Chattanooga), Bills 1962

Tom Henry B (LSU), Rock Island Independents 1920

Gary Henson E (Colorado), Eagles 1963 and pre-season 1964

Ed Heuring G (Maryland), pre-season Broncos 1960

Ralph Heywood E (USC), Rockets (AAFC) 1946, Lions 1947, Boston Yanks 1948, New York Bulldogs 1949

James Higgins G (Trinity of Texas), Chicago Cardinals 1941

Claude "Big" Hipps Jr. B (Georgia), Steelers 1952-53

Elroy Hirsch B (Wisconsin-Michigan), Rockets (AAFC) 1946-48, Rams 1949-57

Herman Hodges B (Howard of Ala.), Dodgers 1939-42

Al Hoisington E (Pasadena JC), pre-season Rams 1959, Raiders and Bills 1960, pre-season Bills 1961, pre-season Raiders 1962

Holly Hollingshead E (Mississippi St.), pre-season Steelers 1962

Fran Holmes B (Santa Clara-Pacific), pre-season Redskins 1947

Earl "Dixie" Howell B (Muhlenburg-Mississippi), Dons (AAFC) 1949

Jim Lee Howell E (Arkansas), Giants 1937-42, 1946-48

Brad Hubbert B (Arizona), Chargers 1967-70

Gene Hubka B (Temple-Bucknell), Steelers 1947

Dick Huffman T (Tennessee), Rams 1947-50

Jay Huffman LB (Penn St.), pre-season Eagles 1962

Weldon Humble G (Rice-Southwestern Louisiana), Browns (AAFC/NFL) 1947-50, Texans 1952

Chuck Huneke T (St. Mary's of Texas-Wyoming-St. Benedict's), Rockets (AAFC) 1946-47, Dodgers (AAFC) 1947-48

Ken Huxhold T (Wisconsin), pre-season Eagles 1951 or 1952, Eagles 1954-58 and pre-season 1959

John Huzvar B (North Carolina St.-Pittsburgh-Georgia), Eagles 1952, Colts 1953-54

Talma "Tut" Imlay B (Cal), Los Angeles Buccaneers 1926, Giants 1927

Duke Iverson B (Oregon), Giants 1947 and pre-season 1948, NY Yankees (AAFC) and Yanks (NFL) 1948-51

Marvin Jacobs T, pre-season Chicago Cardinals 1947, Cardinals 1948 Harry Jefferson B (Illinois), pre-season Giants 1959

Tom Jelley E (Miami of Fla.), Steelers 1951

Jack Jenkins B (Vanderbilt), Redskins 1943, 1946-47

Cornelius Johnson G (Virginia Union), Colts 1968-73 Don Johnson C (Northwestern), Cleveland Rams 1942

Farnham "Gunner" Johnson E (Wisconsin-Michigan), pre-season Bears 1947, Rockets (AAFC) 1948

Howard "Smiley" Johnson G (Georgia), Packers 1940-41 (Killed in action on Iwo Jima.)

William "Bull" Johnson G (SMU-North Carolina), Bears pre-season 1946, Bears 1947

Cleveland Jones B (San Diego CC-Oregon), pre-season Cowboys 1961

Elmer "Buck" Jones G (Wake Forest-Franklin & Marshall), Bisons (AAFC) 1946, Lions 1947-48

Jim Jones E (Kent State), pre-season Lions 1941

Saxon Judd E (Tulsa-Southwestern Louisiana), Dodgers (AAFC) 1946-48

Charles Kalbfleish T (Western Michigan), pre-season Lions 1947

Don "Duke" Karnoscak C-LB (Colorado), pre-season Broncos 1960

Ted Karras T (Purdue-Indiana), Steelers 1958-59, Bears 1960-64 and pre-season 1965, Lions 1965 and pre-season 1966, Rams 1966

Mike Kasap T (Illinois-Purdue), Colts (AAFC) 1947), Bills (AAFC) 1947

Ed Kasky T (Villanova), Eagles 1942

Leo Katalinas T (Catholic), Packers 1938

Eulis Keahey G-T (George Washington), Giants and Dodgers 1942

Bill Kellagher B (Fordham), Rockets (AAFC) 1946-48

Bob Kelley C (West Texas), Eagles 1955-56

Bill Kennedy G (Michigan St.), Lions 1942, Boston Yanks 1947

John Kerns T (Ohio Univ.-Duke-North Carolina), Bills (AAFC) 1947-49

Ed Kesler B (North Carolina), pre-season Steelers 1965

Ken Keuper B (Georgia), Packers 1945-47 and pre-season 1948, Giants 1948

Bob Keyes B (Univ. of San Diego), Raiders 1960, pre-season Chargers 1961

Carl Kilsgaard T (Idaho), Chicago Cardinals 1950

Howard Kindig T-C (Los Angeles St.), Chargers 1965-67, Bills 1967-71, Dolphins 1972-73, Jets 1974

George Kinek B (Tulane), pre-season Rams 1951, Chicago Cardinals 1954

Don King B (Syracuse), pre-season Lions 1963

Don King T (Kentucky), Browns 1954, Eagles and Packers 1956, Broncos 1960, pre-season Patriots 1961

Lafayette King E (Georgia), Bisons (AAFC) 1946, Bills (AAFC) 1947, Rockets (AAFC) 1948, Hornets (AAFC) 1949

Dolph Kissell B (Boston College), Bears 1942

John Klotz T (Penn Military), pre-season Rams 1958, Titans 1960-62, Chargers 1962, Jets 1963 and pre-season 1964, Oilers 1964 and pre-season 1965

Sam Knox G (New Hampshire-Illinois), Lions 1934-36

John Koniszewski T (George Washington), Redskins 1945-46, pre-season 1947, 1948

John Kovatch E (Notre Dame), Redskins 1942, 1946; Packers 1947, pre-season Redskins 1948

John Kreamcheck G (William & Mary), Bears 1953-55

Ray Kuffel E (Marquette-Notre Dame), Bills (AAFC) 1947, Rockets (AAFC) 1948, Hornets (AAFC) 1949

Pat Lahey E (John Carroll), pre-season Lions 1941, Rockets (AAFC) 1946-47

"Big Jim" Landrigan T (Holy Cross-Dartmouth), Colts (AAFC) 1947

Mort Landsberg B (Cornell), Eagles 1941, Dons (AAFC) 1947

MacArthur Lane B (Laney JC-Utah St.), Cardinals 1968-71, Packers 1972-74, Chiefs 1975-78

Gary Larsen T (Concordia of Minn.), Rams 1964, Vikings 1965-74

Denver Latimore DE (Hutchinson CC-Arkansas St.), pre-season Browns 1977

Jimmy Lawson B (Los Angeles St.), pre-season Chiefs 1966-67, pre-season Chargers 1969, pre-season Rams 1970

Bill Lazetich B (Montana), Cleveland Rams 1939, 1942

Eddie LeBaron QB (Pacific), pre-season Redskins 1950, Redskins 1952-53, 1955-59; Cowboys 1960-63

Jack "Whitey" Lee B (Carnegie Tech), Steelers 1939

Reid Lennan G, Redskins 1945, pre-season Redskins 1946, Dons (AAFC) 1947.

Jim Levey B, Steelers 1934-36

Ernie Lewis B (Colorado), Rockets (AAFC) 1946-48, Hornets (AAFC) 1949

"Big Daddy" Lipscomb T, Rams 1953-55, Colts 1956-60, Steelers 1961-62

Dick Loepfe T (Wisconsin), Chicago Cardinals 1948-49

Jim Loflin B (LSU-Southwestern Louisiana), pre-season Browns 1949

Bob Logel E, Bills (AAFC) 1949

Dick Loncar T (Notre Dame-NE Louisiana), pre-season Steelers 1960

Mike Long E (Brandeis), Patriots 1960

John "Tony" Lowden CB, pre-season Patriots 1984

Dick Lucas E (Boston College), pre-season Steelers 1958, pre-season Redskins 1960, Eagles 1960-63

Jack Lummus E (Baylor), Giants 1941 (Medal of Honor winner; killed in action on Iwo Jima.)

Ken Lutterbach B (Evansville), pre-season Bills 1961

Players (NFL, AAFC, AFL)

Ken MacAfee E (Alabama), Giants 1954-58, Eagles and Redskins 1959.
Jack MacKenzie B (Drake-Northwestern), pre-season Chicago Cardinals 1947
Bob MacLeod B (Dartmouth), Bears 1939
"Big Jim" MacMurdo T (Pittsburgh), Boston Braves/Redskins 1932-33, Eagles 1934-37
John Magee G (Rice-Southwestern Louisiana), Eagles 1948-55
Achille "Chick" Maggioli B (Notre Dame-Illinois), Bills (AAFC) 1948, Lions 1949, Colts 1950
Howard "Red" Maley B (Southern Methodist-North Texas Agri.), Boston Yanks 1946-47 and pre-season 1948
Charles Malone B (Texas A&M), Boston Redskins 1934-36, Washington Redskins 1937-40, 1942
Norm Maloney E (Purdue), 49ers (AAFC) 1948-49
Hugo Marcolini B (St. Bonaventure), Dodgers (AAFC) 1948
Bill Marker E (West Virginia), pre-season Redskins 1954
Billy Martin B (Minnesota), Bears 1962-64 and pre-season 1965
Jim Martin C-OG-OT-DE-OLB-MLB-PK (Notre Dame), Browns 1950, Lions 1951-61 and pre-season 1963, Colts 1963 and pre-season 1964, Redskins 1964 and pre-season 1965
John Maskas T (Virginia Tech-North Carolina), Bills (AAFC) 1947, 1949
Earl Maves B (Wisconsin-Michigan), Lions 1948, Colts (AAFC) 1948
Art McCaffray T (Santa Clara-Pacific), Steelers 1946
Willie McClung T (Florida A&M), Steelers 1955-57, Browns 1958-59 and pre-season 1960, Lions 1960-61 and pre-season 1962
Harley McCollum T (Tulane), New York Yankees (AAFC) 1946, Rockets (AAFC) 1947
Len "Tuffy" McCormick C (Baylor-Southwestern of Texas), Colts (AAFC) 1948
Lloyd McDermott T (Kentucky), Lions 1950, Chicago Cardinals 1950-51
Lester McDonald B (Nebraska), Bears 1937-39, Eagles and Lions 1940
Bob McDougal B (Miami of Fla.-Duke), Packers 1947
Thurman "Fum" McGraw T (Colorado A&M), Lions 1950-54
Paul McKee E (Rochester-Syracuse), Redskins 1947-48
John McLaughry B (Brown), Giants 1940
Tuss McLaughry B (Westminster of Pa.), Massillon Tigers in the early 1920s
Frank McPhee E (Princeton), Chicago Cardinals 1955 and pre-season 1956
Jack Meagher E (Notre Dame), Chicago Tigers 1920
Bill Meglen G (Minnesota-Utah St.), pre-season Los Angeles Chargers 1960, pre-season San Diego Chargers 1963
Mike Mercer K (Minnesota-Florida St.-Hardin Simmons-Northern Arizona), Vikings 1961-62, Raiders 1963-66, Chiefs 1966, Bills 1967-68, Packers 1968-69 and pre-season 1970, Chargers 1970
Art Mergenthal T (Xavier of Ohio-Bowling Green-Notre Dame), Cleveland/Los Angeles Rams 1945-46, pre-season Eagles 1947 and pre-season 1948
Ernie Merk B (USC), pre-season Steelers 1959
Bob Meyers B (Stanford), 49ers 1952
"Automatic Art" Michalik G (St. Ambrose), 49ers 1953-54, Steelers 1955-56
Mike Mihalic G (Mississippi St.) pre-season Yanks 1947
Bill Miklich B (Idaho), Giants 1947-48, Lions 1948
Don Miller B (Wisconsin), Packers 1941-42
Paul Miller T (LSU), Rams 1954-57 and pre-season 1958, Texans 1960-61, pre-season Titans 1962, Chargers 1962
Chuck "Bill" Milner T (South Carolina-Duke), Bears 1947-49, Giants 1950
Ed Mioduszewski (also Meadows) B (William & Mary), Colts 1953
Bob Mirth G (Moravian-Muhlenburg), pre-season 49ers (AAFC)
Billy Mixon B (Georgia), 49ers 1953-54
Avery Montfort B (New Mexico), Chicago Cardinals 1941
Mike Montler G-T (Colorado), Patriots 1969-72, Bills 1973-76, Broncos 1977, Lions 1978
George Morris B (Baldwin-Wallace), Cleveland Rams 1941-42
Fred "Curly" Morrison B (Ohio St.), Bears 1950-53, Browns 1954-56
Frank Morze T (Boston College), 49ers 1957-61 and pre-season 1962, Browns 1962-63 and pre-season 1964, 49ers 1964 and pre-season 1965
Kelley Mote E (South Carolina-Duke), Lions 1947-49, Giants 1950-52
Tim Moynihan C (Notre Dame), Chicago Cardinals 1932-33
Joe Muha B (Virginia Military), Eagles 1946-50
Keith Munyan G (Ohio University-William Carey-Louisiana College), pre-season Redskins 1959, pre-season Oilers 1960

305

Jesse Murdock E (California Western), Raiders 1963, Bills 1963 and pre-season 1964
John Murphy T, pre-season Eagles 1947
Jim Musick B (USC), Boston Braves/Redskins 1932-33, 1935-36
Jim Mutscheller E (Notre Dame), Colts 1954-61 and pre-season 1962
Herb Nakken B (Utah), pre-season Rams 1956
Fred "Father" Negus C (Wisconsin-Michigan), Rockets 1947-48 (AAFC), Hornets (AAFC) 1949, Bears 1950
Ernie Nevers B (Stanford), Duluth Eskimos 1926-27, Chicago Cardinals 1929-31
Emery Nix B (Texas Christian), Giants 1943, 1946 and pre-season 1947
Jack Nix B (USC), 49ers 1950
Leo "The Lion" Nomellini T (Minnesota), 49ers 1950-63 and pre-season 1964
John North E (Vanderbilt), Colts (AAFC/NFL) 1948-50
Bob Nussbaumer B (Michigan), Packers 1946, Redskins 1947-48, Chicago Cardinals 1949-50, Packers 1951
Bernie Nygren B (San Jose St.), Dons (AAFC) 1946, Dodgers (AAFC) 1947
Phil Odle E (Brigham Young), Lions 1968-70
Hank Olshanski E (Wisconsin-Michigan), pre-season Colts (AAFC) 1948
James O'Neal G (Texas Christian-Southwestern of Texas), Rockets (AAFC) 1946-47
Tom O'Rourke B (Villanova), pre-season Broncos 1962
Ted Ossowski T (Oregon St.-USC), New York Yankees (AAFC) 1947
Don Owens T (Southern Mississippi), pre-season Steelers 1957, Redskins 1957 and pre-season 1958, Eagles 1958-60, St. Louis Cardinals 1960-63 and pre-season 1964
Darrell Palmer (Texas Christian), New York Yankees (AAFC) 1946-48, Browns (AAFC/NFL) 1949-53
Maurice "Babe" Patt E (Carnegie Tech), Lions 1938, Cleveland Rams 1939-42
Bob Patton T (Clemson), Giants 1952
Charles Pavlich G, 49ers (AAFC) 1946
Jim Pearcy G (Marshall), Rockets (AAFC) 1946-48, Hornets (AAFC) 1949
Bob Peck C (Pittsburgh), Massillon Tigers 1919
Don Penza E (Notre Dame), pre-season Steelers 1956
Bob Perina B (Princeton), New York Yankees (AAFC) 1946, Dodgers (AAFC) 1947, Rockets (AAFC) 1948, Bears 1949, Colts 1950
John Perko G (Minnesota-Notre Dame), Bisons (AAFC) 1946
Claude "Cupe" Perry T (Alabama), Packers 1927-31, Dodgers 1931, Packers 1932-35
Volney Peters T (USC), Chicago Cardinals 1952-53, Redskins 1954-57, Eagles 1958, pre-season Packers 1959, Los Angeles Chargers 1960 and pre-season 1961, Raiders 1961 and pre-season 1962
John Petibon B (Notre Dame), Texans 1952, Browns 1955-56, Packers 1957, pre-season Redskins 1958
Ray Piotrowski C, pre-season Packers 1947
Joyce Pipkin B (Arkansas), Giants 1948, Dons (AAFC) 1949
Bob Polidor B (Temple-Rochester-Villanova), pre-season Chicago Cardinals 1949
Barney Poole E (Mississippi-North Carolina-Army), New York Yankees (AAFC) 1949, New York Yanks 1950-51, Texans 1952, Colts 1953, Giants 1954
Oliver Poole E (Mississippi-North Carolina), New York Yankees (AAFC) 1947, Colts (AAFC) 1948 and pre-season 1949, Lions 1949
Ray Poole E (Mississippi-North Carolina), Giants 1947-52
Al Postus B (Villanova), Steelers 1945
Pat Preston T (Wake Forest-Duke), Bears 1946-49
Frank Quillen E (Penn), Rockets (AAFC) 1946-47
Volney "Skeet" Quinlan B (Texas Christian-San Diego St.), Rams 1952-56, Browns 1956
Stan Quintana B (New Mexico), pre-season Vikings 1966-68
George Radosevich C (Pittsburgh), Colts 1954-56
Frank Ramsey T (Oregon St.), Bears 1945
Ray Ratkowski E (Notre Dame), Patriots 1961
Eddie Rayburn T (Rice), pre-season Giants 1959, pre-season Oilers 1960
Frank Reagan B (Penn), Giants 1941, 1946-48, Eagles 1949-51
Ken Reese B (Alabama), Lions 1947
Bob Rennebohm E (Wisconsin-Michigan), pre-season Packers 1948
Jack Riley T (Northwestern), Boston Redskins 1933
Bill Roberts B (Dartmouth), Packers 1956
Dick Rockenbach B (Illinois St.), pre-season Lions 1949
Hosea Rodgers B (Alabama-North Carolina), Dons 1949, pre-season Eagles 1950
Darryl Rogers B (Long Beach CC-Fresno St.), pre-season Rams 1959, pre-season Broncos 1960

Tom Roggeman T (Purdue), Bears 1955-57

Jay Roundy B (USC), pre-season Rams

Conrad Rucker TE (Southern), Oilers 1978-79 and pre-season 1980, Buccaneers 1980, Rams 1980

Joe Ruetz G (Notre Dame), Rockets (AAFC) 1946, 1948

Pat Ryan QB (Holy Cross), pre-season Packers 1959

Julie Rykovich B (Illinois-Notre Dame), Biiis (AAFC) 1947-48, Rockets (AAFC) 1948, Bears 1949-51, Redskins 1952-53

Joe Sabasteanski C (Fordham), Boston Yanks 1946-48, New York Bulldogs 1949

Jack Sachse C (Texas-Southwestern of Texas), Boston Yanks 1945

Bill Samer E (Pittsburgh), pre-season Steelers

John Sanchez T (Los Angeles CC-Univ. of San Francisco-Redlands), Rockets (AAFC) 1947, New York Yankees (AAFC) 1947, Lions 1947, Redskins 1947-49, Giants 1949-50

John Sanders G (SMU), Steelers 1940-42, Eagles 1945

George Savitsky T (Penn), Eagles 1948-49 and pre-season 1950

Carl Schiller E (Montana-Western Michigan), pre-season Colts 1948

Henry Schmidt T (USC-Trinity of Texas), 49ers 1959-60 and pre-season 1961, Chargers 1961-64 and pre-season 1965, Bills 1965, Jets 1966

Bob Schnelker E (Bowling Green), Eagles 1953, Giants 1954-60, Vikings 1961, Steelers 1961 and pre-season 1962

Bill Schroeder B (Wisconsin), Rockets (AAFC) 1946-47

Carl Schuette C (Marquette), Bills (AAFC) 1948-49, Packers 1950-51

Joe Scott B (Texas A&M, Univ. of San Francisco), Giants 1948-53

Johnny Scott B (Lafayette) Akron Pros 1919, Buffalo All-Americans 1920-23, Frankford Yellowjackets 1924.

John Scott T (Ohio St.), pre-season Steelers 1960, Bills 1960-61

John Seiferling B (Utah St.-Colorado College-Fresno St.), pre-season Bears 1947

Ed Sharkey T (Duke-Nevada), New York Yankees (AAFC) 1947-49, New York Yanks 1950, Browns 1952, Colts 1953, Eagles 1954-55, 49ers 1955-56

Herb Siegert G (Illinois), Redskins 1949-51

Joe Signaigo G (Notre Dame), pre-season Rockets (AAFC) 1948, New York Yankees (AAFC) 1948-49, New York Yanks 1950

Sig Sigurdson E (Pacific Lutheran), Colts (AAFC) 1947

Homer Simmons T (Oklahoma), pre-season Eagles 1947

John Sims B (Tulane), pre-season Boston Yanks 1947

Frank Sinkovitz C (Duke), Steelers 1947-52

Eli Smith B (Grambling), pre-season Rams 1966

Houstin Smith E (Mississippi), Bears 1947-48

Ray Gene Smith B (Cameron-Midwestern), Bears 1954-57

Bill Smyth T (Notre Dame-Cincinnati-Penn St.), Rams 1947-50

Ben Sohn G (USC), Giants 1941

George Speth T (Murray St.), Lions 1942

Ed Stacco T (Colgate), Lions 1947, Redskins 1948

Stan Stapley T (Brigham Young), pre-season Giants 1948

Ernie Stautner T (Boston College), Steelers 1950-63 and pre-season 1964

Odell Stautzenberger G (North Texas Agri., Texas A&M), pre-season Browns (AAFC) 1949, Bills (AAFC) 1949

Jim Still B (Perkinston JC, Georgia Tech), pre-season Dons (AAFC) 1948, Bills 1948-49

Jack Stilwell E (Northwestern), pre-season Patriots 1960

Pete Stout B (Texas Christian, North Texas Agri.), Redskins 1949-50

Jack Sugarman E (Temple), pre-season Redskins 1945

Tony Sumpter G (Cameron), Rockets (AAFC) 1946-47

George Sutch B (Temple-Rochester), Chicago Cardinals 1946

Paul Szakash B (Montana), Lions 1938-39, 1941-42

Walt Szot T (Bucknell), Chicago Cardinals 1946-48, Steelers 1949-50

Paul Terhes B (Bucknell), pre-season Patriots 1961

Ray Terrell B (Mississippi), Browns (AAFC) 1946-47, Colts (AAFC) 1947

Lee Tevis B (Washington of Mo., Miami of Ohio), Dodgers 1947-48

Rupert Thornton G (Santa Clara), 49ers (AAFC) 1946-47

Si Titus E (Holy Cross), Dodgers 1940-42, Steelers 1945

Orv Trask T (Rice), Oilers 1960-61 and pre-season 1962, Raiders 1962

Herb Travenio K (Texas College), pre-season Chiefs 1964, Chargers 1964-65 and pre-season 1966

Bob Trocolor B (Alabama, Long Island), Giants 1942-43, Dodgers 1944
Bob Tulis G (Texas A&M), pre-season Lions 1948
Harold Turner E (Tennessee St.), Lions 1954
James Orville Tuttle G (Phillips, Oklahoma City), Giants 1937-41, 1946
Gasper Urban G (Notre Dame), Rockets (AAFC) 1948
Sam Vacanti QB (Iowa, Purdue, Nebraska), Rockets (AAFC) 1947-48, Colts (AAFC) 1948-49
Vern Valdez B (Antelope Valley JC, Univ. of San Diego), Rams 1960 and pre-season 1961, Bills 1961, Raiders 1962
Carl Valletto E (Alabama), pre-season Steelers 1961
Vic Vasicek G (USC-Texas), Bills (AAFC) 1949, Rams 1950
Norm Verry T (USC), Rockets (AAFC) 1946-47 and pre-season 1948
Walt Viellieu T (Purdue), pre-season Chicago Cardinals 1955
Carroll Vogelaar T (Loyola of LA, Univ. of San Francisco), Boston Yanks 1947-48, New York Bulldogs 1949, New York Yanks 1950
Dewey Wade T (Kansas St.), pre-season 49ers 1956
Larry Wagner T (Vanderbilt), pre-season Titans 1960
Bill Ward G (Washington St.-Washington), Redskins 1946-47, Lions 1947-49
Paul Ward T (Whitworth), pre-season Bears 1961, Lions 1961-62 and pre-season 1963
Caleb "Tex" Warrington C (William & Mary, Auburn), Dodgers (AAFC) 1946-48
George Watts T (Appalachian), Redskins 1942
Jim Weatherall T (Oklahoma), Eagles 1955-57 and pre-season 1958, Redskins 1958 and pre-season 1959, Lions 1959-60 and pre-season 1961
Paul Weaver B (Penn St.), pre-season Steelers 1947
Chuck Weber LB (West Chester), Browns 1955-56, Chicago Cardinals 1956-58, Eagles 1959-61
Tad Weed PK (Ohio St.), Steelers 1955
Jerry Wenzel C (Indiana, St. Joseph's of Ind.), pre-season Redskins 1955
Ben Whaley G (Virginia St.), Dons (AAFC) 1949
Ray Whelan G (LSU-Rochester), pre-season Redskins 1948
Paul White B (Michigan), Steelers 1947
Bob Whitlow C (Arizona), Redskins 1960-61, Lions 1961-65, Falcons 1966, pre-season Rams 1967, Browns 1968
Ray Wietecha C (Michigan St., Northwestern), Giants 1953-62
Wilbur "Wee Willie" Wilkin (St. Mary's of Calif.), Redskins 1938-43, Rockets (AAFC) 1946
Garland Williams T (Georgia-Duke), Dodgers (AAFC) 1947-48, Hornets (AAFC) 1949
Walt Williams B (Boston Univ.), Rockets (AAFC) 1946, Boston Yanks 1947 and pre-season 1948
Kelton Winston B (Wiley), pre-season Bears 1964, pre-season Rams 1966, Rams 1967-68 and pre-season 1969
Pete Wissman C (Washington of Mo., Miami of Ohio, St. Louis Univ.), 49ers (AAFC) 1949, 49ers 1950-52, 1954
Alex Wizbicki B (Holy Cross, Dartmouth), Bills (AAFC) 1947-49, Packers 1950
John Wolff B (Colorado A&M), pre-season Broncos 1960
Lud Wray C (Penn), Massillon Tigers 1919, Buffalo All-Americans 1920-21, Rochester Jeffersons 1922
James Wright G (SMU, North Texas Agri.), Boston Yanks 1947
John Yohn LB (Gettysburg), Colts 1962 and pre-season 1963, Jets 1963 and pre-season 1964
John Yonakor E (Notre Dame), Browns (AAFC) 1946-49, New York Yanks 1950, Redskins 1952 and pre-season 1953
Art Young E (Springfield, Dartmouth), pre-season Steelers 1947
Joe Young E (St. Benedict's, Marquette, Arizona), Broncos 1960-61
Zig Zamlynski B (Villanova), pre-season 49ers 1946
Carroll Zaruba B (Doane, Nebraska), Texans 1960
Frank Zoppetti B (Duquesne), Steelers 1941

Lt. Gen. Ernie Cheatham, Col. Henry Gotard and Lt. Conrad Rucker were on active duty in the mid-1980s.
***

Bob Trocolor played pro ball during World War II while on leave, perhaps the only documented NFL case involving a Marine.
***

Jim Collum (1951), Larry Wagner (1960), Paul Terhes (1961) and Dennis Golden (1963) played with pro teams and Quantico the same seasons. Carl Kilsgaard (1950) did it with San Diego.
***

Frank Reagan and James Higgins were among the few Marine pro footballers on active duty Dec. 7, 1941.

NFL: Jack Adams T, p-s Eagles 1956; Phil Ahwesh B (Duquesne), p-s Redskins 1946; Wendell Bates C (West Texas), p-s Redskins 1951; Howard Perry B (Penn), Rochester 1921-22; Stu Betts B (Northern Michigan), p-s Cowboys 1976; Charlie Carpenter OL (Murray St.), p-s Eagles 1976; Dick Deschaine K, Packers 1955-57, Browns 1958; Tony Elliott NT (Wisconsin-Pratt JC-North Texas), Saints 1982-88; Steve K Fehr (Navy) p-s Bengals 1987, Mike Fisher G (Kansas), p-s Eagles 1962; Sam Fox E (Ohio St.), Giants 1945; Bob Garner T, Giants 1945; Johnny Ray Hatley G (Sul Ross St.), Bears 1953, Cardinals 1954-55, Broncos 1960; Tony Klimek DE (Illinois), Chicago Cardinals 1951-52; Joe Koch HB (Wake Forest), p-s Bears 1953; Mo Latimore G (Hutchinson JC-Kansas St.), p-s Jets; Howard Lehman T (Loyola of L.A., Miss. Southern), p-s Giants 1955; Reed Lennan C (Baltimore CC), Redskins 1945, Dons 1947; Frank Letteri T (Geneva), p-s Steelers 1950, p-s Redskins 1952; John Linnemanstons T (Marquette), p-s Redskins 1956; Glenn Lott (Drake LB), p-s Buffalo, Detroit (mid-'70s).

Jim McCarthy E (Illinois), Dodgers 1946-47, Rockets 1948, Hornets 1949; Eddie Meyers FB (Navy), p-s Falcons 1982-88; Mort Moriarity E (Texas), p-s Eagles 1957; Jim Norman G, p-s Redskins 1955; Phil Pettey OG (Missouri) Redskins 1987; Jim Reynolds B (Auburn), Seahawks 1946; John Rapacz (Oklahoma C), Rockets 1948, Hornets 1949, Giants 1950-54; Jack "Spagyo" Richards E (Arkansas), p-s Redskins 1952; Bob Shann DB (Boston College), Eagles 1965, 1967; Harry Sortal E (Geo. Washington-St. Louis), p-s Chicago Cardinals 1948; Harold Springer E (Central Oklahoma), Giants 1945; Sam Venuto B (Guilford), Redskins 1952; Mike Wilson B (Lafayette), Frankford Yellowjackets 1929; Gus Yahn G (Youngstown), p-s Redskins 1952.

Also: Bob Denton (Pacific), Browns 1960, Vikings 1961-64; Bill LaFleur (Dayton, Penn State), p-s Steelers 1948; Carl Schiller (Montana, Western Michigan), p-s Colts 1948

NFL (6-month)

Erich Barnes DB (Purdue) Bears 1958-60, Giants 1961-64, Browns 1965-71

Lem Burnham DE (Santa Ana JC, USIU) p-s Redskins 1976, Eagles 1977-80 (led team in sacks with 10 in 1977)

Jerry Hillebrand LB (Colorado), Giants 1963-66, Cardinals 1967, Steelers 1968-70

Essex Johnson RB (Grambling) Bengals 1968-75, Bucs 1976

Jacque McKinnon FB-TE (Colgate) Chargers 1961-69, Raiders 1970

Jack Mattox T (Fresno St.) Broncos 1961-62

Rubin "Bud" Whitehead DB-FL (Florida St.) Chargers 1961-68

Football Grand Slam

Linebacker Hardy "Thumper" Brown* played in 4 pro leagues

All-America Football Conference
Dodgers 1948, Hornets 1949

National Football League
Colts 1950, Redskins 1950, 49ers 1951-56

Canadian Football League
Hamilton 1956

American Football League
Broncos 1960

* Brown was a WWII Marine paratrooper.

Sideline Leaders

To some, the selection of Leon "Bud" Carson as the Cleveland Browns' 1989 head coach seemed almost pre-ordained.

For it extended to six the number of seasons that two Marines had been head coaches in the NFL.

In 1984, it was Bum Phillips (Saints) and Les Steckel (Vikings); in 1985, it was Phillips and Darryl Rogers (Lions); in 1986, 1987 and 1988 it was Rogers and Jim Mora (Saints); and in 1989 it was Mora and Carson.

Mora became the fourth former Marine at the Saints' helm.

Actually, the NFL had had a former Marine as head coach each season since 1970 and 1971 when John Mazur was at New England and J.D. Roberts at New Orleans.

There were four in 1972: Mazur, Roberts, Abe Gibron (Bears) and John Ralston (Broncos). It was Gibron, Ralston and John North (Saints) in 1973.

There were five in 1974: Gibron, North, Ralston, Bill Arnsparger (Giants) and Rick Forzano (Lions); and five in 1975: Arnsparger, Forzano, North, Ralston and Phillips (Oilers).

In 1976, Arnsparger, Forzano, Phillips and Ralston returned.

Phillips was the lone Marine at the helm from 1977 through 1983.

Jim Lee Howell had been the most successful of the former Marines, his Giants winning 54 games, three division titles and an NFL title from 1954 through 1960. The New York team with its defense and excitement in the nation's biggest media market also helped popularize the pro sport.

■

For Carson, life began again at 58, hearing aid and all.

In being named the franchise's eighth head coach, his first top job in the NFL, he received a three-year contract worth a reported $400,000 a year.

"I never thought I'd get it (the position)," Carson told the Los Angeles Times. "The last five years I quit worrying about it. I wasn't even thinking about it. I thought it was too late."

He had been a college head coach at Georgia Tech from 1967-71 and an assistant at his alma mater, North Carolina, and South Carolina, Georgia Tech and Kansas. He played with the 1952 Quantico and 1953 Camp Fisher teams.

Things started well at Cleveland. In his first season, the Browns won the AFC Central Division title, beat the Buffalo Bills in the playoffs, 34-30, but lost to the Denver Broncos, 37-21, for the AFC title and a Super Bowl berth.

But an impatient owner (Art Modell) and a battered offensive line led to his firing on Nov. 5, 1990.

But life — and coaching — goes on. Carson was named defensive co-ordinator of the Eagles for the 1991 season.

"He's been an innovator and has made an impact wherever he has gone," Eagles head coach Rich Kotite said, noting Carson had been to the Super Bowl twice with the Steelers and once with the Rams.

■

The role of the former Marine as an assistant coach in the NFL arguably was even more significant.

Carson had helped design Pittsburgh's "Steel Curtain" and been an assistant with the Rams, Colts, Chiefs and Jets.

Don Doll joined the Lions as an assistant in 1963, was with the Rams, Redskins, Packers, Colts and Dolphins before returning to the Lions in 1977.

Brad Ecklund coached with the Cowboys, Falcons, Saints, Eagles and Bears, among others, from 1960 through 1977.

John Idzik was with the Dolphins, Colts, Eagles and Jets 16 seasons.

Bobb McKittrick, beginning in 1971, was with the Rams, Chargers and 49ers, where he shared in their Super Bowl successes.

Jim Myers long was a familiar sight at Tom Landry's side, serving the Cowboys from 1962 until he retired after the 1986 season. He was succeeded by former Marine Jim Erkenbeck. Another longtime Landry aide was Ernie Stautner who, after tours with the Steelers and Redskins, was a Dallas assistant from 1966 through 1988. Dr. Bob Ward joined the Cowboys' staff in 1975.

Bob Schnelker became one of the NFL's most valuable and visible assistants. Beginning in 1963, he was with the Rams, Packers, Chargers, Dolphins, Chiefs, Lions and Vikings.

Dick Voris, from 1961 through 1979, was with the Packers, 49ers, Cardinals, Lions, Colts, Jets and Buccaneers.

Chuck Weber was an aide with the Patriots, Chargers, Bengals, Cardinals, Browns and Colts from 1964 through 1986.

And Ray Wietecha was an assistant with the Rams, Packers, Giants, Bills and Colts from 1963 through 1981.

Arnsparger gained as much fame as an assistant with the Colts and Dolphins as being the Giants' head coach.

Other longtime assistants included Lew Erber, Dick Evans, Jack Faulkner, Chet Franklin and Frank Lauterbur.

■

Dan Topping owned the Brooklyn Dodgers and Tigers, and Joe Foss was the first AFL commissioner, as Marines made their marks, too, in the front offices.

M. Dorland Doyle, Elroy "Crazylegs" Hirsch, Eddie LeBaron and Graham Smith wore general manager's hats.

And a number of others directed personnel, scouting or administrative departments.

Pro Coaches (through 1986)

Bill Arnsparger, New York Giants 1974-76. Assistant Colts 1964-69, Dolphins 1970-73, 1976-80.

Cliff Battles, Brooklyn Dodgers (AAFC) 1946-47.

Hugo Bezdek, Cleveland Rams 1937-38. As a civilian, helped prepare Mare Island for 1918 Rose Bowl game and in 1924 was a consulting coach for All-Marine team.

Marty Brill, Oakland Hornets (AFL) 1944.

Jack Chevigny, Chicago Cardinals 1932. Killed in action on Iwo Jima.

Bob Dove, co-coach Chicago Rockets (AAFC) 1946. Assistant Lions 1958-59, Bills 1960-61.

Chuck Drulis, co-coach St. Louis Cardinals 1961. Assistant Packers 1951-53, Eagles 1954, Cardinals 1968-71 (incomplete)

Jack Faulkner, Denver Broncos 1962-64. Assistant Rams 1955-59, 1966, 1971-79; Chargers 1960-61, Vikings 65, Saints 1967-70, administrator of football operations for Rams 1980-86.

Rick Forzano, Detroit Lions 1974-76. Assistant Cardinals 1966-67, Browns 1968, Lions 1973 (incomplete)

Joe Galat, Montreal (CFL) 1984-85, GM 1986. Assistant at Memphis (WFL) 1974-75, Giants 1977-78, Montreal (CFL) 1979-80, Oilers 1981.

Abe Gibron, Chicago Bears 1972-74. Chicago Wind (WFL) 1975. Assistant Redskins 1960-64, Bears 1965-71, Buccaneers 1976-84, Seahawks (scout) 1985.

Mike Giddings, Hawaii (WFL) 1974-75. Assistant 49ers 1968-73, Broncos 1976. President of Pro Scout Inc., Newport Beach, Cal.

Dick Hanley, Chicago Rockets (AAFC) 1946. Was fired after three games. Sued owner and collected $1 for slander.

Jim Lee Howell, New York Giants 1954-60. Assistant, consultant Giants 1949-53, 1961-86. Record was 54-29-4, including three division titles and one NFL title.

John Mazur, New England Patriots 1970-72. Assistant Bills 1962-68, Patriots 1969-70, Eagles 1973-76, Jets 1977-80.

Jack Meagher, Miami Seahawks (AAFC) 1946.

Jim Mora, Philadelphia Stars (USFL) 1983-84, Baltimore Stars (USFL) 1985, New Orleans Saints 1986. Assistant Seahawks 1978-81, Patriots 1982.

Ernie Nevers, Duluth Eskimos 1926-27, Chicago Cardinals 1929-31, 1939. Assistant Rockets (AAFC) 1946.

John North, New Orleans Saints 1973-75. Assistant Lions 1966-72, Falcons 1977-82, Breakers (USFL) 1984.

O.A. "Bum" Phillips, Houston Oilers 1975-80, New Orleans Saints 1981-85. Assistant Chargers 1967-71, Oilers 1974. Record was 86-80.

John Ralston, Denver Broncos 1972-76. Assistant Eagles 1978; VP/administration 49ers 1979-80; assistant Invaders (USFL) 1983-84; president Breakers 1984-85. Record was 34-33-3.

Vic Ramus, San Francisco (PCFL) 1947-48.

J.D. Roberts, New Orleans Saints 1970-72, Richmond (ACFL) 1969-70. Assistant Jets 1965-66, Saints 1967-68.

Darryl Rogers, Detroit Lions 1985-86.

Maurice "Clipper" Smith, Boston Yanks 1947-48. Rams assistant-scout 1953.

Les Steckel, Minnesota Vikings 1984. Assistant 49ers 1978, Vikings 1979-83, Patriots 1985-86.

Ardell Wiegandt, Calgary (CFL) 1980-81. Assistant Americans (WFL) 1974, Vulcans (WFL) 1975, Calgary 1977-79, Montreal (CFL) 1982, Bills 1985-86.

Also: Sam Rutigliano, Browns 1978-84, assistant with Broncos, Patriots, Jets, Saints

Pro Assistants (through 1986)

Alex Agase, Texans 1952.

Ralph Berlin, trainer, Cardinals 1963-64, Steelers 1968-86.

Jack Bushofsky, scout BLESTO 1977-78, assistant Buccaneers 1979-82, player personnel director Colts 1983-86.

John Butler, Chicago Blitz (USFL) 1984. NFL scout 1981, front office Blitz 1982-83.

Bud Carson, Steelers 1972-77 (helped design "Steel Curtain"), Rams 1978-81, Colts 1982, Chiefs 1983-84 (resigned pre-season), Jets 1985-86.

Owen Dejanovich, Vancouver (CFL) 1973, Wheels (WFL) 1974.

Chuck Dickerson, Toronto (CFL), Fire (WFL), Showboats (USFL) 1984, director of player personnel 1985.

Don Doll, Lions 1963-64, Rams 1965, Redskins 1966-70, Packers 1971-73, Colts 1974, Dolphins 1975-76, Lions 1977-86.

Brad Eckund, Cowboys 1960-64, CEPO scouting 1965, Falcons 1966-67, Saints 1968-70, Eagles 1971-72, Bears 1973, Florida (WFL) 1974, Bears 1975-77.

Lew Erber, 49ers 1975, Raiders 1976-81, Patriots 1982-84, Rams 1985-86.

Jim Erkenbeck, Winnipeg (CFL) 1977, Montreal (CFL) 1978-81, Calgary (CFL) 1982, Stars (USFL) 1983-85, Saints 1986.

Dick Evans, Cardinals 1952, Redskins 1955-56, Browns 1960-63, Eagles 1964-68, Packers 1970, Patriots 1971-72

Dennis Fitzgerald, Steelers 1982-86

Chet Franklin, 49ers 1971-74, Chiefs 1975-77, Saints 1978-79, Raiders 1980-86.

Bob Griffin, Broncos 1966, Falcons 1969-74 (incomplete).

Ron Hudson, Memphis (USFL) 1986.

Tom Hughes, trainer Colts 1955.

John Idzik, Ottawa (CFL) 1955, Dolphins 1966-69, Colts 1970-72, Eagles 1973-76, Jets 1977-79, Colts 1980-81.

Doug Kay, Breakers (USFL) 1983-84.

MacArthur Lane, Invaders (USFL) 1984-85.

Rick Lantz, Patriots 1981.

Frank Lauterbur, Colts 1955-56, 1974-77; Rams 1978-81; Seahawks 1982, Maulers (USFL) 1984, Renegades (USFL) 1985.

"Big Jim" MacMurdo, Eagles 1938-40.

Jim Martin, Broncos 1962, Lions 1967-72, Storm (USFL) 1974, Thunder (USFL) 1975.

Earl Martineau, Dons (AAFC) 1948.

Rod Masterson, strength coach, Raiders 1979.

Thurman McGraw, Steelers 1958-61.

Bobb McKittrick, Rams 1971-72, Chargers 1974-78, 49ers 1979-86.

John McLaughry, Providence (AFL) 1941.

Bill Meyers, Packers 1982-83, Steelers 1984.

Jim Mutscheller, Colts 1963.

Jim Myers, Cowboys 1962-86.

Jim Niblack, Jacksonville (WFL) 1974-75, Bills 1983-84, Renegades (USFL) 1985.

Nick Nicolau, Hamilton (CFL) 1977, Montreal (CFL) 1978-79, Saints 1980, Broncos 1981-86.

Bob Nussbaumer, promotion director Cardinals 1952-53, director of player personnel Lions 1954-56; assistant Lions 1957-64, Browns 1965-71.

Ed Peasley, Hawaii (WFL) 1975, scout Bills 1978.

John Petercuskie, Browns 1978-84.

Frank Reagan, Eagles 1952-53.

Jim Royer, Richmond (ACFL) 1969-70, Saints 1970-72, Redskins 1973, GALAXY 1974, scout Jets 1975-77, personnel director Jets 1978-86.

Joe Sabasteanski, Paterson (AFL) 1943.

Dante Scarnecchia, Patriots 1982-86.

Bob Schnelker, Rams 1963-64, Packers 1965-71, Chargers 1972-73, Dolphins 1974, Chiefs 1975-77, Lions 1978-81, Packers 1982-85, Vikings 1986.

Ray Shands, scout Cowboys 83, assistant Renegades (USFL) 1985.

Ron Smeltzer, British Columbia (CFL) 1984-85.

Bill Smyth, Ottawa (CFL) 1958-62 (incomplete).

Ernie Stautner, Steelers 1963-64, Redskins 1965, Cowboys 1966-86.

Larry Sullivan, Hamilton (CFL).

Mike Sweatman, Edmonton (CFL) 1975-76, Vikings 1984, Giants 1985-86.

Roger Theder, Colts 1982-84, Outlaws (USFL) 1985.

Orville Tuttle, Yankees (AAFC) 1947.

Bubba Tyer, Redskins 1971-76, trainer 1977-

Dick Voris, Rams 1954, Packers 1961-62, 49ers 1963-67, Cardinals 1968-71, Lions 1972, Colts 1973, Jets 1974-75, Buccaneers 1976-79.

Dr. Bob Ward, Cowboys 1975-86.

Chuck Weber, Patriots 1964-67, Chargers 1968-69, Bengals 1970-75, Cardinals 1976-77, Browns 1978-79, Colts 1980-81, Chargers 1982-86.

Ray Wietecha, Rams 1963-64, Packers 1965-70, Giants 1971-77, Bills 1978-79, Colts 1980-81, Blitz (USFL) 1983, Wranglers (USFL) 1984, scout Packers 1985.

Bob Windish, Orlando (CFL) 1969, Jersey City (ACFL) 1970, BLESTO scouting 1971-72, Houston (WFL) 1974.

Andy Woidtke, Dolphins 1971-72, trainer Florida (WFL) 1974.

NFL Game Officials (through 1986)

Jim Blewett, Ron Botchan, Pat Harder, Joe Muha, Jack Nix, Bill O'Brien, Norm Schachter, Frank Sinkovitz.

NFL head coaches 1987, '88

Jim Mora (Saints), Darryl Rogers (Lions)
Rogers was fired at mid-season of 1988

1989 head coaches

Bud Carson (Browns), Mora

NFL assistants 1987

Bud Carson (Jets), Chuck Dickerson (Bills), Don Doll (Lions), Jim Erkenbeck (Cowboys), Dennis Fitzgerald (Steelers), Bobb McKittrick (49ers), Nick Nicolau (Broncos), Dante Scarnecchia (Patriots), Bob Schnelker (Vikings), Ernie Stautner (Cowboys), Les Steckel (Patriots), Mike Sweatman (Giants), Roger Theder (Chargers), Bob Ward (Cowboys)
Ron Eckert, the Redskins' "practice official," was featured in an AP story.
Dr. Lem Burnham was the Eagles' player-relations consultant.

NFL Assistants 1988-89

Dr. Lem Burnham, player-relations consultant, Eagles; Carson, Dickerson, Doll, Erkenbeck, Fitzgerald, McKittrick, Nicolau (Raiders), Paternostro, Scarnecchia, Schnelker, Stautner, Steckel, Sweatman, Ward
McKittrick a member of Super Bowl champion 49ers' staff 1989, 1990.
Erkenbeck ousted in Jones-Johnson-Landry move. Signed by Chiefs 5-89
Fitzgerald's contract not renewed 1-89.
Nicolau fired 1-89; joined Bills 2-89
Scarneccia to Colts, 1989
Steckel's contract not renewed 12-88
Ward ousted by Cowboys 1-90
Dickerson rejoined Bills 3-90

NFL Assistants 1990-91

Burnham, Dickerson, Erkenbeck, McKittrick, Nicolau, Scarnecchia, Schnelker, Sweatman
Schnelker fired 1-91
Scarnecchia fired, signed by Patriots 1-91
Carson signed by Eagles 1-91
Stautner signed by Broncos 2-91

NFL assistants/1992

Arnsparger, to Chargers
Dickerson, released
Erkenbeck, to Rams
Jay Robertson, to Colts

NFL game officials 1987, '88

Ron Botchan (umpire)

Who Was That Man?

Marines have been called many things through the years. But in the old Pacific Coast Football League, some weren't even called by their own names.

No one knows for sure how many Marines played in the league during its 1940-1948 existence. Officially, at least 35 have been identified, but the total could have been twice as high.

Because of military and amateur-athletics regulations, an undetermined number of Marines played under assumed names to avoid a court-martial or protect college eligibility.

A Navy directive issued in late 1944 and reiterated in 1945 said pro opponents were to be played only on military bases and that military athletes were not to compete for pro teams.

As an apparent result, a check of newspaper microfilm showed, a sudden increase in the number of "Smiths" and "Johnsons" playing for PCFL teams took place.

The most extreme cases, perhaps, involved tackle Wilbur "Wee Willie" Wilkin of the Washington Redskins, who anchored the El Toro Marines' line in 1944 and 1945, and Hall of Famer Elroy "Crazylegs" Hirsch, the all-purpose back for the '45 Flying Marines.

Wilkin, a PFC or private or PFC depending on the month, played under the name "Ben Finney" at an all-star game in nearby Orange County. (Maj. Ben Finney was the Flying Marines' business manager.)

The irony, of course, was that Wilkin, a former All-Pro, stood 6-6 and weighed 290. Few — on the field or in the stands — were fooled.

Recalls teammate Pat Lahey: "At the half, we were told that the coach (Dick Hanley), Finney and assistant Ernie Nevers were in the stands, and we were afraid to go out for the second half.

"Willie dressed and left. I went back out and played.

"Thank God, he (Hanley) needed us — especially Willie — or we would have been put in the brig!"

At practice Monday, according to Lahey, Hanley said he "heard rumors of outside employment." From now on, Hanley said, there'll be "two-a-days" (double workouts).

Several players at a 1988 banquet of the Pacific Coast Football League confirmed that Wilkin also played under various names.

Bob Dove, a Notre Dame All-American stationed at El Toro, said Hanley also spotted Wilkin at a post-season all-star game.

"Frank Ramsey, an Oregon State tackle, and Willie played. Hanley and Finney go to the game; here comes Willie out on the field with no headgear. 'Ben, look at that SOB disguised under a Bandaid,' Hanley said. Wilkin used Hanley's name in the game. Finney laughed. Ramsey used Finney's name. Hanley laughed."

The 1987 annual of the Professional Football Researchers Assn. reported that back Jack Sullivan of the 1945 San Diego Bombers might have been Hirsch, also a star at Wisconsin (1942), Michigan (1943) and Camp Lejeune (1944).

315

, "For the record," the publication said, "Sullivan (whose college was listed as Fordham) made the All-PCFL second team for 1945, despite missing almost half the season with injuries."

Asked recently if he had used the name Sullivan, Hirsch answered, "Guilty."

The Flying Marines' travel kept Hirsch out of more San Diego games than any injuries. And it's doubtful the name change fooled many defenders.

Hirsch gave up two years of college eligibility in 1946 to join Hanley, Wilkin, Lahey and much of the 1944 and '45 El Toro teams to form the Chicago Rockets of the new All-America Football Conference.

Several others performed for the Flying Marines' 1944 and '45 teams on Fridays and Saturdays and then for a PCFL team on Sundays, as travel and physical condition permitted.

In addition, the NFL seasons of that era ended in early December, and some players then headed to the West Coast under their names, or others, for late-December or early-January games.

The Marines, of course, weren't the only military personnel employing game aliases. There were soldiers, sailors and airmen doing the same.

An exception was back Steve Bagarus (Notre Dame), a key player on the San Diego Bombers' 1942, 1943 and 1944 champions. He played as Bagarus — with the Army's permission.

Actually, a 9-game schedule in 1944 and 10-game schedule in 1945 had given El Toro players additional chances to play for the PCFL teams from September to January.

"Many of us played under various names for the pro teams in LA and San Francisco," said Lahey. "I played two years with the Hollywood Rangers. I used the name Pat Haley and Mike Haley most of the time."

Lahey, an end from John Carroll, was on El Toro's 1944-45 teams. "Haley" was simply a rearrangement of Lahey.

"The Army was doing it, too," Lahey said. "We had a family and kids and $100 to $140 (a game) was a lot of money."

Dove played two years in the Coast League under the name Bruce Thyberg (Whittier) and the number 82. Sometimes the name and number depended on what jersey was available; the programs already had been printed.

Dove recalled one game in which he, Lahey, Hirsch and Wilkin drove to San Diego to play for the Bombers — an appropriate team nickname for El Toro players — against Oakland. But a fanbelt broke, they hit a storm and arrived late. San Diego already had enough players and needed only Wilkin and Willie, who brought pads and shoes.

Brill, an Oakland coach, was a Notre Dame man, "So he asked Lahey and I to play for Oakland. They gave us jerseys and equipment and we did (play).

"We drove home, of course, in the same car. There were only one or two places then to stop between San Diego and Santa Ana. We hit one, and Willie ordered six bottles of beer. When they arrived, I reached for a bottle. A big arm came down on mine. It was Willie's. 'That's mine.' "

316

That was one of the few people Dove, 6-2 and 222, a former Knute Rockne Trophy winner and future nine-season pro, didn't argue with. He, Lahey and Hirsch had to order their own.

"The first bottle went down," Dove said. "I looked and the second was down; he (Wilkin) had 2½ bottles before his second breath."

San Diego also was the beneficiary in 1942 and 1943 of Marines (principally officers) from the nearby Marine Corps Base as well as just-opened Camp Pendleton, where Hanley's combat-conditioning program was headquartered. They played as duties and regulations permitted.

Once hostilities ended, however, regulations relaxed a little and servicemen awaiting release to civilian life — like guard Ray "Pappy" Crabaugh (Gonzaga) returning from South Pacific combat — started joining PCFL teams in 1945 late in the season and for the post-season.

Besides name changes, there was the hype. In one program Haley (Lahey) not only was listed by the fictitious name but also was said to have played for the Cleveland Rams. (Lahey had a 1941 tryout with the Detroit Lions.) The game, on Sunday, Jan. 13, 1946, pitted the Los Angeles Bulldogs against the National Professional League Stars.

The Service All-Stars (principally El Toro and Fleet City Navy players such as Buddy Young) took on the Hollywood Bears (bolstered by 4th Air Force players) on Sunday, Jan. 20, 1946 at Gilmore Stadium.

W.R. "Bill" Schroeder, co-owner and general manager of the champion Bears, who won, 14-0, recalled: "After the game, I gathered together $11,000 in paper money, placed it in a large market bag, and turned it over to Hirsch, Wilkin and (Paul) Governali. The threesome hustled to a nearby bar, where the remaining service team members gathered and divided up the loot.

"Each of the boys received over $600, which was a sizable sum for the boys who were in service."

Schroeder was founder and director of the former Helms Athletic Foundation museum.

Three weeks later, the 15 El Toro players, Young and several Fleet City players joined forces again as the All-Service All-Stars to oppose the Kenny Washington All-Stars, a collection of 4th Air Force, USC, UCLA and black athletes, to benefit the Veterans Housing Fund.

And to the north, the Marines also had landed. In San Francisco, a city known for its fondness for Leathernecks, the San Francisco Clippers employed a former Marine as coach (Vic Ramus) and at least half a dozen former Marines during parts of the 1946-48 seasons.

Marines listed in the PFRA annual included:

Ray Apolskis C (Marquette), San Diego Bombers 1943

John Barrett B (Georgetown), Bombers 1943 (killed in action)

Marty Brill, coach, Oakland Hornets 1944

Tom Bussjaeger C (Loyola of LA, Arizona-Flagstaff), Bombers 1944, San Francisco Clippers 1946

Wayne Clark E (Utah), Hollywood Bears 1941, Bombers 1942-43, Los Angeles Bulldogs 1945, Salt Lake City Seagulls 1946-47

Ray "Pappy" Crabaugh G (Gonzaga), Bombers 1942-43, Oakland Giants 1945-46

Shan Denniston G-B (St. Mary's), Los Angeles Bulldogs 1942, Hollywood Bears 1942, 1945, 1948

Joe Donohoe T (Navy), Bombers 1942
Hank Ennen C (UCLA), Los Angeles Bulldogs 1948
Chuck Fenenbock B (UCLA), Bombers 1941, Los Angeles Bulldogs 1942-43, 1945
Gene Flathmann T (Clemson-Navy), Bombers 1942
Jack Guthrie B (St. Mary's), Bombers 1941
Bob Herwig C (Cal), San Francisco Packers 1941
Elroy Hirsch (aka Jack Sullivan) B (Wisconsin-Michigan), Bombers 1945
Herman Hodges B (Howard of Ala.), Bombers 1943
Bill Kennedy G (Michigan St.), Bombers 1943
Fred Klemenok B (Univ. of San Francisco, Pacific), San Francisco Clippers 1948
Bob Kurtz G (Cal), San Francisco Clippers 1944, 1946
Francis Mattingly B (Texas A&I), Bombers 1941
Jim Musick B (USC), Los Angeles Bulldogs 1947
Ted Ogdahl B (Willamette), Bombers 1946
Dick Pfuhl B (Missouri, St. Louis), Honolulu Warriors 1946
Vic Ramus B (Univ. of San Francisco), San Francisco Packers 1943, SF Clippers 1946-48 (coach 1947-48)
Gene Riska G (BYU), Salt Lake City Seagulls 1946
Ed Roseborough T (Univ. of San Francisco), San Francisco Clippers 1948
John Sanchez T (Los Angeles CC, USF, Redlands), San Francisco Clippers 1946
Ray "Scooter" Scussell B (Yale), Honolulu Warriors 1947
Sig Sigurdson E (Pacific Lutheran), Tacoma Indians 1946
Bernie Smith E (Tulane), Bombers 1945
Ken Smock B (Purdue), Los Angeles Mustangs 1944
Ben Sohn G (USC), Bombers 1946
Bruce Thyberg (aka Bob Dove) C (Whittier), Bombers 1944
Robert "Bull" Trometter B (St. Mary's), Bombers 1942
Bob Troppmann C (Univ. of San Francisco, Redlands), Oakland Giants 1946, San Francisco Clippers 1946-47
Ray Whelan C (LSU-Rochester), Bombers 1944-45
Wilbur "Wee Willie" Wilkin T (St. Mary's), Hollywood Bears 1945

San Francisco 49ers offensive line coach Bobb McKittrick coached a regimental team at Camp Pendleton.

A Marine Town

Chicago traditionally has been a Marine town. But the fledgling Chicago Rockets and Chicago Hornets of the All-America Football Conference might have overdone the hospitality.

The team had an affinity to signing former Marines, whether just out of service, out of college or after being released by other teams.

The trend started in 1945 even before the league opened when trucking operator John Keeshin signed Coach Dick Hanley and 17 players of the 1944 and '45 nationally ranked El Toro Flying Marines teams.

The Santa Ana Register's headline on Sept. 13, 1946 put it this way: "Rockets (El Toro) Make League Bow."

The Rockets in 1946 had such luminaries as back Elroy "Crazylegs" Hirsch, tackle Wilbur "Wee Willie" Wilkin and end Bob Dove from El Toro. Eight former Marines started against the Buffalo Bills and in the two games against the Los Angeles Dons seven started.

Other former El Toro and Marine players in 1946 were:

Back Walt Clay, back Don Griffin, end Ralph Heywood, tackle Chuck Huneke, back Bill Kellagher, end Pat Lahey, back Ernie Lewis, guard James O'Neal, guard Jim Pearcy, end Frank Quillen, guard Joe Ruetz, back Bill Schroeder, guard Tony Sumpter, tackle Norm Verry and back Walt Williams plus assistant coach Ernie Nevers. Dove and Wilkin were two of the interim tri-coaches after Hanley was fired.

With the coaching changes and a rash of injuries, the Rockets finished with a 5-6-3 record. Because of ownership and organizational problems, the team slumped to 1-13 records in 1947 and '48 but recovered a little to 4-8 in 1949, the final AAFC season.

The signings continued. Chicago (the name was changed to the Hornets for the '49 season) also used these former Marines:

1947 — guard Alex Agase, tackle Alf Bauman, quarterback Angelo Bertelli, Clay, Dove, Hirsch, Huneke, Kellagher, Lahey, Lewis, tackle Harley McCollum, center Fred Negus, O'Neal, Pearcy, Quillen, tackle John Sanchez, Schroeder, Sumpter, quarterback Sam Vacanti, Verry.

1948 — Bertelli, guard Bob David, back Chuck Fenenbock, Hirsch, end Farnham "Gunner" Johnson, Kellagher, end Lafayette "Dolly" King, end Ray Kuffel, Lewis, Negus, Pearcy, back Bob Perina, Ruetz, back Julie Rykovich, Sumpter, guard Gaspar Urban, Vacanti.

1949 — linebacker Hardy "Thumper" Brown, tackle Ted Hazelwood, end Bob Heck, King, Kuffel, Lewis, Negus, Pearcy, tackle Garland "Bulldog" Williams.

Also: Jim McCarthy E (Illinois), Rockets 1948, Hornets 1949; John Rapacz C (Oklahoma), Rockets 1948, Hornets 1949

Super Bowl Marines

The Super Bowls get all the publicity these days. But the NFL and AFL championship games used to be *the* time for former Marines to get together and swap war stories before and after kicking and gouging each other on the gridiron.

At least five Marines played in a Super Bowl and 18 were assistant coaches of participating teams. The first Super Bowl was in 1967.

Jim Lee Howell had been head coach of the New York Giants in 1956, 1958 and 1959 NFL title games. They won in 1956, lost in 1958 and 1959.

At least 34 former former Marines started in NFL or AFL title games. One of the most memorable, the 23-17 overtime victory by Baltimore over New York in 1958, featured Art Donovan, Big Daddy Lipscomb and Jim Mutscheller of the Colts and Charlie Conerly, Ken MacAfee, Bob Schnelker and Ray Wietecha of the Giants.

The 1941 New York Giants had at least seven players bound for the Corps; the 1948 Chicago Cardinals had at least seven former Marines.

And in the USFL of the 1980s, Jim Mora was a head coach in all three title contests (winning two and losing one), and three former Marines were assistants on participating teams.

Super Bowl Participants

Cornelius Johnson, Baltimore Colts 1969, 1971
Howard Kindig, Miami Dolphins 1973
Gary Larsen, Minnesota Vikings 1970, 1974, 1975
Mike Mercer, Kansas City Chiefs 1967
Mike Montler, Denver Broncos 1978

Assistants

Bill Arnsparger, Baltimore Colts 1969, Miami Dolphins 1972-73-74, 1983
Bud Carson, Pittsburgh Steelers 1975, 1976, Los Angeles Rams 1980
Chuck Dickerson, Buffalo Bills 1991-92
Lew Erber, Oakland Raiders 1977, 1981
Jack Faulkner, Los Angeles Rams 1980
Chet Franklin, Oakland/Los Angeles Raiders 1981, 1983
John Idzik, Baltimore Colts 1971
Frank Lauterbur, Los Angeles Rams 1980
Bobb McKittrick, San Francisco 49ers 1982, 1985, 1989-90
Jim Myers, Dallas Cowboys 1971-72, 1976, 1978-79
Nick Nicolau, Buffalo Bills 1991-92
Dante Scarnecchia, New England Patriots 1986
Bob Schnelker, Green Bay Packers 1967-68
Ernie Stautner, Dallas Cowboys 1971-72, 1976, 1978-79
Les Steckel, New England Patriots 1986
Mike Sweatman, New York Giants 1987. 1991
Dr. Bob Ward, Dallas Cowboys 1976, 1978-79
Ray Wietecha, Green Bay Packers 1967-68

Championship Games

Coach

Jim Lee Howell, New York Giants 1956, 1958-59

Starters

Cliff Battles, Boston/Washington Redskins 1936-37
Bill Blackburn, Chicago Cardinals 1947
Ron Botchan, Los Angeles Chargers 1960
Cloyce Box, Detroit Lions 1952
Harold Bradley, Cleveland Browns 1955
Gus Cifelli, Detroit Lions 1952
Charlie Conerly, New York Giants 1959
Mike Connelly, Dallas Cowboys 1967
Bob Dee, Boston Patriots 1963
Steve Filipowicz, New York Giants 1946
George Franck, New York Giants 1941
Hugh Gallarneau, Chicago Bears 1941-42, 1946
Abe Gibron, Cleveland Browns 1951-52-53-54-55
Pat Harder, Chicago Cardinals 1948, Lions 1952
Elroy Hirsch, Los Angeles Rams 1951, 1955
Dick Huffman, Los Angeles Rams 1949-50
Jim Lee Howell, New York Giants 1938-39, 1941, 1946
Weldon Humble, Cleveland Browns 1950
Ted Karras, Chicago Bears 1963
Ken MacAfee, New York Giants 1956
Charley Malone, Boston/Washington Redskins 1936-37, 1940
Jim Martin, Detroit Lions 1952, 1954
Fred "Curly" Morrison, Cleveland Browns 1955
Joe Muha, Philadelphia Eagles 1947-48
Jim Mutscheller, Baltimore Colts 1958-59
Volney Peters, Los Angeles Chargers 1960
Skeet Quinlan, Los Angeles Rams 1955
Hank Schmidt, San Diego Chargers 1961, 1963
Bob Schnelker, New York Giants 1958-59
Bill Smyth, Los Angeles Rams 1949
Orville Trask, Houston Oilers 1960
Orville Tuttle, New York Giants 1938-39
Ray Wietecha, New York Giants 1956, 1958-59, 1961-62
Wee Willie Wilkin, Washington Redskins 1940, 1942

Franck, Howell, Medal of Honor winner Jack Lummus, Frank Reagan, Ben Sohn and Tuttle were members of the New York Giants' 1941 division champion.

Ed Beinor, John Kovatch, Malone and Wilkin were members of the Washington Redskins' 1942 title team.

Filipowicz, Franck, Pete Gorgone, Howell, Reagan and Tuttle were members of the Giants' 1946 division champion.

Ray Apolskis, Blackburn, Harder and Waltz Szot were members of the Chicago Cardinals' 1947 title team.

Apolskis, Blackburn, Bob Dove, Harder, Marvin Jacobs, Dick Loepfe and Szot were members of the Cardinals' 1948 division champion.

Nelson Green, Duke Iverson, Darrell Palmer, Ed Sharkey and Joe Signaigo were members of the New York Yankees 1948 (AAFC) division champion.

Alex Agase, Humble, Palmer and John Yonakor were members of the Cleveland Browns' 1949 (AAFC) title team.

Agase, Gibron, Humble, Martin and Palmer were members of the Browns' 1950 title team.

Paul Barry, Hirsch, Huffman, Smyth and Vic Vasicek were members of the Los Angeles Rams' 1950 division champion.

Box, Cifelli, Don Doll, Harder, Martin and Thurman McGraw were members of the Detroit Lions' 1952 title team.

Box, Dove, Harder, Martin and McGraw were members of the Lions' 1953 title team.

Bradley, Gibron, Don King and Morrison were members of the Browns' 1954 title team.

Box, Dove, Martin and McGraw were members of the Lions' 1954 division champion.

Bradley, Gibron, Morrison, John Pettibon and Chuck Weber were members of the Browns' 1955 title team.

Bob Griffin, Hirsch, Big Daddy Lipscomb and Quinlan were members of the Rams' 1955 division champion.

Howell (coach), Conerly, Gene Filipski, MacAfee, Schnelker and Wietecha were with the Giants' 1956 title team.

Don Bingham, Ed Brown, Tom Roggeman and Ray Smith were members of the Chicago Bears' 1956 division champion.

Art Donovan, Lipscomb and Mutscheller were on the Baltimore Colts' team that defeated the Giants, 23-17, in the famous 1958 overtime title game.

Conerly, MacAfee, Schnelker and Wietecha were members of the Giants' 1958 division champion.

Donovan, Lipscomb and Mutscheller also were teammates on Colts' 1959 championship team.

USFL Title Games

Coach
Jim Mora, Baltimore Stars 1983-84, Philadelphia Stars 1985

Assistants
Jim Erkenbeck, Philadelphia/Baltimore Stars 1983-84-85
MacArthur Lane, Oakland Invaders 1985
Ray Wietecha, Arizona Wranglers 1984

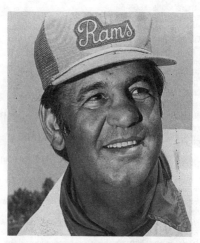

Jack Faulkner, a WW II Marine, is administrator of football operations for the Los Angeles Rams. A former Broncos head coach, he was an assistant with the Chargers, Vikings, Saints and University of Cincinnati. He played at Miami (Ohio).

Marine All-Pros

All-Pro is the top of the ladder.

And at least 20 former Marines reached it. Tackle Leo Nomellini was there six times; back Ernie Nevers five times (he played only five seasons); tackle Art Donovan four; back Cliff Battles, back Pat Harder, tackle Dick Huffman and tackle Big Daddy Lipscomb, three; and end Elroy "Crazylegs" Hirsch, tackle Ernie Stautner and tackle Wilbur "Wee Willie" Wilkin, twice.

Six former Marines — Battles, Donovan, Hirsch, Nevers, Nomellini and Stautner — were elected to the pinnacle, the Pro Football Hall of Fame, and Battles, Nevers and Hirsch to the Helms Pro Hall of Fame.

Another milestone was the Pro Bowl, for which at least 45 Marines were selected.

Nomellini again led the way with 10 appearances; Stautner had 9, Donovan 5, Bob Dee, Don Doll, Abe Gibron, Eddie LeBaron and Ray Wietecha 4, and Hirsch, Lipscomb and Wilkin 3.

And four former Marines were Coaches of the Year.

Battles (twice) and Jim Musick led the NFL in rushing; Ed Brown, Charlie Conerly and LeBaron in passing; Joe Arenas, Al Carmichael, Don Doll and Joe Scott in kickoff returns; Pat Harder (three times) and Hirsch in scoring; Harder, Jim Martin and Mike Mercer (AFL) in field goals; Hirsch in receiving; MacArthur Lane in receptions; Fred "Curley" Morrison and Joe Muha in punting; and Frank Reagan a co-leader in interceptions.

All-Pros

Cliff Battles, HB Boston Braves/Redskins 1933, 1936, Washington Redskins 1937
Cloyce Box, E Detroit Lions 1952
Art Donovan, T Baltimore Colts 1954-55-56-57
Chuck Drulis, G Chicago Bears 1948
Hugh Gallarneau, B Chicago Bears 1946
Joe Geri, HB Pittsburgh Steelers 1950
Abe Gibron, G Cleveland Browns 1955
Pat Harder, FB Chicago Cardinals 1947-48-49
Elroy Hirsch, E Los Angeles Rams 1951, 1953
Dick Huffman, T Los Angeles Rams 1947-48-49
Tut Imlay, B Los Angeles Buccaneers 1926
Big Daddy Lipscomb, T Baltimore Colts 1958-59, Pittsburgh Steelers 1961
Thurman McGraw, T Detroit Lions 1952
Ernie Nevers, FB Duluth Eskimos 1926-27, Chicago Cardinals 1929-30-31
Leo Nomellini, T San Francisco 49ers, 1951-52-53-54, 1957, 1959
Volney Peters, T Los Angeles Chargers 1960
Joe Signaigo, G New York Yanks 1950
Ernie Stautner, T Pittsburgh Steelers 1956, 1958
Ray Wietecha, C New York Giants 1958
Wee Willie Wilkin, T Washington Redskins 1941-42.

Pro Hall of Fame

Cliff Battles, Boston Braves/Redskins 1932-36, Washington Redskins 1937
Art Donovan, Baltimore Colts 1950, New York Yanks 1951, Dallas Texans 1952, Colts 1953-61
Elroy Hirsch, Chicago Rockets (AAFC) 1946-48, Los Angeles Rams 1949-57
Ernie Nevers, Duluth Eskimos 1926-27, Chicago Cardinals 1929-31

Leo Nomellini, San Francisco 49ers 1950-63
Ernie Stautner, Pittsburgh Steelers 1950-63

Helms Pro Hall of Fame

Battles, Nevers, Hirsch

Coaches of the Year

Jack Faulkner, AFL (Denver Broncos 1962) (UPI)
Jim Mora, USFL (Philadelphia Stars 1984) (Sporting News)
Mora, NFL (New Orleans Saints 1987) (AP, Sporting News)
John Ralston, AFC (Denver Broncos 1973) (UPI)

Pro Bowl

Ray Apolskis, Chicago Cardinals 1942
Frank Balasz, Green Bay Packers 1940
Cloyce Box, Detroit Lions 1951, 1953
Ed Brown, Chicago Bears 1956-57
Charlie Conerly, New York Giants 1951, 1957
Bob Dee, Boston Patriots 1962, 1964-65-66
Don Doll, Detroit Lions 1951-52-53, Washington Redskins 54
Art Donovan, Baltimore Colts 1954-55-56-57-58
Bob Dove, Chicago Cardinals 1951
Chuck Drulis, Chicago Bears 1942
Brad Ecklund, New York Yanks 1951-52
Leo Elter, Washington Redskins 1957
Hugh Gallarneau, Chicago Bears 42
Joe Geri, Pittsburgh Steelers 1951-52
Abe Gibron, Cleveland Browns 1953-54-55-56
Rob Goode, Washington Redskins 1952, 1955
Pat Harder, Chicago Cardinals 1951, Lions 1953
Elroy Hirsch, Los Angeles Rams 1952-53-54
Jim Lee Howell, New York Giants 1939
Brad Hubbert, San Diego Chargers 1968
Weldon Humble, Cleveland Browns 1951
Gary Larsen, Minnesota Vikings 1970-71
Eddie LeBaron, Washington Redskins 1956, 1958-59; Dallas Cowboys 1963
Big Daddy Lipscomb, Baltimore Colts 1959-60, Pittsburgh Steelers 1963
Charley Malone, Washington Redskins 1942
Jim Martin, Detroit Lions 1962
Thurman McGraw, Detroit Lions 1951
Art Michalik, San Francisco 49ers 1954
Jim Mutscheller, Baltimore Colts 1958
Leo Nomellini, San Francisco 49ers 1951-52-53-54, 1957-58-59-60-61-62
Volney Peters, Washington Redskins 1956
Skeet Quinlan, Los Angeles Rams 1955
Bob Schnelker, New York Giants 1959-60
Ernie Stautner, Pittsburgh Steelers 1953-54, 1956-57-58-59-60-61-62
Orville Tuttle, New York Giants 1939-40
Jim Weatherall, Philadelphia Eagles 1956-57
Ray Wietecha, New York Giants 1958-59, 1961, 1963

Also: Ed Beinor, Hardy Brown, Dick Huffman, MacArthur Lane, Mike Mercer, Curley Morrison, Hank Schmidt, Wee Willie Wilkin (3)

Doll was the Player of the Game in 1953, Stautner the Lineman of the Game in 1957 and Lipscomb the Lineman of the Game in 1960 and 1963.

League Leaders

Joe Arenas (San Francisco 49ers) led in kickoff returns (16 for a 34.4 average) in 1953.
Cliff Battles (Boston/Washington Redskins) led in rushing (576 yards) in 1932 and (874 yards) in 1937.
Ed Brown (Chicago Bears) led in passing (96 of 168 for 1,667 yards and 11 TDs) in 1956.

Al Carmichael (Green Bay Packers) led in kickoff returns (14 for a 29.9 average with one for 106 yards) in 1955.

Charlie Conerly (New York Giants) led in passing (113 of 194 for 1,706 yards and 14 TDs) in 1959.

Don Doll (Detroit Lions) led in kickoff returns (21 for a 25.5 average) in 1949.

Pat Harder (Chicago Cardinals) led in scoring (102 points) in 1947, (110 points) in 1948 and (102 points) in 1949.

Harder also led in field goals (7) in 1947.

Elroy Hirsch (Los Angeles Rams) led in receiving (66 for 1,495 yards and 17 TDs) in 1951. Hirsch also led in scoring (102 points) in 1951.

MacArthur Lane (Kansas City Chiefs) led in receptions (66 for 686 yards) in 1976.

Eddie LeBaron (Washington Redskins) led in passing (79 of 145 for 1,365 yards and 11 TDs) in 1958.

Jim Martin (Detroit Lions) led in field goals (24) in 1963.

Mike Mercer (Oakland Raiders-Kansas City Chiefs) led in field goals (21) in 1966.

Fred "Curly" Morrison (Chicago Bears) led in punting (57 for a 43.3 average) in 1950.

Joe Muha (Philadelphia Eagles) led in punting (57 for a 47.3 average) in 1948.

Jim Musick (Boston Redskins) led in rushing (809 yards) in 1933.

Bob Nussbaumer (Chicago Cardinals) led in interceptions (12) in 1949.

Frank Reagan (New York Giants) tied for lead in interceptions (10) in 1947.

Joe Scott (New York Giants) led in kickoff returns (20 for a 28.5 average, with one for 99 yards) in 1948.

NFL Game Officials

Jim Blewett, Ron Botchan, Pat Harder, Joe Muha, Jack Nix, Bill O'Brien, Norm Schachter, Frank Sinkovitz.

Lt. Gen. Ernie Cheatham was a tackle and linebacker for Loyola (Cal.), Camp Fisher, Baltimore Colts, Pittsburgh Steelers and MCRD San Diego.

In The Front Offices

There were Marines at the very top, too, in pro football. Dan Topping, for example, was an owner; Clint Murchison Jr., a board chairman; Joe Foss, a league commissioner; and Elroy "Crazylegs" Hirsch, Eddie LeBaron, Fred "Curly" Morrison and Graham Smith, general managers.

Former Marines also served in a variety of other front-office positions. Among them:

Pro Executives (through 1986)

Ed Buckley, director of pro scouting Blitz (USFL) 1983, Wranglers (USFL) 1984. Had been affiliated also with NFL, AFL, CFL, Redskins, Chiefs.

Don Canning, controller Rams 1965-77.

Leo Carlin, Eagles front office 1960-77, business manager Stars (USFL) 1985.

Jim Cipriano, ticket director Bills 1969-86.

J.W. "Wobble" Davidson, personnel evaluator for Cowboys, Rams, Saints, Chargers and 49ers 1969-83.

Bob Dee, VP Quincy (ACFL) 1969.

Mike Dizney, assistant GM Renegades (USFL) 1985.

M. Dorland Doyle, VP Redskins 1942.

Joe Foss, AFL commissioner 1960-66.

Bruce Gelker, owner Storm (WFL) 1974.

Elroy "Crazylegs" Hirsch, GM and assistant to the president Rams.

Carroll Huntress, GALAXY 1973-74, scout Jets 1975-81.

Robert Irsay, owner Colts 1972-86.

Robert Keating, director Schaefer Stadium 1971, executive VP/GM Colonials (ACFL) 1973, Stars (WFL) 1974.

Richard Kitchen, secretary Broncos 1979.

Eddie LeBaron, GM Falcons 1977-82, VP/chief operating officer 1982-84.

Rod MacKenzie, owner Sacramento (California Football League) 1979, commissioner of league 1982.

Joe Mansfield, field security manager Giants 1976-86.

Patrick T. McGahn Jr., partner Stars (USFL) 1984.

Jerry Mickelsen, assistant ticket manager Rams 1968-86.

Jim Milam, equipment manager Oilers 1968-73, Houston (WFL) 1974.

Fred "Curly" Morrison, VP/GM Sun (WFL) 1974, chief operating officer Express (USFL) 1983.

Clint Murchison Jr., chairman of the board Cowboys 1960-83.

Graham Smith, GM Lions 1942.

Stan Springer, scout Redskins 1967-68, scout CEPO 1969.

Joe Sullivan, front office Packers 1957-58, Bears 1959-65, Rams 1966-70, Redskins 1971-72, VP/operations Cardinals 1973-81.

Dan Topping, owner NFL/AAFC Brooklyn Dodgers/Tigers in the 1940s.

Fred Williams, security consultant, assistant to the president, VP/administration Saints 1968-84.

Chuck Ziober, equipment manager Sun (WFL) 1974-75. Also with Chargers, Broncos, Dolphins and Saints organizations 1969-73.

NFL executives 1987

Jack Bushofsky (director of player personnel, Colts), John Butler (director of college scouting, Bills), Jack Faulkner (administrator, football operations, Rams), Chet Franklin (director of player personnel, Chargers), Robert Irsay (president and treasurer, Colts), Eddie LeBaron (NFL Management Council), Jim Royer (pro personnel director, Jets)

NFL Executives 1988-89

Jack Bushofsky, Butler, Faulkner, Franklin, Irsay, Royer
Franklin dismissed 12-89

NFL Executives 1990

Jack Bushofsky, Butler (director of player personnel), Faulkner, Warren "Lockerbox" Jones (asst. to the chairman of the board, San Diego Chargers), Royer

NFL Executives 1991

Eddie LeBaron was one of five Sacramento-area businessmen who submitted an application to bring an NFL expansion team to the Calif. capital.

Frederick W. Smith is founder/chairman/CEO of Federal Express, which is sponsoring Federal Express Orange Bowl football game for 4 years beginning in 1990. Smith formed Mid-America Football Inc. to land an NFL team in Memphis but removed himself as a potential owner

Pervis Atkins was a standout at Camp Pendleton before starring at Santa Ana College, New Mexico State (an All-American) and six years in the pro ranks as a back, flanker and kick returner. Nowadays, he's better known as a movie and TV actor.

327

Their Canadian Club

They sang "North of the Border" as well as "South of the Border" in the late 1940s, the 1950s and the 1960s. The Canadian Football League offered an alternative to the NFL and AFL, and, in some cases, paid more.

Some Marines started their careers up there; others ended it in Canada.

And several stayed for a long look. For example, tackle Dick Fouts played 13 seasons for British Columbia and Toronto. Tackle Bill Frank put in 14 seasons with British Columbia, Toronto and Winnipeg. Guard Lew Golic, whose sons would star for Notre Dame and in the NFL, was with Montreal, Hamilton and Saskatchewan seven seasons. Tackle Dick Huffman was selected to the league's Hall of Fame. He played seven seasons with Winnipeg and Calgary.

Others went north to coach.

At least four Marines were still around to play in the short-lived World Football League.

And there were other leagues to play and coach in, as far back as the 1930s or as recently as the 1980s.

Canadian Football League

Mel Anderson B, pre-season Ottawa 1962

Marv Beguhl T (Idaho), Saskatchewan 1954

Bill Blackburn C (Rice-Southwestern Louisiana), Calgary 1951-52

Tommy Bland E (West Liberty), Toronto 1970

Wayne Bock T (Illinois), pre-season Toronto 1960

Alex Bravo T (Cal Poly SLO), Saskatchewan 1956

Sam Brazinsky C (Villanova), Hamilton

Lem Burnham DE (US International), Winnipeg 1976

Owen Dejanovich, assistant Vancouver 1973

Moses Denson B (Maryland St.), Montreal 1970-72

Chuck Dickerson L (Florida-Illinois), Montreal; assistant with Toronto 1976-79

Joe Eilers T (Texas A&M), Hamilton-Sakatchewan 1966

Jim Erkenbeck, assistant Winnipeg 1977, Montreal 1978-81, Calgary 1982

Gary Fallon B (Syracuse), Hamilton 1963, Toronto 1964

Chuck Fenenbock B (UCLA), Calgary 1950

Gene Filipski B (Army-Villanova), Calgary 1958-61

Lou Florio T (Boston College), pre-season Calgary 1957

Dick Fouts T (Missouri), Toronto 1957-61, British Columbia 1962-66, Toronto 1967, British Columbia 1968-69

Bill Frank T (San Diego CC-Colorado), British Columbia 1963-64, Toronto 1965-68, Winnipeg 1970-76

Joe Galat, coach Montreal 1984-85, general manager 1986; assistant Montreal 1979-80

Tom Gates B (Oceanside JC, San Bernardino JC, Univ. of San Diego, Oregon St.), Toronto-Montreal 1963

Jack Ging B (Oklahoma), Edmonton 1954

Lew Golic G, Montreal 1956, Hamilton 1956-57, Saskatchewan 1958-62

Bob Griffin C (Arkansas), Calgary 1959, assistant Montreal 1967-68

Andy Heck B (Wake Forest), team not available

Ed Heuring T (Maryland), Montreal 1957-59

Conrad Hitchler E (Missouri), Calgary 1963-65

Dick Huffman T (Tennessee), Winnipeg 1951-55, Calgary 1956-57

John Idzik, assistant Ottawa 1955
Bob Kelley C (West Texas), Hamilton 1958
John Kerns T (Ohio Univ., North Carolina, Duke), Toronto 1950-51
Moe Lattimore G (Hutchinson JC-Kansas St.), Calgary 1972-74, Saskatchewan 1974, Hamilton 1974-75
Jimmy Lawson B (Los Angeles St.), Montreal 1965
Eddie LeBaron QB (Pacific), Calgary 1954
Ken Lutterback B (Evansville), pre-season Toronto 1960
Dunn Marteen B (Santa Ana JC, Los Angeles St.), Ottawa 1965
Billy Martin B (Minnesota), Edmonton 1965, Toronto 1966, Winnipeg 1968
Tom Maudlin QB (USC), Toronto 1962, Montreal 1963
Jack Maultsby T (North Carolina), Toronto 1956
John Mazur QB (Notre Dame), British Columbia 1954
Willie McClung T (Florida A&M), Hamilton 1962
Bob Meyers B (Stanford), Calgary 1955
Art Michalik G (St. Ambrose), Calgary 1958
Nick Nicolau, assistant Hamilton 1977, Montreal 1978-79
Jack Nix E (USC), Saskatchewan 1951
Ed Rayburn T (Rice), Montreal 1958
Bill Roberts B (Dartmouth), British Columbia 1957
J.D. Roberts G (Oklahoma), Hamilton 1954
Willie Roberts E (Tulsa), Calgary 1955-57
J.T. Seaholm T (Texas), Calgary 1958 and pre-season 1959
Ed Sharkey G (Nevada-Duke), British Columbia 1957-58
Ron Smeltzer, assistant British Columbia 1984-85
Bill Smyth, assistant Ottawa 1958-62
Larry Sullivan, assistant Hamilton
Mike Sweatman, assistant Edmonton 1975-76
Al Viola G (Northwestern), pre-season Saskatchewan 1958
Dick Washington B (Notre Dame), Calgary 1958, pre-season Hamilton 1959
Jim Weatherall T (Oklahoma), Edmonton 1954
Ardell Wiegandt, coach Calgary 1980-81; assistant Calgary 1977-79, Montreal 1982
John Yonakor E (Notre Dame), Montreal 1951
Joe Young E (St. Benedict's, Marquette, Arizona), pre-season Saskatchewan 1958

Also: Hardy Brown LB (Tulsa), Hamilton 1956, Glenn Lott (Drake DB), Montreal 1976, Emidio Petrarca B (Boston College), p-s Ottawa 1958

Canadian Football League (1987-)

Joe Galat, GM, British Columbia Lions; named coach 8-89
MacArthur Lane, asst. Calgary, 1988
Darryl Rogers, coach, Winnipeg Blue Bombers 1991

***

Dick Huffman was elected to the Candian Football Hall of Fame in 1988.

World Football League

Buck Baker T (Georgia), Jacksonville 1974-75
Lem Burnham DE (US International), Hawaii 1974-75
Glenn Ellison B (Arkansas), Jacksonville 1974
Howard Kindig C-DE (Los Angeles St.), Jacksonville 1974-75

American Association (1936-42)

Chuck Avedisian G (Providence), Long Island 1941 (all-league selection)
Bob Beckwith T (New Britain Tch.), Hartford 1942
Jim Breen T (North Central), Newark 1939
Ronnie Cahill QB (Holy Cross), Holyoke 1942
John "Cowboy" Farris HB (Wyoming), Jersey City 1941
Roger Grove HB (Michigan St.), Brooklyn Bushwicks 1937
Lew Hamity QB (Chicago), Newark 1941
Leo Katalinas T (Catholic), Paterson 1939-42 (assistant 1940)

Eulis Keahy T (Geo. Washington), Jersey City 1940
Jack Lee FB (Carnegie Tech), Long Island 1940
Mike Mazurki T (Manhattan), Passaic 1936
John McLaughry B (Brown), assistant, Providence 1941
Tim Moynihan FB (Notre Dame), Passaic 1936
Keith Topping E (Stanford), Danbury 1937
Bob Trocolor FB (Long Island-Alabama), Paterson 1941
Paul Weaver QB (Penn St.), Springfield 1942, Providence
Larry Yurkonis QB (Niagara), Providence 1941

American Football Leagues (1936-41)

Ed Beinor T (Notre Dame), St. Louis 1939
John "Cowboy" Farris HB (Wyoming), Buffalo 1940
Thel Fisher B (Drake), Boston 1940
Lew Hamity HB (Chicago), East Chicago 1939
Eulis Keahy T (Geo. Washington), New York 1941
Bill Lazetich HB (Montana), Columbus 1939
Nick Padgen C (Creighton), Columbus 1939-41 (2nd team all-league selection 1941)
Claude "Cupe" Perry T (Alabama), Pittsburgh 1936-37
Dave Rankin E (Purdue), Kenosha 1941
Larry Yurkonis HB (Niagara), Buffalo 1941

American Football League (1946-50)

Verlie Abrams G (Missouri-Notre Dame), Wilmington 1949
Phil Ahwesh HB (Duquesne), Jersey City 1947
Chuck Avedisian G (Providence), Long Island 1946-47 (all-league selection 1946)
Angelo Bertelli QB (Notre Dame), coach Paterson 1950
Bob Buel T (Wisconsin-Franklin & Marshall), Paterson 1947
Geo. "Beast" Bytsura T (Duquesne), Bethlehem 1946, Wilkes-Barre 1947
Pete Calcagno C (Panzer-Bucknell), Bloomfield 1947, Newark 1948
Vin Carlesimo G-T (Villanova), Paterson-Newark 1946, Newark 1948
John Dzitko QB (Villanova), Jersey City 1946-47
Weldon "Scratch" Edwards T (TCU-North Texas Agri.), Wilmington 1948
Bill Erickson G (Georgetown), Jersey City 1946-47
Martin Fay G (Manhattan-Dartmouth), Jersey City 1946
Sam Fox E (Ohio St.), Jersey City-Paterson 1946
Geo. Franck HB (Minnesota), Jersey City 1948
Gorham Getchell E (Temple), Bethlehem 1947
Bernard Gillespie E (Scranton), Bethlehem-Scranton 1946, Wilkes-Barre 1947
Pete Gorgone FB (Muhlenburg), Bethlehem 1947-48
Ralph Grant QB (Bucknell), Wilkes-Barre 1947-48
Nelson Greene T (Tulsa), Paterson 1949
Marv Jacobs T (Central Washington), Bloomfield 1947, Wilmington 1949
Bill "Bull" Johnson G (SMU-North Carolina), Akron 1946 (2nd team all-league selection)
Farnham "Gunner" Johnson E (Wisconsin-Michigan), Bloomfield 1947
Ed Kasky T (Villanova), Long Island 1946-47, Richmond 1947
Don Kasprzak HB (Columbia-Dartmouth), Jersey City-Paterson 1949
Leo Katalinas T (Catholic), Paterson 1946
Bill Kellagher HB (Fordham), Bethlehem 1949
Mike Kerns T (Villanova-Penn St.), Bethlehem 1946, Wilmington 1947, assistant Wilmington 1948
Frank Kiesecker QB (Manhattan), Long Island 1946
John Koniszewski T (Geo. Washington), player-assistant Wilkes-Barre 1947
Mike Kostynick HB (Manhattan-Bucknell), Paterson 1946, Long Island 1947
Adam Kretowicz E (Holy Cross), Newark 1946
Bert Kuczynski E (Penn), Bethlehem 1946-47, Wilmington 1947-49
Earl Lambert FB (Manhattan-Dartmouth), Long Island-Jersey City 1947, Jersey City 1949
Reid Lennan G (Baltimore CC), Wilmington 1946, 1949
Bob Logel E Bethlehem 1949
Leo Long HB (Duke), Newark 1948
Len "Tuffy" McCormick C (Baylor-Southwestern of Texas), Wilmington 1947
Bob McDougal FB (Miami of Fla.-Duke), Richmond 1948

Bob Mirth T (Moravian-Muhlenburg), Richmond 1949-50 (all-league selection 1949)
Dom Papaleo G (Boston College), Erie 1950
Keith Parker HB (Missouri-Purdue), Paterson 1947
Al Perl B (Youngstown-Georgia), Erie 1949
Joe Polce E (Indiana), Richmond 1950
Bob Polidor HB (Villanova), Wilmington 1949 (2nd team all-league selection)
Jim Reynolds B (Auburn), Jersey City 1947
Joe Sabasteanski C (Fordham), Long Island 1946, player-assistant Paterson 1950
Geo. Speth T (Murray St.), Charlotte 1948-49
Chris Stefan QB (Ohio Univ.), Erie 1949
Bob Thalman G (Richmond), Richmond 1947-48
Si Titus C (Holy Cross), Jersey City 1946-49
Bob Trocolor B (Long Island-Alabama), coach Paterson 1946
Jim Worst E (Manhattan-Bucknell), Paterson 1946, Jersey City 1948

Continental Football League

Tommy Bland B (West Liberty), Wheeling 1962-64, Fort Wayne 1965, player-coach Orlando 1968-69
Don Christman E (Richmond), Richmond 1966
Chuck Dickerson, assistant, Toronto 1964-66
Alvin Hall S, Providence 1965 (all-league selection)
Cleveland Jones B (San Diego CC-Oregon St.), Orange County Ramblers 1967
Mike Kasap, assistant, Charleston 1966
Tony Koszarsky B (North Carolina St.), Richmond 1965
Jimmy Lawson B (Los Angeles St.), Orlando 1968
Dunn Marteen QB (Santa Ana JC-Los Angeles St.), Montreal 1966-67
Stan Quintana B (New Mexico), Las Vegas 1969
Jerry Ward QB (Bowling Green), Richmond 1965
Bob Wilson T (West Chester), Pottstown 1971
Bob Windish (Villanova), coach-executive, Orlando

Atlantic Coast Football League

Bob Dee, vice president, Quincy 1969
Danny Hale G (West Chester), Pottstown 1968
Robert Keating, executive VP/general manager, Colonials 1973
Leonard Moore T (Jackson St.), Richmond 1968-69
J.D. Roberts (Oklahoma), coach, Richmond 1969-70
Jim Royer (Navy), assistant, Richmond, 1969-70
Bob Windish (Villanova), coach-executive, Harrisburg, Jersey and Westchester

Other leagues

Dave Culmer E, Costa Mesa Raiders (Western) 1964
Mike Dau, coach, Lake County Rifles (Central States) 1965
Dick Deschaine K Marinette Hornets 1952
Dan Droze B (North Carolina), Virginia Sailors
Brad Ecklund (Oregon), coach, Orange Empire Outlaws (California) 1981
Joe Fowlkes E, Providence Steam Roller 1962
Walt Herron B, Costa Mesa Raiders (Western) 1964
Al Hoisington E (Pasadana JC), Orange County (Cal.) Rhinos 1958 (Pacific Coast Football Conference)

Cleveland Jones B (San Diego CC-Oregon), Orange County Rhinos (Western) 1965
Jimmy Lawson B (Los Angeles St.), Costa Mesa Raiders (Western) 1964
Charlie Malone E (Texas A&M), St. Louis Gunners 1933
Rod McKenzie, owner, Sacramento (California) 1981; commissioner, California League 1982
Ernie Merk B, Orange County Rhinos (Western) 1964
Palmer Mitchell LB (East Los Angeles JC), Orange County Rhinos (Western) 1964
Steve Noe G, Costa Mesa Raiders (Western) 1964
Jim Norris E, Costa Mesa Raiders (Western) 1964
Terry O'Brien, Baltimore Eagles (Interstate Football League)
Ray Piotrowski B, Honolulu Bears 1944

Johnny Scott B (Lafayette), Philadelphia Quakers (American) 1926
Dave Shuford, assistant, San Diego Sharks (California) 1981-82
Jerry Stens E, Costa Mesa Raiders (Western) 1964
Bob Tougas B (Providence), Providence Steam Roller
Bob Windish (Villanova), coach-executive, San Diego Sharks (California), and Bologna, Italy
Joe Young E (St. Benedict's-Marquette-Arizona), Tucson Rattlers 1958 (Pacific Coast Football Conference)

***

Tommy Bland was elected to the Semi Pro/Minor League Football Hall of Fame in 1982, Bob Windish in 1987.

Arena League

1987: Larry Zierlein, asst., Washington Commandoes
1988: Lew Erber, assistant, Los Angeles Cobras; Jim Niblack, assistant, Chicago Bruisers
1990: Ernie Stautner, head coach, Dallas Texans

NFL Alumni Inc.

Gen. Paul X. Kelley, elected to advisory Board of Governors.
Elroy Hirsch was second vice president, and he and Charles Weber were on Board of Directors.
Art Donovan received group's Career Achievement Award on March 8, 1989.

World League of American Football 1991

Rich Apolskis G (Arkansas), Barcelona Dragons (Ray's grandson)
Chet Franklin, co-ordinator, pro scouting/reserve team
Doug Kay, assistant, Raleigh-Durham Sykhawks
Larry Zierlein, assistant, New York-New Jersey Knights

***

Inaugural season of International League of American Football was set in Europe, but league folded 5-90.
ILAF founder and commissioner was Carroll P. Huntress.
John Idzik was to have been a head coach had the league started.
Otto Kofler was to have been defensive coordinator of London Lightning.

World League/1992

Chet Franklin, GM, Montreal Machine; Jim Niblack, assistant, Sacramento Surge; John Petercuskie, scout, Ohio Glory; Joe Viadella, assistant, Ohio Glory; Larry Zierlein, assistant, New York-New Jersey Knights

On the Move

John Ralston visited Russia to teach Soviet athletes the techniques of pro football.
He also coordinated the World League of American Football's "Operation Discovery," a search for talent in Europe.
He also coached Fresno Bandits to 42-0 victory over Moscow Bears at Fresno 7-4-90

Dixie League

Fran Holmes B (Santa Clara, Pacific), Norfolk 1946; Tim Moynihan C (Notre Dame), Baltimore, 1937; George Speth T (Murray St.), Charlotte 1946-47; Eddie Teague B (N.C> State, North Carolina) Greensboro 1946; Bob Thalman G (Richmond), Richmond 1947.

APFA

Ernest Watson (Olivet) B Detroit 1920

Miscellaneous

Jean "Cheesie" Neil, at the time a Marine, played with Ernie Pinckert's College All-Stars against the Chicago Bears in the 1930s during their West Coast rivalry.

1992 / Darryl Rogers, coach, Arkansas Miners, Pro Spring Football League (folded)

A Draft They Liked

What Marine team had the most players drafted by the NFL, AAFC or AFL?

Surprisingly, the 1945 Fleet Marine Force Pacific team in Pearl Harbor that posted a disappointing 0-4 record. It had 36.

Seventeen players on the 1944 El Toro team were drafted, as were 23 on the '45 team. The numbers would have been higher but a number of players already had been signed by the new All-America Football Conference and NFL teams were reluctant to waste a draft choice.

Three of the New York Giants' first seven picks in 1941 would serve in the Marines.

The Corps corraled the cream of the nation's sophomores and juniors in the 1942-43 school year in the V-12 program. As a result, 9 of the Brooklyn Dodgers' first 17 picks in '44 were Marines; 11 of the Green Bay Packers' choices in '44 were Marines; three of the Pittsburgh Steelers' first four choices in '44 were Marines; 8 of the Washington Redskins' first 15 picks in '44 were Marines; and three of the Philadelphia Eagles' first four picks in '45 were Marines.

Ten of the Giants' 20 picks in 1946 were Marines.

The popularity of Marines and former Marines also extended to No. 1 picks, with at least 18 chosen in the first round:

Harry Agganis, Angelo Bertelli, Tony Butkovich (KIA), Al Carmichael, George Franck, Rob Goode, Paul Governali, Pat Harder, Elroy "Crazylegs" Hirsch, Jack Jenkins, MacArthur Lane, Bob MacLeod, Les McDonald, Fred Morrison, Joe Muha, Leo Nomellini, Johnny Podesto and John Yonakor.

(At least three other No. 1's, Steve Filipowicz, Mike Micka and Frank Sinkwich, signed for Marine duty but did not serve a full tour for various reasons.)

Second-round choices included:

Blondy Black, Lamar Blount, Earl Cook, Alvin Dark, Tom Dean, Tom Farmer, Bob Griffin, Elmer "Buck" Jones, Jim Martin, Thurman McGraw, John McLaughry, Mike Montler, Frank Morze, Frank Reagan, Julie Rykovich, Dave Schreiner (KIA), Joe Scott, Ernie Stautner, Marv Stewart, Keith Topping, Jim Weatherall, Mac Wenskunas and Ralph Wenzel.

(Three other No. 2's, Bob Nussbaumer, Bob Odell and Wayne Williams, signed for Marine duty but did not serve a full tour for various reasons.)

Third-round choices included:

Alf Bauman, Charlie Conerly, Bob Dethman, Bob Dove, Jackie Fellows, Bill Gray, Nelson Greene, Ralph Heywood, Saxon Judd, Lloyd Merriman, Billy Mixon, Don Owens, Hosea Rodgers and George Savitsky.

(Another No. 3 pick, Earl Audet, signed for Marine duty but did not serve a full tour.)

Draftees

A partial list includes:

Alex Agase 44 (Packers, 6), Harry Agganis 52 (Browns, 1), Al Akins 44 (Rams, 4), John Aland 45 (Rams, 13), Tom Alberghini 43 (Rams, 13), Bob Albrecht 46 (Rams, 18), Billy Aldridge 45 (Packers, 30), Wilson Allison 61 (Colts, 18), Cliff Anderson 44 (Packers, 20), Joe Andrejco 44 (Rams, 9), Dee Andros 50 (Cards, 14), Ray Apolskis 41 (Cards, 5), Joe Arenas 51 (49ers, 8), Ron Aschbacher 55

(49ers, 10), Walt Ashcraft 53 (Redskins, 26), Pervis Atkins 60 (Raiders), Johnny August 45 (Rams, 8), Bo Austin 57 (Redskins, 13), Jim Austin 45 (Eagles, 15).

Tommy Bailes 54 (Eagles, 20), John Baklarz 43 (Redskins, 16), Frank Balasz 39 (Packers, 16), Ken Barfield 52 (Redskins, 23), Bobo Barnett 43 (Packers, 8) and 45 (Cards, 14), John Barrett 43 (Redskins, 20) (KIA), Paul Barry 49 (Rams, 13), Bob Bauman 43 (Bears, 22) (KIA), Frank Bauman 46 (Bears, 12), Lloyd Baxter 45 (Packers, 22), Ron Beagle 56 (Cards, 17), Wendell Beard 46 (Bears, 7), Ed Beinor 39 (Bears, 4), Relden Bennett 44 (Boston, 16), Gordon Berlin 47 (Bears, 22), Ed Berrang 49 (Redskins, 5), Angelo Bertelli 44 (Boston, 1), John Bicanich 44 (Dodgers, 11), Gene Bierhaus 43 (Packers, 23), Don Bingham 53 (Bears, 7), Blondy Black 43 (Dodgers, 2), Bill Blackburn 44 (Cards, 5), Bill Bledsoe 43 (Dodgers, 20), Allen Bliss 57 (Browns, 26), Lamar Blount 44 (Giants, 2), Wayne Bock 57 (Cards, 5), Fred Boensch 44 (Rams, 7), Rex Boggan 52 (Giants, 20), Don Boll 53 (Redskins, 48), John Bond 44 (Boston, 13), Harry Botsford 46 (Boston, 26), Cloyce Box 48 (Redskins, 18), Jack Boyd 45 (Bears, 10), Pat Boyle 44 (Bears, 27), Jim Bradshaw 45 (Redskins, 17), Alex Bravo 54 (Rams, 9), Tom Brock 43 (Packers, 11), Ed Brown 52 (Bears, 6), Gail Bruce 46 (Steelers, 30), Nick Burke 43 (Cards, 16), Al Bush 46 (Giants, 12), Tony Butkovich 44 (Rams, 1)

Ralph Calcagni 44 (Boston, 29), Gus Camarata 47 (Lions, 32), Jim Camp 48 (Cards, 6), Fred Campbell 55 (Cards, 18), Jerry Carle 47 (Packers, 28), Al Carmichael 53 (Packers, 1), Ernie Cheatham 51 (Steelers, 21), Andy Chisick 40 (Cards, 7), Don Christman 62 (Patriots, 24), Gus Cifelli 50 (Lions, 19), Walt Clay 46 (Giants, 10), Tom Coll 43 (Rams, 21), Tom Colella 42 (Lions, 7), Spot Collins 44 (Boston, 25), Chas. Conerly 45 (Redskins, 11), Manny Congedo 60 (Rams, 17, and Patriots), Zuehl Conoly 43 (Eagles, 10), Earl Cook 48 (Yanks, 2), Russ Cotton 41 (Steelers, 11), Hugh Cox 44 (Packers, 16), Jim Cox 44 (Packers, 19), John Coyne 56 (Rams, 20), Jim Crawford 50 (Bears, 20), Dick Creavy 43 (Bears, 28), Bill Cromer 47 (Bears, 18), Jim Cullom 49 (Redskins, 24) and 50 (Redskins, 17)

Joe D'Agostino 54 (Colts, 15), Bob Dal porto 47 (Rams, 23), Don Daly 55 (Lions, 17), John Damore 55 (Giants, 13), Alvin Dark 45 (Eagles, 2), Bob David 47 (Rams, 25), Jim Davis 60 (Patriots), Warren Davis 50 (Giants, 23), Joe Day 43 (Redskins, 14), Tom Dean 45 (Boston, 2), Bill DeChard 51 (Redskins, 11), Bob Dee 55 (Redskins, 19), Owen Dejanovich 64 (Oilers, 11) and (Colts, 19), Chuck Dellago 45 (Eagles, 4), Moses Denson 71 (Oilers, 16) and 72 (Redskins, 26), Don Deskins 60 (Raiders), Don Doll 48 (Lions, 9), Art Donovan 47 (Giants, 20) and 51 (Browns, 4), Tom Dorais 45 (Lions, 30), Bob Dove 43 (Redskins, 3), Wally Dreyer 47 (Bears, 15), Phil Dupler 58 (Bears, 18)

Brad Ecklund 47 (Packers, 18), Don Edmiston 42 (Bears, 15), Weldon Edwards 47 (Redskins, 12), Virgil Eikenberg 45 (Dodgers, 18), Bump Elliott 47 (Lions, 10), Vern Ellison 57 (Steelers, 12), Ken Elmore 55 (Rams, 22), Mike Enich 41 (Packers, 10), Bill Erickson 48 (Giants, 6), Jesus Esparza 54 (Colts, 26), Jay Dale Evans 61 (Broncos, 6)

Terry Fails 55 (Eagles, 19), Gary Fallon 62 (Vikings, 12), Jack Faris 58 (Redskins, 14), Tom Farmer 43 (Rams, 2), John Feltch 52 (Cards, 10), Jackie Field 43 (Steelers, 16), Steve Filipowicz 43 (Giants, 1), Pat Filley 44 (Rams, 10), Gene Filipski 53 (Browns, 7), Willis Fjerstad 59 (Steelers, 30), Pat Flanagan 51 (Giants, 14), Wayne Flanigan 45 (Lions, 14), Royce Flippin 56 (Redskins, 27), Dick Fouts 56 (Rams, 22), Jerry Fouts 55 (Bears, 30), Terry Fox 41 (Steelers, 15), George Franck 41 (Giants, 1), Bill Frank 64 (Dallas, 18) and (Chargers, 24), Neal Franklin 51 (Eagles, 21), Herman Frickey 44 (Giants, 7), Fred Fugazzi 65 (Patriots, 20), Lou Futtrell 45 (Dodgers, 7) and 49 (Eagles, 21)

Vern Gagne 47 (Bears, 14), Bernie Gallagher 47 (Lions, 6), Hugh Gallarneau 41 (Bears, 4), Mike Garzoni 47 (Redskins, 4), Tom Gates 60 (Rams, 18) and (Texans), John Genis 44 (Dodgers, 14), Joe Geri 49 (Steelers, 4), Ted Ghelman 51 (Steelers, 17), Bart Gianelli 44 (Rams, 23), Abe Gibron 48 (Steelers, 27) and 49 (Giants, 6), Dennis Golden 63 (Cowboys, 16), Rob Goode 48 (Bears 13) and 49 (Redskins, 1), Zig Gory 45 (Boston, 24), Paul Governali 43 (Dodgers, 1), Bob Graiziger 44 (Dodgers, 7), Ralph Grant 45 (Steelers, 29) and 46 (Packers, 19), Bill Gray 45 (Dodgers, 3) and 47 (Redskins, 5), Stan Green 45 (Lions, 23), Nelson Greene 47 (Giants, 3), John Gremer 60 (Oilers), Bob Griffin 51 (Rams, 2), Don Griffin 44 (Packers, 12), Geo. Grimes 48 (Rams, 4), Al Grubaugh 44 (Packers, 25), Dick Guy 57 (49ers, 18)

Bill Hachten 47 (Giants, 11), Chet Haliski 41 (Rams, 5), Van Hall 44 (Cards, 14), Sid Halliday 45 (Redskins, 19), Lou Hallow 55 (Rams, 26), Ed Hamilton 49 (Rams, 22), Fred Hamilton 47 (Steelers, 19), Roscoe Hansen 51 (Eagles, 29), Bob Hanzlik 44 (Eagles, 11), Pat Harder 44 (Cards, 1), Chuck Harris 54 (Browns, 8), Dave Hayes 63 (Colts, 8) and (Patriots, 11), Jack Hays 59 (49ers, 11), Bob Hazelhurst 46 (Giants, 14) and 47 (Boston, 10), Ted Hazelwood 46 (Bears, 16), Holley Heard 45 (Cards, 11), Bob Heck 48 (Rams, 11), Carey Henley 62 (Bills, 21), Gary Henson 62 (Rams, 14) and (Oilers, 28), Bob Herwig 38 (Cards, 2), Ed Heuring 57 (Bears, 16), Claude Hipps 52 (Steelers, 7) Paul Hirsbrunner 43 (Cards, 12), Elroy Hirsch 45 (Rams, 1), Willard Hofer 39 (Packers, 19), Earl Howell 49 (Rams, 5), Brad Hubbert 66 (Chargers-future, 7), Dick Huffman 45 (Rams, 9), Tom Hughes 45 (Steelers, 19), Weldon Humble 43 (Cards, 24), Dan Hunter 54 (Eagles, 8), Ken Huxhold 51 (Cards, 27)

Bill Iannicelli 45 (Boston, 25) and 46 (Eagles, 9), Larry Isbell 52 (Redskins, 1), Duke Iversen 47 (Giants, 5)

Harold Jackson 55 (Giants, 29), Dick Jamison 44 (Bears, 21), Tom Jelley 51 (Bears, 4), Jack Jenkins 43 (Redskins, 1), Wm. "Bull" Johnson 43 (Bears, 20), Cornelius Johnson 67 (Colts, 8), Wayne Johnston 45 (Bears, 29) (KIA), Buck Jones 46 (Giants, 2), Saxon Judd 44 (Cards, 3)

Mike Kasap 45 (Lions, 10), Dan Kasprzak 45 (Boston, 10), Bob Kelley 52 (Eagles, 25), Dick Kelley 46 (Giants, 20), Ed Kensler 52 (Redskins, 6), John Kerestes 51 (Redskins, 20), John Kerns 46 (Eagles, 13), Ed Kessler 64 (Steelers, 16) and (Oilers, 22), Hal Kilman 50 (Rams, 27), Carl Kilsgaard 50 (Cards, 5), Howard Kindig 64 (Chargers, 14; 1st future) and (Eagles, 13), Geo. Kinek 51 (Rams, 4), Lafayette King 46 (Rams, 5), Tom Kingsford 51 (49ers, 24), Dolph Kissell 42 (Bears, 19), Kit Kittrell 44 (Giants, 21), Earl Klapstein 44 (Eagles, 22), Fred Klemenok 49 (Rams, 24), John Klotz 56 (Rams, 18), Gene Konopka 45 (Rams, 25), Andy Kosmac 46 (Packers, 21), John Kovatch 42 (Redskins, 11), John Kreamchek 53 (Bears, 8), Bert Kuczynski 43 (Lions, 19), Ray Kuffel 44 (Cards, 20), Vic Kulbitski 44 (Eagles, 5).

LeRoy Labat 53 (Colts, 18), Jim Lalikos 46 (Giants, 6), Earle Lambert 45 (Boston, 9), Jim Landrigan 45 (Steelers, 19), Mort Landsberg 41 (Steelers, 20), MacArthur Lane 68 (Cards, 1), Gary Larsen 64 (Rams, 10), Bill Lazetich 39 (Lions, 14), Eddie LeBaron 50 (Redskins, 10), Jack Lee 39 (Steelers, 10), John Lee 55 (Colts, 14), Ernie Lewis 46 (Eagles, 7), Chas. Lively 45 (Dodgers, 20), Jim Loflin 46 (Giants, 19), Jim Lohr 56 (Colts, 26), **Dick Loncar** 59 (Steelers, 29), Leo Long 47 (Boston, 14), Herman Lubker 47 (Packers, 24), Dick Lucas 56 (Rams, 10), Buddy Luper 45 (Cards, 13), Ken Lutterbach 57 (Bears, 24)

Jack MacKenzie 46 (Cards, 24), Bob MacLeod 39 (Bears, 1), John Magee 45 (Eagles, 20), Chick Maggioli 46 (Redskins, 9), Red Maley 44 (Dodgers, 17), Chas. Malmberg 44 (Steelers, 26), Norm Maloney 46 (Lions, 19), Bob Mangene 45 (Boston, 27), Hugo Marcolini 47 (Boston, 16), Bill Marker 54 (Redskins, 8), Billy Martin 61 (Bills, 30), Grady Martin 45 (Redskins, 21), Jim Martin 50 (Browns, 2), John Maskas 44 (Boston, 12), Bob Mathias 53 (Redskins, 30), Jack Maultsby 54 (Rams, 12), Earl Maves 47 (Lions, 26), Art McCaffray 44 (Steelers, 4, Mickey McCardle 44 (Packers, 4), Pat McCarthy 63 (Patriots, 19), Harley McCollum 42 (Redskins, 4), Lloyd McDermott 50 (Packers, 6), Lester McDonald 37 (Bears, 1), Bob McDougal 47 (Packers, 7), Jim McDowell 48 (Bears, 9) and 50 (Lions, 24), Thurman McGraw 50 (Lions, 2), Paul McKee 45 (Redskins, 10), Carl McKinnon 46 (Boston, 29), John McLaughry 40 (Giants, 2), Ralph McLeod 53 (49ers, 27), Frank McPhee 53 (Redskins, 13), Bill Meglen 59 (Rams, 22) and (60 Patriots), Mike Mercer 61 (Vikings, 15), Lloyd Merriman 47 (Cards, 3), Bob Meyers 52 (49ers, 16), Art Michalik 51 (49ers, 17), Mike Micka 44 (Redskins, 1), Bill Miller 44 (Steelers, 20), Paul Miller 53 (Rams, 60), Bill Milner 44 (Bears, 13), Ed Mioduszewski 53 (Lions, 18), Billy Mixon 51 (49ers, 3), Mike Montler 69 (Patriots, 24), Mort Moriarity 57 (Eagles, 15), Fred Morrison 50 (Bears, 1), Frank Morze 55 (49ers, 2), Kelly Mote 46 (Lions, 14), Vince Mroz 45 (Giants, 22), Joe Muha 43 (Eagles, 1), Billy Murphy 44 (Dodgers, 15), Ed Murphy 43 (Steelers, 7), Jim Mutscheller 52 (Texans, 12), Jim Myers 44 (Steelers, 15)

Herb Nakken 56 (Rams, 5), Bob Nanni 44 (Cards, 24), Bob Neff 43 (Eagles, 26), Fred Negus 45 (Rams, 7), Jack Nix 50 (49ers, 20), Leo Nomellini 50 (49ers, 1), John North 45 (Redskins, 4), Bob Nussbaumer 46 (Packers, 2)

Fran O'Brien 48 (Boston, 20), Ed O'Connor 53 (Steelers, 22), Bob Odell 44 (Steelers, 2), Phil Odle 68 (Lions, 6), Chet Ostrowski 52 (Redskins, 10), Lloyd Ott 44 (Cards, 30), Don Owens 57 (Steelers, 3).

Paul Paladino 44 (Packers, 27), Darrell Palmer 43 (Bears, 4), Dom Papaleo 50 (Bears, 4), Bob Patton 52 (Giants, 5), Frank Pavich 55 (Eagles, 25), Tom Payne 50 (49ers, 14), Don Penza 54 (Steelers, 18), Bernie Pepper 44 (Bears, 28), John Perko 44 (Eagles, 8), Al Perl 46 (Steelers, 16), Johnny Perry 44 (Packers, 21) (KIA), Volney Peters 51 (Cards, 13), Emidio Petrarca 56 (Lions, 18), John Pettibon 52 (Texans, 7), Joe Pezelski 45 (Boston, 13), Sam Pino 55 (Packers, 29), Joyce Pipkin 45 (Giants, 27), Howie Pitt 54 (Cards, 12), Jim Pittman 50 (Cards, 26), Johnny Podesto 44 (Steelers, 1), Bob Polidor 48 (Cards, 29), Vic Pollock 52 (Steelers, 23), Barney Poole 45 (Giants, 4), Oliver Poole 44 (Giants, 15), Ray Poole 44 (Giants, 13), Al Postus 44 (Eagles, 20), Jim Powers of St. Mary's 43 (Packers, 16), Jim Powers of USC 50 (49ers, 26), Art Preston 52 (Rams, 21), Pat Preston 43 (Bears, 15), Steve Pritko 43 (Rams, 28)

Skeet Quinlan 52 (Rams, 4), Stan Quintana 66 (Vikings, 11)

Frank Ramsey 38 (Bears, 5), Dave Rankin 41 (Bears, 9), Chas. Rapp 52 (Dallas, 14), Ray Ratkowski 61 (Patriots, 17), Ed Rayburn 56 (Browns, 10), Frank Reagan 41 (Giants, 2), Ken Reese 45 (Eagles, 29), Bill Renna 49 (Rams, 12), Bob Rennebohm 48 (Packers, 12), Dale Rennebohm 36 (Lions, 8), Art Renner 46 (Packers, 5), Dick Reynolds 61 (Colts, 12) and (Oilers, 7), Allen Richards 46 (Bears, 25), Moe Richmond 44 (Boston, 21), Vic Rimkus 53 (Packers, 10), Stan Ritinski 43 (Giants, 27), J.D. Roberts 54 (Packers, 17), Willie Roberts 53 (Rams, 4), Roger Robinson 46 (Redskins, 20), Sam Robinson 45 (Eagles, 6), Tom Roche 53 (Colts, 30), Hosea Rodgers 46 (Giants, 3), Darryl Rogers 57 (Rams, 24), Hal Roise 39 (Bears, 10), Jay Roundy 50 (Giants, 11), Julie Rykovich 46 (Bears, 2), John Ryland 39 (Rams, 14), Lou Rymkus 43 (Redskins, 5)

John Saban 52 (Browns, 30), Joe Sabasteanski 43 (Dodgers, 11), Jack Sachse 44 (Dodgers, 8), Otis Sacrinty 47 (Redskins, 25), Joe Sadonis 45 (Eagles, 8), John Sanchez 44 (Giants, 9), Geo. Savitsaky 47 (Eagles, 3), Hank Schmidt 58 (49ers, 6), Walt Schneiter 57 (Colts, 28), Bob Schnelker 50 (Browns, 29), Dave Schreiner 43 (Lions, 2), Carl Schuette 47 (Lions, 22), John Schuetzner 52 (Lions, 24), Joe Scott 48 (Giants, 2), John Scott 59 (Steelers, 26), J.T. Seaholm 54 (Bears, 13), Len Seelinger 44 (Steelers, 30), Jack Seiferling 46 (Steelers, 5), John Shearer 56 (Colts, 28), Herb Siegert 49 (Redskins, 18), Joe Signaigo 46 (Rams, 8), Rudy Sikich 44 (Dodgers, 4), Frank Sinkwich 43 (Lions, 1), Houstin Smith 47 (Bears, 6), Ken Smock 46 (Bears, 27), Bill Smyth 47 (Rams, 5), Ben Sohn 41 (Giants, 7), Geo. Speth 42 (Lions, 18), Ed Stacco 45 (Redskins, 16) and 46 (Lions, 23), Ray Stackhouse 48 (Cards, 26), John Staples 45 (Giants, 30), Stan Stapley 46 (Giants, 15), Ernie Stautner 50 (Steelers, 2), Odell Stautzenberger 47 (Boston, 27), Harold Steed 46 (Eagles, 22), Gene Stewart 51 (Eagles, 26) , Marv Stewart 37 (Bears, 2), Bert Stiff 43 (Dodgers, 13), Jim Still 48 (Cards, 14), Jack Stilwell 57 (Browns, 20), Pete Stout 46 (Giants, 5), Jay Stoves 43 (Giants, 12), Ray Suchy 52 (Texans, 30), Pete Susick 43 (Packers, 25), Geo. Sutch 43 (Cards, 22), Paul Szakash 38 (Lions, 5), Walt Szot 44 (Cards, 18)

Joe Tepsic 46 (Steelers, 4), Paul Terhes 61 (Colts, 80) and (Patriots, 7), Ed Tokus 55 (Browns, 28), Keith Topping 36 (Boston, 2), Jack Tracy 44 (Packers, 5), Orv Trask 56 (Cards, 24), Ben Trickey 45 (Lions, 12), Bob Trout 52 (Lions, 27), Bob Tulis 47 (Lions, 29), Jim Turner 47 (Bears, 12)

Gaspar Urban 46 (Rams, 15)

Sam Vacanti 45 (Giants, 19), Vic Vasicek 49 (Redskins, 10), Norm Verry 43 (Packers, 7), Jack Verutti 45 (Lions, 20), Al Viola 57 (Redskins, 23), Carroll Vogelaar 47 (Boston, 5)

Dewey Wade 55 (49ers, 25), Larry Wagner 60 (Patriots), Ben Wall 46 (Lions, 16), Tex Warrington 44 (Boston, 7), Jim Weatherall 52 (Eagles, 2), Bill Weeks 51 (Eagles, 18), Howard Weldon 46 (Bears, 28), Mac Wenskunas 46 (Cards, 2), Ralph Wenzel 40 (Steelers, 2), Bob Werckle 52 (Lions, 24), Barney Werner 45 (Eagles, 14), Don Whitmire 44 (Packers, 7), Jerry Whitney 45 (Dodgers, 25), Ray Wietecha 50 (Giants, 12), Garland Williams 45 (Dodgers, 280, Wayne Williams 45 (Dodgers, 2), Windell Williams 45 (Lions, 13), Jack Wink 45 (Giants, 13), Kelton Winston 62 (Bears, 9), Pete Wismann 49 (Boston, 70), Jerry Witt 54 (Redskins, 19), Alex Wizbicki 45 (Steelers, 18), Jim Woodside 44 (Steelers, 19), Harry Wright 43 (Redskins, 11), Jim Sid Wright 44 (Dodgers, 13), Clay Wynne 43 (Steelers, 22)

Ray Yagiello 48 (Rams, 20), John Yonakor 45 (Eagles, 1), Art Young 47 (Steelers, 25), Joe Youⁱg 55 (Bears, 24)

Zig Zamlynski 44 (Rams, 16), Carroll Zaruba 60 (Texans), John Zeigler 46 (Bears, 8), Geo. Zellick 43 (Packers, 22), Wally Ziemba 43 (Redskins, 4)

Also: Doug Ahlstrom, Lions 1944-20; Earl Audet, Redskins 1944-2; Alf Bauman, Lions 1942-2; Karl Bays, Cardinals 1955-23; Stu Betts, Patriots 1976-8; Matt Bolger, Lions 1944-9; Hardy Brown, Giants 1946-10; Kermit Davis, Packers 1944-17; Tom Davis, Redskins 1944-15; Bob Dethman, Lions 1942-3; Fraser Donlan, Dodgers 1942-9; Jackie Fellows, Redskins 1944-3; Harold Fischer, Redskins 1944-5; D.J. Gambrell, Rams 1946-24; Bob Hatch, Giants 1948-13; Herb Hein, Lions 1944-10; Ralph Heywood, Lions 1944-3; Bill Joslyn, Redskins 1944-10; Adam Kretowicz, Giants 1942-18; Dick Loepfe, Chicago Cardinals 1946-11; Glenn Lott, Bills 1976-2.

Geo. Makris, Packers 1943-24; Walt Mayberry, Rams 1938-6; Ted Ogdahl, Redskins 1944-7; Ted Ossowski, Redskins 1944-14; Maurice Patt, Lions 1937-5; John Rapacz, Boston 1947-3, Browns 1947-7; Bob Riddell, Eagles 1939-17; Judd Ringer, Chicago Cardinals 1942-10; Jack Sanders, Giants 1939-15; Bob Shann, Eagles 1965-20; Rupert Thornton, Chicago Cardinals 1942-7; Paul White, Lions 1944-11.

Bob Denton (Pacific), Browns 1959-6.

All-America Football Conference Draftees

Special selection: Bernie Gallagher (Chicago)
Second round: Charley Conerly (Brooklyn)
Third round: Ray Kuffel (Buffalo), Lloyd Merriman (LA), William "Spot" Collins (NY)
Fourth round: Weldon Humble (Miami), Joe Andrejco (Buffalo), Jim Sid Wright (Brooklyn)
Sixth round: Jack Bush (Cleveland)
Seventh round: Garland Williams (Brooklyn), Geo. Savitsky (LA)
Eighth round: Matt Bolger (Chicago), Bob Hazelhurst (Cleveland)
Ninth round: Virgil Eikenberg (Chicago), Ted Ossowski (NY)
10th round: John Maskas (Buffalo), Bill Milner (Brooklyn)
11th round: Martin Chaves (Chicago)
13th round: John Miklich (NY)
14th round: Joe Signaigo (Cleveland)
16th round: John North (Miami)
18th round: Mac Wenskunas (Chicago)
19th round: John Sims (Miami)
21st round: George Watkins (Chicago)
22nd round: Sam Vacanti (Chicago)
25th round: Jim Landrigan (Miami)
  (Miami a few days later became Baltimore.)

For 1948 season

Seventh round: Weldon Edwards (LA), Pete Stout (NY)
Eighth round: Jim Turner (Chicago)
Ninth round: Barney Poole (NY)
12th round: Jim Camp (Brooklyn)
13th round: George Grimes (Buffalo)
15th round: Bill Erickson (LA)
19th round: Bill Cromer (Brooklyn)
20th round: Don Doll (Chicago)
22nd round: Bob Heck (SF)
23rd round: Jim McDowell (Cleveland)
25th round: Bob Rennebohm (Buffalo)
26th round: Jim Still (Buffalo)
29th round: Herb Siegert (SF)

For 1949 season

Secret draft: Abe Gibron (Buffalo), Ernie Stautner (SF). But Stautner was declared ineligible because he was not a senior.
Third round: Earl Cook (Baltimore), Hosea Rodgers (LA)
Sixth round: Joe Geri (LA)
Seventh round: Bill Renna (LA)
Eighth round: Vic Vasicek (Buffalo)
13th round: Roland Dale (Brooklyn), Ed Berrang (NY)
15th round: Pete Wismann (SF)
16th round: Rob Goode (Buffalo)
17th round: Art Donovan (Buffalo)
27th round: Vern Gagne (Cleveland)
  Also: Dee Andros, Los Angeles 1947-20; Earl Cook, Baltimore 1948-3; Dick Loepfe, San Francisco 1948-21; Chas. Malmberg, San Francisco 1947-8; John Rapacz, Cleveland 1947-7; Joe Scott, San Francisco 1948-1; Tony Stalloni, Miami 1947-21

A No-Man's Land

The what-might-have-been will always be with Eddie Meyers, a record-setting Naval Academy back and Marine captain.

Meyers set a host of records at Annapolis and was co-captain of the 1981 team. The 5-9, 210-pounder could run the 40 in 4.55 seconds and appeared to have a promising pro career ahead of him after his tour of duty ended.

He was signed as a free agent by Atlanta and worked out each summer during leave time with the Falcons and even applied in 1985 for a year off to join the NFL team, saying he'd serve three years for each pro season. But the request was turned down by the commandant, Gen. P.X. Kelley (who had played football at Villanova and Quantico).

He also unsuccessfully requested a transfer in 1986 from Camp Pendleton to a recruiting station in Georgia so he could play with Atlanta. Secretary of the Navy John Lehman had said Meyers could play pro football if it didn't interfere with Marine duties.

Meyers was a supply officer with the 1st Service Support Group at Pendleton.

"Lt. Meyers incurred his military obligation to his country when he sought and accepted a free, four-year education at the Naval Academy and a commission in the Marine Corps," Kelley said, adding a transfer "would be a shameful waste of scarce defense dollars and a violation of the public trust."

A third request — for a transfer to the Marine Reserve — also had been rejected.

"I figured I'd have a 7-year football career and then serve 21 years in the Marines," Meyers told the Los Angeles Daily News. "Thinking back, that was crazy. ... Anything I ever offered I always got a flat no."

According to former Falcons coach Dan Henning, the military "held Eddie hostage for five years."

"It crossed my mind that I could have broken loose from the Marines," Meyers told The Sporting News. "The Marine Corps has very strict rules, and I could have broken any of them to get out early. But my pride wouldn't let me belittle myself just to play pro ball."

"If he wasn't obligated to the U.S. Marines, he would probably play in the NFL," Falcons General Manager Tom Braatz said.

In a 1984 exhibition against Tampa Bay, Meyers carried five times for 30 yards and a TD.

Finally, his five-year tour over and with a master's degree from National University in San Diego, he joined the Falcons at age 28 in 1987 only to be hurt and put on injured reserve.

He tried out again in 1988 but was cut by the Falcons on July 27.

His Naval Academy records included 43 carries against Boston College in 1981. He also had rushed 42 times that season against Syracuse and against Army in 1979.

His season-record 277 carries of 1981 was broken two years later by Napoleon McCallum, who as a Long Beach-based ensign briefly played with the Los Angeles Raiders. McCallum's 908 career carries at Navy also broke Meyer's mark of 589.

Meyers rushed for 100 yards or more eight times in 1981 and 14 in his Navy career. Twice, he rushed for more than 200. He rushed for four TD's against Syracuse in 1981.

Meyers held single-game rushing marks of 298 yards against Syracuse in 1981 and 278 against Army in 1979. For a season, he is third to McCallum with 1,318 yards in 1981. For a career, he is second to McCallum with 2,935 yards.

And the Middies posted 7-4, 8-3 and 7-3-1 regular-season records from 1979-81, including 2-0-1 against Army, but losing to Houston, 35-0, in the 1980 Garden State Bowl and to Ohio State, 31-28, in the 1981 Liberty Bowl.

■

Starting late in the pro ranks is nothing new to Marines, however.

Kicker Herb Travenio (Texas College, 1st Marine Division, MCRD San Diego) debuted at 33 with the San Diego Chargers in 1964.

Back Moses Denson (Maryland State, Quantico) was a 30-year-old rookie with the Washington Redskins in 1974.

Tackle Harley McCollum and backs Alvin Hall and Jim Levey, like Meyers, were 28 when breaking into the pro ranks.

End John North, tackle Alf Bauman, center Brad Ecklund and back Hosea Rodgers were 27 as rookies.

And breaking in at 26 were tackle Don Boll, Bill Frank, Willie McClung and Hall of Famer Leo Nomellini; guards/linebackers Weldon Humble, Elmer "Buck" Jones and Charles Weber, backs Brad Hubbert, Bill Kellagher, MacArthur Lane and Achille "Chick" Maggioli, and end-kicker Jim Martin.

In addition, tackle Alvin "Moose" Wistert was an All-American at Michigan in 1948 at age 32, and again in 1949 and was captain in '49.

MofH Winner Remembered

The city of Augusta, Ga., dedicated a memorial Sept. 17, 1990, commemorating the 50th anniversary of the activation of the 19th Infantry Battalion of WW II and to honor Medal of Honor recipient Lt. Col. A.J. Dyess, a former Clemson player.

A Tony Award

Anthony Robert "Tony" Elliott, unfortunately, might be the answer to this trivia question: Who was the last Marine athlete to stick in the NFL?

The 6-2, 295-pound nose tackle played for the New Orleans Saints from 1982-88 and started all but one game in 1987, a season in which he had two sacks and 22 tackles (15 of them unassisted).

He is "extremely strong, quick and aggressive, (and) is a prototype nose tackle," said a Saints media guide.

In 1986, he started the first 15 games for Coach Jim Mora, a former Marine, missing the other because of a knee injury, a season in which he had 47 tackles and 3½ sacks.

"He's always hollering," Mora told the Washington Post. "But you have to admire him because the results are showing everybody that what he's doing is successful."

Elliott started all 16 games in 1985 and recovered two fumbles. He had been waived by the Saints prior to the '84 season but was re-signed for the last four games. As a reserve in 1983, he had six sacks in 12 games. He appeared in nine games in 1982, his rookie season, when another former Marine, Bum Phillips, was coach.

Elliott "came to the Saints smallish at 247 pounds but weightlifting and roadworking helped him bulk up," the guide said.

"Being in the Marine Corps seems to give a man something that enables him to go beyond what you think he can do," Elliott told the Post.

Elliott had attended Harding High in Bridgeport, Conn., Wisconsin, Pratt (Kan.) CC and North Texas. He was a fifth-round Saints draft choice.

In the off-season, he "helped organize and direct a developmental league for aspiring pro footballers in New Orleans," the guide said, "and continues to work in the community, lecturing to school children."

The "often-stormy relationship" between Elliott and the Saints was terminated in April 1989 when the team gave the 7-year veteran his outright release, The Sporting News reported. An unprotected free agent without a contract, he was not offered a 1989 contract.

"Let's just call it philosophical differences and leave it at that," said Saints General Manager Jim Finks.

Elliott seemed happy about the release, The Sporting News said. "It's good, it's real good. Because it gives me an opportunity to move on. It's a positive thing for me. I know I'm going to be playing somewhere in this league."

But Elliott did not sign with any team in 1989. He earned $275,000 in 1988.

He had fallen "out of favor with Saints coaches because of what they perceived to be his lackadaiscal off-season training habits," The Sporting News reported.

He was involved also in at least four other off-the-field controversies.

Pettey Shows Them

Phil Pettey spent four years as a Marine, attaining the rank of sergeant.

But his long-term goal had been to play major-college football.

"Out of high school, I guess I didn't have a good attitude, and for that reason my (high school) coach and I didn't get along," Pettey told a spokesman at Missouri, where he played three seasons before an NFL stint.

"I told myself that I'd go into the Marine Corps and get bigger, stronger and faster, and work my way up to get a scholarship."

He entered the Corps at 6-4, 225, and added 50 pounds.

With about 90 days to serve, he caught the eye of a Marine lieutenant who steered him toward the Tigers. The officer was Shep Cooper, son of the Missouri recruiting coordinator.

Two weeks later, Pettey looked over the Columbia, Mo., school — and liked it. The coaching staff signed him to a scholarship without seeing him play.

Pettey sat out his freshman season but started as a 23-year-old offensive guard in 1984 and lettered also in 1985 and 1986.

It took acclimating to the complex formations of college football. "Most of the dudes on my Marine team weren't so smart," Pettey told a reporter, "so we had to keep the offense simple."

He gave up his senior season to try out with the Atlanta Falcons in 1987, and was signed by the Washington Redskins.

Pettey had played high-school ball in Kenosha, Wisc., and was the star of a 13-1 Marine team at Camp Lejeune in 1981 besides being a VIP driver.

He'd eat 12 eggs sunnyside up with 10 links of sausage for breakfast.

"I just got a deal going with them (the mess hall)," he told a reporter. "I could get just about anything I wanted."

He also served on Okinawa and in Japan and was recruited by East Carolina, North Carolina and Florida State.

LES STECKEL

DENNIS FITZGERALD

BUD CARSON

JIM NIBLACK

DARRYL ROGERS

NICK NICOLAU

These former Marines served as head coaches and assistant coaches in pro football

Marines At The Helm

The leader stands in front of his men, giving and barking directions, exhorting them to a greater or, at least, definable goal and then supervising their actions.

Sound like a DI? Or maybe a college-football coach?

The similarities are there, and perhaps because of the former there are the latter.

Whatever the case, former Marines have made their marks as head coaches in college football.

The peak might have been the 1964 season when at least 43 former Marines handled the reins.

It had taken a decade or two for the WWII and Korean War Marines to mature and work their way up the ladders.

And former Marines were successful into the 1970s and 1980s as some of their teams were nationally ranked and selected for bowl games.

The 1964 coaches were:

Alex Agase (Northwestern), Al Akins (Southern Oregon), Rolla Anderson (Kalamazoo), Dee Andros (Idaho), Charlie Bradshaw (Kentucky), Jim Camp (George Washington), Jerry Carle (Colorado College), Robert Carroll (Tennessee-Martin), Bill Dando (John Carroll), Russ De Vette (Hope), Vince Dooley (Georgia), Bill Doolittle (Western Michigan), Bob Dove (Hiram), Wally Dreyer (Wisconsin-Milwaukee), Chalmers "Bump" Elliott (Michigan), Rick Forzano (Connecticut), Hayden Fry (Southern Methodist), Bob Hatch (Bates), Don Henderson (Mars Hill), John Idzik (Detroit), Ted Keller (Randolph-Macon), Chuck Klausing (Indiana of Pa.), Howie Kolstad (St. Norbert's)

Also, Frank Lauterbur (Toledo), Mike Lude (Colorado State), George Makris (Temple), John McLaughry (Brown), Jim Mora (Occidental), Billy Murphy (Memphis State), Bob Odell (Bucknell), Ted Ogdahl (Willamette), Forrest Perkins (Wisconsin-Whitewater), Orville "Potch" Pottenger (Southwest Missouri), John Ralston (Stanford), Roger Robinson (Cortland), John Simpson (Colby), Max Spilsbury (Northern Arizona), Ralph Starenko (Augustana of Ill.), Bill Tate (Wake Forest), Eddie Teague (The Citadel), Bill Weeks (New Mexico), Ben Whaley (Hampton) and Jack Wink (St. Cloud)

Among the Rose Bowl coaches were Bernie Bierman (Tulane), 1932; Elliott, 1965; Ralston, 1971 and 1972, and Fry (Iowa), 1982 and 1986.

Agase was the Football Writers Assn. of America Coach of the Year in 1970; Bierman had national championships at Minnesota in 1934, 1936, 1940 and 1941; Bradshaw was The Associated Press' Coach of the Year in 1965; Dooley was the American Football Coaches Assn. and Football Writers Assn. Coach of the Year in 1980; Tuss McLaughry received the Amos Alonzo Stagg Award in 1951 and the Touchdown Club of New York Award in 1965; Perkins was the NAIA Coach of the Year in 1966; and Darryl Rogers (Michigan State) was the Sporting News' Coach of the Year in 1978.

Bierman, "Navy Bill" Ingram and McLaughry are in the College Hall of Fame and Bierman and McLaughry in the Helms College Hall of Fame.

Bierman, Harold "Red" Drew, Dick and Pat Hanley, Ray Hanson, Earl Martineau and Jack Meagher served in as WWI Marines and made coaching headlines in the 1930s and early '40s. All but Meagher (a Navy Pre-Flight coach) served as WWII Marines, primarily as athletic directors, instructors or coaches, although Pat Hanley received the Silver Star on Saipan.

In additiion, coaches in their late 30s and 40s such as Ingram, Tuss McLaughry, Ernie Nevers, Roy Randall and Maurice "Clipper" Smith came aboard in WWII.

Jack Chevigny, coach of the Chicago Cardinals in 1932 and at the University of Texas from 1934-36, was killed in action the second day on Iwo.

College coaches (through 1986)

Alex Agase, Northwestern 1964-72, Purdue 1973-76; record 50-83-2; assistant at Iowa St., Northwestern

Al Akins, Southern Oregon 1955-69; record 71-61-3

Phil Ahwesh, Duquesne 1949-50 (school dropped football in 1951)

Kim Alsop, Samford 1984-86; asst. at Richmond

Rolla Anderson, Kalamazoo 1953-66; record 56-56-1

Dee Andros, Idaho 1962-64, Oregon St. 1965-75; record 62-80-2; asst. at Oklahoma, Kansas, Texas Tech, Nebraska, California, Illinois

Bill Arnsparger, LSU 1984-86; asst. at Miami of Ohio, Ohio St., Kentucky, Tulane

Ed Baker, Kalamazoo 1967-84; record 61-81-3

Harold Ballin, Duquesne 1923-24; asst. at Princeton, Lafayette

Larry Bemol, Mt. San Antonio (Cal.) JC 1956-58

Walt Bergman, Ft. Lewis (Colo.) JC 1947-49, Mesa (Colo.) JC 1950-65; record 102-63-9

Bernie Bierman, Montana St. 1919-21, Mississippi St. 1925-26, Tulane 1927-31, Minnesota 1932-41, 1945-50; recalled to active duty in World War II; record 146-62-12

Ron Botchan, Los Angeles CC 1966-71

Charlie Bradshaw, Kentucky 1962-68, Troy St. 1976-82; record 85-68-6; asst. at Kentucky, Alabama, Texas A&M, Vanderbilt

Marty Brill, La Salle 1933-39, Loyola of LA 1940-41; record 40-35-6; asst. at Columbia

Jack Bushofsky, Austin Peay 1973-76; asst. at Villanova

Jim Camp, George Washington 1961-66 (school dropped football in 1967); record 22-35; asst. at Mississippi St., Minnesota, USC

Jerry Carle, Colorado College 1957-85; record 129-130-5; asst. at Iowa St., Colorado College

Vince Carlesimo, St. Peter's 1972-73; asst. at Upsala

Gene Carpenter, Adams St. 1968, Millersville 1970-86; record 118-49-4; asst. at Adams St., Utah

Robert Carroll, Tennessee-Martin 1957-74; record 85-82-4

Bud Carson, Georgia Tech 1967-71; record 27-27; asst. at North Carolina, South Carolina, Georgia Tech, Kansas

Ron Case, Carson-Newman 1978-79; asst. at Richmond, Carson-Newman, Maryville, West Texas

Jim Chapman, Case-Western Reserve 1982-86; record 36-7-1

Jack Chevigny, Texas 1934-36; a Notre Dame graduate, he took his Texas team to South Bend in 1934 and won, 7-6; asst. at Notre Dame; killed in action on Iwo Jima

William "Spot" Collins, Southwestern of Texas 1948-50 (school dropped football in 1951)

Ralph Cormany, Rockhurst 1949 (school dropped football in 1950); asst. at Gustavus-Adolphus

Bruce Craddock, Northeast Missouri 1979-82, Western Illinois 1983-86; record 44-41-1; asst. at Vermont, Northeast Missouri

John "Biff" Crawley, Imperial Valley (Cal.) JC 1951; asst. at Kansas St.

Roland Dale, Southeast Louisiana 1972-73; asst. at Mississippi, Jones County (Miss.) JC, Southern Mississippi, Tulane

Bill Dando, John Carroll 1964, Buffalo 1977-86; record 54-47-1; assistant at SMU, Buffalo, John Carroll

Tom Danna, Michigan Tech 1985-86; asst. at James Madison, Michigan Tech

Mike Dau, Lake Forest 1966-86; record 71-91; asst. at Lake Forest

Don Davis, Santa Ana (Cal.) JC 1955-56

DuWayne Dietz, St. Thomas (Minn.) 1970-80; record 52-52-2

Shan Deniston, U.S. International 1977-78; asst. at Pepperdine, Drake

Russ DeVette, Hope 1955-69; record 62-64-1

Don Doll, West Contra (Cal.) JC 1956; asst. at Washington, USC, Notre Dame

Vince Dooley, Georgia 1964-86; record 183-71-10; asst. at Auburn

Bill Doolittle, Western Michigan 1964-74; record 58-49-2; asst. at Army, Brown

Bob Dove, Hiram 1962-68; record 22-34; asst. at Detroit

Harold "Red" Drew, Trinity (Conn.) 1921-23, Birmingham Southern 1924-27, Chattanooga 1929-30, Mississippi 1946, Alabama 1947-54; record 95-66-14; asst. at Alabama

Wally Dreyer, Wisc.-Milwaukee 1960-69; record 25-58-2

Les Dugan, Buffalo St. 1981-85; record 19-24

Chalmers "Bump" Elliott, Michigan 1959-68; record 51-42-2; asst. at Iowa, Oregon St., Michigan

Charles Erb, Nevada 1924, Idaho 1926-28

Lew Erber, Imperial Valley (Cal.) JC 1968; asst. at Wichita St., Iowa St., Cal Western, San Diego St., California

Jim Erkenbeck, Grossmont (Cal.) JC 1962-64; asst. at San Diego St., Utah St., Washington St., California

Gary "Falcon" Fallon, Washington & Lee 1978-86; record 45-41; asst. at Princeton, Ithaca

Harold Fischer, Stephen F. Austin 1956-58; asst. at S.F. Austin

Dennis Fitzgerald, Kent St. 1975-77; asst. at Michigan, Kentucky, Kent St., Syracuse, Tulane

Rick Forzano, Connecticut 1964-65, Navy 1969-72; record 17-43-1; asst. at Navy, Wooster, Kent St.

Hayden Fry, SMU 1962-72; North Texas St. 1973-78, Iowa 1979-86; record 150-122-5; asst. at Baylor, Arkansas

Vernon Gale, Valley City 1955-59, Wayne (Mich.) 1965-71; record 45-43-1; asst. at Iowa St.

Mike Giddings, Glendale (Cal.) JC 1960, Utah 1966-67; asst. at USC

Pete Glick, National Agriculture 1950 (recalled to active duty in 1951)

Dennis Golden, Framingham 1972-81; record 47-35

Paul Governali, San Diego St. 1956-60; record 11-27-4

Herb Grenke, Northern Michigan 1983-86; asst. at Wisc.-Milwaukee, Northern Illinois, Wisc.-Platteville

Danny Hale, West Chester 1984-86; asst. at Colgate, Bucknell, Vermont, West Chester

Dick Hanley, Haskell Institute 1923-26, Northwestern 1927-34; record 74-33-8; recalled to active duty in World War II

Leroy B. "Pat" Hanley, Boston Univ. 1934-41; record 35-24-5; asst. at Haskell Institute, Northwestern; recalled to active duty in World War II

Ray "Rock" Hanson, Macomb Teachers/Western Illinois 1926-41; record 58-58-12; recalled to active duty in World War II

Web Harrison, Bates 1978-86; record 33-37-2

Bob Hatch, Bates 1952-72; record 59-93-8

Jim Helms, Cameron 1976-78; asst. at Texas, Oklahoma, Oklahoma St., SMU

Don Henderson, Mars Hill 1950-62; became a four-year school in 1963; record 6-30-4

Bob Herwig, American River (Cal.) JC 1963-65; asst. at California, Cal Poly, Arizona

James Higgins, Lamar 1953-62; record 56-31-4

Gib Holgate, Hillsdale 1948; asst. at Yale

Jim Lee Howell, Wagner 1947-53; record 24-30-3

Tom Hughes, Cal-Santa Barbara 1956; asst. at North Dakota, Oregon

Carroll Huntress, Bucknell 1965-68; asst. at Maryland, Kentucky

John Idzik, Detroit 1962-64; asst. at Tennessee, Maryland, Tulane, Detroit

"Navy Bill" Ingram, Indiana 1923-25, Navy 1926-30, Cal 1931-34; record 69-39-9; asst. at William & Mary

William "Sonny" Jackson, Nicholls 1981-86; record 39-28-1; asst. at Northeast Louisiana

Norwood Jaqua, John Muir (Cal.) JC 1947-50

Bill Jennings, Nebraska 1957-61; record 15-34-1; asst. at Oklahoma, Kansas

Doug Kay, Olivet 1971-75; record 23-20-1; asst. at Western Illinois, Indiana St., San Jose St., UCLA, Hawaii

Ted Keller, Randolph-Macon 1964-81; record 104-57-6; asst. at Randolph-Macon

Tom Kingsford, Southern Utah 1967-77; record 50-52; asst. at Montana

Chuck Klausing, Indiana (Pa.) 1964-69, Carnegie-Mellon 1976-85; record 123-26-2; asst. at Rutgers, Army, West Virginia, Pittsburgh.

Howard Kolstad, St. Norbert's 1960-78; record 96-76-5

Ed "Moose" Krause, St. Mary's (Minn.) in the 1930s; asst. at Notre Dame, Holy Cross

Tom Kurucz, Chicago 1979; asst. at South Carolina, New Mexico, Tenn-Chattanooga, Millersville, Kentucky

345

Emory "Swede" Larson, Navy 1939-41; as a player and coach, beat Army six straight times

Frank Lauterbur, Toledo 1963-70, Iowa 1971-73; record 52-60-3; asst. at Kent St., Army, Pitt

Jim Lawson, Los Angeles CC 1983-84; asst. at Occidental, Azusa Pacific, Pomona-Pitzer, UCLA, Morris Brown, Santa Ana (Cal.) JC, Cal Poly Pomona, Cal State Fullerton, LA CC

Jim Lohr, Southeast Missouri 1974-83; record 52-53-4

Mike Lude, Colorado St. 1962-69; record 29-51-1; asst. at Hillsdale, Maine, Delaware

George Makris, Temple 1960-69; record 45-44-4

Earl Martineau, Kalamazoo Teachers 1924-28; record 26-10-2; asst. at Purdue, Princeton, Michigan; returned to active duty in World War II

Cecil McGehee, Palomar (Cal.) JC 1963-66; asst. at Arizona

DeOrond "Tuss" McLaughry, Westminster (Pa.) 1916-21; Amherst 1922-25, Brown 1926-40; Dartmouth 1941-42, 1945-54; record 140-132-12; joined Marine Corps at age 50

John McLaughry, Union (N.Y.) 1947-49), Amherst 1950-58, Brown 1959-66; record 78-80-8

Jay McNitt, Fort Lewis (Colo.) 1971-81; record 46-56-1

Jack Meagher, St. Edward's (Texas) 1924-28, Rice 1929-33, Auburn 1934-42; record 92-82-14

Jim Mora, Occidental !964-66; asst. at Occidental, Stanford, Colorado, UCLA, Washington

Billy "Spook" Murphy, Memphis St. 1958-71; record 91-44-1; asst. at Mississippi St., Minnesota

Jim Myers, Iowa St. 1957, Texas A&M 1958-61; record 16-29-5; asst. at Wofford, Vanderbilt, UCLA

Walt Nadzak, Juniata 1969-76, Connecticut 1977-82; record 69-65-5; asst. at Muskingum

Ernie Nevers, Lafayette 1936; asst. at Stanford, Iowa

Nick Nicolau, Bridgeport 1965-69; record 24-22; asst. at Southern Connecticut, Springfield, Bridgeport, Massachusetts, Connecticut, Kentucky, Kent St.

Ed Nyden, Citrus (Cal.) JC 1950

Bernard Nygren, Visalia (Cal.) JC 1948-50

Bill O'Brien, Southern Illinois 1952-54

Tom O'Connor, College of the Desert (Cal.) CC 1965-68

Ted Ogdahl, Willamette 1952-70; record 93-61-10

Fred Pancoast, Tampa 1962-63, Memphis St. 1972-74, Vanderbilt 1975-78; record 40-52-4

George Paterno, Merchant Marine 1965-68, 1971-75; record 46-32-3; asst. at Michigan St.

Ed Peasley, Northern Arizona 1971-74; asst. at Long Beach St., Washington, Stanford

Forrest Perkins, Wisc.-Whitewater 1956-84; record 185-93-8

Bum Phillips, Tex-El Paso 1962; asst. at Texas A&M, Houston, SMU, Oklahoma St.

Russ Picton, Wilkes 1955-56

Jim Pittman, Tulane 1966-70, TCU 1971 (died during a game); record 24-32-2; asst. at Texas, Washington, Mississippi St.

Ray Poole, Northwest Mississippi JC 1979-80; asst. at Mississippi

Orville "Potch" Pottenger, Southwest Missouri 1961-64; record 24-12-2; asst. at SW Missouri

Lou Quint, Grant Tech (Cal.) JC 1947-54, American River (Cal.) JC 1955-57

John Ralston, Utah St. 1959-62, Stanford 1963-71; record 86-47-4; asst. at California

Roy Randall, Haverford 1933-42, 1946-62; recalled to active duty during World War II; record 63-108-10

Frank Reagan, Villanova 1954-59; record 17-41

Joe Reutz, St. Mary's (Cal.) 1950 (school dropped football in 1951); asst. at St. Mary's, Stanford

Fred Rice, Colgate 1957-58; asst. at Colgate, Marquette

Roger Robinson, Cortland 1963-79; record 70-77-3; asst. at Harvard, Lebanon Valley

Darryl Rogers, Hayward St. 1965, Fresno St. 1966-72, San Jose St. 1973-75, Michigan St. 1976-79, Arizona St. 1980-84; record 129-84-7; asst. at Fresno (Cal.) CC.

Vern Rosene, Cuesta (Cal.) JC 1965-66; asst. at Chico St., Idaho St., San Diego St., Wenatchee Valley (Wash.) CC

Joe Sabasteanski, Adelphi 1952-53

Carl Schiller, Cypress (Cal.) JC 1967-69

Dal Shealy, Mars Hill 1969, Carson-Newman 1970-73, Richmond 1980-86; record 68-62; asst. at Auburn, Carson-Newman, Baylor, Tennessee, Iowa St.

John Simpson, Colby 1962-66; record 8-32; asst. at Colby

Maurice "Clipper" Smith, Gonzaga 1925-28, Santa Clara 1929-35; Villanova 1936-42, Univ. of San Francisco 1946, Lafayette 1949-51; record 108-76-12; joined the Marines at age 45

Max Spilsbury, Northern Arizona 1956-64; record 59-24-5

Ralph Starenko, Concordia (Neb.) 1959-63, Augustana (Ill.) 1964-68, Augustana (S.D.) 1969-76; record 84-77-6

Paul Straub, Tampa 1946

Larry Sullivan, McGill (Canada) 1954-58; asst. at Boston College

Bill Sylvester, Butler 1970-84; record 84-65-2; asst. at Purdue, Butler

Steve Szabo, Edinboro 1985-86; asst. at Western Michigan, Ohio St., Iowa St., Johns Hopkins, Toledo, Iowa, Syracuse

Bill Tate, Wake Forest 1964-68; record 17-32-1; asst. at Illinois

Eddie Teague, Guilford 1949-50, The Citadel 1957-65; record 52-53-3; asst. at Guilford, Maryland, North Carolina

Bobby Thalman, Hampden-Sydney 1956-59, Virginia Military Institute 1971-84; record 80-103-4; asst. at North Carolina

Roger Theder, California 1978-81; asst. at Bowling Green, Northern Illinois, Stanford, Cal

Bob Trocolor, Bergen (N.J.) JC 1947-48; Stetson 1949 (school dropped football in 1950), William Paterson 1974; asst. at William Paterson

Bob Troppmann, Marin (Cal.) JC 1981; asst. at San Francisco St.

James Orville Tuttle, Oklahoma City 1948-49 (school dropped football in 1950); asst. at Oklahoma

Bob Vanatta, Central of Missouri 1948-49; asst. at Southwest Missouri, Army

Norm Verry, El Camino (Cal.) JC 1952-60

Dick Voris, Salinas (Cal.) JC 1952-53, Virginia 1958-60; asst. at Army

Bill Weeks, New Mexico 1960-67; record 40-41-1

Mac Wenskunas, Quincy 1947-49, North Dakota St. 1950-53; record 30-27-1

Forrest "Frosty" Westering, Parsons 1962-63, Lea (Minn.) 1966-71, Pacific Lutheran 1972-86; record 160-59-3

Ben Whaley, Hampton 1957-64; record 34-38-1

Dick Wheaton, Rochester Tech 1974; asst. at Ithaca, Cortland

Neil Wheelwright, Colgate 1968-75, Holy Cross 1976-80; record 61-72-2; asst. at Colgate, Hofstra

Duane Whitehead, San Mateo (Cal.) JC, 1953

Jack Wink, Wayne (Neb.) 1949-51, Stout 1952-56, St. Cloud 1956-64; record 52-75-8

Al Woods, Maryland 1940-41 (was a tri-coach); asst. at Maryland

Harry Wright, Portland Univ. 1949 (school dropped football in 1950), Merchant Marine 1958-63; record 35-28-1

Bill Yeagle, Salisbury St. 1979-81; asst. at Wisc.-Eau Claire, Northern Colorado

1987 head coaches

Jerry Carle (Colorado College), Gene Carpenter (Millersville), Bruce Craddock (Western Illinois), Bill Dando (Buffalo Univ.), Tom Danna (Northwood), Mike Dau (Lake Forest), Vince Dooley (Georgia), Gary Fallon (Washington & Lee), Hayden Fry (Iowa), Bob Green (Montana Tech), Herb Grenke (Northern Michigan), Danny Hale (West Chester), Web Harrison (Bates), Sonny Jackson (McNeese), Dal Shealy (Richmond), Steve Szabo (Edinboro), Frosty Westering (Pacific Lutheran)

Georgia (9-3) beat Arkansas, 20-17, in the Liberty Bowl
Iowa (10-3) defeated Wyoming, 20-19, in the Holiday Bowl
Northern Michigan (10-2) lost in second round of NCAA Division II playoffs
Pacific Lutheran (10-1-2) tied for NAIA Division II championship
Richmond (7-5) lost in first round of NCAA Division I-AA playoffs
West Chester (9-2) lost in a Pennsylvania playoff

1988 head coaches (Division I-A, I-AA)

Craddock, Dooley, Fry, Jackson, Shealy

Division II, III

Ed Baker (returned at Kalamazoo), Carle, Carpenter, Dando, Dau, Fallon, Grenke, Hale, Harrison.

NAIA

Danna, Green, Westering

Dooley collected his 200th coaching victory Nov. 26, beating Georgia Tech, 24-3. He retired as coach after the Bulldogs defeated Michigan State, 34-27, in the Gator Bowl. His overall record was 201-77-10.

Iowa lost to North Carolina State, 28-23, in the Peach Bowl
Western Illinois lost to Western Kentucky, 35-32, in the NCAA Div. 1-A playoffs
West Chester lost to Jacksonville State, 63-24, in the NCAA Div. II playoffs.
Millersville defeated Indiana (Pa.), 27-24, but lost to North Dakota State, 36-26, in the NCAA Division II playoffs.
Pacific Lutheran lost to Oregon Tech, 56-35, in the NAIA Div. II playoffs.
Fry was a coach in the Ricoh Japan Bowl all-star game Jan. 15 in Yokohama.
Hale resigned despite a four-year, 31-11 record because of differences with the school administration
Shealy resigned to become executive vice president of the Fellowship of Christian Athletes

Szabo stepped down after the '88 season.

1989 head coaches

Divisions I-III: Craddock, Fry, Jackson, Sam Rutigliano (Liberty); Baker, Carle, Carpenter, Dando, Dau, Fallon, Grenke, Harrison; **NAIA:** Danna, Green, Westering
Jackson resigned, effective 1-15-90
Darryl Rogers and Tom O'Brien, among others, were interviewed for the 1990 Navy coaching job.
Bill Meyers was an unsuccessful candidate for the 1990 Long Beach State position.
Jerry Carle stepped down 12-89 after 33 seasons at Colorado College
Ed Baker stepped down 12-89 after 19 seasons at Kalamazoo.
Bill Dando stepped down 12-89 after 14 seasons at Buffalo.

1990 head coaches

Jim Chapman returned to college coaching at Mercyhurst. He had posted a 36-7-1 record at Case-Western Reserve before returning to the high-school ranks.
Others: Fry, Rutigliano; Carpenter, Dau, Fallon; Grenke, Harrison; Danna, Green, Westering
Fry's Iowa team tied for the Big Ten title and was selected for the 1991 Rose Bowl game against Washington because it had beaten Illinois, Michigan and Michigan State. He was named 1990 Dave McClain Big Ten Football Coach of the Year. Iowa lost to the Huskies, 46-34.
Grenke retired after the 1990 season.

1991 head coaches

Stan McGarvey, Missouri Western. Previously, William Jewell 1978-80, Austin 1983, William Jewell 1987-88

Also: Tom Brock, Kings (Pa.) 1946-48, asst. at Omaha; Cecil "Tonto" Coleman, Long Beach CC, Fresno St. 1959-63; Ron Cote, Panhandle 1972-74, asst. at UC Santa Barbara, Moorpark JC, Imperial Valley JC; Kermit Davis, Sunflower JC 1949; Dr. Wm. E. "Bud" Davis, Colorado 1962; Bud Dawson, Fullerton CC 4 seasons, Chas. Erb, Humboldt St. 1935-37; Jim "Red" McCarthy, Lewis (1952-56; school dropped football); Maury McMains, Drexel 1944-45; John Merricks, Gallaudet 1956-57; Sam Rutigliano, Liberty 1990-91, asst. at Maryland, Connecticut; Bill Steers, California (Pa.) 1929-40; Duane Whitehead, Cal Poly San Dimas 1948-50, 1952

One could write an entire book about Dick Hanley, the veteran and controversial coach of the El Toro Flying Marines in 1944 and 1945

Assistance League

They didn't get the headlines that were reserved for the head coaches, but former Marines as assistant college football coaches might have had as much influence on the game.

The job as assistant, of course, was a springboard for many to the head-coaching position.

But a number remained as assistants during their careers.

Joe Arenas, for example, was an assistant at Houston from 1964 to 1986. Bert Baston was at Minnesota from 1932 to 1950. Cliff Battles was a Columbia assistant 17 seasons, J.W. "Wobble" Davidson at Mississippi 23 seasons, Frank Foster at Navy 28 seasons, Renzie Lamb at Williams 21 seasons and Norm Maloney at Purdue 26 seasons.

Some were pro assistants as well.

College assistants (through 1986)

Murray Adler, Fordham; Dwight Adams, Florida, The Citadel, Clemson; Bruno Andruska, Wisconsin; Joe Arenas, Houston (1964-86).

Jim Baldinger, Navy; (Col.) Charles L. "Gus" Banks, Utah; Gary Barnett, Southwest Missouri, Southeast Missouri, Western Kentucky; Bert Baston, Minnesota (1932-50); Cliff Battles, Columbia (1938-43, 1946-56); Harold "Indian Joe" Bauer, Navy (Medal of Honor winner; KIA); Fred Beans, Navy; John Beckett, Navy; Marv Bell, Marquette (1936-42, 1946-49), Carl Benton, San Diego St.; Steve Bernstein, Virginia Tech, Utah St., Wake Forest; Jess Berry, Georgia Tech, South Carolina; Stu Betts, Hamline, New Mexico State, Wisconsin; Tommy Bland, Central Florida; Matt Bolger Jr., Rutgers, Brown; Harry Botsford, Boston Univ.; Bill Boyarsky, Pacific; Chuck Boyer, Navy; Leon Bramlett, Navy; Rich Browning, Michigan St., Oregon St., New Mexico St.; John Butler, Evansville

Glenn Cafer, Washburn; Tony Calwhite, Missouri Southern; Bob Carew, Hamline; Charlie Carpenter, Cumberland; Dave Carson, Long Beach St., San Francisco St.; Gus Cifelli, Notre Dame; Tom Coll, St. Mary's; Frank Condini, Ashland, West Virginia, East Stroudsburg; (Gen.) Lou Conti, Cornell; Charlie Cooke, Pacific; Ron Cote, UC Santa Barbara; Denzil Cox, Nicholls, Northeast Louisiana; Joe Cribari, Colorado St.; Tom Cruickshank, Nevada-Las Vegas, Boise St.; Jim Cullom, California; Ed Czekaj, Johns Hopkins

Don Daly, Eastern Kentucky; J.W. "Wobble" Davidson, Mississipi (1942, 1946-68); Tom Dean, SMU; Tucker Debetaz, McNeese; Owen Dejanovich, Tulsa; Chuck Dickerson, Minnesota, Eastern Illinois; Emerson Dromgold, Delaware Valley, Michigan St., Olivet, Boston College, Rhode Island; Dan Droze, Georgetown, Catholic

Jack Eatinger, North Carolina A&T, Santa Barbara CC, Nevada-Reno, Weber State, Lincoln; Brad Ecklund, Oregon, Chapman; Jerry Elliott, Tennessee, Vanderbilt, Auburn, Kansas St.; Vern Ellison, Palomar JC; Elmer Engel, Illinois; Hank Ennen, Los Angeles St.; Don Erusha, Northern Iowa, Coe, Iowa; Dick Evans, Long Beach CC, Nevada, Notre Dame

Jack Faulkner, Cincinnati; Ed Ferem, San Francisco St.; Steve Filipowicz, Mt. St. Mary's; Pat Filley, Cornell 1945-55 (with athletic dept. until 1984); Don Fleming, Creighton, Washington; Lou Florio, Boston College; Mark Edsel Ford, Alabama St.; Frank Foster, Navy (1924-51); Chet Franklin, Stanford, Oklahoma, Colorado

Joe Galat, Miami (Ohio), Yale, Kentucky, Youngstown; Joe Geri, Chattanooga; Ken Germann, Columbia; Don Green, Cal Lutheran; Mike Green, Iowa St.; Bob Griffin, Arkansas, Tulsa

Lee Hanley, South Carolina; Bill Hannah, Cal State Fullerton (killed with other coaches in 1971 plane crash on way to scout an opponent), Dave Hare, Western Montana; Hal Harwood, Navy; Ted Hazelwood, North Carolina; McCoy "Hoss" Hewlett, Auburn; Bill Hofer, Iowa; Ron Hudson, Notre Dame, UCLA, Oregon, California, Stanford

Bill Iannicelli, Franklin & Marshall; Frank Inman, Georgia

John Jackson, USC, Dartmouth, Illinois, Hofstra; Ron Jeziorski, Santa Clara; Buddy Jones, Lake Forest; Bob Joye, Tennessee Tech; Saxon Judd, Tulsa

Mike Kasap, Vermont; John Kavanagh, Ferris, St. Thomas; Fred Kelley, Virginia Military; Frank Kemp, Navy; Bill Kennedy, Univ. of San Francisco; Ed Kensler, North Carolina, Washington & Lee, Virginia Military, Maryland, Miami (Fla.); Keith Kephart, Kansas, Iowa St., Northern Iowa; John Kerr,

Navy; Clark King, Virginia Military; Tom Kisselle, Bowling Green; Otto Kofler, Stanford, San Diego St., Washington; John Kopka, Navy

Renzie Lamb, Williams (1968-86); Richard Lantz, Notre Dame, Georgia Tech, Boston Univ., Rhode Island, Buffalo, Navy, Miami (Fla.); Denver "Mo" Latimore, Kansas St.; Paul Lentz, Guilford; Ernie "Buddy" Lewis, Cal Western, Mira Costa JC; Mickey Lile, Northwestern, Eastern Illinois; Jim Lindholm, Texas-Arlington, Emporia St.; Terry Looker, Oklahoma

Don MacKay, Montclair; Don Magee, San Diego St.; Eddie Mahan, California, Harvard, Boston College; Mike Malham, Arkansas St.; Ned Maloney, Purdue (1951-86); Bob Mangene, Boston College; Jim Martin, Idaho St.; John Mazur, Tulane, Marquette, Boston Univ.; M.L. "Mac" McBride, Carthage, Arizona Western; Thurman McGraw, Colorado St.; Paul McKee, Rochester, Harvard; Bobb McKittrick, Oregon St., UCLA; Norm McNabb, Oklahoma; Tracy Mehr, Boston College; Ernie Merk, San Diego St.; John Merricks, Maryland, Gallaudet; Lonnie Messick, Navy; Bill Meyers, Missouri, California, Santa Clara, Notre Dame; Art Michalik, Golden West CC; Phil Monahan, Navy; Alan Mooney, Notre Dame; Lloyd Moore, Wichita St., Stephen F. Austin, New Mexico Highlands; John Morello, San Diego St., Pacific; Paul Moret, Navy (KIA); Kelley Mote, Colgate, Columbia; Barrett Murphy, McNeese, Nicholls

John Nelson, Southern Connecticut; Jim Niblack, Kentucky, Florida; John North, Tennessee Tech, Kentucky, LSU

Carl Oakley, Murray St., Morehead St., Eastern Kentucky; Tom O'Brien, Navy; Joe O'Hara, Cal State Fullerton (killed in crash with Hannah); Joe Ososki, Fordham; Tom Owen, Vanderbilt

Thom Park, Maryland, Connecticut, West Chester, The Citadel; Mike Parker, Texas, SMU, Southern Mississippi, Wyoming; John Parry, Penn; Duane "Pat" Patterson, Allegheny; Bob Patton, Vanderbilt, The Citadel, West Virginia, Clemson; John Petercuskie, Dartmouth, Boston College, Princeton; Robert Pfeifer, Middlebury, Colby, New Hampshire; John Pinter, Concord; Don Plato, Drake; Barney Poole, Alabama, LSU, Southern Mississippi; Pat Preston, North Carolina, Wake Forest; Daynor Prince, Parsons; Frank Prusch, Moravian.

Terry Quast, Northwest Louisiana, Southern Arkansas, Delta St.; Stan Quintana, New Mexico

J.D. Roberts, Denver, Oklahoma, Navy, Auburn, Houston; Jay Robertson, Notre Dame, Wisconsin, Northern Illinois, Northwestern; Don Roby, William & Mary; Herbert Rogers, Alabama St.; Tom Roggeman, Arizona, Purdue; Jim Royer, Navy, Buffalo, Tulane, Pittsburgh; Jim Ruehl, Bowling Green

Ruben Sanchez, Fordham; Dante Scarnecchia, SMU, Cal Western, Iowa St., Pacific, Northern Arizona; Carl Schuette, Navy; Ray Segale, Oregon; W. Levi Shade, Gettysburg; Ray Shands, Indiana, Navy, Louisville; Gerard Shea, Notheastern; Dave Shuford, Montana Tech; William Simon, Yale; Ralph Sinke Jr., St. Leo; Ron Smeltzer, UC Santa Barbara, Colorado; Don Smith, Texas-El Paso, Southwestern Louisiana; Eli Smith, East Stroudsburg; Bill Smyth, Xavier (Ohio); Roger Socoli, Hofstra; Stan Springer, Coast Guard; Les Steckel, Colorado, Navy; Mike Sweatman, Tennessee, Kansas, Tulsa; Paul Szakash, Montana

Nick Teta, Rochester, Alfred; Forest G. "Red Eye" Thompson, Navy; Jim Thrasher, Idaho St.; Joe Till, Penn St., San Diego St.; Jim Trickett, New Mexico, Southern Mississippi, Southern Illinois, West Virginia, Indiana, Glenville St.; Lon Troxel, San Jose St., Idaho St., Idaho, Cal State Northridge; Harvey Tschirgi, Navy; Fred Tullai, North Carolina, Maryland

Ted Unbehagen, Houston, Rice, Texas A&I, Texas Tech

Joe Viadella, Kentucky, Rhode Island

Mike Waufle, Utah St., Alfred; Terry Weatherald, Indiana Central; Dean Westgaard, California JCs; Paul White, Connecticut; Don Whitmire, Navy; Ardell Wiegandt, Wyoming, North Dakota St.; Bob Windish, Villanova, Upsala, Georgetown, Merchant Marine, Lehigh, Susquehanna

Dick Yoder, West Chester; Cliff Yoshida, Virginia Tech, Utah St., Wake Forest, Duke; Art Young, Dartmouth, Amherst, Yale

Larry Zierlein, Houston, Fort Hays; Mike Zoffuto, Texas Tech; Tony Zullo, Columbia

1987 football assistants

Alex Agase (Michigan), Kim Alsop (Louisiana Tech), Joe Arenas (Rice), Steve Bernstein (Colorado), Stu Betts (Navy), Rick Browning (Edinboro), Charlie Carpenter (Murray St.), Ron Case (Ole Miss), Frank Condino (Indiana of Pa.), Tib Csik (Occidental), Russ DeVette (Hope), Tony DiPaolo (Franklin & Marshall), Chuck Doty (St. John Fisher), Bob Dove (Youngstown), Dan Droze (Georgetown of D.C.), John Falvey (St. Lawrence), Mike Green (William Penn), Jim Helms (Texas A&M), Don Henderson (Mars Hill), Ron Hudson (Illinois), Fred Kelley (Dartmouth), Keith Kephart (South Carolina), Otto Kofler (Stanford), Tom Kurucz (Texas Tech), Renzie Lamb (Williams), Rick Lantz (Louisville), Denver "Mo" Latimore (Texas-El Paso), William "Chick" Leahy (Bates)

Don Maines (Bentley), Mac McBride (Carroll of Wisc.), Tracy Mehr (Amherst), Bill Meyers (Pitt), John Nelson (New Haven), Terry O'Brien (Towson St.), Tom O'Brien (Virginia), Willie Ragan

(Northeast Louisiana), Ron Roberts (Virginia), Jay Robertson (Army), Tom Roggeman (USC), Rick Trickett (Memphis St.), Ted Unbehagen (Texas Tech), Joe Viadella (Bloomsburg), Jack Ward (USC), Mike Waufle (Fresno St.)

1988 assistants

Bernstein (to Illinois); Jim Goodman (to Missouri Southern), Hudson (to Ohio State); Kephart (to Texas A&M), John Petercuskie (to Harvard), Szabo (to Northern Colorado), Cliff Tierney (Lawrence), Bill Yeagle (Montana Tech), Larry Zierlein (to Tulane).

1989 changes

Latimore (to Missouri), Petercuskie (to Liberty), Les Steckel (to Brown), Szabo (to Colorado State), Waufle (to UCLA)
Waufle dismissed 12-89

1990 changes

Steckel left Brown; Trickett (to Mississippi St.), Waufle (to Oregon St.)

1991 changes

Case (to Vanderbilt), Helms (to Mississippi State), Lantz (to Virginia), Steckel (to Colorado)
Szabo, to Boston College
Lt. Chad Van Hulzen, Navy

1992 Assistants

Bernstein, to Texas
Waufle, to Cal

Also: John F. "Jack" Collins, former athletic equipment manager, UC Irvine, Orange Coast College (Cal.); Al Howard (Hampden-Sydney), Tom Hughes, Oregon trainer, East-West Game trainer; Buddy Parker (Baylor), Lee Sargent (Tufts, Davidson), J.F. Simmons (Yale), Geo. Yablonsky, athletic equipment manager, USC, Orange Coast CC (Cal.) and Rancho Santiago CC (Cal.)

Charlie Wike, Western Carolina, Dewey Wade, Buffalo, Maryland, Utah St., Kansas St.

**Longtime Dallas Cowboys
assistant Jim Myers played at
Duke as a Marine V-12 trainee
and won a Silver Star for
heroism on Iwo Jima**

Who's Who In AD's

The role of former Marines with football and basketball backgrounds as major-college and university athletic directors came to the fore in the 1980s.

In the West, for example, Dee Andros was the AD at Oregon State, Mike Lude at Washington, Thurman McGraw at Colorado State and Joe Ruetz at Stanford.

In the Midwest, Alex Agase was the AD at Eastern Michigan, Bill Doolittle at Western Michigan, Chalmers "Bump" Elliott at Iowa, Lew Hartzog at Southern Illinois, Elroy "Crazylegs" Hirsch at Wisconsin, Ed "Moose" Krause at Notre Dame and Hank Raymonds at Marquette.

In the South and Southwest, Bill Arnsparger was the AD at Florida, Dutch Baughman at Furman, Roland Dale at Southern Mississippi, King Dixon at South Carolina, Vince Dooley at Georgia, Billy Murphy at Memphis State, Bill Olsen at Louisville, Eddie Teague and Walt Nadzak at The Citadel, Emery Turner at Tulsa and Bob Vanatta at Louisiana Tech.

In the East, John Parry and Bob Seiple were AD's at at Brown, Ron Perry at Holy Cross, Richie Regan at Seton Hall, John Simpson at Boston University and Carl Ullrich at Army.

Athletic directors (through 1986)

Alex Agase, Eastern Michigan; Rolla Anderson, Kalamazoo; Dee Andros, Oregon St.

Dutch Baughman, Furman, Virginia Tech, asst. AD at Northwestern; Bob Brennan, asst. AD at Tenn.-Chattanooga

Jerry Carle, Colorado College; Gene Carpenter, Millersville; Ron Case, Carson-Newman; Ed Czekaj, Penn St.

Roland Dale, Southern Mississippi; Bill Doolittle, Western Michigan

Royce Flippin, Princeton, MIT; Hayden Fry, North Texas

Ken Germann, Columbia; Don Green, Cal Lutheran

Ray "Rock" Hanson, Macomb Tch./Western Illinois (1926-42, 1946-64); Lew Hartzog, Southern Illinois; Don Henderson, Mars Hill; Elroy Hirsch, Wisconsin; Gib Holgate, Hillsdale, associate AD at Yale

Jack Jaquet, York (Pa.) CC; Martin Johnson, Mayville

Chuck Klausing, Indiana (Pa.); Ed "Moose" Krause, Notre Dame

Mike Lude, assistant at Kent State

Thurman McGraw, Colorado St.; M.E. McMains, La Salle; Billy "Spook" Murphy, Memphis St.

Walt Nadzak, Juniata

Tom O'Connor, Butte JC

Bob Peck, Williams; Forrest Perkins, Wisc.-Whitewater; Jim Phelan, Mt. St. Mary's; Ray Poole, Northwest Mississippi JC; Pat Preston, Wake Forest

Roy Randall, Haverford; Richie Regan, Seton Hall; Thomas Rosandich, Wisc.-Milwaukee and Wisc.-Parkside; Joe Ruetz, Stanford

Bob Seiple, Brown; John Simpson, Boston Univ.; Ralph Starenko, Concordia (Nebr.); Dave Strack, associate AD at Arizona

Eddie Teague, The Citadel; Bobby Thalman, Hampden-Sydney; Emery C. Turner, Tulsa

Carl Ullrich, Western Michigan, assistant AD at Navy

Bob Vanatta, Louisiana Tech and Oral Roberts

Forrest Westering, Parsons.

Also: Cecil "Tonto" Coleman, Fresno St., Illinois, Wichita St.; Bud Dawson, Fullerton CC, Russ DeVette, Hope; Mike Fisher, academic counselor, Kansas; John Glassmire, manager of athletic teams, Ohio University; Harold McElhaney, Allegheny; Ray "Hap" Spuhler, George Mason; Bill Wall, asst. AD/business manager, Tulsa

(Includes former football, basketball, baseball and track coaches who, as ADs or executives, exercised authority over or assisted the football program.)

352

1987 athletic directors, administrators

Dee Andros (special Beaver Club assistant, Oregon St.), Bill Arnsparger (Florida), Warren Benson (athletic business manager, Wyoming), Don Bryant (asst. AD, SID and Bob Devaney Sports Center director, Nebraska), Gene Carpenter (Millersville), Mike Dau (Lake Forest), Vince Dooley (Georgia), Joe Dunn (director of sports promotions and marketing, Akron), Bump Elliott (Iowa), Tom Fields (executive director of Educational Foundation, Maryland), Royce Flippin (MIT), Gus Ganakas (assistant to AD, Michigan St.), Bud Haidet (asst. AD, Miami of Ohio), Robert W. Hatch (Bates), Ray Hewitt (athletic business manager, US International Univ.), James H. Higgins (AD emeritus, Lamar); Elroy Hirsch (consultant to athletic department, Wisconsin), Clayne Jensen (dean and faculty representative, Brigham Young), Ted Keller (Randolph-Macon), Mike Lude (Washington)

Dan Magill (asst. AD, Georgia), Harold McElhaney (Ohio Univ.), Cecil McGehee (associate AD, Colorado), Walt Nadzak (The Citadel), Joe O'Brien (associate AD, Notre Dame), Bill Olsen (Louisville), John Parry (Brown), George Paterno (Merchant Marine), Bob Peck (Williams), Ron Perry (Holy Cross), Jim Phelan (Mt. St. Mary's), Jack Rainey (special administrative assistant, Oregon St.), Hank Raymonds (Marquette), Richie Regan (director, athletic fund-raising, Seton Hall); Russell Rice (assistant to AD, Univ. of Kentucky); Dave Smalley, asst. AD, Navy), John Stevenson (asst. director, Maryland Educational Foundation), Bill Sylvester (Butler), Bill Toohey (ticket manager, East Tennessee), Carl Ullrich (Army), Bill Yeagle (director of special projects/athletics; Montana Tech); Dick·Yoder (West Chester).

1988 AD's

(Division I-A, I-AA)
Arnsparger, A. King Dixon II (South Carolina), Dooley, Elliott, Lude, McElhaney, Nadzak, Olsen, Thurman Owens (interim at Cincinnati), Parry, Perry, Raymonds, Ullrich.

Division II, III AD's
Bud Haidet (Wisconsin-Milwaukee); Bill Helm (Albright), Hewitt, Phelan, Sylvester (incomplete)

NAIA AD's
(incomplete)

1989 AD's
Dutch Baughman (senior associate athletic director, Oregon St.)

1988 AD's

Division I-A, I-AA: Arnsparger, A. King Dixon II (to South Carolina), Dooley, Elliott, Lude, McElhaney, Nadzak, Olsen, Thurman Owens (interim at Cincinnati), Parry, Perry, Raymonds, Ullrich.

Division II, III: Bud Haidet (to Wisconsin-Milwaukee); Bill Helm (to Albright), Hewitt, Edwin Muto (associate director, Univ. of Buffalo), Phelan, Sylvester

NAIA: (not available)

1989 AD's

Division I: Arnsparger, Dixon, Dooley, Elliott, Lude, McElhaney, Nadzak, Olsen, Parry, Perry, Ullrich

Divisions II-III, NAIA: not available

Dutch Baughman (senior associate athletic director, Oregon State); Darryl Rogers (fund-raiser, Arizona St.)

Ed "Sarge" Dennison (athletic operations coordinator, Fordham)

Bob Green (Montana Tech)

Mike Lude, AD at Washington, received James J. Corbett Memorial Award, given annually by National Association of Collegiate Directors of Athletics.

Parry resigned effective 1-90

C.A. "Sandy" Smith Jr. (assistant AD/marketing and promotion, Davidson)

1990 AD's

Divisions I-III (NCAA): Arnsparger, Baughman (AD, Oregon St.), Carpenter, Dau, Dixon, Dooley, Elliott, Flippin, Haidet, Helm, Keller, Lude, McElhaney, Nadzak, Olsen, Parry (Butler), Perry

NAIA: (not available)

Tom Fields, consultant/adviser, Dept. of Intercollegiate Athletics, Univ. of Maryland

Elliott retired 8-91

Lude (retired 1-91 but remained at school thru mid-90)

A longtime supporter of University of Washington sports planned to remove from his will a $1 million donation to the Huskies' athletic department because he was angry over how Lude was removed as AD. "It was unfair — he only had a few months to go," said Will Thomas, 78.

Lude joined National Association of College Directors of Athletics as Division I-A executive director 1-91

1991 AD's
Dave Roach, Brown
Ken Ober, Elizabethtown
John Randolph, William & Mary
Sylvester, commissioner, Midwest Intercollegiate Football League
Ulrich, executive director, Patriot League

1992 AD's
Lude, to Auburn

National Association of Collegiate Directors of Athletics
Hall of Fame: James B. Higgins (Trinity of Texas)
Past presidents: Cecil Coleman, Mike Lude

Georgia's Vince Dooley got his coaching start at Parris Island in the 1950s after playing football at Quantico

354

Roads Lead to Huron

You've heard of the French Connection. But how about the Huron connection?

In the late 1980s, the four-year, 500-student nonsectarian university in South Dakota and its coach, Cary Radisewitz, welcomed a few good Marines to its football program.

For example, three former Marines were All-South Dakota Intercollegiate Conference selections in 1989:

Linebacker Pat Rhodes, senior, 6-0, 205, Louisville

Defensive tackle Marv McCann, sophomore, 6-4, 235, Billings, Mont.

Free safety Bobby Lovett, sophomore, 5-10, 163, Chapel Hill, N.C.

In addition, seven other former Marines were on the team, which won four and lost six:

Freshman quarterback Greg Robillard, Minneapolis; junior defensive back Darryl Spruill, Newark; freshman defensive back Damon Pullens, Cincinnati; freshman fullback David Gratton, Brantford, Ont.; freshman fullback Harvey Enalls, South Bound Brook, N.J.; freshman linebacker David Farley, Barboursville, W.Va.; and defensive tackle Jack Reid, Brooklyn.

J.D. Rice of Roanoke, "a native Virginian and also a Marine," was among the first to publicize the influx of Marines in a November 1988 letter to the Leatherneck.

Huron has "16 former Marines attending. They dominate the sports scene. Coach Radisewitz recruits Marines whose enlistment is up and offers them a good education along with the opportunity to play sports."

Radisewitz, Rice wrote, said he is pro-Marine because they are "well disciplined and in excellent physical shape."

The coach said many of the players were the result of contacts at Camp Lejeune, Cherry Point and Twentynine Palms.

Rhodes came aboard in 1986 and the train began to roll in 1987 with running back Roman Holliday, Rhodes, defensive lineman Don Rice, linebacker Chris Sullivan, defensive lineman Gary Terwilleger and quarterback Toulmin Williams III.

Huron went 6-4 in 1987 and 7-3 in 1988 under Radisewitz, who had a 32-17-1 record in six seasons at Huron.

"We like to bring in four to six Marines a year," he said.

In addition, running back Marv Cox, a former Huron player, transferred to Memphis State after his Marine tour for the 1987, '88 and '89 seasons.

"We watched him in a game on television," Radisewitz said.

Like Father ...

Names such as Baldinger, Golic, Hofer, Lazetich and MacAfee have come around not once but twice.

End Jim Baldinger (Navy) played at Quantico in 1953 and NAS Pensacola in 1954. His sons, Brian (Duke), a center and guard; Rich (Wake Forest), a tackle, and Gary (Wake Forest), a defensive end, played in the NFL in the mid- and late 1980s.

Lew Golic was a tackle at Camp Lejeune in 1951-52. Sons Bob and Mike were standouts at Notre Dame and NFL nose tackles in the '80s and son Greg a tackle at Notre Dame from 1981-83.

Back Bill Hofer (Notre Dame) was a 19th-round draft choice of the Green Bay Packers in 1939. Son Paul was a back at Mississippi and with the San Francisco 49ers from 1976-80.

Back Bill Lazetich (Montana), a 14th-round pick of the Detroit Lions in 1939, played for the Cleveland Rams in 1939 and 1942. Son Pete (Stanford) was a defensive lineman with the San Diego Chargers in 1972-74 and Philadelphia Eagles in 1976-77.

End Ken MacAfee (Alabama) was a standout end at Parris Island in 1952, Quantico in 1953 and for six seasons in the NFL. Son Ken Jr. was a standout tight end at Notre Dame, runner-up for the Heisman Trophy in 1977 and played two seasons with the 49ers.

Sons of other Marines also made their mark in football, among them:

Fred Baston (Minnesota 1946), son of Bert Baston, Minnesota All-American and WWI Navy Cross winner

John Beckett (Pensacola 1946, NAS Jacksonville 1947, Camp Pendleton 1948), son of Gen. John Beckett (All-Marines coach and standout tackle and elected to the College Football Hall of Fame)

Sidney Bond (TCU 1971-73), son of Mendle "Big John" Bond (TCU, North Texas Agricultural, tryout with Boston Yanks)

Bill Boyle (Richmond 1980-83), son of Bill Boyle (Massachusetts-Coast Guard Academy-Parris Island)

Greg Castignola (Ohio State 1977-79), son of Jack Castignola (Dayton-Penn St.)

Paul Debetaz (McNeese 1982-83), son of Tucker Debetaz (Notre Dame, Camp Pendleton, Southeastern Louisiana, assistant at McNeese)

Steve Doolittle (Western Michigan 1971-72), son of Bill Doolittle (Ohio State, coach at Western Michigan)

Dan Dooley (Dallas Cowboys' scouting department 1988), son of Vince Dooley (Auburn, Quantico, assistant at Parris Island, coach at Georgia 25 seasons)

Derek Dooley (Virginia 1987-), son of Vince Dooley

Bob Dove (Ohio State), son of Bob Dove (Notre Dame, El Toro, 9 seasons in the NFL)

Tim Dove (Wittenberg), son of Bob Dove

Chuck Drulis Jr. (Duke 1963-65, pre-season St. Louis Cardinals 1966), son of Chuck Drulis (Temple, Camp Lejeune, seven seasons in the NFL, co-coach of Cardinals)

Bobby Elliott (Iowa 1972, 1974-75, assistant coach at Iowa, Kent State, Ball State, Iowa St., North Carolina), son of Chalmers "Bump" Elliott (Purdue, FMF Pacific, Michigan All-American, coach at Michigan, Iowa athletic director, College Hall of Fame)

Bob Evans (Penn 1945-47, third-team All-American in 1945), son of Bob Evans (Ursinus, college referee)

Kelly Fry, Randy Fry and Zach Fry, all at North Texas, sons of Hayden Fry (Baylor, Quantico, 9th Marines; coach at Baylor, North Texas, Iowa)

Greg Gagne (Wyoming 1970), son of Vern Gagne (Minnesota, El Toro, Olympic and pro wrestler)

Mike Giddings Jr. (Illinois 1984-85), son of Mike Giddings (California, Quantico, Camp Pendleton, MCAF Tustin, coach at Utah and of Hawaii-WFL, pro assistant, pro scout)

Dennis Golden (Holy Cross 1987-), son of Dennis Golden (Holy Cross, Quantico, tryouts with Dallas Cowboys and New England Patriots)

Roman Hale (letter of intent at Temple 1988), son of Danny Hale (West Chester, Quantico, coach at West Chester five seasons)

Jason Helm (letter of intent at SMU 1988), son of Jim Helms (coach at Cameron three seasons, college assistant)

John "J.J." Jackson (USC 1986-89; set school career record in 1989 for receptions; drafted by California Angels 1989), son of John Jackson (college assistant)

Tony Karras (Northwestern 1985-86, Washington Redskins 1987), son of Ted Karras (Purdue, Indiana, MCRD San Diego, nine seasons in the NFL)

Ted Karras, Northwestern 1983-86, son of Ted Karras

Marty Kennedy (Eastern Michigan 1977-78), son of Bill Kennedy (Michigan St., El Toro, Detroit Lions, Boston Yanks)

Matt Kofler (San Diego St. 1980-81, five seasons in NFL), son of Otto Kofler (Camp Pendleton, Washington State, college assistant)

Emory Larson Jr. (Yale 1946-48), son of Emory "Swede" Larson (Navy, All-Marines, famed Annapolis and Marine coach)

John Loncar (Kansas 1981-84), son of Dick Loncar (Notre Dame, Camp Pendleton, Northeast Louisiana, tryout with Pittsburgh Steelers)

Mark Loncar (Augustana of Ill.), son of Dick Loncar

Ladd McKittrick (Oregon State 1983-84), son of Bobb McKittrick (Oregon State, assistant with San Francisco 49ers)

John McLaughry (Brown 1937-39; No. 2 draft pick; N.Y. Giants 1940, coach 20 years at Union, Amherst and Brown), son of Tuss McLaughry (College Hall of Fame coach who joined Marines at age 50)

Bob McLaughry (Dartmouth 1946, DFC), son of Tuss McLaughry

Jim Mora (Washington 1981-84), son of Jim Mora (Occidental, Quantico, Camp Lejeune, and coach in the USFL and NFL)

Tim Norman (Illinois 1977-78, 1980; Hamilton-CFL, Chicago Bears, Chicago Blitz), son of Bob Norman (Quantico)

Ken Norton (UCLA 1984-87; selected on Football News and Walter Camp All-American team, and 3rd team Associated Press All-American. Drafted in second round by Dallas Cowboys), son of Ken Norton (Northeast Missouri, Camp Lejeune, boxing champion)

Matt Odle (Brigham Young 1988-), son of Phil Odle (MCRD San Diego, BYU, Detroit Lions)

Toby Page (USC 1966-67), son of Chuck Page (USC, El Toro, UCLA)

Jerry Petercuskie (college assistant), son of John Petercuskie (East Stroudsberg, college and pro assistant)

Gary Petercuskie (Penn St. 1975-77), son of John Petercuskie

Wade Phillips, interim coach of New Orleans Saints 1985, pro assistant, son of Bum Phillips (coach of Houston Oilers and New Orleans Saints)

Tom Polce (Indiana 1984-87), son of Joe Polce (Cherry Point, Indiana)

Ray S. Poole Jr. (Mississippi 1976), son of Ray Poole Sr. (Mississippi, North Carolina, FMF Pacific, six seasons in the NFL)

R. Scott Robinson (Nassau CC, Syracuse 1971-72; college assistant), son of Roger Robinson (Syracuse, Rochester, coach at Cortland State 17 seasons)

Tim "Buck" Roggeman (Stanford 86-89), son of Tom Roggeman (Purdue, Quantico, 1st MarDiv, Chicago Bears, college assistant)

Tom "Rock" Roggeman (Notre Dame 1983-84, college assistant, son of Tom Roggeman

Vic Shealy (college assistant), son of Dal Shealy (Carson-Newman, Quantico, coach at Mars Hill, Carson-Newman, Richmond; executive VP of Fellowship of Christian Athletes)

William Shofner (Harvard 1970-72), Robert Stewart Shofner (Harvard 1976-78), Michael Shofner (Southwestern of Tenn. 1976-79), son of Gen. Austin Shofner (Tennessee, MCB San Diego, POW, coach at Quantico)

Rick Theder (Stanford 1986-88), son of Roger Theder (Western Michigan, coach at Cal, pro assistant)

Jim Troppmann (Stanford, assistant at Quantico 1970), son of Bob Troppman (USF, Redlands)

David Valletto (Tennessee-Martin 1980-81, Alabama 1983-85), son of Carl Valletto (Camp Pendleton, 1st MarDiv, Alabama, tryout with Steelers)

Rick Venturi (1966-67, coach at Northwestern 1978-80, pro assistant), son of Joe Venturi (St. Mary's of Texas, El Toro)

Tom Venturi (college assistant), son of Joe Venturi.

John Wilkin (Stanford 1963), son of Wilbur "Wee Willie" Wilkin (St. Mary's, Washington Redskins, El Toro)

Grandsons

Rick Apolskis (Arkansas 1986-). Grandson of Ray Apolskis (Marquette, eight seasons in the NFL)

Michael Dove entered Tulane on a football scholarship in 1989. Grandson of Bob Dove.
Robert Page, was a Dartmouth linebacker in the late '80s. Grandson of Chuck Page.

Also: Joe Bushofsky, former director, player personnel, Lions 1990 (Jack's son)
Wade Phillips, Broncos assistant 1989 (Super Bowl), Eagles assistant 1986-88; interim head coach of Broncos 8-90 during Dan Reeves' recovery (Bum's son); Bonner Montler (Mike's son), a sophomore (football) center at San Diego State; Brig. Gen. Mike Neil USMCR, a San Diego lawyer (son of Marine athletic great Jean "Cheesie" Neil) was recalled for the Kuwait crisis 9-90 and commanded Camp Pendleton; tackle-center Jim Sweeney (Pittsburgh), with N.Y. Jets (father a staff sergeant in Korea)

BOB GOLIC

RICH BALDINGER

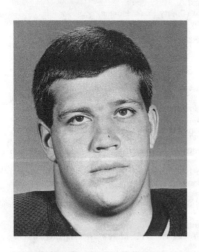

TIM NORMAN

RICK VENTURI

They Served, Again

T
he Korean War required a massive callup of Marine reservists to fight as well as man operational and staff positions in the Pacific and the United States.

The callup was about as popular as a Marine saying something nice about the Army.

In some cases, the men had been civilians only a few months after being separated from active duty.

Others — especially the aviators — at least had drilled with Reserve units and remained proficient in their MOS's.

But in many cases, the men had not served on active duty for almost five years and, in the meantime, had returned to school or begun civilian careers.

"If you can walk, you can fight," was one greeting the reservists received on reporting for physicals.

The Marine Corps, not North Korea, was the villain.

Among those recalled and who volunteered in heavy numbers were officers commissioned through the V-12 and OCS programs in the latter stages of World War II. If baseball had its Ted Williams and Jerry Coleman, football had its:

Harry Agganis (Boston University), Henry Armstrong (Rice-Southwestern Louisiana), Doug Arndt (St. Cloud and Minnesota), Walt Ashcraft (USC), Joe Bartos (Navy), Lloyd Baxter (SMU), J. Ainslie Bell (UCLA-USC-Stanford), Carl Benton (Northwest State-Southwestern Louisiana-UCLA), Fred Beyrouty (Loyola of LA-Flagstaff), Harry Botsford (Boston University), Cloyce Box (West Texas), Joe Brady (Columbia-Dartmouth), Bob Buel (Wisconsin-Franklin & Marshall), Gus Camarata (Wartburg-Western Michigan-Iowa Teachers), Jerry Carle (Minnesota-Northwestern), Paul Chess (Pitt), Jim Cloud (SMU-Southwestern Louisiana), W.H. "Spot" Collins (Texas-Southwestern of Texas), Carl·Cooper (Howard of Ala.), Ralph Cormany (Loras), Joe Cribari (Denver), Jim Cullom (Cal), Ed Czekaj (George Washington-Penn State), Lou Darnell (North Carolina), Chuck Dellago (Minnesota-Northwestern), Al Denham (Howard of Ala.), Wally Dreyer (Wisconsin-Michigan), Dick Enzminger (Miami of Ohio), Joe Ferem (St. Mary's-Pacific), Charles Getchell (Temple), Pete Glick (Pendleton), Ken Gould (Monmouth), Bob Heck (Purdue), Herb Hein (Minnesota-Northwestern), McCoy "Hoss" Hewlett (Auburn-Duke), Ralph Heywood (USC), Tom Hoffman (Monmouth), Dick Howard (Utah State), Earl Howell (Muhlenburg-Mississippi), Weldon Humble (Rice-Southwestern Louisiana), Jack Hussey (North Carolina), John Huzvar (North Carolina State-Pitt-Georgia), Fritz Jackson (Maryland-Colgate), Bill Justice (Rollins), Carl Kilsgaard (Idaho), Clark King (Nebraska State), Dick Kitchen (a Broncos' official), Bill LaFleur (Dayton-Penn State), "Big Jim" Landrigan (Holy Cross-Dartmouth), Don Lehmkuhl (Iowa-Purdue), Paul Lentz (Guilford), Frank Letteri (Geneva), Jim Loflin (LSU-Southwestern Louisiana)

Doug MacLachlan (UCLA-USC), Joe Mansfield (a Giants' official), Grover Martin (William & Mary), Art McCaffray (Santa Clara-Pacific), Mickey McCardle (USC), Len "Tuffy" McCormick (Baylor-Southwestern of Texas), Ed McFarland (Southwestern of Texas), Bill McLain (North Carolina), Bob McLaughry (Dartmouth), Bob McNeil (Michigan State), Lloyd Merriman (Stanford), Chuck Milner (South Carolina-Duke), Bob Mirth (Moravian-Muhlenburg), John Murphy (Holy Cross), Ralph Noble (Rice-Southwestern Louisiana), Ed O'Connor (Maryland), Don O'Neil (Denison-Missouri Valley), Wil Overgaard (Idaho), Thurman Owens (Tulane-Southwestern Louisiana-Cincinnati), Charles Pavlich (St. Mary's Pre-Flight), Ken Peck (Flagstaff-Southwestern Louisiana-Stanford), Jack Pevehouse (SMU), Ray Pfeifer (Rice), Bayard Pickett (South Carolina), Russ Picton (Temple-Wilkes), Dick Piskoty (Miami of Ohio), Jack Place (William & Mary), Johnny Podesto (St. Mary's-Pacific), Bill Pottenger (Springfield Teachers of Mo.), Skeet Quinlan (Texas Christian-San Diego State), Art Ramage (Coffeyville JC-Tulsa), Ken Reese (Alabama), Hosea Rodgers (Alabama-North Carolina), George Rusch (Dartmouth), John Seiferling (Utah State-Colorado College-Fresno State), Joe Signaigo (Notre Dame), Ken Smock (Purdue), Harvey Solon (South Dakota-Minnesota), Harry Sortal (St. Louis), John Staples (Alabama-North Carolina), Wayne Steele (Syracuse-Bucknell), Rube Swanson (St. Cloud), Walt Szot (Bucknell), Eddie Teague (North

Carolina State-North Carolina), Al Thomas (Northwestern), Gaspar Urban (Notre Dame), Sam Vavcanti (Iowa-Purdue-Nebraska), George Vercelli (Loyola of LA-Flagstaff), Guy Way (UCLA), Rex Wells (Idaho State-Michigan), Don White (Fresno State), Duane Whitehead (USC), Billy Willard (Rice-Southwestern Louisiana), Wally Williams (Boston University), Bob Winship (Loyola of LA-Southwestern Louisiana-Flagstaff), Jim Woodside (Temple-Rochester), Art Young (Springfield-Dartmouth).

Also: Everette Carlton, Russ DeVette, Bill Jones, Lloyd Lewis, Ken McLennan, Spencer Moseley, Chuck Page, Karl Schwelm (Kuwait)

Despite the unpopularity of the war — and the recall — the men served and fought with distinction.

For example, Bartos, Camarata, Landrigan and Thomas (twice) were awarded the Silver Star in Korea; McLaughry, Merriman, Pavlich and Smock the Distinguished Flying Cross; and Landrigan, LeBaron, Overgaard and Williams the Bronze Star.

On the home front, the recall of reservists saved the football program at Camp Lejeune in 1950. But Camp Pendleton dropped the sport for one season.

There was no doubting the impact key players had: Agganis at Lejeune, LeBaron at Quantico and Quinlan at San Diego in 1950, and Box and Szot at Pendleton, Humble and McCaffray at Quantico and Vacanti at Parris Island in 1951.

More pronounced was the impact on coaching.

The 1950 staff at Lejeune included Botsford, Landrigan and Williams, and the '51 staff had Jackson, King, Milner, Piskoty and Urban.

At Pendleton, Crawley was to have been the coach in 1950 had there been a team. Cormany was the coach in 1951 and Carle in 1952. On the staff were Howard and Pottenger in 1951, and Armstrong, Cloud and Cribari in '52.

Bill Justice was the coach at Quantico in 1951, and the staff included Benton, McNeil, Rodgers and Woodside.

Charles Getchell was the coach at El Toro in 1951, and Crawley the head man at Lejeune in 1953. San Diego went with Ramage in 1953, Crawley in 1954 and Heywood in 1955.

And as late as 1954, the staff at Parris Island included Brady, Cooper, Hewlett and Overgaard.

Go back, go back, go back to the woods!
You haven't, you haven't, you haven't got the goods!
You haven't got the rythmn,
You haven't got the jazz,
You haven't got the team
That Quantico has!

A Quantico cheer

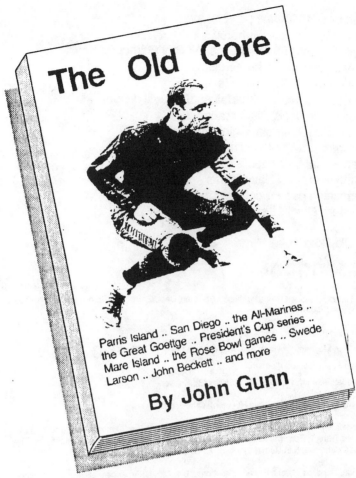

The Old Core

Parris Island .. San Diego .. the All-Marines ..
the Great Goettge .. President's Cup series ..
Mare Island .. the Rose Bowl games .. Swede
Larson .. John Beckett .. and more

By John Gunn

Features include:
* Marine football players killed in action
* Mare Island's two Rose Bowl teams
* All-Marine teams of 1920s, '30s
* The Great Goettge
* Quantico teams of late 1930s, early '40s
* San Diego's powerhouse of 1930s, 1940
* Parris Island's early teams
* Other Marine teams
* Football in Shanghai

* The Best 40 Marine players, ever
* The Marines' Four Hundred
* Hall of Fame, All-Americans, All-Star Games
* Players decorated for heroism
* The generals, the colonels
* The Last Game on Guadalcanal; 12 will die on Okinawa
* Jack Lummus: A Giant Marine
* Football in Australia, China, Nagasaki
* Marines steal 1943 college headlines
* Marines land Annapolis' Best
* Marines play on Navy teams
* Launching pad for colleges, pros
* Western Illinois' Leathernecks

The Old Core/1992

Addendum

Killed in action: Robert Brenton (Missouri) Saipan, Capt. Grant Ellis (Cornell-Penn) Korea, Lt. Lester Smith (Idaho) Guam.

Silver Star: Bob Blevins (Houston) Korea.

DFC: Tom Meehan, Vietnam; Spencer Moseley (Yale), Korea.

Bronze Star: Meehan, Vietnam.

Air Medal: Meehan 18, Vietnam; Moseley (3), Korea

Generals: Claude Reinke (Sam Houston), Quantico

Colonels:Bruno Andruska (Iowa), Joe Donahoe (Navy), Fred Jones (Oregon St.), Randy Lawrence (Navy), Tom Meehan (Boston College), Bob Mirth (Moravian-Muhlenburg), Ray Powell (Oklahoma), Earl Roth (Maryland), Mitch Sadler (Rice).

Top Four Hundred: C John Rapacz, Oklahoma. 6-4, 230. All-American. All-Star Game. Seven pro seasons.

East-West Game: Bob Denton (Pacific). College All-Star Game: Denton.

Foes of Long Standing: Quantico beat Xavier, 34-0, in its last game, 1972.

They Also Served: Bert Bacharach (Sr.), VMI

Education: Dr. Willis Holcombe, president, Broward (Fla.) CC.

Government: Alan D. Fiers Jr. (Ohio St.), former head of CIA covert operations in Latin America: Robert Fisher (Missouri), mayor of Fulton, Mo.; William Tuck (William & Mary), former Virginia governor, congressman.

Navy teams: Robert Fisher (Missouri), NAS Memphis 1955, Atsugi Flyers 1956.

$19.95, plus $2 handling, J&J Publishing, 404 Brighton Springs, Costa Mesa, CA 92627